Preservation of Archaeological Remains *In Situ*

Preservation of Archaeological Remains In Situ*: A Reader* reveals to the heritage practitioner and student, as well as to archaeologists, conservators and inspectors of ancient monuments, the issues surrounding the preservation of archaeological remains *in situ*. It considers a wide range of terrestrial sites, including graves, caves, castles, earthworks and battlefields as well as the artefacts and ecofacts buried at such sites. Identifying contemporary and classic papers from across the subject, Caple combines them with a series of introductions that contextualize specific problems and approaches to enable a greater understanding of contemporary preservation practice. The book illustrates the wide variety of threats to *in situ* archaeological remains, developing the concept of a holistic appreciation of the threats, and recognizing the need to prioritise appropriate forms of response and to develop appropriation mitigation strategies. Using a careful balance of sources, some technical, some theoretical, some practical as well as case studies which explore these threats and their mitigation, it provides a holistic statement on preserving archaeological remains *in situ*.

Chris Caple, currently a Senior Lecturer at Durham University, has been director of the postgraduate programme in artefact conservation at Durham since 1988. He is active teaching, researching and publishing in conservation, analysing and researching ancient artefacts and has been directing and publishing archaeological excavations since 1982.

Preservation of Archaeological Remains *In Situ*

Chris Caple

Routledge
Taylor & Francis Group

LONDON AND NEW YORK

First published 2016
by Routledge
2 Park Square, Milton Park, Abingdon, Oxon OX14 4RN

and by Routledge
711 Third Avenue, New York, NY 10017

Routledge is an imprint of the Taylor & Francis Group, an informa business

© 2016 C. Caple

The right of the editor to be identified as the author of the editorial material, and of the authors for their individual chapters, has been asserted in accordance with sections 77 and 78 of the Copyright, Designs and Patents Act 1988.

All rights reserved. No part of this book may be reprinted or reproduced or utilised in any form or by any electronic, mechanical, or other means, now known or hereafter invented, including photocopying and recording, or in any information storage or retrieval system, without permission in writing from the publishers.

Trademark notice: Product or corporate names may be trademarks or registered trademarks, and are used only for identification and explanation without intent to infringe.

Unless otherwise specified, all figures are taken from original articles.

British Library Cataloguing-in-Publication Data
A catalogue record for this book is available from the British Library

Library of Congress Cataloging-in-Publication Data
Names: Caple, Chris, 1958– editor.
Title: Preservation of archaeological remains in situ : a reader / edited by Christopher Caple.
Description: New York, NY : Routledge, 2016.
Identifiers: LCCN 2015042830 | ISBN 9780415832533 (hardback : alk. paper) | ISBN 9780415832540 (pbk. : alk. paper)
Subjects: LCSH: Antiquities – Collection and preservation. | Archaeology | Archaeological sites – Conservation and restoration. | Historic sites – Conservation and restoration. | Cultural property – Protection. | Historic preservation.
Classification: LCC CC135 .P716 2016 | DDC 930.1 – dc23
LC record available at http://lccn.loc.gov/2015042830

ISBN: 978-0-415-83253-3 (hbk)
ISBN: 978-0-415-83254-0 (pbk)

Typeset in Sabon and Bell Gothic
by Florence Production Ltd, Stoodleigh, Devon, UK

Contents

List of figures	*x*
List of tables	*xvi*
Preface	*xviii*
Acknowledgements	*xx*

Introduction to preservation *in situ*   1

SURVIVAL, LOSS AND IDEAS OF PRESERVATION   11

1 Survival: a history of the perception of the survival of archaeological remains   13

     1.1 Excavation reports   21
         ALISON E. COOLEY AND M.G.L. COOLEY

     1.2 An Egyptian treasure: great find at Thebes: Lord Carnarvon's long quest from our Cairo correspondent   26
         THE TIMES

     1.3 The bog people: Iron Age man preserved   30
         P.V. GLOB

2 Threats and losses: the spur to preservation   35

     2.1 The preservation of archaeological sites by environmental intervention   48
         JOHN COLES

	2.2	MARS: the Monuments at Risk Survey of England, 1995 TIMOTHY DARVILL AND ANDREW K. FULTON	70
	2.3	Estimating artefact loss MELANIE B. RIMMER AND CHRIS CAPLE	77
	2.4	Decay of delicate organic remains in shallow urban deposits: are we at a watershed? HARRY KENWARD AND ALLAN HALL	84

APPROACHES TO PRESERVATION AND CONSERVATION — 89

3	**Knowledge of the burial environment**		**91**
	3.1	The formation of vegetable mould through the action of worms with observations of their habits CHARLES DARWIN	105
	3.2	Soils for the archaeologist IAN W. CORNWALL	109
	3.3	The Experimental Earthwork Project, 1960–1992: discussion and conclusions MARTIN BELL	113
	3.4	Limits of the natural environment in terms of pH and oxidation-reduction potentials L.G.M. BAAS BECKING, I.R. KAPLAN AND D. MOORE	125
	3.5	Chemical and microbiological aspects of the preservation process in *Sphagnum* peat T.J. PAINTER	134
4	**Legislation and organisations**		**144**
	4.1	Introduction: the rationale of archaeological heritage management HENRY CLEERE	159
	4.2	Archaeological resource management and preservation WILLEM J.H. WILLEMS	171
5	**Conservation theory**		**179**
	5.1	Manifesto of the Society for the Protection of Ancient Buildings WILLIAM MORRIS	194

	5.2	International Charter for the Conservation and Restoration of Monuments and Sites (The Venice Charter 1964): IInd International Congress of Architects and Technicians of Historic Monuments, Venice, 1964. Adopted by ICOMOS in 1965 ICOMOS	196
	5.3	European Convention on the Protection of the Archaeological Heritage (Revised) COUNCIL OF EUROPE	200
	5.4	The Nara Document on Authenticity UNESCO	205
	5.5	The Burra Charter (1999) AUSTRALIAN NATIONAL COMMITTEE OF ICOMOS	209

PROBLEMS OF DECAY AND CONSERVATION MEASURES BY SITE TYPE — 219

6 Decay and mitigation of stone ruins — 221

6.1	Short story: the demise, discovery, destruction and salvation of a ruin JOHN ASHURST AND ASI SHALOM	235
6.2	Philosophy, technology and craft JOHN ASHURST AND COLIN BURNS	242
6.3	Setting and structure: the conservation of Wigmore Castle GLYN COPPACK	269

7 Decay and mitigation of earthen architecture remains — 275

7.1	Conservation approaches to earthen architecture in archaeological contexts LOUISE COOKE	285
7.2	Preservation of earthen sites in remote areas: the Buddhist Monastery of Ajina Tepa, Tajikistan ENRICO FODDE, KUNIO WATANABE AND YUKIYASU FUJII	290

8 Decay and mitigation of earthworks — 304

8.1	Managing ancient earthworks: diagnosis, cure and prevention of erosion ANTHONY D.F. STREETEN	318

9 Decay and mitigation of fragile and buried sites — 329

9.1 The study of impacts on archaeological sites — 343
LESLIE E. WILDESEN

10 Decay and mitigation of rock art and cave sites — 358

10.1 The consequences of allowing unrestricted tourist access at an Aboriginal site in a fragile environment: the erosive effect of trampling — 372
ALANA M. ROSSI AND R. ESMÉE WEBB

11 Decay and mitigation of waterlogged sites — 383

11.1 Results of the characterisation of the anoxic waterlogged environments which preserve archaeological organic materials — 396
CHRIS CAPLE, DAVID DUNGWORTH AND PHIL CLOGG

11.2 Steps towards the heritage management of wetlands in Europe — 408
BRYONY COLES

GENERIC MITIGATION MEASURES: VISITOR AND LAND MANAGEMENT — 419

12 Generic mitigation measures: visitor management — 421

12.1 Sustainable visitation at the Mogao Grottoes: a methodology for visitor carrying capacity — 426
MARTHA DEMAS, SHIN MAEKAWA, JONATHAN BELL, AND NEVILLE AGNEW

13 Generic mitigation measures: shelters — 438

13.1 Methodology, conservation criteria and performance evaluation for archaeological site shelters — 450
NEVILLE AGNEW

14 Generic mitigation measures: reburial — 462

14.1 Preservation of the Laetoli hominid trackway in Tanzania — 476
MARTHA DEMAS, NEVILLE AGNEW, SIMON WAANE, JERRY PODANY, ANGELYN BASS AND DONATIUS KAMAMBA

14.2 Saving the Rose Theatre: England's first managed and monitored reburial — 484
MIKE CORFIELD

14.3 Chaco Canyon Reburial Programme 493
DABNEY FORD, MARTHA DEMAS, NEVILLE AGNEW, ROBERT BLANCHETTE,
SHIN MAEKAWA, MICHAEL ROMERO TAYLOR AND KATHERINE DOWDY

15 Conclusion **510**

Index *514*

Figures

1.2.1	Tutankahmen's tomb, just after the tomb was opened, showing the disordered grave goods piled one on another in the ante-chamber	28
1.3.1	The Tollund man, who died 2,000 years ago	32
2.0.1	Fenced off monuments, either short-term or long-term, may be necessary physical protection, but also create a visual barrier to seeing, understanding and appreciating the monument	45
2.1.1	Iron Age fortification at Arbur, Northants being ploughed away	51
2.1.2	Erosion damage from overgrazing and tourism	52
2.1.3	Trees root disturbance of barrows – Iron Age Square Barrow in Broxa Forest, North Yorkshire	54
2.1.4	The Church of Breedon on the Hill, eighth-century centre of Mercian religious life, isolated by a stone quarry	55
2.1.5	Water erosion: the incoming tide erodes away the prehistoric ritual site of 'Seahenge'	57
2.1.6	Rock art at Vastervik in Sweden, buried during the winter period to reduce ice damage	58
2.1.7	Scheme for intervention to preserve shipwrecks in the polders of the Netherlands	60
2.1.8	The large numbers of visitors walking on and over Hadrian's wall take their toll on the monument	61
2.1.9	Development road slicing through Olcote kerbed cairn, Isle of Lewis	61
2.1.10	Early Neolithic wood trackway, the Sweet Track, in the Somerset Levels, England	65
2.1.11	Sketch map to show part of the alignment of the Sweet Track as it passes through a National Nature Reserve and the barriers, ditches and irrigation system details which maintain moisture levels in the Reserve	66
2.2.1	Pie chart showing the main causes of monument destruction to 1995	72

2.2.2	Pie chart showing the main causes of piecemeal loss and damage to MARS Monuments in 1995, including instances where more than one cause of damage was recorded	74
3.0.1	Typical composition of soil, major constituents	98
3.0.2	Build-up of corrosion/decay layers	99
3.0.3	Generalised rate of loss of archaeological remains over time	99
3.2.1	Soil-profiles to show nomenclature of horizons	112
3.3.1	The section of Wareham Experimental Earthwork showing its changing profile between 1963 and 1980	115
3.3.2	The section of Overton Down Experimental Earthwork showing its changing profile between 1960 and 1992	117
3.3.3	Diagram summarizing the preservation of buried materials (textiles, leather and goatskin) in the earthworks on a scale of 0–4	119
3.3.4	Diagram summarizing the preservation of buried materials (rope, wood, bone and pottery) in the earthworks on a scale of 0–4	120
3.4.1	Stability fields of some important naturally occurring non-metallic compounds in terms of oxidation-reduction potentials and pH framed within the limits suggested by this work	127
3.4.2	Eh-pH characteristics of peat bogs	128
3.4.3	Eh-pH characteristics of soils	129
3.4.4	Suggested stability fields of various soil types	129
3.4.5	Eh-pH characteristics of fresh-water sediments	130
3.4.6	Approximate areas of Eh-pH for the photosynthetic organisms studied in this work	131
3.4.7	Approximate areas of Eh-pH for the geologically important bacteria studied in this work	132
4.2.1	The organisational principles of archaeological resource management systems in different countries	173
4.2.2	The relations between the government, archaeological contractors and developers	174
4.2.3	The cyclical process of archaeological resource management	177
5.0.1	Stages in the Conservation-Based Research and Analysis (CoBRA) approach advocated by English Heritage for conservation work on historic buildings	188
5.0.2	Flow chart showing values-based planning methodology for conservation and management planning advocated by Getty Conservation Institute (GCI)	189
5.0.3	Simplified sequence of values-based planning activities for site preservation	190
5.5.1	The Burra Charter process: sequence of investigations, decisions and actions	217
6.0.1	Roman stonework at Cardiff Castle outlined during the nineteenth-century restoration work of the Marquis of Bute and William Burges	225
6.0.2	Internal elevation of Round Tower (Area D) of Dryslwyn Castle, Carmarthenshire, drawn by Mr R.F. Caple circa 1982 and 1986	231
6.1.1	The complete building	236
6.1.2	Phase one deterioration	236

6.1.3	Phase two deterioration	237
6.1.4	Phase three deterioration	237
6.1.5	Phase four deterioration	238
6.1.6	Archaeology as an informing force	239
6.1.7	Archaeology as a destructive force	239
6.1.8	Ignorant repair as a destructive force	240
6.1.9	Correct conservation as a benign intervention	240
6.1.10	Reburial	241
6.2.1	The west front of Tintern Abbey c.1860	243
6.2.2	William Harvey's drawing of the north chancel wall showing the drift of the masonry to the west	244
6.2.3	William Harvey's drawn plan showing the proposed installation of reinforced concrete wall head beam linked to a ring beam at the head of the tower	245
6.2.4	Reinforcement of the corbelled masonry of the broken nave arcade	245
6.2.5	Tintern Abbey – north-west pier showing timber shoring under broken nave arcade	246
6.2.6	Reinforcement required to support overhanging masonry – Tintern Abbey	247
6.2.7	Ruin profiles, broken wall heads	249
6.2.8	Broken wall heads in masonry and core	250
6.2.9	End profile and overhangs	251
6.2.10	Treatments of low-lying walls	253
6.2.11	Wall head treatments	254
6.2.12	Perfect protection for this roofless ruin is provided by a mature mat of turf and wild flowers	256
6.2.13	Characteristics of different kinds of core in ruined contexts	257
6.2.14	Grouting masonry walls	259
6.2.15	This replacement stone has been set in a damaged medieval entrance arch still used by vehicular traffic	261
6.2.16	Massive, unmortared stones at Cuzco illustrate some of the most accurately worked masonry seen anywhere, and virtually indestructible except through severe seismic activity, deliberate demolition or artillery fire	266
6.2.17	Masonry of water-washed boulders at Tel Dan, northern Israel	267
6.3.1	Wigmore Castle from the south prior to being taken into guardianship	270
6.3.2	The north wall of the shell keep before repair	270
7.1.1	Maintenance of earthen architecture	285
7.1.2	Erosion factors affecting un-maintained earthen architecture	286
7.1.3	Erosion factors affecting eroded but still extant earthen architecture	287
7.1.4	Erosion factors affecting unexcavated archaeological sites	289
7.2.1	Schematic plan of the monastery of Ajina Tepa	291
7.2.2	Diagram showing grading envelope or reference area of soil particle sizes for historic *pakhsa* and mudbrick	297
7.2.3	Drawing conventions in English and Russian employed for the documentation of damage and conservation threats	299
7.2.4	Documentation of damage using the conventions in Figure 7.2.3	299

7.2.5	Local master builders and labourers, trained during the project, applying a shelter coat of mudbrick to the most endangered walls (2007)	301
7.2.6	Shelter coating of mud plaster following the morphology of the earthen walls	301
7.2.7	The structural consolidation of leaning walls was undertaken with thick mudbrick buttresses	301
8.0.1	A decay profile based on excavated data from the long barrows at Hazelton, Giants Hill and Tiverton	305
8.0.2	The isolated motte of Castell Dyffryn Mawr, Pembrokeshire, covered with trees	308
8.0.3	Gravestone outside York station	309
8.0.4	Cattle scrape in a twelfth-century ringwork castle, Castell Pengawsai, Pembrokeshire	310
8.1.1	Dinedor Camp, Hereford and Worcester, inappropriate siting of picnic tables	321
8.1.2	Herefordshire Beacon repairing erosion scars	324
8.1.3	Bryn Amwlg Castle, Shropshire, specification for modest earthwork repairs	325
9.0.1	Mathewson's matrix of differing site information sources against the decay mechanisms that can afflict them	332
9.0.2	Wind Rose: monitoring the direction of wind for a year enables a diagram that shows the percentage of time (distance from the centre) the wind comes from a particular direction	337
10.0.1	(a) Peterborough petroglyph as initially recorded and as infilled with wax crayon, identified as a picture of a snake and three snake eggs. (b) The same petroglyph as it appears when examined closely and recorded (photographed) in oblique light	359
10.1.1	Location of Hyden on the Yilgarn Block, a craton of Archaean granite, in south-central Western Australia	373
10.1.2	Estimated rate of erosion at the cave mouth graphed against visitor numbers	374
10.1.3	Four views of the walkway installed at Mulka's Cave (May 2006)	375
10.1.4	Monthly wind speed and rainfall patterns and annual rainfall at Hyden for the last seventy years	377
10.1.5	Reconstruction of the ground level within Mulka's Cave between 1952 and 2006	379
11.0.1	Model of hydrology and water chemistry of Bryggen, Bergen	386
11.1.1	The redox potential (Eh) readings (mV) following insertion of the monitoring probe into the anoxic waterlogged burial environment at Lanchester	400
11.1.2	Representative Eh and pH values for waterlogged anoxic environments from archaeological sites monitored 'in situ' using a Water Quality Monitoring system	401
11.1.3	The Eh readings for 'in situ' monitoring and for samples removed immediately and after purging from a dipwell, in the anoxic deposits at Lanchester	402

11.1.4	Changes in the Eh and pH of sediment samples from Lanchester which are undergoing dehydration and rehydration	404
11.1.5	The changes in Eh and pH of an anoxic waterlogged sediment sample from Lanchester which has oxygenated water flowing over it for days 0–6 and through it for days 7–15	405
11.2.1	Map of Western Europe to show the location of the three case studies discussed in the text	410
11.2.2	Archaeological and palaeoenvironmental investigations at Muldbjerg I in the Åmose	411
11.2.3	Aerial view of the Federsee, showing the area of the shrunken lake in the foreground, with the peat-moor zone of archaeological and nature conservation interest clearly visible surrounding the remaining water-body	413
11.2.4	Aerial view of the Lac de Chalain	415
12.1.1	The Grotto Zone is the protected, narrow strip along the cliff face into which the caves were carved	428
12.1.2	Ongoing deterioration of the wall paintings can be activated by elevated external humidity entering the caves, especially during periodic rain events in the summer months	429
12.1.3	Laboratory investigations showed that salts identified in the wall plaster at Mogao begin to absorb a large amount of water vapor at approximately 67 percent RH	431
12.1.4	Clay coupon, simulating the structure, composition, and pigments of the wall paintings, showing typical salt-related deterioration after 26 cycles of high and low RH fluctuations in an environmental chamber	432
12.1.5	The physical capacity of a cave, based on usable area of the main chamber, varies markedly	435
13.0.1	Shelters at Strata Florida Abbey (Ceredigion) above and North Leigh Roman Villa (Oxfordshire) below	443
13.1.1	Roof at Lark Quarry in 1981, prior to the erection of a perimeter fence to prevent kangaroos sheltering under the roof	454
13.1.2	Loss of part of the dinosaur trackway at Lark Quarry	454
13.1.3	Shelter building over the DK hominid site in Olduvai Gorge, Tanzania	456
13.1.4	Hexashelter at Fort Selden, New Mexico	459
14.0.1	Reburial protection involves the insertion of a buffer between the erosive agents of an aggressive environment and the archaeological remains	469
14.0.2	Conceptual protective reburial system	470
14.1.1	Laetoli trackway, Site G	477
14.1.2	Reburial profile to show six of the ten layers of the composite: coarse sand layer (foreground), second layer of Biobarrier, Enkamat, coarse sand, local soil, and lava boulder capping	481
14.2.1	The Terram barrier has been laid over the site, the joins sealed with lime mortar and the sand cover is being delivered through a pipeline to minimize activity on the theatre remains	487
14.2.2	The monitoring scheme, as designed by Huntings Technical Services	488
14.2.3	Soil moisture content measured by TDR (Time Domain Reflectometry), 2001–2002	489

14.2.4	Redox potential, 1994–1996	490
14.3.1	Aerial view of Pueblo Bonito, the largest of the great houses at Chaco	494
14.3.2	Room 62 in Pueblo Bonito during its excavation in the 1890s	495
14.3.3	Differential fills in partly reburied or excavated structures result in lateral pressure and salt crystallization on the exposed wall	496
14.3.4	Room 62 partially backfilled after excavation and re-excavated in 1992	499
14.3.5	Rooms 54, 53 and 46 during their excavation in 1932	500
14.3.6	Phase 1 rooms prior to reburial	502
14.3.7	Basic stratigraphy of the reburial, incorporating features of the redesign for the Phase 1 rooms	504
14.3.8	Phase 1 rooms after reburial, looking west	505
14.3.9	Well preserved wood post reburial, Room 59, Chetro Ketl	506

Tables

0.1	Defined terms	2
2.0.1	Causes of loss or damage to archaeological sites (ancient monuments)	43
2.1.1	Pressures on archaeological environments	50
2.1.2	Priorities in the selection of monuments and nature conservation sites for protection in England	63
2.2.1	Identified hazards causing wholesale loss of MARS monuments since 1940 in relation to MARS regions	73
2.3.1	Site types used in MARS and this research	78
2.3.2	Average artefact density by monument type	78
2.3.3	Number of monuments and area in MARS sample	79
2.3.4	Total number of artefacts in England	79
2.3.5	Total number of artefacts destroyed by wholesale monument loss in MARS sample	80
2.3.6	Artefact loss per year from piecemeal loss in MARS sample	80
2.3.7	Total artefact loss per year in England	80
2.3.8	Corrosion rate ranges for copper and iron	81
2.3.9	Artefact loss per year from corrosive decay	82
3.0.1	Decay of archaeological materials	94
3.4.1	Organisms and their associated environmental conditions	126
4.0.1	Principles for scheduling archaeological remains under the 1979 Ancient Monument and Archaeological Areas Act, guidance issued by DCMS (2013)	145
4.0.2	A history of heritage legislation and organisations in England and Wales	148
4.0.3	A history of heritage legislation in the USA	155
6.0.1	Examples of different approaches to preserving and displaying ancient remains	227
6.2.1	Mortar type 'A' – lime putty and pozzolan	264

6.2.2	Mortar type 'B' – hydraulic lime	264
9.1.1	Definitions of surface disturbance categories	349
11.0.1	Oxidising/reducing environment	386
11.0.2	Reported burial environment of selected urban and rural sites	387
11.1.1	Conductivity levels, in microsiemens, of various waters and waterlogged anoxic burial environments	403
12.1.1	Summer monthly percentile rank of surface relative humidity at the west wall of cave 29 based on data collected over a five-and-a-half-year period	434
13.0.1	Shelter types	444

Preface

One bright Saturday morning, when I was 14 years old, I accompanied my father to a local excavation being run by Dr Peter Webster and Cardiff Archaeology Society, uncovering a medieval monastic grange at Merthyrgeryn in Monmouthshire (Gwent) (Parkes and Webster 1975). I spent the morning working with other local volunteers removing the turf and revealing rows of the thin split sandstone slates – the collapsed roof of one of the thirteenth-century barns. As the day passed, I lost all awareness of time. At its end, I was physically exhausted, but I was fascinated; the act of discovering the past was magical. I was hooked and have spent the whole of my subsequent professional life unearthing, cleaning and preserving archaeological and historic remains, or teaching others how to do so.

At the end of that weekend of excavation, there was what felt like a bitter sting in the tail, our carefully revealed barn was to be reburied, covered up with the earth from which we had so carefully excavated it. Why couldn't this fascinating glimpse of the past remain exposed so that friends and colleagues could see what had been found? Older and wiser councils prevailed; and now covered by a foot of topsoil, the remains of the grange at Merthyrgeryn are still preserved safe beneath the turf. I now realise that had they been left exposed, frost would have shattered the stone, cattle trampled the earth to a quagmire and plants taken hold, roots tearing the stone walls apart, turning the ruins to an overgrown wilderness.

The excitement of discovery and revelation of archaeological remains is a powerful driving emotion. But the frustration and despair upon seeing remains that had survived, buried in the soil for hundreds or thousands of years, being damaged and decayed by animals, vegetation and weather in just a few brief years of exposure, is heartbreaking. It is no good railing about the lack of resources to fence, shelter and maintain the site; with so much past, we simply cannot preserve it all as exposed monuments. The need is for good decision-making, selecting and conserving that small fraction of these remains that can be effectively and efficiently displayed and recording and reburying the rest. This book explores the subject of preservation of archaeological remains in situ. It is what I needed to read when I was 14, so I write this book to my younger self.

I also write this book for the thousands of archaeology students studying and emerging from universities around the world every year; educated in period culture, typologies, archaeological theory and techniques of excavation, subjects that reflect the interests of their lecturers. They are focused on uncovering and interpreting information from our past, educated and partially skilled for careers in commercial archaeology or academia. What they lack is any real idea of how to preserve the remains they find. This knowledge and these skills remain scarce – almost non-existent in our universities and barely present in the archaeological literature. Until we give this subject prominence in education and practice, our archaeologists will continue to be good legislators and interpreters but poor preservers. This book seeks to make students of and graduates in archaeology aware of this subject and give them an entry into the ideas and literature of the preservation of archaeological remains in situ.

Acknowledgements

Several groups of people deserve acknowledgement here. The first group: my late father Ray Caple, who helped me get started in archaeology and who actively supported my efforts throughout my career, Peter Webster, the excavation director under whom I learnt to dig and with whom I continue to work to the present day, and the late Richard Avent, who, as a senior colleague and Principal Inspector for Wales, supported me directing excavations at Dryslwyn Castle. All these people taught me not merely to retrieve and understand the archaeological record through excavation, but to take seriously my responsibilities towards the remains that I unearthed.

The second group are those who raised my interest in the burial environment and how we could analyse and understand it. Leo Biek for showing me that the most important thing was not analytical equipment, but accurate observation and an enquiring mind, Mike Corfield, the godfather of preservation in situ in the UK, so active in supporting the early English Heritage research into waterlogged environments and who still has the best grasp of this subject of anyone I have ever worked with.

The third group includes David Leigh, Dave Watkinson, Em. Prof. Rosemary Cramp and my colleagues in conservation, all of whom have given me the opportunity to learn or practise archaeological conservation. It is their efforts that supported and guided my understanding of the decay of materials and the processes of artefact conservation.

The fourth group facilitated the creation of this book: Jim Spriggs, who so ably covered my teaching, the Dept of Archaeology and Durham University, who enabled me to take research leave to complete this book, and all colleagues who read chapters and gave sage advice; Prof. Charles Augard, Dr Mary Brooks, Prof. John Chapman, Mike Corfield, Will Davies, Dr Prof. Chris Gerrard, Andrew Millard, Ian Panter, Dr Kate Sharpe and the late Prof. Tony Wilkinson.

The final group are the students who have sat through and so actively contributed to the half module 'In situ and on site conservation' (Specialised Aspects in Archaeology), that I have run at Durham University for the last seven to eight years. They have provided me with references, examples and ideas. It is the need to provide them with a textbook and reader for studying this subject that has spurred me on to complete this work.

Introduction to preservation *in situ*

THIS BOOK IS CONCERNED with the preservation of archaeological remains, which includes all types of terrestrial archaeological site: graves, caves, castles, stone and earth buildings, earthworks and battlefields, as well as the artefacts (coins, ceramics, weapons, etc.) and ecofacts (bones, seeds, shells, etc.) buried at such sites. Different types of site and artefact are often the concern of different groups of specialist archaeologists and curators, each generating different literatures, working in different materials and different craft traditions. However, heritage agencies are required to deal with a wide range of sites, have a consistent approach and apply ethical standards equitably in the preservation of a wide range of archaeological remains. This book identifies some key published works in the different areas of the subject, and by combining them with a series of 'Introductions' to the various problems and approaches to preservation, it is hoped to create a single volume that will lead to greater awareness of the subject. By drawing from widely differing sites, materials and approaches, I seek to show that although the problems are substantial, there are a range of options available and a more coherent approach to the subject is emerging. To aid this process, a number of commonly used terms are defined in Table 0.1.

The nature of the past

Why is the past so important that we seek to preserve it? We only know things by reference to what we have seen and experienced in the past; therefore, a personal past is essential to us to identify and understand our present. A more distant past also appears to be an essential human requirement, since it provides us with a wider sense of belonging. This manifests itself in many ways such as the need to trace one's ancestors or the need of immigrants to maintain the traditions of their homeland: 'I like roots. Plants don't grow well without them. People are the same' (Emmott 1994: 28). These requirements stem from the need for humans, as social animals, to have points of contact, shared experiences or beliefs so that there is some basis for communication. The unknown is feared, but things that fit into existing schemes of

Table 0.1 Defined terms

Term	Definition
Archaeological remains	(in this book often contracted to the term 'remains') All types of archaeological site: graves, caves, caverns, castles, buildings, earthworks, landscapes and wrecks, as well as the artefacts (coins, jewellery, pottery, tools, weapons) and ecofacts (bones, shell, seeds, charcoal, pollen) buried at such sites.
Artefact	Anything formed by a human being, from a nail to a cathedral. Normally, it refers to smaller items such as tools, ceramics, statues, jewellery, coins, etc. The term is used interchangeably with object.
Conservation	Activity undertaken to preserve, investigate and reveal (uncover, clean, restore) a site, construction or artefact (Caple 2000).
Construction	A building, shelter, barrier, monument, etc. erected of any material for any purpose.
Cultural heritage	The physical remains (sites, artefacts, etc) and intangible attributes of a society or culture.
Damage	The loss of integrity of archaeological remains, often occurring quickly and as a result of impacts caused by human actions. 'The immediate consequences of traumatic events' (Cather 2003).
Decay	The physical, chemical or biological processes that change (destroy, corrode, dissolve, corrupt) archaeological remains. Decay processes normally occur slowly. 'A gradual cumulative process due to inherent and/or prevailing conditions' (Cather 2003).
Delamination	Material splitting in thin layers (lamella), usually upon drying.
Groundwater	Water present in the soil.
In situ	The place where the remains have been located since antiquity, often the site where constructions and artefacts were created or used.
Maintenance	Continuing regular care of the remains, preventing the build-up of harmful agents or correcting minor damage and decay.
Mitigation	Reducing the impact of damage and decay (preservation) and recovering from it through appropriate conservation methods.
Monument	A physical, visible structure or signifier that has meaning or is associated with a specific person, idea or people from the past.
Preservation	The act of ensuring that no further significant change occurs to archaeological remains.
Reconstruction	Intervening with archaeological remains to return them, partially or completely, to an almost certain original form. Post-Burra Charter, it refers to reconstructing with new materials what was certainly known (supported by evidence) to have originally been present.
Recreation	Intervening with archaeological remains to return them, partially or completely, to a likely original form. Post-Burra Charter, it refers to reconstructing with new materials what was very likely to have been originally present.

Table 0.1 Defined terms—*continued*

Term	Definition
Relative humidity	The water vapour (gas) present in the air, expressed as a percentage of the total amount of water vapour the air can contain at the same temperature.
Repair	Intervening with archaeological remains to correct past damage to return some level of function to the remains.
Restoration	Intervening with archaeological remains to partially or completely return them to their original form, where there is clear evidence for the original form.
Site	A place in which remains (construction or artefacts) or evidence of human past activity are present.
Stabilisation	Halting, or slowing to a barely perceptible level, the physical, chemical or biological decay processes that degrade archaeological remains.
Western	The culture and ideas that have emanated from Western Europe and North America from the seventeenth century and the Age of Enlightenment onwards. They include secular rational ideas based on logical deduction that are evidence-based.
Windthrow	Vegetation, normally a tree blown (thrown) down by the wind, which often tears up archaeological remains in its roots.

1 The term conservation/restoration is often used in international charters to describe the activities of preserving the physical substance and nature of structures/objects. In this book, I use conservation as the all-embracing term while restoration refers specifically to material added to the original fabric of a site or object in order to reintegrate the whole and be able to see and understand (read) the form and purpose of the original site/object.

understanding are explicable and thus not frightening or threatening. Denial of an individual's past, like the denial of an individual's beliefs, has always been seen as a restriction on individual liberty; UNESCO identifies a cultural heritage as an essential human right, as it does access to food and water (Lowenthal 1996).

In a similar manner to individuals, groups appear to cherish a past; indeed they invariably define themselves and their traits or qualities by reference to their past. Thus, regiments record their battle honours, sports teams record their victories and people erect monuments to their past heroes and leaders. No sooner is a country created than efforts are made to preserve the places and objects associated with its inception and its past. The house of Chairman Mao was a national monument before his death and Americans sought to preserve Colonial Williamsburg barely 175 years after it had been the capital city of Virginia. A past legitimises the present, while the new is not trusted since it shows things are easily changed. Thus, 'heritage' (Lowenthal 1996) goes beyond an individual's desire to have a past, to be an essential component of almost every social and political organisation.

Studies of societies around the world suggest that many of them divide the past into three or four divisions (Layton 1994: 5–7):

- present;
- recent past;
- ancient or distant past; and
- origins.

Examples include the Inuit (Anawak 1994), Hadza (Ndagala and Zengu 1994), peoples of north-west Portugal (Pina-Cabral 1994: 62), classical Greeks (Sparkes 1994: 126–7) and the Aboriginal peoples of North East Queensland (Chase 1994: 172–6). For many such groups, the past is seen as a series of events that occurred in a specific sequence, even if there is no separate concept of time. In Europe, historians and archaeologists have, since the Age of Enlightenment, developed a hugely detailed factually based 'culture history' account of the past based on written history and archaeological material. Crucially, this has an independent chronometric system (years) determined by radiometric measurement, annual environmental and astronomical phenomena, and calendars of historic events. This allows multiple separate pasts to be understood as happening at the same or different absolute times, and there is an understanding of differing amounts of time occurring between events. However, the public grasp of the past, even in the developed countries of Europe, is often little more than the basic three or four divisions of past; their visits to castles, Roman forts, country houses and prehistoric monuments are often lumped together as things in the 'ancient' past.

When talking of the past, as understood by ancient Egyptians, Baines (1994: 131) remarked, 'Like any other society they constructed their present and projected their future out of their past'. He also noted that for them, 'the past legitimates the present order'. This correspondence between the future, the past and the present was most succinctly noted by George Orwell in the novel *Nineteen Eighty Four*: 'Who controls the past, controls the future; who controls the present controls the past' (Orwell 1949: 31). Recordings of the oral history of tribes such as the Tiv of Nigeria attest changes in their recounted oral history tradition in order to better explain the present (Lowenthal 1996). This has led Malinowski and others to see myths and oral history traditions as functioning entirely to support present needs (Layton 1994: 1). This is unlikely to be true given the prevalence of physical remains, which act as mnemonics for these accounts. Many oral history and written traditions make reference to, or draw hugely from, the landscape. Examples include the Paez of the Colombian highlands (Rappaport 1994: 88), the Aboriginal peoples of North East Queensland (Chase 1994: 177), the people of north-west Portugal (Pina-Cabral 1994: 65) and the Inuit (Anawak 1994: 48), where prominent features in the landscape anchor the accounts of creation and the distant past. Their pasts, like all pasts, are made up of physical remains, and the narrative (oral or written), including associated beliefs, activities and traditions, that explain them. In Geoffrey of Monmouth's *History of the Kings of Britain* (1154), Arthur's father Uther Pendragon is buried at Stonehenge, while in William Caxton's *Chronicles of England* (1480) the Neolithic chambered tomb of Wayland's Smithy is associated with Volund the smith from Norse mythology.

The oral history tradition, prior to written records, is what binds these monuments into a past; but the oral tradition is potentially both long-lived and inaccurate. Evidence exists for its ability to transmit information from a distant past; Panday (1994) suggests that even prehistoric past is recalled and written down in eleventh-century AD India. However, Pina-Cabral (1994: 60) has shown that oral traditions of north-west Portugal are all recent, failing to record significant changes between the fifteenth and nineteenth centuries. Written texts can be similarly accurate and inaccurate. In such cases, the sites or artefacts mentioned were seen as physical proof of the written or oral account of the past. These remains were valued for their associations with significant individuals or supernatural beings and for being proof of the truth of the past. Indeed, the need for such physical 'touchstones' of the past was so great that they were sometimes recreated – as at the step pyramid of Djoser at Saqqara where a symbolic south tomb alludes to older burials in Upper Egypt. Funerary structures, originally temporary, were symbolically rebuilt in sturdy form and stone vases, inscribed with kings' names of the first- and second-dynasty were buried in galleries beneath the pyramid to create the illusion of history, power and the sanctity that is attendant on a distant past (Baines 1994: 134).

Artefacts are both hugely emotive symbols conveying messages powerfully to people and physical evidence, proof of the past. They were frequently used as mnemonics to invoke the past and support, even legitimise, the present; wearing the crown made you king. Many non-Western cultures consider the spirit of the maker or owners of objects to be suffused into the fabric of the object. Archaeologists recognised that artefacts provide a detailed record of society, providing, through changes in object form and decoration, a means to identify culture, date, wealth, status, beliefs and activities of peoples of the past, though context provides crucial evidence for accurate interpretation (Caple 2006).

Memorials identify particular events, people or ideas from the past that are important to a present society. They can take many forms, from buildings and objects of the past, to newly created statues, columns, plaques and structures (websites to museums). It is their meaning and their ability to invoke/reflect the past that is crucial. As with gravestones, memorials are often not concerned so much with the physical entity of the past; rather, they are 'sacred to the memory of'. Examples include the ruins of buildings preserved and sacred to the ancestors who 'inhabit' the place, though in reality they come from an entirely different period or culture. This is certainly true for many traditional/non-Western cultures.

Though the term 'the past' is used to describe the objects and events of earlier times, Lowenthal, Michalski and others (Michalski 1994; Lowenthal 1996) distinguish between two forms of the past:

- *History*: The whole of the past, raw unrefined events. History is ever-expanding and all-inclusive. It explores and explains the past; its purpose is simply to be and be known. This is the past that is taught in classrooms and in books.
- *Heritage*: A personal inheritance of the past, a past that can be used in the present. It is that subsection of the past that an individual inherits, their family, their ancestry and the traditions of their nation. It is exclusive, it is biased and its purpose is to benefit the individual. It is personal memory, an attachment to people, places and things, a past that can be used.

Archaeological remains in a distant part of the country are part of a large data set, a dot on a distribution map, that we call history. But to local people, that same site is where they played as children, told stories and carved their initials on the trees; this is part of peoples' heritage, a deeply personal past (Lowenthal 1996). While it can reasonably be argued there is some continuum between heritage and history, personal heritages morph into local and regional cultural memory and even national identities; for many people, the heritage/history division applies to much of the past.

The landscape, sites, monuments and artefacts of the past can all act as mnemonics accessing the past, triggering memories and stories. However, the value placed on ancient remains is far more than this. It is complex altered by context, ownership and other associated sites and artefacts; they frequently form the focus of ceremonies, festivals and other social activities. Objects and sites can be valued in many different ways by different groups of people. It is important for heritage practitioners to understand these tangible and intangible values before they alter, improve or conserve the remains. Even if they act to preserve, they can unintentionally destroy key relationships and meanings of the monument/artefact of which they are unaware. Preservation *in situ* aims to preserve as many of these physical and spiritual relationships as possible. Even the peoples who inhabit remote landscapes from the Canadian arctic to the Australia, whether Inuit or Aboriginal, are becoming conscious of their changing lifestyles and the need to preserve these sites as a connection to the past, taking conscious actions to preserve the past, both the oral accounts and the physical sites, natural and human made (Anawak 1994; Chase 1994).

Starting to preserve remains

The hunter-gatherer communities of the European Palaeolithic and Mesolithic, like more recent Aboriginal and Bushman groups, were mobile and transient; they had to carry everything. Their material culture was functional and they could not retain old, non-functional artefacts. Consequently, their past existed as an oral history, a past preserved through memory and invigorated through traditional practices such as retelling stories, performing ceremonies, dances and redecorating places in nature such as repainting rock art – effectively, they created and maintained '*in situ*' memorials within the landscape.

Some of the earliest evidence of ancestry in the archaeological record of Britain is suggested by Bradley (1998), who noted the visual similarity between megalithic tomb structures, portal dolmens and the natural stone outcrops, known as *tors*, in areas such as Cornwall. These Neolithic tombs do not appear to have developed through copying the natural rock outcrops since they occur at earlier dates elsewhere on the Atlantic seaboard. However, since some of the natural rock outcrops appear to be incorporated within man-made enclosures, Bradley has reasoned that the Neolithic people appropriated the natural rock outcrops, treating them as ancestral places, perhaps seeing them as tombs of gods or ancestors. Thus, they appear to have created a past for themselves and incorporated this physical evidence of that past into their culture.

The importance of this concept of ancestry in artefacts is also suggested by Gillings and Pollard (1999) when discussing the biography of the Grey Wether Stone, from Avebury. They suggest that polished areas on the stone were initially created while it was still a natural boulder in the sarsen stone fields of Salisbury Plain when it acted as an abrasive block for smoothing and shaping flint axes. Over time, it acquired meaning, a powerful place associated with activities and people of the past. Subsequently, when the large ritual monument of Avebury was created, these sarsen boulders were used to form a megalithic ring, whose significance was initially derived from the accumulated power and meaning of the ancestral stones of which it was composed. A similar example of a valued ancestral stone is provided by the decorated capstones of the Neolithic dolmen at Gavrinis in Brittany, which can be joined to capstones of dolmens of Table des Marchand and Er Vinglé at Locmariaquer more than 4 km distant; an earlier ancestor object, which had clearly been highly valued and decorated then deliberately fragmented and the pieces moved and reused in new locations (Bradley 2002: 36–7).

Once you have permanent dwellings, you can retain (protect) objects that are important to you or your society. In the sixth century BC, En-nigaldi-Nanna, the daughter of Mesopotamian king Nabonidus, had a collection of ancient objects in a building that has been interpreted as a school (Lewis 1992), and is perhaps the earliest museum, a collection used to educate others. Objects were also collected into the temples of ancient Greece and Rome, such as that established in 490 BC in the Temple of Delphi to celebrate the victory of the

Athenians at Marathon. This collection and preservation of artefacts continued at places of worship, resulting in the treasuries of medieval cathedrals, mosques and Shinto shrines. These objects were venerated not for their age, but because they provided physical proof of the people and events mentioned in holy books and texts. These objects were sometimes such powerful symbols that they could have had miraculous powers to heal, cause unusual happenings or sanctify the area around them or things they touched. Objects of the past were also collected by medieval monarchs, and later classical antiquities were acquired and displayed by the princes of the Renaissance to demonstrate the power, prestige, wealth, knowledge and taste of their owner (see Chapter 5). These collections developed into museums by the nineteenth century as they developed research and educative roles, and were eventually seen and used by the public (Lewis 1992). The sites from which these antiquities came survived through neglect, benevolent ownership or a socially perceived ancestral value (see Chapter 8). Legal protection for sites of antiquity only started to develop from the mid-seventeenth century (see Chapter 4).

The present-day philosophical basis for preserving archaeological remains finds its origins in the Age of Enlightenment, which sought evidence from observation of the natural, physical world rather than religious texts, and believed that, through reason, humankind could find knowledge and happiness. Sites and artefacts of antiquity began to be preserved in order that they could be studied and classified, such as mounted butterflies or animals preserved in spirit jars. This is part of the larger process of collecting and preserving evidence from the natural world, through which we have built up a detailed cultural history understanding, a factual past into which new specimens and sites can be fitted. We also preserve sites and artefacts, from earthworks to weapons, so that future generations can study them and reassess, reorganise and rewrite our past. Though numerous other personal and national motives have become involved with collecting, preserving and presenting archaeological remains, the need to create an evidence-based understanding of the past to match our understanding of the biology, physics and chemistry of the natural world remains at the heart of the Enlightenment ideal. Every society has a past, one it creates to help support its belief system and social structure. From the seventeenth century, European society developed one based on physical evidence and reason.

The emergence of the concept of preservation *in situ*

Medieval monarchs such as Henry I and Henry III had menageries, collections of wild and exotic animals from around the world (Blunt 1976), as well as collections of unusual, ancient and artistic objects (Lewis 1992). In the centuries that followed, the menageries became zoos, owned by nations, cities and learned societies. They were retained or re-established as symbols of civic and national pride and to inform the members of the zoological societies who supported them. By the late nineteenth century, they developed the role of entertaining the general public as they became larger and increasingly funded through paid admission (Blunt 1976; Vevers 1976). However, by the late twentieth century, public attitudes had changed, and for many people in Europe and North America capturing and caging wild animals was seen as cruel and oppressive. Through education, film, television and travel, the public has become interested in the lives of animals, their actions and interactions, and their role in the natural world. Indeed, this could be described as the 'purpose' or 'meaning' of wild animals to much of modern society. The removal of wild and exotic animals from their natural habitats is no longer seen as justifiable. Consequently, zoos in the present century have emphasised their educational role and their involvement in breeding programmes to support endangered species. The expectation now is that animals will be preserved in the wild. Even if we cannot see them, we believe it is important that they are there and safeguarded (legal protection and reserves or national parks) for future generations. Present-day nature conservation measures are focused on preserving and even recreating natural habitats such as wetlands, which are widely understood as essential to maintain wildlife.

Ancient archaeological and historic artefacts are following the same public expectations. Antiquities were initially seen as rare and precious curiosities. European archaeologists such as Austin Henry Layard roamed through the ruins of ancient Middle Eastern civilisations like explorers in a jungle, sending back specimens to European museums. In 1848–1850, he sent the winged beast gate portals from the palace at Nimroud back to the British Museum, to be, in his words, the 'wonder stock to the busy crowd of a new world' (Chamberlin 1979: 124). However, again through the mediums of education, film, television and travel, the subject of archaeology is developing. The public has become interested in the people of the ancient world and, through their art and artefacts, their ideas and actions can be identified and understood. The archaeological context from which the objects have come is, like an animal's habitat, frequently the key mechanism to understanding its role or purpose. The efforts of many developing countries to retain and display sites and artefacts from their past, as well as banning the export of archaeological artefacts and controlling foreign excavations in their countries, have greatly enhanced this. Such developments are widely supported by the public in the developed world. Increasingly, antiquities are preserved in their original context, their 'natural habitat'. Mosaics, for example, are now rarely lifted, but are preserved in the shattered remains of the villas in which they were constructed, a setting in which their shape, orientation, patterns and materials have obvious meaning. Preservation of archaeological remains *in situ* is a product of changing social values of the past and its role in national and regional identity. Though it can be detected early in the subject's history, it is only in the last 20 years that preservation *in situ* has become the dominant social presumption for archaeological remains.

Though this subject has deep roots in the concerns of the nineteenth century, and is increasingly emphasised in the charters that have characterised the twentieth century (see Chapter 5), much of the literature that relates to this subject is more recent. The Getty Conservation Institute, an organisation that has recognised preservation *in situ* and reburial as a key approach to archaeological conservation held and published the proceedings of conferences on this subject in Cyprus in 1983 (Stanley Price 1984), Ghent in 1985 (ICCROM 1986), Mexico in 1986 (Hodges 1987), the Mediterranean region in 1995 (de la Torre 1997), Corinth in 2000 (Teutonico and Palumbo 2000) and Santa Fe in 2003 (Burch and Matero 2004). It has additionally supported a range of preservation *in situ* projects such as the Laetoli Trackways (see Chapter 14) and the Mogao Grottoes (see Chapter 10). British and European practitioners held and published a series of Preservation of Archaeological Remains *In Situ* (PARIS) conferences: PARIS 1 in London in 1996 (Corfield *et al.* 1998), PARIS 2 in London in 2001 (Nixon 2004), PARIS 3 in Amsterdam in 2006 (Kars and van Heeringen 2008) and PARIS 4 in Copenhagen in 2011 (Gregory and Matthiesen 2012). These conferences initially started with a focus on waterlogged sites but are developing to cover the full range of archaeological sites and burial environments. The journal that covers this subject, *Conservation and Management of Archaeological Sites* (CMAS), started in 1998. Specific types of sites, such as earthen architecture (adobe) (see Chapter 7), and mosaics have held regular conferences on their subject, which invariably featured papers on preservation *in situ*.

Much of the literature on this subject up to 1999 was summarised in the GCI Project Bibliography: Conservation and Management of Archaeological Sites (www.getty.edu/conservation/resources/archaeology bib.pdf), while Sullivan and Mackay (2012) have recently produced a substantial reader on the conservation and management of archaeological sites.

My perception of the past and preservation

Archaeology was created by a European post-Enlightenment response to the past (Bahn 1996: xi); consequently, in exploring the development of the preservation of archaeological remains, this book will have a considerable European bias. As this book is written by an archaeologist and conservator who has worked exclusively in Britain, it uses many British examples. However, as the subject develops, it meets an increasing range of societies and differing attitudes to the past – generating new approaches to how and why archaeological remains can be revealed, understood and preserved. In this book, the subject has been initially divided into different types of evidence, archaeological, scientific, legal and conservation, whose origins and history are explored (see Chapters 1–5). Subsequently, six different types of building material or burial environments are identified, which is how most archaeologists will focus on the subject, and their decay and damage problems and the efforts that have been made to mitigate such degradation is described (see Chapters 6–11). Finally, a number of mitigation strategies, visitor management, shelters, reburial and some concluding remarks (see Chapters 12–15) are outlined.

Bibliography

Anawak, J. (1994) 'Inuit perceptions of the past', in R. Layton (ed.), *Who Needs the Past? Indigenous Values and Archaeology*, London: Routledge, pp. 45–50.
Bahn, P. (1996) *The Cambridge Illustrated History of Archaeology*, Cambridge: Cambridge University Press.
Baines, J. (1994) 'Ancient Egyptian concepts and uses of the past: 3rd and 2nd millennium BC evidence', in R. Layton (ed.), *Who Needs the Past? Indigenous Values and Archaeology*, London: Routledge, pp. 131–49.
Blunt, W. (1976) *The Ark in the Park*, London: Hamish Hamilton.
Bradley, R. (1998) 'Ruined buildings, ruined stones: enclosures, tombs and natural places, in the Neolithic of South West England', *World Archaeology*, 30(1): 13–22.
Bradley, R. (2002) *The Past in Prehistoric Societies*, London: Routledge.
Burch, R. and Matero, F. (eds) (2004) 'Special issue on site reburial', *Conservation and Management of Archaeological Sites*, 6: 3–4.
Caple, C. (2000) *Conservation Skills: Judgement, Method and Decision Making*, London: Routledge.
Caple, C. (2006) *Objects: Reluctant Witnesses to the Past*, London: Routledge.
Cather, S. (2003) 'Assessing causes and mechanisms of detrimental change to wall paintings', in R. Gowing and A. Heritage (eds), *Conserving the Painted Past: Developing Approaches to Wall Painting Conservation*, London: James & James, pp. 64–74.
Chamberlin, E.R. (1979) *Preserving the Past*, London: Dent & Sons.
Chase, A.K. (1994) 'Perceptions of the past among north Queensland Aboriginal people: the intrusion of Europeans and consequent social change', in R. Layton (ed.), *Who Needs the Past? Indigenous Values and Archaeology*, London: Routledge, pp. 169–79.
Corfield, M., Hinton, P., Nixon, T. *et al*. (1998) *Preserving Archaeological Remains In-Situ, Proceedings of the Conference of 1st–3rd April 1996*, London: Museum of London.
de la Torre, M. (ed.) (1997) *The Conservation of Archaeological Sites in the Mediterranean Region*, Los Angeles, CA: The Getty Conservation Institute.
Emmott, K. (1994) 'A child's perspective on the past: influences of home, media and school', in R. Layton (ed.), *Who Needs the Past? Indigenous Values and Archaeology*, London: Routledge, pp. 21–44.
Gillings, M. and Pollard, J. (1999) 'Non-portable stone artefacts and contexts of meaning: the tale of Grey Wether', *World Archaeology*, 31(2): 179–93.

Gregory, D. and Matthiesen, H. (eds) (2012) 'Special issue: preserving archaeological remains in situ', *Conservation and Management of Archaeological Sites*, 14: 1–4.

Hodges, H. (ed.) (1987) *In-Situ Archaeological Conservation*, Mexico: Instituto Nacional de Antropologia e Historia & J. Paul Getty Trust.

ICCROM (1986) *Preventive Measures During Excavation and Site Protection. Conference Ghent 6–8 November 1985*, Rome: ICCROM.

Kars, H. and van Heeringen, R.M. (2008) *Preserving Archaeological Remains In-Situ? Proceedings of the 3rd Conference 7–9 December 2006, Amsterdam*, Geoarchaeological and Bioarchaeological Studies 10, Amsterdam: Vrije Universiteit Amsterdam.

Layton, R. (1994) 'Introduction: who needs the past?', in R. Layton (ed.), *Who Needs the Past? Indigenous Values and Archaeology*, London: Routledge, pp. 1–18.

Lewis, G. (1992) 'Museums and their precursors: a brief world survey', in J.M.A. Thompson (ed.), *Manual of Curatorship*, 2nd edn, Oxford: Butterworth-Heinemann, pp. 5–21.

Lowenthal, D. (1996) *Possessed by the Past*, New York: The Free Press.

Michalski, S. (1994) 'Sharing responsibility for conservation decisions', in W.E. Krumbein, P. Brimblecombe, D.E. Cosgrove and S. Staniforth (eds), *Durability and Change*, Chichester: Wiley, pp. 241–59.

Ndagala, D.K. and Zengu, N. (1994) 'From the raw to the cooked: Hadzabe perceptions of their past', in R. Layton (ed.), *Who Needs the Past? Indigenous Values and Archaeology*, London: Routledge, pp. 51–6.

Nixon, T. (ed.) (2004) *Preserving Archaeological Remains In-Situ, Proceedings of the 2nd Conference 12–14 September 2001*, London: Museum of London.

Orwell, G. (1949) *Nineteen Eighty Four*, London: Penguin.

Panday, D.P. (1994) 'An 11th century reference to prehistoric times in India', in R. Layton (ed.), *Who Needs the Past? Indigenous Values and Archaeology*, London: Routledge, pp. 57–8.

Parkes, L.N. and Webster, P.V. (1975) 'Merthyrgeryn: a grange of Tintern', *Archaeologia Cambrensis*, 123: 140–54.

Pina-Cabral, J. de (1994) 'The valuation of time among the peasant population of the Alto Minho, Northwestern Portugal', in R. Layton (ed.), *Who Needs the Past? Indigenous Values and Archaeology*, London: Routledge, pp. 59–68.

Rappaport, J. (1994) 'Geography and historical understanding in indigenous Colombia', in R. Layton (ed.), *Who Needs the Past? Indigenous Values and Archaeology*, London: Routledge, pp. 84–94.

Sparkes, B. (1994) 'Classical Greek attitudes to the past', in R. Layton (ed.), *Who Needs the Past? Indigenous Values and Archaeology*, London: Routledge, pp. 119–30.

Stanley Price, N. (ed.) (1984) *Conservation on Archaeological Excavations*, Rome: ICCROM.

Sullivan, S. and Mackay, R. (2012) *Archaeological Sites: Conservation and Management*, Readings in Conservation, Los Angeles, CA: GCI.

Teutonico, J.M. and Palumbo, G. (2000) *Management Planning for Archaeological Sites*, Los Angeles, CA: The Getty Conservation Institute.

Vevers, G. (1976) *London's Zoo*, London: The Bodley Head.

Survival, loss and ideas of preservation

Chapter 1

Survival

A history of the perception of the survival of archaeological remains

Survival and decay

IDEAS OF DECAY AND PRESERVATION are not human constructs; we observe them as phenomena in the natural world, microbes break down wood and textiles, metals (save gold) tarnish and corrode, glass and ceramics shatter when dropped and frost fractures stone; eventually, all things turn to dust. But the world around us is also peppered with artefacts and monuments from the past. Thus, we understand that much of our world decays but fragments survive. Humankind had developed food preservation as one of its earliest technologies; cooking, smoking, salting, drying, pickling, freezing and sealed storage were essential to the survival of hunter-gatherer and early agricultural communities. These techniques presumably developed through experimentation and copying the preservation mechanisms seen in nature, though these varied depending where you were in the world and the nature of local resources available. The Bible, the principal source of intellectual ideas for Europe from the fifth to seventeenth centuries AD, established that decay was the ordained norm and the efforts of God (or man) were needed to preserve what was valuable: 'Man decays like a rotten thing, like a garment that is moth-eaten' (Job 13:27–8); 'God raised him from the dead so that he will never be subject to decay' (Acts 13:33–4). Thus, where preservation occurred without human intervention, it was miraculous and divinely ordained. When the body of Cuthbert was retrieved from beneath the altar of the monastery church of Lindisfarne, it was found to be 'uncorrupted', proof of divine intervention, and as such part of the evidence that led to Cuthbert's beatification.

Our awareness of the survival of archaeological remains is derived from the discovery of ancient remains (through excavation or accidental discovery) and those remains coming to public attention (through visits, letters, books, newspapers, magazines, exhibitions, film, TV and the Internet). Throughout the history of archaeological discoveries, both antiquarians and the general public have been more focused on what archaeological remains tell us about the past than what they tell us about survival. However, it is possible to see that the preserved remains of certain archaeological sites, such as those mentioned in this chapter, have unconsciously formulated our perceptions/expectations about the survival of archaeological remains.

The earliest antiquarians

The frequency of ancient metal ancient artefacts in later graves, or the siting of graves close to ancient remains, indicates that ancient monuments and artefacts had a value to prehistoric, Roman and medieval humans that appears to derive from their age, scarcity or perceived apotropaic traits (White 1988; Greenhalgh 1989; Williams 1998). The realisation that ancient artefacts were often preserved in ancient tombs or in the ground beside ruined walls was widely appreciated and exploited, though often for mercenary rather than altruistic motives. Strabo records excavators ransacking and selling off antiquities from ancient Greek tombs in Corinth when the Romans established a colony on the site (Bahn 1996: 5). However, it was the enthusiasm for the classical past by the princes and aristocrats of Renaissance Italy that led to excavations to uncover and retain ancient Roman remains in Rome and other cities in the fifteenth and sixteenth centuries.

In the seventeenth and eighteenth centuries, Europe's elite received a classical education, learning to read Latin and Greek. Fed a diet of Homer and Pliny, it is hardly surprising that the gentlemen of England, princes of Germany and counts of France sought to view and retain the aesthetic treasures of the classical world. Fuelled by the publications of early collectors of marble statues and inscriptions, such as the Earl of Arundel's *Marmora Arundeliana* (1628), throughout the eighteenth century, young men from England and France toured Europe, in particular Italy and Greece, to see the beauties of classical civilisation that still remained. Frequently, they bought statues and other classical relics to grace their country houses or chateaux. These antiquities particularly complemented the rash of new country houses being built in the Palladian style throughout Britain in the eighteenth century. This grand tour created and maintained a market for antiquities that fuelled archaeological excavation in the Mediterranean lands.

The most influential of these excavations for classical antiquities were those of Herculaneum (1738 on) and Pompeii (1748 on). Pompeii in particular produced an endless stream of antiquities for the King of Naples' private museum, and the numerous visitors, especially the important ones, were shown the site and the recovered antiquities. Edited extracts from the journal *Pompeianarum Antiquitatum Historia* recording activities on the site of Pompeii by Giuseppe Fiorelli (Cooley and Cooley 2002) (see Chapter 1.1) reveal that visits to the site by aristocracy and royalty, or their representatives, led to written and oral accounts that circulated throughout the aristocratic and intellectual elite of mid-eighteenth-century Europe. The emphasis on collecting classical art meant that the wall paintings were often cut off the walls of the Pompeian villas for display in the royal collections. This could, to later eyes, appear to be vandalism, but as many of those wall paintings that were left *in situ*, such as those in the Pompeii amphitheatre, were lost due to frost, this removal to a museum was in reality a crude but effective conservation strategy. Equally damaging to the antiquities exposed at the surface was the effect of visitors. In Fiorelli's journal, there are several examples of soldiers and other visitors damaging the ruins with acts of mindless vandalism and taking 'souvenirs'. Uniquely, the hot volcanic ash covered organic objects, which did not ignite, but carbonised from lack of oxygen. This enabled the excavators to identify the fruits ready to be eaten by the first-century AD inhabitants of Pompeii and discover a library of carbonised papyri in a house in Herculaneum, now known as the Villa of Papyri. The continued emphasis on recovering art objects meant that although buildings of the first-century AD were being cleared and seen for the first time, the journal entries simply record: 'nothing of note' was revealed.

The visit and personal letter could not meet the increasing European-wide interest in antiquities. The demand was sufficient to make it financially viable to publish books and enable antiquarian societies to publish journals. Starting in the late eighteenth century, the number and range of these publications increased; through the nineteenth century, they became the primary means of information transmission.

Antiquarians to archaeologists; private collections to public museums

Napoleon's military expedition to Egypt in 1798 brought French scholars to recover and study ancient Egyptian remains. Following Nelson's victory at the Battle of the Nile, many of the recovered Egyptian antiquities were deposited and displayed in the British Museum. The arrival of these antiquities and the drawings and written accounts of antiquarians such as Baron Vivant Denon's *A Journey Through Upper and Lower Egypt* (1802), as well as early work by Claudius Rich and the success of his book *Memoir on the Ruins of Babylon* (1815), stimulated British public interest in, and awareness of, the remains of ancient civilisations present in the Middle East. Subsequently, excavations in Mesopotamia, such as those by Botta between 1842 and 1848 at Ninevah and Khorsbad, and by Layard between 1845 and 1851 at Nimrud, Ninevah and Ashur, yielded treasures that were brought back to Europe and displayed in Paris, London and Berlin. Layard's book *Ninevah and its Remains* was published in 1849 and became a bestseller, which further promoted interest in archaeology and the preserved remains of Mesopotamia. The enthusiastic excavation of numerous ancient cities, temples, etc. in ancient Egypt, Syria and Mesopotamia from the 1850s to the 1930s produced a stream of finds and inscriptions to fill the museums of Europe. The sheer volume of this material and the lack of later disturbance were key factors in the survival of such large numbers of artefacts of stone, metal, glass and ceramics.

The fact that artefacts were often preserved in the ground associated with ruined walls or earth mounds drew the earliest antiquarians of Britain and north-western Europe to trench through prehistoric mounds, to unearth the fragments of pots, stone and bronze artefacts, and gold jewellery. In Britain, antiquarians such as William Stukely, William Cunnington, Thomas Bateman and Canon William Greenwell could indulge their Victorian obsessions of collecting and classification using these finds. These men both competed and cooperated as they sought to build up their collections, which were both a status symbol and, given the lack of public collections, the only way for these self-funded amateurs to accurately research the past. It was through their collections and their publications, such as Greenwell and Rolleston's *British Barrows* (1877), that these men made sense of their obsession as well as the past. They defined cultures in terms of the objects – pottery styles or bronze or stone weapon types, naming them after sites where those distinctive object forms had been found. Lacking the dates provided by classical literature, it was through stratigraphy and the correspondences between object type and monument form that they established the chronological sequence of these prehistoric cultures. Stereotypes of early antiquarians as grave robbers reveals a lack of awareness of the fragmentary state of knowledge and of the cultural, social and academic norms in which they worked (Schnapp 2008); the early antiquarian collectors were intent on answering the questions 'who' and 'when'. After the 1880s, the improved archaeological excavation techniques of Flinders Petrie and General Pitt Rivers meant that questions such as 'how' and 'why' also started to be asked.

Proud of their collections, early antiquarians frequently sought to display them; recognition was often important, though this was usually sought from their peers rather than the public. They also sought to preserve their collections, bequeathing them to longer-lived institutions (cities, universities or nations), so creating museums. The British Museum was established in 1759 for the collections of Sir Hans Sloane, and rapidly built up its holding by adding the collections of antiquarians such as Canon William Greenwell. The British Museum was initially only available by appointment to approved people and visitor numbers were small. However, ideas of public improvement, fused with higher levels of literacy, education and the increased interest in the artefacts recovered from Egyptian, classical and Mesopotamian civilisations (Layard's bestselling *Ninevah and its Remains*), created a demand for public access to museums. By the late nineteenth century, the British Museum and an increasing number of museums around Europe were opening to the general public. The level of public interest in the remains of the past is reflected by sites discovered during building work in London. 33,000 people queued over three days to see the Roman mosaic, the Bucklersbury Pavement, when it was unearthed in 1869, while in 1954, 30,000 people saw the Roman Temple of Mithras in just nine days when it too was unearthed (Siddell 2012). Fed by objects from the latest excavations, the public flocked to see treasures that had survived for millennia, leading 1.65 million visitors to see the Tutankhamen exhibition during its nine-month stay in 1972 at the British Museum. Through the growth of museums by the late nineteenth century, awareness of the survival of archaeological artefacts had been greatly enhanced; the real, rare and precious ancient objects were just inches away on the other side of the glass.

Waterlogged deposits

Since the 1840s, extensive organic remains, even food and clothing, had been found by European antiquarians in the remains of prehistoric villages preserved in the mud of alpine lakes (Munro 1890). Results of excavations published by Keller in 1878, *The Lake Dwellings of Switzerland*, brought information about these sites to wider attention. However, the archaeologists, antiquarians, museums and collectors who sponsored investigations of these sites principally sought and collected metal and stone tools and ceramics, since they could use them to define 'periods' and 'cultures' of the past. Although archaeologists drew, measured and described the organic material objects of wood, basketry and textiles that survived, only blackened fragments appeared in museums around Europe since they lacked the means to preserve them 'as found'. They were also of limited interest to collectors since they were not valued by other collectors and they did not help date or culturally code the site. Building their collections and determining the chronology of the past remained the focus of antiquarians.

The reasons for the survival of organic materials and the uncorroded condition of much of the metalwork was clearly understood by the more perceptive antiquarians, such as Munro, who identified the presence of minerals, such as vivianite, in the deposits, which were only formed in reducing (anoxic) conditions (i.e. devoid of oxygen) (Munro 1890: 38, 319). 'The peat has, in some instances, actually engulfed entire villages with the accumulated debris of their industrial equipments, thus hermetically sealing up everything in one of the best antidotes to natural decay' (Munro 1890: 110).

In Britain, Augustus Lane Fox (Pitt-Rivers), who excavated in the waterlogged deposits of London in 1866, noted that wooden structures and antiquities were preserved in these deposits (Munro 1890: 460–4). Similarly, wooden finds had been regularly unearthed in Scottish and Irish crannogs excavated during the nineteenth century. It was, however, the quality of evidence unearthed in Bullied and Gray's excavation of Glastonbury and later Meare Lake Villages from 1878 onwards, excavations that were visited by most of the influential

English antiquarians of the period, that made the archaeological community and many beyond aware both that waterlogged deposits were present throughout Britain and of the informative nature of the archaeological remains that survived. However, the problems of long-term preservation of these remains continued until the development and spread of conservation techniques and facilities occurred in the 1970s. The discovery of waterlogged sites throughout the twentieth century, such as the defended Iron Age settlement of Biskupin in Poland (containing over 100 houses and thousands of domestic artefacts), the Roman fort and vicus at Vindolanda in Northumberland, England (writing tablets) and Ozette, Washington State, USA (a complete Native American Makah Indian village filled with artefacts buried 'Pompeii-like' beneath a mud slide, buried in AD 1560 or 1750 – depending on cited source) have continued to remind people of the potential quality of the preserved information present on waterlogged sites.

Desiccation and fossilisation

The survival of archaeological sites in ancient Egypt and Mesopotamia were associated in the public imagination with sandy desert. The discovery of intact buildings with roof timbers, basketry, food remains, etc. at Chaco Canyon in 1852 and later at Mesa Verde by Richard Wetherill in 1888, as well as the survival of silk road sites in the Takla Makan desert in Turkmenistan, from which Aurel Stein acquired early Chinese and Buddhist documents on birch bark, silk, paper and wood in the period 1900–1920, led to an appreciation that dry conditions preserved traces of civilisations around the world. More recently, recognition of the extensive collections of manuscripts, made in the thirteenth to seventeenth centuries from around the Islamic world, preserved in the libraries of Timbuktu, have demonstrated the beneficial nature of these conditions to survival.

In burial environments, such as the lime-rich soils or limestone caves, the process of fossilisation occurs; in archaeological remains such as bone, the organic component (collagen) decays away slowly while minerals such as calcium carbonate are deposited from groundwater within the archaeological remains, creating a hard, lithified material. This process has enabled bone fragments to survive in cave sites such as Kent's Cave and Paviland. In different burial environments, minerals such as silica or even iron minerals fossilise ancient remains. This process has been crucial in preserving bones for millions of years, especially early fossil hominid bones from around the world, especially in the East African Rift Valley, areas such as Koobi Fora (Turkana Boy), Olduvai Gorge and Hadar in Ethiopia (Lucy).

Physical protection

The discovery of drawings by prehistoric man in the caves at Altamira in the 1860s emphasised not only how human and artistic prehistoric humans were, but how protective cave environments could be, a point reinforced by later Palaeolithic cave art discoveries at Pech Merle (1922) and Lascaux (1940). The survival of these images demonstrated that it was physical protection from the action of wind, weather, frost and, above all, animals and human beings that preserved the fragile fragments of the past. Where this protection was synergistically enhanced by desiccation, waterlogging or sealed (oxygen-free) environments, the levels of preservation were even greater. Examples include the disassembled boat of Khufu in a chamber beside the Great Pyramid (excavated 1954) and the Dead Sea Scrolls – parchment scrolls in jars preserved dry in caves in the cliffs above the Essene settlement of Qumran close to the Dead Sea (discovered 1947, 1952–1955); the dry/desiccated conditions inside the physical protection of the rock enabled organic materials such as wood and parchment to survive.

Burial chambers had long been sought by antiquarians and archaeologists for the rich grave goods deposited within them. The physical protection of a chamber often resulted in the preservation of complete and unbroken vessels, while the soil or a mound over the tomb could prevent animal and human disturbance and sometimes created sealed (oxygen-free) or waterlogged (also oxygen-free) conditions. Between 1871 and 1875, excavation of the Bronze Age burial mound of Borum Eshøj in Jutland yielded three intact oak coffins containing bodies with surviving flesh and hair. Their woolen clothing was well preserved, as were their processions such as a wooden scabbard, bark box and horn combs. Excavations of the mounds at Tune in 1867 and Gokstad in 1880 produced perfectly preserved Viking ships beneath mounds composed of the local 'blue' boulder clay; this contrasted with the earlier excavated mound of sand and gravel at Borre in 1850–1852, where little trace of the boat had remained. The later find of the ship and burial at Oseberg (1904), under a similar blue clay mound, revealed a hugely rich burial with carved sleighs, cart, bucket, clothing, metalwork and tapestries. In more recent times (1974), chambers forming part of the grave complex of the first emperor of China Qin Shi Huangdi were uncovered near Xi'an in Shaanxi Province. They revealed an army of life-size fully painted terracotta statues of warriors. Subsequently, other collapsed chambers have yielded similar statues of courtiers and entertainers, providing a detailed picture of the people present in the Chinese court of the third century BC. Initially protected from physical harm by the chamber, if the chamber is made of wood, subsequent collapse usually leaves the objects requiring extensive conservation before the remains can be displayed. Such displays, however, reinforce the idea that rare, fragile archaeological remains are preserved in buried chambers.

The protective nature of chambers cut into, or formed of stone, and the quality of the protected remains was firmly fixed in the public imagination with the discovery of the tomb of Tutankhamun (see Chapter 1.2), remarkable for the nature of materials, the completeness and opulence of the objects that survived. This site also demonstrated that as late as 1922, archaeology was still primarily supported by wealthy European aristocracy and industrialists, or learned societies from America and Europe. However, newspapers were now the prime means of informing the public who had an appetite for spectacular, new sites filled with ancient treasures. Given the popularity of photographs and film, reports of these discoveries increasingly needed to be supported by images. Though Tutankhamun's tomb was opened on 29 November 1922 and reported in *The Times* newspaper on 30 November (see Chapter 1.2), the photographic images of inside the tomb had to be physically transported from Egypt and so were not published in *The Times* until 30 January 1923 (see Figure 1.2.1). As the damaged fragments of archaeological remains can often be uninspiring and difficult to understand, drawn images, especially reconstructions of the site as it would have looked in antiquity, were often used. This is seen in the work of Alan Sorrell (Perry and Johnson 2014), and were an important element of newspaper reports of archaeological sites, especially the *London Illustrated News*, a significant source of information on archaeological sites during the late nineteenth and early twentieth centuries (Bacon 1976).

Bog bodies

From the *Sphagnum* peat bogs of Denmark, Ireland, Scotland and northern England, bodies, or parts of bodies, had been retrieved for centuries (Glob 1969; Turner and Scaife 1995). Whenever recovered, bog bodies would decay, and thus were normally quickly given Christian burial in a local churchyard. Eighteenth- and nineteenth-century antiquarians had little interest in bog bodies as they were not accompanied by pottery or bronze weapons so they could not be fitted into the emerging culture history of the past. However, as shown in P.V. Glob's book *The Bog People* (see Chapter 1.3), by the late nineteenth century archaeologists such as Worsae were examining the archaeological evidence objectively and not simply fitting the archaeology to the existing historical narrative. By the 1950s, the world had changed. When Tollund man was unearthed, archaeologists were among the first people to be contacted. Science had advanced to the point that forensic information could be recovered about the body, yielding information about his life, his death and from botanical analysis of his stomach content the nature of his last meal. It was also now possible to attempt to preserve the human remains. In the case of Tollund man, just the head was preserved, but in 1952 the whole body of Graubelle Man was preserved. These conserved bodies could now go on public display and with photographic images of the faces of these Iron Age men seen on the world's media, a large number of people had the experience of being face-to-face with someone who lived over 2,000 years ago (see Figure 1.3.1). The development of radiocarbon dating during the 1960s and the expanded ideas of period and culture of the past now allow bog bodies and other isolated finds to be tied into a much fuller picture of ancient cultures.

Frozen

Though the ability of freezing to preserve food and other perishables was well understood by the eighteenth century, this was not thought of in archaeological terms until the twentieth century. The first frozen archaeological remains to come to international attention were found in 1924 in the frozen Pazyryk (Scythian) tombs of the fourth to fifth centuries BC, in the Altai Mountains of the Russian steppes. Tombs were excavated in 1929 and 1947–1949 (Rudenko 1970), and further examples were unearthed on the Ukok Plateau in 1990–1995 (Bogucki 1996). The frozen conditions in the tombs had been quickly established after the burial since the tomb is in the permafrost layer. Consequently, all organic material, textiles (including complete Persian carpets), wood, leather and metal items were preserved frozen and undecayed. Frozen bodies of Inca sacrifices had been discovered high in the Andes in 1954 and 1964, but it was the frozen body in 1995, the 'Ampato Maiden', with its coverage in the *National Geographic* magazine, that drew worldwide attention to this frozen survival (Schreiber 1996). However, it was in 1991 that a body, together with clothing, copper axe, bow and arrows, and other accoutrements, revealed by a retreating glacier in the Alps, drew worldwide attention to frozen archaeological remains. Recovered and studied at Innsbruck University, the corpse (Ötzi the Iceman) proved to be a late Neolithic man (3365–2940 BC) (Spindler 1994). Other notable discoveries have included the frozen bodies of Thule culture people from Qilakitsoq in Greenland, discovered in 1977, the dramatic corpses preserved through being 'freeze-dried', protected under a rock overhang. By the late twentieth century, for newspapers and magazines such as *National Geographic*, dramatic colour photographic images had become such an important element of the story and such a powerful tool for showing the survival of archaeological remains that the report of the discovery now waited for the images (Hart Hansen et al. 1985).

Expectations

Awareness that ancient sites and artefacts could be preserved *in situ* came from high-profile examples that permeated people's consciousness, from Pompeii to Ötzi the Iceman. In the eighteenth century, it was the crowned heads of Europe, members of their court and their ambassadors who were aware of the latest archaeological discoveries. From the late eighteenth century, an educated elite, taking the newly established archaeological journals, would have been aware, but it was only in the late nineteenth and early twentieth centuries that newspapers brought such discoveries to widespread public awareness. Eventually, from the late twentieth century, television and the Internet became the primary means of communicating image-based news.

The survival of such archaeological remains has raised expectations, initially among an educated elite and later among the general public, that archaeological remains would be in that 'as first seen' condition. Where objects were removed to museums and where resources were made available for conservation work, it has proved possible to preserve almost all archaeological remains. In practice, this has largely been from the mid-twentieth century to the present. However, from the early records of Pompeii to the present, it has often proved much more difficult, frequently impossible, for archaeological remains to survive *in situ*, without damage. The power of the image and mass media that can associate finds with a site has arguably created an unrealistic expectation that all archaeological remains recovered can be preserved on site for public view – an unsustainable expectation, as described in the Preface.

Bibliography

Bacon, E. (1976) *The Great Archaeologists*, London: Book Club Associates.
Bahn, P. (1996) *The Cambridge Illustrated History of Archaeology*, Cambridge: Cambridge University Press.
Bogucki, P. (1996) 'Pazyryk and the Ukok Princess', in P. Bahn (ed.), *Tombs, Graves and Mummies*, London: Weidenfeld & Nicolson, pp. 146–51.
Cooley, A.E. and Cooley, M.G.L. (2002) *Pompeii: A Sourcebook*, Abingdon: Routledge.
Glob, P.V. (1969) *The Bog People*, London: Faber & Faber.
Greenhalgh, M. (1989) *The Survival of Roman Antiquities in the Middle Ages*, London: Duckworth.
Hart Hansen, J.P., Meldgaard, J. and Nordqvist, J. (1985) 'The mummies of Qilakitsoq', *National Geographic*, 167(2): 191–207.
Munro, R. (1890) *The Lake Dwellings of Europe*, London: Cassell.
Perry, S. and Johnson, M. (2014) 'Reconstruction art and disciplinary practice: Alan Sorrell and the negotiation of the archaeological record', *Antiquaries Journal*, 94: 323–52.
Rudenko, S.I. (1970) *Frozen Tombs of Siberia: The Pazyryk Burials of Iron Age Horsemen* (trans. M.W. Thompson), London: Dent.
Schnapp, A. (2008) 'Between antiquarians and archaeologists: continuities and ruptures', in T. Murray and C. Evans (eds), *Histories of Archaeology*, Oxford: Oxford University Press, pp. 392–405.
Schreiber, K. (1996) 'Inka mountain sacrifices', in P. Bahn (ed.), *Tombs, Graves and Mummies*, London: Weidenfeld & Nicolson, pp. 160–3.
Siddell, J. (2012) 'PARIS London: One Hundred and Fifty Years of Site Preservation', *Conservation and Managements of Archaeological Sites*, 14(1–4): 372–83.
Spindler, K. (1994) *The Man in the Ice*, London: Phoenix.
The Times (1922) 'An Egyptian treasure', 30 November, p. 19.
Turner, R.C. and Scaife, R.G. (1995) *Bog Bodies: New Discoveries and New Perspectives*, London: British Museum Press.
White, R. (1988) *Roman and Celtic Objects from Anglo-Saxon Graves: A Catalogue and an Interpretation of Their Use*, BAR Brit. Ser. 161, Oxford: Archaeopress.
Williams, H. (1998) 'Monuments and the past in early Anglo-Saxon England', *World Archaeology*, 30(1): 90–108.

Chapter 1.1

Excavation reports

Alison E. Cooley and M.G.L. Cooley

Source: Cooley, A.E. and Cooley, M.G.L (2002) *Pompeii: A Sourcebook*, Abingdon: Routledge.

THIS CHAPTER CONTAINS TRANSLATED excerpts from contemporary excavation daybooks. *Pompeianarum Antiquitatum Historia (PAH: History of Pompeian Antiquities)* is a three-volume work (1860–1864) that published transcriptions of the manuscript notes kept by the excavators from 1748 onwards (**J1–58**). It was compiled by Giuseppe Fiorelli while he was a political prisoner in 1849. He is better known for his introduction of a more scientific approach to digging at Pompeii after he had become inspector of the excavations in 1860. His system of numbering every building with three numbers – region, *insula* and doorway – remains the foundation of how buildings at Pompeii are still identified today. This supplemented the previous custom of giving names to houses, some of which would accumulate more than a dozen names over the years, which could result in confusion. One of the most memorable features of visits to the site today is seeing plaster casts of Vesuvius' victims, a technique that Fiorelli adopted extensively.

[. . .]

J2: 6 April 1748

In the excavation which we have begun at Torre Annunziata, the first thing which we have discovered is a painting 11 ft long and 4½ ft tall, which contains two large festoons of fruit and flowers; a very large and well-executed head of a man; a helmet; an owl; various birds and other things. I think that it is one of the better pieces of painting found up until now. And after the sculptor had come here this morning to see it, I gave instructions for it to be cut out on Tuesday. His Majesty was informed of this in the afternoon and he ordered a stretcher to be brought to take it, as the Officer has arranged, since this is the most convenient way of avoiding damaging it.

[. . .]

J6: 8 June 1765

What is believed to be a small temple on the estate of Montemurro at Civita has been completely uncovered. This has already been mentioned in the report of 4 May this year. It is part of a larger building, which is included in the hall, already mentioned elsewhere. This second small structure is still entirely decorated with stuccowork on all sides {a description follows . . .}. This building remained uncovered, and inside nothing was found except for a small staircase, which led underground, whose function still could not be discovered because of the mofette (fumarole).

To the sides of the entrance to this building, outside, there are two small altars of soft stone, and in front of these is another larger one, on which there are still ash and small pieces of burnt bones of sacrificial victims. Near to this temple, in the soil of the courtyard, is seen a square hole full of a large quantity of black ash, or of the remains of burnt fruit. At the bottom of this pit was found an iron nail, an Egyptian idol lacking its legs and broken into various pieces, and from its belt downwards decorated with many hieroglyphs . . . Among the remains of burnt fruit which were seen in the aforementioned pit, the following were extracted from them: various pieces of figs, many pine seeds with their shells and pieces of pine-bark, some pieces of walnut, some hazelnut-shells, and two dates. All of the things described above, as well as the remains of the little idol, and the pictures that have been found so far, reveal that this temple was dedicated to some Egyptian deity.

[. . .]

A royal visit (J24)

The year 1748 heralded the start of official excavations at Pompeii (J1–5), under the authority of the Bourbon King Charles VII of Naples. On the death of his half-brother Ferdinand VI in 1759, he handed over this realm to his son, so that he could return to Spain as King Charles III.

The following account illustrates how the young King Ferdinand IV (about 18 years old at this time) had to be prodded into showing much interest in the excavations, which his father had eagerly initiated. The Hapsburg Emperor Joseph II (his brother-in-law) was much more aware of the kudos which could be derived from canny exploitation of the excavations, and played an important role in trying to convince his younger relation of this, even by appealing to Ferdinand IV's obsession with hunting.

Access to the site by visitors was severely restricted, so it is no surprise to find the antiquity-mad English Ambassador to Naples (from 1764 to 1800), Sir William Hamilton, taking the opportunity to join in this inspection. Marquis Bernardo Tanucci, formerly a professor in law at Pisa University, was an influential figure in the Naples court: he founded the Royal Herculaneum Academy in 1755 and acted as Regent for Ferdinand IV.

Entries like this one, recording visits to the excavations by royal dignitaries, are often accorded more space in the excavation diary than actual episodes of archaeological digging!

J24: 7 April 1769

Yesterday at about the 20th hour, His Majesty the King {Ferdinand IV} came to observe the excavation of Pompeii, together with the Queen {Maria Carolina} and Emperor

Joseph II. Besides their entourage were Count Kaunitz, the English Ambassador {Sir William Hamilton}, and that ambassador's antiquary Mr. D'Ancrevil. When the King saw the antiquary entering the site, he told him to carry out his duties, and did me (F. La Vega) the honour of saying that I should follow the King himself; whereas the aforementioned antiquary was there for the express purpose, to explain things to the Emperor en route. Their Majesties first entered the Barracks; they wanted to give all parts of it special attention, as well as the material with which it had been overwhelmed. The Emperor asked how this excavation had had its beginnings, which I answered, and I also added, that it had not been carried out in earlier times because a forest had stood in this place, which had been cut down about 28 years ago. The Sovereign examined this building with pleasure and disapproved of the fact that the earth in the middle of the courtyard had not also been cleared. From this place, their Majesties proceeded to the west to a house, where they admired the vaults still intact, the stairs and plaster. In this site they found work proceeding in four rooms and they observed the digging with pleasure. Through the previous instruction of His Excellency Marquis Tanucci, the number of workers had been increased for some days, in anticipation of the visit. In these rooms the earth remained at a height of only 2 feet, and a good part of this had been cleared, where it was less probable that one could find something. After a short time a bronze vase began to be excavated, and so from one thing to another there was uncovered in the 2 rooms all that which is noted down here in order by material, with the exception of some small things which had already been found. {List of finds includes 12 pieces of silver plaque with relief figures; bronze objects – basin, vases, coins, door-hinges, brooches; items in iron, lead, glass, bone, and pottery.}

And the following pieces of plaster had been found in the same rooms shortly before ... {description follows}. The Emperor was surprised, and even wondered whether all these things had been placed there artificially in order to flatter their good fortune; but he came to realize the truth as I pointed out the position of the finds, the type of earth that contained them, and when I reported what had been done. He then congratulated the King on such a good day's hunting, which was in effect to apologize; and I added that such a pleasure had been reserved for him alone of all Sovereigns. The English Ambassador, Sir William Hamilton, with his passion for antiquity, did not fail in the midst of this to make known the value of the discoveries with the most detailed observations. The King displayed the greatest pleasure in this encounter, and was so enthused that, besides not wanting to move a step from the place where excavations were being carried out, he actually said two or three times to La Vega to let him know when places were ready to be uncovered, because he wanted to be present when discoveries were being made; and he would be very happy for a day to be set aside for seeing discoveries being made. The Queen was also very joyful at these finds and impatient to see them soon. In the other two rooms nothing was found except for a skeleton, and two coins of the type already described. Afterwards their Majesties went to see some rooms, which had been exposed, where an intact skeleton was still preserved. From this place they proceeded to the Theatre ... The Emperor asked La Vega how many workmen were employed in this task, and having been informed that there were 20, asked the King how he allowed such a task to proceed so slowly. When he said that little by little it would all be done, the Emperor added that this was a job for employing 3,000 men, and that he would have thought that nothing like this existed in Europe, Asia, Africa, and America, and that this created a special honour for the

Kingdom; and he asked the King who was looking after these antiquities; he replied that it was the Marquis Tanucci. Her Majesty expressed disapproval of this, and joined in urging the King to devote some energy to such a task. From this place they continued, after having observed the signs that an Odeion had been found, to a whole private house, to see the Temple of Isis, which brought forth praise from the Emperor; and in the meanwhile he did not cease to encourage the King in the most vigorous manner to value these things most highly. In the temple, La Vega showed to their Majesties the drawings, which he had made, towards which the King graciously condescended to show favour. The Emperor particularly enjoyed seeing what remained as an impression of the wooden door, preserved as an imprint on the ground. After having examined all these buildings, which formed a unit as it were, they proceeded to the town gate, where the Emperor was displeased not to see any workmen. La Vega showed to the Sovereigns the plan, which fixes the location of all the buildings excavated in Pompeii, and what had been done at other times, to make them understand the situation and the shape. The Emperor asked what there was of those buildings which they had not seen, and was assured that they had been covered over again (as perhaps Ancrevil had told him, as he was coming together with the rest of the Emperor's retinue). And he asked the King why he had allowed this. His Majesty replied to this that it had been done in the time of his Esteemed Father {Charles VII}; and La Vega added that it had been done 20 years ago when there was no sign that the site could be a town; but being assured about 6 years ago that it was Pompeii from an inscription found near the site where they were, they had left buildings uncovered, no measures having been taken before this other than for creating the Museum. Their Majesties after this departed at around the 22nd hour and a quarter.

[. . .]

J27: 15 April 1809

Last week between 12 and 15 soldiers came to Pompeii, of those who are stationed at Torre Annunziata. They did not want to be escorted by anyone, and among their fooling about and drunkenness they knocked over some pilasters at the entrance to the Theatre, and they tore out and seized two bronze letters of the inscription, which remains on the paving of the Odeion, an R and an O. The veterans assigned to this part of the site did not believe in worrying themselves about them; the curators were afraid of their sabres.

[. . .]

J33: 10 August 1816

While working in excavating the Forum with 2 carts and 7 workmen, nothing to report happened last week.

J39: 5 October 1816

In the excavations, last week, nothing to report. The usual 8 workmen, 2 carts and 5 men were employed for taking off the useless pieces and putting back those pieces which belong to various sites, and a craftsman for restoring the pavings. Curators were employed in cleaning the cleared areas.

[. . .]

J41: 7 June 1817

Last week we worked in the usual places indicated many times, with 73 workmen and 4 carts, without anything noteworthy happening. On day 3 of the current month, contrary to Aquila's contractor and the supervisors, we set about searching the small cellar which remains beneath the upper rubble of the Forum, in accordance with instructions of Your Most Noble Lordship. After various searches we finally found a most beautiful bronze statue, broken into 3 pieces, and lacking the right foot, an arm, and a hand. It depicts a young nude male, 5{1/2} feet tall, with a small piece of drapery, which he holds hanging down over his arms, and which covers his loins; this is being kept safe by supervisor Imparato.

Chapter 1.2

An Egyptian treasure

Great find at Thebes: Lord Carnarvon's long quest from our Cairo correspondent

The Times

Source: *The Times*, (1922) 'An Egyptian treasure', 30 November, p. 19.

VALLEY OF THE KINGS (by runner to Luxor), Nov. 29.

THIS AFTERNOON LORD CARNARVON and Mr. Howard Carter revealed to a large company what promises to be the most sensational Egyptological discovery of the century.

The find consists of, among other objects, the funeral paraphernalia of the Egyptian King Tutankhamen, one of the famous heretic kings of the Eighteenth Dynasty, who reverted to Amen worship. Little is known of the later kings, including Tutankhamen, and the discovery should add invaluably to our knowledge of this period and of the great city of Tel-el-Amarna, which was founded in the fifteenth century BC by Amenhotep IV., the first of the heretic kings.

The remarkable discovery announced to-day is the reward of patience, perseverance, and perspicacity. For nearly sixteen years Lord Carnarvon, with the assistance of Mr. Howard Carter, has been carrying out excavations on that part of the site of the ancient Thebes situated on the west bank of the Nile at Luxor. From time to time interesting historical data were unearthed, but nothing of a really striking character was found, although Deir el Bahari and Drah Abul Neggar were diligently explored. Seven years ago work was started in the Valley of the Kings, after other excavators had abandoned the Valley. Here, again, the excavators had little success. At times they almost despaired of finding anything, yet they did not lose heart.

The search was continued systematically, and at last the dogged perseverance of Mr. Carter, his thoroughness, above all his *flair*, were rewarded by the discovery, where the Royal Necropolis of the Theban Empire was situated, directly below the tomb of Rameses VI., of what looked like a *cache*. Mr. Carter covered up the site, and telegraphed to Lord Carnarvon, who at once came out from England.

By this time news of the find had got about. The whole of Luxor, where everyone down to the smallest urchin is an antiquity hunter, was agog. Great was the speculation in regard to the contents of the chamber. Would one of the missing kings be found inside? Was it the tomb of a queen or a high member of the Court of ancient Egypt (for the region is the burial place not only of many celebrated early Egyptian kings, but also of their wives and high officials)? Little, however, did Lord Carnarvon and Mr. Carter suspect the wonderful nature of the contents of the chambers—for there are more than one—as they stood outside. The sealed outer door was carefully opened; then a way was cleared down some sixteen steps along a passage of about 25ft. The door to the chambers was found to be sealed as the outer door had been, and, as on the outer door, there were traces of reclosing. With difficulty an entrance was effected, and when at last the excavators managed to squeeze their way in an extraordinary sight met their eyes, one that they could scarcely credit.

The treasure within

First they saw three magnificent State couches, all gilt, with exquisite carving and heads of Typhon, Hathor, and lion. On these rested beds, beautifully carved, gilt, inlaid with ivory and semi-precious stones and also innumerable boxes of exquisite workmanship. One of these boxes was inlaid with ebony and ivory, with gilt inscriptions; another contained emblems of the underworld; on a third, which contained Royal robes, handsomely embroidered, precious stones, and golden sandals, were beautifully painted hunting scenes.

There was a stool of ebony inlaid with ivory, with the most delicately carved duck's feet: also a child's stool of fine workmanship. Beneath one of the couches was the State Throne of King Tutankhamen, probably one of the most beautiful objects of art ever discovered. There was also a heavily gilt chair, with portraits of the King and Queen, the whole encrusted with turquoise, cornelian, lapis, and other semi-precious stones.

Two life-sized bituminized statues of the King, with gold work holding a golden stick and mace, faced each other the handsome features, the feet, and the hands delicately carved with eyes of glass and head-dress richly studded with gems.

There were also four chariots, the sides of which were encrusted with semi-precious stories and rich gold decoration. These were dismantled, with a charioteer's apron of leopard's skin hanging over the seat.

Other noteworthy objects were Royal sticks, one of ebony with the head of an Asiatic as a handle in gold, another of the handsomest filigree work; also a stool for a throne with Asiatics carved on it, denoting that the King had placed his foot on the neck of the Asiatic prisoners taken in war. There were some quaint bronze-gilt musical instruments and a robing dummy for Royal wigs and robes.

There were also some exquisite alabaster vases with very intricate and unknown design, all of one piece, and some handsome blue Egyptian faience, and enormous quantities of provisions for the dead, comprising trussed duck, haunches of venison, etc., all packed in boxes according to the custom of the time. There were some remarkable wreaths, still looking evergreen, and one of the boxes contained rolls of *papyri*, which are expected to render a mass of information.

A further chamber revealed an indescribable state of confusion. Here furniture, gold beds, exquisite boxes, and alabaster vases similar to those found in the first chamber were piled high one on top of the other, so closely packed that it has been impossible to get inside yet.

Numbers of these treasures are in a fairly good state of preservation, but others are in a somewhat precarious condition. The greatest care is being taken in handling them, however, and there is every hope that under Mr. Carter's capable direction most of them will be preserved.

On the occasion of the official, opening of the chambers, Lord Carnarvon's daughter, Lady Evelyn Herbert, entertained a large party at luncheon at the Valley of Kings, including Lady Allenby and Abdel Aziz Bey Yehia, Governor of Kena Province, who has given invaluable assistance in safeguarding the treasures.

From the manner in which its contents were disposed it is evident that this *cache* has not remained untouched since it was buried. There seems no doubt that this wonderful collection of objects formed part of the funeral paraphernalia of King Tutankhamen, whose *cartouche* is seen everywhere, in both its forms, and that they were moved from the tombs where they were originally placed, and in order to preserve them from thieves were transferred for safety to these chambers.

The sealing and blocking of the doors and passages which have so far been opened suggest that metal robbers had attacked these chambers and that inspectors of Rameses IX. had reason to enter to reclose them. From the famous Abbott and other *papyri* it is known that these Royal tombs suffered at the hands of robbers. But, whatever the chambers may have contained originally, their contents today are sufficient cause for

Figure 1.2.1 Tutankahmen's tomb, just after the tomb was opened, showing the disordered grave goods piled one on another in the ante-chamber. This picture was published with others in *The Times* on January 30, 1923, the first images to be seen of the tomb, two months after it was opened.

Source: © Heritage Image Partnership Ltd/Alamy

sensation in the Egyptological world. They considerably increase our knowledge of Ancient Egyptian history and art, and experts who were present at today's opening consider that the discovery will probably rank as the most important of modern times.

[. . .]

What adds interest to this discovery is that there is still yet a third sealed chamber, which, significantly, the two figures of the king discovered are guarding, and which may possibly turn out to be the actual tomb of King Tutankhamen, with, members of the heretic's family buried with him. Until the vast amount of material in the other chambers has been completely removed it will be impossible to ascertain the contents of this third chamber.

Chapter 1.3

The bog people
Iron Age man preserved

P.V. Glob

Source: Glob, P.V. (1969) *The Bog People,* London: Faber. Translated from the Danish by Rupert Bruce-Mitford.

Bog people in Denmark

[. . .]

IN 1797 IN UNDELEV FEN (south-west Jutland) (the body) of a man of short stature, but strong and broad, (was discovered) during peat-cutting. This man was exceptionally well preserved. He had curly red hair and long fingernails, and was covered with two skin capes—an inner, with hair on the inside, and an outer, with the hair to the outside. On one foot was a cowhide shoe sewn at the back with leather strips, instead of thread, and having holes by means of which it could be strapped to the foot. Alongside the body lay three hazel rods. The find naturally aroused much attention and it was conjectured that the man must be a Tartar, or a Gipsy, or perhaps one of the ancient Cimbri. In the hot summer's day, however, the body began to disintegrate, affected by the sun's rays. Such a peculiar smell arose from it that it had to be covered up again. The local authorities had some planks knocked up into a coffin and the next day the dead man and the three hazel rods were buried in Holbøl churchyard.

As the years passed many bog finds went the same way. When the peat-cutters and local inhabitants had gazed at the dead person and marvelled at the 'well-nigh miraculous power of iron-containing bog water to preserve not only all manner of objects of antiquity but even parts of the human body', so well-known today, the corpse was carted to the nearest churchyard and buried there. Only on one occasion, in 1886 at Rønbjerg, in West Jutland, where three discoveries took place in the course of one year, was it arranged that the objects accompanying the body—the sheath for a knife, a cap and a sheepskin coat—should be sent to the National Museum, before the re-burial was carried out.

On two occasions the dead person was dug up again after re-interment. This happened in the case of a find made at Corselitze, on Falster, in 1843. The find itself is outstanding as the only bog burial to yield ornaments—a bronze pin and seven glass beads, which date it to about AD 300. It had already been re-interred in the churchyard when the Crown Prince Frederick came to the spot and personally had it dug up again and sent to the National Museum. Crown Prince Frederick, who became King Frederick VII in 1848, had shown an interest in archaeological discoveries from his earliest youth, and had himself undertaken the excavation of ancient burial-mounds. He, more than anyone else, helped to arouse the wide interest in Danish antiquities which has persisted to this day.

[...]

In the last century the most important discoveries of Iron Age people were of two women from bogs in Jutland. The one which caused the greatest stir was the woman found in Juthe Fen, in central Jutland, on the ancient estate of Haraldskjaer, south of Denmark's oldest royal seat, Jelling, in East Jutland. She was said by a certain Professor and several eminent scholars to be none other than the Norse Queen Gunhild, the cruel consort of King Erik Bloodaxe. Historical sources describe Gunhild as a beauty, refer to her love of pomp, and characterize her as shrewd, witty, clever, merry and eloquent, friendly and open-handed to everyone who would do what she wanted, but cruel, false, malevolent and cunning if anyone crossed her. She seems also to have been dissolute and domineering to a high degree. Of the death of Gunhild the Queen Mother, the sources tell us that she was enticed from Norway to Denmark by King Harald on the understanding that he wanted to marry her; but when she arrived, with a stately retinue, she was met by a party of slaves and house-carls whom he had sent against her. After being grossly maltreated she was drowned and sunk in miserable fashion in a terrifyingly deep bog. This would have been about a thousand years ago. The stories of Queen Gunhild's fate, however, are fantasy rather than historical fact.

The learned gentleman who identified the woman in Juthe Fen as Queen Gunhild had accepted the historical records uncritically. He had also assumed that the happenings described must have taken place at one of the ancient Danish royal seats, either Lejre on Zealand, or Jelling on Jutland. Jelling was preferred because the body had turned up near it, only six miles south of the royal site. In due course it was said that King Harald had been the founder of the Haraldskjaer estate. The woman from Juthe Fen was clad in rich garments, but perhaps the decisive point in favour of the identification was that the bog where the discovery had taken place, or at any rate the area around, had earlier borne the name of 'Gunnelsmose', that is 'Gunhild's bog'.

All these arguments were vigorously contested by a young student, J. J. A. Worsaae, destined to become a very famous scholar and the founder of modern Danish archaeology as a science. Worsaae maintained that it was not historically established that Queen Gunhild had been murdered by Harald Blue-tooth (King Harald), by being drowned in a bog. He identified the discovery as one of a particular group of Iron Age bog finds.

[...]

The Tollund man

An early spring day—8 May, 1950. Evening was gathering over Tollund Fen in Bjaeldskov Dal. [...] He lay on his damp bed as though asleep, resting on his side, the head inclined a little forward, arms and legs bent. His face wore a gentle expression—

the eyes lightly closed, the lips softly pursed, as if in silent prayer. It was as though the dead man's soul had for a moment returned from another world, through the gate in the western sky.

The dead man who lay there was two thousand years old. A few hours earlier he had been brought out from the sheltering peat by two men who, [. . .] were occupied in cutting peat for the tile stove and kitchen range.

As they worked, they suddenly saw in the peat-layer a face so fresh that they could only suppose they had stumbled on a recent murder. They notified the police at Silkeborg, who came at once to the site. The police, however, also invited representatives of the local Museum to accompany them, for well-preserved remains of Iron Age men were not unknown in Central Jutland. At the site the true context of the discovery was soon evident. A telephone call was put through straightaway to Aarhus University, where at that moment I was lecturing to a group of students on archaeological problems. Some hours later—that same evening—I stood with my students, bent over the startling discovery, face to face with an Iron Age man who, two millennia before, had been deposited in the bog as a sacrifice to the powers that ruled men's destinies.

The man lay on his right side in a natural attitude of sleep. The head was to the west, with the face turned to the south; the legs were to the east. He lay fifty yards out

Figure 1.3.1 The Tollund man, who died 2,000 years ago.
Source: © Granger, NYC./Alamy.

from firm ground, not far above the clean sand floor of the bog, and had been covered by eight or nine feet of peat, now dug away.

On his head he wore a pointed skin cap fastened securely under the chin by a hide thong. Round his waist there was a smooth hide belt. Otherwise he was naked. His hair was cropped so short as to be almost entirely hidden by his cap. He was clean-shaven, but there was very short stubble on the chin and upper lip.

The air of gentle tranquillity about the man was shattered when a small lump of peat was removed from beside his head. This disclosed a rope, made of two leather thongs twisted together, which encircled the neck in a noose drawn tight into the throat and then coiled like a snake over the shoulder and down across the back. After this discovery the wrinkled forehead and set mouth seemed to take on a look of affliction.

[. . .]

The Tollund man's head was especially well preserved, the best-preserved human head, in fact, to have survived from antiquity in any part of the world. Majesty and gentleness still stamp his features as they did when he was alive. His cropped hair, up to two inches long, was not dressed in any way. His eyebrows were partially preserved, and the very short stubble already mentioned covered his upper lip, chin and cheeks. It is the dead man's lightly-closed eyes and half-closed lips, however, that give this unique face its distinctive expression. [. . .]

As to the condition of the body, Dr Thorvildsen writes that most of its upper part was still covered with skin. The left part of the chest and the left shoulder, however, were slightly decomposed, the epidermis being absent from considerable areas. A succession of sharp cuts could be seen down the back. These had been caused by peat-cutting. The left hip-bone protruded from the skin and the stomach lay in folds. The sexual organs were in a good state of preservation.

The naked body was clad only in cap and girdle, with a skin rope fastened tightly around the neck. The pointed cap was made of eight pieces of leather sewn together, the hair side inwards, and was fastened to the head by two thin leather laces, fixed at the temples with knots and tied off in a bow, which was tucked in under the cap at the right temple. The belt lay low on the hips, in folds at the back but tight across the stomach. Made of thin hairless skin, it had one end drawn through a slot in the other and wider end and was secured with a slip-knot on the left side.

The plaited skin rope round the dead man's neck was knotted at one end to form an eyelet through which the other end was drawn, forming a noose which could be tightened from the back. It had left clear impressions in the skin under the chin and at the sides of the neck, but no mark at the nape of the neck, where the knot rested. The rope was skilfully plaited from two strips of hide about half an inch wide, and measured five feet from the curve of the eyelet to the opposite extremity. It had, however, been cut at this point and must originally have been longer.

The Tollund man most probably met his death by means of this rope. The vertebrae of the neck did not appear to be damaged, but the doctors and medico-legal experts who took part in the examination judged, nevertheless, from the way the rope was placed that the Tollund man had not been strangled, but hanged. An attempt was made to decide the point by radiography, carried out by a senior medical officer at Bispebjerg Hospital, Dr Baastrup. The result was indeterminate, because of the decalcified state of the vertebrae. A radiograph of the skull was taken at the same time. This showed clearly that the head was undamaged. The wisdom teeth had developed, indicating that the man must have been appreciably over twenty years old. The brain was intact but shrunken. An autopsy showed that the inner organs such as the heart, lungs and liver were very well preserved. So was the alimentary canal, which was removed by the palaeo-botanist, Dr Hans Helbaek, with the object of determining the nature of the dead man's last meal. This was still contained in the stomach and in the larger and smaller intestines which, though somewhat flattened by the weight of the overlying peat, were otherwise intact.

[. . .]

In collaboration with the anatomists, Drs Bjøvulf Vimtrop and Kay Schaurup, a point of great interest was established. Investigation showed that although the contents of the stomach consisted of vegetable remains of a gruel prepared from barley, linseed, 'gold-of-pleasure' (*camlina sativa*) and knotweed, with many different sorts of weeds that grow on ploughed land, it could not have contained any meat at the time of death, since recognizable traces of bone, sinew or muscular tissue would certainly have remained. It was further established, from the degree of digestion of the remains of the meal in the alimentary canal, that the Tollund man had lived for between twelve and twenty-four hours after eating his last meal.

In addition to the varieties of cultivated grain, it is worth noticing the unusual quantity of knotweed (*pale persicaria*) in the stomach. It must have been gathered deliberately and other plants represented may have been gathered along with it incidentally; for example, blue and green bristle-grass, dock, black bindweed, camomile and gold-of-pleasure. The gruel made from this mixture of cultivated and wild grains was no doubt the normal diet in the early Iron Age, around the time of Christ, when the Tollund man was alive. Fish and meat were also eaten. Rich furnishings of bowls and dishes, with ribs of ox and sheep, and carving knives lying ready, are known in the graves of the time. But meat was certainly not the daily diet as it was in the time of the Stone Age hunters. Milk and cheese, on the other hand, probably were, as the forms of the pottery vessels would seem to indicate.

[. . .]

When the exhaustive study of the Tollund man had been concluded, a decision was taken on preserving him for the future. Unfortunately it was only thought practicable to undertake the conservation of the splendid head. This was first of all placed for six months in a solution of water to which formalin and acetic acid had been added. The solution was then changed for one of 30 per cent alcohol, which was later replaced by one of 99 per cent alcohol to which toluol (toluene) had been added. Finally, it was put into pure toluol progressively mixed with paraffin, for which wax heated to different temperatures was later substituted. After more than a year's treatment the head was sent to the Silkeborg Museum in Central Jutland, a bare six miles from the spot where it had come to light in Tollund fen. It can be seen there, alongside other discoveries of the Iron Age.

In the process of conservation the proportions of the head and the features of the face were happily completely retained, but the head as a whole had shrunk by about 12 per cent. In spite of this it has emerged as the best preserved head of an early man to have come down to us so far. The majestic head astonishes the beholder and rivets his attention. Standing in front of the glass case in which it is displayed, he finds himself face to face with an Iron Age man. Dark in hue, the head is still full of life and more beautiful than the best portraits by the world's greatest artists, since it is the man himself we see.

Chapter 2

Threats and losses
The spur to preservation

As DESCRIBED IN THE INTRODUCTION, the past is composed of physical remains (sites and artefacts) and the oral narrative (later written), including traditions and associated beliefs, which explain the remains. The memory of this oral tradition is perhaps the most vulnerable, easily lost or altered aspect of the past (Pina-Cabral 1994: 60), though it is routinely recreated to benefit the present (Lowenthal 1996). In this book, however, we focus on the damage and decay of the physical remains, how and why this occurs and if it can be mitigated.

Loss of sites: anthropogenic causes

One of the earliest written descriptions of loss or damage to an archaeological site was by William Stukeley, the eighteenth-century English antiquarian, who observed the prehistoric stones of Avebury being set upon by a local man, Tom Robinson, and his accomplices. They dug pits beneath the recumbent stones, lit fires of straw in the pits heating the stones, shattered them by throwing on cold water, then collected and sold the stone fragments to local builders as building stone. Stukeley was unable to stop this irreparable act of destruction; he could only record what remained (Piggott 1985). In this case, as so many others, the archaeological remains are destroyed because they have such little value to their present owners or the local community. The value of the standing stones was less than that of building stone. However, Stukely notes that for earlier generations the stones still had a value, and in the medieval period men dug large holes into which the upright stones were toppled, so burying them. This may have cleared the land for growing more crops, but given the level of effort this required it seems likely that they still respected the power of the stones, burying them as they would their own relatives (Piggott 1985: 94). The monumental stone had changed from a highly valued component of a ritual site in prehistory to one of respect in the medieval period to a value below that of building stone by the eighteenth century; though it also clearly varied from individual (Tom Robinson) to individual (William Stukeley).

Changes in present-day realities can alter the value of archaeological remains very quickly. This is exemplified by the sculptures from the Hittite city of Carchemish. They had been retrieved during the long-running British excavation on the site, but had to be left when the site was abandoned in 1914 when the First World War broke out. After the war, the site straddled the new Turkish–Syrian border and a Turkish officer had many of the stones broken up and used to strengthen a railway embankment. Subsequently, some pieces were looted and at least one was recovered to the British Museum (Bahn 1996: 160).

Conflict

As the bomb-damaged Coventry Cathedral and the Neus Museum in Berlin vividly remind us, wars demonstrate that one set of values, dealing with the immediate social and political control of the nation, outweigh those of the preservation of the heritage. Religious and civil conflicts, such as those currently (2014) raging in Syria, Iraq and Afghanistan damage and destroy cultural property through:

- *Collateral damage*: archaeological sites unintentionally damaged by weapons, especially ordnance and fire, as fighting rages around them. The castle at Falaise and the monastery at Monte Casino were heavily damaged in the Second World War by artillery and bombing that was intended to kill the soldiers taking cover within the ruins. Similarly, the building of bases and fortifications after the war in Iraq damaged the ruins of ancient Babylon (Kila 2012: 119).
- *Looting*: the breakdown of law and order leaves individuals physically and socially unconstrained. Their motives for removing valuable archaeological remains can range from the extremes of starvation (Hollowell 2006) to simple personal gain. Immediate needs or desires overcome any perception of the social value of antiquity. Sites of antiquity in Iraq were pockmarked with the holes of looters following the Iraq War (Kila 2012).
- *Iconoclasm*: the deliberate destruction of sites or artefacts either by the state or individuals. This ranges from the vandalism as a form of disrespect (Kila 2012: Figure 4) through the defacing of the figurative carvings in the Chapter House of Ely Cathedral by the believers of the English Reformation, to the complete obliteration of an individual, people or places from history, such as the eradication of any mention of the pharaoh Akhenaten by later generations (Quirke and Spencer 1992: 82) or the Nazi destruction of large parts of Warsaw; an act of total domination. It can extend to the suppression of national or group identity through capture or obliteration of the symbols of nationhood or cultural uniqueness, as for example practised by the conquistadors in Central and South America. It has been used by invading armies throughout human history to make conquered peoples easier to control.

The looting and damage to cultural heritage during the Second World War led to the creation of military agencies as MFAA (Monuments, Fine Arts and Archives), 'the Monuments Men' (Edsel 2009), who sought to mitigate the effects of the conflict on cultural heritage. It also established the concept of Cultural Property Protection (CPP). This found expression in the 1954 (Hague) *Convention for the Protection of Cultural Property in the Event of Armed Conflict* and its 1954 and 1999 protocols (UNESCO 1954), which was intended to signify the value that ancient remains and cultural heritage now have for the majority of people on the planet, though this convention has yet (2014) to be ratified by a number of countries, including the UK. The 1954 Hague Convention specified a Blue Shield symbol to denote cultural property subject to international protection during armed conflict; this was designed to receive the recognition and respect of the Red Cross. The benefit of swift and knowledgeable action while areas are still in military control to minimise the impact of war on cultural heritage, established in 1944/5 by MFAA, has led a number of armies to have appropriately trained individuals and units (Kila 2012; Kila and Zeidler 2013). Post-war rebuilding also invariably leads to a loss of archaeological remains; the need for functional new buildings and infrastructure can sweep away the surviving historic buildings (see Chapter 4), which also acts to remove the shattered remains of a painful conflict.

The deliberate demolition of the Babri Masjid mosque at Ayodhya in northern India on 6 December 1992 by a mob of Hindu fundamentalists, since they believed that it stood on the site of a Hindu temple (Layton and Thomas 2001), or the blowing up of the Bamiyan Buddhas in March 2001 by Muslim fundamentalists, demonstrates that religious or any other beliefs, held beyond the point of tolerating the symbols and beliefs of others, will lead to the destruction of human heritage.

Excavation

Archaeological remains become extremely vulnerable when they are excavated and removed from the physically and chemically supportive burial environment with which they have achieved near equilibrium. The remains are desiccated, shattered, delaminated or dissolved by the weather and damaged by the incursion of humans, animals and vegetation. Cleland (1932), a US professor of geology, upon visiting sites in the Mediterranean in the 1930s, bitterly decried the exposed and degraded stonework and pleaded for reburial:

> When Delphi was excavated the archaeologists did a splendid piece of work, judged by their standards. They uncovered every column, every inscription, every carving and foundation stone that nature had so carefully preserved. Everything, in fact, is exposed and the destructive work of the weather is at a maximum. The interesting notices in small Greek characters which tell of the freeing of the slaves, are in walls where they must inevitably rapidly become illegible.
> At Carthage not only are the mosaics exposed to the sun, but some of them are the stamping grounds for herds of goats.
> (Cleland 1932: 169–70)

The archaeological process itself raises questions of loss and the relative value of physical remains and information. Botta, the French consul, who excavated in both Nineveh and the palace of Sargon II at Khorsabad, described the problem of balancing information against loss. Many Assyrian palaces had been burnt down, calcining the finely carved gypsum reliefs that decorated the palaces and temples. When excavated, they were revealed for a few hours or days before they crumbled (the drying action of the sun and salt crystallisation damage) (Bahn 1996). Recognising that they would have to be reburied to be preserved, the excavator was frequently left with the choice of expose and destroy or leave unexcavated and thus unknown but preserved. This conundrum remains to the present day for many excavators who often lack the resources to preserve what they uncover. Again and again, the question is which is the greater value: knowledge of the sites and artefacts, or the presence of the remains?

Many of the organisations who accept responsibility for sites find that as a result of poor project planning, the increased costs of conservation and maintenance, increased workloads, reduced budgets or declining interest (value) in a site, they are trapped between initial aspirations and the realities of decaying sites, and are unable to effectively bridge the gap. Solutions have included reburial (see Chapter 14), reducing the amount of excavation or reducing expectations about what the site should be like when it becomes a visitable monument (see Chapter 6.3). Even when conservation is undertaken, work that is inexpertly done (does not properly identify the causes of decay, prevent or manage them) or uses inappropriate materials can lead to further problems: 'today's solution may be tomorrow's damage' (Sullivan and Mackay 2012: 3). Extensive restoration works have often led to regret in later years over the loss of original fabric, William Morris commenting in 1877 of the restoration of historic building in the nineteenth century, 'We think that those last fifty years of knowledge and attention have done more for their destruction than all the foregoing centuries of revolution, violence and contempt' (Miele 1996b: 52–3). The reactions to such losses have, however, developed the subject of conservation.

Loss of sites: natural events

Natural forces fall into three groups:

- Sudden violent geological, climatic and hydrological activities such as earthquakes, volcanoes, tidal waves, winds, flooding and landslip. These occur frequently in specific regions of tectonic activity but are sudden and unpredictable, damaging to sites and objects alike. Pliny the Younger witnessed and described the destruction of Herculaneum and Pompeii through earthquakes and volcanic eruption: 'The buildings all round were shaking and though we were in the open, it was confined space and our fear of falling buildings became great and definite' (Walsh 2006: 148).
- Periodic events, often climate-driven, such as coastal erosion, rain and water erosion, frost damage and desiccation, all damage sites and artefacts.
- Gradual biological, physical and chemical activity effects, such as plant growth, fungal and insect infestation, salt crystallisation, and light, temperature and humidity fluctuation. Ancient Roman and Greek authors were well aware of the potential damage that natural agencies such as light, damp and insects could do to antiquities (Strong 1973; Caple 2011: 3).

In all cases, these natural forces appear to be considered inevitable. Though there is risk associated living near geological faults and volcanoes or even on the coast, people continue to inhabit these locations to the present day, considering the benefits of such locations outweigh the risks. In the case of some threats, the risk can be mitigated through human intervention constructing shelters, improving drainage and erecting protective barriers. However, this protection only lasts as long as the threat is appreciated and protective measures maintained. Most human agencies fail after a few years or decades, often due to loss of memory and inaccurate reappraisal of the risk, but these threats are ever-present.

The IPCC (Intergovernmental Panel on Climate Change) established under the auspices of the UN has, through it reports in 1990, 1995, 2001, 2007 and 2014, shown that the world's climate is changing, warming due in large part to greenhouse gas emissions, resulting in melting of the polar ice caps, rising seas levels and, with increased energy in the system, greater degree of variation in the world's climate. Over the next few decades, it predicts this will result in an increase in the number and scale of severe events throughout the world.

The UKCIP (UK Climate Impacts Programme) have created projections such as UKCIP02 about what this could mean in terms of changes in the weather of the different regions of the UK, data that were assessed for their impact on heritage in 2005 (Cassar 2005) and informed the current advice given by English Heritage (2008). Envisaged effects for UK heritage include:

- Increased rainfall during winters will result in greater levels of soil erosion on sites.
- Increased summer temperatures will lead to increased drying out of wetlands, with the associated threat to waterlogged archaeological sites, and cracking and shrinkage of clay soils, leading to subsidence and changes in the burial environment.
- Greater variation in rainfall levels, leading to increasingly fluctuating water levels and greater disturbance of 'the metastable equilibrium between artefacts and soil' (Cassar and Pender 2005).
- Vegetation change resulting from increased summer temperatures may lead to changes in farming practice and disturbance to sites, and some vegetation dieback on dry sites, leading to increased erosion.
- Increased threat to sites as flood defences for towns are constructed and sites will be lost to the sea through 'managed coastal realignment', which utilises salt marshes rather than hard coastal defences.
- Increased temperature and water cycling on stone surfaces will increase decay rates.
- Increased risk of storm activity resulting in windthrow damage.

The speed and extent of climate change vary depending where you are in the world. At present, the greatest threat is the warming summer temperature in the polar and tundra regions, leading to loss of permafrost for longer periods and thawing to increasing depth every summer. This is leading to the loss of organic artefacts and ecofacts in archaeological sites in Greenland, Alaska and Siberia, such as the 4,000-year-old kitchen midden at Qajaa in Greenland (Hollesen *et al.* 2012).

Loss of sites: holistic approach

From the earliest antiquarian accounts, there has been mention of the loss of ancient remains by specific natural or human agencies. Evidence to a joint parliamentary committee in 1912, by the Royal Commission on Ancient and Historic Monuments (established in 1908), reported that 20 per cent of all monuments in Hertfordshire and South Buckinghamshire were damaged, including 50 per cent of the earthworks (Champion 1996: 45). In 1969, the Walsh Committee on the management of field monuments revealed figures showing extensive destruction of field monuments in rural England; of 640 monuments in Wiltshire, 250 had been severely damaged or destroyed, and 150 had suffered lesser damage (Champion 1996: 52). The first holistic appraisal of the causes for the damage or loss of archaeological remains *in situ* was that by Coles (1987) at the In Situ *Archaeological Conservation Conference* in Mexico in 1986 (Hodges 1987: 5). Coles grouped man-made (anthropogenic) losses by economic activity and natural agencies were grouped by water or land erosion (see Chapter 2.1). A number of natural events such as earthquakes and hurricanes did not appear on this list because major geological and climatic events in the UK, the principal source of the data used by Coles, are small-scale and have minimal impact on archaeological sites and artefacts.

Later authors have tended to record Coles' 'Tourism and Urbanism' category as two separate activities and consider these separately (Burnham 1991; Rees 1994).

- *Development*: construction of houses, factories, roads and other infrastructure, it is actually difficult to distinguish if they are for tourism or the indigenous population.
- *Visitors*: damage done largely to monuments by the presence of people, erosion (see Chapter 8), vandalism and changing cave environments (see Chapter 10).

We invariably undervalue threat and overvalue loss. To try to gain a more objective assessment of site loss in 1995, English Heritage commissioned Tim Darvill and his colleagues to undertake a 'Monuments at Risk Survey' (MARS) for England (Darvill and Fulton 1998). This study undertook a detailed objective assessment of the loss and damage to ancient monuments in England between 1945 and 1995, using the aerial photography record and site visits to give precise figures on the complete loss and partial damage of archaeological monuments (see Chapter 2.2). The losses were again looked at holistically, grouped in a similar manner to Coles (see Figures 2.2.1 and 2.2.2), though with more detailed breakdown of man-made activities. This work moved on from simply looking at threats in a holistic manner, to evidence-based quantification of the destruction activity.

Building on Coles (1987) and Darvill and Fulton (1998), a more comprehensive classification for damage to archaeological sites can be proposed (see Table 2.0.1) that takes account of natural threats seen elsewhere in the wider world.

In many cases, damage is synergistic, one form of damage induces and promotes other forms of damage greatly exacerbating the overall effect; farming leads to heightened erosion exposing masonry remains that are damaged by frost action.

A similar study to MARS for wetlands, MAREW Monuments at Risk in England's Wetlands (van de Noort *et al.* 2002), drew together evidence from the Wetland Studies commissioned by English Heritage – Somerset Levels, Fenland Project, North West Wetland Survey and the Humber Wetlands Project. The results from these surveys and the Site and Monuments Record for England showed that there had been substantial loss and damage to wetland monuments in the latter half of the twentieth century, a minimum of 10,450 sites lost in the last 50 years, 78 per cent of the total resource. Since many sites are buried beneath peat on prehistoric land surfaces or within the wetland soils, especially in urban contexts in cities such as London, Hull and York (not included in MAREW), far higher numbers of sites remain undetected. The MAREW figures are thus a minimum. It remains impossible to know the extent of loss of wetlands prior to the soil and aerial surveys of the 1940s and 1950s. Clearly, there would also have been substantial losses in the eighteenth-, nineteenth- and early twentieth-century from land improvement schemes. Only when a site is unearthed can it be protected through legislative process (scheduling) and this often does not maintain the water levels necessary to preserve the waterlogged wood and other organic materials (see Chapter 11). Similar figures probably apply for many European countries.

In the Mediterranean region, Palumbo (2002) and the ICOMOS document 'Heritage at Risk' (ICOMOS 2000) highlighted a number of threats:

- Development that often surrounded and isolated ancient remains, so decontextualising them.
- Bulldozing monuments for infrastructure projects to promote development in rural areas or to service expanding urban areas.
- Pollution from cars and other vehicles, fertilisers and sewage.

- Tourism both in terms of developing visitor facilities and the effects of vandalism. Their potential economic benefit causes authorities to develop sites and infrastructure damaging remains as they do so and over-restoring the remains. Johnson (2001) suggested the ancient monuments of the Vietnamese city of Hue were at risk of more damage from tourism development and restoration than they had received during the Tet offensive of the war in Vietnam.
- Social unrest, which can lead to collateral damage from conflict and deliberate targeting of iconic sites (e.g. bridge at Mostar as well as religious buildings, mosques and synagogues).
- Looting of sites.
- Neglect after sites have been excavated and they are abandoned. Underfunded or uninformed conservation/restoration work.

Recognising the benefits of sharing problems and potential solutions and the need to identify global threats or areas of the world suffering particular problems (e.g. as a result of natural disasters), ICOMOS commenced a series of annual reports (starting in 1999) to highlight heritage at risk. Individual threatened heritage places, monuments and sites or wider issues are identified by ICOMOS National Committees, International Scientific Committees and the ICOMOS worldwide professional network and submitted to the report.

Surveys of site loss and damage such as MARS and MAREW identify and quantify the total loss or damage occurring between surveys, often expressing it in terms of an annual loss rate. This:

- Enables them to use a wide range of surveys and other data over different time intervals to give a single comparable figure.
- Objectively establishes the activities that represent the greatest threat to the existing ancient monument population and which types of site are most at risk. This enables legislation to be framed effectively to protect the types of site most at risk or the greatest threats to be identified and mitigated. Limited resources can be targeted to provide the greatest level of protection.
- Expresses loss in a figure understandable to the public and in a form likely to draw attention to this problem.

However, surveys are hardly ever repeated. This is essential if we are to establish preservation measures are working or the nature of the threat is changing. Annual loss rates are also a useful way of quantifying the loss of artefacts (see Chapter 2.3).

Loss of artefacts

It is possible to argue that archaeological information is unevenly distributed through any artefact.

- *Loss of surface*: the colour and decoration of an object is often contained in the outer painted or gilded surface layer. These paper-thin coatings are the first to degrade in burial environments, and thus an awareness of the original appearance is quickly lost. The marble statues of the Greeks and Romans were partially painted, as were Roman alters and the internal surfaces of many buildings, including churches. Almost all have now been stripped back to stone through the effects of decay or subsequent cleaning and restoration processes.

- *Loss of exterior*: the outer couple of millimetres of an artefact's surface contain key elements of the decoration, inlaid, punched or incised into the surface. Some objects such as coins have images and lettering stamped into their outer layer, crucial information allowing their identification and dating; the loss of this information eliminates their use to the archaeologist.
- *Loss of substance*: the bulk of the artefact that forms its shape usually degrades slowly. The loss of this material is seen most usually in iron or copper alloy artefacts or bones in acid soils. Eventually, it reaches the point where the original form is no longer discernible. Only the fact that there was once an artefact is apparent.
- *Loss of the artefact*: the object is entirely lost so no trace of its presence remains.

This means that far more of the detailed archaeological information is lost in the initial periods of decay than later in the process. The differential rates of survival of artefacts are dependent on the materials of which they are made and the soil/burial conditions in which they are buried. These are highly variable. In 'normal' aerobic topsoil burial conditions, organic materials (wood, leather, textiles, etc.) will decay within the initial decades of burial due to microbial action (Caple 2001); metals corrode steadily in most (but not all) cases; stone, ceramics and glass decay even more slowly (see Table 3.0.1). Since the majority of artefacts in our lives are made of organic materials (just look around you), in terms of the total number of artefacts, the majority are lost within the first few years of burial, making it increasingly difficult to gain an accurate picture of the past the longer the site has been buried. Rare survivals such as Ötzi the Iceman, in frozen conditions that preserved the huge range of organic garments and equipment he possessed (Spindler 1994), emphasise the poverty of the archaeological record from normal soil environment.

It is not just the artefact itself that is important, but the relationship to the archaeological context in which it occurs. The metal-detected object, or artefact ploughed to the surface, may still be recognisable, but ripped from its burial context it has lost much of its archaeological value and information. Thus, artefacts are lost through:

- damage and destruction of sites where objects remain buried;
- damage and decay within the burial environment; and
- removal from site without relationship to the surrounding archaeology (e.g. metal-detected or looted).

The only attempt to establish the loss of artefacts through partial and complete site destruction and decay *in situ* was the work of Rimmer and Caple (2008), who calculated loss rates of iron and copper alloy artefacts from ancient monuments (see Chapter 2.3). They determined that in England between 1945 and 1995, around 14 million objects per year were being lost through damage and destruction of sites, as compared to only 5 million from the corrosion of artefacts on those sites.

These figures do not include metal-detecting, though Darvill and Fulton (1998: 139) suggested only 1 per cent of the monuments showed evidence of metal-detecting. Though metal-detecting could be seen to be a loss of archaeological artefacts and information, and is banned in countries such as Ireland, it is legal in the UK, with the landowner's permission and excepting scheduled ancient monuments, and has produced archaeologically useful results through its voluntary reporting scheme, the Portable Antiquities Scheme (http://finds.org.uk/) (see Chapter 9).

Table 2.0.1 Causes of loss or damage to archaeological sites (ancient monuments)

	Damage type	Includes
Anthropogenic		
	Construction and development	House, industry, road and infrastructure construction.
	Quarrying and mineral extraction	Gravel, sand, clay, coal, stone and metal ore extraction.
	Farming	Ploughing out or exposing monuments to other damage, roots of crops, spreading fertiliser, terracing or flattening for ease of exploitation.
	Forestry	Planting of trees and associated drainage creation, felling and clearing activities, root damage, windthrow.
	Drainage/flooding	Drainage of wetlands or the wetting (irrigation) of previously dry soils, flooding.
	Pollution	Spread of people and their waste products, either industrial or domestic, acid rain.
	Visitors and vandalism	Erosion of sites from high visitation rates (unconscious damage), construction of paths and other facilities. Deliberate despoliation for gain (metal detecting, looting), wilful acts (e.g. graffiti)
	Military and warfare	Accidental damage from vehicles, collateral damage from explosives and constructing defences or deliberate destruction to damage and treatments and looting.
	Archaeology and conservation	Unconserved and exposed archaeological remains, ineffective conservation, poor conservation materials, excessive cleaning or restoration.
Natural		
	Flora and fauna	Natural vegetation growth – root damage and soil disturbance from tree collapse. Burrowing animals, trampling by larger animals.
	Erosion	Soil and the sites it contains removed through the actions of wind, water and downslope movement.
	Weather/climate (water)	Soluble salts, damp, rotting of wood.
	Weather/climate (temperature)	LOW – Frost damage. HIGH – Desiccation of earthen architecture, killing off vegetation and subsequent soil loss, wildfires.
	Seismic and volcanic activity	Cracking and collapse of buildings, raising or submerging land, changes in drainage patterns, covering in volcanic materials (lava, ash), tsunami, pyroclastic flows.

Loss of ecofacts

In a similar manner to artefacts, the ability of ecofacts (bones, wood, seeds, other plant material, pollen, snails shells, phytoliths and insect remains) to tell us about the human past (archaeological potential) depends on the level of external surface detail that survives. The rate of loss of this organic material varies depending on the soil type and burial conditions. The lack of surviving material in all but waterlogged, frozen or desiccated sites (Caple 2001) means that the loss of ecofactual information, apart from bone, is normally 100 per cent for aerobic sites over 50 years old. The experimental work at Overton Down and Wareham Bog (see Chapter 3.3) has provided some data for the speed of such loss. No agreed quantified scale for the extent of decay has been established, though scales based on the loss of external visible detail for insect and seed remains have been published (Murphy and Wiltshire 1994; Kenward and Large 1998). Kenward and Hall (2004), exploring the sequence of events from initial burial to the establishment of the anoxic waterlogged conditions, have emphasised the need for anoxic waterlogged conditions to form quickly if labile and delicate organic matter is to survive. The subsequent drying out and oxygenation of these waterlogged anoxic deposits leads to loss of information, and the acidification of soil leads to the loss of bone (Millard 2001). This desiccation and oxygenation process has been observed in recent years in cities such as York, where the upper metre of the waterlogged black deposits are oxidising, turning red and losing their environmental evidence (Kenward and Hall 2000) (see Chapter 2.4). This process is occurring to all the deposits identified as drying out in the MAREW report (see Chapter 11).

Benefits from loss

The threat of loss is a galvanising force; it often triggers efforts to protect and retain that which still remains; this leads to the establishment of laws and organisations (see Chapter 4). In the case of Britain, the 'restoration' of thousands of medieval churches between 1840 and the 1870s gave rise to concerns about the loss of historic building fabric. The religious zeal that drove forward Anglican missionary work in the nineteenth century was also evident in the restoration of medieval churches (Fawcett 1976; Pevsner 1976). Eventually, plans by George Gilbert Scott to restore Tewksbury Abbey galvanised William Morris to write about the issue to *The Athenium* in March 1877, a letter that led to the formation of SPAB (Society for the Protection of Ancient Buildings) on 22 March 1877 (Miele 1996a: 21). 'One of the ironies of the Gothic revival is that it largely destroyed the very buildings from which it drew inspiration', 'considerably more architecture was lost through restoration than through demolition' (Fawcett 1976: 75).

The driving force of loss for initiating change has also occurred for artefacts. On 4 May 1802, a thief stole the two solid gold Gallehus horns from the Danish royal collections in Copenhagen. Subsequently melted down to make fake jewellery and coins, the loss triggered an enquiry that recommended the establishment of a National Museum and legal protection for field monuments. Similarly, in the 1890s, in the USA, Richard Wetherill was retrieving finds from Mesa Verde and the Chaco Canyon sites for collectors such as the Swedish Baron Gustaf Nordenskiöld, whose attempt to return to Sweden with painted pottery and probably at least one mummy from the Mesa Verde site is suggested as the event that prompted the US 1906 Antiquities Act and the creation of the Mesa Verde National Park (Bahn 196: 189).

THREATS AND LOSSES 45

Figure 2.0.1 Fenced off monuments, either short-term (as in this case at Les Petits Fradets, a megalithic tomb on the Ile d'Yeu off the west coast of France) or long-term, may be necessary physical protection, but also create a visual barrier to seeing, understanding and appreciating the monument.

Source: Photo by Prof. C. Scarre

The threat of loss has continued to be a galvanising force. The spread of urbanism and industrialisation, leading to a loss of rural Britain, generated an increased appreciation of nature throughout the late eighteenth and nineteenth centuries. Visiting the scenic sites of Britain became an increasingly accepted social norm and the wish to avoid its destruction led to the establishment of organisations such as the National Trust (1895) and National Parks (1949/1951) dedicated to its preservation. The loss of traditional farming practices and methods, especially working with horses, with the coming of machinery, was cited as the reason for the interest in folk art and museums in the 1930s. It led to the establishment of the Welsh National Folk Museum at St Fagans in 1951 and many others in the 1960s. In each case, specific threats of loss galvanised action, but there was often a general feeling of concern of gradual loss prior to the incident, which created the environment in which specific actions were enthusiastically received and supported. In Chapter 4, the loss of specific buildings is shown in several instances to be the key driver for enhancements in protective legislation. In many cases, organisations are also established or agencies created and funded to enact the legislation. The highlighting of loss has proved effective in raising public concerns, generating funding, providing impetus for using existing legislation and mobilising local and national government action.

Loss in many forms

The interest in the antiquarian past in the nineteenth century brought visitors flocking to monuments such as Stonehenge (Chippindale 1997: 159–61). Here, they dropped litter, chipped fragments off the stones as souvenirs and carved their names into the megaliths, irreparably damaging the monument (Chippindale 1997: 159; Oliver and Neal 2010; Baird and Taylor 2011). The build-up of rubbish and the wearing away of the monument surface threatened the archaeological traces still present in the ground, as did antiquarian digging. However, steps to protect ancient monuments by shielding them with railings, even in the present day (see Figure 2.0.1), have resulted in a loss of understanding of the monument, the loss of the image (you see the fence before you see the stones) and separation from both the landscape of which it was part and the society that made and preserved it. So measures designed to protect and preserve physical remains can also lead to a loss of less tangible properties.

Bibliography

Bahn, P. (1996) *The Cambridge Illustrated History of Archaeology*, Cambridge: Cambridge University Press.
Baird, J.A. and Taylor, C. (eds) (2011) *Ancient Graffiti in Context*, London: Routledge.
Burnham, H. (1991) 'A survey of the condition of scheduled ancient monuments in Wales: part 7, overall review', Cadw and Welsh Historic Monuments Internal Report, Cardiff: Cadw.
Caple, C. (2001) 'Degradation, investigation and preservation of archaeological evidence', in D.R. Brothwell and A.M. Pollard (eds), *Handbook of Archaeological Science*, Chichester: Wiley, pp. 287–95.
Caple, C. (2011) *Preventive Conservation in Museums*, London: Routledge.
Cassar, M. (2005) *Climate Change and the Historic Environment*, London: Centre for Sustainable Heritage.
Cassar, M. and Pender, R. (2005) 'The impact of climate change on cultural heritage: evidence and response', in A. Paterakis et al. (eds), *ICOM-CC 14th Triennial Meeting The Hague 12–16 September 2005*, London: James & James, pp. 610–16.
Champion, T. (1996) 'Protecting the monuments: archaeological legislation from the 1882 Act to PPG 16', in M. Hunter (ed.), *Preserving the Past*, Stroud: Alan Sutton, pp. 38–56.
Chippindale, C. (1997) *Stonehenge Complete*, rev. edn, London: Thames & Hudson.
Cleland, H.F. (1932) 'The crime of archaeology: a study of weathering', *The Scientific Monthly*, 35(2): 169–73.
Coles, J.M. (1987) 'The preservation of archaeological sites by environmental intervention', in H. Hodges (ed.), *In-Situ Archaeological Conservation*, Mexico: Instituto Nacional de Antropologia e Historia & J. Paul Getty Trust, pp. 32–55.
Darvill, T. and Fulton, A. (1998) *The Monuments at Risk Survey of England 1995*, London: Bournemouth University & English Heritage.
Edsel, R.M. (2009) *Monuments Men*, London: Arrow Books.
English Heritage (2008) *Climate Change and the Historic Environment*, London: English Heritage.
Fawcett, J. (1976) 'A restoration tragedy: cathedrals in the eighteenth and nineteenth centuries', in J. Fawcett (ed.), *The Future of the Past: Attitudes to Conservation 1174–1974*, London: Thames & Hudson, pp. 75–116.
Hodges, H. (1987) 'Preface', in H. Hodges (ed.), *In-Situ Archaeological Conservation*, Mexico: Instituto Nacional de Antropologia e Historia & J. Paul Getty Trust, pp. 4–10.
Hollesen, J., Jensen, J.B. and Matthiesen, H. *et al.* (2012) 'The future preservation of a permanently frozen kitchen midden in western Greenland', *Conservation and Management of Archaeological Sites*, 14(1–4): 159–68.
Hollowell, J. (2006) 'Moral arguments on subsistence digging', in C. Scarre and G. Scarre (eds), *The Ethics of Archaeology: Philosophical Perspectives on Archaeological Practice*, Cambridge: Cambridge University Press, pp. 69–93.
ICOMOS (2000) *ICOMOS World Report 2000 on Monuments and Sites in Danger*, available at: www.icomos.org/en/get-involved/inform-us/heritage-alert/heritage-at-risk-reports (accessed September 2014).
Johnson, M. (2001) 'Renovating Hue (Vietnam): authenticating destruction, reconstructing authenticity', in R. Layton, P.G. Stone and J. Thomas (eds), *Destruction and Conservation of Cultural Property*, London: Routledge, pp. 75–92.

Kenward, H. and Hall, A. (2000) 'Decay of delicate organic remains in shallow urban deposits: are we at a watershed?', *Antiquity*, 75: 519–23.

Kenward, H. and Hall, A. (2004) 'Actively decaying or just poorly preserved? Can we tell when plant and invertebrate remains in urban archaeological deposits decayed?', in T. Nixon (ed.), *Preserving Archaeological Remains In-Situ?*, London: Museum of London Archaeological Service, pp. 4–10.

Kenward, H. and Large, F. (1998) 'Recording the preservational condition of archaeological insect fossils', *Environmental Archaeology*, 2: 49–60.

Kila, J.D. (2012) *Heritage Under Siege: Military Implementation of Cultural Property Protection Following the 1954 Hague Convention*, Leiden: Brill.

Kila, J.D. and Zeidler, J.A. (2013) *Cultural Heritage in the Crosshairs: Protecting Cultural Property During Conflict*, Leiden: Brill.

Layton, R. and Thomas, J. (2001) 'Introduction: the destruction and conservation of cultural property', in R. Layton, P.G. Stone and J. Thomas (eds), *Destruction and Conservation of Cultural Property*, London: Routledge, pp. 1–21.

Lowenthal, D. (1996) *Possessed by the Past*, New York: The Free Press.

Millard, A. (2001) 'The deterioration of bone', in D.R. Brothwell and A.M. Pollard (eds), *Handbook of Archaeological Sciences*, Chichester: Wiley, pp. 637–48.

Miele, C. (1996a) 'The first conservation militants: William Morris and the Society for the Protection of Ancient Buildings', in M. Hunter (ed.), *Preserving the Past: The Rise of Heritage in Modern Britain*, Stroud: Alan Sutton, pp. 17–37.

Miele, C. (1996b) *William Morris on Architecture*, Sheffield: Sheffield Academic Press.

Murphy, P.L. and Wiltshire, P.E.J. (1994) 'A proposed scheme for evaluating plant macrofosssil preservation in some archaeological deposits', *Circaea*, 11: 1–6.

Oliver, J. and Neal, T. (eds) (2010) *Wild Signs: Graffiti in Archaeology and History*, BAR International Series 2074, Oxford: Archaeopress.

Palumbo, G. (2002) 'Threats and challenges to the archaeological heritage in the Mediterranean', in J.M. Tuetonico and G. Palumbo (eds), *Management Planning for Archaeological Sites*, Los Angeles, CA: GCI, pp. 3–12.

Pevsner, N. (1976) 'Scrape and anti-scrape', in J. Fawcett (ed.), *The Future of the Past: Attitudes to Conservation 1174–1974*, London: Thames & Hudson, pp. 35–54.

Piggott, S. (1985) *William Stukeley: An Eighteenth Century Antiquary*, rev. edn, London: Thames & Hudson.

Pina-Cabral, J. de (1994) 'The valuation of time among the peasant population of the Alto Minho, Northwestern Portugal', in R. Layton (ed.), *Who Needs the Past? Indigenous Values and Archaeology*, London: Routledge, pp. 59–68.

Quirke, S. and Spencer, J. (1992) *The British Museum Book of Ancient Egypt*, New York: Thames & Hudson.

Rees, S. (1994) 'Erosion in Wales: the extent of the problem', in A.Q. Berry and I.W. Brown (eds), *Erosion on Archaeological Earthworks: Its Prevention, Control and Repair*, Mold: Clwyd County Council.

Rimmer, M.B. and Caple, C. (2008) 'Estimating artefact loss: a comparison of metal artefact loss rates through in-situ decay and loss of ancient monument sites in England', in H. Kars and R.M. van Herringen (eds), *Preserving Archaeological Remains In-Situ, Proceedings of the 3rd Conference, 7–9 December 2006, Amsterdam*, Amsterdam: VU University Amsterdam, pp. 65–74.

Spindler, K. (1994) *The Man in the Ice*, London: Phoenix.

Strong, D.E. (1973) 'Roman museums', in D.E. Strong (ed.), *Archaeological Theory and Practice*, London: Seminar Press.

Sullivan, S. and Mackay, R. (eds) (2012) *Archaeological Sites: Conservation and Management*, Readings in Conservation, Los Angeles, CA: GCI.

UNESCO (1954) *Convention for the Protection of Cultural Property in the Event of Armed Conflict with Regulations for the Execution of the Convention 1954*, available at: http://portal.unesco.org/en/ev.php-URL_ID=13637&URL_DO=DO_TOPIC&URL_SECTION=201.html (accessed September 2014).

van de Noort, R., Fletcher, W. and Thomas, G. *et al.* (2002) *Monuments at Risk in England's Wetlands*, Exeter: English Heritage and Exeter University.

Walsh, P.G. (2006) *Pliny the Younger: Complete Letters*, Oxford: Oxford University Press.

Chapter 2.1

The preservation of archaeological sites by environmental intervention

John Coles

Source: Coles, J.M. (1987) 'The preservation of archaeological sites by environmental intervention', in H. Hodges (ed.), *In-Situ Archaeological Conservation*, Mexico: Instituto Nacional de Antropologia e Historia & J. Paul Getty Trust, pp. 32–55. For reasons of clarity and copyright, some images have been changed.

> The nation behaves well if it treats the natural resources as assets which it must turn over to the next generation, increased not impaired in value ... Conservation means development as much as it does protection
>
> Theodore Roosevelt

WITH THESE WORDS, the American naturalist and statesman Theodore Roosevelt formulated a principle of conservation that has often been neglected and sometimes willfully ignored. A nation's natural resources include its cultural heritage—those surviving traces of past human endeavor that mark the individual character of a nation and its people. Such visible signs of identity provide cohesion and help establish relationships that may otherwise be difficult to recognize in the makeup of society. Archaeologists have a primary obligation to identify, explain, and conserve the heritage of the past and to present it to the public not merely as a collection of antiquarian curiosities, but as a valuable and important resource for education and for the development of an awareness of human existence, struggle, and achievement. It is in the patterns of the past that we see our present state, and our aspirations for the future are conditioned by such patterns.

One of the more obvious ways in which our archaeological purposes and obligations may be met is through the presentation of important sites and monuments to society as a whole. It could be argued that such presentations, accompanied by explanations of the significance of the monuments, constitute the particular aspect of archaeological endeavor that justifies the continued existence of our discipline. All our other work could be seen as mere internal reorganization of the database, satisfying only to those few who have the time to participate in the endless assembling and sorting of evidence. Whether or not this is true, almost every nation that has developed a policy for its heritage has emphasized the fundamental importance of preserving those monuments that have been identified as significant to society as a whole. In 1985, ICCROM (1985: 315–316) agreed to principles that concur with such aims, recognizing the need for the development of strategies to identify and protect monuments, for adequate controls on the restoration of sites, and for suitable conservation measures both during and subsequent to excavation. For too long, passivity and neglect have led to the gradual deterioration of important and unique sites.

The examples of environmental control in this paper are drawn from Europe, where there are particular problems perhaps not encountered in other regions of the world. These problems derive from the dense settlement of Europe over a very long period of time. Today, large areas are being intensively cultivated or otherwise worked, which makes the need for environmental management extremely urgent. In northern and western Europe in particular, damp conditions lead to special problems affecting vegetation growth, land fertility, and (for archaeology) wet-site conservation. This is not to say that other regions of the world do not have other, even more severe, problems. Isolation of sites, lack of documentation and monitoring, vandalism, pollution, land erosion, and the like are among these major threats. The European examples may help to throw some of these into perspective and may suggest possible action.

All my information indicates that sites and monuments can be preserved successfully only under the following conditions: (1) legal intervention—protective orders, often incapable of application and imperfectly framed; (2) cultural intervention—management of human activities, including public education; and (3) environmental intervention—the establishment of suitable survival conditions for sites based on natural features of the landscape.

Sites and landscapes

No archaeological monument has ever existed divorced from its environment, no site was ever established in the past without a landscape setting, and no society has ever contemplated placing a structure at random. Every site we deal with has, or had, a landscape that was a part of the monument, that provided not only a base for the structure but also an environment in which it functioned. In most cases, each site was designed to suit its contemporary environment; the occasional cracked and slipped castle provides ample proof of the results for those who neglected to assess the situation. Lakeshore settlements set on deeply driven piles, massive stone monuments set on living rock or on wide flat rafts of stone or wood, structures at high altitudes strongly built to withstand snow and frost, fortress earthworks laced with timber and engineered against landslip, and burial platforms and pathways made of wood and pegged into marsh or swamp all demonstrate the ancient acknowledgment of the intimate relationship of site and setting. But the monuments of ancient societies—constructed to suit a particular environment and a specialized regime of human behavior—have often survived beyond those humans and now face conditions that threaten their very existence. Many monuments that were lost perished through the ignorant or willful actions of people who had not acknowledged the importance of the cultural heritage. The loss of thousands of burial mounds by ploughing in Denmark and Poland, the demolition of stone monuments for building materials in Ireland and France, and the destruction of settlements by quarrying in Germany and Britain are examples of such cultural annihilation.

Table 2.1.1 Pressures on archaeological environments

Farming	Clearance, cultivation, biocides, drainage, grazing
Forestry and vegetation	Planting, harvesting, drainage, scrubland
Quarrying	Rock, sand, gravel; on land and underwater
Water erosion	Lake levels, wave action, rivers
Land erosion	Temperature, precipitation, leaching, landslip
Tourism and urbanism	Erosion, housing, industry, pollution, transport
Wetland drainage	Desiccation, erosion, biochemical degradation

The pressures on archaeological sites are very great, yet measures can be taken to prevent or redress their destruction. Some of the pressures exerted on archaeological monuments in recent years are listed in Table 2.1.1, and those for which environmental intervention is possible are discussed below. A few comments on cultural intervention are also given, although this is a separate subject, much concerned with education.

Farming

Probably the greatest threat to archaeological monuments is posed by farming, that fundamental activity that has dominated the landscapes of many parts of the world for at least 6,000 years. It is only in the past few decades, however, that farming has changed from a relatively stable operation with non-cumulative effects to an aggressive and relentlessly extractive process systematically damaging many traditional aspects of the land (Lowe et al. 1986).

The clearance of hitherto untouched woodland, including hedgerows and bands of vegetation, has caused erosion and deteriorated a stable environment. Deep ploughing and pan-breaking has removed the traces of untold numbers of ancient sites already reduced to mere shadows by natural processes of decay (Hinchliffe and Schadla-Hall 1980). The negative impact of agricultural activity on monuments has increased substantially with the advent of national or international agencies charged with the mandate of producing food at any cost. The European Economic Community (EEC) has a particularly bad record here, with millions of tons of excess grain in storage awaiting disposal either through natural means (deterioration beyond use) or uneconomic means (by sale below cost of production).

The ploughing of earthen monuments gradually levels sites until their significance, in terms of heritage, is gone. There are almost too many examples of this phenomenon to choose from, but instructive aerial photographs of the deserted medieval village earthworks of Burreth Tupholme, England, show the immaculate precision of identifiable streets, houses, and small fields in 1963, and only their flattened, distorted images in 1976 (Baker 1983). The fact that earthen monuments, particularly burial mounds and hillforts, are often protected by law does not necessarily mean that agricultural pursuits already in operation can be stopped (see Figure 2.1.1), nor does it deter erosion or the effect of animals. This seems to be the case in many countries, such as Britain, France, Switzerland, Germany, and The Netherlands. Even sites as important as the Wauwilermoos in Germany, where Mesolithic and Neolithic settlements

Figure 2.1.1 Iron Age fortification at Arbur, Northants being ploughed away.

cluster around a gradually shrinking wetland, cannot effectively be protected from activities related to farming, although major disturbances of the underlying layers are prevented (Wyss 1979).

Agricultural damage to sites results from land drainage, which leads to desiccation; the spreading and spraying of fertilizers and biocides directly on the site or by drift from adjacent land; and uncontrolled grazing by livestock. Drainage in certain environments, such as marshlands and moorlands, can have disastrous effects on buried waterlogged monuments (as we will see below), and only firm environmental policies and interventions can control this practice. Although the deteriorating effect of acidic fertilizers on monuments is not fully accepted or understood, biocidal sprays designed to clear unwanted wildlife are known to affect adversely natural agents that aid archaeological conservation (see below). Ancient earthworks, as well as stonestructures, suffer severely from overgrazing by cattle or sheep (see Figure 2.1.2); the damage to an earthwork caused by rooting pigs may be compared to the impact of uncontrolled tourists.

There are, however, hopeful signs amid these scenes of disaster. If an agency with jurisdiction over the land is sympathetic to the conservation of archaeological sites and monuments, opportunities for preservation exist, even if the land is being worked for agricultural purposes. Denmark's Conservation of Nature Act (1978) recognizes that cultural/historical features in the landscape are as important as its natural attributes, and preservation must take into account both scientific and recreational needs (Ministry of the Environment 1978). The Ancient Monument Act of Sweden (1942) protects every monument (about 450,000); approval is required for any action that could damage or alter a site (Hyenstrand 1979). In Britain, agencies, such as English Heritage, Cadw (Wales), the Scottish Development Department, and the Department of the Environment for Northern Ireland have statutory requirements for the protection of ancient monuments, but their powers are limited; until adequate surveys are conducted and

Figure 2.1.2 Erosion damage from overgrazing and tourism. Livestock have eroded the ground around standing stone used as a rubbing post.
Source: Photo by Alan Simkins

sites are assessed, the listing of "Scheduled Ancient Monuments" will be incomplete. In England alone, for example, of 635,000 known ancient sites only 12,600 are currently protected in this way. Moreover, this legal protection may have no effect on normal ploughing (if it is already practiced on the site); erosion by cattle; rock fall, river, or wave action; scrub clearance or tree growth; or a decline in the water table (Wainwright 1985).

Many other countries have such policies, and, indeed, some embrace the entire landscape. Nonetheless, damage to sites still occurs in every country. Unfortunately, in France the problem is even worse because only formal acquisition of the land can ensure control over agriculture. Official policy statements seem to be universally rejected by French farmers, and while this reaction may be laudable, it rarely benefits archaeology.

The cooperation (or at least acquiescence) of landowners and landusers is crucial to the provision of appropriate environmental conditions for monuments. Such protection can sometimes take the form of environmental intervention. For example, the National Trust in the United Kingdom was originally established to acquire places of historic and natural beauty in order to allow the "preservation of their natural aspect, features and animal and plant life." The Trust is one of the largest landowners in the U.K., and among its holdings are perhaps as many as 20,000 archaeological sites (Thackray and Hearn 1985). In many cases the lands held are worked under tenancy agreements, and conservation interests are negotiated with each successive tenant. On the Isle of Wight, a strip-field system, rich in wildlife and ancient hedgerows, is managed along traditional, nonintensive farming lines in order to preserve both human and wildlife features. In Cornwall at West Penwith, part of a very ancient land-use pattern (probably Iron Age in origin, ca. 500 BC–AD 100) is preserved by stone fences forming small fields. The stone walls support specialized wildlife forms, while the fields are generally rather sparsely occupied by plant species. The archaeological interests, however, are paramount and the tenancy agreements restrict changes in farming patterns. Broadly comparable stone-lined holdings in other regions (western Ireland, for example) have lost up to 80 percent of their monuments because of changes in traditional farming practices inspired by the expansionist policies of the EEC.

The perpetuation of traditional, non-innovative agricultural practices—by inducement, agreement, or law—represents a form of environmental intervention that often comes close to the aims of other agencies, particularly nature conservancy interests. So much land in Europe has now been taken for agriculture, and the methods are so artificial—broad deep sweeps for the plough and heavy use of fertilizers and biocides—that few areas remain for remnant colonies of traditional wildlife, plant or animal. Earthworks of many kinds provide habitats for these relict survivors, and increasingly there has developed a common ground between archaeologists and nature conservationists. For example, several Bronze Age barrows (ca. 1000 BC) in Zealand, Denmark, have been studied as habitats for plant communities that rarely survive elsewhere in the area (Ravnsted-Larsen 1983). Shade and temperature preferences for a wide variety of these plants were studied on the Hagbards Høj, a round barrow, which by definition offers all aspects to the sun. The preservation of such monuments through environmental control is thus desirable for both wildlife and archaeological interests (see also Kelly 1981).

In a few cases, these interests may diverge. Archaeologists will want a light and uniform grazing pattern on large earthen monuments and landscapes of ancient fields, but environmentalists might prefer a varied grazing pattern that allows dense turf to develop, enabling the support of certain insects (e.g., butterflies). Archaeologists are keen to prevent the erosion of earthworks and the exposure of subsoil, but others may see areas of erosion as an ideal environment for boring invertebrates. Burrowing animals in earthworks are another problem for archaeologists; unwelcome, but some are protected by law. Notwithstanding, the association of archaeological and natural conservationists is a logical outcome of their overwhelmingly common aim: the preservation of the landscape.

[. . .]

Forestry and vegetation

In assessing the impact of environmental change on archaeological sites, it is clear that we must deal with landscapes. The historic evidence of human occupation and activity has often survived in tangible form, readily visible and understandable to all. The Roman frontier walls and forts, often restored, represent the earliest of these historic monuments, but medieval field systems, villages, and farms are equally preserved, if less heavily intrusive, in the landscapes of today. Their European predecessors—prehistoric sites and monuments—are less apparent and often survive only as shadow or cropmark sites. They are easily overlooked by both archaeologists and those working the land, and when obscured by heavy plant growth, they are defenseless.

Few surveys have been carried out on the effects of forestry operations on ancient landscapes, but the evidence suggests a very heavy loss of archaeological information. Forestry involves the clearing and uprooting of trees and scrub, machine planting and, sometimes, ploughing to depths of nearly 1 meter and widths of almost 2 meters.

Figure 2.1.3 Trees root disturbance of barrows – Iron Age Square Barrow in Broxa Forest, North Yorkshire.
Source: Photo by Chris Collyer, www.stone-circles.org.uk

Environmentally, the effects are severe; there can be an alteration in intensity or direction of drainage, monuments can be truncated, and upper deposits can be weathered and eroded (Lowe et al. 1986). In such cases, archaeological intervention can only consist of attempts to educate forestry operators, the surveying and marking of monuments, and the planning of subsequent action. I know of no examples (1986) in this field of an adequate archaeological response, or a successful environmental intervention, although in parts of Scotland there is a clear awareness of the problem and attempts are being made to inform operators and prevent damage (Jackson 1978).

Scrub vegetation is a natural result of the abandonment of land, whether it be farmland or archaeological sites. In Europe, scrub can involve both trees and shrubs, and its encroachment over a site can be serious, masking contours and disturbing underground features. The Iron Age forts of Badbury Rings and Hembury in southern England have been overwhelmed by scrub woodland and bracken; they are now being cleared, mostly by hand, and seeded with grass to permit grazing. Sheep and cattle will have an intervention role here, but only strict management will prevent the recurrence of the problems.

The common practice in some European regions of planting trees on conspicuous burial mounds (e.g., the Bronze Age barrow at Olhøj in Denmark) had profound effects on the survival of such monuments, particularly where secondary burials were inserted into barrow sides (see Figures 2.1.3 and 8.0.2) (Thorsen 1982). These were easily disturbed by roots and, in addition, the dense foliage of tall trees, such as elms or oaks,

THE PRESERVATION OF ARCHAEOLOGICAL SITES 55

Figure 2.1.4 The Church of Breedon on the Hill, eighth-century centre of Mercian religious life, isolated by a stone quarry.
Source: Photo by Andy Mabbett

discouraged the regeneration of grasses and herbaceous plants, which would have stabilized the mound surface and provided a habitat for other plants and animals.

[. . .]

Quarrying

Many modern operations have a more direct and wholly irreparable effect on monuments and landscapes than the pressures of agriculture or forestry. There is an understandable, yet indefensible, attitude on the part of many agencies that, while some sites may have archaeological significance and should be left alone, their immediate surroundings do not deserve consideration and can be razed or otherwise damaged. Environmental decay around a monument will seriously damage the site, in the sense of loss of information and loss of appreciation of the place and role of the site within an ancient world (see Figure 2.1.4). Perhaps the best example of such a relationship, and of such blatant damage, is the landscape of a hilltop enclosure at Navan in Northern Ireland (Mallory n.d.). Navan was the focus of Celtic rituals in 600–100 BC and had an elaborate central monument overlooking a ritually important lake and earthworks. The site later became the capital of the Kingdom of Ulster. The limestone rock upon which Emain Macha (its Irish name) sits is now being quarried away in perhaps the greatest act of heritage destruction in Europe. Archaeologists are resisting extensions to the quarry, which now approaches the outer bank of the monument itself in an immense cutting about 25 meters deep. The spoil from the quarry is dropped in the lake (which contains many Iron Age and Celtic artifacts), thereby separating the two ritual sites and truncating the landscape. Only environmental intervention can stop this total destruction. [. . .]

The law must sometimes intervene in order that environmental and cultural control can be achieved over such nationally significant sites. A recent application to extend the quarry at Navan even further onto the site has been refused, through the vigorous efforts of a group of archaeologists; but the present damage remains unchecked.

Quarrying is not restricted to rock alone, and many archaeological monuments are at risk because of such operations, both on land and under water. Gravel digging by dredger, combing of fossil oyster beds for fertilizer, and channeling work along the coasts of western Europe (and sometimes in inland lakes, as in Switzerland) have yielded many archaeological finds. Only in Denmark does there seem to be an adequate environmental response. Off the coast of southern Fyn, for example, diving surveys have located more than forty Mesolithic and Neolithic sites, some with good organic preservation (Skaarup 1983: 137–161; and see Fischer and Sørensen 1983: 104–126 for other surveys). All of these are now protected by legislation, but environmental control over adjacent dredging is necessary to prevent erosion and currents that could damage the sites. Similar procedures have to be imposed to protect the many submerged wrecks known to exist in some of the fjords and harbor approaches in Denmark, such as the scuttled Viking boats in the Roskilde fjord. Although there are agencies for protecting sites by legislation, there are great difficulties in imposing and maintaining particular environmental conditions underwater (see Muckelroy 1980 for notes on sites and protection).

Water erosion

An underwater environment may seem to offer no problems requiring intervention, but erosion and shifting deposits can be severe, difficult to detect, and almost impossible to prevent (see Figure 2.1.5). Yet, in some circumstances, shallow waters can be controlled. In Finland, rock painting sites along lake shores are usually above the water level, although some northern sites are subject to water damage caused in part by storm action, but primarily by changes in lake levels. Erosion may be partially prevented by building rock walls to break the force of the waves. The rocks for the walls are brought to the sites across the frozen lakes in winter, a good example of an environment aiding in its intervention.

Elsewhere, archaeological monuments are more severely threatened by lake waters. In western Switzerland, many Neolithic and Bronze Age settlements were constructed on the shores of lakes Neuchâtel and Bienne. Overwhelmed by rising lake waters, these sites were protected by sands and chalk silts and kept waterlogged, thereby preserving unique evidence about structures, industries, and economies of the period circa 3000–500 BC. Adjustments to the overall water sources in the Jura in 1880 lowered the lake levels; falls of more than 2 meters exposed the protective sands and silts. Storms and wave action began to erode the deposits, and further adjustments of the Jura waters stabilized the lake waters at the level of the ancient structures. This shoreline erosion led to the exposure of thousands of wood piles from the prehistoric sites, some of which are now destroyed. Others, like Cortaillod-les-Esserts, are "leached" and most of the organic components

THE PRESERVATION OF ARCHAEOLOGICAL SITES 57

Figure 2.1.5 Water erosion: the incoming tide erodes away the prehistoric ritual site of 'Seahenge'.
Source: Photo © Historic England

have been lost. Several attempts to conserve the surviving sites have been made. One popular approach is to bury the site under sand and rocks. The overall effect of this procedure has been to deform and damage the structures and to introduce decay of the organic elements that made these sites so important. Neuchâtel-Bains du Crêt, a very large Bronze Age settlement, has suffered in this way, as have Neolithic Saint-Blaise and the leached site of Cortaillod-les-Esserts. Here, then, a policy amounting to environmental intervention has not succeeded (see Egloff 1982: 109–118 for a survey of the problems).

A further development, seemingly of destructive character, has had surprisingly positive results. The planned construction of a motorway along the north shore of Lake Neuchâtel led to an archaeological survey that revealed complete Bronze Age villages submerged in the deeper waters of small bays. An archaeological service was set up to conduct a major excavation program, and one of its tasks was to devise measures to protect sites still buried by sands and silts that lie perilously close to the erosion-line of the lakes. At Corcelettes, a Bronze Age settlement, some piles are already exposed and decaying in the water (Vaud 1983: 223–251). Intervention in 1983 consisted of a curtain of wood poles driven into the lake-bed just off shore, with the pole tops level with the average height of the lake. Behind the curtain, a beach of cobblestones has been laid up to the present shore, providing added protection against erosion. The aim is to stabilize the beach with vegetation, maintaining the water-saturation of the ancient deposits beyond, but preventing any further erosion. To date, the intervention appears to be successful.

Where archaeological sites lie near marine waters, added difficulties may well occur, not only through tidal and wave action, but also through the action of salt. At Lothal, for example (a city of the Indus culture, ca. 2500–2000 BC; see Sankalia 1974 for a general survey), the mudbrick structures have suffered from salt spray and atmosphere. Experiments are underway to solve the problem internally, as environmental change is hardly possible.

Land erosion

The effects of erosion and weathering by climatic events are similarly difficult to counter. Archaeological sites at high altitudes, subject to severe frost and heavy snow, need special measures to ensure their survival. The Great Moravian sites of Staré Mesto and Mikulcice (Poulik 1960: 24–29) in Czechoslovakia have ancient stone walls with upper courses of modern stonework that strengthen and protect the older remains from winter frost. More elaborate intervention at the thirteenth-century monastery of Oujon in Switzerland has involved the excavation and reburial of some walling, with overlying deposits of soil shaped to depict the wall lines and provide protection against frost and snow at the 1,000-meter altitude (Weidmann 1985). New forms of concrete and cement for use under these conditions fall more properly into the category of restoration.

Even at lower altitudes, sites may suffer damage through severe climatic conditions. Some Bronze Age engravings on rocks in Sweden have been affected by frost and snow. When snow melts, water covers the rock surfaces and severe frosts may then crack the rock, detaching flakes or small "plates" (see Figure 2.1.6). The interventionist action here involves burying the sites at risk by piling earth over the engraved areas; this also helps protect the monuments from vandalism. But there are thousands of such rock art sites in Sweden, Norway, and Denmark, and it is impossible to protect them all.

A variant approach to monuments, in a totally different environment, has been adopted in The Netherlands. For centuries, the Zuiderzee was an important body of water for transport and fishing. The shallow waters were usually calm, but mud banks and occasional storms often proved fatal for small and large ships. Since 1930, reclamation of the Ijesselmeer polders has taken place (see van der Heide 1959 for a historical survey), and as these lands have emerged through damming and pumping, hundreds of wrecks have appeared, the oldest so far dating back to the thirteenth century. Many await investigation and their conservation poses problems. Basic, of course, is the loss of the water that constituted their environment both during use (as boats) and after sinking. Drying the deposits would be disastrous to the survival of these sites.

Over the past ten years, about twelve wreck sites have been protected by environmental intervention. While the polder is still damp, the site is surrounded by a vertical wall of plastic foil extending from the surface down into the thick clay subsoil. As this base is impermeable, the effect of the wall is to create a "tub" of water, keeping the shipwreck and its enclosing silts and clays waterlogged (see Figure 2.1.7). Where the wreck lies partially exposed on the surface, deposits of 1 to 2 meters of clay have been placed on top to help seal the site, making it possible to continue to introduce new water from time to time. In this way, the wreck may survive for ten to twenty years.

Figure 2.1.6 Rock art at Vastervik in Sweden, buried during the winter period to reduce ice damage.
Source: Photo: Magdalena Kaliszewska

The reburial of sites of all kinds is increasingly accepted as a form of environmental and cultural intervention.

[. . .]

Tourism and urbanism

There are few sites stable and strong enough to withstand an excess of popularity (see Figure 2.1.8); sometimes environmental control, rather than intervention, is necessary. Take for example Stonehenge, one of the best-known prehistoric sites in the world. The small central megalithic monument (only 30 meters in diameter) received about 500,000 annual visitors until 1978 when entry to the circle of stones was barred. By then, the land surface of the monument had been seriously flattened and eroded. Even with barely any access to the monument's stones, there are now about 750,000 visitors to Stonehenge each year, and the pressures on the land, roads, and facilities are overwhelming (English Heritage n.d.).

[. . .]

Human pressures on monuments are not restricted to tourism alone, of course, and whereas farming can sometimes be regulated to permit the survival of sites within their landscapes, this is not the case with urban or industrial development. Such pressures

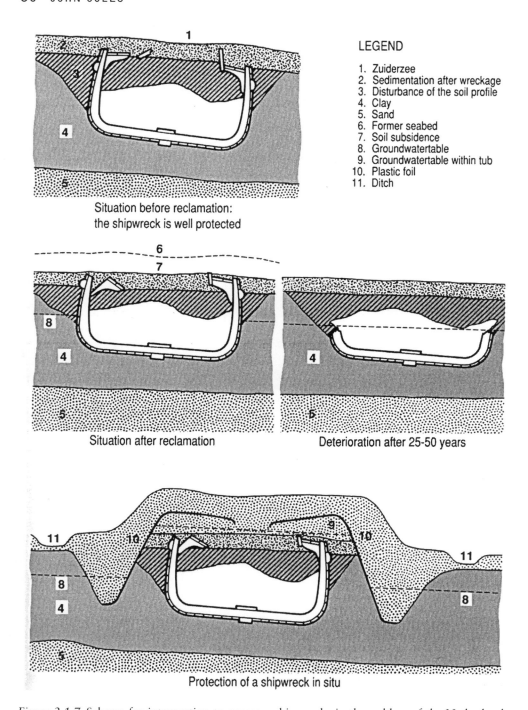

Figure 2.1.7 Scheme for intervention to preserve shipwrecks in the polders of the Netherlands.

THE PRESERVATION OF ARCHAEOLOGICAL SITES 61

Figure 2.1.8 The large numbers of visitors walking on and over Hadrian's wall take their toll on the monument.
Source: Photo courtesy of ncjMedia

Figure 2.1.9 Development road slicing through Olcote kerbed cairn, Isle of Lewis.
Source: Photo: Dr Sandy Gerrard: copyright reserved

usually lead to serious damage (see Figure 2.1.9), almost certain loss of the cultural environment of the site (e.g., Tredegar Camp, Wales, is almost totally surrounded by houses), and sometimes the initiation of decay by pollution or subsidence. [...]

The public and conservation interests

It is not appropriate here to consider the wider implications of "public archaeology," but what is important to note is that in the long run it is the public who will determine the fate of all monuments of the past. Education at all levels is crucially important—about the past, about the monuments of the past, and about the duty of all to treat the cultural heritage with respect.

Legislation for the protection of monuments, as enacted in most European countries, rarely allows or makes provision for environmental intervention in the classic sense of those words, but some of the examples above demonstrate that opportunities for protection have been seized by archaeologists in certain circumstances. In Bavaria, for example, although sites and areas of archaeological interest are protected in general (*Grabungsschutzgebieten*), each case also requires separate negotiation in order to ensure its survival and appropriate management. The wide public interest in restoration, particularly of Roman forts and towers (Weber 1984; Bayerisches Staatsministerium 1983), as well as of other monuments (e.g., Iron Age ramparts; Abels 1984), show the genuine value of a broadly interpreted monuments protection act (*Denkmalschutzgesetz*; Bayerisches Staatsministerium 1974; Schwarz 1977).

To the north, in Schleswig-Holstein, conditions for the survival of monuments are different, and restrictions on agricultural and other practices for areas of archaeological interest are strict and legally enforced. Recognition of the unique habitats that ancient monuments provide for wildlife has already been noted, and here there is excellent collaboration between nature conservation and the archaeological authorities—to such an extent, in fact, that complete protection of monuments, such as the Danewerk, is made possible (Müller and Neergaard 1908). The Danewerk, or Danevirke—an earthen rampart more than 7 kilometers long, in parts 6 meters high, and 30 meters wide—protected the Danish north from the Saxon south in the eighth century AD. It was used again in 1864 and in 1945, both times unnecessarily. This massive fortification has required protection by legislation and by the combined efforts of archaeological and nature conservation interests. The environmental regime for the monument has thus been controlled so that both disciplines benefit.

[...]

This Schleswig-Holstein example demonstrates the success of good documentation of resources, of careful use of legislation, and of close collaboration with nature conservation interests. The two subjects are, of course, included in the Conservation of Nature Act in Denmark, embodying an ideal toward which others are striving, and which was foreseen by the true pioneer of collaboration, Gudmund Hatt (Hansen 1984). It may be of some interest to note the comparable ideas for conservation of both sites and wildlife in Denmark and Germany (e.g., Solvang 1983; Glutz, Grewe, and Müller 1984). That the interests of archaeology and nature conservancy are very closely linked is also borne out by a recently published list of priorities for conservation in England (see Table 2.1.2).

Table 2.1.2 Priorities in the selection of monuments and nature conservation sites for protection in England

Archaeology	Nature conservation
Survival/condition (quality)	Survival: quality and extent
Period: all types	Habitat type: all types
Rarity (unique sites)	Rarity value: rare species
Fragility/vulnerability	Fragility or vulnerability
Diversity (multiple or single features)	Diversity of interest (plants and animals)
Documentation: adequacy of data	Documentation: species records
Group value: landscape association	Group value: wildlife reservoirs
Potential (anticipation of importance)	Potential: future value

Note: Bracketed comments are paraphrased from the original.
Source: Based on Wainwright (1985) and Vittery (1985)

Wetland drainage

While some archaeological monuments and sites exist in advantageous circumstances, there are also certain problems. Many sites are in wetlands—flat expanses of marsh and moor, often with peat deposits laying over rock, clays, and sands, all the result of glacial outwash and ice sheet withdrawal. Archaeological monuments in such environments are often well preserved (e.g., the midfirst millennium AD). Feddersen Wierde settlement with house walls, sheds, and fences standing 1 meter high in places (Haarnagel 1979), and the still-intact wood roads from the Neolithic and Bronze Age (Hayen 1986). Such wetlands are rich in wildlife and thus attract nature conservation interests. In Lower Saxony, evidence of settlement since Neolithic times may be found in the peatbogs. Wetland wildlife is abundant, and traditional rural pursuits are still practiced (e.g., peat cutting, moor burning, water-meadow grazing, and special cropping of reeds). All combine in efforts to conserve monuments, wildlife, and human traditions in the same areas (Hayen 1980, 1981).

On the other hand, however, all these interests are brought together by one element—water. High water levels are necessary for organic preservation on sites, for specialized wildlife habitats, and for traditional wetland farming sustenance. Environmental intervention to retain sites is therefore a subsidiary benefit to more widespread interests in the conservation of nature and of traditions. Thus the priorities for the preservation of particular ancient monuments cannot be selected independently.

There is, however, one fundamental difference in the effect of the outcome of any combined nature conservation and archaeological action in a wetland. Wetlands attract specialized wildlife that evolve and change according to environmental dictates. A drying wetland supports certain life forms, but if re-wetted, the land will again attract the specialized forms common to a true wetland. In other words, with nature conservation, wetlands may be restored to previous levels and even enhanced in some cases. This is not the case for waterlogged archaeological remains. Once they begin to dry out, they cannot be returned to their original well-preserved condition. The loss is permanent, and no future wetting of the environment can restore the archaeological elements.

[...]

Just as wetlands are probably the most threatened archaeological environment, their physical survival as a land form is also in jeopardy (Coles 1987a). Wetlands are repositories for peat (the partial decay of centuries of reeds, sedges, mosses, and other plants) and are a valuable fertilizer for impoverished soils. The quarrying of peat in Ireland, Lower Saxony, and England has removed millions of tons of organic deposits, often containing or protecting waterlogged archaeological remains. Settlements, platforms, trackways, and countless prehistoric and early historic artifacts have been discovered; sometimes they have been examined, but generally they have been destroyed. In the Irish and northern German boglands, it has not been possible to conserve any monuments in situ, either because of the lack of an archaeological strategy or because of the difficulties of water retention (Coles 1987b; Hayen 1980).

In England, comparable problems exist for the huge wetland of the Fenland. Here, centuries of drainage have succeeded in transforming a wet organic peat and silt land into a dry fertile landscape suitable for cultivation. As a result, meters of organic soils have been lost through wind erosion and shrinkage, and the whole landscape has been lowered, except for the embanked watercourses that carry water above the surrounding land. Previously, the land was both wet and dry, with streams, marshes, islands, and peninsulas that supported many populations from Neolithic to recent times. As the land shrunk and eroded, the archaeological monuments that were buried by peats and silts have begun to emerge. Thus, some flat, featureless fields have become richly varied cultural landscapes, distinguished by protruding Bronze Age barrows (Hall 1985, 1986). Such sites may still have waterlogged deposits in their lower sections—uneroded, unexposed, and unexamined; in other words, they offer a virtually intact prehistoric landscape. The great and urgent need is for some measure of environmental intervention to ensure the survival of this unique evidence. How this can be achieved is not at all clear. For individual sites not truncated by drainage ditches, some form of walled enclosure (as used in The Netherlands for shipwrecks) might help to hold waterlogged structures for several decades. In areas with settlement patterns and ritual activities still intact, the procedures would involve the use of existing ditches to bring water to the area, barriers to retain high water tables and prevent shrinkage of the peat body, and grassland regimes to curtail erosion. The costs for such an operation would be high, but the results would justify them.

The same wetland problems have been encountered and overcome in the Somerset Levels in England, where archaeologists have identified hundreds of prehistoric structures built in the swamps and moors of a wide basin (Coles and Coles 1986). The earliest known structure circa 3900 BC is a Neolithic trackway, the Sweet Track, built of many varieties of wood (see Figure 2.1.10). Detailed environmental and dendro-chronological analyses, excavations, and experimental work have revealed that this 1,800-meter-long track was built in a very short period of time (perhaps only one or two days!) by two groups of Neolithic farmers and gatherers using huge oaks and other trees from different managed woodlands on the hills and islands of the Levels. The many studies of this structure inform us about local and regional environmental conditions, climatic change, the elm decline that often signals the onset of farming practices in western Europe, carpentry and craftsmanship in wood, refinements in tree-ring dating, and sophisticated use wear analysis of flint tools found beside the structure.

Figure 2.1.10 Early Neolithic wood trackway, the Sweet Track, in the Somerset Levels, England. The track was overwhelmed by water and then peat formation, and all its components are immaculately preserved. The entire structure is organic. Peat removal and drainage now threaten survival.
Source: Images provided by Dr Richard Brunning courtesy of Prof. John Coles and the Somerset Levels Project

[. . .]

Some of this unique monument has been destroyed by peat cutting, and parts have been damaged by drainage that has allowed the fragile Neolithic wood to decay beneath the ground. Our overall aim in the Levels has been to conserve whatever sites we can, and for the Sweet Track a collaborative effort was undertaken involving archaeology and nature conservancy. This is yet another example of the importance of combined interests working toward a common goal, as we have seen in northern Germany and Denmark. For the Sweet Track, matters were taken a stage further with the purchase of 16.8 hectares of peatland from the major peat-cutting company in the area at a cost (£95,000) well below the commercial price. This company (Fisons plc) had a fifteen-year record of cooperation with archaeologists. The funds for the purchase were

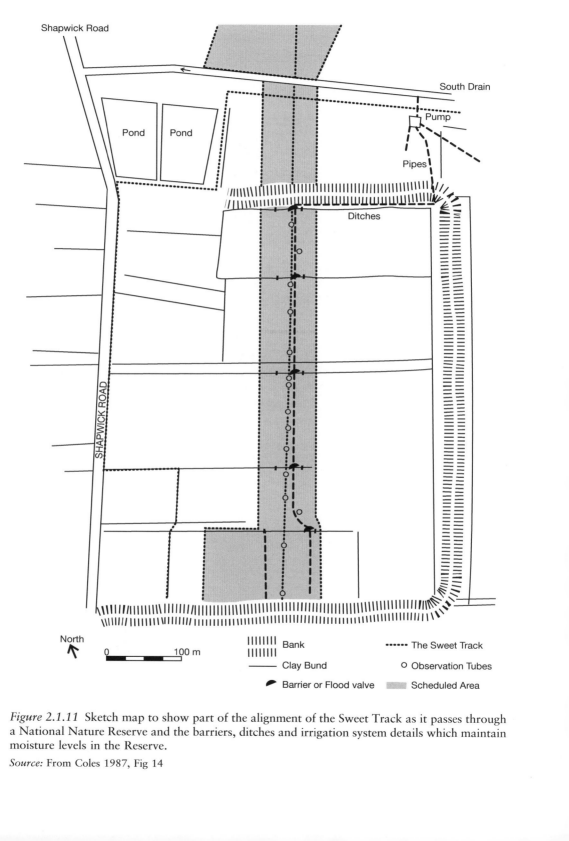

Figure 2.1.11 Sketch map to show part of the alignment of the Sweet Track as it passes through a National Nature Reserve and the barriers, ditches and irrigation system details which maintain moisture levels in the Reserve.

Source: From Coles 1987, Fig 14

obtained from the National Heritage Memorial Fund by a combined approach from the Nature Conservancy Council, English Heritage, and the Somerset Levels Project (the archaeological unit). This action prevented any further peat cutting and thus preserved about 500 meters of the track (see Figure 2.1.11). However, drainage around much of this reserve was drying out the peat, affecting the unique wetland wildlife of the reserve (which was of the highest grade of nature reserves in Great Britain), and decaying the prehistoric wood structure (a scheduled ancient monument). It must be emphasized again that legislation protecting a nature reserve or an archaeological monument is ineffective if the adjacent land is not also managed and controlled in sympathy with scientific and cultural interests. Thus, we had an association of interests in organisms as variable as butterfly orchid, royal fern, nightingale, and silver-washed fritillary, and the 6,000-year-old wood monument of the Sweet Track, with all its planks, pegs, pottery, seeds, flints and wood artifacts—all requiring protection.

The solution involved environmental intervention on a massive scale. An additional grant (£35,000) was obtained from the same fund and this was used to construct a clay bank (bund) around part of the reserve and to reinforce peat banks on the other sides. These measures prevented drainage onto the adjacent lower lands. Near the line of the monument, which lies buried about 1 meter below the peat surface, narrow flow channels were dug by hand, and, on the surface. a 20-centimeter-diameter pipe with a series of flood valves was laid. (This effort was funded separately by national archaeological and nature conservancy agencies.) The flood valves were placed over cross-ditches with barrier walls to retain high levels of water within the central area where the monument lies. Water is regulated by a timing device (with manual override for special conditions). All the ditches and flow channels are kept filled with water, thereby soaking the peat, encouraging the wetland wildlife for the nature reserve, and keeping the monument waterlogged. Small observation tubes have been inserted into the peat beside the track, and measurements are taken at least weekly throughout the year to monitor the water level by direct sighting; any lowering can then by corrected by additional pumping. Since this work was done in 1984, the monument has been maintained in a satisfactory condition, and the wetland plants and animals have been attracted back to the reserve. The environmental intervention here has been entirely successful; it must surely provide another example of the opportunities for archaeologists to combine with other interests in taking positive action to preserve significant parts of our cultural heritage for the future.

Conclusion

For too long, monuments have been neglected, stemming from the belief that legislative orders alone will somehow guarantee their unchanged survival. This virtual abandonment cannot halt, and sometimes cannot even delay, the processes of attrition and decay that threaten the monuments of the past. Such passive attitudes are unconscionable when they affect monuments of national significance. Cultural intervention requires positive management and public control, but often little can be done beyond delaying deterioration. Environmental intervention is a more fundamental and dynamic process that can positively affect the preservation of monuments, at least retaining their condition upon discovery.

No archaeologist today could deny the contributions of the natural sciences to the understanding of ancient sites—their environments and economies—as well as to the conservation of artifacts. Collaborating with natural scientists would yield not only a broader knowledge of ancient environments, but also of present environments; this would aid in the development of appropriate environmental controls to protect the sites from the effects of modern climatic, geographical, and human pressures. The financing for such efforts is often more easily obtained by nature conservation interests than by archaeologists, whose contact with the public in some regions is less well established.

The enormous public interest in nature conservation as it relates to plant life and animal life in nature reserves and national parks, the public enthusiasm for archaeological monuments, and the overwhelming concern with destruction and pollution of all kinds, could be channeled by archaeologists into efforts to establish environmental intervention on sites and monuments.

Education plays a major role in the preservation of the cultural heritage. It is, after all, the public who will make the decisions affecting the survival of the heritage. Without adequate education, particularly for the young, efforts at archaeological preservation cannot succeed. Education can provide the key to solving problems of archaeological destruction, but the public must be in a position, both socially and economically, to receive and accept that education.

Finally, all efforts to conserve the environment must take into account and accept the natural evolution of the world. All monuments and all sites cannot remain untouched. Choices regarding the preservation of monuments and landscapes must be based on adequate documentation of the cultural record and presented to an educated public and an informed government. This will require positive action on the part of archaeologists and conservators in making available our results and in asserting our beliefs.

References

Abels, B.-U. (1984). Ausgrabungen und rekonstruktion der spatlatènezeitlichen Befestigungsmauer auf dem Staffelberg. *Das archäologische Jahr in Bayern 1983.*
Baker, D. (1983). *Living with the past. The historic environment.* Bedford.
Bayerisches Staatsministerium (1974). *Bayerisches Denkmalschutzgesetz.* Munich.
Bayerisches Staatsministerium (1983). *Flurbereinigung und Denkmalpflege. Ein Mosaik aus Mittelfranken.* Munich.
Coles, B. and J. Coles (1986). *Sweet Track to Glastonbury.* London.
Coles, J.M. (1987a). Precision, purpose and priorities in wetland archaeology. *Antiquaries Journal* 66. Oxford.
Coles, J.M. (1987b). 'Irish bogs. The time is now.' *North Munster Antiquarian Journal* 28.
Egloff, M. (1982). 'Un avenir _our notre passé? L'archéologie Neuchâteloise entre trax et truelle.' *Musée Neuchâteloise* 3. Colombier, Switzerland.
English Heritage (n.d.). *Stonehenge study group report.* London.
Fischer, A. and S.A. Sørensen (1983). 'Stenalder på den danske havbund.' *Antikvariske studier* 6.
Glutz, R., K. Grewe and D. Müller (1984). *Zeichenrichtlinien für topographische Pläne der archäologischen Denkmalpflege.* Cologne.
Haarnagel, W. (1979). *Die Grabung Feddersen Werde. Methode, Hausbau, Siedlungs-und Wirtschaftsformen sowie Sozialstruktur.* Wiesbaden.
Hall, D.N. (1985). 'Survey work in eastern England.' In S. Macready and E.H. Thompson (eds.), *Archaeological field survey in Britain and abroad.* London.

Hall, D.N. (1986). *Fenland landscape and settlement between Peterborough and March.* East Anglian Archaeology, Fenland Monograph 2. Norfolk.
Hansen, S.S. (1984). 'Gudmund Hatt—The individualist against his time.' *Journal of Danish Archaeology* 3. Odense.
Hayen, H. (1980). *Gedanken zum Schutz von Moor-Resten.* Oldenburg.
Hayen, H. (1981). *Moorarchäologie und Naturschutz.* Oldenburg.
Hayen, H. (1986). 'Peat bog archaeology in Lower Saxony, Germany.' In J.M. Coles and _.J. Lawson (eds.), *European Wetlands in Prehistory.* Oxford.
Hinchliffe, J. and R.T. Schadla-Hall (eds.) (1980). *The Past under the Plough.* Directorate of Ancient Monuments and Historic Buildings. Occasional Paper 3. London.
Hyenstrand, A. (1979). *Ancient monuments and prehistoric society.* Stockholm.
ICCROM (1985). *Preventive Measures During Excavation and Site Protection.* Rome.
Jackson, A.M. (1978). *Forestry and Archaeology. A study in survival of field monuments in south west Scotland.* Hertford.
Kelly, E.P. (1981). 'A short study of the botanical zones on a ringfort at Simonstown, Co. Meath, used as an aid to the recovery of archaeological features.' In D.Ó Corráin (ed.), *Irish Antiquity.* Cork.
Lowe, P., G. Cox, M. MacEwen, T. O'Riordan, and M. Winter (1986). *Countryside conflicts. The politics of farming, forestry and conservation.* Aldershot.
Mallory, J.P. (n.d.). *Navan fort. The ancient capital of Ulster.* Belfast.
Ministry of the Environment (1978). *Conservation of Nature Act.* National Agency for the protection of nature, monuments and sites. Copenhagen.
Muckelroy, K. (ed.) (1980). *Archaeology under water. An atlas of the world's submerged sites.* London.
Müller, S. and C. Neergaard (1908). 'Danevirke.' *Nordiske Fortidsminder* 1.
Poulik, J. (1960). 'Découvertes dans le bourgwall de l'époque de l'Empire Grand-morave à Mikulcice en Moravie méridionale.' *Nouvelles fouilles archéologiques en Tchécoslovaquie.*
Ravnsted-Larsen, L. (1983). 'Fortidsminder og botaniske interesser. Gravhøje er andet end oldsager og skeletter!' *Antikvariske studier* 6.
Sankalia, H.D. (1974). *The prehistory and protohistory of India and Pakistan.* Poona.
Schwarz, K. (1977). 'Denkmalschutz.' *Jahresbericht der bayerischen Bodendenkmalpflege* 15/16, 1974/75.
Skaarup, J. (1983). 'Submarine stenalderbopladser i Det sydfynske Ohav.' *Antikvariske studier* 6.
Solvang, G. (1983). 'Fredningsplanlægning og kulturhistorie. Metoder og resultater fra et pilotprojekt i Vestsjællands amt.' *Antikvariske studier* 6.
Thackray, D.W.R. and K.A. Hearn (1985). 'Archaeology and nature conservation: the responsibility of the National Trust.' In G. Lambrick (ed.), *Archaeology and nature conservation.* Oxford.
Thorsen, S. (1982). 'Olhøj ved Asnæs. Lidt om en ganske almindelig gravhøj, og om dens tilstand gennem de sidste to hundrede år.' *Antikvariske studier* 5.
van der Heide, G.D. (1959). 'Dijkbouw door de eeuwen heen.' In J.E. Bogaers, W. Glasbergen, P. Glazema, and H.T. Waterbolk (eds.), *Hondred eeuwen Nederland.* Gravenhage.
Vaud (Canton de Vaud) (1983). 'Chronique des fouilles archéologiques 1983.' *Revue historique vaudoise* 1983.
Vittery, A. (1985). 'Wildlife and the Countryside.' In G. Lambrick (ed.), *Archaeology and nature conservation.* Oxford.
Wainwright, G.J. (1985). 'The preservation of ancient monuments.' In G. Lambrick (ed.), *Archaeology and nature conservation.* Oxford.
Weber, L. (1984). *Konseivierte Geschichte?* Kempten.
Weidmann, D. (1985). 'Un manteau de terre pour protéger la chartreuse d'Oujon à Arzier.' *Chantiers/Suisse* 16.
Wyss, R. (1979). *Das mittelsteinzeitliche Hirschjägerlager von Schötz 7 in Wauwilermoos.* Archäologische Forschungen. Zurich.

Chapter 2.2

MARS

The Monuments at Risk Survey of England, 1995

Timothy Darvill and Andrew K. Fulton

Source: Darvill, T. and Fulton, A. (1998) *The Monuments at Risk Survey of England 1995*, London: Bournemouth University & English Heritage.

Summary

MARS, THE MONUMENTS AT RISK SURVEY, is the first census of England's rich and diverse archaeological resource. [...]

MARS had two primary aims: first to provide a general picture of the survival and condition of England's archaeological monuments; and, second, to set benchmarks against which future changes can be monitored. The census date for the survey is 1995. [...]

The starting point for MARS was the information held in local and national archaeological records. A representative sample of 14,591 monuments distributed through 1,297 randomly selected sample transects was examined. Work was carried out through four linked programmes: Field Survey to record the survival and current land-use of all MARS Monuments; Aerial Photography to examine land-use change and monument decay for a sub-sample of 7,005 MARS Monuments in 646 transects; National Survey to collate information about existing local and national archaeological records; and Case Study Research to investigate the archaeological history of select monuments and landscapes.

[...]

MARS defined monuments in general terms as: any definable structure, building or work that has archaeological integrity because it represents the contemporary embodiment of the physical context, setting or result of one or more activities that took place in the past. Extrapolating from the MARS sample there are approximately 300,000 monuments recorded in England. Collectively, these cover about 6.5% of the country's land area. No account is taken of monuments not yet discovered.

About 12% of recorded monuments are of prehistoric date, 7% Roman, 22% medieval, and 37% post-medieval and modern; the remainder are of unknown date.

Over half of all monuments are small single monuments (e.g. barrows and enclosures under 3 ha in extent), 9% are large single monuments (e.g. hillforts, deserted villages), 22% are standing buildings and structures, 8% are linear monuments (e.g. roads, boundaries), and 5% are field systems. About 49% of monuments were visible at ground level. There is public access to about 25% of monuments; payment for access was recorded for only 1% of monuments.

Monument survival: half a century of change, 1945–95

England's archaeological resource is constantly changing, not only in its composition and definition, but also in terms of what survives physically and how well. It is a dynamic non-renewable resource. [. . .] All monuments begin to deteriorate from the moment of their creation. If, following its creation, a monument was left entirely alone its deterioration could be described as a natural decay trajectory. The speed of deterioration, the steepness of the decay curve, would be determined by the materials used in construction and the environment in which the monument was set. However, natural decay trajectories seldom if ever occur. There are two opposing forces at work that deflect the course of natural decay trajectories on their inevitable downward path.

First, active curation, whether in the past through repair and reconstruction, or in recent times through conservation and management, may slow down the decay trajectory of a given monument. Second, the effects of hostile land-use or other forms of degradation accelerate the decay process. Because of these forces, the steepness and form of decay profiles, whether natural, semi-natural or accelerated, and the processes that cause decay, are the principal interests of archaeological resource management.

[. . .]

Wholesale monument loss

[. . .] out of 13,488 MARS Monuments examined by the Field Survey Programme, 2,145 (16%) were found to have disappeared. Examination of available records and work by the Air Photographic Survey programme revealed that about half all losses occurred prior to c.1945 (8.3% of the MARS sample), the remainder (7.7%) having been lost between c.1945 and 1995. With an estimated recorded resource of 300,000 monuments, a 16% destruction means that the extant recorded resource in 1995 comprised an estimated 253,000 monuments. [. . .]

Forces of wholesale destruction

During the MARS Project 16 different main hazards which gave rise to monument destruction were recognized. As Figure 2.2.1 shows, five of these hazards account for nearly 80% of all wholesale monument destruction: development and urbanization (27%); demolition and building alteration (20%); mineral extraction and industry (12%); agriculture (10%); and road-building (9%). Of the remainder, 17% of losses could not be attributed to particular forces, while 5% of losses were attributable to a range of relatively minor factors including natural processes, vandalism, visitor erosion, military damage and forestry operations.

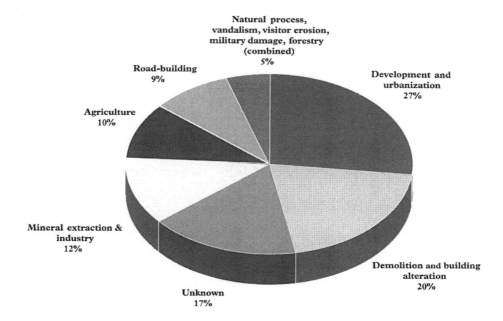

Figure 2.2.1 Pie chart showing the main causes of monument destruction to 1995.
Source: MARS Field Survey Programme (sample: $n = 2{,}145$)

Regional trends are also evident (see Table 2.2.1). Mineral extraction, for example, accounts for a higher percentage of losses in the South West than elsewhere in England. Losses through development and urbanization are highest in the North West and East Midlands, lowest in the West Midlands and South West. Some causes of wholesale monument destruction are more evenly spread around the country, for example losses through road-building and natural processes.

Piecemeal loss and damage

Wholesale destruction is only part of the story. The nibbling away of monuments is less noticeable, less sensational, but cumulatively more destructive. [...]

Out of the extant MARS Monuments checked by the Field Survey Programme, 95% were found to have some evidence of damage or destruction. In some cases this was relatively minor, for example animal burrowing; in other cases it was very considerable and involved the disappearance of large parts of the monument. Subtracting the Current Area 1995 (CA95) of extant MARS Monuments from the projected archaeological extent for the population of extant MARS Monuments reveals that piecemeal loss on extant monuments amounts to 149.3 km², 35% of all the land recorded as containing archaeological monuments or deposits in the sample transects. Extrapolated out, this suggests the piecemeal loss of 2,975 km² of recorded archaeology in England to 1995.

Table 2.2.1 Identified hazards causing wholesale loss of MARS monuments since 1940 in relation to MARS regions

Hazard/cause of destruction	North West	North East	East Midlands	West Midlands	South West	South East	Total
Development and urbanization	6.46	3.56	1.45	4.79	2.86	3.43	22.54
Demolition	5.36	1.10	1.49	3.78	1.71	1.63	15.07
Agriculture	1.10	1.89	0.57	1.80	1.93	1.23	8.52
Road-building	1.32	1.54	1.01	1.58	1.27	0.57	7.29
Mineral extraction	0.35	1.19	0.66	1.49	2.81	0.57	7.07
Industry	0.22	0.53	0.40	0.92	0.88	0.09	3.03
Natural process	0.48	0.97	0.31	0.53	0.35	0.40	3.03
Building alteration	0.09	0.48	0.13	0.70	0.04	0.22	1.67
Forestry	0.09	0.26	0	0.04	0	0	0.40
Military damage	0	0	0	0.13	0.09	0	0.22
Visitor erosion	0	0.04	0	0.04	0	0.04	0.13
Vandalism	0	0	0.04	0.04	0	0	0.09
Unknown	1.89	4.92	1.84	5.36	4.79	12.12	30.94
Total	17.36	16.48	7.90	21.20	16.73	20.30	100%

Source: MARS Aerial Photographic Programme with SMR information (sample: $n = 2,276$)

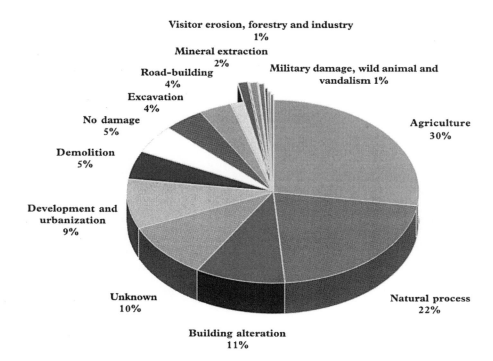

Figure 2.2.2 Pie chart showing the main causes of piecemeal loss and damage to MARS Monuments in 1995, including instances where more than one cause of damage was recorded.
Source: MARS Field Survey Programme (sample: n = 14,639)

Causes of piecemeal loss and damage

At any time the recorded resource is vulnerable to damage or destruction from a very wide range of activities: natural and anthropogenic, legal and criminal. Sometimes they can be hard to detect from field observation, and talking to local people and landowners does not always help. The study of aerial photographs sometimes provides valuable clues, especially where they have been taken at or near to the time when monuments were being damaged.

The causes of piecemeal loss to archaeological monuments are numerous and various, with all 16 defined hazards being recorded. Figure 2.2.2 shows the overall observed incidence of each as a percentage of all recorded observations of damage. At some monuments more than one form of damage was observed. Only 10% of observations could not be tied back to particular hazards or causes.

Four main factors account for nearly 80% of recorded instances of piecemeal loss: agriculture; natural processes and related erosion; building alterations and demolition; and development and urbanization. The balance between these differs considerably from the pattern of forces involved in wholesale destruction. This is because some highly destructive activities such as road-building and mineral extraction do not figure prominently here as their impact is usually wholesale rather than piecemeal. Equally, forces such as agriculture and natural process are well represented here because their effect is accretional and gradual.

The impact of natural and accelerated decay is clear from the figure, with natural processes accounting for 22% of the total incidence of monument loss. The direct effect of anthropogenic causes is clearest, with agriculture and building alteration accounting for 30% and 11% of the total respectively.

At a general level, causes of damage and destruction can be related to the defined monument states. Among earthworks, for which there were 4,315 observations from 5,180 MARS Monuments, agricultural damage was the most frequently reported (53.7% of observations). It is important to recognize, however, that 72% of observations relating to agricultural damage on earthworks relate to flattened monuments whereas only 31% relate to upstanding earthworks. By contrast, 35% of observations related to natural erosion on upstanding earthworks whereas only 7.4% of observations related to natural erosion on flattened earthworks. 2% of observations related to no damage on upstanding earthworks, but only 0.4% of observations recorded no damage on flattened earthworks.

Among buildings and structures, for which there are 5,033 observations relating to 5,229 MARS Monuments, the two largest causes of reported damage are building alterations (39.6%) and natural processes (34%). No damage was recorded in 11.6% of observations.

Landcut monuments are represented by 5,293 observations relating to 5,168 MARS Monuments. The pattern here, as with earthworks, is dominated by natural damage to upstanding examples, but this class also has the highest incidence of no recorded damage (12.5%). Road-building, vandalism and development are observed as more frequent causes of damage in this class.

Detailed analyses of damage to MARS Monuments by form, based on 15,963 observations relating to 14,639 monuments, highlights the fact that standing buildings suffer from quite different causes of damage from other forms of monument. Agriculture is the single biggest cause of damage to all forms except standing buildings, followed by natural processes.

Agriculture is a particular problem for field systems, and within this class it accounted for 66% of losses through piecemeal destruction. This is borne out by a detailed study of medieval ridge and furrow field systems in Northamptonshire where losses of between 63% and 87% were recorded in six sample parishes (Hall 1993: 25). The impact of road-building is also notable: it accounts for 3.6% of observed losses to monuments taken as a whole, but 16.3% of cases affecting linear monuments. Interestingly, forestry accounts for only 1.09% of all instances of observed destruction, and seems to affect large single monuments more than other forms.

There are also regional differences in the pattern of damaging activities, with reference to the three categories of monument character. Among earthworks damage from agriculture is far higher in the East Midlands and South East than in the North West, while natural processes appear to have the greatest effect in the North West and South West. For buildings, natural processes are more prevalent in the West Midlands and South West. [. . .]

Summary (cont.)

The destruction of archaeological monuments has been considerable and widespread. Numerically, 16% of recorded monuments had been completely destroyed prior to 1995,

8% within the last 50 years. In real terms this represents the loss of one recorded monument every day. Piecemeal destruction was recorded at all but 5% of surviving monuments. In total, piecemeal losses amounted to 35% of recorded archaeologically sensitive land. Five main hazards account for over 80% of losses: agriculture, urbanization and development, mineral extraction, demolition and building works, and road construction.

Over the last 50 years there have been considerable changes in monument survival. It was estimated that 95% of earthwork monuments had very good survival in the 1940s; by 1995 only 76% of monuments fell into this category, a decrease of nearly 20%.

Land-use is a critical factor for the survival of archaeological remains. Together, arable, pasture, developed land, semi-natural land and forestry contain about 95% of recorded monuments. Some 87% of monuments lie under a single land-use regime, but only 58% have the same land-use around about as over the monument itself. About 43% of monuments which survived in 1995 had changed land-use at least once since 1945. Attention is given to the implications of projected land-use changes in relation to the survival of the archaeological resource.

About 6% of monuments are protected in law as Scheduled Monuments. They were found to have suffered a lower than average rate of destruction. Consideration is given to other site-based and area-based designations. It was found that many extensive area-based designations, for example National Parks and Areas of Outstanding Natural Beauty, contain some of the best-surviving monuments in the country.

Risk is defined in terms of the probability of particular hazards having a detrimental effect in relation to the impact of such effects. All surviving monuments were assessed. Nationally, about 2% of monuments were found to be at high risk and are considered likely to suffer destruction or serious damage in the next three to five years.

Bibliography

Hall, D. (1993) *The Open Fields of Northamptonshire: The Case for Preservation of Ridge and Furrow*, Northampton: Northampton County Council.

Chapter 2.3

Estimating artefact loss

Melanie B. Rimmer and Chris Caple

Source: Rimmer, M.B. and Caple, C. (2008) 'Estimating artefact loss: a comparison of metal artefact loss rates through in-situ decay and loss of ancient monument sites in England', in H. Kars and R.M. van Herringen (eds), *Preserving Archaeological Remains In-Situ, Proceedings of the 3rd Conference, 7–9 December 2006, Amsterdam*, Amsterdam: VU University Amsterdam, pp. 65–74.

Introduction

[...]

TO ASCERTAIN THE EFFECTIVENESS of ancient monument protection English Heritage commissioned Prof. Tim Darvill to undertake a survey in the 1990s; MARS (Darvill & Fulton 1998). This sought to determine the rate of monument loss since 1945. Five percent of the land area of England was surveyed in order to calculate loss and damage rates for ancient monuments. No estimate has ever been made of the number of archaeological artefacts buried within the ancient monuments of England, nor the rate of object loss through the destruction of these monuments. We have used the information within the MARS report such as estimates of the size and nature of sites, combined with calculations of artefact densities on sites from published archaeological excavation reports, to calculate well founded estimates of:

- The number of metal objects (iron and copper alloy) buried in ancient monuments in England.
- The number of metal objects (iron and copper alloy) lost every year through the destruction of ancient monuments.

[...] Using an innovative differential three-rate estimate for corrosion and data from excavation reports on minimum object dimension it was possible to calculate a well founded estimate of:

- The number of metal objects (iron and copper alloy), buried in England's ancient monuments, lost every year due to corrosion.

Table 2.3.1 Site types used in MARS and this research

Site type	Examples
Field systems	
Large single monuments (more than 3 hectares in area)	causewayed camps, large enclosures, hillforts, oppida, small towns, deserted medieval villages, stone circles
Linear monuments	cursus monuments, avenues, tracks, roads, linear earthworks, pit alignments, linear boundaries, dykes, railways, tramways, canals
Small single monuments (less than 3 hectares in area)	long barrows, bowl barrows, henges, small enclosures, stone circles, Roman villas, moats, moot mounds, castles, farmsteads
Standing buildings	castles, churches, manor houses

MARS Survey

The *Monuments at Risk Survey* (MARS) undertaken by English Heritage in 1995 [...] sought to define the extent of the resource, its condition now and in the past, and the identification of the factors threatening sites (Darvill & Fulton 1998: 4–5) [...]. For calculation purposes sites were grouped into five categories (see Table 2.3.1).

Artefact densities

[...] A series of 48 sites, typical of the period and monument type and with published excavation reports giving the size of the excavated area and listing the metal finds were selected (Rimmer 2006: Appendix One) and metal artefact densities calculated for each monument type (see Table 2.3.2). Standing buildings were excluded. [...]

The MARS survey consisted of a 5% sample of England's total area, estimated at 130,035 km^2. [...] Within the MARS sample area, 14,591 monuments were recorded, covering 425 km^2 or 6.5% of land, suggesting that in England as a whole, 8,500 km^2 are occupied by archaeological sites. The MARS sample area is distributed among the monument forms, as shown in Table 2.3.3.

Using the average object density per square metre figures in Table 2.3.2 and the MARS information on the total area of each monument type, it is possible to calculate an estimate of the total number of copper alloy and iron objects buried in monuments in England.

Table 2.3.2 Average artefact density by monument type

Monument type	Number of sites	Mean artefact density (artefacts/m^2)	Artefact density range (artefacts/m^2)
Field system	4	0.0014	0–0.00542
Large single monument	21	0.8172	0.00176–9.567
Linear monument	9	0.0353	0–0.257
Small single monument	14	0.3933	0.00206–3.345
All	48	0.4789	0–9.567

Table 2.3.3 Number of monuments and area in MARS sample

Monument form	No. of monuments	% of area	Area (km²)
Field systems	751	30	127.50
Large single monuments	1,243	51	216.75
Linear monuments	1,243	7	29.75
Small single monuments	8,276	11	46.75
Standing buildings	3,077	1	4.25
Total	14,590	100%	425

Table 2.3.4 Total number of artefacts in England

Monument form	Total site area in England (m²)	Average density (artefacts per m²)	Total no. of artefacts
Field system	2,550,000,000	0.0014	3,570,000
Large single monument	4,335,000,000	0.8172	3,542,562,000
Linear monument	595,000,000	0.0353	21,003,500
Small single monument	935,000,000	0.3933	367,735,500
Total	8,500,000,000		3,934,871,000

Artefact loss from monument loss

The MARS survey showed that a total of 187 km² of archaeological land in the sample had disappeared, representing 44% of the total area of the MARS sample (Darvill & Fulton 1998: 125) [...] MARS found that the wholesale loss of monuments accounted for 20% or 37.7 km² of the total area loss, while piecemeal loss was much more important, contributing nearly 80% of the total area loss.

Wholesale loss

Of the 14,591 monuments in the survey, 13,488 were examined by the Field Survey programme, and 2,145 of these were found to be totally destroyed, representing 16% of the surveyed sample (Darvill & Fulton 1998: 113). MARS states that just over 48% of the wholesale loss took place between 1945 and 1995 (Darvill & Fulton 1998: 113). This information allows the average loss per year for this time period to be calculated (see Table 2.3.5).

Piecemeal loss

[...] Assuming that piecemeal loss follows the same distribution pattern as that established for wholesale loss, when combined with total area lost through piecemeal loss and the artefact densities, this allows the artefact loss from piecemeal destruction of sites to be calculated in total numbers and yearly loss rate (see Table 2.3.6).

Table 2.3.5 Total number of artefacts destroyed by wholesale monument loss in MARS sample

Monument form	MARS area lost (km^2)	Artefact density (artefacts/m^2)	Estimated total artefact loss	Estimated artefact loss per year
Field system	13.2	0.0014	18,480	177
Large single monument	14.6	0.8172	11,931,068	114,850
Linear monument	3.3	0.0353	116,490	1,115
Small single monument	6.6	0.3933	2,596,045	24,926
Total	37.7		14,662,083	141,068

Table 2.3.6 Artefact loss per year from piecemeal loss in MARS sample

Monument form	Total piecemeal area loss (km^2)	Artefact density (artefacts/m^2)	Estimated total artefact loss	Estimated artefact loss per year
Field system	52.275	0.0014	73,185	703
Large single monument	57.819	0.8172	47,249,687	453,597
Linear monument	13.069	0.0353	461,336	4,429
Small single monument	26.137	0.3933	10,279,682	98,685
Total	149.3		58,063,890	557,414

Table 2.3.7 Total artefact loss per year in England

Monument form	Piecemeal artefact loss per year	Wholesale artefact loss per year	Total artefact loss per year
Field system	14,060	3,540	17,600
Large single monument	9,071,940	2,297,000	11,368,940
Linear monument	88,580	22,300	110,880
Small single monument	1,973,720	498,520	2,472,240
Total	11,148,300	2,821,360	13,969,660

When the two types of loss are combined, it becomes clear that destruction of archaeological land in the MARS survey area alone results in nearly 700,000 metal artefacts being lost per year. Table 2.3.7 shows the extrapolation from the 5% MARS sample to the whole of England. This provides an estimate of nearly 14 million metal artefacts destroyed in England per year.

The loss of 14 million artefacts per year represents approximately 0.36% of the total resource of 4 billion metal artefacts buried in monuments (Table 2.3.4), lost per year between 1945 and 1995.

Artefact loss from corrosion

Corrosion rate

[...] Corrosion rate data from Romanoff (1957) shows [...] the range of corrosion rates of the differing soil types can be divided into three rate bands, with most soil types corroding metal at the slower rate (Rimmer 2006: 34–37). Assuming that this is also true for soils on archaeological sites, corrosion rates for archaeological iron and copper alloy can be represented using three smaller ranges centred on three means. The majority of Romanoff's soil corrosion rates (71%) fall into the first, slowest, range, with the other two holding 13% and 12% respectively. Therefore, three ranges were calculated from a range of archaeological corrosion rates (Rimmer and Caple 2008: Table 10) for both iron and copper alloy (see Table 2.3.8).

Table 2.3.8 Corrosion rate ranges for copper and iron

Rate	Iron		Copper	
	Range (mm year^{-1})	Mean (mm year^{-1})	Range (mm year^{-1})	Mean (mm year^{-1})
Band 1	0.000025–0.00335	0.0016875	0.00003–0.00045	0.00024
Band 2	0.00335–0.006675	0.0050125	0.00045–0.00087	0.00066
Band 3	0.006675–0.0100	0.0083375	0.00087–0.0013	0.00108

Object size

Of primary importance is the point at which an artefact loses its archaeological information value. This point will be reached at different times for different objects. Large iron objects may still provide information on shape and function even when totally mineralised, whereas coins may lose most of their archaeological value with the corrosion of the upper few millimeters, where the dating information lies. For the purposes of estimation, therefore, a figure of 75% mineralisation, based on the experience of conservators and archaeologists, was assigned at which an object is considered to have lost all its value and is no longer part of the useful retrievable archaeological record. [...] The dimensions of (230 copper and iron) artefacts from the sites of Deansway and Orton's Pasture were taken [...] and the smallest dimension that was continuous throughout the artefact, estimated to the nearest millimetre. Using this information and knowing the corrosion rate, it is possible to calculate the lifespan of an artefact, since when the smallest dimension has corroded through, the object has effectively corroded away. [...]

Object loss rate

Using the total number of artefacts calculated from the MARS data (see Table 2.3.4) and assuming that the distribution of the object sizes from Deansway and Orton's

Table 2.3.9 Artefact loss per year from corrosive decay

	Total no. of artefacts	Artefacts lost per year at Rate 1	Artefacts lost per year at Rate 2	Artefacts lost per year at Rate 3	Total estimated artefacts lost per year
Iron	2,457,657,312	1,864,000	1,013,775	1,556,542	4,434,317
Copper	1,474,702,030	292,676	147,369	222,599	662,644
All	3,934,871,000	2,156,676	1,161,144	1,779,141	5,096,961

Pasture were representative of the whole buried objects population, the number of artefacts of each size and material was calculated. Then the number of artefacts falling into each of the three rate bands (71% of artefacts in rate band 1, 13% in band 2, 12% in band 3) as suggested by Romanoff's study above, could be calculated and, assuming that 75% loss of thickness meant loss of all archaeological information, it was possible to calculate the average 'useful' lifespan of artefacts of each size at each of the mean corrosion rates. When the number of artefacts in each category is divided by the expected life span for that category an estimate of object loss rate per year is achieved (see Table 2.3.9).

These calculations suggest that corrosive decay accounts for an average loss of over 5 million objects per year. This represents approximately 0.13% of the total resource.

Conclusion

In this study, the data from the *Monuments at Risk Survey* of 1995 were used as a baseline for understanding the number and loss rate of metal artefacts (iron and copper alloy) buried in the monuments of England. This was calculated using average artefact densities of the various site types. It was calculated that in 1945, the archaeological area of England contained nearly 4 billion iron and copper artefacts. This number represents only the area of known archaeological monuments and does not include single findspots, as these were not part of MARS (Darvill & Fulton 1998: 31). The same artefact densities were then used to calculate the number of artefacts being lost per year from macro scale destruction of archaeological sites. This was found to be approximately 14 million artefacts per year across England. It has been shown that it is possible to apply corrosion rate data to calculate object loss rates. [. . .]This resulted in estimates of artefact loss from corrosion of around 5 million artefacts per year, representing approximately 0.13% of the total resource. These figures would suggest that corrosive decay accounts for around one third as much loss as monument damage.

Measures such as monument scheduling make the protection of vulnerable archaeological sites possible on a legal basis. [. . .]

An alternative approach to legal protection is to identify risk, an approach that has been explored by Jonathan Ashley-Smith for museum objects (Ashley-Smith 1999). By identifying the extent of object loss and the mechanisms responsible, it should be possible to target resources to minimise loss and, if necessary, archaeologically recover those objects in the potentially most damaging environments. This study has provided the first estimates of metal artefact numbers in England and their loss rates, showing the potential scale of the resource and the level of risk it is at. Though annual loss rate is a simplistic device – it does powerfully demonstrate the scale of artefact loss.

Though this work would suggest that presently larger numbers of objects are being lost through monument destruction than corrosion, this probably reflects the large loss of monuments in the post war building boom. The present rate of monument loss and thus artefact loss rate is likely to be far lower, due to the increasing awareness of archaeological remains following the introduction of PPG16. However, until the MARS survey is repeated there is no proof that the rate of monument loss has declined. [. . .] Recent work suggests that corrosion rates are increasing due to air pollution, the use of fertilisers, climate, changing soil water contents, road salting, fertilisers and soil disturbance. Consequently, the figure for object loss due to corrosion *in situ* may well be increasing. [. . .] These figures do indicate that there is an appreciable loss rate for archaeological metal artefacts buried in the soil of England and that the term 'preservation *in situ*' is potentially misleading, since while remaining buried *in situ*, metal artefacts are not all being preserved.

Bibliography

Ashley-Smith, J. (1999). *Risk Assessment for Object Conservation*. Oxford: Butterworth-Heinemann.

Darvill, T. and A. Fulton (1998). *The Monuments at Risk Survey of England 1995: Main Report*. Bournemouth and London: Bournemouth University & English Heritage.

Rimmer, M. (2006). Modeling the Destruction of the Archaeological Resource, unpublished BSc dissertation, Dept. of Archaeology, Durham University.

Rimmer, M.B. and C. Caple (2008). 'Estimating Artefact Loss: A comparison of metal artefact loss rates through in-situ decay and loss of ancient monument sites in England.' In H. Kars, R.M. van Herringen (eds.), *Preserving Archaeological Remains In-Situ, Proceedings of the 3rd Conference, 7–9 December 2006, Amsterdam*. Amsterdam: VU University Amsterdam, 65–74.

Romanoff, M. (1957). *Underground Corrosion (National Bureau of Standards Circular 579)*. Houston, Texas: National Association of Corrosion Engineers.

Chapter 2.4

Decay of delicate organic remains in shallow urban deposits
Are we at a watershed?

Harry Kenward and Allan Hall

Source: Kenward, H. and Hall, A. (2000) 'Decay of delicate organic remains in shallow urban deposits: are we at a watershed?', *Antiquity*, 74: 519–25.

URBAN OCCUPATION DEPOSITS containing organic materials preserved by anoxic waterlogging offer an extraordinarily valuable source of information about past life in many European towns, from Dublin to Novgorod, and from Tromsø to Zürich. Such deposits present an enormous challenge to those who wish to preserve the below-ground cultural heritage since there is very little understanding of the way they will react to human interference, or to both local and global environmental change. York, England, is one of the richest repositories of such deposits, as shown by a quarter-century of excavation and research by the York Archaeological Trust and others. In much of the city centre richly organic deposits are 2–5 m in thickness and contain abundant plant and animal remains as delicate as leek leaf epidermis and lice (Kenward & Hall 1995), as well as a wealth of artefacts of biological origin. These deposits are, of course, very vulnerable to damage through changing ground conditions, particularly reduction in water content, and any evidence that they are endangered must be taken most seriously. This is not a new issue; as long ago as 1994 Martin Biddle drew attention to the possibility that the insertion of piles—widely seen as an acceptable mitigation strategy—might cause physical destruction to surrounding deposits through disturbance and also lead to irreversible damage to archaeological evidence through dewatering and oxidation (Biddle 1994). A series of observations suggests that deposits in York may be at risk, and in particular that there is a slice of shallower deposits which are undergoing active decay.

The first steps towards addressing the problem of in-ground decay are being made (see, for example, papers in Corfield *et al.* 1998), but with emphasis on survival of organic artefacts and monitoring using groundwater chemistry. Some studies of decay of biological remains have been made at rural sites but we would suggest that urban deposits present a rather more complex set of problems. We would also argue that it cannot be assumed that easily monitored groundwater properties, the normal measure of the well-being of deposits, can necessarily be directly related to the preservation of delicate biological remains.

Is there a general problem of decay in near-surface deposits?

A long series of observations (mostly made before current awareness of in-ground decay issues) have led the authors to suspect that recent or current decay of urban organic deposits may be widespread. Because the problem has only been recognized in the past few years, the evidence from York all remains circumstantial and has rarely been systematically recorded. It may be summarized as follows. First, biological remains suspected of having undergone recent severe decay have been observed at 44–45 Parliament Street (Davis *et al.* 2002; Oxley 1998). The remains showed an unusual kind of preservation, indicated by yellow-brown to orange-brown colours, which were also locally evident in the raw organic sediment and in concretions formed from faecal material. Outside York, a striking example of preservation of insect remains close to the point of destruction was provided by material from an 18th century pit at Berrington Street, Hereford (Kenward 1985); with hindsight, it is hard to believe that the pale filmy 'ghosts' of insects found at this site could have survived for very long in what, when sampled, appeared to be a well-drained layer. Recent dewatering of deposits which were formerly saturated by static water and therefore anoxic surely represents a far more plausible explanation for the condition of the fossils.

A second kind of evidence for decay of organic sediments in recent decades is the observation that there has been shrinkage of deposits beneath modern concrete slabs—noted at the Parliament Street site and at an excavation within the premises of British Home Stores in Feasegate (Carrott *et al.* 1998), 150 m away. A brief survey of field archaeologists suggests that other examples have gone unremarked in York and elsewhere, their significance to the problem of recent in-ground decay not having been recognized.

A third likely indicator of changing ground conditions is deposition of calcium sulphate within sediments, positively identified at Parliament Street (Carrott *et al.* 1996a: 5). Very similar white crystalline deposits were seen in voids at the Feasegate site. It has been suggested that this is the result of water laden with calcium (from a slab of poor concrete) interacting with dewatering sulphide-rich deposits which had until recently been anoxic.

Perhaps the commonest and most significant circumstantial evidence for recent decay is the widespread occurrence of abundant but poorly preserved delicate remains in shallow deposits. It is with the fate of remains in deposits of this kind, rather than with local effects such as those caused by cellars, piles, and crushed limestone backfills, that we are primarily concerned in this note.

Before discussing this phenomenon further, it will be useful to define three categories of biological remains. The first, *labile* material such as muscle, fat, and plant cell contents, will normally decay very quickly through autolysis and fermentation. *Delicate* remains, such as plant cell walls and insect cuticle, with which we are mainly concerned here, are generally preserved only under conditions of anoxia. The last category, *robust* remains, comprises mineralized tissue such as bone, shell and plant silica, and charred or mineral-replaced remains of more delicate fossils, able to survive in a much wider range of depositional environments.

Why are poorly preserved delicate remains a cause for concern?

Deposits containing poorly preserved, often reddened, delicate macrofossil plant and invertebrate remains are common in the upper parts of the stratigraphy in York. Indeed, they are regarded as normal, and the archaeological community, including the present authors, appears to have accepted rather unquestioningly that it is quite natural that these remains were simply preserved in poor condition and that they would remain so indefinitely. Sites in Swinegate, The Bedern and Coffee Yard (Carrott *et al.* 1994; Hall *et al.* 1993; Robertson *et al.* 1989) provide excellent examples, where insect remains were often on the borderline of identifiability and plant remains were limited to the more decay-resistant types and ghosts of less robust kinds. Such remains have been assumed to be strongly decayed either because they were deposited under rather dry conditions or because they were in sediments with a low organic content which favoured degradation of organic matter. But, as will be argued below, both of these assumptions may be unfounded.

Preservationally sensitive biological remains such as seeds, wood and insect fragments are able to survive without charring or mineralization in suitable anoxic deposits for very long periods of time. There are examples of such materials which are millions of years old (e.g. Andrews 1961; Elias 1994; Matthews 1970), and plant and insect fossils a few thousand years old preserved by anoxia are of course common place in northern Europe, and elsewhere in the world. Post-burial change (diagenesis) of these remains in stable anoxic deposits is evidently extremely slow. It is thus not surprising that urban archaeological deposits—which are relatively extremely young—often give remains which are quite stunningly well preserved. Where insects occur at all they are mostly in rather good condition, retaining roughly their original colours and surfaces, and often hairs and scales (e.g. Kenward 1978: plate IV), although with characteristic changes in texture; very delicate fossils such as lice and wings of bees and flies are often present in urban deposits (e.g. Kenward & Hall 1995: 705–7; Schelvis 1998). Plant remains vary more in their state of preservation, perhaps because of the greater likelihood of a variable degree of preburial decay and certainly because of the less robust nature of many non-lignified plant tissues. Despite this, what survives—seeds, leaves, stems and even very delicate tissues such as fragments of epidermis—often retains many diagnostic features (e.g. Tomlinson 1985). Such plant and insect remains can mostly be identified very easily, given appropriate experience and reference material, and they yield important archaeological evidence. [. . .]

Having established that preservation of delicate remains by anoxic waterlogging in deeper deposits is often superb, the occurrence of typically much more decayed fossils in near-surface layers becomes the more striking and in need of explanation. The same contrast is seen at some rural sites, and in natural deposits, but here it may be quite clear that recent and identifiable changes in ground conditions (through drainage) have caused the damage, e.g. at Seamer Carr, North Yorkshire (Carrott *et al.* 1996b; Kenward & Large 1997) and at various sites in England identified during the series of large-scale wetland surveys funded over the past quarter-century by English Heritage.

[. . .]

No systematic record of the condition of fossils in such deposits has been made, although a proposal to make detailed recording of preservational condition a matter of routine has been put forward (Kenward & Large 1998).

When did decay occur in York's shallow stratigraphy?

[...]

The slow and synchronous decay of organic matter over large areas, or the occurrence of slightly adverse conditions leading to widespread stable but poor preservation, both seem most improbable. It is hard to see how an 'equilibrium' state of decay could be maintained in an oxidizing burial environment; decay is a 'ratchet' process which can only move in one direction. If conditions are not suited to long-term preservation, we suggest, then the remains will surely decay quickly and completely, although at different rates for different deposits of the same age.

It is difficult to make a case for gradual long-term decay. Casual observations suggest that aerobic decay of most biological materials of the kind we are considering here in modern soils and other media (such as compost heaps) is quite fast. It is suggested that, for archaeological remains, the main phase of decay occurred before, during and for a short period after deposition. At this stage labile remains disappeared unless conditions were right for rapid mineral-replacement (Briggs & Kear 1993a, 1993b). Soon after burial, ground conditions typically became more or less stable. If the chemistry of an archaeological sediment was suitable for long-term preservation of delicate remains, they should still exist for us to find, unless ground conditions subsequently changed. If conditions were not right, then the delicate fossils were quickly lost and only robust remains survived. Only very rarely is decay likely to have progressed, but slowly enough for fossil assemblages to be only partly down the trajectory after several centuries.

[...]

If we rule out slow continuous decay mechanisms we are led to the conclusion that the reddened insect and other remains in superficial layers are currently undergoing fairly rapid decay, having *until recently* been subject to conditions which were suitable for long-term survival, but which have altered, probably through reduction in water content.

[...]

For the present we can at least flag up the possibility that there is widespread recently initiated decay of delicate remains (and the organic matrix) in superficial urban archaeological deposits, in the hope that all archaeologists, whether engaged in excavation or working on recovered organic materials, are aware that it may exist, and that they will collect and disseminate relevant evidence whenever it appears.

References

Andrews, H.N. (1961). *Studies in palaeobotany*. New York: Wiley.

Biddle, M. (1994). *What future for British archaeology?* Oxford: Oxbow. Lecture 1.

Briggs, D.E.G. and A.J. Kear (1993a). 'Fossilisation of soft tissue in the laboratory.' *Science* 259: 1439–42.

Briggs, D.E.G. and A.J. Kear (1993b) 'Decay and preservation of polychaetes: taphonomic thresholds in soft-bodied organisms.' *Paleobiology* 19: 107–35.

Carrott, J., K. Dobney. A. Hall, D. Jaques *et al*. (1994). 'Assessment of biological remains from excavations at 12–18 Swinegate, 8 Grape Lane, and 14, 18, 20 and 22 Back Swinegate/Little Stonegate, York (YAT/Yorkshire Museum site codes 1989-90.28 and 1990.1).' *Environmental Archaeology Unit Report 94/13*. York: Environmental Archaeology Unit.

Carrott, J., A. Hall, M. Issitt *et al*. (1996a). 'Suspected accelerated in situ decay of delicate bioarchaeological remains: a case study from medieval York.' *Environmental Archaeology Unit. Report 96/15*. York: Environmental Archaeology Unit.

Carrott, J., H. Kenward and M. Issitt (1996b). 'Seamer Carr landfill extension: evaluation of the archaeological potential of insect remains.' *Environmental Archaeology Unit Report 98/16*. York: Environmental Archaeology Unit.

Carrott, J., P. Huches, D. Jaques *et al.* (1998). 'Assessment of biological remains from BHS store, Feasegate, York (site code YORYM1998.2).' *Environmental Archaeology Unit Report 98/16*. York: Environmental Archaeology Unit.

Corfield, M., P. Hinton, T. Nixon *et al.* (ed.) (1998). *Preserving Archaeological Remains In-Situ?*. London: Museum of London Archaeological Service.

Davis, M., A. Hall, H. Kenward *et al.* (2002). 'Preservation of Urban Archaeological Deposits: monitoring and characterisation of archaeological deposits at Marks and Spencer, 44–45 Parliament Street, York.' *Internet Archaeology* 11, available at: http://intarch.ac.uk/journal/issue11/oxley_index.html.

Elias, S.A. (1994). *Quaternary insects and their environments*. Washington (DC): Smithsonian Institution Press.

Hall, A.R., H.K. Kenward and A. Robertson (1993). 'Investigation of medieval and post-medieval plant and invertebrate remains in The Bedern', *Ancient Monuments Laboratory Reports* 56–8/93.

Kenward, H.K. (1978). 'The analysis of archaeological insect assemblages: a new approach.' *The Archaeology of York* 19(1): 1–68. London: Council for British Archaeology.

Kenward, H.K. (1985). 'The insect fauna: Berrington Street site 4.' In R. Shoesmith, *Hereford City Excavations 3: The Finds*, CBA Research Report 56, (and microfiche M9.B4–11). London: Council for British Archaeology.

Kenward, H.K. and A.R. Hall (1995). 'Biological evidence from Anglo-Scandinavian deposits at 16–22 Coppergate.' *The Archaeology of York* 14(7): 435–797. York: Council for British Archaeology.

Kenward, H. and F. Large (1997). 'Insect remains from Seamer Carr landfill site: ecological reconstruction of a Mesolithic shore.' *Environmental Archaeology Unit Report 97/30*. York: Environmental Archaeology Unit.

Kenward, H. and F. Large (1998). 'Recording the preservational condition of archaeological insect fossils.' *Environmental Archaeology* 2: 49–60.

Matthews, J.V. (1970). 'Two new species of *Micropeplus* from the Pliocene of western Alaska with remarks on the evolution of Micropeplinae (Coleoptera: Staphylinidae).' *Canadian Journal of Zoology* 48: 779–88.

Oxley, J. (1998). 'Planning and the conservation of archaeological deposits.' In M. Corfield, P. Hinton, T. Nixon *et al.* (ed.), *Preserving Archaeological Remains In-Situ?*. London: Museum of London Archaeological Service. 51–4.

Robertson, A., P. Tomlinson and H.K. Kenward (1989). 'Plant and insect remains from Coffee Yard, York.' *Environmental Archaeology Unit Report 89/12*. York: Environmental Archaeology Unit.

Schelvis, J. (1998). 'Remains of sheep ectoparasites as indicators of wool processing in the past.' In M. Dewilde, A. Ervynck and A. Wielemans (ed.), *Ypres and the medieval cloth industry in Flanders*, Archeologie in Vlaanderen Monografie 2. Asse-Zellik: Instituut voor het Archeologisch Patrimonium, 89–98.

Tomlinson, P. (1985). 'Use of vegetative remains in the identification of dyeplants from waterlogged 9th-10th century AD deposits at York.' *Journal of Archaeological Science* 12: 269–83.

Approaches to preservation and conservation

Chapter 3

Knowledge of the burial environment

Soil and stratigraphy

THE CONCEPTS OF THE WEATHERING of rock to form sands and silts, their transportation deposition and lithification to form new rocks, as well as the concept of stratigraphy, were described by James Hutton in *Theory of the Earth* in 1785, though it was Charles Lyell's *Principles of Geology* of 1833 that brought these ideas to wider attention. Japetus Steenstrup (1836) showed that stratigraphy applied to bogs, and since trees and other plant remains survived in such waterlogged conditions, a vegetation history of the past could be established. Only when it was appreciated that pollen was preserved in bogs could the full potential for creating detailed vegetational history sequences be fully realised (Erdtman 1924). A sketch of the vertical section through his excavations made by William Stukeley in 1722 (Piggott 1985: Figure 18) suggests that a basic understanding of the stratigraphic concept, and that it could be applied to soils and cultural remains, was appreciated by at least some of the earliest antiquarians, though it would be later that archaeologists such as Pitt-Rivers who routinely use it as an archaeological tool for relative dating of sites and associated artefacts.

Generations of farmers and gardeners from the Neolithic to the present have been aware of the nature of soil, its structure and the decay of materials buried within it. It was only in the nineteenth century that such phenomena began to be recorded systematically and theories about the physical, biological and chemical activities taking place advanced. In his book *The Formation of Vegetable Mould Through the Action of Worms with Observations of Their Habits* (1881) (see Chapter 3.1), Darwin showed, from repeated experiments and observations, how earthworms sifted the soil, gradually transporting it to the surface through their casts, and thus buildings and large objects appeared to slowly sink as the ground around them rose 0.2 of an inch per year (Atkinson 1957).

Soils have principally been studied and discussed as the medium in which crops grow; consequently, research has focused on plant nutrition, the cycling of elements and the activities of soil organisms. Work by Boussingault in France in the 1830s, Liebig in Germany in the 1840s and Laws and Gilbert in England in the 1970s established the principles of plant nutrition and the importance of the chemistry of soil as a medium for plant growth. Soil has also been studied as an engineering material in, on or of which structures such as buildings, dams or roads are constructed. The physical properties such as the particle size distribution or the compressive strength of different soils were measured and studied by engineers. Farmers and mining engineers and administrators were aware of water in the soil and could use it to supply cities with water, as Julius Sextus Frontinus did for Rome after AD 97, or remove it from mines as described by Georgius Agricola (*De re metallica*) in 1556. It was William Smith (1769–1839) who started to apply stratigraphic principles to water holding capacities of rocks and soils, but only after 1856 when Frenchman Henry Darcy determined a generalised relationship for flow of liquids in porous media (Darcy's Law) (rate at which groundwater flows is equal to the product of the hydraulic conductivity multiplied by the hydraulic gradient) did it become possible to plan and predict the behaviour of water in soils, and the science of hydrology (a term coined by Lucas in 1874) had begun.

By the twentieth century, particular types of soil were seen to develop in specific climatic conditions, on specific bedrocks, in specific topographies and under specific types of vegetation. The presence of different types of soil was mapped across the world, exemplified by Kubiëna's classification of *The Soils of Europe* (1953). The development of soil classification systems, such as the ABC horizon format initially developed by Dukochaev in Russia in the 1870s and widely promulgated by Curtis Marbut in the USA in the 1920s, was an essential prerequisite to such mapping.

This evolving understanding of the nature of soil appreciated that it was not only dependent on vegetation, climate and parent rock type, but also on human activity. Since soil is a medium that retains a record, through the different colours and textures in the soil, a history of past events can be read and interpreted. Phenomena such as the stratigraphic build-up of human debris on continuously occupied sites, soil stains from decayed organic matter (e.g. postholes) and distinctive changes in soil texture and orientation derived from human excavation of pits and ditches could all be understood and associated with the distinctive artefacts they contained to provide a relative sequence of human activities. These events can be seen at the human scale in groupings such as settlements. They can also be seen on a larger scale, where evidence of soil exhaustion speaks of widespread unsustainable agriculture, and at a regional/landscape scale, where blanket peat formation speaks of climate change. These phenomena could also be detected on the micro-scale, where the size and shape of soil grains and the presence of seeds and charcoal fragments are evidence of agriculture and other human activities. Environmental archaeologists and soil scientists have encouraged archaeologists to interpret land use through soil analysis both at a macro and more recently at a micro level: Ian Cornwall's (1958) *Soils for the Archaeologist* (see Chapter 3.2), Susan Limbrey's (1975) *Soil Science and Archaeology* and more recently the work of Davidson and Simpson (2001). However, it is through drawing from ethnography, experimental archaeology and archaeological excavation that the correlation between soil features and their causative human activities are established (Schiffer 1987).

Experiment and decay

Disciplines such as chemistry, biology and physics can perform experiments to test their hypotheses. The corrosion and decay processes of numerous materials, iron, glass, copper, silver, wood, bone and even modern polymers, have been investigated in the laboratory and the key factors and mechanisms identified. Modern studies are largely concerned with short-term performance of materials, ensuring objects do not fail in use; they are rarely extrapolated to longer time frames. Disciplines such as climatology, astronomy, geology and archaeology rely primarily on observations of the natural world and the principle of uniformatarianism (the processes that we observe today are the same as those that occurred in the past and gave rise to features in the environment that surround us) to explain their observations.

Both these approaches have been used to understand the degradation (diagenesis) processes that affect archaeological remains buried in the soil:

1 *Laboratory-based studies*: ascertaining the mechanisms of decay of modern materials in the laboratory and modelling the data from short-term laboratory experiments with a limited number of variables to predict rates of decay in the longer term for more complex archaeological burial situations. The work by Pollard et al. (2006) and Wilson et al. (2006) demonstrated the difficulty in correlating data from laboratory studies with readings from field studies or creating accurate predictive models. The short time frames available for modern laboratory work make it difficult to accurately mimic archaeological time frame processes.
2 *Evidence from the burial environment*: examining ancient artefacts retrieved from archaeological excavations. Pedologists, biologists, geologists and chemists have measured aspects of the burial environment and analysed archaeological materials retrieved from these contexts (Davy 1826; Schweizer 1994; Fjaestad et al. 1996). However, assumptions have to be made about the starting conditions, which can never truly be known, in order to offer any interpretation about what has occurred over archaeological time.

There are a small number of examples where 'known' modern materials have been buried in different natural soils. In almost all these short-term experiments, samples have been retrieved after a few years – so results can be published (Romanoff 1957; Pollard et al. 2004). In all these approaches, high levels of variation have been found, which reflects the complexity we see in the natural environment and the synergistic nature of decay processes (one process influencing the rate of another). Using information from all these sources, the basic principles of decay for all archaeological materials have been ascertained (see Table 3.0.1) and published (Cronyn 1990; Huisman 2009).

To date, archaeology has conducted few 'ground truthing' experiments, recording the resultant archaeological traces of the decay or destruction of known structures, after undertaking known activities or burying known materials for long periods. Apart from the experiments at Lejre (Denmark), the most well known and longest running is the Experimental Earthwork Project (Bell et al. 1996) (see Chapter 3.3), which, in 1960, constructed a short section of bank and ditch at Overton Down identical to the prehistoric chalk-land earthwork monuments seen throughout southern England. A similar earthwork was dug in 1963 on the acidic sandy soil at Wareham Heath, Dorset. Both these earthworks had materials buried beneath their banks and had sections to be excavated at intervals of 2, 4, 8, 16, 32, 64 and 128 years in order to:

- ascertain the time and manpower needed to construct prehistoric earthworks;
- establish the nature, speed and mechanisms of physical alteration of the bank and ditch, in order to better interpret the forms of monument that had been excavated;
- obtain accurate figures for the movement of archaeological artefacts due to the action of earthworms and other mechanisms; and
- establish the rate of loss of materials and ascertain the mechanisms of decay.

Table 3.0.1 Decay of archaeological materials

Material	Decay	References
General	Physical damage occurs at macro levels. Animals trample apart earth and stone structures and artefacts. Human beings vandalise or alter and adapt all forms of artefact and structure for new uses. Root action from vegetation gradually tears apart stone structures and punches holes through waterlogged materials. Weathering; the effects of rain, wind, sun wear away all exposed materials at different rates.	Cronyn (1990); Florian *et al.* (1990)
Ceramics Clays (hydrated alumino-silicates) e.g. kaolin with added temper (crushed stone, vegetable material, shell, etc.) fired between 700 and 1,300°C.	Vessels are brittle breaking into fragments (sherds) when dropped. Porus earthernware ceramic: poorly fired ceramics soften in damp conditions (rehydration of meta kaolin). Sherds, suffer distortion, physical fracture and abraision. Poorly attached glaze and slip can detach due to expansion and contraction at differing rates to the ceramic body. Ceramics from marine and many arid environments contain soluble salts which are drawn to the surface due to evaporation and capillary action, where they form crystals which break up the surface or cause it to spall off. High fired porcelains and stonewares are generally chemically stable.	Buys and Oakley (1993: 18–28)
Glass Non-crystalline solid based on silica normally with sodium, potassium and calcium oxide additions.	Vessels are brittle, breaking into fragments (sherds) when dropped. In damp soil, sodium and potassium ions dissolve from the outer edge of the glass, replaced by hydrogen ions from water in the burial environment. This outer 'hydrogen glass' layer forms fine lamella over the surface, which flakes off easily. The sodium and potassium can form strong alkalis, which breaks down the glass network, which gradually becomes porous. The rate of decay depends on the glass composition. Poor composition, too much potassium or too little silica ('forest glass' found in Medieval Europe) leads to glass that decays quickly. Too much lime in the glass composition can lead to the formation of a hard white crust, which, if it adsorbs dirt and dust, appears black.	Newton and Davison (1989: Chapter 4)
Stone Sedimentary rock (sandstone, limestone) typically formed of rock fragments held together with a cement and	All rocks, split along lines of weakness – bedding planes. In freezing conditions, water forms ice crystals in the pores of the stone that, if they are of varying sizes, lead to growth of large ice crystals which shatter the stone. In oscillating wet and dry conditions, lime, silica and iron oxides, which often bind together the mineral grains in sedimentary rocks, can partially dissolve and be drawn to the	Price (1996); Porter (1991); Webster (1992)

Table 3.0.1 continued

Material	Decay	References
containing voids (pores) or lithified organic materials (coal, amber). Igneous rocks (granite, basalt) formed of solidified molten rock from the earth's core. Metamorphic rocks (marble, slate) formed from heat affecting sedimentary rocks.	stone exterior where they redeposit. This leads to a dense surface with a weakened area behind. This surface can split off since it expands and contracts at different rates to the rest of the stone. In many cases, a crust of redeposited mineral and dust can form on the stone surfaces (often black from soot). This is likely to spall off from differential thermal or hydration expansion and contraction. Permanently wet stone surface support algae. Stone in contact with groundwater can contain soluble salts that break up the surface (see ceramics). Chalk or lime-rich rocks can be dissolved by acidic groundwaters. Some stones such as amber gradually hydrolyse with water. Stones such as jet and shale crack and surfaces spall off when water reacts with clay particles expanding them and minerals such as iron sulphide oxidise. Igneous and metamorphic rocks generally have lower porosity and are usually more stable than sedimentary rocks.	
Metals Archaeological metals; iron (steel, cast iron) and copper alloys (bronze, brass, quaternary alloys), lead, tin, silver gold and its alloys.	In oxidising conditions, metals, with the exception of gold, react with oxygen and water (and dissolved gases and other soluble ions) to form a range of corrosion minerals. Iron corrodes readily, especially in marine environments (chloride ions catalyse its corrosion), forming a range of yellow to red to black iron oxides. Copper alloys corrode more slowly, normally forming red (cuprite) and green (copper carbonate) corrosion products. Lead corrodes slowly, principally forming white-grey (lead carbonate) minerals, save in the presence of decaying organic material when it can corrode quickly. Tin forms a brown mineral coating (cassiterite) and corrosion slows almost to a halt. Silver corrodes slowly, producing grey corrosion products (silver sulphide and silver chloride). In reducing (anoxic/anaerobic) conditions (without oxygen), metals do not corrode; some have thin dense black sulphide coatings.	Selwyn (2004); Cronyn (1990)
Leather Tanned form of animal skin (hide) formed of fibres of the protein collagen.	Only survives in waterlogged, desiccated or frozen conditions as insect and microbial attack will consume it within months in normal damp oxygenated soils. Vegetable tanning agents (normally used) dissolve out slowly in waterlogged conditions. The collagen gradually	Kite and Thomson (2006: Chapter 5); Calnan and Haines (1991)

Table 3.0.1 continued

Material	Decay	References
	breaks down under the effect of water (hydrolysis), leaving a weak material plumped up with water. If it dries out, the leather shrinks, distorts and cracks.	
Bone Matrix of the mineral hydroxyapatite and protein collagen.	In normal damp aerobic burial conditions, bone degrades slowly as the mineral limits the access to the collagen, which is consumed by microbes. In acidic soils, the hydroxyapatite is dissolved by the groundwater and the bone degrades much more quickly. In chalky conditions, lime deposits build up on and in the bone. Over long time periods, groundwater containing dissolved minerals can deposit these minerals in the porous bone, gradually replacing the collagen, leading to fossilised bone.	Millard (2001)
Wood Material with a hollow tubular cellular structure, cell walls composed of cellulose (long glucose-based polymer), lignin (aromatic alcohol polymer) and hemicelluloses (shorter branched cellulose).	Only survives in waterlogged, desiccated or frozen conditions as fungal attack will consume it within months in normal damp oxygenated soil conditions. In waterlogged conditions, bacterial attack and the hydrolysis of cellulose weakens the wood, whose structure is maintained through the presence of water. Loss of the water upon excavation and the associated capillary tension effects cause cellular collapse, cracking, warping and shrinkage of the wood. Eventually, water loss from the cell walls leads to irreversible shrinkage.	Rowell and Barbour (1990: Chapters 2, 3, 5, 6)
Textiles Primarily woven sheet materials of threads formed of twisted animal and plant fibres. Animal fibres = hair from sheep (wool) or other animals, also silk. Plant fibres = either baste fibres (linen from flax plant) or seed fibres (cotton).	Cellulosic fibres (cotton, linen) only survive in waterlogged, desiccated or frozen conditions as fungal attack will consume them within months in normal damp oxygenated soil conditions. In waterlogged conditions, bacterial attack and hydrolysis weaken the cellulose chains, leading to a loss of strength. The structure is supported by water, which, upon evaporation, causes the material to shrink and break up. Proteinaceous fibres (wool, silk) only survive in waterlogged, desiccated or frozen conditions as insect and microbial attack will consume them within months in normal damp oxygenated soil conditions. In waterlogged conditions, hydrolysis weakens the protein chains (keratin for wool, fibroin for silk), leading to a loss of strength. The structure is supported by water, which, upon evaporation, causes the material to shrink and break up.	O'Connor and Brooks (1990); Timár-Balázsy and Eastop (1998: Chapter 1)

Initially conceived to ascertain information on the first three points, the materials' decay was added to this experiment and was consequently less well planned. The work at Overton Down (Bell et al. 1996) has thus far shown:

- An initially vertical-sided flat bottom ditch, cut into chalk or sand, developed a shallow V-shaped profile. The bank lost height and spread at the base (see Figure 3.3.2).
- The rate of soil movement was initially high, though the rate of silting thereafter was slow. This confirms observations on similar earthworks made by Pitt-Rivers in 1897 at Wor Barrow and later by Curwen at Thundersbarrow hill (Jewell 1963: 9, 10).
- The biological activity in the soil significantly affected the rate of loss of organic materials (wood, textile, skin). Earthworm activity accounted for the gradual loss of stratigraphy and vertical movement of finds (see Figures 3.3.3 and 3.3.4).
- pH was a significant factor in decay of bone, dissolving in the lower pH 4.5–5.1 of Wareham and preserved thus far, though slightly degraded, at Overton Down (see Figure 3.3.4).
- Movement of water is seen as significant in removing tanning agents, a key factor in the survival of leather.
- Variability (e.g. in the survival of linen) that is not yet explicable.

Subsequent experimental earthworks at Wroughton (Wiltshire), Little Butser (Hampshire), Boscombe (Hampshire), Fishbourne (Sussex), L'Esquerda, Vic (Catalonia, Spain) and Butser Ancient Farm reveal how different prehistoric construction forms on chalk soils weather/age. There is no burial environment information (known materials in known buried conditions) being derived from these sites (Bell et al. 1996: 225–7). However, small animal body and bone burial studies (Janaway 1987; Gill-Robinson 2002) have been undertaken, and these have emphasised the variation that differences in deposition, a coffin, clothing or, in the case of food, heating can make in the short term to decay (diagenetic) rates and processes.

The next generation of reburial experiments (post-2000) has often focused on waterlogged deposits, burying known materials and monitoring the water chemistry (Eh, pH, conductivity) of sites such as Fiskerton (Williams et al. 2008), Firestone Copse, Isle of Wight (Hogan et al. 2006), Nydam, Denmark (Matthiesen et al. 2007) and beneath the seabed at Marstrand Harbour, Sweden (Peacock et al. 2008). This work often seeks to establish the capacity of existing archaeological artefacts to remain preserved or the potential to rebury archaeological artefacts in these saturated anoxic environments.

Soil composition

The soil is composed of:

- inorganic fragments of rock and mineral;
- water containing dissolved salts (either bound to particles, capillary attracted to their surface or free water moving through the pore spaces between the particles);
- organic material decaying vegetable matter and the resultant polymeric humus material;
- living organisms; and
- gases filling the pores not occupied by water (see Figure 3.0.1).

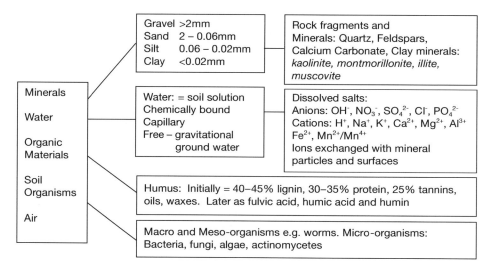

Figure 3.0.1 Typical composition of soil, major constituents.

There is huge variation in the composition of soil depending on the underlying geology, the vegetation and the history of soil formation.

All chemical reactions occur between the soil solution and the archaeological remains or particles (mineral or organic) present. Soil solution slowly reaches equilibrium with the particles. When the soil is disturbed (agriculture/archaeological excavation), chemical and biological equilibria are changed and must re-establish. When artefacts or building materials are inserted into the soil, they start reacting with the soil solution or the microorganisms of the soil. A reaction zone develops around the artefact/archaeological material, which we normally refer to as decay, or corrosion for metals (see Figure 3.0.2). Though the rate of reaction will depend on the chemistry/biology or physical nature of the soil, the rate of reaction slows as the decay zone builds around the archaeological material.

The formation of the decay/corrosion zone creates a partial record of the burial environment (Schweizer 1994). If excavation occurs, the equilibrium is broken and a new biological/chemical and physical environment applies. Consequently, new reactions start; these are initially relatively fast, but again slow as a new reaction/decay zones builds up (Dowman 1970; Caple 2000) (see Figure 3.0.3). Rimmer (2006: 31), Matthiesen *et al.* (2007: 290) and Neff *et al.* (2007: 71–2) have all noted that fresh metal samples buried in the ground initially have much higher rates of reaction than archaeological materials – which normally decay/corrode at much slower rates. Kenward and Hall (2004: 7) have mapped this changing loss rate on to the biological decay process.

The capacity to preserve artefacts and building materials *in situ* requires an understanding of the chemistry and microbiology of the burial environment; only then can mitigation actions be planned to reduce the rate of loss of archaeological remains. Conservation normally focuses on the material of which the artefacts are constructed (see Table 3.0.1); preservation *in situ* also needs to consider the burial environment. This is normally described in terms of a series of key variables.

KNOWLEDGE OF THE BURIAL ENVIRONMENT

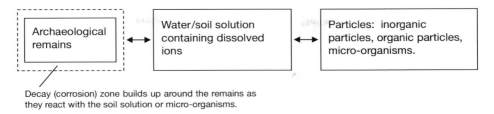

Figure 3.0.2 Build-up of corrosion/decay layers.

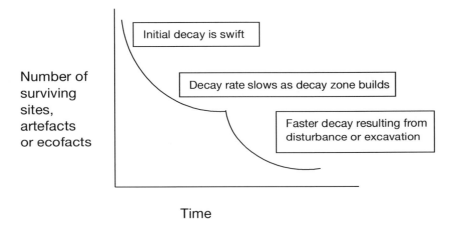

Figure 3.0.3 Generalised rate of loss of archaeological remains over time.

Burial chemistry

Dissolved salts

Soil water contains dissolved salts/minerals. Any change in physical or chemical parameters can lead to precipitation of the minerals out of solution. For partially soluble minerals, these can include changes in pore size, dissolved gas levels, concentration of ions, temperature, changes in pH, oxidation/reduction level, etc. The most common minerals that precipitate out include iron oxides (iron pan), calcium carbonate (lime) and calcium sulphate (gypsum). These coat or cover materials or deposit inside porous materials. At or near the surface where water is lost through evaporation, the concentration of even highly soluble salts such as potassium nitrate or sodium chloride can occur. Repeated dissolution and recrystallisation of highly soluble salts (efflorescence and cryptoflorescence) gives rise to surface damage.

Though there is a focus in the literature on the soil solution, it exists in equilibrium with the soil particles, with considerable ion exchange between the two, especially smaller clay particles with high surface area. These can buffer pH changes in soil solution. Thus, a solution of fertiliser rich in nitrogen, potash and phosphate when poured over a typical farmland soil from West Yorkshire produced clean run-off water, with just slightly elevated calcium content (Pollard et al. 2006: 228). This buffering capacity is important in maintaining the mid range pH of most soils.

pH

The concentration of hydrogen ions (H^+) has the most significant effect on the chemistry of the soil water. Soil pH affected the ability of soil to grow crops, and acidic soils were being treated with lime to neutralise them and increase crop yields centuries before testing of soil pH became common. The concentration of hydrogen ions present in soil solutions is normally determined by the ammonium, bicarbonate and iron oxyhydroxide chemical equilibria (Caple 1994), with additional inputs from decaying organic matter, rainwater, etc. The stability of many archaeological materials varies with pH (van de Noort and Davies 1993), though most soil waters are in the mid pH range and most archaeological materials are relatively stable. Acidic waters (low pH) can lead to the dissolution of lime (mortar and plaster) and the mineral content of bone. Hydrolysis (polymer breakdown through reaction with water) of organic materials increases with high pH (i.e. basic or alkaline conditions) or very low pH (i.e. acidic). This can be a significant factor in weakening organic material not degraded by microbes.

Eh/oxygen

The basic characterisation of the chemistry of the burial environment, and in particular the soil solution, was only determined on a large scale in the 1950s. The seminal publication on this subject was provided by Bass Becking *et al.* (1960) (see Chapter 3.4), which utilised 6,200 measurements of the two key parameters:

- Redox potential (electron availability), often referred to as Eh, which is a measure of how oxidising or reducing the environment is. Surface soil is oxygen-rich and highly oxidising and has a high Eh; deep soils and stagnant-water-saturated soils such as bogs and mires are reducing and have a low Eh.
- Hydrogen ion (H^+, proton) availability (measured as pH) determining the acidic or basic (alkaline) nature of the soil water.

These two parameters create a measure of the possible burial chemistry (see Chapter 11). On to graphs of Eh and pH it was possible to plot measurements that defined the soils of the world, all of which supported biological life. Within this area, it was possible to show areas where certain minerals were stable and areas where they were not; areas where certain organisms were found and areas where others were not. Burial conditions were found to correspond with soil types in which specific minerals and organisms were found. Eh/pH graphs were used in pedology and hydrology from the 1960s to describe soil conditions and predict reactions, and from the 1970s to describe corrosion of metals in archaeological deposits (Pourbaix 1977). Only in the 1990s did archaeological scientists start to measure and describe waterlogged archaeological burial environments using these graphs and start to use scientific data to predict the ability of burial environments to preserve archaeological remains *in situ* (Caple *et al.* 1997) (see Chapter 11.1). The Eh/pH level can be determined either by direct *in situ* measurements (this requires saturated soil), or a sample of soil solution measured in a laboratory. In practice, it is often determined by noting the presence of specific minerals or the changes undergone by known archaeological materials (see Chapter 11).

In practice

Though it is possible to monitor pH, dissolved salts and redox potential (Eh) using electrodes in the soil or take samples of soil and identify the minerals present through X-ray diffraction, in practice virtually no archaeological projects have the funding to do so. In Sweden, Germany and Denmark in the 1990s, there was concern that the acid rain pollution might increase the corrosion of copper alloy artefacts in the ground. Consequently, large surveys of the extent of the corrosion of copper alloy archaeological artefacts excavated by earlier generations were compared to the levels of corrosion of those artefacts excavated in recent years (Fjaestad et al. 1996, 1998; Gerwin et al. 1998; Wagner et al. 1998; Mattsson et al. 1999; Madsen et al. 2004). These suggested that there were increasing rates of corrosion, accelerated by acid rain, agrochemicals, road salting and ground disturbance. Subsequent experiments demonstrated that while some fertilisers containing potassium chloride did appear to enhance corrosion rates, phosphate-rich fertilisers may reduce corrosion rates (Pollard et al. 2004, 2006; Wilson et al. 2006). Work by Gerwin et al. (1998) and Galliano et al. (1998) emphasised the site-specific nature of metal corrosion both in terms of soil pH and also soil saturation (redox potential).

Burial biology

In soils where water and nutrients are present, thriving microbial populations exist. The primary consumers of organic matter are fungi and bacteria that perform the key role of consuming and recycling organic material by the soil. Archaeological deposits are normally either aerobic/oxic or anaerobic/anoxic.

Aerobic/oxic

In soils with oxygen, aerobic organisms exist in an oxic environment. Organic matter based on cellulose, such as wood (also linen, cotton, paper) is primarily eaten by white and brown rot fungi. Huisman (2009: 22) suggests this fungal attack can have a velocity of 100 mm per year; most authorities quote a few decades for wooden posts surviving in soil, a rate matched by the decline evident in the Overton Down and Wareham Heath wood samples. For protein-based materials such as keratin (wool) and collagen (bone, skin, body tissue), both fungal and bacterial attack is suggested (Millard 2001: 640; Jans 2005: 10). Microbial decay of stone surfaces by organisms such as lichens or bacteria is invariably slow (Price 1996: 9–11). All wet or damp surfaces (stone, plaster, even glass) that receive light can host algae, but remain free of algae while dark and buried.

Anaerobic/anoxic

Wood appears preserved in waterlogged conditions. In saturated soils with low levels of oxygen present, soft rot fungi and fungi imperfecti are the primary degradation agents. Bacteria (tunnelling and especially erosion) have been seen as key degraders of wood in near anoxic conditions (Rowell and Barbour 1990). Anaerobic bacteria can be active degraders (Painter 1995: 89); however, in fully stagnant anoxic conditions, their breakdown products appear to limit activity for both protein and cellulose degradation (Caple 1994: 69; Huisman 2009: 23). The presence of sulphate-reducing bacteria (MacFarlane and Gibson 1991) in anaerobic environments is key in determining the nature of the burial chemistry and the deposition of sulphide minerals as corrosion products for metals or within porous organic materials such as waterlogged wood.

Specific environments

The biology and chemistry of specific preservative environments is still being uncovered, both by observation and monitoring of soil burial conditions and laboratory analysis. Painter (1995) (see Chapter 3.5) has shown how the chemistry of sphagnan (5-keto-D-mannuronic acid) released by the breakdown of *Sphagnum* peat acts within the anoxic, mineral-poor pH conditions (5.5–6.5) of raised bogs to act as a 'tanning' agent to the collagen of human tissues and so preserves human bodies sacrificed in these locations. These natural environments are not common, but where they occur they have the power to preserve, but are invariably more complex and subtle than initially appreciated, often preserving through a series of synergistic processes.

Bibliography

Atkinson, R.J.C. (1957) 'Worms and weathering', *Antiquity*, 31: 219–33.
Bass Becking, L.G.M., Kaplan, I.R. and Moore, D. (1960) 'Limits of the natural environment in terms of plant and oxidation and reduction potentials', *The Journal of Geology*, 68: 243–84.
Bell, M., Fowler, P.J. and Hillson, S.W. (1996) *The Experimental Earthwork Project 1960–1992*, CBA Research Report 100, York: CBA.
Buys, S. and Oakley, V. (1993) *The Conservation and Restoration of Ceramics*, Oxford: Butterworth-Heinemann.
Calnan, C. and Haines, B. (1991) *Leather, Its Composition and Changes with Time*, Northampton: Leather Conservation Centre.
Caple, C. (1994) 'Reburial of waterlogged wood: the problems and potential of this conservation technique', in *International Biodeterioration Biodegradation*, 34(1): 61–72.
Caple, C. (2000) *Conservation Skills: Judgement, Method and Decision Making*, London: Routledge.
Caple, C., Dungworth, D. and Clogg, P. (1997) 'The assessment and protection of archaeological organic materials in waterlogged burial environments', in P. Hoffmann, T. Grant, J.A. Spriggs and T. Daley (eds), *Proceedings of the 6th Waterlogged Organic Archaeological Materials Conference, York 1996*, Bremerhaven: ICOM-CC WOAM Working Group, pp. 57–72.
Cornwall, I.W. (1958) *Soils for the Archaeologist*, London: Phoenix House.
Cronyn, J.M. (1990) *The Elements of Archaeological Conservation*, London: Routledge.
Darwin, C. (1881) *The Formation of Vegetable Mould Through the Action of Worms with Observations on Their Habits*, London: Faber & Faber.
Davidson, D.A. and Simpson, I.A. (2001) 'Archaeology and soil micromorphology', in D.R. Brothwell and A.M. Pollard (eds), *Handbook of Archaeological Sciences*, Chichester: Wiley, pp. 167–78.
Davy, J. (1826) 'Observations on the changes that have taken place in some ancient alloys of copper', *Phil. Transactions of the Royal Society of London*, 116: 55–9.
Dowman, A. (1970) *Conservation in Field Archaeology*, London: Methuen & Co.
Erdtman, G. (1924) 'Studies in micropalaeontology of post-glacial deposits in northern Scotland and the Scotch Isles, with special reference to the history of woodlands', *Journal of the Linnaen Society (Bot.)*, 46: 4–49.
Fjaestad, M., Nord, A.G. Tronner, K. *et al.* (1996) 'Environmental threats to archaeological artefacts', in *Preprints, ICOM-CC 11th Triennial Meeting, Edinburgh, Scotland, 1–6 September 1996*, London: James & James, pp. 870–5.
Fjaestad, M., Ullen, I., Nord, A.G. *et al.* (1998) 'Are recently excavated bronze artefacts more deteriorated than earlier finds?', in W. Mourey and L. Robbiola (eds), *Metal 98, Proceedings of the International Conference on Metals Conservation*, London: James & James, pp. 71–9.
Florian, M-L. E., Kronkright, D.P. and Norton, R.E. (1990) *The Conservation of Artifacts Made from Plant Materials*, Marina Del Rey, CA: Getty Conservation Institute.
Galliano, F., Werner, G. and Menzel, K. (1998) 'Monitoring of metal corrosion and soil solution at two excavation sites and in the laboratory', in W. Mourey and L. Robbiola (eds), *Metal 98, Proceedings of the International Conference on Metals Conservation*, London: James & James, pp. 87–91.

Gerwin, W., Scharff, W. and Baumhauer, R. (1998) 'Corrosive decay of archaeological metal finds from different soils and effects of environmental pollution', in W. Mourey and L. Robbiola (eds), *Metal 98, Proceedings of the International Conference on Metals Conservation*, London: James & James, pp. 100–5.

Gill-Robinson, H. (2002) 'This little piggy went to Cumbria, this little piggy went to Wales: the tales of 12 piglets in peat', in J.R. Mathieu (ed.), *Experimental Archaeology: Replicating Past Objects, Behaviours, and Processes*, BAR International Series 1035, pp. 111–26.

Hogan, D., Jones, M. and Simpson, P. (2006) *Reburial of Organic Remains: Final Report to English Heritage 2006*, Archaeology Data Service, available at: http://archaeologydataservice.ac.uk/archives/view/reburial_eh_2007/ (accessed September 2014).

Huisman, D.J. (ed.) (2009) *Degradation of Archaeological Remains*, Den Haag: Sdu Uitgevers b.v.

Janaway, R.C. (1987) 'The preservation of organic material in association with metal artefacts deposited in inhumation graves', in A. Boddington, A.N. Garland and R.C. Janaway (eds), *Death, Decay and Reconstruction*, Manchester: Manchester University Press, pp. 127–48.

Jans, M.M.E. (2005) *Histological Characterisation of Diagenetic Alteration of Archaeological Bone*, Geoarchaeological and Bioarchaeological Studies 4, Amsterdam: Vrije Universiteit Amsterdam.

Jewell, P.A. (ed.) (1963) *The Experimental Earthwork at Overton Down, Wiltshire, 1960*, London: British Association for the Advancement of Science.

Kenward, H. and Hall, A. (2004) 'Actively decaying or just poorly preserved? Can we tell when plant and invertebrate remains in urban archaeological deposits decayed?', in T. Nixon (ed.), *Preserving Archaeological Remains In-Situ?*, London: Museum of London Archaeological Service, pp. 4–10.

Kite, M. and Thomson, R. (2006) *Conservation of Leather and Related Materials*, Oxford: Butterworth Heinemann.

Kubiëna, W.L. (1953) *The Soils of Europe: Illustrated Diagnosis and Systematics with Keys and Descriptions for Easy Identification of the Most Important Soil Formations of Europe with Consideration of the Most Frequent Synonyms*, London: Thomas Murb.

Limbrey, S. (1975) *Soil Science and Archaeology*, London: Academic Press.

MacFarlane, G.T. and Gibson, G.R. (1991) 'Sulphate reducing bacteria', in P.N. Levett (ed.), *Anaerobic Microbiology: A Practical Approach*, Oxford: IRL, pp. 221–2.

Madsen, H.B., Andersen, J.H. and Andersen, L.B. (2004) 'Deterioration of prehistoric bronzes as an indicator of the state of preservation of metal antiquities in the Danish agrarian landscape: preliminary results', in T. Nixon (ed.), *Preserving Archaeological Remains in Situ?*, London: Museum of London Archaeology Service, pp. 50–7.

Mattsson, E., Nord, A.G., Tronner, K. *et al.* (1999) *Deterioration of Archaeological Material in Soil: Results on Bronze Artefacts, Rapport RIK 10*, Stockholm: The Central Board of National Antiquities and the National Historical Museums.

Matthiesen, H., Gregory, D., Sorenson, B. *et al.* (2007) 'Long term corrosion of iron at the waterlogged site of Nydam in Denmark: studies of environment, archaeological artefacts and modern analogues', in P. Dillmann, G. Beranger, P. Piccardo and H. Matthiesen (eds), *Corrosion of Metallic Heritage Artefacts*, Cambridge: Woodhead, pp. 272–92.

Millard, A. (2001) 'The deterioration of bone', in D.R. Brothwell and A.M. Pollard (eds), *Handbook of Archaeological Science*, Chichester: Wiley, pp. 637–48.

Neff, D., Vega, E., Dillmann, P. *et al.* (2007) 'Contribution of iron artefacts to the estimation of average corrosion rates and the long term corrosion mechanisms of low carbon steel buried in soil', in P. Dillmann, G. Beranger, P. Piccardo and H. Matthiesen (eds), *Corrosion of Metallic Heritage Artefacts*, Cambridge: Woodhead, pp. 41–76.

Newton, R. and Davison, S. (1989) *Conservation of Glass*, London: Butterworths.

O'Connor, S. and Brooks, M. (1990) *Textiles for the Archaeological Conservator*, UKIC Occasional Paper No 10, London: United Kingdom Institute for Conservation.

Painter, T.J. (1995) 'Chemical and microbiological aspects of the preservation process in *Sphagnum* peat', in R. Turner and R. Scaife (eds), *Bog Bodies: New Discoveries and New Perspectives*, London: BMP, pp. 88–99.

Peacock, E., Bergrstrand, T., Godfrey, I.N. *et al.* (2008) 'The Marstraand reburial project: overview, phase 1 and future work', in H. Kars and R.M. van Heeringen (eds), *Preserving Archaeological Remains In Situ? Proceedings of the 3rd Conference 7–9 December 2006, Amsterdam*, Geoarchaeological and Bioarchaeological Studies 10, Amsterdam: Vrije Universiteit Amsterdam, pp. 253–63.

Piggott, S. (1985) *William Stukeley: An Eighteenth Century Antiquary*, rev. edn, London: Thames & Hudson.

Pollard, A.M., Wilson, L., Wilson, A.S. *et al.* (2004) 'Assessing the influence of agrochemicals on the rate of copper corrosion in the vadose zone of arable land – part 1: field experiments', *Conservation and Management of Archaeological Sites*, 6: 363–76.

Pollard, A.M., Wilson, L., Wilson, A.S. *et al.* (2006) 'Assessing the influence of agrochemicals on the rate of copper corrosion in the vadose zone of arable land – part 2: laboratory simulations', *Conservation and Management of Archaeological Sites*, 7: 225–39.

Pourbaix, M. (1977) 'Electrochemical corrosion and reduction', in B.F. Brown, H.C. Burnett, W.T. Chase, M. Goodway, J. Kruger and M. Pourbaix (eds), *Corrosion and Metal Artefacts: A Dialogue between Conservators and Archaeologists and Corrosion Scientists*, NBS Special Publication 479, Washington, DC: US Dept of Commerce – National Bureau of Standards, pp. 1–16.

Porter, J. (1991) 'Stonecleaning', *Conservation News*, 46 (November): 16–20.

Price, C. (1996) *Stone Conservation: An Overview of Current Research*, Santa Monica, CA: GCI.

Rimmer, M. (2006) 'Modelling the destruction of the archaeological resource', unpublished BSc dissertation, Dept. of Archaeology, Durham University.

Romanoff, M. (1957) *Underground Corrosion* (National Bureau of Standards Circular 579), Houston, TX: National Association of Corrosion Engineers.

Rowell, R.M. and Barbour, R.J. (1990) *Archaeological Wood: Properties, Chemistry and Preservation*, Advances in Chemistry 225, Washington, DC: American Chemical Society.

Schiffer, M.B. (1987) *Formation Processes of the Archaeological Record*, Albuquerque, NM: University of New Mexico Press.

Schweizer, F. (1994) 'Bronze objects from lake sites: from patina to biography', in D.A. Scott, J. Podany and B.B. Considine (eds), *Ancient and Historic Metals, Conservation and Scientific Research*, Marina del Ray, CA: GCI, pp. 33–50.

Selwyn, L. (2004) *Metals and Corrosion: A Handbook for the Conservation Professional*, Ottawa: Canadian Conservation Institute.

Steenstrup, J. (1836) 'Geognostisk-geologisk undersagelese af Skovmoserne Vines-og Lillemosse. Videnskop Selskap naturvidenskap og methematic', *Athundling IX*.

Timár-Balázsy, A. and Eastop, D. (1998). *Chemical Principles of Textile Conservation*, Oxford: Butterworth-Heinemann.

van de Noort, R. and Davies, P. (1993) *Wetlands Heritage: An Archaeological Assessment of the Humber Wetlands*, Hull: University of Hull.

Wagner, D., Kropp, M., Fischer, W.R. *et al.* (1998) 'A systematic approach to the evaluation of the corrosion load of archaeological metal objects', in W. Mourey and L. Robbiola (eds), *Metal 98, Proceedings of the International Conference on Metals Conservation*, London: James & James, pp. 80–6.

Webster, R.G.M. (1992) *Stone Cleaning and the Nature, Soiling and Decay Mechanisms of Stone*, London: Donhead.

Williams, J., Fell, V., Graham, K. *et al.* (2008) 'Re-watering of the Iron Age Causeway at Fiskerton, England', in H. Kars and R.M. van Heeringen (eds), *Preserving Archaeological Remains In Situ? Proceedings of the 3rd Conference 7–9 December 2006, Amsterdam*, Geoarchaeological and Bioarchaeological Studies 10, Amsterdam: Vrije Universiteit Amsterdam, pp. 181–97.

Wilson, L., Pollard, A.M., Hall, A.J. *et al.* (2006) 'Assessing the influence of agrochemicals on the rate of copper corrosion in the vadose zone of arable land – part 3: geochemical modelling', *Conservation and Management of Archaeological Sites*, 7: 241–60.

Chapter 3.1

The formation of vegetable mould through the action of worms with observations of their habits

Charles Darwin

Source: Darwin, C. (1881) *The Formation of Vegetable Mould Through the Action of Worms with Observations on Their Habits,* London: Faber.

The amount of fine earth brought up by worms to the surface

[. . .]

WE NOW COME TO the more immediate subject of this volume, namely, the amount of earth which is brought up by worms from beneath the surface, and is afterwards spread out more or less completely by the rain and wind. The amount can be judged of by two methods,—by the rate at which objects left on the surface are buried, and more accurately by weighing the quantity brought up within a given time. [. . .]

Near Mael Hall in Staffordshire, quick-lime had been spread about the year 1827 thickly over a field of good pasture-land, which had not since been ploughed. Some square holes were dug in this field in the beginning of October 1837; and the sections showed a layer of turf, formed by the matted roots of the grasses, 0.5 inch in thickness, beneath which, at a depth of 2.5 inches (or 3 inches from the surface), a layer of the lime in powder or in small lumps could be distinctly seen running all round the vertical sides of the holes. The soil beneath the layer of lime was either gravelly or of a coarse sandy nature, and differed considerably in appearance from the overlying dark-coloured fine mould. Coal cinders had been spread over a part of this same field either in the year 1833 or 1834; and when the above holes were dug, that is after an interval of 3 or 4 years, the cinders formed a line of black spots round the holes, at a depth of 1 inch beneath the surface, parallel to and above the white layer of lime. Over another part of this field cinders had been strewed, only about half-a-year before, and these either still lay on the surface or were entangled among the roots of the grasses; and I here saw the commencement of the burying process, for worm-castings had been heaped on several of the smaller fragments. After an interval of 4.75 years this field was re-examined, and now the two layers of lime and cinders were found almost everywhere at a greater depth than before by nearly 1 inch, we will say by 0.75 of an inch. Therefore mould to an average thickness of 0.22 of an inch had been annually brought up by the worms, and had been spread over the surface of this field.

[...]

At Stonehenge, some of the outer Druidical stones are now prostrate, having fallen at a remote but unknown period; and these have become buried to a moderate depth in the ground. They are surrounded by sloping borders of turf, on which recent castings were seen. Close to one of these fallen stones, which was 17 ft long, 6 ft. broad, and 28.5 inches thick, a hole was dug; and here the vegetable mould was at least 9.5 inches in thickness. At this depth a flint was found, and a little higher up on one side of the hole a fragment of glass. The base of the stone lay about 9.5 inches beneath the level of the surrounding ground, and its upper surface 19 inches above the ground.

[...]

Summary of the thickness of the mould accumulated over objects left strewed on the surface, in the course of ten years

- The accumulation of mould during 14.75 years on the surface of a dry, sandy, grass-field near Maer Hall, amounted to 2.2 inches in 10 years.
- The accumulation during 21.5 years on a swampy field near Maer Hall, amounted to nearly 1.9 inch in 10 years.
- The accumulation during 7 years on a very swampy field near Maer Hall amounted to 2.1 inches in 10 years.
- The accumulation during 29 years, on good, argillaceous pasture- land over the Chalk at Down, amounted to 2.2 inches in 10 years.
- The accumulation during 30 years on the side of a valley over the Chalk at Down, the soil being argillaceous, very poor, and only just converted into pasture (so that it was for some years unfavourable for worms), amounted to 0.83 inch in 10 years.

[...]

We have no means of judging how great a weight of earth a single full-sized worm ejects during a year. Hensen estimates that 53,767 worms exist in an acre of land; but this is founded on the number found in gardens, and he believes that only about half as many live in corn-fields. How many live in old pasture land is unknown; but if we assume that half the above number, or 26,886 worms live on such land, then taking from the previous summary 15 tons as the weight of the castings annually thrown up on an acre of land, each worm must annually eject 20 ounces. A full-sized casting at the mouth of a single burrow often exceeds, as we have seen, an ounce in weight; and it is probable that worms eject more than 20 full-sized castings during a year. If they eject annually more than 20 ounces, we may infer that the worms which live in an acre of pasture land must be less than 26,886 in number.

[...]

The part which worms have played in the burial of ancient buildings

[...]

Archaeologists are probably not aware how much they owe to worms for the preservation of many ancient objects. Coins, gold ornaments, stone implements, etc., if dropped on the surface of the ground, will infallibly be buried by the castings of worms in a few years, and will thus be safely preserved, until the land at some future time is turned up. For instance, many years ago a grass-field was ploughed on the northern side of the Severn, not far from Shrewsbury; and a surprising number of iron arrow-heads were found at the bottom of the furrows, which, as Mr. Blakeway, a local antiquary, believed, were relics of the battle of Shrewsbury in the year 1403, and no doubt had been originally left strewed on the battle-field.

[...]

Abinger, Surrey.— Late in the autumn of 1876, the ground in an old farm-yard at this place was dug to a depth of 2 to 2.5 feet, and the workmen found various ancient remains. This led Mr. T. H. Farrer of Abinger Hall to have an adjoining ploughed field searched. On a trench being dug, a layer of concrete, still partly covered with tesserae (small red tiles), and surrounded on two sides by broken-down walls, was soon discovered. It is believed, that this room formed part of the atrium or reception-room of a Roman villa. The walls of two or three other small rooms were afterwards discovered. Many fragments of pottery, other objects, and coins of several Roman emperors, dating from 133 to 361, and perhaps to 375 AD, were likewise found. Also a half-penny of George I., 1715.

[...]

When the concrete and tesserae were first cleared over a space of 14 by 9 ft., the floor which was coated with trodden-down earth exhibited no signs of having been penetrated by worms; and although the overlying fine mould closely resembled that which in many places has certainly been accumulated by worms, yet it seemed hardly possible that this mould could have been brought up by worms from beneath the apparently sound floor.

[...]

Although the concrete floor did not at first appear to have been anywhere penetrated by worms, yet by the next morning little cakes of the trodden-down earth had been lifted up by worms over the mouths of seven burrows, which passed through the softer parts of the naked concrete, or between the interstices of the tesserae. On the third morning twenty-five burrows were counted; and by suddenly lifting up the little cakes of earth, four worms were seen in the act of quickly retreating. Two castings were thrown up during the third night on the floor, and these were of large size. The season was not favourable for the full activity of worms, and the weather had lately been hot and dry, so that most of the worms now lived at a considerable depth. In digging the two trenches many open burrows and some worms were encountered at between 30 and 40 inches beneath the surface; but at a greater depth they became rare. One worm, however, was cut through at 48.5, and another at 51.5 inches beneath the surface. A fresh humus-lined burrow was also met with at a depth of 57 and another at 65.5 inches. At greater depths than this, neither burrows nor worms were seen.

[...]

Conclusion

Worms have played a more important part in the history of the world than most persons would at first suppose. In almost all humid countries they are extraordinarily numerous, and for their size possess great muscular power. In many parts of England a weight of more than ten tons (10,516 kilogrammes) of dry earth annually passes through their bodies and is brought to the surface on each acre of land; so that the whole superficial bed of vegetable mould passes through their bodies in the course of every few years. From the collapsing of the old burrows the mould is in constant though slow movement, and the particles composing it are thus rubbed together. By these means fresh surfaces are continually exposed to the action of the carbonic acid in the soil, and of the humus-acids which appear to be still more efficient in the decomposition of rocks. The generation of the humus-acids is probably hastened during the digestion of the many half-decayed leaves which worms consume. Thus the particles of earth, forming the superficial mould, are subjected to conditions eminently favourable for their decomposition and disintegration. Moreover, the particles of the softer rocks suffer some amount of mechanical trituration in the muscular gizzards of worms, in which small stones serve as mill-stones.

[. . .]

It has been shown that a layer of earth, 0.2 of an inch in thickness, is in many places annually brought to the surface; and if a small part of this amount flows, or rolls, or is washed, even for a short distance, down every inclined surface, or is repeatedly blown in one direction, a great effect will be produced in the course of ages. It was found by measurements and calculations that on a surface with a mean inclination of 9 degrees 26 seconds, 2.4 cubic inches of earth which had been ejected by worms crossed, in the course of a year, a horizontal line one yard in length; so that 240 cubic inches would cross a line 100 yards in length. This latter amount in a damp state would weigh 11.5 pounds. Thus a considerable weight of earth is continually moving down each side of every valley, and will in time reach its bed. Finally this earth will be transported by the streams flowing in the valleys into the ocean, the great receptacle for all matter denuded from the land. It is known from the amount of sediment annually delivered into the sea by the Mississippi, that its enormous drainage-area must on an average be lowered .00263 of an inch each year; and this would suffice in four and half million years to lower the whole drainage-area to the level of the sea-shore. So that, if a small fraction of the layer of fine earth, 0.2 of an inch in thickness, which is annually brought to the surface by worms, is carried away, a great result cannot fail to be produced within a period which no geologist considers extremely long.

Archaeologists ought to be grateful to worms, as they protect and preserve for an indefinitely long period every object, not liable to decay, which is dropped on the surface of the land, by burying it beneath their castings. Thus, also, many elegant and curious tesselated pavements and other ancient remains have been preserved; though no doubt the worms have in these cases been largely aided by earth washed and blown from the adjoining land, especially when cultivated. The old tesselated pavements have, however, often suffered by having subsided unequally from being unequally undermined by the worms. Even old massive walls may be undermined and subside; and no building is in this respect safe, unless the foundations lie 6 or 7 feet beneath the surface, at a depth at which worms, cannot work. It is probable that many monoliths and some old walls have fallen down from having been undermined by worms.

Chapter 3.2

Soils for the archaeologist

Ian W. Cornwall

Source: Cornwall, I. (1958) *Soils for the Archaeologist,* London: Phoenix.

[...]

WHATEVER THE SOIL OR CLIMATE, hill-top sites are constantly subject to denudation. All material loosened by weather or by man's operations tends to wash or blow away downhill. In the case of prehistoric hill-sites, therefore, it is unlikely that a complete stratigraphical record will be preserved *in situ* unless the section happens to lie in a natural depression or in an artificial feature, such as a ditch or a pit cut into the subsoil. Prehistoric and later ploughing, besides the work of earthworms, has been responsible for much widespread mixing of the upper 6 inches of soil and weathering and rainwash have often completed the work of levelling eminences, filling depressions and carrying away much that once may have lain there. Heavier and bulkier objects, such as quernstones, may remain in the place where they were once used, but not *in situ* in contemporary deposits, for these will long since have been removed by natural agencies.

An extreme case of this was to be seen at an Iron-Age site on the summit of a rounded limestone hill at Dainton, S. Devon. The section was seldom more than a few inches deep, consisting of a thin turf, perhaps two inches of red-brown soil and the unaltered bedrock. In these circumstances any examination of the soil was clearly valueless. What was left merely represented the balance between present-day soil-formation and the contemporary processes of denudation. There was nothing to show that any of the soil was more than a few years old. Some collapsed dry-stone structures, perhaps hut-foundations, yielded a few finds, the preservation of which was eloquent of these conditions. Potsherds were small and their edges were eroded both by weather and by having long lain loose on the surface, under the feet of the human and animal traffic on the site. Animal and human bones, though in actual contact with the limestone, were marked and deeply etched by rootlets, having been only just below the turf ever since they were left there. The edges of ancient fractures (and, like the pottery, the bones were much comminuted) were so worn that even manifest joins could only be made to fit with great difficulty.

[...]

Preservation of organic matter in archaeological deposits

Under certain conditions, not always easily defined, original organic substances or breakdown-products of them can survive for very long periods in the soil.

Some instances of such remarkable preservation have been (seen) it will be useful here to summarize the known facts and to point out directions in which further research might yield valuable results.

A rather special case is presented by the wooden objects and leather garments preserved from the Bronze Age in the copper-mining sites of Upper Austria. These owe their survival to the inability of organisms of decay to live in the presence of certain concentrations of copper salts, a well-known property used by horticulturists when they spray their fruit-trees against fungi with 'Bordeaux Mixture', a suspension of copper and calcium hydroxides in water. In such cases, the actual objects and substances have been preserved sufficiently well for their recognition by archaeologists and their nature is not in doubt.

Even when the actual substance of the object has not persisted, there will be little doubt possible as to its original nature when it has been preserved as a natural cast or mould. This is generally due to the deposition of some other substance in or round it while it still retained sufficient shape to leave an impression. Such are the leaf-impressions in travertine or lake-clays, the natural internal cast of the braincase in the first-discovered *Australopithecus* skull, grain-impressions in pottery and textile-weaves preserved in the corrosion-products of iron or bronze objects, with the surface of which the original material was in contact as it decayed.

An outstanding case, not alas, saved from destruction before it could be properly treated, was reported in connection with the discovery of the skull and bones of the Rhodesian Man, at Broken Hill Mine. Not only the bones were in reasonably good condition, impregnated with preservative metallic salts, but a mould of the entire body, in the flesh, was formed round it by the matrix of the cave-filling before decay.

The preservation of vegetable substances in peat-bogs and other waterlogged situations is, by now, common knowledge, though the chemistry involved has never been fully expounded, but it is less well known that even animal remains, apart from the bones, can, in certain circumstances, survive.

Some fairly general principles can be laid down to explain the observed phenomena.

With free access of moisture and oxygen, most organic matter quite quickly undergoes chemical and bacterial decomposition, which results in the breakdown of its complex constituents (proteins, fats, etc.) into simple substances such as water, carbon dioxide, nitrogen and mineral salts. If either oxygen or water is excluded, the processes of decay slow down and may, eventually, come to a halt. In poorly aerated surroundings animal substances like leather can survive almost unchanged, to all appearances, fats may be converted into adipocere and, in the absence of oxygen, decay be unable to proceed any further. Ammonia and hydrogen sulphide are typical products.

The other condition, lack of moisture, is seen in the wonderful state of preservation of archaeological objects of wood, fabrics and foodstuffs in the extremely dry rock-tombs of Egypt, or even in desert sands. Here the decaying organisms cannot live without water.

An unusual intermediate set of conditions was apparently shown by the Bronze-Age tombs at Jericho, which are not by any means completely dry. Nevertheless, wooden furniture, textiles, joints of meat left as offerings and even the shrivelled brains still in the skulls of the dead, had been preserved to some extent through the millennia. The reason here seems to lie in gaseous emanations from the limestone rock in which the tombs were cut—carbon dioxide and methane seeping in from depth through fissures and replacing the air which would have permitted full decay. Even the insects attacking the wood had perished—wood-worms and termites—and had been preserved.

In our less favourable conditions, it is clear that whereas alkaline surroundings favour the preservation of bone, it is above all in acid waterlogged conditions that horn, hide, leather, hair and wool may survive. Beyond this we are no longer on sure ground, but the known evidence suggests that, in special cases, much more than this can be preserved.

The Siberian frozen mammoths present a fairly simple case of perennial refrigeration in frozen ground which has never thawed since the carcases became buried, thousands of years ago, but the case of the woolly rhinoceros of Starunia is more complicated. The surroundings were acid and peaty, for the beast's hide and even the hair, though loosened from it, were preserved, as were the remains of grasshoppers and other insects living at the same time as the rhinoceros. Salt water seems to have played the part of a preservative while the presence of mineral oil helped in the exclusion of air.

[...]

The soil-profile

A vertical section through a soil, from the surface with its vegetation down to unaltered bedrock, is termed its profile.

The profile may be more or less clearly subdivided into zones, not due to successive changes in deposition, as in the strata of a geological section, but formed in situ from the parent rock by processes of weathering which have caused the translocation in the profile of certain soil-constituents, resulting in local enrichment or impoverishment in respect of these substances. Such zones, normally extending horizontally, are called soil-horizons.

Soil-profiles are subdivided into three main kinds of horizons, designated by the first three letters of the alphabet:

- A-horizons, characterized by the presence of humus and by the washing out by percolating moisture of certain soluble components—eluvial horizons.
- B-horizons, zones into which some materials washed out of an A-horizon are conveyed and re-deposited—illuvial horizons.
- C-horizons, the chemically-unaltered parent rocks.

With the advance of our knowledge of soils and the description of numerous varieties of the main types, finer subdivision of profiles has become necessary. Subsidiary levels in the main horizons are denoted by subscript figures, as 'B_2-horizon', 'A_1-horizon'.

Transitional layers, where the boundaries between main horizons are not clearly defined, are called, for example, A/B or B/C horizons.

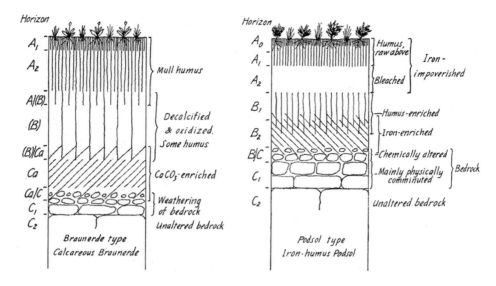

Figure 3.2.1 Soil-profiles to show nomenclature of horizons.

An horizon which is not manifestly an illuvial horizon, but which occupies the position of one and is due to deep weathering and oxidation is called a (B)-horizon (pronounced 'B-bracket').

Additional letters are used for special cases to designate layers of particular character: 'G-horizon' (G for 'gley'), an intermittently waterlogged part of the profile showing alternating oxidation- and reduction-phenomena; 'Ca-horizon', 'Fe-horizon', for those enriched with calcium or ferric compounds, respectively.

Grouping of soils according to profile-types

In his *Soils of Europe* (1953), Kubiena recognizes five distinct types of profile:

- (A)C-soils, with humus development not yet to be distinguished by the naked eye, but bearing sparse vegetation and faunal life close to the very surface. This includes the very youthful stages of temperate soils and those which, in desert, high-alpine or arctic environments are arrested in development owing to lack of moisture or constant low temperatures, both of which hinder the progress of chemical weathering.
- AC-soils, having clear humus-horizons but no B-horizons (e.g. ranker, rendsina).
- A(B)C-soils, having visible B-horizons which are chemically weathered but are not true illuvial-horizons (e.g. brownearths and redearths).
- ABC-soils, with true eluvial and illuvial horizons (e.g. podsols and bleached brown- and red-loams).
- B/ABC-soils, having crusts irreversibly precipitated at the surface owing to capillary rise of dissolved or peptized constituents and intense hot-season evaporation (e.g. lateritic and salt-soils, mainly of tropical and semi-desert environments).

Chapter 3.3

The Experimental Earthwork Project, 1960–1992
Discussion and conclusions

Martin Bell

Source: Bell, M., Fowler, P.J. and Hillson, S.W. (eds) (1996) *The Experimental Earthwork Project 1960–1992*, CBA Research Report 100, York: CBA.

Summary

THIS MONOGRAPH [...] provides a synthesis of and assesses the results of the first 32 years of the Experimental Earthwork Project. The experiment is designed to last for over a century. It is principally concerned with two earthworks, one on Overton Down, Wiltshire, the other on Morden Bog near Wareham, Dorset, England.
[...]
A basic manual described the project, its design and expectation (Jewell 1963). Early work on the Overton Earthwork was published by Jewell and Dimbleby (1966).
[...]

Comparison of the buried soils and turf stacks

The Wareham Earthwork buries an acid humus/iron podzol, the Overton Earthwork buries a rendzina profile. The original soil surface at Wareham, still sharply defined on photos from the 1972 and 1980 sections, even below the turf stack (Evans and Limbrey 1974, Plate 17), shows no indications of the mixing at this boundary which was such a feature of the Overton Earthwork. Each individual turf of the turf stack was also very clearly defined by comparison with Overton. After 17 years plant material was still recognizable in the Wareham soil, whereas at Overton traces of plant material were only found on the leather at 16 years and only vestigial traces remained in soil samples after 32 years. Pottery discs on the old ground surface at Wareham had also undergone little movement by comparison with Overton, where some of those on the ditch side had been moved by moles The only possible evidence noted of faunal activity within the bank at Wareham was the absence of one of the placed steel discs and the presence of arthropod faecal pellet residues from the decomposition of rope (Evans and Limbrey 1974, 191). In the Wareham ditch faunal activity was noted behind the vegetation curtain overhanging the ditch. Generally, however, there was a very much lower level of faunal reworking and biological activity in the more acid Wareham soils. The main change in the Wareham soil had been compaction, partly brought about by a reduction in void spaces from c.50–60% to 16% (Scaife and Macphail 1983; Fisher and Macphail 1985). Compaction was mainly in the first two years and it has remained relatively stable since the eight year stage. At Overton the main change to the morphology of the earthwork was compression of the turf stack and the overlying topsoil (B). This occurred mainly during the first four years or so. The Overton buried soil has also become very thin in places because some soil has been abstracted by moles and some has been moved upward into the bank by earthworms. It is noteworthy that the upward reworking of more shallowly buried soils had been predicted by Atkinson (1957), prior to the experiment, on the basis of his observations at Stonehenge. Micromorphological and chemical analysis was first carried out on the Wareham buried soil from the 17 year section. This was partly to facilitate comparison of this 17 year old buried soil and turf stack with essentially comparable features preserved in the cores of Bronze Age round barrows (Scaife and Macphail 1983). That demonstrated the potential of analytical work on the earthwork buried soils. When the time came to excavate the 32 year section at Overton a more ambitious programme of micro-morphological and linked chemical analysis was planned. Soil micro-morphology had, by this stage, developed into an important technique in archaeology (Courty *et al.* 1989) but interpretations were often hampered by a limited knowledge of processes occurring after burial. The extent of earthworm reworking of the buried soil at Overton is remarkable and evidenced both by the visible signs of upward topsoil movement into the interstices of the bank and by evidence for the movement of *Lycopodium* spores both upwards and downwards. Macphail and Cruise (1996, 101) also postulate, on the basis of micromorphological evidence, a subsequent phase of reworking by enchytraeid worms.

Comparison of the banks

The development of the two earthworks is illustrated in two comparative diagrams: Figure 3.3.1 which shows Wareham over 17 years and Figure 3.3.2 which shows Overton over 32 years. The two earthwork banks have adopted very contrasting profiles. Overton has a steeper bank in comparison with the low spread bank of Wareham. The reason is the smaller particle size and consequent lower angle of rest of the Wareham sediments. The Overton earthwork has not spread at all to the north and only some 0.3 m to the south whereas the Wareham Earthwork has spread 0.9 m to the south and 1.3 m to the north. This contrast is emphasized by the greater downslope curvature of the upper part of the polythene tubes in the Wareham bank indicating slope processes operating on the surface of that bank.

There is a marked contrast in the extent to which the two earthworks have stabilized over the experimental period. After 5 months the Wareham bank was found to be deeply gullied, some gullies subsequently filling with wind-blown sediment. No gullies ever developed on the more permeable Overton bank. The latter also vegetated and stabilized more quickly, within about 15 years (Fowler 1989, 94). Although on parts of the bank top there was still only a patchy vegetation cover after 32 years there is no evidence of

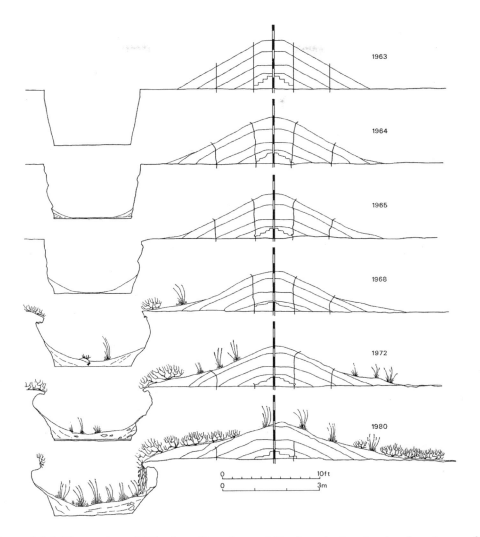

Figure 3.3.1 The section of Wareham Experimental Earthwork showing its changing profile between 1963 and 1980.

active erosion and the bank surface is a compacted ACu horizon representing the early stages of soil formation. By contrast, after 31 years, the upper part of the Wareham bank is more sparsely vegetated and, despite evidence for the formation of a surface 'crust', there are also signs of active erosion: coarser particles, such as the roadstone chips, tend to be left on little pedestals reflecting perhaps the effect of deflation or rainsplash.

[. . .]

Comparison of the ditches

Ditches form one of the most common features on archaeological sites. They form traps for many of the artefacts which we recover, so it is clearly important to think about how ditch sediments form and how the artefacts relate to the timescale of ditch sedimentation. One early result of the experiment was to emphasize that material of widely differing dates can easily become associated in the primary fill of a ditch. The earthwork experiments showed how rapidly primary ditch silts form. The experiment facilitated the definition of a three-fold sequence of ditch sedimentation: primary (physical weathering), secondary (stability and soil development) and tertiary (overploughing and colluviation). This sequence is outlined by Evans (1972), Limbrey (1975) and Proudfoot (1965).

[. . .]

Earthworms and soil fauna

On the acid soil at Wareham there was little evidence for faunal disturbance and earthworm activity, virtually no movement of *Lycopodium* spores had taken place between construction and 1972 (the 1980 samples were lost). By contrast at Overton there were many signs of faunal changes. Locally, moles had burrowed into the Old Land Surface and abstracted soil, and earthworms seem to have reworked most of the fine sediment in the buried soil and bank over the last 32 years. Their activities had obliterated any clear boundary between the old land surface and the turf stack, making it difficult to define the surface on which the lower group of buried materials had been placed. Old land surface material had been moved by earthworms into the base of the bank and the *Lycopodium* spore evidence of Dimbleby and Crabtree confirms the existence of upward and downward movement from the old land surface.

[. . .]

At Overton a distinct concentration of earthworm casts was noted in 1968 and 1992 around many of the buried materials in the chalk environment. Earthworm activity was confirmed by the discovery of aestivating worms in contact with some of the buried materials. There was no obvious sign that earthworms were feeding on the buried materials; they could have been feeding on fungi or other organisms involved in decomposition (Edwards and Lofty 1977). It seems more probable that they were attracted by a more favourable, e.g. moister, microenvironment created by the buried materials.

Biological evidence

At Wareham some plant material was still recognizable in the turves at the 16 year stage. At Overton plant material on the old land surface only survived at 16 years above and below the leathers presumably because tannins had inhibited decay. By the 32 year stage at Overton no macroscopically visible plant material remained on the old landsurface. [. . .]

The extensive reworking seen at Overton does not, however, seem to apply everywhere. Some old land surfaces on chalk in the Avebury area clearly preserve good palaeoenvironmental sequences in an apparently stratified form, as illustrated by the old land surfaces below long barrows at South Street (Ashbee *et al.* 1979) and Easton Down (Whittle *et al.* 1993). Both soils have a thin earthworm-sorted surface, clearly succeeding cultivation at South Street, and the soils at both sites preserve well stratified

THE EXPERIMENTAL EARTHWORK PROJECT 117

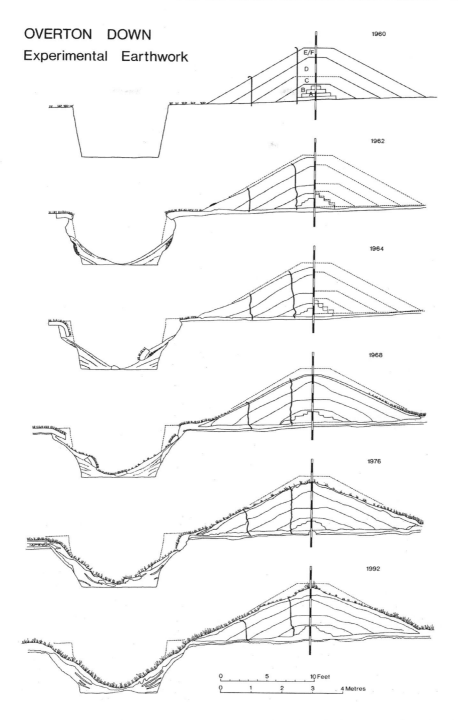

Figure 3.3.2 The section of Overton Down Experimental Earthwork showing its changing profile between 1960 and 1992.

Note: For 1962 and 1964 the bank section to the right of the central pole shows the original profile in dotted form. No section of this part of the bank is available for these two years.

molluscan sequences. Photographs of South Street (Ashbee *et al.* 1979, Plate 35b) show an exceptionally clearly-defined old land surface with no evidence of blurring by earthworm activity. At Easton Down, however, a photograph of the buried soil (Whittle 1993, Fig 5) hints at some upward movement of soil material into the bank as at Overton [...]

At Overton there was unfortunately no opportunity to investigate the effects of reworking on land mollusc sequences because the old land surface was found to be decalcified and virtually no molluscs survived except in the very much earlier subsoil hollow at the base of the profile. This evidence, however, serves to remind us that decalcification arising from periods of stability, or particular vegetational changes such as the development of a thick turf mat, can produce conditions which are poor for both mollusc life and survival.

[...]

The buried materials

The approach to the buried materials has changed dramatically during the project's life. Peter Jewell (pers comm 14.7.94) writes:

> 'The original idea and intention was to provide a set of references for *field excavators* to help them make reliable interpretations. The inclusion of buried materials and their subsequent examination was an afterthought.'

Even then, during the planning stage, the emphasis was more on the recovery and interpretation of the buried materials in the field, rather than on the laboratory investigations of the materials which have become such an important aspect of the project today. This helps to explain why, during the early decades, the buried materials proved to be the most problematic aspect of the project (Evans and Limbrey 1974; Fowler 1989, 92). The records of observations in the field are not always as complete as required and some materials were lost, for example all the buried materials from Wareham 1965 except for the wood. Comparability between individual sections is made more difficult because of variations and improvements in recovery techniques.

[...]

Despite problems with the buried materials aspects, much worthwhile information is available from earlier years and some consistent patterns emerge. To help clarify these, evidence for preservation on the two sites is summarized graphically in Figures 3.3.3 and 3.3.4. Preservation is categorized on a scale of 0–4: 4 = well preserved; 3 = localized degradation; 2 = general degradation; 1 = traces only; 0 = no trace. Inevitably the classification is somewhat subjective but it does help to identify the main trends and the chief contrasts, both between the different burial environments (turf and bank) and the Overton and Wareham sites.

Overton buried materials

The preservation of organics is much poorer in the more biologically active turf than the chalk environments.

THE EXPERIMENTAL EARTHWORK PROJECT 119

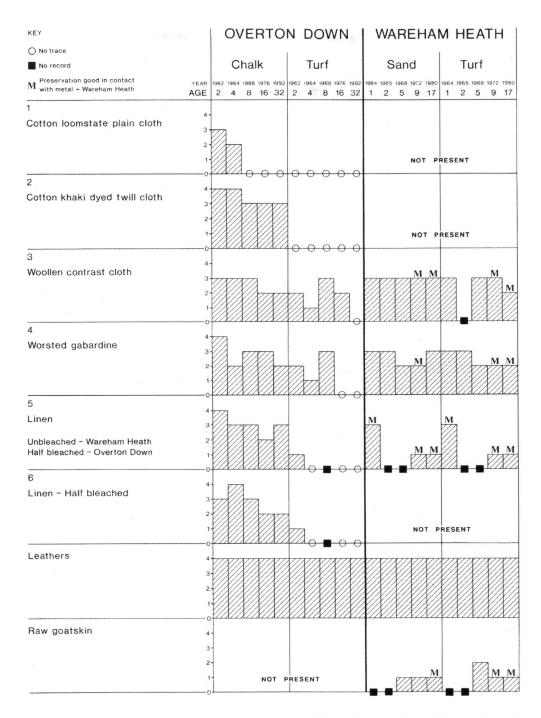

Figure 3.3.3 Diagram summarizing the preservation of buried materials (textiles, leather and goatskin) in the earthworks on a scale of 0–4. 4 = well preserved; 3 = local degradation; 2 = general degradation; 1 = traces only; 0 = no trace.

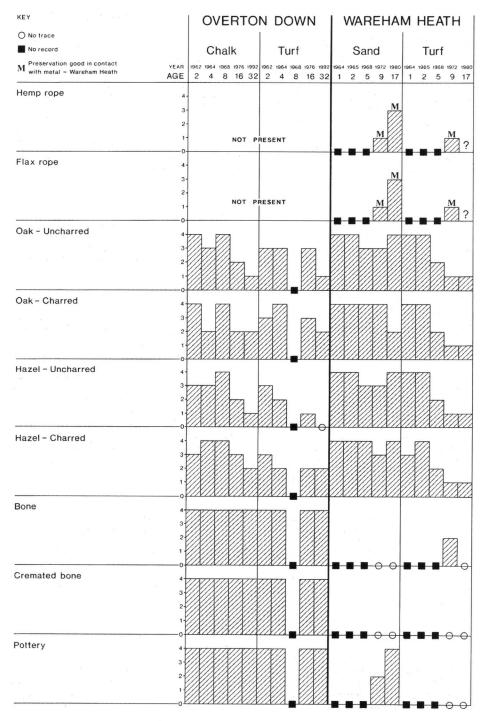

Figure 3.3.4 Diagram summarizing the preservation of buried materials (rope, wood, bone and pottery) in the earthworks on a scale of 0–4. 4 = well preserved; 3 = local degradation; 2 = general degradation; 1 = traces only; 0 = no trace.

Textiles

In the turf, Textile 1, cotton loomstate plain cloth, and Textile 2, cotton khaki dyed twill cloth, were not recovered, even in the first section after 2 years. The linen textiles were represented by traces up to, but not beyond the two year section. The wools survived rather longer. Textile 3, woollen contrast cloth, was present in a degraded form up to 16 years. Despite careful searching no trace remained of any textiles in the 32 year section. In the chalk environment, Textile 1, cotton loomstate plain cloth, only survived to the 4 year section but the khaki was still well preserved after 32 years. Both wool textiles survived in a fragmentary condition up to 32 years and the linens were also present in a degraded form. Chalk blocks placed on the surfaces of textiles to hold them in place had clearly helped to protect the underlying textiles in the chalk environment.

Leather

These survived very well in both burial environments and all samples were recovered with little macroscopically visible deterioration after 32 years.

Wood

All woods were intact up to the 8 year section in the chalk environment but there is no information about this stage from the turf. At the 16 year stage the hazel in the turf environment was more degraded than in the chalk and conversely the oak was more degraded in the chalk than in the turf. By 32 years no trace remained of the uncharred hazel and of the other woods only fragments or 'charcoal tubes' remained. In the chalk environment at both the 16 and 32 year stages hazel was better preserved than oak. Blanchette suggests that the fibre cells of hazel may be more resistant to soft rot fungi than those of oak.

Bone

All the bones survived in both the turf and chalk environments up to the 32 year stage when, on excavation, preservation appeared to be very good. Scanning Electron Microscope examination has, however, produced evidence of significant post-burial modification including cracking and dissolution by saprotrophic fungi and percolating water. The results of phosphate analysis confirm the effects of dissolution and indicate that it is occurring to a greater extent in the lower pH turf environment.

Wareham buried materials

Here the record only relates to the first 17 years, since the 32 year section will not be cut until 1996. The buried materials record is less complete for the early years than at Overton. A smaller range of textiles and leathers was buried at Wareham but additional objects included goatskin and ropes of hemp and flax. On each organic material a halfpenny and a steel disc were placed making possible consideration of the effects of metal corrosion products on preservation. By the 5 year stage it was clear that preservation was greater below the metals and by the 9 year stage some organics were only preserved where they were in contact with metal. This clearly relates to the well-known decay-inhibiting properties of copper and indicates iron decay products are having a similar effect. Preservation was generally better in the sand than in the turf environment.

Textiles

In the turf environment, the woollen contrast cloth survived in a partly decayed form up to the 17 year stage as did the worsted gaberdine. Linen only survived in contact with the metals. In the sand environment a similar picture obtains. It would be expected that materials such as linen and hemp, which are largely composed of cellulose, would not survive long in acid environments (R. Janaway pers comm).

Leather and hide

Leather survived well in both environments at the 17 year stage but there was evidence that in the more freely draining sand environment it was being detanned more rapidly than in the turf where, unlike the other organics, it was better preserved. Of the goat hide the skin had decayed by the fifth year except where it was in contact with the metals but in all cases a deposit of hairs remained in the 17 year section.

Rope

The first records relate to the 9 year excavation by which time the rope was only preserved in contact with the metal discs, similarly after 17 years.

Wood

Changes in wood density over the first 9 years bring out interesting contrasts (Evans and Limbrey 1974, Table 2). Only slight reductions in density are apparent in the 1 and 2 year sections. After that in the sand environment density gradually reduces. By the 17 year stage the uncharred oak and hazel samples were still well preserved, the charred hazel likewise; the charred oak was not so well preserved. In contrast each of the wood samples from the turf shows a sudden reduction in density at the 5 year stage and only residues and fragmentary 'charcoal tubes' remained in the 9 and 17 year sections.

Bone

In the 9 and 17 year sections bone was no longer preserved in the sand environment at Wareham. Even cremated bone appeared to have been lost which is a surprise in view, for instance, of the survival of cremated bone from Iron Age contexts in acid soils of Wales (Austin *et al.* 1986; Gilchrist and Mytum 1986). In the turf environment bone did survive but dissolution of the upper surfaces had occurred.

Comparison between buried materials at Overton and Wareham

Burial contexts in both earthworks are generally aerobic and have probably remained damp but not waterlogged since construction. It is noted that even at the height of the

1976 drought the Overton buried materials were still damp enough to sustain biological activity. Evans and Limbrey (1974) noted the possibility of some anaerobism in the turf at Wareham.

The Wareham site has lower pH values, in the range 4.5–5.1 in both environments, compared to Overton, with 5.5 from the turf environment, and 7.5 in the chalk environment. The contrast between the pHs of the two old ground surfaces is probably less than would have been expected by the project's founders. The extent of decalcification at Overton does not seem to have been recognized until 1992; furthermore the process has probably increased over the last 32 years. Figures 3.3.3 and 3.3.4 show that, as a generalization, the decay of organics is occurring at a comparable rate in the two earthworks, although there are also some interesting contrasts.

In making comparison between preservation at the two sites we must note that the inclusion of coins and steel disc on the Wareham organics has introduced a variable not present at Overton, but one can assume that areas of textile not underneath metals share equivalent conditions with Overton. Even a difference in the number of layers of textile, 6 at Overton and 4 at Wareham, could prove to be significant, because it is clear that inner layers tend to be better preserved.

Up to the 32 year stage at Overton and the 17 year stage at Wareham preservation of organic samples is generally better in the bank environment, which in both cases is better drained and more aerobic than in the turf. The probable explanation is the higher rates of biological activity in the turf environments. Microbiological study of the Overton 32 year section showed that both bacterial and fungal counts were higher in the turf than in the chalk environments. It suggested that fungal activity may have been supressed in the chalk environment by high pH and a paucity of nutrients. The only cases from the two sites where preservation seems to have been better in the turf seem to relate to processes involving dissolution at Wareham where bone was lost and leather more leached in the more freely draining sand environment.

Other aspects of preservation reveal major contrasts between the two earthworks. All the bone samples were well-preserved in both environments at Overton but at Wareham all the bone, cooked, uncooked and cremated, had vanished by the 17 year stage. Even at Overton the amount of damage to the bone, apparently as a result of fungal activity, suggests that if the present rate of damage continues the bone is unlikely to survive over archaeologically relevant timescales. This indicates that we need to give greater consideration to the possibility of spatial contrasts in bone preservation even on those sites where, generally speaking, conditions for preservation appear to be good.

Pottery was well-preserved at Overton but at Wareham was only preserved in the sand environment and had vanished in the turf after just 9 years or less. The apparent speed of pottery destruction at Wareham is remarkable and must go some way towards explaining the paucity of poorly fired prehistoric pottery on acid and upland soils. This makes the identification of aceramic cultures in the west and north of Britain more open to debate.

Charred and uncharred wood billets had been included in the earthworks to establish whether the traditional practice of charring the ends of posts before putting them in the ground aids preservation. The results suggest that, generally speaking, it has little effect. Tubes of charcoal were all that remained after 16 and 17 years respectively. However, in one instance charring had created a sufficient seal to prevent decay.

[. . .]

Problems with the experiment

The buried materials were said to be similar to those used in prehistoric times (Jewell 1963, 43). That applies to most inorganic materials (with the exception of the choice of metal alloys used at Wareham), but not the organic materials, many of which had been treated in ways which differ significantly from prehistoric practice. Ryder remarks on the inappropriateness of the wool types used. Of the leathers, only the oak-bark tanned example is directly archaeologically relevant and textile preservation seems to be very much related to the presence, absence and nature of dyes such as the modern chromium based khaki which probably has a greater preservative effect than the dyes and mordants which were used in antiquity (R Janaway pers comm).

[...]

Bibliography

Ashbee, P., I.F. Smith and J.G. Evans (1979). 'Excavation of three long barrows near Avebury, Wiltshire.' *Proceedings of the Prehistoric Society* 45: 207–300.

Atkinson, R.J.C. (1957). 'Worms and weathering.' *Antiquity* 31: 219–233.

Austin, D., M.G. Bell, B.C. Burnham *et al.* (1986). *The Caer Cadwgan Project: Interim Report for 1985*. Lampeter: University of Wales.

Courty, M.A., P. Goldberg and R.I. Macphail (1989). *Soils, Micromorphology and Archaeology*. Cambridge: Cambridge University Press.

Edwards, C.A. and J.R. Lofty (1977). *Biology of Earthworms*. London: Chapman & Hall.

Evans, J.G. (1972). *Landsnails in Archaeology*. London: Seminar Press.

Evans, J.G. and S. Limbrey (1974). 'The experimental earthwork on Morden Bog, Wareham, Dorset, England: 1963–1972.' *Proceedings of the Prehistoric Society* 40: 170–202.

Fisher, P.J. and R.I. Macphail (1985). 'Studies of archaeological soils and deposits by micromorphological techniques.' In N. Feiller, D.D. Gilbertson and N.G.A. Ralph (eds), *Palaeoenvironrnental Investigation: Research Design, Methods and Data Analysis*, BAR IS258. Oxford: British Archaeological Reports, 93–112.

Fowler, P.J. (1989). 'The Experimental Earthworks: A summary of the project's first thirty years: The thirteenth Beatrice de Cardi Lecture.' *Annual Report of the Council for British Archaeology* 39, 83–98.

Gilchrist, R. and H.C. Mytum (1986). 'Experimental archaeology and burnt bone from archaeological sites.' *Circaea* 4: 29–38.

Jewell, P.A. (ed.) (1963). *The Experimental Earthwork at Overton Down, Wiltshire 1960*. London: British Association for the Advancement of Science.

Jewell, P.A. and G.W. Dimbleby (eds) (1966). 'The Experimental Earthwork on Overton Down, Wiltshire, England: the first four years.' *Proceedings of the Prehistoric Society* 32: 313–342.

Limbrey, S. (1975). *Soil Science and Archaeology*. London: Academic Press.

Macphail, R.I. and G.M. Cruise (1996). 'Soil micromorphology.' In M. Bell, P.J. Fowler and S.W. Hillson (eds), *The Experimental Earthwork Project 1960–1992*, CBA Research Report 100, York: CBA, 95–106.

Proudfoot, V.B. (1965) 'The study of soil development from the construction and excavation of experimental earthworks.' In E.G. Hallsworth and D.V. Crawford (eds), *Experimental Pedology*. London: Butterworths, 282–294.

Scaife, R.G. and R.I. Macphail (1983) 'The post-Devensian development of heathland soils and vegetation.' In C.P. Burnham (ed.), *Soils of the Heathlands and Chalklands*, Journal of the South East Soils Discussion Group 1. Wye: SEESOIL, 70–99.

Whittle, A., A.J. Rouse and J.G. Evans (1993). 'A Neolithic downland monument in its environment: excavations at the Easton Down Long barrow, Bishops Canning, North Wiltshire.' *Proceedings of the Prehistoric Society* 59: 197–239.

Limits of the natural environment in terms of pH and oxidation-reduction potentials

L.G.M. Baas Becking, I.R. Kaplan and D. Moore

Source: Bass Becking, L.G.M., Kaplan, I.R. and Moore, D. (1960) 'Limits of the natural environment in terms of plant and oxidation and reduction potentials', *The Journal of Geology*, 68: 243–84.

Introduction

THE NATURAL ENVIRONMENT, taken as a unit, contains so many variables that it may seem impossible to ascribe limits to it. However, modern methods of measurement have made it possible to compare the two fundamental components of the natural environment in remarkably easy fashion. These two components—protons and electrons—are omnipresent in the natural environment; their concentrations, or more precisely their activities, can be measured electrometrically as electrode (oxidation-reduction or redox) potential and pH; and these activities may be plotted one against the other in an Eh-pH diagram. The total area of such a diagram contained by measurements delineates the natural environment.

[. . .]

Distribution of results

The total number of sets of measurements used in this paper is 6,200, of which our own contribution is about 3,500. The bulk of all measurements on organisms was made by us (1,700 of 2,100), and the measurements on environment are divided into 1,800 from us and 2,300 from the literature and unpublished sources. [. . .]

Work on organisms has been confined to those of geological importance—algae and a few groups of bacteria. These organisms and their environment are mutually dependent and the environmental limits are set by the activities of the organisms as shown in Table 3.4.1.

Table 3.4.1 Organisms and their associated environmental conditions

Conditions	Organisms
Low pH, high Eh	Iron bacteria
High pH, high Eh	Algae
High pH, medium Eh	Purple bacteria
High to medium pH, low Eh	Green bacteria, sulfate reducers, heterotrophic anaerobes
Low pH, medium Eh	Thiobacteria

Natural environments

General

In the course of gathering the data on environments, which are presented in the following pages, it soon became clear that many of the geologically distinct environments could not be differentiated by their Eh-pH characteristics. This is because the factors which affect Eh-pH are complex, and the components preserved in the rocks are often not those exerting the greatest influence (see Figure 3.4.1).

[...]

In any particular environment there are several outstanding controls, all related to water. Water is the universal carrier of gases, ions, and un-ionized solutes. It carries, in suspension, organisms as well as less-soluble minerals on which numerous microbes may be adsorbed. The quantity and the quality of the above environmental controls determine the nature of the milieu. This milieu is further determined by the topography of the site and by its geographical location, although in the description of the various inorganic environments it will appear that these last factors are of minor importance only.

[...]

Meteoric waters

There was considerable variation of Eh-pH characteristics in the rains studied. The variation was on two levels, within rains and between rains. Electrical storms were found to show rapid fluctuations of both Eh and pH, often as much as 2 pH units within ten minutes. Steady rain, on the other hand, was much more uniform.

[...]

Peat bogs

Peat bogs are of two types—low moors and high moors; the names have nothing to do with geographical situation, they refer to the bog topography. High moors build themselves up into low mounds composed entirely of plant material; low moors are depressions. The two types of bog reflect differences in the source of their water. High moors derive their water almost entirely from rain (ombrogenic) and are characterized by very low salt concentrations. In these conditions decay is very slow, and a thick peat deposit can accumulate. Low moors, on the other hand, are fed by waters which have

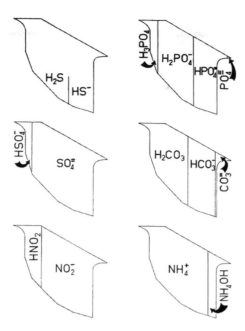

Figure 3.4.1 Stability fields of some important naturally occurring non-metallic compounds in terms of oxidation-reduction potentials and pH framed within the limits suggested by this work. Distribution of these compounds in un-ionized and ionized states is governed by their dissociation constants. The equilibrium pH for each dissociation is as follows:

$H_2S \rightleftharpoons HS^-$
  pH 7.0

$H_3PO_4 \rightleftharpoons H_2PO_4^- \rightleftharpoons HPO_4^{2-} \rightleftharpoons PO_4^{3-}$
  pH 2.1   pH 7.2   pH 12.0

$HSO_4^- \rightleftharpoons SO_4^{2-}$
  pH 1.9

$H_2CO_3 \rightleftharpoons HCO_3^- \rightleftharpoons CO_3^{2-}$
  pH 6.4   pH 10.3

$HNO_2 \rightleftharpoons NO_2^-$
  pH 3.3

$NH_4 \rightleftharpoons NH_4OH$
  pH 9.4

been in contact with soil and rock and hence contain much greater amounts of soluble salts. Decay is enhanced in these conditions, and many low-moor bogs deposit very little peat.

[...]

The differences in the two types of bog are reflected in pH as well as mineralogy. Low-moor peats have pH's from 7 to 8, apparently the upper limit of peat formation. High moors, on the other hand, have pH values generally below 6, and, in extreme cases, as low as 2.8 (Pearsall, 1938). *Sphagnum*, the major contributor to many modern

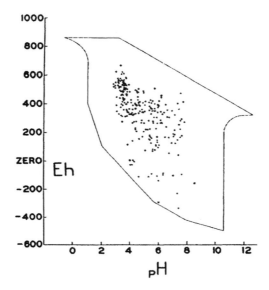

Figure 3.4.2 Eh-pH characteristics of peat bogs.

peat bogs, can actively lower the pH by cation exchange on its cell walls (Baas Becking and Nicolai, 1934) (see Figure 3.4.2).

[. . .]

Soils

Rain water which strikes the ground most frequently falls upon soil of one type or another. Surprisingly little reaches stream channels by direct runoff. It is fitting, therefore, that soils should be the next environment to study. [. . .]

Mineral soils range in pH from 2.8 to over 10, and in Eh from +750 mV to −350 mV. Our data are probably quite adequate in terms of Eh range, and in the acid limit of pH, but our most alkaline pH reading for which we have an Eh value as well is 9.0, at least one pH unit too low. Unfortunately, soils of such high pH are not found in Australia, so that we are unable to remedy the deficit.

[. . .]

From observations in the literature, soils may be divided into three categories: normal, wet, and waterlogged. Wet soils are those subject to seasonal waterlogging but which may be quite dry at other times of the year. These types can be divided from each other, as in Figure 3.4.3.

The other categories of soil are clearly marked by their pH range on the acid side, where our information is concentrated, and there is a suggestion of a similar division on the poorly documented alkaline side (see Figures 3.4.3 and 3.4.4). One may state the differences as follows: Normal soils range in pH from 2.8 to 10+; wet soils range from 3.7 to 8.5(?); and waterlogged soils range from 5.0 to 8.0. [. . .]

In waterlogged soils lime persists indefinitely, thus limiting the pH at 5; in wet soils the occasional draining is sufficient to remove lime but not enough to remove iron and

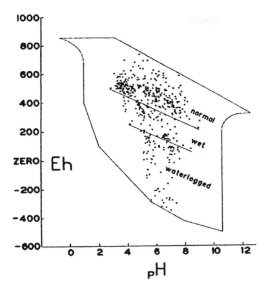

Figure 3.4.3 Eh-pH characteristics of soils.

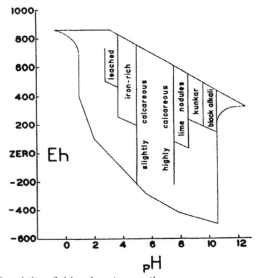

Figure 3.4.4 Suggested stability fields of various soil types.

alumina. A second limit at pH 3.7 seems to operate. Where conditions are well drained so that complete leaching can take place, even the iron and alumina are removed, and the pH can fall to 2.8. Completely leached soils of this nature are called 'podsols' and are often associated with peat development. Mineral acids from the peat waters may be responsible for the very low pH's.

Alkaline soils occur predominantly in arid regions. They differ from acid soils in the direction of ground-water movement, downward in acid soils, upward in alkaline soils. The upward movement is accompanied by precipitation of calcium and sodium salts in the soil profile. These salts are responsible for the high pH. The correlation of high pH and arid conditions of formation suggests that soils of high pH would not form under waterlogged conditions, and the scanty evidence at our disposal agrees with this postulate.

[. . .]

Fresh-water sediments

As may be expected, fresh-water sediments (see Figure 3.4.5) show close comparison in their Eh-pH distribution with the waters in which they are deposited. There is a much more obvious pH control in the sediments, at least in the data available to us, and, although a T-shaped catena occurs, the vertical stroke is much stronger than the crossbar. This is a consequence of the type of sediment prevalent in fresh water. The soluble mineral matter content of most fresh waters is dominated by calcium carbonate, which is generally sufficiently concentrated as a nutrient for plants. A controlling factor in the precipitation of limestone (or marl) is, according to Kindle (1929), the depth of the thermocline beneath the water surface.

The Eh of fresh-water sediments shows considerably more variation than the pH. In the intermittent Lake George, New South Wales, a 10-foot auger hole put down at the northern end of the lake showed consistently high Eh's, varying from a maximum of +586 mV at a depth of one foot to a minimum of +460 mV at a depth of eight feet. Eh readings above +500 mV are exceptional in other lakes, where permanent water bodies have encouraged the development of stagnation in the depths and the consequent onset of reducing conditions. The lowest Eh's recorded are −150 mV, but it is quite

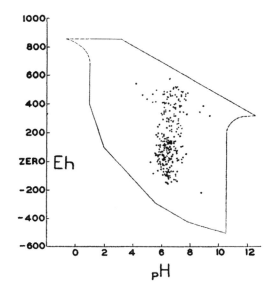

Figure 3.4.5 Eh-pH characteristics of fresh-water sediments.

likely that much lower values exist in eutrophic lakes well below the mud surface. The majority of cores from lake sediments do not penetrate the mud for more than three feet.

[...]

Evaporites

Evaporites may arise by solar concentration from most of the foregoing environments, with the exceptions of rain water and peat bogs. They often, at the present time, receive contributions from geothermal waters. In view of their complex origin, it is scarcely surprising that they cover a wide range of both pH and Eh.

[...]

The Eh range responds to the state of the iron in the evaporite body. Reducing conditions in the form of fetid black muds are reported from many evaporite lakes (Strøm, 1939); in Searles Lake, California, we have found potentials as low as −500 mV at pH 10.48. At the other extreme lie the coquimbite evaporites of Peru and Australia. Measurements made on Australian coquimbite by one of us (Baas Becking) in 1936 gave a pH 2.6, and measurements made on saturated ferric sulfate solutions in equilibrium with the air gave Eh's of +860 mV.

It seems likely that evaporites may fill almost the whole area of the natural environment, as we have outlined it. The data so far recorded do no more than suggest

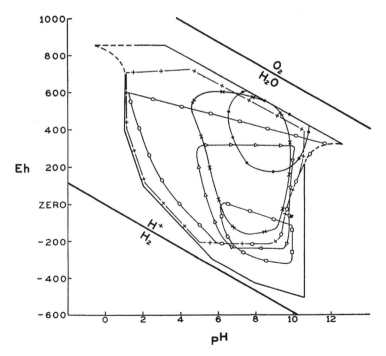

Figure 3.4.6 Approximate areas of Eh-pH for the photosynthetic organisms studied in this work. The 'area' for each environment is bounded by a different symbol: ○○○ = green algae and diatoms; ●●● = *Dunaliella*; ××× = *Enteromorpha*; +++ = blue-green algae; ▲▲▲ = purple bacteria; □□□ = green bacteria.

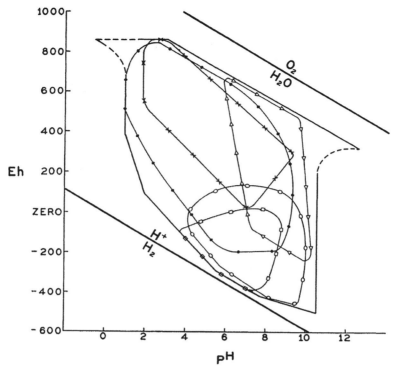

Figure 3.4.7 Approximate areas of Eh-pH for the geologically important bacteria studied in this work. The 'area' for each environment is bounded by a different symbol: ○○○ = sulfate-reducing bacteria; ●●● = thiobacteria; ××× = iron bacteria; ▲▲▲ = denitrifying bacteria; □□□ = heterotrophic anaerobic bacteria.

the wideness of the range. It can readily be seen that this environment, originally suggested by Krumbein and Garrels (1952) as being oxidative, can also be highly reducing. It is often true that, while the surface waters may give high positive Eh-values, the bottom mud is black and highly reducing.

[...]

Organisms

To summarize the findings, the approximate outlines of the various limits for environments and organisms are represented in Figures 3.4.6 and 3.4.7. It is within these boundaries that the results of our measurements lie. Although it is quite possible that future work may expand these limits, especially for the environments and organisms on which few readings have been made, they will serve to illustrate at a quick glance the potential range covered by the more typical of examples studied. It is further possible, by comparing Figures 3.4.1 to 3.4.6 with Figures 3.4.6 and 3.4.7, to estimate what organisms one would expect to find in the environment with corresponding Eh-pH characteristics. It should be noted that the limits are drawn at a maximum pH range.

[...]

References cited

Baas Becking, L.G.M. and M.F.E. Nicolai (1934). 'On the ecology of a *Sphagnum* bog.' *Blumea* 1: 10–45.

Kindle, E.M. (1929). 'A comparative study of different types of thermal stratification in lakes and their influence on the formation of marl.' *Jour. Geology* 37: 150–157.

Krumbein, W.C. and R.M. Garrels (1952). 'Origin and classification of sediments in terms of pH and oxidation-reduction potential.' *Jour. Geology* 60: 1–33.

Pearsall, W.H. (1938). 'The soil complex in relation to plant communities.' *Tour. Ecol.* 26, 180–193, 194–209, 298–315.

Strøm, M.K. (1939). 'Land-locked waters and the deposition of black muds.' In P.D Trask (ed.), *Recent marine sediments*. Tulsa, Oklahoma: Am. Assoc. Petroleum Geologists Bull., 357–372.

Chapter 3.5

Chemical and microbiological aspects of the preservation process in *Sphagnum* peat

T.J. Painter

Source: Painter, T.J. (1995) 'Chemical and microbiological aspects of the preservation process in *Sphagnum* peat', in R. Turner and R. Scaife (eds), *Bog Bodies: New Discoveries and New Perspectives*, London: BMP, pp. 88–99.

WHY DO BODIES, and other biodegradable things, get preserved in peat? [...] Why does peat exist at all? Why do *Sphagnum* mosses grow, year after year, upon the dead remains of previous generations, while deriving little, if any, sustenance from them (Clymo and Hayward 1982)? Why do these residues decay so slowly, when a heap of grass clippings, for example, will rot so quickly that it becomes hot?

Many traditional uses of *Sphagnum* moss and peat point to an antimicrobial property. Bandages made from dried *Sphagnum* have been used in folk medicine since the Bronze Age [...] In past centuries, seafarers took peat-bog water with them on long voyages, because they had found that it would stay 'fresh' much longer than ordinary spring or well water.

[...]

The 'sphagnol' hypothesis

It is natural to suspect that *Sphagnum* mosses contain some kind of antimicrobial substance.
[...]
The distinguished soil microbiologist Selman Waksman (Nobel Prize, 1952) vigorously contested the notion that peat possessed any significant antimicrobial activity, after finding 10^7–10^8 cells per gram (dry weight) of aerobic bacteria, microscopic fungi and actinomycetes in the surface layer of a lowmoor peat bog. Deeper down, where the conditions were anoxic (oxygen-lacking), 10^4–10^6 cells per gram of anaerobic bacteria were found (Waksman 1930). Although these figures are very low compared with the 10^{10} cells per gram that may be found, for example, in a rotting heap of grass

(Kononova 1961), they are hardly evidence of toxicity; they could be due simply to a lack of nutrients.

Aerobic v. anaerobic bacteria as agents of decay

The fact that there is virtually no molecular oxygen below the top 30–50 cm of a peat bog does not mean that there would be no decay. On average, anaerobic bacteria are just as effective as aerobic ones in breaking down the proteins in animal remains and the polysaccharides in vegetable ones, because these are hydrolytic reactions that require only the presence of water. Likewise, fats can be hydrolysed to give glycerine and long-chain fatty acids, but further breakdown of the latter entails repeated oxidation.

Even oxidative reactions can be carried out by anaerobic bacteria, but only by reducing other substances such as carbon dioxide (to methane), sulphate (to sulphur or hydrogen sulphide), or nitrate (to nitrogen or ammonia). When these are lacking, or when the bacteria derive too little energy from the oxidation to meet their metabolic requirements, the reaction will not go, and incompletely oxidised substances accumulate as end-products.

Typical end-products of the anaerobic breakdown of cellulose are lactic acid, succinic acid, ethyl alcohol, and short-chain fatty acids. Those from proteins include short chain fatty acids and toxic, foul-smelling amines such as putrescine, cadaverine, and skatole. The long-chain fatty acids released by hydrolysis from fats and waxes can be reduced when they are unsaturated, but instances of their oxidation under anoxic conditions are rare. Sulphur-metabolising bacteria in marine sediments provide one exception to this rule (McInerney 1988).

Lignin and humic acids are polymers that anaerobic bacteria find it particularly hard to cope with, probably because their breakdown entails oxidative steps right from the beginning. Some researchers claim to have observed a very slow breakdown, with release of carbon dioxide and methane, but others have been unable to confirm this (Colberg 1988). Ancient, waterlogged woods, which seem at first sight to have been 'preserved' in anoxic sediments, often prove to be no more than a fragile honeycomb of lignin, from which the cellulose and hemicelluloses have been hydrolysed selectively away. It would, therefore, be correct to state that the anoxic conditions in a peat bog contribute to the preservation of lignin and humic acids, and also of the fatty acids liberated from fats and waxes, but not of the bodies or the carbohydrates in plant residues.

Acidify as a disinfectant

Another theory that has gained wide acceptance is that preservation is due to the acidity of peat-bog water, combined with the anoxic conditions beneath the surface layer. It is based essentially upon the well-known fact that foods can be preserved by pickling in vinegar (and usually also salt) at a pH of about 2.5. This kind of preservation makes use of the fact that anaerobic, putrefactive bacteria (such as *Clostridium*, for example) usually grow best under nearly neutral conditions (pH 5.5–7.5). Acid-tolerant strains are known, but they do not usually mean trouble in the kitchen.

The acidity of peat has, however, been exaggerated, possibly because of a misconception that will be explained in the next section. It is necessary to distinguish between two different kinds of peat. Lowmoor peat (fens) as its name implies, is flushed continuously by groundwater that has run off from higher terrain, and is buffered by the salts (especially calcium bicarbonate) dissolved in it. Its pH is typically 5.5–6.5 (Waksman 1930). This is close to the *optimum* pH for growth of most normal strains of putrefactive bacteria. It is also a typical pH range for unpolluted rainwater, and for many kinds of soil that have rich microbial floras and no preservative properties.

Highmoor peat (blanket bog), on the other hand, is watered almost exclusively by precipitation. Its pH is typically 3.2–4.5, with most readings close to the average of 4.0 (Waksman 1930; Clymo 1984). The acidity arises because *Sphagnum* mosses contain a cation exchanger which absorbs the cations of salts dissolved in rain water, liberating mineral acid (Clymo 1963; Brehm 1970, 1971; Clymo 1984). The cation exchanger is the holocellulose, which is the total polysaccharidic fraction of the cell walls of the moss, consisting of cellulose, hemicellulose and pectic acid (Schwarzmaier and Brehm 1975; Painter and Sørensen 1978). The traces of salts in rain water originate mainly from the oceans and deserts, from which they are swept up by strong winds. They consist mainly of the chlorides of sodium and magnesium, and hence the acidity is due mainly to hydrochloric acid.

Intermediate between these two extremes is the special case of 'raised' bogs on low terrain. As the name implies, the surfaces of these bogs have grown up above the level of the surrounding land. That part of the peat which lies above the upper limit of the water table resembles highmoor peat in that it is watered mainly by rainfall. In periods of dry weather, however, groundwater rises by capillary action to replace water lost from the surface by evaporation, like oil climbing the wick of a lamp. It is hard to give a statistically reliable average, but the present author has never found a pH lower than 5 in this sort of lowmoor peat. Lindow Man, Tollund Man, and Grauballe Man were found in peat of this kind (Turner, personal communication).

Even in highmoor peat, however, acid-tolerant bacteria, both aerobic and anaerobic, have been found (Waksman 1930; Waksman and Stevens 1929). It is worth remembering that most wines and ciders are produced by anaerobic fermentation at pH 3.0–3.8. The special strains of yeast that do this are, of course, genetically adapted to grow on fruits and their juices; most yeasts, like most bacteria, grow best under neutral conditions. It should not, therefore, be a surprise to learn that millions of years of natural selection have likewise ensured that peat bogs have their own, special, microbial floras, uniquely adapted to exploit whatever opportunities for growth they offer.

Attention is drawn to a special, microbiological investigation of Lindow Man's body, and samples of peat associated with it (Ridgway *et al.* 1986). The most prominent micro-organisms were bacteria of the genus *Pseudomonas*. These are typical saprophiles, widely distributed in soils and water, and capable of adaptation to both aerobic and anaerobic growth. They were evidently growing on nutrients derived from the peat or the bog water, but not from the body.

Sequestration of multivalent metal cations

One of the most consistent observations on bog bodies is that they are extensively decalcified. The British Museum's previous report is especially clear on this point (Connolly *et al.* 1986). In exceptional cases, the bones have dissolved completely (Coles and Coles 1989; Ross and Robins 1989). Everybody knows that vinegar softens and dissolves fish bones as well as preserving the flesh, so the inference in the minds of the discoverers must have seemed quite compelling: peat-bog water is acidic, and quite strongly so.

There are, however, other substances in peat that will decalcify bones and teeth much more efficiently than a trace of acidity. *Sphagnum* holocellulose will sequester calcium and other multivalent metal cations with high selectivity compared to monovalent cations such as sodium (Smidsrød and Painter 1984). It will do this at any pH above 3, but it does so most efficiently at pH 7 (Andresen *et al.* 1987). The anionic groups that take part in this binding are concentrated in polysaccharidic chains that are chemically related to pectic acid, but which also contain building units of an unusual keto-uronic acid, namely 5-keto-D-mannuronic acid, which is abbreviated to 5KMA.

In the living moss, the pectic acid is chemically linked, through its 5KMA units, to the other cell-wall polysaccharides in the holocellulose (cellulose and hemicellulose), and also to lignin. As the dead moss is slowly transformed into peat, these chemical linkages are gradually broken by a reaction known as 'autohydrolysis', and the pectic acid, still containing most of the original 5KMA units, is released in soluble form (Painter and Sørensen 1978; Painter 1983a, 1983b, 1991). The properties of this polysaccharide are so different from those of ordinary pectic acid that it has been given a special name, sphagnan (Painter 1991).

Sphagnan is the refined and concentrated form of the cation exchanger in *Sphagnum* holocellulose and the living moss, and it has the same affinity for calcium and other multivalent metal cations. Because of its content of 5KMA it is, however, an unstable substance – most keto-acids are unstable. Under mildly acidic conditions, and especially in the presence of ammonia or an amine, it is slowly converted into a brown, anionic polymer that is familiar to everyone, namely, aquatic humus or humic acid (Painter 1983b, 1991). [Note: When completely neutralised, humic acids should, strictly speaking, be called 'humâtes', but it is more convenient to call them 'humic acids' all the time, and to specify the pH separately. In peat with a pH range of 3.2–6.5, they would be only partly neutralised.]

Humic acids also sequester multivalent metal cations. They do this so efficiently under mildly acidic, neutral, or even alkaline conditions, that they will even erode and dissolve rocks (Kononova 1961). Bog bodies are permanently immersed in a solution containing sphagnan, intermediates in the conversion of sphagnan into humic acids, and the humic acids themselves. There can be no doubt that this is why they are decalcified. Decalcification is not evidence of acidity, and in fact the sequestering properties of these polymers would be impaired by too much acidity.

Humic acids as regulators of microbial growth

Micro-organisms cannot grow without trace elements (micro-nutrients), which include multivalent metal cations such as those of copper, iron, manganese, molybdenum and zinc. Since these are sequestered by *Sphagnum* holocellulose, sphagnan, and humic acids, it is to be expected that microbial growth in peat would be suppressed. [. . .]

The ancient mariners' belief in the 'keeping' properties of bog water was well founded!

[. . .]

Possibilities for tanning by polymeric polyphenols

Another consistent observation on peat-bog bodies is that the best-preserved parts are the connective tissues, and especially the skin. In these tissues, the collagen fibres are remarkably intact, and they seem to be *tanned*, as in leather (Connolly *et al.* 1986). Bourke (1986) likens the skin of Lindow Man to soft, suede leather.

Polyphenolic tannins are widely but not equally distributed in the vegetable kingdom. They occur most abundantly in the bark, leaves and heartwood of woody dicotyledons ('dicots') such as acacia (bark, 36%), eucalyptus (bark, 40%), mangrove (bark, 46%), oak (bark and wood, 15%), and sumac (leaves, 25%; galls, 64%). In *Sphagnum* mosses, polyphenolic tannins are completely absent (Hegnauer 1962).

It should be emphasised that all of the plants including *Sphagnum*, contain other kinds of phenolic compounds that do not tan. Only a special kind of polymeric (or oligomeric) phenol will bind to the collagen fibres of skin in such a way as to protect them from microbial attack, toughen them physically, and stabilise them to heat (which would convert untreated collagen into gelatin).

What is it, then, that tans the bodies? [...]

In a 15 cm thick band of peat surrounding Lindow Man, *Calluna* was absent, but fragments of *Vaccinium* were stated to be either 'rare' or 'occasional'. The rest of the peat was dominated by *Sphagnum*, especially *S. imbricatum*, but fragments of the cotton sedge (*Eriophorum vaginatum*, order Cyperales) in different samples were stated to be 'absent', 'rare', or 'occasional'. A report on the chemical composition of this and other *Eriophorum* species makes no mention of the presence of polyphenolic tannins, as expected for a sedge (Hegnauer 1963).

[...]

Two pieces of direct evidence likewise oppose the idea that polyphenolic tannins contribute significantly to the preservation of bodies in *Sphagnum* peat. Direct, chemical tests on samples of soft tissue from Lindow Man gave negative results (Omar *et al.* 1989). The significance of this observation is unfortunately diminished by the possibility than any polyphenols initially present could have changed chemically during 2,000 years of interment.

The other piece of evidence is the colour of the bodies. Leathers produced by conventional vegetable tannage are light, brownish-yellow, brownish-orange or brownish-red ('tan', or 'tawny', in fact). In contrast, the bodies are roughly the colour of black coffee – all well-authenticated, modern reports affirm that this is the case.

A final word is needed about sedge peats, especially as they often form strata in and under *Sphagnum* peats. Pure sedge peats do not seem to preserve bodies. In Great Britain, at least, all bodies found in sedge peats are represented only by bones (Turner 1995, 115–17).

Tanning by sphagnan

Leather can be formed by many other kinds of organic compounds besides polymeric polyphenols. In theory, any compound containing a reactive carbonyl (>C = O) group should tan under mildly acidic conditions. In the leather industry, formaldehyde, glyoxal, pyruvaldehyde, glutaraldehyde, acrolein, and periodate-oxidised starch ('dialdehyde starch') are all used (Gustavson 1956; Nayudamma 1978; Clark and Courts 1977).

Dialdehyde starch is especially interesting, because it is a polysaccharide into which numerous reactive carbonyl groups have been introduced artificially by selective oxidation. Sphagnan already contains reactive carbonyl groups in its 5KMA residues, and is therefore a naturally-occurring tanning agent of the same kind. It is very unusual for naturally-occurring polysaccharides to contain keto-sugars, but *Sphagnum* is an unusual plant. It is believed from fossil discoveries to have separated from the mainstream of evolution sometime in the Permian Period, 220–280 million years ago, when, instead of developing roots, it specialised in absorbing nutrients through its leaves (Andrews 1961).

Chemically speaking, 'aldehyde tanning' consists in the building of polymeric 'bridges' between the free amino ($-NH_2$) groups on different collagen molecules, rather like threads of spider's silk stretched between the twigs of a tree. When the tanning agent contains two or more carbonyl groups in the same molecule, the 'bridges' themselves may be 'bridged', and a kind of 'cobweb' develops. If one now thinks of the molecules of proteolytic enzymes as flies, one has a simple picture of how aldehyde tanning prevents decay.

There is a lot of empty space in the 'cobweb', and leathers produced by aldehyde tanning alone are correspondingly porous. They are soft and turgid when wet, but shrink markedly and become hard on drying. Chamois leather, used for washing windows, is produced by formaldehyde tanning. Leather produced by tanning with sphagnan would be even more hydrophilic (water attracting) and lipophobic (fat-repelling) than other aldehyde leathers, because sphagnan is chemically related to pectin, which has a high affinity for water.

Experiments on the tanning of pigskin (chosen because of its similarity to human skin) have confirmed these expectations, and have shown as well that the leather produced is dark brown, like the bodies. This very dark, coffee colour is so characteristic of tanning by sphagnan that one could confidently assert that any body of a different colour must have been preserved in some other way.

The colour is the product of a 'Maillard', or 'melanoidin' reaction. This is a well-known, but complex, chemical transformation that occurs whenever reducing carbohydrates, and certain other aldehydes and ketones, react with proteins, amino acids or other amines under mildly acidic conditions (Maillard 1916, 1917; Ellis 1959). The pigments in soya sauce and black treacle are authentic products of a Maillard reaction.

Preservation of non-collagenous tissue

The word 'tanning' implies the conversion of hide into leather, so it may be incorrect to apply it to proteins other than collagen. Sphagnan does, however, react with other proteins by the same mechanism, and with the same effect of protecting them from microbial attack. In this section we consider other water-insoluble proteins such as myosin, the principal fibrous protein of muscle.

It is seldom realised that the preservation of fish and meat by 'smoking' (exposure to wood smoke or treatment with an oil condensed from wood smoke) is identical in principle with aldehyde tanning. Wood smoke does contain phenolic compounds with antimicrobial properties, but the most active preservatives are a group of at least 133 different aldehydes and ketones referred to in the industry as 'carbonyls'. These include formaldehyde, glutaraldehyde and acrolein, three of the aldehydes actually used in leather manufacture. In addition, smoke contains formic, acetic and many other organic acids that would catalyse the reaction with protein (Maga 1988).

[...]

The non-collagenous tissues of Lindow Man had decomposed much more than the connective tissues (Connolly 1986), and in Damendorf Man they had dissolved completely, along with the bones, leaving only skin and hair (Coles and Coles 1989). This must be partly because the sphagnan in the bog water took longer to reach them; it is a fairly big molecule, and it diffuses slowly.

It should be noted, however, that the degradation of animal tissues that commences immediately after death has nothing to do with invasion from without by micro-organisms in the first instance. It is caused by a special group of digestive enzymes contained in cell organelles called 'lysosomes'. In living tissues, these serve to remove dead or damaged cells, so that they can be replaced by new ones. Lysosomes are present in all the tissues of the body, including the skin, but they are most abundant in the cells of organs such as the liver, pancreas and kidneys; it is therefore to be expected that these would be the first to disintegrate after death. Interestingly, the embalmers of ancient Egypt must have known from experience that these organs would disintegrate first, because otherwise it is hard to explain why they used to remove them, and preserve them separately in jars (Harmer 1979).

[...]

Tanning as a cause of adipocere formation

Turner (1988) following Thomson (1984), defines 'adipocere' as a 'condition where the tissues (of a bog body) are converted into a mixture of soaps, fatty acids and volatile substances, which exude on to the body surface'. In a report on Meenybraddan Woman, Omar et al. (1989) state that 'there were deposits of adipocere distributed over the body and under the skin. Adipocere is produced by the prolonged storage of animal fat under anaerobic, cool conditions'.

Certain fish, such as salmon, mackerel and herring, become oily when smoked. The oil does not come from the smoke (cod and haddock do not become oily when smoked) but from polyunsaturated fat stored in the muscle. It gets physically squeezed out as the muscle contracts. The contraction is due partly to the loss of water by evaporation, but also to the cross-linking of the myosin fibres by the carbonyl compounds in the smoke.

In leather manufacture, the hide is always de-fatted before tanning (Nayudamma 1978). If this step were to be omitted, the leather produced would exude fat for a long time afterwards. The present author has confirmed this by doing experiments with chicken skin (chosen for its high fat content). The exudation occurred both with sphagnan and with a polyphenolic tannin as the tanning agent.

In the anoxic region of a peat bog, the exuded fat would be broken down to a limited extent by anaerobic bacteria. The initial reaction would be hydrolysis of triglycerides to give first diglycerides, then monoglycerides, and finally glycerine and long-chain fatty acids. At the pH of the bog (probably 5–6), the latter would be present partly as soaps. The bacteria would then ferment the glycerine, with the formation of volatile, short-chain fatty acids such as acetic and propionic acids, but they would not break down the long-chain fatty acids (McInerney 1988).

It has been suggested (Thomson 1984) that adipocere contributes to the preservation of the bodies, but the facts listed above indicate that adipocere formation and preservation are two separate consequences of tanning.

Binding and inactivation of soluble proteins and enzymes

The binding of soluble (globular) proteins such as serum albumin, gelatin and haemoglobin, and of enzymes such as pepsin, trypsin, amylase, pectinase and cellulase by *Sphagnum* holocellulose, has now been observed in the author's laboratory. Once bound, the enzymes lost their activity completely in about 3–10 days at 20° C, whereas in aqueous solution they were considerably more stable. These observations imply that any enzyme secreted by any micro-organism into the ambient water would become trapped and inactivated on the surface of the insoluble fragments of *Sphagnum* in peat, and prevented from attacking its substrate.

The enzymes would include proteases capable of hydrolysing the proteins in animal remains and woollen artefacts, and the cellulases, hemicellulases and pectinases that hydrolyse the polysaccharides in wooden artefacts and the remains of higher plants, as well as the cell walls of *Sphagnum* moss itself. This implies that the bio-degradation of *any* polymeric substrate (that is, molecules that are too big to be ingested whole by bacterial cells) would be suppressed in peat, even when it cannot be tanned.

The binding and inactivation of water-soluble enzymes do not, however, occur so rapidly as to preclude any possibility of decay in *Sphagnum* peat. Moreover, enzymes bound to bacterial cell walls can also act on polymeric substrates. It is quite clear that bio-degradation does occur, very slowly, in peat (consider the case of adipocere, for example). Collagen and keratin (the fibrous protein in hair, wool and nails) seem to survive particularly well because they are protected in several different ways.

[...]

Conclusions

- The low density of bacterial cells in the anoxic region of a *Sphagnum* peat bog is due to deprivation of essential metal cations and amino-nitrogen. Both kinds of nutrient are sequestered by a pectin-like polysaccharide (sphagnan) in the cell walls of *Sphagnum* mosses.
- Bodies are preserved in *Sphagnum* peat partly because they are tanned by sphagnan, and also because sphagnan reacts with the digestive enzymes secreted by putrefactive bacteria, immobilising them on the surface of *Sphagnum* fragments in the peat, and causing them to lose their activity. Wooden artefacts and the remains of higher plants are also preserved for the latter reason.
- Because of the solubility of sphagnan in water, collagen and other proteins in preserved bodies could bind sphagnan photosynthesised at a different, and normally later, period in history. This could lead to errors in radiocarbon dating unless a tissue component, such as cholesterol, which does not bind sphagnan, is utilised.
- Adipocere is fat, squeezed out of the tissues of a bog body by the tanning process, and then partially hydrolysed and fermented by anaerobic bacteria.

Bibliography

Andresen, K., H. Grasdalen, K.A. Holsen et al. (1987). 'Structure, properties and potential applications of *Sphagnum* holocellulose.' In S.S. Stivala, V. Crescenzi and I.C.M. Dea (eds), *Industrial Polysaccharides: The Impact of Biotechnology and Advanced Methodologies*. London: Gordon and Breach.
Andrews, H.N. (1961). *Studies in Paleobotany*. New York: Wiley.
Bourke, J.B. (1986). 'The medical investigation of Lindow Man.' In Stead et al. 46–51.
Brehm, K. (1970). 'Kationenaustausch bei Hochmoorsphagnen: Die Virkung von an den Austauscher gebunden Kationen in Kulturversuchen.' *Beitr. Biol. Pfanzen* 47: 91–116.
Brehm, K. (1971). 'Ein *Sphagnum*-Bult als Beispiel einer natürlichen Ionenaustauschersäule.' *Beitr. Biol. Pflanzen* 47: 287–312.
Clark, R.C. and A. Courts (1977). 'The chemical reactivity of gelatin.' In A.G. Ward and A. Courts, *The Science and Technology of Gelatin*. London: Academic Press.
Clymo, R.S. (1963). 'Ion-exchange in *Sphagnum* and its relation to bog ecology.' *Ann. Bot.* 27: 309–24.
Clymo, R.S. (1984). '*Sphagnum*-dominated peat bog: a naturally acid ecosystem.' *Phil. Trans. R. Soc. Lond.* B305: 487–99.
Clymo, R.S. and P.M. Hayward (1982). 'The ecology of *Sphagnum*.' In A.J.E. Smith (ed.), *Bryophyte Ecology*. London: Chapman and Hall.
Colberg, P.J. (1988). 'Anaerobic microbial degradation of cellulose, lignin, oligolignols, and monoaromatic lignin derivatives.' In A.J.B. Zehnder (ed.), *Biology of Anaerobic Microorganisms*. New York: Wiley.
Coles, B. and J. Coles (1989). *People of the Wetlands*. London: Guild Publishing.
Connolly, R.C. (1986) 'The anatomical description of Lindow Man.' In Stead et al. 54–62.
Connolly, R.C., R.P. Evershed, G. Embery et al. (1986). 'The chemical composition of some body tissues.' In Stead et al. 72–6.
Ellis, G.P. (1959). 'The Maillard reaction.' *Adv. Carbohydr. Chem.* 14: 63–134.
Gustavson, K.H. (1956). *The Chemistry of Tanning Processes*. New York: Academic Press.
Harmer, R.M. (1979). 'Embalming, burial and cremation.' *Encyclopedia Britannica*, 15th edn. Macropaedia 6: 735–41.
Hegnauer, R. (1962). *Chemotaxonomy of Plants 1*. Birkhauser Verlag, Basel and Stuttgart, 181–3, 347–50.
Hegnauer, R. (1963). *Chemotaxonomy of Plants 2*. Birkhauser Verlag, Basel and Stuttgart, 128.
Kononova, M.M. (1961). *Soil Organic Matter*. Oxford: Pergamon.
Maga, J.A. (1988). *Smoke in Food Processing*. Boca Raton: CRC Press.
Maillard, L.C. (1916). 'Synthesis of humic substances.' *Ann. Chim. (Paris)* 5: 258–317.
Maillard, L.C. (1917) *Ann. Chim. (Paris)* 7: 113–52.
McInerney, M.J. (1988). 'Anaerobic hydrolysis and fermentation of fats and proteins.' In A.J.B. Zehnder (ed.), *Biology of Anaerobic Microorganisms*. New York: Wiley.
Nayudamma, Y. (1978). 'Leather and Hides.' *Encyclopaedia Britannica*, 15th edn, Macropaedia 10: 759–64.
Omar, S., M. McCord and v. Daniels (1989). 'The conservation of bog bodies by freeze-drying.' *Stud. Conserv.* 34: 101–9.
Painter, T.J. (1983a). 'Residues of D-*lyxo*-5-hexosulopyranuronic acid in *Sphagnum* holocellulose, and their role in cross-linking.' *Carbohydr. Res.* 124: C18–C21.
Painter, T.J. (1983b) 'Carbohydrate origin of aquatic humus from peat.' *Carbohydr. Res.* 124: C22–C26.
Painter, T.J. (1991) 'Lindow Man, Tollund Man and other peat-bog bodies: the preservative and antimicrobial action of sphagnan, a reactive glycuronoglycan with tanning and sequestering properties.' *Carbohydr. Polymers* 15: 123–142.
Painter, T.J. and N.A. Sørensen (1978). 'The cation exchanger of *Sphagnum* mosses: an unusual form of holocellulose.' *Carbohydr. Res.* 66: C1–C3.
Ridgway, G.L., M. Powell and N. Mirza (1986). 'The microbiological monitoring of Lindow Man.' In Stead et al., 21.
Ross, A. and D. Robins (1989). *The Life and Death of a Druid Prince*. London: Guild Publishing.

Schwarzmaier, U. and K. Brehm (1975). 'Detailed characterisation of the cation exchanger in *Sphagnum magellanicum* Brid.' *Z. Pflanzenphysiol.* 75: 250–5.

Smidsrød, O. and T.J. Painter (1984) 'Contribution of carbohydrates to the cation-exchange selectivity of aquatic humus from peat-bog water.' *Carbohydr. Res.* 127: 267–81.

Stead, I.M., J.B. Bourke and D. Brothwell (1986). *Lindow Man: The Body in the Bog.* London: British Museum Press.

Thomson, W.A.R. (1984). *Black's Medical Dictionary*, 746–7.

Turner, R.C. (1988) 'A Cumbrian bog body from Scaleby.' *Trans. Cumb. & Westmorland Antiq. & Archaeol. Soc.* 88: 1–7.

Turner, R.C. (1995). 'Recent Research into British Bog Bodies.' In R. Turner and R. Scaife (eds), *Bog Bodies: New Discoveries and New Perspectives.* London: BMP, 108–22.

Waksman, S.A. (1930) 'Chemical composition of peat and the role of micro-organisms in its formation.' *Am. J. Sci.* 19: 32–54.

Waksman, S.A. and K.R. Stevens (1929). 'The role of microorganisms in peat formation and peat decomposition.' *Soil Sci.* 28: 315–38.

Chapter 4

Legislation and organisations

Heritage legislative protection

POPULATED LAND MASSES ARE divided into countries or states that have laws that govern the conduct of their peoples. Such laws invariably provide protection for cultural heritage assets such as archaeological remains. The extent and nature of the protection, any associated punitive sanctions against transgressors and any agency charged with protection are defined in law and are appropriate to the culture and the other laws of that country. International organisations concerned with heritage such as UNESCO and ICOMOS (which can be composed of member states or qualified individuals) pass charters, conventions and resolutions (see Chapter 5) that represent the intentions and aspirations of the international community. In the case of organisations such as UNESCO or the EU, when such conventions have been ratified by sufficient member states, it is expected that the policy of the international organisation will be incorporated into the laws and statutes of the individual member countries. Only then does it become legally binding, enforceable by law and result in sanctions against those who do not obey it (Stanley-Price 2009: 34).

Legislation is not effective without clear definitions and awareness of what is being legislated. So archaeological sites must be surveyed, classified and an inventory created before any heritage legislation can define what is being protected and why (DCMS 2013) (see Table 4.0.1). Threats must also be understood and the measures proposed to protect sites must be effective in preventing damage. An agency/organisation responsible for national heritage is invariably required to manage the legal protection, extend it to protect new sites, advise governments on changes to legislation and enforce legal protection. Given its awareness and structure, it is invariably also an appropriate body to engage in measures other than legal protection such as physical protection, education and raising social value, appropriate for preserving/protecting heritage sites. With the exception of a few wealthy individuals who have saved specific sites, it is only through organisations that most countries can effect preservation of their heritage. Organisations are either brought into existence by legislation (National Parks), are created by another organisation (UNESCO or ICCROM) or are formed by a group of like-minded people coming together (National Trust).

A brief history of legal protection and the processes of managing heritage sites on a worldwide scale is given by Henry Cleere (1989) (see Chapter 4.1). He shows that the legislative process is just one of many steps a society takes to care for its heritage. He articulates the situation present in 1989, before the 'preservation *in situ*' conventions and wider definitions of heritage started to be adopted.

As countries formed in Europe evolving from the fiefdoms of medieval monarchs to 'nation states' during the sixteenth to nineteenth centuries, the emerging national identity invariably drew on the historical narrative about people and events and the associated physical remains – artefacts, buildings and places to form their nations' story. In the case of England, the emergence of the use of written and spoken English in the fourteenth century, the schism of the Reformation and the threats of foreign invasion in the sixteenth century had helped to create a concept of England that could be articulated by Shakespeare at the end of the sixteenth century as a 'green and pleasant land' and a 'sceptred isle'. As early as 1540, John Leland was starting to catalogue and describe the ancient sites and monuments of England, and in 1586, William Camden, probably using some of Leland's notes, published *Britannia*, the first guide to the antiquities of England, in fact of any single country. This gave the emerging nation state a past, though valued ancient places continued to be protected

Table 4.0.1 Principles for scheduling archaeological remains under the 1979 Ancient Monument and Archaeological Areas Act, guidance issued by DCMS (2013)

Significant archaeological remains can be protected from the damaging actions of human beings through legal protection, which in Britain is achieved through adding them to a list or schedule of protected ancient monuments. These are the criteria (indicators) currently (2014) in use to define archaeological significance in England.

	Monuments should be considered from legal protection which/where:
Period	Characterise a period.
Rarity	Best portray the typical and commonplace classes of monument as well as the rare, taking account of their national and regional distribution.
Rarity	Are so scarce that all surviving examples retain some significance.
Documentation	Have records of previous investigations, contemporary records or related artefacts or ecofacts that enhance the significance of the monument.
Group value	Have association with related contemporary monuments and/or those of different periods and/or associated land.
Survival/condition	Have significant features above and/or below ground and/or underwater whose surviving condition is of concern.
Fragility/ vulnerability	Can be destroyed by a single ploughing or standing structure of particular form or complexity whose significance can be severely reduced by neglect.
Diversity	Possess a combination of high-quality features or a single important attribute.
Potential	There is reason to anticipate the existence of important evidence of the past, especially where it is likely such evidence would be revealed through expert investigation.

as they had since prehistory by local tradition (see Chapter 8) rather than any formal laws. For England, aspects of nationhood such as resolving political and economic power that led to the English Civil War, the Commonwealth and the Restoration, an empire and an industrialised society resulted in the continued presence of a strong landowning governing class well into the twentieth century that effectively delayed any formal protective heritage legislation in England and Wales until 1882 (see Table 4.0.2).

For new countries emerging in the nineteenth century, heritage legislation became an early act of establishing identity. Mexico passed heritage protection legislation in 1825 (independence in 1821), Peru in 1825 (independence in 1822) and Greece in 1834 (independence from Turkish rule in 1830). Typical wording from Greek legislation illustrates the nationalistic dimension of these acts: 'all objects of antiquity in Greece being the productions of the ancestors of the Hellenic people, are regarded as the common national procession of all Hellenes' (Cleere 2002). This powerful idea of the past belonging to the people of a nation and representing the identifiable communal achievement of a nation was an ideology that corresponded with ideals of socialism and communism; in October 1918, the USSR declared all its cultural property as owned by the people. Similar legislation was subsequently passed by Cuba, China and the countries that formed the communist bloc after World War II (Cleere 2002). The countries of sub-Saharan Africa that emerged from colonial control after the Second World War were similarly keen to enact laws that protected their cultural patrimony (Ndoro *et al*. 2008: 114–15), but as Négri (2008) points out, there are considerable elements of pragmatism in the legislation. Portraying all the traditional sites and artefacts as the heritage and property of the newly independent country helps mitigate tribal rivalries and affinities that always threaten to split apart newly formed countries. Many former colonies also retained elements of the colonial heritage legislation that was effective and, especially in former British colonies such as Kenya and Tanzania, was relevant to local needs. Sullivan (2012: 645) has drawn on successful legislation to create a key series of objectives for heritage protection legislation.

Concern over national identity has not been the only driving force for legislation to protect archaeological remains. In 1666, Olof Verelius was appointed Swedish Royal Antiquary and in the same year a royal proclamation decreed that all ancient monuments in Sweden were the property of the crown, which undertook to protect and preserve them in the name of the Swedish people (Cleere 2002). In 1669, this royal decree was extended to cover artefacts. This is the earliest protective cultural heritage legislation in the world, but occurs at the height of the Swedish empire when there was no threat to national identity and appears to spring from royal concern not the will of the people. Elsewhere, the King of Naples and Sicily was prompted to declare royal ownership of all buried materials and sites in his kingdom in 1738, probably by the start of excavations at Herculaneum. The Danes established protection for ancient monuments and archaeological finds in 1807, though it is unclear if this was prompted by concern over national identity (defeat of the fleet by the English at the battle of Copenhagen) or by a royal or national consciousness about the heritage following the report in 1806 on the chaotic state of the internationally renowned collections of antiquities of Olaf Worm, by Professor Rasmus Nyerup – *Survey of the National Monuments of Antiquity Such as May Be Displayed in a Future Museum*. German states followed the Danish lead, passing heritage/monument legislation based on the Swedish model, in the early nineteenth century, Mechlenburg (1807) to Baden (1837) (Cleere 2002), in what appears to be a copycat process.

History of English legislative protection

As suggested in Chapter 2, the principal spur to preservation is threat or loss. The succession of legislation passed in the nineteenth and twentieth centuries to protect the archaeological remains of England and Wales (Breeze 1993; Champion 1996) and the establishments and actions of organisations (Miele 1996; Stamp 1996; Thurley 2013) is prompted by threat and loss (see Table 4.0.2). Though the initial growth of the preservation movement in the nineteenth century can be related to wider social phenomena, concerns over industrialisation and the growth of the romantic movement (Hunter 1996: 4), most authors, including William Morris, point to the loss of ancient buildings in general and to the threat to a specific much loved building or site as the spur that drove them to action. In the case of Morris, he was concerned about the excessive restoration of churches in the mid-nineteenth century, but it was the threat to Tewksbury Abbey in particular that triggered action (see Chapter 2). As early as 1841, a House of Commons Select Committee considered establishing national monuments and made a proposal to parliament. In 1845, following the smashing of the Portland Vase, the Protection of Works of Art and Scientific and Literary Collections Act was passed, giving legal protection against damage to museum collections (Caple 2000: 56). The 1854 Public Statues Act extended protection to public statues, but the attempt to create a commission for the Conservation of National Monuments failed and the period of concern about safeguarding national identity/heritage passed. The difficulty in passing legislation dealing with ancient monuments such as earthworks was due to the powerful political interests of landowners on whose lands they were located. Since the Saxon period, English law had been focused on land ownership and associated rights. Though they were happy to pass laws about statues and museum objects, the rights of the landowners, who peopled the Houses of Commons and Lords in the nineteenth and early twentieth centuries, were not so quickly given up.

Following the threat to the prehistoric earthworks and standing stones of Avebury, which he personally safeguarded through purchasing part of the site, Sir John Lubbock tried several times in the 1870s to introduce robust legislation to protect prehistoric monuments. However, the threat of compulsory acquisition when a monument was threatened in that legislation meant that the landowners in parliament would not support it until 1882, when George Shaw Lefevre succeeded in getting the first Ancient Monuments legislation passed, which had no legal powers of compulsory purchase. There were subsequent pieces of legislation that increasingly strengthened legislation protecting ancient remains (see Table 4.0.2). The most notable changes occurred in the 1913 Ancient Monument Consolidation and Amendment Act shortly after the threat of Tattershall Castle being demolished and rebuilt in the USA emerged (Thompson 2006: 49–59; Thurley 2013: 72–5), and whilst concern for the nation's past was high with the threat of the First World War looming. The French similarly passed legislation protecting archaeological monuments in 1913.

The acceptance of a greater role for the state following WWI, coupled with concerns for the loss of rural England, led to the establishment of the Council for the Preservation of Rural England in 1926. This relationship between the people and the countryside was further emphasised by developments such as aerial photography utilised by Crawford in the 1930s, where soil and crop marks indicated extensive archaeological remains and identified that people had lived in all areas of highland and lowland Britain in the past. This changed the thinking about legislation, which, until that point, had been based on single monuments. The 1931 Ancient Monuments Act protected areas around monuments and groups of archaeological features. However, it required the Second World War and the further increase

Table 4.0.2 A history of heritage legislation and organisations in England and Wales

Time	Legislation	Organisations
1500–1600	**1560**: Royal proclamation against breaking or defacing monuments. Attempt to stop the destruction of monuments, which commenced with the Reformation and destruction of church memorials and fabric, which continued under reigns of Edward VI and Mary.	**1533**: Leland = King's Antiquary (Henry VIII).
1600–1700		**1751**: Society of Antiquaries of London founded. Raised the profile of ancient sites and created an organisation that sought to preserve them. Developing knowledge about them was key to that process.
1700–1750		
1750–1800	**1845**: The Protection of Works of Art and Scientific and Literary Collections Act made it an offence to destroy or damage any museum object, glass or statue in a chapel or public statue. {11}	**1842**: The Archaeological Institute founded. 1844: The British Archaeological Association founded. Both seeking to investigate and preserve 'works from ancient times'.
1800–1850	**1854**: Public Statues Act, making it an offence to damage or deface a schedule of royal statues in London, the Commissioners of Works = guardians of the statues.	
1860s		**1865**: Commons Preservation Society.
1870s		**1877**: Society for the Protection of Ancient Buildings (SPAB) established by artists and aesthetes. SPAB drew attention to the historic value of all the phases of ancient building and gradually established greater respect for historic fabric, especially in churches bringing to an end a rampant phase of destructive church restoration. {1}
1880s	**1882**: The Ancient Monuments Protection Act – the Commissioners of Works could take ancient monuments (largely prehistoric) into guardianship (with the owner's permission) and ancient monuments could be maintained at public expense. A professional Inspector of Ancient Monuments post established to enact these processes. Vandalism or damage of ancient monuments (other than by the owner) was punishable by a fine or imprisonment.	

Table 4.0.2 continued

Time	Legislation	Organisations
1890s	**1890**: London County Council (LCC) comes into existence, its 1889 LCC General Powers Act gave LCC powers to acquire and maintain 'buildings and places of historic and architectural interest or works of art'. In 1893, it acquires first historic building York Water Gate in order to preserve it.	**1895**: The National Trust established by Octavia Hill and colleagues to own and maintain in perpetuity places of historic interest and natural beauty. Given legal status by act of parliament in 1907, properties could not be sold or significantly altered.
1900s	**1900**: Ancient Monuments Protection Act – extended act to cover medieval buildings, excluding occupied and ecclesiastical property.	**1908**: Royal Commission on Historic Monuments for England, Scotland and Wales established an inventory of important buildings and monuments up to AD 1700, fully researched and recorded.
1910s	**1913**: Ancient Monuments Consolidation and Amendment Act – Commissioners to create and publish a schedule of nationally important monuments. Owners of scheduled monuments had to apply for permission to damage or demolish the monument. The Commissioners had power to issue preservation orders and protect monuments, through guardianship or ownership, from damage or destruction. Ancient Monuments Board (experts) established to advise the Commissioners. {2}	
1920s		**1926**: Council for the Preservation of Rural England established.
1930s	**1931**: The Ancient Monuments Act – authorised local authorities to set up preservation schemes to protect monuments and areas around monuments (effectively conservation areas). {3}	**1937**: National Trust country house scheme.
	1932: Town and Country Planning Act – local authorities authorised to set up preservation schemes to protect buildings or groups of buildings of architectural and historic interest. No requirement for owner to inform authority of intention to damage or demolish.	**1937**: The Georgian Group – the destruction of Georgian buildings in the 1930s caused those concerned to form a society to seek to protect these buildings. {4, 5, 6, 7, 8}
1940s	**1944 and 1947**: Town and Country Planning Acts – ministry required to draw up lists of buildings of architectural or historic interest	**1941**: National Buildings (later Monument) Record – established to record buildings damaged in WWII. This developed into the listing process.

Table 4.0.2 continued

Time	Legislation	Organisations
	(Graded I or II), inform local authorities and owners, who were legally required to inform of intention to damage or demolish. The authority could issue building preservation order to prevent such actions. In practice, almost all original buildings pre-1725 were listed, as were most pre-1800.	**1949**: Cathedral's Advisory Committee – established to give guidance on the repair and development of cathedrals.
1950s	**1953**: Historic Buildings and Ancient Monuments Act – grants made available from public funds to maintain or repair buildings (including churches) of outstanding interest and their contents in private or public ownership. Funds also available to take such buildings and their contents into public ownership. Established Historic Buildings Council (experts and owners) to advise and enact.	**1952**: Waverley Rules introduced to control the export of artefacts from the UK if over a certain value, present in the UK for over 50 years or recovered from UK soil or territorial waters, enabling price paid to be matched in which case the object stays in the UK. **1957**: The Civic Trust – founded by Duncan Sandys to promote and facilitate the sensitive redevelopment and use of historic towns and their buildings. **1958**: The Victorian Society – the destruction of Victorian buildings caused those who valued such architecture to form a society to protect Victorian buildings. {9, 10}
1960s	**1967**: Civic Amenities Act – required local authorities to create and maintain lists areas of architectural and historic interest to be designated 'conservation areas'. **1968**: The Town and Country Planning Act – unlimited fines or imprisonment for demolition or damage of listed buildings, formal requirement to inform and consult specialist preservation group (e.g. Georgian and Victorian societies). Spot listing allowed instant protection for historic buildings under threat. Compulsory purchase of neglected listed buildings and approval of alterations to listed buildings through listed building consent introduced.	**1968**: Advisory board for redundant churches set up to advise the Church Commissioners on architectural and historic importance of churches.
1970s	**1972**: Field Monument Act – instituted a system of payments to landowners of scheduled ancient monuments for appropriate management of their monument.	

Table 4.0.2 continued

Time	Legislation	Organisations
	1974: Town and Country Amenities Act – alterations, demolition of any building within a conservation area required local authority approval. Church buildings brought within the authority of historic buildings legislation.	**1975**: SAVE British Heritage – high-profile pressure group formed following destruction of historic housing in cities such as Bath to preserve historic buildings through mobilising publicity and public opinion.
	1979: Ancient Monument and Archaeological Areas Act – made metal detecting on scheduled ancient monuments illegal, introduced 'archaeological areas' where archaeological access was guaranteed and consents for archaeological sites – similar to those for listed buildings. {13}	**1979**: Thirties (now 20th Century) Society established, seeking to preserve architecture of this period. {11}
1980s	**1980**: National Heritage Memorial Act – trustees and funding created to acquire, preserve and help maintain buildings of national importance.	**1984**: English Heritage and Historic Scotland take over the roles of the Historic Buildings Council and Ancient Monuments Board.
	1987: Any building over 30 years old can be listed.	
1990s	**1990**: PPG16 – embeds archaeological assessment into the planning process, established the presumption that archaeological remains should be preserved *in situ*, the polluter/developer is responsible for assessment and recovery by record if remains are not preserved.	**1999**: English Heritage appoints Regional Science Advisors to advise archaeologists in each English region on scientific techniques, including means of preserving archaeological remains *in situ*.
	Managing Our Past published.	
	1994: PPG15 – similar to PPG16 but for historic buildings.	
	1996: The Treasures Act.	
2000s	**2010**: PPS5 replaces PPG16.	
	2012: National Planning Policy Framework – replaces PPS5.	

The establishment of many conservation and preservation organisations was triggered by the threat or loss of specific buildings or monuments.

{1 = Tewksbury Abbey, 2 = Tattershall Castle, 3 = Hadrian's Wall, 4 = Waterloo Bridge, 5 = Bedford Square (west side), 6 = Royal Pavilion, Brighton, 7 = Adelphi Terrace, 8 = Abingdon Street, 9 = The Euston Arch, 10 = London Coal Exchange, 11 = Portland Vase, 12 = Rose and Globe Theatres, 13 = Baynards Castle, 14 = Firestone factory}

in power of centralised government to generate money for national institutions and legislation with significant powers for national protection of heritage – though many of these post-WWII developments have their origins in the 1930s:

- The Town and Country Planning Acts 1944 and 1947, which gave the state power to list, and thus protect historic buildings, occurred just after World War II when national identity was at its height and landowning classes had less political power.
- A government enquiry in 1931 had recommended the establishment of National Parks, but the legislation was not passed until 1949 and the first parks established in 1951–1957.
- The 1930s also saw the rise of the folk museum, exemplified in the collecting of rural artefacts by people such as the Reverend Dr John Kirk, whose collection was on display in the Female Prison in York, now the York Castle Museum, by late 1938. But the larger national folk museums were established later; the Welsh National Folk Museum at St Fagans in 1951 and the Ulster Folk Museum in 1958 (opened 1964).

The rise of the modern heritage movement after the Second World War, which has shaped modern concerns over historic buildings and arguably dragged archaeological remains in its wake, was again triggered by loss. The frustration at the loss of the Georgian and Victorian buildings in the period 1945–1975 was voiced for many by John Betjeman: 'In fact it might be said that more destruction to English cities and towns was wrought by so-called modern architects than by German bombs' (Betjeman 1976: 62).

Despite the establishment of the Victorian Society in 1958, buildings continued to be demolished in the post-war reconstruction of Britain. The destruction of the Georgian terraces of Bath, insufficiently unique to be listed, featured in the *The Sack of Bath* by Adam Fergusson (1973), was followed in 1975 by the publication of Colin Amery and Dan Cruickshank's book *The Rape of Britain*, which highlighted the loss of historic housing and the redevelopment of almost every town centre in Britain in the late 1960s and early 1970s. Marcus Binney's exhibition *The Destruction of the Country House* at the Victoria and Albert Museum raised concerns about the loss of grander historic buildings throughout Britain at this period. The continued loss of historic buildings was, by the mid-1970s, running at one listed building lost every day. Continued concerns resulted in the establishment of SAVE Britain's Heritage in 1975, a small active group that campaigned to preserve Britain's historic building structures. This organisation stressed the economic benefits for tourism and cost-effectiveness of retention and conversion of historic buildings. These themes have become regularly repeated in the present by national heritage agencies (Andreae 1996: 143–7). The increasing value placed on historic buildings led to a continuing toughening up of the stream of legislation, which ushered in conservation areas: the 1967 Civic Amenities Act, the 1968 Town and Country Planning Act and the 1974 Town and Country Amenities Act (see Table 4.0.2). The public's desire for new housing and clearance of pre-war slums had started to decline as problems with tower blocks and newly built estates emerged. Now, removed from the post-war emergency need for housing, the loss of history and dislocation of people from their past became a significant issue. Urban redevelopment slowed and the values of historic properties rose; however, demolition continued. On Friday 2 August 1979, just before it was to be listed, the Firestone factory was demolished, causing public controversy and providing impetus to the emerging Thirties Society, later the 20th Century Society, who held their inaugural meeting on 13 December 1979 (Stamp 1996: 94). This was another clear example where loss of a notable piece of heritage triggered a preservative response.

Arguably, the most significant change to legislation, which ushered in the focus on preservation *in situ* for archaeological remains, emerged not from concern for national identity, but a wider world and a pan-European concern about the extent of development and the wider loss of 'our' heritage. This was articulated in the 1990 *ICOMOS Charter for the Protection and Management of the Archaeological Heritage* – Lausanne and the *1992 European Convention on the Protection of the Archaeological Heritage* – Valletta (see Chapter 5.3). These both identified that the appropriate state for archaeological remains was that they should be preserved *in situ* and that any potential developer who proposed disturbing those remains should be seen as disturbing/polluting the natural environment, and as such should pay for assessment of the nature and extent of archaeological remains and for full archaeological excavation if development occurred and the archaeological remains were destroyed. This approach was articulated by English Heritage in *Exploring Our Past: Strategies for the Archaeology of England* (1991) and introduced into the English planning (legal) process in November 1990, PPG 16 (Planning Policy Guidance, note 16) (Department for the Environment 1990). This was advice to all local planning authorities on how to protect archaeological remains that could be damaged or destroyed by development, through the planning process. This was later replaced (March 2010) by 'Planning Policy Statement 5: Planning and the Historic Environment' (Department for Communities and Local Government 2010). While the phrase 'preservation *in situ*' appeared in PPG16, the revised planning guidance PPS5 simply refers to 'conservation of heritage assets'. This change has reduced the emphasis on preservation *in situ* in England in recent years (Malim and Panter 2012). The reason for the change was, in part, due to the 1995 Public Inquiry into the development at 82–90 Park Lane, Croydon (O'Sullivan 1996). While English Heritage and the developer sought preservation of the remains of an early Anglo-Saxon burial ground *in situ* beneath a car park following PPG16 (point 8), many archaeologists, including the British Museum, favoured excavation. Concerned (but unable to prove) that preservation *in situ* was far from likely given the proposed building work, the PPG16 wording limited the options available at the Public Enquiry and the car park was constructed. The subsequent PPS5 required a holistic consideration of the significance of the remains and the impacts of development; it did not use the term 'preservation *in situ*' or identify this as the normal, preferred or appropriate state for archaeological remains.

From March 2012, PPS5 was replaced by National Planning Policy Framework, which, while requiring developers to assess the significance of heritage assets, including archaeological remains, indicated that they should do so at a level of detail that is '*proportional to the asset's importance*'. There is no longer any presumption of the preservation of archaeological remains *in situ*, but an acknowledgement of their value – which must be weighed against the value for any proposed development that damages or impinges on those remains.

The aim through PPG16 (and PPS5 and NPPF) is to move away from a central heritage agency enacting and policing heritage preservation to a system where assessment of archaeological remains is a routine part of the planning process (Wainwright 1993). The operation of the post-Valetta and Lausanne environment established an extensive archaeology industry in Britain and most European countries, with similarities to the CRM (cultural resource management) and salvage archaeology industry established in the USA in the 1970s following the 1960 Reservoir Salvage Act, the 1964 Wilderness Act, the 1966 Department of Transportation Act and the 1966 National Historic Preservation Act (see Table 4.0.3). This industry, together with preservation *in situ*, was reviewed by Willem Willems in 2006 (Willems 2008) (see Chapter 4.1). Key concerns are the appropriate balance between the developer, archaeological contractor and heritage authority in a contracting archaeology environment, which has no defined standards regarding preservation of archaeological remains *in situ* and little relevant research (see Chapter 11).

History of American legislative protection

Based on a series of federated states, the USA has a similar regard for land ownership as Britain but lacking the crises of WWI and WWII or (since 1906) the threat of people from other countries purchasing significant parts of the nation's heritage, they have been reluctant to see federal interference with landowning rights or personal possessions. Legislation (see Table 4.0.3) started in 1906 following the concerns over the removal of artefacts from Mesa Verde. It was primarily a concern to preserve the natural beauty of the American wilderness, which led to the establishment of the National Park Service in 1916, though through its landholding and legislation NPS has been key to preserving sites of cultural heritage. The beneficial role of a centralised state was brought home to some in the 1930s with the efforts of federal government to relieve unemployment (New Deal). Subsequently, legislation affecting federal lands such as the Archaeological Resources Protection Act and NAGPRA has mirrored wider world approaches to heritage, but such laws only apply on federal lands. With the exception of the National Historic Preservation Act, which created State Historic Preservation Officers in every US state who identify and seek to protect significant historic sites, which they can nominate to add to a national register, and any federally funded project that must 'take into account' historic sites and minimise harm to them from the project, the US has not created legislation to protect heritage that limits the rights of the individual landowner. A number of private individuals have been instrumental in saving historic sites in the US: Ann Pamela Cunningham through creating the Mount Vernon Ladies Association saved George Washington's House for the nation in the 1850s while J.D. Rockerfeller funded the preservation and restoration of Colonial Williamsburg in the 1920s and 1930s.

Long-term protection through purchase

Given that fragile sites are most vulnerable to human impact, it may be thought that leaving them in the wilderness might be an appropriate response, but the increasing level of human activity even in wastelands has meant such sites are not safe without protection. The central role of land ownership in the legal system of Britain and countries such as the United States of America and Australia that draw their legal systems from Britain has historically invested landowners with considerable rights/control over their land, powers that are retained to this day. This led individuals concerned with the loss of ancient monuments to purchase the land on which the monument was situated (e.g. Keiller – Windmill Hill, Libbock part of Avebury, Putnam and the ladies of Boston – the Great Serpent Mound in Ohio and Stephens the Mayan site of Copan) (Barnes 1981). Though this rescued the monument from immanent destruction, its protection was confined to the lifespan of the individual owner. Longer-term organisations were required to preserve in perpetuity, and when heritage agencies emerged they were given such protected sites. However, those organisations funded by central governments have increasingly had an educational and fundraising role – leading to the emphasis on displayable monuments, rather than preserving buried archaeological remains that may have no display potential.

Table 4.0.3 A history of heritage legislation in the USA

Date	Legislation
1906	Antiquities Act: protected archaeological sites on federal lands, preventing excavation or damage without permission. Excavations only by approved bodies for research purposes and all objects to be preserved in public museums. Empowered the President to declare historic landmarks, historic and prehistoric structures on land under governmental control as national monuments.
1916	National Park Service established to preserve and manage designated public spaces, including several historic monuments (e.g. Statue of Liberty). Now over 26 million acres contolled by the NPS, including many national parks and cultural heritage sites.
1935	Historic Sites Act: developed a national policy of preservation and permitted programmes to preserve the heritage to be funded. It facilitated the American Historic Building Survey and other programmes.
1949	National Trust for Historic Preservation Act: intended to facilitate public involvement in preserving sites of national significance, it initially (though no longer) lacked funds to be effective.
1960s	1960 Reservior Salvage Act, 1964 Wildernesss Act, 1966 Department of Transportation Act: provide policy, procedures and funding to carry out programmes of archaeological survey and recording ahead of specific developments.
1966	National Historic Preservation Act: created a National Register of Historic Places, the formal designation of nationally important sites opening access for funding, though no legal protection. Created State Historic Preservation Office and officers to aid preservation of historic places in each state. Required all projects with federal funding to 'take into account' their impact on historic places (Section 106 Review Process). Effectively started the cultural resource management (CRM) industry.
1969	National Environment Policy Act: the NEPA process consists of an evaluation of the environmental effects (including historic and cultural heritage) of a federal project or action.
1974	The Archaeological and Historic Preservation Act: required archaeological assessment finding and characterising sites, for land use projects with elements of federal funding, and assessing the effect the proposed land use would have on them. This provided further impetus for the developing cultural resource management (CRM) industry.
1979	Archaeological Resources Protection Act: gave increased protection to archaeological sites on federal land. It is a crime to disturb such sites. Native American tribes must now be involved in approving work done on their lands or involving remains of their predecessors.
1987	Abandoned Shipwreck Act: makes it illegal to salvage or remove anything from an embedded (anything but recent) shipwreck in US waters as they are a national historic resource.
1990	Native American Graves Protection and Repatriation Act: defines ownership of Native American remains and grave goods, defines procedures for analysing and returning grave goods to appropriate tribes.

Objects

The 1956 UNESCO Recommendations on International Principles Applicable to Archaeological Excavations encouraged all states to create legal protection of archaeological remains, establish appropriate state agencies that could license archaeological excavation and 'ensure the protection of the archaeological heritage'. In the Scandinavian countries, the countries in Eastern Europe, Greece, Italy, Turkey, Cyprus, Tunisia, Belize and Kenya, indeed most of the countries of the world, all archaeological artefacts recovered from the soil are legally the property of the state (Longworth 1993; O'Keefe 1995). In countries such as France, the state can acquire archaeological objects through compulsory purchase, while in countries such as Spain or Australia exporting archaeological objects is illegal (O'Keefe 1995). This means that almost any trade in newly excavated archaeological artefacts is illegal. In many of these countries, illegal excavation and removal of objects from the ground automatically constitutes a crime – either theft of state property or excavating without a licence; however, there is evidence of extensive illegal excavation and looting in countries such as Turkey, Greece and Italy. In contrast, in England and Wales, all artefacts (save those of gold and silver, which are covered by the Treasure Act 1996) are the property of the landowner; this is consistent with the legal system that has the rights of landowners as one of its fundamental tenants. In England and Wales, archaeological excavation on land with the owner's permission is legal and metal detecting is legal, though from 1997 a voluntary Portable Antiquities Scheme (PAS) for reporting all archaeological, especially metal-detected, finds has been in force. The safeguards for archaeological remains lie in the concerns of the landowner, the legal protection afforded scheduled ancient monuments, which can only be excavated with a consent (i.e. a licence), and the requirements of the planning system (NPPF) outlined above for remains disturbed by building and development work, which requires planning permission. Illegal metal-detecting and damage to protected sites, night-hawking, occur occasionally (Dobinson and Denison 1995).

Trade in antiquities is illegal in many countries, but legal in the US and Britain, though both with limitations on export. International conventions attempting to restrict or prevent trade in antiquities have only been slowly accepted by the international community:

- 1970 UNESCO 'Convention on the Means of Prohibiting and Precluding the Illicit Import, Export and Transfer of Ownership of Cultural Property' has now (1 April 2013) been ratified or accepted by 123 countries including the UK (in 2002) and the USA (in 1983).
- European Council Directorate on 'Return of Cultural Objects Unlawfully Removed from the Territory of a Member State and Regulations on the Export of Cultural Goods' requires that all EU states will, when requested by another state, recover and return national treasures (artistic, historic and archaeological) removed from the host country at any time after 1 January 1993. The host country is required to reimburse the expenses of the country undertaking the recovery. This legislation is cumbersome and must be conducted on a state-to-state basis.
- 1995 UNESCO 'Convention on Stolen and Illegally Exported Cultural Objects' UNIDROIT has now (1 April 2013) been ratified or accepted by 44 countries, though not the UK or USA.

Given the extensive limitations on excavation and export of objects from other countries, it has been suggested that 60 per cent, or even 80 per cent, of the antiquities in the antiquities trade come from illegal excavations or are illegally exported (Elia 1995).

Bibliography

Amery, C. and Cruickshank, D. (1975) *The Rape of Britain*, London: Elek.

Andreae, S. (1996) 'From comprehensive development to Conservation Areas', in M. Hunter (ed.), *Preserving the Past: The Rise of Heritage in Modern Britain*, Stroud: Alan Sutton, pp. 135–55.

Barnes, M.R. (1981) 'Preservation of archaeological sites through acquisition', *American Antiquity*, 36(3): 610–18.

Betjeman, J. (1976) 'A preservationists progress', in J. Fawcett (ed.), *The Future of the Past: Attitudes to Conservation 1174–1974*, London: Thames and Hudson, pp. 53–64.

Breeze, D.J. (1993) 'Ancient monuments legislation', in J. Hunter and I. Ralston (eds), *Archaeological Resource Management in the UK*, Stroud: Alan Sutton, pp. 44–55.

Caple, C. (2000) *Conservation Skills: Judgement, Method and Decision Making*, London: Routledge.

Champion, T. (1996) 'Protecting the monuments: archaeological legislation from the 1882 Act to PPG 16', in M. Hunter (ed.), *Preserving the Past*, Stroud: Alan Sutton, pp. 38–56.

Cleere, H. (1989) 'Introduction: the rationale of archaeological heritage management', in H. Cleere (ed.), *Archaeological Heritage Management in the Modern World*, London: Routledge, pp. 283–9.

Cleere, H. (2002) 'Preserving archaeological sites and monuments', in *Encyclopaedia of Life Support Systems*, Paris: UNESCO.

Darvill, T. and Fulton, A. (1998) *The Monuments at Risk Survey of England 1995*, London: Bournemouth University and English Heritage.

Department for Communities and Local Government (2010) *PPS5 Planning for the Historic Environment: Historic Environment Planning Practice Guide*, London: Department for Communities and Local Government.

Department for Communities and Local Government (2012) *National Planning Policy Framework*, London: Department for Communities and Local Government.

Department for Culture Media and Sport (2013) *Scheduled Monuments – Policy Statement 10, 2013*, available at: www.gov.uk/government/uploads/system/uploads/attachment_data/file/249695/SM_policy_statement_10-2013__2_.pdf (accessed September 2014).

Department for the Environment (1990) *Archaeology and Planning: Planning Policy Guidance 16*, London: DoE.

Dobinson, C.S. and Denison, S. (1995) *Metal Detecting in Archaeology*, London: English Heritage and CBA.

Elia, R. (1995) 'Conservators and unprovenanced objects: preserving the cultural heritage or servicing the antiquities trade?', in K.W. Tubb (ed.), *Antiquities: Trade or Betrayed*, London: Archetype, pp. 244–55.

English Heritage (1991) *Exploring Our Past*, London: English Heritage.

Fergusson, A. (1973) *The Sack of Bath: A Record and Indictment*, Salisbury: Compton Russell.

Hunter, M. (1996) 'Introduction: the fitful rise of British preservation', in M. Hunter (ed.), *Preserving the Past: The Rise of Heritage in Modern Britain*, Stroud: Alan Sutton, pp. 1–16.

Longworth, I. (1993) 'Portable antiquities', in J. Hunter and I. Ralston (eds), *Archaeological Resource Management in the UK: An Introduction*, Stroud: Allan Sutton, pp. 56–64.

Malim, T. and Panter, I. (2012) 'Is preservation in situ and unacceptable option for development control? Can monitoring prove the continued preservation of waterlogged deposits?', *Conservation and Management of Archaeological Sites*, 14(1–4): 429–41.

Miele, C. (1996) 'The first conservation militants: William Morris and the Society for the Protection of Ancient Buildings', in M. Hunter (ed.), *Preserving the Past: The Rise of Heritage in Modern Britain*, Stroud: Alan Sutton, pp. 17–37.

Négri, V. (2008) 'Introduction to heritage law in Africa', in W. Ndoro, A. Mumma and G. Abungu (eds), *Africa 2009 Conservation of Immovable Cultural Heritage in Sub-Saharan Africa*, ICCROM Conservation Studies 8, Rome: ICCROM, pp. 7–12.

Ndoro, W., Mumma, A. and Abungu, G. (2008) *Africa 2009 Conservation of Immovable Cultural Heritage in Sub-Saharan Africa*, ICCROM Conservation Studies 8, Rome: ICCROM.

O'Keefe, P. (1995) 'Conservators and actions for recovery of stolen or unlawfully exported cultural property', in K.W. Tubb (ed.), *Antiquities: Trade or Betrayed*, London: Archetype, pp. 73–82.

O'Sullivan, H. (1996) '82–90 Park Lane, Croydon: a planning case study', *London Archaeologist*, 7(16): 424–31.

Stamp, G. (1996) 'The art of keeping one jump ahead: conservation societies in the twentieth century', in M. Hunter (ed.), *Preserving the Past*, Stroud: Alan Sutton, pp. 77–98.

Stanley-Price, N. (2009) 'The reconstruction of ruins: principles and practice', in A. Richmond and A. Bracker (eds), *Conservation Principles, Dilemmas and Uncomfortable Truths*, London: Butterworth-Heinemann, pp. 32–46.

Sullivan, S. (2012) 'Conservation policy delivery', in S. Sullivan and R. Mackay (eds), *Archaeological Sites: Conservation and Management*, Readings in Conservation, Los Angeles, CA: GCI, pp. 640–52.

Thompson, M. (2006) *Ruins Reused: Changing Attitudes to Ruins Since the Late Eighteenth Century*, Kings Lynn: Heritage.
Thurley, S. (2013) *Men from the Ministry: How Britain Saved its Heritage*, London: Yale University Press.
Wainwright, G.J. (1993) 'The management of change: archaeology and planning', *Antiquity*, 67: 416–21.
Willems, W.J.H. (2008) 'Archaeological resource management and preservation', in H. Kars and R.M. van Herringen (eds), *Preserving Archaeological Remains In-Situ: Proceedings of the 3rd Conference, 7–9 December 2006, Amsterdam*, Geoarchaeological and Bioarchaeological Studies 10, Amsterdam: Vrije Universiteit Amsterdam, pp. 283–90.

Chapter 4.1

Introduction
The rationale of archaeological heritage management

Henry Cleere

Source: Cleere, H. (1989) 'Introduction: the rationale of archaeological heritage management', in H. Cleere (ed.), *Archaeological Heritage Management in the Modern World*, London: Routledge.

Historical introduction

[...]

ARCHAEOLOGICAL HERITAGE MANAGEMENT may be deemed to have begun with the Swedish Royal Proclamation of 1666, declaring all objects from antiquity to be the property of the Crown. This was a departure from the widespread medieval fiscal prerogative of Treasure Trove, or the Royal Fifth of the Spanish monarchy that operated in the Americas, which saw gold and silver objects from antiquity solely in terms of their financial convertibility; for the first time the intrinsic importance of the remains of the past was acknowledged in a national legal code. The despoliation of the remains of Herculaneum in the mid-18th century provoked the Bourbon king of Naples to issue a decree to bring the buried heritage of his realm under juridical control a century later (D'Agostino 1984), and Denmark followed suit in the first decade of the 19th century (Kristiansen 1984). By the end of the century the ancient monuments of most of Europe were covered by protective legislation of varying degrees of efficacy, and the USA enacted its first Federal Antiquities law in 1906 (McGimsey & Davis 1984). The UK passed its first Ancient Monuments Protection Act in 1882 (Cleere 1984), although this was, somewhat surprisingly, a relatively toothless measure compared with the earlier (1863) law that had been enacted in Imperial India (Thapar 1984).

Although legislation was in force over much of the world by the outbreak of World War II, the profession of archaeological heritage manager was still embryonic in many countries. The few names which come immediately to mind from the 19th century – J. J. A. Worsaae in Denmark, General Pitt Rivers in the UK, Prosper Merimée, the saviour of Carcassonne, in France, and Auguste Mariette in Egypt – were all full-time directors of antiquities services, but they were usually working either alone or at best with a handful of paid and largely untrained assistants. Excavation was a part-time activity, for the most part in the hands of university teachers, museum curators or gentleman amateurs, and the maintenance and presentation of great monuments, particularly those outside Europe, was generally entrusted to officials with little, if any, awareness of or concern for archaeology. [. . .] Decisions regarding excavations or presentation were often taken for ideological reasons – witness the archaeological policies of Italy during the Mussolini regime in, for example, Rhodes (or Rome, for that matter). Few countries outside Scandinavia had developed policies towards the archaeological heritage, based on equal concern for public interest and academic priorities.

The end of World War II saw the beginnings of archaeological heritage management as an integral component of social and economic planning. The devastation of 1939–45 provided boundless scope for archaeological initiatives in many countries. Excavations took place in many of the war-torn cities of Europe, of which the work on Roman Cologne around the Dom is probably the most outstanding. Many opportunities for the investigation of historic town centres in Europe were lost: in London, for example, municipal avarice meant that much of its history was obliterated without any recording (Grimes 1968). Nevertheless, the concept of 'rescue' or 'salvage' archaeology in advance of development or redevelopment became firmly rooted in the archaeological consciousness – and, more reluctantly perhaps, in that of officialdom.

It has been, however, the immense economic, political, social and technological changes since 1945 that have done most to foster the development of archaeological heritage management. Postwar reconstruction was followed by the worldwide economic boom of the later 1950s and 1960s. This was accompanied by the coming to nationhood of many colonial territories, notably in Africa and Asia. Economic prosperity in the older nations resulted in substantial investment in and aid to the developing countries, making use of the technological and scientific advances triggered by the strategic exigencies of the war years.

Suddenly, in the 1960s, development became the dominant theme. In the developed countries major highways spread in all directions, historic town centres became the prey of property developers and speculators (not infrequently the civic authorities themselves), mineral extraction tore gaping holes in the landscape, the new 'agribusiness' converted areas of traditional countryside or wilderness into cereal prairies, and new towns were built to house expanding populations. With the growth of affluence tourism became a major industry, long stretches of quiet coastlines were submerged under ribbon hotel development, and the visitor pressure on major historic sites such as Stonehenge and the Athenian Acropolis began to put the monuments themselves in jeopardy from sheer physical attrition. Affluence, along with the availability of relatively inexpensive detection and earth-moving equipment, also created a new form of threat to the archaeological heritage: the long-established *tombaroli* of Etruria and the *huaqueros* of Central and South America were joined by legions of pot-hunters, often working with mechanical back-hoes, in the American Southwest and the treasure hunters of Europe, with their electronic metal-detectors. [. . .] The spoils of this commercialized looting has swelled the illicit trade in cultural property, which was the subject of a UNESCO Convention in 1970. [. . .]

[. . .]

The end of the period of unremitting economic growth in the early 1970s did little to relieve this pressure. The need to maximize agricultural yields all over the world meant that erosion of the non-urban environment continued apace, while the demand for alternative sources of energy to replace oil stepped up mineral extraction in certain areas: the fate of the medieval town of Most in northern Bohemia, sacrificed to reach the rich deposits of lignite on which it was built, is a paradigm of this situation (though in fairness to the Czechoslovak Government it should be recorded that the state energy organization financed a long and detailed archaeological investigation as the town was being quarried away). The availability of abundant natural gas from the North Sea and the need to build long pipelines created a new source of threat to the archaeological heritage (Catherall *et al.* 1984).

Suddenly environmental protection became a major international preoccupation. Following a major conference in Helsinki in 1972, the United Nations established the UN Environmental Programme (UNEP), and funds became available to mitigate the impact of development. The USA had enacted its National Environmental Policy Act (NEPA) in 1969, and this was followed by a series of measures, one of which, the Archaeological and Historic Preservation Act of 1974, provided substantial funding for archaeological work in advance of all Federally financed projects (McGimsey and Davis 1984). The official adoption of environmental protection policies had followed a swell in grass-roots public opinion, which has now become a significant political force in some countries as the Green Movement.

In most countries, however, the importance of archaeological conservation as the historical dimension of the heritage was largely overlooked. It had long been conceived as such in countries such as Denmark, where the archaeological heritage managers constitute one branch of *Fredningsstyrelsen*, the environmental agency, alongside their wildlife and landscape conservation colleagues (Kristiansen 1984), and the USA adopted the historical element as an essential component of all Environmental Impact Assessment in respect of Federal projects. Over much of the world, however, antiquities services stand apart from other governmental environment protection agencies. It is significant that the breakthrough in the UK which led to significantly increased funding for rescue excavations, under sustained pressure from the archaeological community, both amateur and professional through the ginger group *Rescue*, was directed almost exclusively to urban archaeology (Schofield & Leech 1987).

Nevertheless, the development pressures of the 1960s and the environmental movement of the 1970s had a profound effect on archaeological heritage management. It is significant that almost every European country enacted new antiquities legislation during the 1970s, to replace the outdated and ineffectual statutes of a less stressful pre-war era. To meet the increased demands of this legislation, there was a substantial increase in personnel to carry out the necessary operations of recording, designation and excavation, while the pressures of increased tourism led to a radical reappraisal of presentation methods in several countries. All of these changes took place, however, under extreme pressure; only in the USA was there initially any apparent awareness of the growth of a new profession with a need to establish its own philosophical and ethical framework, to identify its academic and social relationships and obligations, and to evolve its own methodologies. For the most part archaeologists were plunged headlong into routines that were laid down in a more leisurely age and woefully inadequate to cope with the pressures of the later-20th century.

The concepts of 'cultural resource management' (CRM), 'public archaeology' and 'conservation archaeology' (which are largely synonymous, or at least overlapping) were developed in a series of important studies published in the USA in the 1970s (McGimsey 1972, Lipe and Lindsay 1974, McGimsey and Davis 1977, King *et al.* 1977, Schiffer & Gumerman 1977, Dickens & Hill 1978), all based almost exclusively on US practice. The ethical problems associated with heritage management have been tackled by the professional bodies established in the USA (the Society of Professional Archaeologists) and the UK (the Institute of Field Archaeologists) in their respective Codes of Conduct but the most extensive treatment of this important subject so far to appear in print again emanates from the USA (Green 1984).

The first attempt to study archaeological heritage management on a supranational, comparative level was in 1978, an initiative taken by archaeologists and heritage managers in the German Democratic Republic (Herrmann 1981). At the same time valuable work was being done by the International Council of Museums (ICOM) and the Council of Europe (Burnham 1974, Hingst & Lipowschek 1975, Council of Europe 1979) in bringing together legislative texts relating to the protection of antiquities and monuments, with commentaries. UNESCO is currently publishing the texts of legislation relating to the protection of movable cultural property from all of its member countries (UNESCO 1985 onwards), but the most important publication in this field is probably the ambitious series of volumes being produced by two distinguished Australian jurists (O'Keefe & Prott 1984).

[...]

Why manage the archaeological heritage?

An awareness of the past is a characteristic that is unique to *Homo sapiens*. In less-developed societies myth and history intermingle to create a tradition that is a living reality – the Dreamtime of the Australian Aborigines (Flood 1983) is a vital element in creating social awareness and cohesion, for example, whereas ancestor worship is an important component of many religions. This is not to imply that in such societies there is no awareness of the linear dimension of time: it is highly developed and continuously renewed through oral transmission. The past is a living component of present-day life in such societies. This identity of past and present is often closely associated with specific locations and structures, which may be devoid of any tangible human artefacts, such as many Aboriginal ritual sites. However, even without this spiritual foundation, an interest in the past is manifested widely among contemporary 'developed' societies. Many treasure-hunters are genuinely motivated in this way, robbing archaeological sites not for financial gain, but solely to build up personal collections of 'relics' – not dissimilar to the 17th and 18th century 'cabinets of curiosities' that formed the basis of so many great European museums. The greater mobility of modern developed societies leads to a search for roots, which may take many forms – an interest in the previous owners of a dwelling-house or in the history of an adopted community, or a concern to delve into family history.

The formation of attitudes towards the past has been the subject of several recent studies in the UK (Lowenthal & Binney 1981, Lowenthal 1985), but these attitudes are so ill-formulated in the minds of most individuals that it is difficult to draw any valid analytical conclusions. The one element that seems to be common to them all involves the concept of identity or identification – a sense of belonging to a place or a tradition.

In less-developed societies this is enshrined in religious or spiritual beliefs. The members of a tribe or clan are bound together by their religion, which embodies the corporate traditions of the group and is usually expressed in tangible terms by association with certain sites or constructions. In such cases, however, the identification is restricted to those material elements that have a direct significance in connection with the spiritual apparatus; thus a ritual or funerary site may be sacrosanct and inalienable, but other manifestations of the group's social development, such as dwellings or fortifications, or elements of this kind lying within their territory that have no cultural associations with the group, may be demolished or neglected as having no significance, even though from an archaeological point of view they are equally meaningful.

This restricted concern for archaeological and historical artefacts can, of course, be identified in more developed societies. In Europe, the remains of classical antiquity were used as quarries for the great medieval palaces and cathedrals; the medieval and Renaissance pontiffs ransacked Imperial Rome to bedeck their constructions, only the Pantheon surviving intact, and that by virtue of being converted into a church. The Reformation in England saw a similar disregard for the magnificent abbeys and monasteries of the outlawed Roman Catholic orders, which were for the most part deliberately slighted to provide building materials for their new secular masters, where they were not used as the cores of new private dwellings. It is change of use that has ensured the survival of many of the masterpieces of antiquity, the most famous being perhaps Constantine's Santa Sophia, in Istanbul.

It was probably the Renaissance and the ensuing Enlightenment, with the revival of historical studies as a branch of learning, stemming from the classical historians, that created the relatively modern notion of cultural continuity – the linear view of history – as distinct from the spiritual continuity of other communities. Contemporary societies were perceived as having cultural links extending back over time, so the relics of earlier phases were seen to be important documents in recording that continuity, and as such they became worthy of care and preservation. This concept was slow to achieve recognition: the debates in the British Parliament during the passage of the first Ancient Monuments Protection Act in 1882 were notable for some remarkably reactionary views. One Conservative aristocrat queried the concept of 'national monuments', which he dismissed as the 'absurd relics' of the 'barbarian predecessors' of the English, 'who found time hanging heavily on their hands and set about piling up great barrows and rings of stones' (Kennet 1972, p. 25)! Nevertheless, this basic philosophical tenet is now widely accepted in many countries of the world, and it underlies much modern heritage management.

Few, if any, countries can, however, lay claim to unbroken cultural continuity of any kind. In some there is a serious problem stemming from traumatic cultural discontinuities. For example, in the USA a European culture was abruptly and fiercely imposed upon an indigenous culture. The earlier European settlers were openly contemptuous of the Native Americans, and they made every effort, either deliberately or out of indifference, to erase the monuments of the pre-contact societies. Of the many thousands of earthworks of all kinds in the Mississippi valley that were surveyed by early antiquaries such as Caleb Atwater or the famous partnership of Ephraim Squier and Edwin Davis in the 19th century, only a minute proportion have survived to the present, and even the Great Serpent Mount, nearly 400 m long and 4 m wide, was only saved from obliteration by the dedication of an archaeologist, Frederick Putnam (Fagan

1977). Further south many great pre-Columbian monuments in Central and South America were either obliterated for political motives (as was the case with Moctezuma's great capital of Tenochtitlán) or slighted and left for the tropical forests to engulf.

A situation of this kind can be exacerbated by political considerations. Ex-colonial powers often left their newly independent ex-colonies a legacy of excellent heritage management legislation. During their two centuries of rule the British endowed India with excellent protective legislation and a well-organized antiquities service, both of which continued after Independence in 1947 (Thapar 1984). India's record in protecting and preserving its monuments stands in comparison with that of any country in the world at present, with one exception. The British were in India for more than two centuries and, whatever the ethical considerations involved, this period constitutes a significant phase in the history of the subcontinent, one that left its mark in the form of tangible monuments. Sadly, until comparatively recently monuments of the Raj have been accorded the lowest priority in heritage management in India, except where they have been taken over for contemporary functions, as in New Delhi or in military cantonments. As a result the task of conservation involved in dealing with the surviving colonial monuments is of considerable proportions. A comparable situation obtains in many other ex-colonial territories, such as Togo.

The end of colonialism in the postwar period and the birth of new nations has seen the promotion of archaeological heritage management in a more positive sense, however. Colonialism created a discontinuity in many of these countries, which is being counteracted by the use of monuments to demonstrate a continuous cultural identity within which the colonial period was no more than an irrelevant episode. The supreme example of this phenomenon must surely be that of the former British colonial territory of Southern Rhodesia, which elected on achieving its independence to take the name of its greatest archaeological monument, Zimbabwe. This use of the archaeological heritage to establish cultural identity in former colonial territories is widespread, and not solely a 20th century phenomenon; the Spanish ex-colonies of Latin America, notably Mexico, have made extensive use of their pre-colonial antiquities to consolidate the sense of cultural continuity and identity, as a visit to the Anthropological Museum in Mexico City quickly confirms. The importance of archaeological remains in establishing cultural identity in Latin America has been powerfully stated by Sanoja.

With older nations which have survived as discrete political entities for many centuries, such as France or England in Europe, the innate awareness of cultural identity is such that material symbols of this kind are perhaps hardly needed. The average French or English man or woman does not need archaeological or historical monuments as a reminder of his or her Frenchness or Englishness; this is inborn and reinforced daily in many ways. Language is perhaps the primary and most obvious carrier of this tradition. The secure cultural identity of such nations contrasts with that of others, such as the Poles or the Jews, for whom monuments are potent symbols of nationhood: one only has to think of the reconstruction of the Old City in Warsaw, or the excavations at Masada.

[...]

An important factor underlying the protection of monuments is their educational value. The teaching of national history is universal, and modern teaching methods call for the use of aids of many kinds. Especially for younger children, the appeal of an historic site or structure visited in connection with formal classroom teaching of a specific period or topic is strong. The imagination of the child can be stimulated much more effectively by ruined castle walls or ancient burial mounds than by any amount of formal teaching or reading. The value of archaeological sites and monuments is now recognized universally as being an incomparable teaching aid (PACT 1985, 1986, 1987, Cracknell & Corbishley 1986, Council of Europe 1988) which is widely used in all parts of the world.

At a less-elevated level but of rapidly growing importance is the role of monuments in tourism. Mass tourism is a feature of modern economic life, both nationally and internationally; although much of it is directed exclusively towards sunny beaches or snow-covered pistes, historical and archaeological monuments and sites form an important element in much tourism. 'Cultural tourism', visiting primarily monuments and art galleries, represents only a minor proportion of the visitors to such monuments: for every 'cultural' tour group visiting Ephesus or the Pyramids at Teotihuacan and spending several hours studying them in detail there are 20 groups arriving by bus *en route* between one visit and the next, spending half an hour in a hurried and unprepared tour before buying their souvenirs and boarding their buses for their next destination. The value of such tours is debatable; for the individuals concerned it is probably minimal, since they will have little time to absorb even the basic facts about these important and complex sites. Nevertheless, there is an intangible benefit in that many of them will be almost subconsciously influenced by a feeling of respect for the past and for the human achievement that such monuments represent – though few are likely to be able to articulate these feelings in such terms – and as a result they may well be instinctively sympathetic to 'archaeology' when they are confronted with it in their home environments, whether in a television programme or an excavation in their home town. Archaeological heritage managers should not be too dismissive of mass tourism of this kind, since it can only serve to improve public attitudes towards their work, at the same time probably contributing financially to their continued work. It is vital, however, that the quality of presentation at monuments should be high and that it should be directed at more than one level of visitor, otherwise it may prove to be counterproductive by sending visitors away with a sense of disgruntlement and dissatisfaction.

The final justification for archaeological heritage management – at the same time by no means the least important, but equally not the most important – is the protection of the database for the academic discipline of archaeology. Archaeologists are always avid for data, both qualitative and quantitative. Without any form of heritage management the stock of sites and monuments would dwindle rapidly: the rate of destruction from all sources of prehistoric monuments in the UK in the past decades has led some heritage managers to estimate that all save the most outstanding, such as Stonehenge or Maiden Castle, would have disappeared by the end of this century through the usual processes of destruction without the protection of the legislation and its administrative infrastructure. The intensity of industrial and agricultural development in the *Land* of Nordrhein-Westfalen, in the Federal Republic of Germany, and the difficulties of achieving preservation under the *Land* land-use planning and monuments legislation have meant that the annual expenditure on rescue excavation in recent years has regularly exceeded the total rescue budget for the whole of the UK. Inadequate or underfunded archaeological heritage management in a country with a high level of development can quickly result in the almost total disappearance of the archaeological database without record, an ever-present danger in the Third World.

To summarize, therefore, archaeological heritage management has an ideological basis in establishing cultural identity, linked with its educational function, it has an economic basis in tourism, and it has an academic function in safeguarding the database.

How should the archaeological heritage be managed?

Since the archaeological heritage is governed by legislation, which must be deemed to have been enacted in the public interest, and is in most countries in the ownership of the state or other public institutions, it must be accepted as axiomatic that it should be managed in the public interest.

There are, however, many problems in defining that public for whose benefit the heritage is being managed, which is multifaceted. In its broadest sense, the public must be seen as the body of taxpayers whose money is being used in its name to finance antiquities services, survey and excavation, compensation for taking monuments out of cultivation, the conservation, presentation and promotion of monuments, and much more. Then there is the tourist public, whose entrance fees and purchases of souvenirs and guidebooks make a substantial contribution to maintenance and promotional costs. There is the public that visits monuments and sites for educational purposes – schoolchildren, students and vocational archaeologists. In many countries there is that public for whom archaeological sites and monuments are potent symbols of an indigenous culture that is threatened or submerged by an alien intrusive culture. There is the academic public for whom the archaeological heritage forms an essential resource base. The demands of these disparate groups on the archaeological heritage differ in quality and in degree, and not infrequently they come into conflict with one another.

In many countries further complications are introduced by the existence of property rights under the law. Those countries with fully socialist constitutions experience no difficulties in this respect: all land and property are owned by the state, which can manage them in any way that it sees fit. In the Common Law countries such as the UK and many of its former dominions and colonies (including the USA), however, property rights in land are absolute, without the fundamental legal concept of all of the territory of a sovereign nation being vested in the state which exists in other legal systems. A frequently recurring motif in debates on successive protection measures introduced into the British Parliament is encapsulated in the description by a Conservative landowner of the 1882 Act as 'a measure of spoliation ... legalising burglary by daylight ... invading the right of private property' (Kennet 1972, p. 24). Only in the Scandinavian countries, with their long traditions of heritage protection, does the ideal enunciated by Lord Curzon in a Parliamentary debate on the 1913 UK Ancient Monuments Act seem to have become deeply rooted in the national consciousness: 'Owners now recognise that they are not merely owners of private property, but trustees to the nation at large' (Kennet 1972, p. 35).

Given the differing constraints under which archaeological management organizations have to work, it is not an easy task to lay down general principles. Certain common determining factors can, however, be identified.

The basis for all archaeological heritage management must be the identification and recording of that heritage. In some countries the mere act of registration constitutes legal protection, but this is an exceptional situation. There are archaeological managers who take the view that all archaeological resources must be considered to be relevant until they are proved to be irrelevant and so some form of protection must be given to all antiquities. By far the majority of national heritage management services are compelled by legal, political or financial constraints to operate some form of selectivity in respect of monuments protection and management. If the selection is to be valid in academic and cultural terms, then it must be representative, and a representative sample can only be decided on the basis of a knowledge of something approaching the total stock, which can then be evaluated according to carefully formulated objective criteria for selection Darvill (1987). Fundamental to this process is systematic and comprehensive field surveying and recording, of the type begun in Denmark by Worsaae as early as 1873 (Kristiansen 1984, p. 22).

The popular perception of archaeology is that of excavation, and that of the archaeologist as excavator. This is hardly surprising, since major excavations such as the tomb of Tutankhamun, the terracotta warriors of Xi'an or the 16th-century English warship, the *Mary Rose*, provide the 'stories' so beloved of the media. For archaeologists themselves excavation is perhaps the most enjoyable aspect of their work, too. Excavation must obviously continue to be a major source of basic archaeological data, but its role in heritage management is a somewhat ambivalent one. The pressures of modern society have created a demand for 'rescue' or 'salvage' excavations that soak up most of the available archaeological manpower, whether in major international projects such as those in Sri Lanka, in Nubia or at Carthage, prestige excavations such as those at the Louvre in Paris or the Parliament building in Stockholm, or the more run-of-the-mill mitigation excavations occasioned by pipeline projects or urban redevelopment. Government finance for non-rescue excavations, initiated with solely research objectives, is severely limited in every part of the world, and the obligatory funding of excavations by developers, that is an expanding feature of the world scene, is by definition applicable only in a rescue context.

[...]

The second determining factor in relation to heritage management that does seem to have universal applicability is the need for it to be closely integrated with land-use planning. The Danish system (Kristiansen 1984) is an admirable paradigm of this aspect of heritage management, and similar systems apply in the UK and in federally owned territories in the USA (Newcomb 1979 contains a perceptive comparison of the three systems). In each of these countries – and, indeed, in several other countries – all planning decisions are passed in review to determine their impact on the archaeological heritage, and appropriate action is taken to mitigate that impact. This may take the form of intensive survey and selective excavation, as exemplified by the UNESCO-sponsored Nubia Project (Säve-Söderbergh 1987) or on a slightly more modest scale by the Cache River project in Arkansas (Schiffer & House 1975). [...]

Land-use planning as practised in most countries relates to every aspect of the landscape, and man has left his imprint over much of the world's surface. The current environment must be conceived of as possessing more than one dimension. It is inhabited not only by man, but also by countless biological species, living in a state of delicate balance. It also has aesthetic qualities of especial significance to modern man. Human operations of all kinds – forestry, agriculture, road-building, mineral extraction, industrial activity, etc. – can disturb this balance and degrade these aesthetic qualities, to the detriment of future generations. It is often forgotten – not least by archaeologists – that the sites and monuments of antiquity constitute the historical dimension of this global environment, and that their interests are intimately bound up with those of the wildlife and aesthetic dimensions. Ancient woodland may preserve high-standing archaeological remains of an ancient landscape that has everywhere else been obliterated by ploughing, for example, whereas certain types of ruined archaeological site may form havens for endangered species of animals and plants. There is thus a strong community of interest between the different conservation agencies, yet in so many parts of the world this interdependence has not been appreciated and the conservation agencies operate in isolation from one another. A third significant factor in any archaeological heritage management operation must therefore be the establishment of close links and common policies between the different facets of environmental protection. The Danish model is admirable, with the ancient monuments protection service completely integrated into a conservation agency that covers every aspect of environmental heritage protection, including wildlife, landscape, coastal protection, and much more (Kristiansen 1984).

So much for the less-visible, though nonetheless fundamental, aspect of heritage management. Its more conspicuous face, in terms of the general public, is represented by the sites and monuments that are managed and promoted for public enjoyment and edification. It has to be assumed that these are adequately conserved and maintained, out of respect to the monuments themselves as much as in the interests of their potential visitors. The debate on the level of restoration and reconstruction that is permissible is an endless one. The philosophy behind the stringent criteria applied for over a century in the UK is admirably summarized by Thompson (1981), and will not be recapitulated here. The Venice Charter, which enshrines the basic doctrine of ICOMOS, sets its face resolutely against any level of reconstruction beyond anastylosis (the replacement of elements in locations from which they can be demonstrated to have derived).

It is undeniable that reconstruction of archaeological monuments has proceeded considerably further in many parts of the world, from the Wilhelmine excesses of the Saalburg in western Germany to that triumph of scholarly re-creation, Colonial Williamsburg. Although the academic objections to high levels of reconstruction on inadequate evidence are wholly valid, it cannot be gainsaid that many archaeological sites make impossible intellectual and imaginative demands on the lay visitor. Little effort is required to appreciate Chichén Itzá, Herculanaeum or the Great Wall of China, perhaps, but many visitors with high expectations must leave Troy, Carthage or the Roman Forum with a sense of disappointment coupled with bafflement and, even more serious, a loss of sympathy towards the archaeological heritage.

The onus upon archaeological heritage managers to make those components of the heritage of which they are public guardians accessible, both physically and intellectually, to the whole range of needs that the public embraces is therefore another common factor. This obligation to present and interpret is overriding, and it should involve making the fullest use of modern techniques of mass communication. There is the thinnest of dividing lines here between effective interpretation and the creation of what have been described as 'archaeological Disneylands'. This does not mean that the methods of Orlando have no place in archaeological interpretation: the remarkably effective Jorvik Viking Centre in York has successfully adapted the electric cars of Disney world to take visitors around its re-created 10th century street and the excavations upon which this was based. The York experiment has succeeded, largely thanks to the predominant role assigned to professional archaeologists in its conception and execution.

At Stonehenge two approaches to the problem of presenting and interpreting a great prehistoric monument which attracts nearly a million visitors each year could be taken (Addyman 1989, Golding 1989). The English Heritage approach is cautious in its innovations, conscious of the fragility of the monument under the impact of increased visitor numbers, it has chosen to remove its interpretation centre and parking facilities some distance from the monument itself, and to require visitors to proceed to the monument on foot, a solution which will inevitably result in a constraint being placed upon visits (and consequently on potential revenue). The emphasis in the proposals from Heritage Projects (whose experience was gained with the Jorvik Viking Centre) is placed, by contrast, on maximizing visitor numbers by ensuring a smooth and rapid throughput (though allowing for a more leisurely and extensive tour by more-serious visitors). There is no doubt that the English Heritage solution will be more in harmony with the ambience of the monument itself: it may prove worthy of study by those heritage managers wrestling with the problem of other 'honeypot monuments', such as the Athenian Acropolis or the Taj Mahal.

The interpretation of the heritage has wide ramifications, going beyond the presentation of monuments. It requires the archaeologist involved in its management to ascertain the requirements of the public in its many different guises, and to ensure that there is printed and audio-visual material available to explain the significance of the heritage and to help visitors, whether tourists or local residents, schoolchildren or professionals, to understand what they are seeing. The excavation monograph must be prepared for the scholar, the worksheet for the schoolchild, the card guide for the general tourist, and the works of synthesis and survey for the informed layman and the 'cultural tourist'. It is too much to expect professional heritage managers to produce such a broad spectrum of publications, but their expertise must be available to the professionals in the field of communications who have the requisite skills.

[...]

References

Addyman P.V. (1989). 'The Stonehenge we deserve.' In H. Cleere (ed.), *Archaeological heritage management in the modern world*. London: Routledge, 265–274.

Burnham, B. (1974). *The protection of cultural property: Handbook of national legislations*. Paris: International Council of Museums.

Catherall, P.D., M. Barnett and H. McClean (1984). *The southern feeder: the archaeology of a gas pipeline*. London: British Gas Corporation.

Cleere, H.F. (ed.) (1984). *Approaches to the archaeological heritage*. Cambridge: Cambridge University Press.

Council of Europe (1979). *Monument protection in Europe*. Deventer: Kluwer.

Council of Europe (1988). *A future for our past* 31, 3–21 (issue devoted to the theme 'Young people and heritage').

Cracknell, S. and M. Corbishley (1986). *Presenting archaeology to young people*, CBA Research Report No. 64. London: Council for British Archaeology.

D'Agostino, B. (1984). 'Italy.' In H.F. Cleere (ed.), *Approaches to the archaeological heritage*. Cambridge: Cambridge University Press, 73–81.

Darvill, T.C. (1987). *Ancient monuments in the countryside: an archaeological management review*. London: English Heritage.

Dickens, R.S. and C.E. Hill (eds) (1978). *Cultural resources: planning and management*. Boulder, Colorado: Westview Press.

Fagan, B.W. (1977). *Buried treasure: the story of early archaeologists in the Americas*. London: Macdonald & Jane's.

Flood, J. (1983). *Archaeology of the Dreamtime*. Sydney and London: Collins.
Golding, F.N. (1989). 'Stonehenge – past and future.' In H. Cleere (ed.), *Archaeological heritage management in the modern world*. London: Routledge, 256–263.
Green, E.L. (ed.) (1984). *Ethics and values in archaeology*. New York: Free Press.
Grimes, W.F. (1968). *The excavation of Roman and mediaeval London*. London: Routledge and Kegan Paul.
Herrmann, J. (ed.) (1981). *Archäologische Denkmale und Umweltgestaltung*, 2nd edn. Berlin: Akademie Verlag.
Hingst, H. and A. Lipowschek (1975). *Europäische Denkmalschutzgesetze in deutscher Übersetzung*. Neumünster: Karl-Wachholz Verlag.
Kennet, W. (1972). *Preservation*. London: Temple Smith.
King, T.F., P.P. Hickman and G. Berg (1977). *Anthropology in historic preservation: caring for culture's clutter*. New York: Academic Press.
Kristiansen, K. (1984). 'Denmark.' In H.F. Cleere (ed.), *Approaches to the archaeological heritage*. Cambridge: Cambridge University Press, 21–36.
Lipe, W.D. and A.L. Lindsay (eds) (1974). *Proceedings of the 1974 Cultural Resource Management Conference, Federal Center, Denver, Colorado*. Flagstaff, Arizona: Northern Arizona Society of Science and Art.
Lowenthal, D. (1985). *The past is a foreign country*. Cambridge: Cambridge University Press.
Lowenthal, D. and M. Binney (eds) (1981). *Our past before us: why do we save it?* London: Temple Smith.
McGimsey, C.R. (1972). *Public archeology*. New York and London: Seminar Press.
McGimsey, C.R. and H.A. Davis (eds) (1977). *The management of archaeological resources: the Airlie House report*. Washington, DC: Society for American Archaeology.
McGimsey, C.R. and H.A. Davis (1984). 'United States of America.' In H.F. Cleere (ed.), *Approaches to the archaeological heritage*. Cambridge: Cambridge University Press, 125–31.
Newcomb, R.M. (1979). *Planning the past*. Folkestone: Dawson/Hamden, Connecticut: Archon Books.
O'Keefe, P.J. and L.V. Prott (1984). *Law and the cultural heritage*. Vol. 1: Discovery and excavation. Abingdon: Professional Books.
PACT (1985). 'Acts of the First Meeting on "Making children aware of the existence, study and conservation of the archaeological cultural heritage", Ravello, 11–13 June 1985.' *PACT News* 15, 23–100; 16, 14–82.
PACT (1986). 'Communications of the Second Meeting on "Making adolescents (10–16 years old) aware of the existence, study and preservation of the archaeological heritage". *PACT News* 17, 36–104.
PACT (1987). 'Communications of the Second Meeting on "Making adolescents (10–16years old) aware of the existence, study and preservation of the archaeological heritage". *PACT News* 18, 33–148.
Säve-Söderbergh, T. (ed.) (1987). *Temples and tombs of Ancient Nubia: the International Rescue Campaign at Abu Simbel, Philae and other sites*. London: Thames & Hudson/UNESCO.
Schiffer, M.B. and G.L. Gumerman (1977). *Conservation archaeology: a guide for cultural resource management studies*. New York: Academic Press.
Schiffer, M.B. and J.H. House (eds) (1975). *The Cache River Archeological Project: an experiment in contract archeology*. Fayetteville, Arkansas: Arkansas Archeological Survey.
Schofield, J. and R.H. Leech (eds) (1987). *Urban archaeology in Britain*, CBA Research Report No. 61. London: Council for British Archaeology.
Thapar, B.K. (1984). 'India.' In H.F. Cleere (ed.), *Approaches to the archaeological heritage*. Cambridge: Cambridge University Press, 63–72.
Thompson, M.W. (1981). *Ruins: their preservation and display*. London: British Museum Publications.
Unesco (1985 onwards). *The protection of movable cultural property: collection of legislative texts* (23 published to December 1987). Paris: UNESCO.

Archaeological resource management and preservation

Willem J.H. Willems

Source: Willems, W.J.H. 'Archaeological resource management and preservation', in H. Kars and R.M. van Herringen (eds), *Preserving Archaeological Remains In-Situ: Proceedings of the 3rd Conference, 7–9 December 2006, Amsterdam*, Amsterdam: VU University Amsterdam, pp. 283–90.

[...]

THE ADOPTION – IN 1992 – of the European Convention on the Protection of the Archaeological Heritage, or the Malta (Valletta) Convention as it is better known, which has been ratified by most European countries, will prove to have been a watershed, at least in Europe. It defines a standard for the management of archaeological properties and provides a frame of reference for countries that have not ratified the convention yet and also for countries outside Europe, where a comparable international standard is lacking.

Development of archaeological resource management

[...]

In the 20th century academic archaeological research and protecting and conserving archaeological heritage became very different lines of work. It is not difficult to see why this occurred, despite the common roots. After all, archaeology is about studying the past. Although archaeology may be used or abused for political purposes, completely unconsciously for lack of theoretical reflection, to 'colour' a story in a politically desirable way, to leave out elements that are considered undesirable, or even to falsify evidence, it is about discovering and interpreting material remains from the past. Although there always is some pseudo-science, most archaeological research is done in a scientific manner and is normally considered by its practitioners as apolitical and as 'pure research'.

By contrast, the activity of 'taking care of the past' (the German concept of *Denkmalpflege*, or the Dutch *monumentenzorg*) or its modern form of archaeological heritage management is something which is done in the present. It is always a political activity, which is traditionally dominated by legal issues and practical concerns of conservation methods. For a very long time, therefore, there has been this increasing gap between on the one hand academic research into the history of man and necessarily having an international perspective, and on the other the protection and management of heritage, almost entirely from a national viewpoint and primarily coping with political, legal, administrative and technical issues.

[...]

While it is understandable why academic research and heritage management became separated to varying degrees, it remains curious that until fairly recently there was nothing in archaeology comparable to the role of archival sciences as a sub discipline of historical sciences. The preservation of its study material was apparently not a great concern to archaeology.

From the 1960s onwards, many changes occurred. The environmental movement started, that would result in the green debate and the recognition that the world's natural and cultural resources are in danger. This became the basis for the birth of archaeological heritage or 'resource' management in the modern sense. Archaeological monuments, in the sense of movable as well as immovable parts of the cultural heritage, are no longer seen primarily as objects of study but as cultural resources to be of use and benefit in the present and future. In some ways, '*resource* management' is more suitable than '*heritage* management' because resource is more value-free than 'heritage' and refers to the idea of seeing the material remains of the past as a resource: for society as a whole as well as for research by archaeologists.

Archaeologists have become aware that their source material is rapidly disappearing while only a tiny fraction of the information can be recorded. We now know that its survival needs a different approach that requires communication with the outside world, influencing the political and socio-economic decision-making process, and enlisting the support of the general public. In most of the Western world, existing notions of historic preservation through protection of ancient monuments have gradually been replaced by more dynamic concepts of managing archaeological resources in the framework of spatial planning systems. This happened first in the US in the 1970s; it started a decade or so later in many parts of Europe.

In Europe the pace of this development varied strongly in different countries with different traditions and legal regimes.

The Scandinavian countries, for example, were way ahead and did not really need the Malta Convention when it was adopted in 1992. The result has been that the rescue archaeology, which had dominated fieldwork in much of Europe, came to an end (on developments in the UK, see Thomas 1993).

It started with small-scale excavations during the post-war reconstruction effort and culminated in unprecedented operations accompanying infrastructure development in the 1970s and 1980s. Archaeology became part of the planning process and in a non voluntary manner. Although the scope of the legal obligations varies from country to country, the impact of development on archaeological resources must be taken into account. This has created a vast increase in archaeological fieldwork that used to be referred to as contract archaeology and is nowadays described as 'consulting', 'development-led', 'developer-funded', or 'compliance-driven' archaeology. See also Willems and Van den Dries (2007).

Implementation models of the Malta Convention

There are significant differences in the way in which the Malta Convention is being implemented in various European countries. In my view, there are three models of how this is being done. These are related to political views and to legal notions about the role of the state and about private property. In addition, there are different opinions about the nature of archaeological work. In France, for example, all archaeological work is seen as *research* on behalf of the state. In a country such as the UK, archaeological work is seen as a *service*, not unlike many other services that can be bought and sold; see the recent discussion between Demoule (2002a, 2002b) and Thomas (2002), Hunter and Ralston (1993) or Demoule (2007). Related to this are different political views on the usefulness of such things as a free market and the desirability to allow 'market principles' to operate in the field of culture; and also on the need for, and the degree to which a market needs to be regulated, or the quality of work controlled.

These differences have led to different systems by which the Malta Convention is being implemented. Sometimes, as in Germany, Switzerland or Spain, where cultural autonomy lies with the states and not the federation, there are even considerable differences within one country. If you look at what different systems seem to exist, there are two relevant basic questions:

- Does the state consider archaeological work to be a service, or does it not?
- Does the state wish to control the quality of archaeological work, or does it not?

If these are put into a diagram (see Figure 4.2.1), there are four different options but one of the boxes is empty: I do not know of any situation where a country does *not* consider archaeological work to be a service and at the same time is *not* interested in exercising control over the work that is being done, by whatever means.

In practice, there are thus three different systems in existence. I shall begin with a model that was adopted in a very explicit form in The Netherlands but that exists in many other countries.

Is archeological work considered to be a service?

YES	NO	Does the state want to control the quality of archeological work?
Germany (partial) Ireland Netherlands Sweden	Austria France Germany (partial) Greece	YES
Canada United Kingdom USA		NO

Figure 4.2.1 The organisational principles of archaeological resource management systems in different countries.

Source: After Willems & Van den Dries (2007)

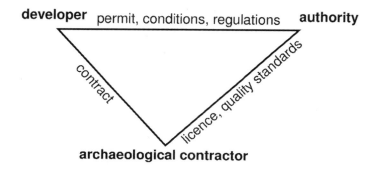

Figure 4.2.2 The relations between the government, archaeological contractors and developers.

In view of the increase of archaeological work in The Netherlands, the political decision was taken to create a market for archaeological services, in which 'market principles' apply. Private excavation companies are allowed to offer their services in competition with each other. However, this is only one aspect of the decision. The complementary part is that, while it is acknowledged that archaeological work may be a service, it is also acknowledged that its result is important for the understanding and valuation of the national archaeological heritage. Therefore, market principles can only be allowed to operate when the quality of the necessary work has been ascertained. Otherwise, there is too big a risk that commercial and financial considerations will prevail. Therefore, a free market system was introduced *in combination with* a system of quality assurance which is based on the law.

This is illustrated in Figure 4.2.2, which shows the triangular relationship that exists between the authority, which can be a local or national government, the developer of plans, and the archaeological contractor. The upper line of the triangle gives the relation between the competent authority and the developer: their relation takes the form of a permit, or usually a whole series of permits, which the developer needs to realise his plans. The main issue here is the ordered use of space and control of the impact of the proposed development.

The right part of the triangle gives the relation between the competent authority and the contractor. The main issue in this case, is the way in which we acquire knowledge about the past. Archaeological sites are an important source of information about our past and it is also a fragile resource which makes it a government's responsibility to ascertain that it is properly handled. In the Dutch view, this cannot be guaranteed by the mechanisms on the left part of the triangle: the issue there, is time and money: when the developer has the right permit, he becomes a principal to the archaeological contractor and their relationship takes the form of a contract by which the principal seeks to ascertain that the work is being done as economically as possible and within a specified period of time. *That*, and nothing else, is the product which the developer wants from the contractor. The government, however, wants the contractor to produce something very different, namely relevant knowledge about the past and for that reason the government needs its own control in the process, which is a licence requiring, among others, work under quality standards.

The whole point of the Malta Convention is that the permit which the developer needs should preferably not be given if valuable archaeological remains are at stake.

If he *does* get it, because other interests are considered to be more important, archaeological investigation should be a condition and it is up to the authority to guarantee that this investigation is properly done. Therefore, the system of quality standards must be backed by the law, so that it will not be easily circumvented.

Comparable systems are in use in other European countries, although explicit archaeological standards are only one way in which the State controls quality. In Germany, for example, in those German states where commercial archaeology is permitted, no explicit standards exist but control is exercised by control of the market: the state archaeological service selects the firm that will do the work. Another variant to this type of control can be a licensing system, in which it is somehow established which contractors are, and which are not considered capable of doing the work.

This is the essential difference with similar systems elsewhere, notably in England where – in principle – the right part of the triangle is lacking. There are exceptions, and I know I am simplifying matters, but in principle only the upper and the left part of the relationship exists: what is being done about archaeology is largely determined by the conditions imposed by the authority on the developer and, second, by what that developer, in his role as principal, agrees with the contractor. There are no legal provisions covering the relationship on the right. In the 1980s, archaeology was privatised without safeguards in the same way as was done in the USA and Canada a decade earlier, and this is precisely what most European countries want to avoid.

Before I go on, I would like to add that I am not implying by this, that archaeological contractors in the UK do not have standards. As you may know the IFA has quite good ones, but these are not backed by legal demands although their use is often encouraged by county archaeologists; for an analysis, see Hinton & Jennings (2007) or Lawson (1993). Nor do I wish to imply that there can't be developers – in the UK or elsewhere – who do in fact take great care to ensure that the archaeological work they commission is properly done. But the basis of the system remains that most archaeological work is being done without an enforceable mechanism for control by the government and much depends on the contract between developer and contractor.

The French system is in fact just the opposite. Although again a simplification, in principle the left part of the triangle is lacking there. The French law has an archaeology tax, which is imposed on developers as compensation for the damage inflicted on the national heritage and which is used to pay for archaeological work. In France, it is the government that determines what the developer should pay and what he should comply with before the development can take place, and it is *also* the government that controls the archaeological work. This is being done by a public administrative institution called INRAP, and although there will in reality surely be contractual arrangements with the developer almost all archaeological work is a state monopoly.

This system does not have explicit standards and provides guarantees for the quality of the work being done because that is ascertained by INRAP. Moreover, there is no direct connection between the tax yield from any given development and the amount that INRAP will in practice spend on the excavation. From an archaeological point of view, this is a very good mechanism to ensure that money is being spent where it is needed most. On the other hand, there is obviously some contradiction here with the way in which the developer pay principle in the Malta Convention was intended. Elsewhere, a development might simply become too expensive and be relocated because of archaeology. In the French system, that requires other mechanisms.

This kind of comparison illustrates what the strengths and weaknesses can be. In the Dutch type of system, for example, the archaeological contractor can get in a very difficult position, because that contractor always has to serve two masters. In the English type of system, there is inadequate government concern for the quality of archaeological work and a strong risk that financial considerations will prevail. And in the French type of system, there is no market competition with a drive for innovation, there is the risk of an inefficient bureaucracy, and there is an assumption that if the work is being done by a semi-governmental organisation, it is done well. Of course each system also has its advantages, and I would like to stress that none of these systems is necessarily superior. Much depends on the way in which archaeological heritage management in a given national context actually works in practice. Some theoretical disadvantages or weaknesses can be remedied by the way in which things are being done in real life. In Sweden, for example, there used to be a French type of system which is currently shifting towards a more commercial, market adjusted practice with more archaeological contractors and no longer a state monopoly (Lekberg 2007). But this is still being done in a controlled way. The alternative for competitive tendering is that a County Board decides who is to carry out the contract archaeology and how much this should cost, and it instructs the developer to make a deal with the chosen archaeological unit. So there you have a system that moves from the 'French' to the 'Dutch' model, but without market competition.

Preservation

Although it may seem that discussion so far has mostly been about preservation *ex situ* and not so much about *in situ* preservation, this is not the case. After all, when states are interested in preserving archaeological resources, the work involved can be done through a state monopoly on archaeological work as well as through a commercial system or any type of hybrid system.

However, even though research on preservation in situ can be commissioned to private enterprise and universities, it is clear that organising preservation in situ is always a core activity of the state. Even in the most commercialised systems, those of the Anglo-Saxon countries, it is semi-governmental organisations such as Parks Canada, the National Park Service or English Heritage that are primarily responsible. This is because on the one hand, preservation in situ is closely connected to legal protection of sites, and on the other it is normally only national level organisations that are equipped to either carry out, or to commission research.

It has become clear that for a sensible archaeological resource management that includes preservation *in situ*, archaeology needs better tools. We have become aware that new types of research are needed to provide such tools. Much of this research is in fact being done by national bodies charged with archaeological heritage management, which are diverting their core business from traditional research of the past, through excavation, to research which is specifically aimed at creating knowledge that is needed for effective management of the remains *from* the past. For example, research into the conditions which determine the survival of artefacts in the soil, which is the subject of the PARIS conference, research into conservation methods, also relevant for this conference, or research aimed at integration of the disciplines which are concerned with the historic environment, among which archaeology is only one, and with their

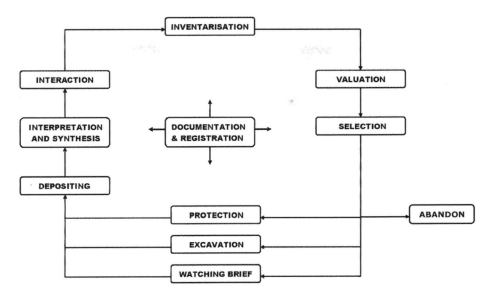

Figure 4.2.3 The cyclical process of archaeological resource management.

integration into such fields as landscape designing and spatial planning. [. . .] Research in conservation methods is of course not a new development. It is in fact a traditional research topic that has been highly developed in countries with an abundance of architectural remains such as in southern Europe, China, India and the southern United States. Very often, this research deals with archaeological remains *after* excavation. By contrast, research into the preservation of buried remains is still an emerging field that as far as I am aware is being developed mostly in Northwestern Europe and in the US.

It is, however, useful to consider that this type of research is not just suitable to underpin preservation *in situ*. Figure 4.2.3 shows a model of the archaeological resource management cycle. All except one of these steps are archaeological. That is selection: the decision to select sites for protection, excavation, to be monitored during destruction (watching brief) or to be given up completely, is not archaeological. Selection is of course completely political. It is a governmental decision and authorities depend on research to underpin what they decide, and even to legitimise it.

Very often nowadays, decisions are taken to preserve sites or parts of sites in situ, because this appears to be the most economically feasible. As archaeologists, we used to be in the business of research of the past and in particular we used to do that by excavation. Nowadays, as archaeological heritage managers we have established a new principle, a conservation ethic, that says that we should try and preserve sites, and not just because they are our primary sources but also because they are such a fragile and non renewable resource. Of course it is wonderful when our governments accept this principle and when there are official policies in place, backed up by research, to preserve important elements of the archives contained in the soil.

But at the same time, in everyday practice, one sees that this conservation ethic is increasingly being used almost as a blind pretext to limit the cost of excavation. There are often situations where there appear to be no good prospects for long-term physical preservation but nevertheless that decision is taken. There are also situations where only a small part of a site is excavated with very limited research value, while the rest is left for investigation sometime in a very uncertain future. It seems to me that in such cases, our ethic is being used against us, by politicians that want to save face as well as to save money and that are being helped by some of us that are so blinded by it that they appear to have forgotten what archaeology is all about. Of course some archaeological sites have important intangible values that ought to automatically make preservation the preferred option, but for the normal type of invisible buried site, preservation should not be a goal in itself but a means to an end. Admittedly, however, and no matter what anyone thinks about preservation, in many cases we really just do not know if what is decided or what we recommend to be decided, is really the best possible option. We simply lack the information to make a well-founded recommendation or decision.

References

Demoule, J-P. (2002a). 'Rescue Archaeology. The French way.' *Public Archaeology* 2: 170–7.
Demoule, J-P. (2002b). 'Reply to Roger Thomas.' *Public Archaeology* 2: 239–240.
Demoule, J-P. (2007). 'Scientific quality control and the general organisation of French archaeology.' In W.J.H. Willems and M.D. van den Dries (eds), *Quality management in Archaeology*. Oxford: Oxbow, 135–47.
Hinton, P. and D. Jennings (2007). 'Quality management of archaeology in Great Britain: present practice and future challenges.' In W.J.H. Willems and M.D. van den Dries (eds), *Quality management in Archaeology*. Oxford: Oxbow, 100–12.
Hunter, J. and I. Ralston (1993). 'The structure of British archaeology.' In J. Hunter and I. Ralston (eds.), *Archaeological Resource Management in the UK. An Introduction*. Stroud: Alan Sutton Publishing, 37–55.
Lawson, A.J. (1993). 'Professional practices in archaeology.' In J. Hunter and I. Ralston (eds), *Archaeological Resource Management in the UK. An Introduction*. Stroud: Alan Sutton Publishing, 194–214.
Lekberg, P. (2007). 'Making it matter: towards a Swedish contract archaeology for social sustainability.' In W.J.H. Willems and M.D. van den Dries (eds), *Quality management in Archaeology*. Oxford: Oxbow, 148–59.
Thomas, R. (2002). 'Comment. Rescue Archaeology. The French way. By Jean-Paul Demoule.' *Public Archaeology* 2: 236–8.
Thomas, R.M. (1993). 'English Heritage funding policies and their impact on research strategy.' In J. Hunter and I. Ralston (eds), *Archaeological Resource Management in the UK. An Introduction*. Stroud: Alan Sutton Publishing, 179–93.
Willems, W. and M. van den Dries (2007). 'The origins and development of quality assurance in archaeology.' In W.J.H. Willems and M.D. van den Dries (eds), *Quality management in Archaeology*. Oxford: Oxbow, 1–12.

Chapter 5

Conservation theory

ARCHAEOLOGICAL REMAINS ARE preserved where they are naturally protected from the destructive power of man or nature (see Chapters 1 and 2). The only other form of preservation is where conscious efforts are made to protect the remains; this is conservation. For any society to provide resources for preserving remains, they have to have a value to that society. Different societies have valued different things from the past. Since the Age of Enlightenment, 'Western' societies have valued the original material, archaeological evidence. Chinese and other Eastern and traditional societies have valued the 'spirit of the place' (Wei and Aass 1989: 6). The concept of 'preservation of archaeological remains *in situ*' has emerged from the archaeological and historic buildings conservation strands of the 'Western' conservation tradition, discussed below. This tradition is, through documents such as the Burra Charter (see Chapter 5.5), seeking to broaden its scope.

Conservation history

Though there is evidence for the 'conservation' of both objects and monuments in the Roman world (Strong 1973; Caple 2011: 3–4), the theories and ideas we practise in conservation today are traditionally considered to have started with the Renaissance interest in classical remains. Throughout the Middle Ages, European scholars had been aware of classical antiquities, especially in Rome. Petrarch (1304–1374) wrote both of the ideals of classical antiquity and the damage being done to classical remains in Rome. Conscious of the emerging importance of the classical world to the Renaissance world, Pope Pius II issued a bull in 1462 ordering the preservation of ancient remains. Subsequent Popes issued similar edicts though their masons continued to use classical ruins as a source of stone. By 1466, the papal or municipal administrators (conservatori) of Pope Paul II were repairing ancient monuments such as the Arch of Septimius Severus, and by the sixteenth century it had become fashionable for princes and cardinals to collect classical statuary and architectural details recovered from excavations around Rome and classical ruins elsewhere in Italy. These pieces were cleaned and displayed in gardens, private rooms and display galleries. Following the examples of the

Medici in Florence who had employed Donatello, in the early sixteenth century Cardinal Andrea della Valle (1463–1534) commissioned the sculptor Lorenzo di Ludovico to complete some of his broken classical statues, adding heads, arms and legs as required. This appears to have set a trend for restoration; Vasari commented in 1550, 'Antiquities thus restored certainly possess more grace than those mutilated trunks, members without heads or figures in any other way maimed and defective' (Jokilehto 1999: 23). This 'restored work' is today more accurately termed 'aesthetic integration' since the sculptors did not know the exact form of the original, but they created what seemed appropriate and was aesthetically pleasing to their patron. This continued the medieval tradition of craftsmen artists fulfilling the artistic wishes of their clients (Thomas 1998: 6).

It should not be imagined that this was the only conservation approach being taken. From the very first, some statues, such as 'The Belvedere Torso of Hercules', were displayed in that broken state in which they had been found (Jokilehto 1999: 24). Artists and sculptors such as Cannova refused to restore the figures carved by Phidias that Lord Elgin brought back from the Parthenon, claiming it would be sacrilege to touch them (Podany 1994). This duality of approach, some objects restored, others preserved 'as found', continues to the present day.

In the period of the sixteenth to nineteenth centuries, antiquities collectors continued to seek aesthetic qualities in their objects and sites. In addition to the tradition of classical beauty, the concept of the picturesque, a trait perceived in many ruins, which contrasted beauty (the fair of form) with the sublime (the vastness and power of nature), was increasingly sought. By the mid- to late nineteenth century, the fashion for Gothic architecture was sweeping through Britain. Fired with Anglican missionary zeal and funding, under the banner of 'restoration' many English churches, in particular, were altered, removing earlier features and recreating imagined 'gothic' interiors and exteriors, a process sometimes derogatively termed 'scrape'. The alteration of much loved places of worship caused widespread disquiet. Following a letter to the *Athenium* to complain about the plans by George Gilbert Scott to 'restore' Tewksbury Abbey, William Morris (designer and manufacturer), together with like-minded artists and aesthetes, formed SPAB (Society for the Protection of Ancient Buildings), issuing a manifesto published in the magazine *Builder* on 25 August 1877 (Morris 1877) (see Chapter 5.1). This statement, which built upon the ideas of Ruskin (1849) and Robert Willis's building narrative (Thompson 1981; Buchanan 2013), argued:

- decayed structures were picturesque and aesthetically pleasing;
- the evidence of age (patina, 'golden glow') was both aesthetically pleasing and informed the viewer of the truth of the object; and
- the 'truth' of the object's history should be preserved; everything from marks of manufacture and evidence of wear to alterations, additions and redecoration.

The building fabric was recognised as an important document of the past, a witnessed testimony to the history of the building. The idea of stripping away such evidence in the name of restoration was anathema to SPAB members. The Ruskinian 'romantic' ideal was to leave the building untouched and unaltered (termed anti-scrape); only maintenance to preserve functionality was seen as appropriate.

SPAB gained support from academics, artists and the public; schemes to renovate the tomb of Edward the Confessor in Westminster Abbey or the front of San Marco in Venice were eventually halted in part through SPAB pressure (Chamberlin 1979); these views gained wide acceptance throughout Europe (Riegl 1903).

Though artefact conservation had started as a craft skill, repairing and cleaning classical antiquities, the challenges provided by the large number of objects being unearthed by archaeological excavations of the nineteenth century increasingly required scientific knowledge to solve their problems. Nineteenth-century scientists such as Humphrey Davy (1821 – charred papyri of Herculaneum), Michael Faraday (1843 – red rot in leather) and David Brewster (1861 – iridescence on glass) sought to ascertain the nature of the decay processes with a view to developing means of preventing further decay. By 1888, Friedrich Rathgen, a young chemist employed as a conservator by the Royal Museums in Berlin, was using his scientific knowledge to desalinate stonework and electrochemically strip and stabilise corroding iron and 'bronze' antiquities (Gilberg 1987).

The increased capacity that technical and scientific knowledge provided encouraged interventive procedures to halt decay and stabilise decaying objects and collapsing buildings. After the Second World War, the boom in visitor numbers to museums and heritage sites, the development of cultural heritage tourism and the financial power that brought encouraged hasty and sometimes ill-judged conservation practice. As the 1960s proceeded, the failures of conservation, polymers such as soluble nylon that could not be removed, the loss of information as original surfaces present in the corrosion crusts of metal objects were stripped off, the cracking and failure of concrete and the corroding and splitting of ancient stones dowelled with steel rods, reminded us of the damage that could be caused to unique antiquities by inappropriate but well-intentioned conservation work. As scientific and technical understanding and resources were increasingly available, conservation became increasingly focused not on 'how', but on 'what' and 'why'. In artefact conservation, these changes were reflected in the frequent alterations to the codes of ethics for professional conservators, in buildings conservation in the agreements of a series of international charters (Athens 1931, Venice 1964, etc.).

From the 1960s to the 1990s, a number of ideas, true nature, reversibility, minimum intervention and stewardship swept through the conservation world (Appelbaum 2007), leading to changes in ethical guidelines of professional artefact conservation organisations such as the American Institute for Conservation (AIC) and the United Kingdom Institute for Conservation (UKIC) (now ICON). Though they are all useful concepts and continue to be used, none could completely encapsulate the theory and practice of conservation.

The conservation concept

As a number of authors have noted, conservation has effectively dwelt between two extremes or 'ideals' (Jokilehto 2007):

- The Ruskinian ideal of preserving the past 'as found', untouched, with just 'the golden glow of time'. This concept remains appealing to many authors (Eggert 2009); however, unchecked, it leads inexorably to Miss Haversham, the poster girl of the Ruskinian ideal, and Satis House, which, in Charles Dickens's *Great Expectations*, remained preserved, untouched throughout the long years since Miss Haversham's wedding day:

    > everything within my view which ought to be white had been white long ago, and had lost its lustre and was faded to yellow. I saw that the bride within the bridal dress had withered like the dress and like the flowers had no brightness left.
    >
    > (Dickens 1875: 65)

Dickens' characters describe Satis House as a place where decay, rather than the past, is what is actually seen. Taken to its logical extreme, *reducto ad absurdum*, leave physical remains 'as found' and eventually you see nothing but piles of dust, fragments, indecipherable corrosion, nothing that you can recognise and interpret; you are no wiser about life in the past. In reality, it is never possible to 'freeze in time' and see a picture of the past; decay processes continue to entropy and obliterate all structure and meaning.

- The ideal of aesthetic restoration, which saw extensive 'stylistic' recreation of historic sites and artefacts from the Renaissance to the mid-nineteenth century (which we might today call reconstruction). It damages or removes the evidence of the past and turns historic sites and artefacts into a new style imitating an imagined past. Here, the *reducto ad absurdum* is the mythical 'grandfather's axe', where endless restoration leaves only the tradition, no physical evidence of the original remains: 'If I replace the handle of the axe and my father had already replaced the head, is it still my grandfather's axe?' (Caple 2000: 132). Through the twentieth century, there has been increasing emphasis on a more exacting standard of restoration, restoring only that which was certainly originally present exactly as it was but in a manner detectable from the original by careful observation.

Neither extreme fully represents conservation, which needs to preserve the evidence of the past intact, so with new knowledge every generation can recreate a new and more accurate understanding of the past, a concept of the Enlightenment. But, as few present day observers have the scholarship to interpret the fragmentary, dirty, decayed, multi-period sites or objects that survive, those caring for the heritage are required to aid its interpretation for the benefit of the public; frequently the owners of the remains. There is thus an ever-present balance between preserving the past and cleaning/revealing it, to make it readable. This is encapsulated in the 1984 ICOM-CC definition of a conservator-restorer: 'the activity of the conservator-restorer (conservation) consists of examination, preservation and conservation-restoration of cultural property'. The need to explicitly retain this balance of competing requirements can still be seen as the essential core of the subject (Caple 2009).

Charters

International organisations were founded after both the First and Second World Wars, seeking to establish a common basis of standards, processes and understanding on which the people of the different countries of the world could deal with one another. These organisations established agencies to deal with issues such as cultural heritage. In 1959, the United Nations Educational, Scientific and Cultural Organisation (UNESCO) founded the International Centre for the Study of the Preservation and Restoration of Cultural Property (ICCROM) in Rome, which in turn supported the International Council of Museums (ICOM) in an attempt to develop international standards in the care of cultural property and provide a forum for interchange of ideas on best practice in all aspects of curating cultural heritage. In 1965, the International Council on Monuments and Sites (ICOMOS), 'a professional association that works for the conservation and protection of cultural heritage places around the world', was established following the conference that presented the Venice Charter (1964). These organisations were able to advise national governments and international agencies, as well as providing intellectual leadership for the subject, spur on the development of training programmes, and foster international communication between conservators, architects, archaeologists, curators and others. They also help establish standards and best practice to which the international community work. This is achieved through publications, guidelines, charters and encouraging professional associations that have codes of ethics and practice. Language, terminology and cultural differences have provided problems for international agreements (see Table 0.1).

Following the influence of SPAB and Ruskin in the last quarter of the nineteenth century, in 1904 the International Congress of Architects 4th Meeting in Madrid adopted an anti-restoration framework, espousing concern for the historical, technical and aesthetic values of historic buildings (Cooke 2010: 52). Subsequently, in 1931, the First International Congress of Architects and Technicians of Historic Monuments produced the Athens Charter on the Restoration of Historic Monuments, which produced a series of seven resolutions (ICOMOS Charters website n.d.):

- to establish organisations for restoration advice;
- to ensure projects are reviewed with knowledgeable criticism;
- to establish national legislation to preserve historic sites;
- to rebury excavations that were not to be restored;
- to allow the use of modern techniques and materials in restoration work;
- to place historical sites under custodial protection; and
- to protect the area surrounding historic sites.

The idea of common world heritage, the importance of the setting of monuments and the principle of integration of new materials were highlighted.

Meanwhile, the increase in the number of archaeological excavations around the world and the concerns of new and developing countries about 'foreign' excavations in their country led UNESCO to adopt *Recommendation on International Principles Applicable to Archaeological Excavations* at its meeting in New Delhi in 1956 (UNESCO 1956; Stanley-Price 1995: 143–9). This built on the 1937 Cairo Act drafted by the League of Nations and the *Manual on the Techniques of Archaeological Excavation*, published by the International Museums Office in 1940 (Egloff and Comer 2012). It established principles that should underpin archaeological excavation, defining the responsibilities of both the excavator and the state. The document was aimed primarily at framing laws in developing countries to ensure the ethical conduct of foreign archaeologists undertaking excavations, with the intention to prevent illicit export of objects from host countries. It also required each nation to create 'an appropriate authority' to regulate (approve) excavations, to protect sites, create archives and facilitate the creation of collections of comparative material (museums). This document is the first international document to refer to preservation '*in situ*': 'Prior approval should be obtained from the competent authority for the removal of any monument which ought to be preserved *in situ*'. Nicholas Stanley-Price (1995: 138) has suggested that these words may not fully correspond to modern reading of that phrase. However, the desirability of preserving cultural material or ancient monuments where found is stated, and there is recognition that there is a loss when the objects are removed from their cultural/archaeological context.

A further meeting was held in Venice in 1964, the Second International Congress of Architects and Technicians of Historic Monuments (ICOMOS Charters website n.d.). It was this that produced arguably the most influential document for the preservation of historic sites and monuments: the Venice Charter (1964) (see Chapter 5.2). Since the nineteenth century, the grandest buildings of Europe had been 'restored' in the aesthetic manner, though the Ruskin and Morris philosophy advocated through SPAB had greatly increased awareness of the value of the history present within a buildings fabric and the value that 'original' or authentic material possessed. Venice opened up a far wider interpretation of what an 'historic monument' was, encompassing humble structures and group of structures, internal decorative features, and urban and rural settings, as well as the grand buildings. It enshrined both historic evidence as well as aesthetic criteria as important. Many best practices were established in this document; 'restoration must stop when conjecture begins', all new materials should be identifiable and bear a 'contemporary stamp', material should not be removed unless what is revealed is of exceptional importance, additions should not falsify and must be distinguishable and be harmonious (in scale, colour, etc.) with the original structure. It was, however, recognised that continued social use of a building facilitated its conservation and was to be encouraged, and though it was desirable for conservation to use traditional techniques, modern materials that had proved effective could be used. It also urged that all scientific and technical means of investigation should be used and that records of all work done should be made, and these records be made available, ideally as a published report. Though concerned to avoid restoration, especially the wholesale restoration of the nineteenth century practised by Sir Gilbert Scott or Violet-le-Duc, the Venice Charter recognised the benefit of anastylosis, the joining together of original pieces into their original position as seen in the re-erection of the columns on the north side of the Parthenon or the Library at Ephesus. This equates with the rejoining of fragments of pottery or broken artefacts, where the fit of the pieces or the shape or external design allow the original position and relationship to be re-established with certainty. The concept of preservation *in situ* was described, though the term was not used in the Venice Charter. All ICOMOS documents on heritage, post-1964, follow on from Venice, often enhancing and clarifying definitions.

The initial focus of conservation was the fabric of buildings and artefacts in Europe. However, as increasing numbers of countries and cultures, especially indigenous peoples, accessed conservation and became involved in international organisations, broader definitions of cultural heritage began to be adopted. This is reflected in the 1972 World Heritage Convention (Convention Concerning the Protection of the World Cultural and Natural Heritage) (UNESCO 1972), which defined cultural heritage as:

> monuments: architectural works, works of monumental sculpture and painting, elements or structures of an archaeological nature, inscriptions, cave dwellings and combinations of features, which are of outstanding universal value from the point of view of history, art or science;
>
> groups of buildings: groups of separate or connected buildings which, because of their architecture, their homogeneity or their place in the landscape, are of outstanding universal value from the point of view of history, art or science;
>
> sites: works of man or the combined works of nature and man, and areas including archaeological sites which are of outstanding universal value from the historical, aesthetic, ethnological or anthropological point of view.

This convention established that national governments had a duty of 'identification, protection, conservation, presentation and transmission' of the cultural (and natural) heritage, on lands belonging to the state, for the benefit of the people of the future. It required states to establish 'services for the protection, conservation and presentation of the cultural and natural heritage with an appropriate staff and possessing the means to discharge their functions'. It also established a list of World Heritage sites, the 'most important' cultural heritage sites on the planet.

The next charters that dealt with preservation of archaeological remains *in situ* were the Lausanne Charter for the Protection and Management of the Archaeological Heritage (1990) (ICOMOS Charters website n.d.) and the Valletta (1992) European Convention on the Protection of the Archaeological Heritage (Council of Europe 1992) (see Chapter 5.3). The Valletta, or Malta, Convention proved a significant spur to legislation for European countries, and advocates 'the conservation and maintenance of archaeological heritage, preferably *in situ*'. It recognised that damage and loss of information occurred through unprotected exposure of archaeological remains and that there were benefits to reburial or even not excavating archaeological remains.

The themes of the Lausanne Charter included:

- Archaeological heritage was fragile and non-renewable; their protection was a moral obligation and should be resourced and protected through policies and legislation.
- The public, especially indigenous peoples, should be involved in developing policies.
- An archaeological authority should need to approve work on protected sites; unauthorised damage should be penalised.
- Sites should be maintained, surveyed and investigated (preferably non-destructively); their significance and information about them should be available on an inventory.
- Protection of archaeological heritage should be integrated into the planning process and developers should minimise impact on archaeological remains and pay for impact assessments of their developments on archaeological heritage.
- Excavation should only occur on threatened sites or for well justified research reasons. A report with the results of the excavation should be created and published.
- Archaeological remains should remain *in situ*, maintained or reburied, and ideally be presented to the public in an appropriate format.

'The overall objective of archaeological heritage management should be the preservation of monuments and sites in-situ' (Lausanne Charter, Article 6).

Though there have been further ICOMOS charters focusing on specific issues (e.g. *Charter for the Protection and Management of the Archaeological Heritage 1990, International Cultural Tourism Charter 1999, Principles for the Analysis, Conservation and Structural Restoration of Architectural Heritage 2003, The Interpretation and Presentation of Cultural Heritage Sites 2008, Safeguarding and Management of Historic Cities, Towns and Urban Areas 2011*), they have reinforced the ideals outlined in earlier documents and provided specific details in the areas of the charter's subject, highlighting the importance of these aspects of cultural heritage. More significantly, however, three recent 'charters' have broadened the concept of cultural heritage to cover the more diverse cultural understandings present in the world, especially for intangible cultural heritage.

- *Nara Document on Authenticity* (ICOMOS Charters website n.d.) (see Chapter 5.4). This document (declaration) recognised that 'the responsibility for cultural heritage and the

management of it belongs in the first place to the cultural community that has generated it'. Cultural heritage can have tangible and intangible forms. Conservation of cultural heritage is 'rooted in the values attributed to the heritage', and thus there is a need to know and understand these values that need to be credible and truthful, and can thus speak to the authenticity of the cultural heritage.
- The Burra Charter (1999) (see Chapter 5.5). Created by ICOMOS Australia in 1979, it was revised in 1981 and 1988 before the 1999 version, which is widely referenced by heritage authorities around the world. In addition to the 34 'Articles', there are a number of guidelines to 'cultural significance', 'conservation policy' and 'procedures for undertaking studies and reports', as well as a 'code of ethics for co-existence in conserving significant places' (ICOMOS Australia n.d.). The emphasis is again on the intangible attributes of cultural heritage, and the term 'place', rather than site, is used to describe a location and its cultural heritage. Some Aboriginal sites have no physical structure but are locations in the landscape; the intangible aspects of the place, what can be seen, heard and experienced at that location, when understood within the Aboriginal cultural historical tradition, may be significant.
- The UNESCO *Convention for the Safeguarding of Intangible Heritage* (UNESCO 2003) recognises that aspects of the heritage that do not have physical remains, such as oral traditions (language, oral history, etc.), performing arts (ceremonies, dance, music or sounds), social activities (rituals and festivals), traditional crafts and practices and traditional knowledge (of nature, human beings and the wider universe), are valuable, and seeks to ensure that such activities, places or experiences are safeguarded.

The principles enshrined in the Lausanne Charter (1990) and the Valetta Convention (1992), as well as in the Nara Document on Authenticity and the Burra Charter, are slowly being incorporated into updated and revised procedures, legislation and guidance by heritage organisations of various countries around the world, such as English Heritage's 2008 *Conservation Principles, Policies and Guidance*. Professional conservation organisations such as AIC and ICON have also changed their guidelines and codes of ethics to reflect these broader definitions of cultural heritage. These documents reflect the increased sensitivity of archaeologists, curators and conservators to intangible heritage and cultural identity issues. They have primarily impacted the initial site/object assessment process. Where work on the fabric now proceeds, it is done with greater awareness of the cultural impact. In many cases, when dealing with archaeological sites and objects, there are no living cultures to articulate the intangible aspects of the remains. Consequently, interventionist conservation work that takes place often appears similar to that done in previous decades; the initial assessment process is, however, more formalised and detailed (Cooke 2010: 58).

Values

The idea that ancient sites or artefacts were preserved because they possessed value to the present society has long been understood. The statue of Marcus Aurelius is the only surviving full-height equestrian bronze statue of a Roman emperor because the medieval kings and popes, who later ruled Rome, removed all other idolatrous images. They preserved this statue as it was believed to be Constantine, the first Christian Roman emperor, and thus it had value or significance for them. After the Second World War, developments in materials, technology and science had created the ability to explain decay processes and had led conservation to a focus on 'how'. The growth in the identification and conservation of archaeological and heritage sites throughout the world in the 1970s–1990s and the increasing awareness of the limitations of resources, as the economic expansion following the Second World War slowed, led to an increase in the managerial approach to all aspects of heritage with greater emphasis on 'what' and 'why'. At the same time, an increase in the rights of indigenous peoples and diminution of power of national governments in Europe gave rise to the increased recognition of many people as 'stakeholders' in decisions regarding the heritage. The need for a wider society to be involved in articulating the 'significance' of archaeology was voiced by Graham Clark (1957), and more specifically by William Lipe (1974), who recognised that all society, including groups such as native peoples, had a role in this process. All this led to the creation of statements about the significance of archaeological remains (Schiffer and Gumerman 1977: 239–47) as the norm.

Since the 1990s, heritage organisations such as GCI, CCI, English Heritage and Cadw have developed managerial and planning approaches to conserving heritage assets (conservation planning) that emphasise the need to start the process by ascertaining the values of the remains to all who have a stake in that asset (site) (Clark 2001; Cadw 2011) (see Figure 5.0.1). Demas (2000) and de la Torre (2002) have explored the concept in a more rounded sense as a fundamental approach to conservation: 'Many of the problems facing archaeological sites today ... are rarely capable of being solved definitively, but can be managed' (Demas 2000: 27) (see Figure 5.0.2).

Though the term value is used in documents such as the Venice Charter (1964), it becomes explicit in the 1980s with the development of cultural resource management (CRM), the work of Lipe (1974, 1984) and the Burra Charter process (1979–1999) (Clark 2012). The term value is normally used to refer to some measure of the importance that present-day human beings ascribe to an object. Mason and Avrami (2000) suggested that this list included: historic value, aesthetic value, social (or civic) value, spiritual or religious value, symbolic or identity value, research value, nature value and economic value. English Heritage (2008) suggests that the 'significance' of a place will be established through its heritage values, which are considered in four categories:

- *Evidential values*: the capacity to provide physical evidence of the human past.
- *Historical values*: the associations that people and events have with the place including connecting the past to the present.
- *Aesthetic values*: sensory and intellectual stimulation the place provides.
- *Communal values*: what the place means to those who live there, those who use it and those who have memory or experience of it.

From these values spring a series of specific heritage significances; the fabric and how it formed, who values the place and why, the heritage value of the fabric, the contribution that objects, landscape and context make to the place, the relative importance of these values in comparison to similar places. These can be summarised in a statement of overall heritage significance. If the assessment of value is to be accurate, all stakeholders (those who value the remains) need to contribute to the valuation process. But, who is a valid stakeholder, just someone with an opinion? Does there need to be some test of validity or worthiness before you can be considered a stakeholder? Who decides (Grabow et al. 2007)? Also, what is the scale/framework on which such values are articulated? Values are highly subjective – as Riegl noted in 1903, 'It is modern viewers rather than the works themselves by their original purpose

Stages in Conservation-Based Research and Analysis

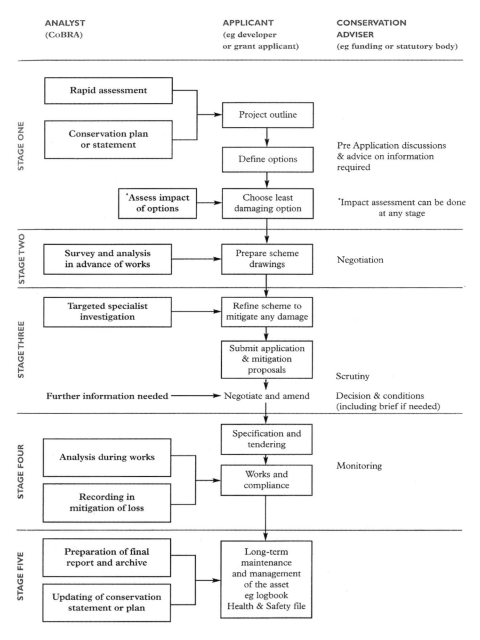

Figure 5.0.1 Stages in the Conservation-Based Research and Analysis (CoBRA) approach advocated by English Heritage for conservation work on historic buildings.

Source: Clark (2001: 43)

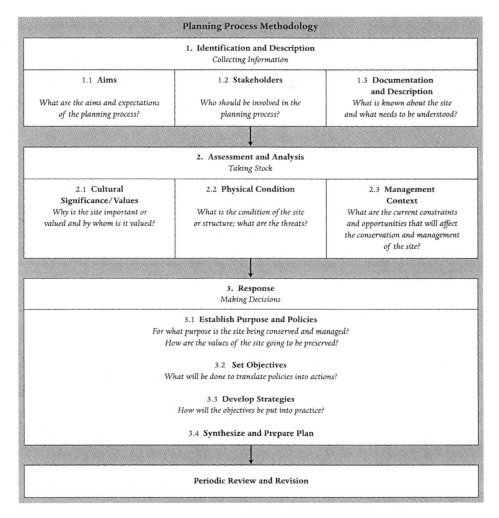

Figure 5.0.2 Flow chart showing values-based planning methodology for conservation and management planning advocated by Getty Conservation Institute (GCI).

Source: Demas (2000: 30)

that assign meaning and significance to a monument'. These individual values are invariably expressed in different ways: financial (dollars, euros, yen), popularity (visitor numbers), influence (citations or references), emotional response (statements about beauty), etc. How do you assess, relate or balance such differing values to reach a conclusion (Mason and Avrami 2000: 25)? This is part of a larger issue about how governments place 'value' on culture (Holden 2004).

At a crude level, heritage organisations need to distribute resources among a number of sites, thus there is a need to rank them based on an appropriate value system. Since we are used to using numbers, all values may be converted into a numerical equivalent and then summed and ranked. An example is provided by English Heritage's assessment of archaeological sites for legal protection (Monument Protection Programme) in the early 1990s. Here, academic/historic values were the key aspect of the sites that needed consideration. In what is a relatively straightforward example, a series of subcategory values, survival, information potential, diversity of features, documentation (archaeological), documentation (historic), associations, group value and the site's amenity value, were considered. It was recognised that giving a 'financial' value to the various categories was inappropriate, so a simple numerical relative scale (1–3) or (1,2) was used. These simple numerical values, which were squared to increase numerical separation, were considered equally important, so they could be totalled and the result used as a basis for selection. Subsequently, any additional 'important' information was added to the process before a final selection was made (Startin 1993). This is termed the site's 'national importance', in order to meet the terms of the 1979 Ancient Monuments Amendment Act.

The importance of identification, classification and inventorisation of sites cannot be overemphasised. Any attempt at a 'values-based' conservation planning process needs to understand how many sites of different types there are, their different features and scarcity. Such knowledge increases objectivity and transparency ensuring that scarce resources are focused on the most significant (valued) sites. Aspects such as sustainability (consuming minimal resources to continue the preservation of the remains into the future) can also be thought of as a value, and incorporated into the valuation process (Throsby 2002).

One of the crucial steps in this process is the creation of a clear statement of significance about the site that accurately reflects the values of various individuals and groups of the site. This statement, such as the one for Chan Chan (Castellanos 2000), provides a rallying point for future plans and actions, as well as a departure point for planning conservation actions. However, as sites such as Petra show, having reports and plans does not guarantee the appropriate protection from development (Akrawi 2000). Legal and economic powers must be provided if an organisation is to be truly effective, or else the plans will not be fully implemented and the site will suffer encroachment and exploitation.

Though much debated, determining values is only one step in the decision-making process (Nardi 1994). Considerable effort is also required to fully record the surviving remains and understand the decay processes, which, as Cather (2003), using the example of wall paintings, has noted, have often been poorly understood in the past.

In previous generations, it can be suggested that values-based 'planning methodology for conservation and management' occurred naturally in the heads of experienced archaeologists,

INITIAL PHASE	SECOND PHASE	FINAL PHASE
A: Identify stakeholders and ascertain values (tangible and intangible) Create a statement of significance (value) **B:** Record physical remains Research / analyse remains Identify decay processes Determine threats and prognosis Identify relevant laws, charters, organisations, codes Ascertain resources available	**A**: Create clear **aims** and **objectives** for the remains / project Achieve agreement of all stakeholders to aims and objectives **B**: Create a **plan** (strategy) to achieve stated aims and objectives (This normally includes costs and times) Access resources	**A**: Undertake work Review and amend plan as required **B**: Upon completion write report identifying the work done Amended record of the physical remains Review process – have all the values been preserved or enhanced?

Figure 5.0.3 Simplified sequence of values-based planning activities for site preservation.

heritage architects and inspectors of ancient monuments who were responsible for archaeological sites. They worked out who had interests in the site, consulted them, ascertained what resources were available, initiated any research and recording required for the site, then drew up a plan and initiated activity. All of this could happen quickly, with little record, sometimes just hastily scribbled on the back of an envelope. The experience is now formalised and transparent in this values-based planning approach. This enables it to be taught to new practitioners, seen and shown to have occurred to those who do not trust large heritage agencies. It can appear a slow, costly cumbersome process, with large levels of management and paperwork, especially in large organisations. For smaller-scale sites and projects, a simplified form of values-based planning can be used (see Figure 5.0.3).

The skill of the heritage professional in conservation planning is often in dealing with the conflicts that emerge during the valuation process (Clark 2012), as well as the traditional problems of accurately determining the decay mechanisms, coping with limited resources to enact conservation, and ensuring maintenance and long-term sustainability of the remains.

Conservation practice

The recording and analysis process determines the physical nature of the remains; the valuation process reveals what we perceive them to be and to mean. Conservation activities have traditionally been focused on meeting the physical, chemical and biological threats to the integrity of the remains. In practice, since many threats (see Chapter 2) are created by present-day society, changing the value these remains have to the present (e.g. increasing knowledge and awareness of them and their importance in the past may affect preservation without the need for costly physical intervention). Raising such social/cultural valuation may be particularly valuable in ensuring sustainability, capable of generating sufficient value to local, regional or national organisations or individuals that resources are allocated to secure its physical and cultural future.

A simple example of knowledge changing values is provided by the doors of Durham Cathedral. In 1991, as the 900th anniversary celebrations for the founding of Durham Cathedral approached, the cathedral authorities sought to enable the north doors to be opened for processions and to give them an impressive new coat of black paint. Conservation work comprised dating of the doors. They were shown to be twelfth century, original and as old as the stonework which surrounded them. On their exterior were paint layers dating back to the seventeenth century (Caple 1999, 2006). This evidence of original fabric dissuaded the authorities from repainting. A preservation process had been affected simply by generating new information; the value of the doors had been changed. Knowledge is a highly effective tool for enacting 'conservation', and thus, for example, excavation of a site revealing its antiquity or important architectural features could potentially be the most effective tool in preserving it. Undertaking an oral history project or creating a good guidebook making local people aware of their ancient remains could be equally effective. Research is, like recording the physical remains, an essential prerequisite to any conservation work. Subsequent mitigation and protection activities, which emerge as necessary for the preservation of the remains from the planning process, are then enacted. These may include legal protection (see Chapter 4) or mitigation measures to preserve the physical remains, which are explored in greater detail in Chapters 6–14.

Bibliography

Akrawi, A. (2000) 'Petra, Jordan', in J.M. Teutonico and G. Palumbo (eds), *Management Planning for Archaeological Sites*, Los Angeles, CA: GCI, pp. 98–112.
Appelbaum, B. (2007) *Conservation Treatment Methodology*, Oxford: Butterworth-Heinemann.
Buchanan, A. (2013) *Robert Willis and the Foundation of Architectural History*, Woodbridge: Boydell Press.
Cadw (2011) *Conservation Principles*, Cardiff: Cadw, available at: http://cadw.wales.gov.uk/docs/cadw/publications/Conservation_Principles_EN.pdf (accessed February 2015).
Caple, C. (1999) 'The cathedral doors', *Durham Archaeological Journal*, 14–15: 131–40.
Caple, C. (2000) *Conservation Skills: Judgement, Method and Decision Making*, London: Routledge.
Caple, C. (2006) *Objects: Reluctant Witnesses to the Past*, London: Routledge.
Caple, C. (2009) 'The aims of conservation', in A. Braker and A. Richmond (eds), *Conservation: Principles, Dilemmas and Uncomfortable Truths*, London: Butterworth-Heinemann, pp. 25–31.
Caple, C. (2011) *Preventive Conservation in Museums*, London: Routledge.
Castellanos, C. (2000) 'Chan Chan, Peru', in J.M. Teutonico and G. Palumbo (eds), *Management Planning for Archaeological Sites*, Los Angeles, CA: GCI, pp. 68–82.
Cather, S. (2003) 'Assessing causes and mechanisms of detrimental change to wall paintings', in W. Gowing and A. Heritage (eds), *Conserving the Painted Past: Developing Approaches to Wall Painting Conservation*, London: James & James, pp. 64–71.
Clark, G. (1957) *Archaeology and Society*, 3rd edn, London: Methuen.
Chamberlin, E.R. (1979) *Preserving the Past*, London: J.M. Dent & Sons.
Clark, K. (2001) *Informed Conservation*, London: English Heritage.
Clark, K. (2012) 'The bigger picture: archaeology and values in long-term cultural resource management', in S. Sullivan and R. Mackay (eds), *Archaeological Sites: Conservation and Management*, Readings in Conservation, Los Angeles: GCI, pp. 105–19.
Cooke, L. (2010) 'Conservation, management and heritage studies', in *Conservation Approaches to Earthen Architecture in Archaeological Contexts*, BAR International Series 2147, Oxford: Archaeopress, pp. 50–60.
Council of Europe (1992) *Details of Treaty No. 143*, available at: conventions.coe.int/Treaty/en/Treaties/Html/143.htm (accessed August 2014).
de la Torre, M. (2002) *Assessing the Values of Cultural Heritage*, Los Angeles, CA: GCI.
Demas, M. (2000) 'Planning for conservation and management of archaeological sites: a values based approach', in J.M. Teutonico and G. Palumbo (eds), *Management Planning for Archaeological Sites*, Los Angeles, CA: GCI, pp. 27–54.
Dickens, C. (1875) *Great Expectations*, London: Chapman & Hall.
Eggert, P. (2009) *Securing the Past*, Cambridge: Cambridge University Press.
Egloff, B. and Comer, D.C. (2012) 'Conserving the archaeological soul of places: drafting guidelines for the ICAHM Charter', in S. Sullivan and R. Mackay (eds), *Archaeological Sites: Conservation and Management*, Readings in Conservation, Los Angeles, CA: GCI, pp. 149–61.
English Heritage (2008) *Conservation Principles Policies and Guidance*, London: English Heritage, available at: www.english-heritage.org.uk/professional/advice/conservation-principles/ConservationPrinciples/ (accessed August 2014).
Gilberg, M. (1987) 'Friedrich Rathgen: the father of modern archaeological conservation', *Journal of the American Institute for Conservation*, 26(2): 105–20.
Grabow, S., Hull, D. and Waterton, E. (2007) *Which Past, Whose Future?* BAR International Series 1633, Oxford: Archaeopress.
Holden, J. (2004) *Capturing Cultural Value: How Culture Has Become a Tool of Government Policy*, London: Demos.
ICOMOS Australia (n.d.) *Charters*, available at: http://australia.icomos.org/publications/charters/ (accessed August 2014).
ICOMOS Charters website (n.d.) www.icomos.org/en/charters-and-texts (accessed August 2014).
Jokilehto, J. (1999) *A History of Architectural Conservation*, Oxford: Butterworth Heinemann.
Jokilehto, J. (2007) 'Conservation concepts', in J. Ashurst (ed.), *Conservation of Ruins*, Oxford: Butterworth-Heinemann, pp. 1–9.
Lipe, W.D. (1974) 'A conservation model for American archaeology', *Kiva*, 39(3/4): 213–45.
Lipe, W.D. (1984) 'Value and meaning in culture resources', in H. Cleere (ed.), *Approaches to the Archaeological Heritage*, Cambridge: Cambridge University Press.
Mason, R. and Avrami, E. (2000) 'Heritage values and challenges of conservation planning', in J.M. Teutonico and G. Palumbo (eds), *Management Planning for Archaeological Sites*, Los Angeles, CA: GCI, pp. 13–26.

Morris, W. (1877) 'The principles of the Society (for the Protection of Ancient Buildings) as set forth upon its foundation', *Builder*, 35, 25 August. Republished as 'Manifesto of the Society for the Protection of Ancient Buildings', in N. Stanley Price, M. Kirby Talley Jr. and A.M. Vaccaro (eds), *Historical and Philosophical Issues in the Conservation of Cultural Heritage*, Los Angeles, CA: The Getty Conservation Institute, pp. 319–21.

Nardi, R. (1994) 'The first steps in preventive conservation: the analysis of the problem', in A. Alarcao, V.H. Correia and C. Beloto (eds), *Conservation Protection Presentation: Fifth Conference of the International Committee for the Conservation of Mosaics, Conimbriga 1994*, Lisbon: Instituto Portugues Museus, pp. 185–94.

Podany, J. (1994) 'Restoring what wasn't there: reconsideration of the eighteenth-century restorations to the Lansdowne Herakles in the collection of the J Paul Getty Museum', in A. Oddy (ed.), *Restoration: Is It Acceptable?* British Museum Occasional Paper No. 99, London: British Museum, pp. 9–18.

Riegl, A. (1903) *Der modern Denkmalkultus: Sein Wesenund seine Entstehung*, Vienna: W. Braumuller. Republished as 'The modern cult of monuments: its essence and its development', in N. Stanley Price, M. Kirby Talley Jr. and A.M. Vaccaro (eds), *Historical and Philosophical Issues in the Conservation of Cultural Heritage*, Los Angeles, CA: The Getty Conservation Institute, pp. 69–83.

Ruskin, J. (1849) *The Seven Lamps of Architecture*, London: Allen & Sons.

Schiffer, M.B. and Gumerman, G.J. (1977) *Conservation Archaeology: A Guide for Cultural Resource Management Studies*, London: Academic Press.

Stanley-Price, N. (1995) *Conservation on Archaeological Excavations*, Rome: ICCROM.

Startin, W. (1993) 'Assessment of field remains', in J. Hunter and I. Ralston (eds), *Archaeological Resource Management in the UK*, Stroud: Alan Sutton, pp. 184–96.

Strong, D.E. (1973) 'Roman museums', in D.E. Strong (ed.), *Archaeological Theory and Practice*, London: Seminar Press, pp. 247–64.

Thomas, A. (1998) 'Restoration or renovation: remuneration and expectation in Renaissance "acconciatura"', in C. Sitwell and S. Staniforth (eds), *Studies in the History of Painting Restoration*, London: Archetype, pp. 1–14.

Thompson, M. (1981) *Ruins: Their Preservation and Display*, London: British Museum.

Throsby, D. (2002) 'Cultural capital and sustainability concepts in the economics of cultural heritage 2002', in M. de la Torre (ed.), *Assessing the Values of Cultural Heritage*, Los Angeles, CA: GCI, pp. 101–17.

UNESCO (1956) *Recommendation on International Principles Applicable to Archaeological Excavations*, available at: http://portal.unesco.org/en/ev.php-URL_ID=13062&URL_DO=DO_TOPIC&URL_SECTION=201.html (accessed August 2014).

UNESCO (1972) *The World Heritage Convention*, available at: http://whc.unesco.org/en/convention/ (accessed August 2014).

UNESCO (2003) *Text of the Convention for the Safeguarding of the Intangible Cultural Heritage*, available at: www.unesco.org/culture/ich/index.php?lg=en&pg=00006 (accessed August 2014).

Wei, C. and Aass, A. (1989) 'Heritage conservation East and West', *ICOMOS Information*, 3: 3–8, ICOMOS website, available at: www.icomos.org/publications/ICOMOS_Information/1989-3.pdf (accessed December 2014).

Chapter 5.1

Manifesto of the Society for the Protection of Ancient Buildings

William Morris

Source: Morris, W. (1877) 'The principles of the Society (for the Protection of Ancient Buildings) as set forth upon its foundation', *Builder*, 35.

[...]

No DOUBT WITHIN THE LAST FIFTY YEARS a new interest, almost like another sense, has arisen in these ancient monuments of art; and they have become the subject of one of the most interesting of studies, and of an enthusiasm, religious, historical, artistic, which is one of the undoubted gains of our time; yet we think that if the present treatment of them be continued, our descendants will find them useless for study and chilling to enthusiasm. We think that those last fifty years of knowledge and attention have done more for their destruction than all the foregoing centuries of revolution, violence, and contempt.

For Architecture, long decaying, died out, as a popular art at least, just as the knowledge of mediaeval art was born. So that the civilized world of the nineteenth century has no style of its own amidst its wide knowledge of the styles of other centuries. From this lack and this gain arose in men's minds the strange idea of the Restoration of ancient buildings; and a strange and most fatal idea, which by its very name implies that it is possible to strip from a building this, that, and the other part of its history—of its life that is—and then to stay the hand at some arbitrary point, and leave it still historical, living, and even as it once was.

In early times this kind of forgery was impossible, because knowledge failed the builders, or perhaps because instinct held them back. If repairs were needed, if ambition or piety pricked on to change, that change was of necessity wrought in the unmistakable fashion of the time; a church of the eleventh century might be added to or altered in the twelfth, thirteenth, fourteenth, fifteenth, sixteenth, or even the seventeenth or eighteenth centuries; but every change, whatever history it destroyed, left history in the gap, and was alive with the spirit of the deeds done midst its fashioning. The result of all this was often a building in which the many changes, though harsh and visible enough, were, by their very contrast, interesting and instructive and could by no possibility mislead. But those who make the changes wrought in our day under the name of Restoration, while professing to bring back a building to the best time of its history, have no guide but each his own individual whim to point out to them what is admirable and what contemptible; while the very nature of their task compels them to destroy something and to supply the gap by imagining what the earlier builders should or might have done. Moreover, in the course of this double process of destruction and addition the whole surface of the building is necessarily tampered with; so that the appearance of antiquity is taken away from such old parts of the fabric as are left, and there is no laying to rest in the spectator the suspicion of what may have been lost; and in short, a feeble and lifeless forgery is the final result of all the wasted labour.

It is sad to say, that in this manner most of the bigger Ministers, and a vast number of more humble buildings, both in England and on the Continent, have been dealt with by men of talent often, and worthy of better employment, but deaf to the claims of poetry and history in the highest sense of the words.

For what is left we plead before our architects themselves, before the official guardians of buildings, and before the public generally, and we pray them to remember how much is gone of the religion, thought and manners of time past, never by almost universal consent, to be Restored; and to consider whether it be possible to Restore those buildings, the living spirit of which, it cannot be too often repeated, was an inseparable part of that religion and thought, and those past manners. For our part we assure them fearlessly, that of all the Restorations yet undertaken the worst have meant the reckless stripping a building of some of its most interesting material features; while the best have their exact analogy in the Restoration of an old picture, where the partly-perished work of the ancient crafts master has been made neat and smooth by the tricky hand of some unoriginal and thoughtless hack of today. If, for the rest, it be asked us to specify what kind of amount of art, style, or other interest in a building, makes it worth protecting, we answer, anything which can be looked on as artistic, picturesque, historical, antique, or substantial: any work in short, over which educated, artistic people would think it worthwhile to argue at all.

It is for all these buildings, therefore, of all times and styles, that we plead, and call upon those who have to deal with them to put Protection in the place of Restoration, to stave off decay by daily care, to prop a perilous wall or mend a leaky roof by such means as are obviously meant for support or covering, and show no pretence of other art, and otherwise to resist all tampering with either the fabric or ornament of the building as it stands; if it has become inconvenient for its present use, to raise another building rather than alter or enlarge the old one; in fine to treat our ancient buildings as monuments of a bygone art, created by bygone manners, that modern art cannot meddle with without destroying.

Thus, and thus only, shall we escape the reproach of our learning being turned into a snare to us; thus, and thus only can we protect our ancient buildings, and hand them down instructive and venerable to those that come after us.

Chapter 5.2

International Charter for the Conservation and Restoration of Monuments and Sites (The Venice Charter 1964)

IInd International Congress of Architects and Technicians of Historic Monuments, Venice, 1964. Adopted by ICOMOS in 1965

ICOMOS

Source: ICOMOS (1966) *International Charter for the Conservation and Restoration of Monuments and Sites (The Venice Charter 1964)*.

IMBUED WITH A MESSAGE from the past, the historic monuments of generations of people remain to the present day as living witnesses of their age-old traditions. People are becoming more and more conscious of the unity of human values and regard ancient monuments as a common heritage. The common responsibility to safeguard them for future generations is recognized. It is our duty to hand them on in the full richness of their authenticity.

It is essential that the principles guiding the preservation and restoration of ancient buildings should be agreed and be laid down on an international basis, with each country being responsible for applying the plan within the framework of its own culture and traditions.

By defining these basic principles for the first time, the Athens Charter of 1931 contributed towards the development of an extensive international movement which has assumed concrete form in national documents, in the work of ICOM and UNESCO and in the establishment by the latter of the International Centre for the Study of the Preservation and the Restoration of Cultural Property (ICCROM). Increasing awareness and critical study have been brought to bear on problems which have continually become more complex and varied; now the time has come to examine the Charter afresh in order to make a thorough study of the principles involved and to enlarge its scope in a new document.

[...]

Definitions

Article 1

The concept of a historic monument embraces not only the single architectural work but also the urban or rural setting in which is found the evidence of a particular civilization, a significant development or a historic event. This applies not only to great works of art but also to more modest works of the past which have acquired cultural significance with the passing of time.

Article 2

The conservation and restoration of monuments must have recourse to all the sciences and techniques which can contribute to the study and safeguarding of the architectural heritage.

Article 3

The intention in conserving and restoring monuments is to safeguard them no less as works of art than as historical evidence.

Conservation

Article 4

It is essential to the conservation of monuments that they be maintained on a permanent basis.

Article 5

The conservation of monuments is always facilitated by making use of them for some socially useful purpose. Such use is therefore desirable but it must not change the layout or decoration of the building. It is within these limits only that modifications demanded by a change of function should be envisaged and may be permitted.

Article 6

The conservation of a monument implies preserving a setting which is not out of scale. Wherever the traditional setting exists, it must be kept. No new construction, demolition or modification which would alter the relations of mass and colour must be allowed.

Article 7

A monument is inseparable from the history to which it bears witness and from the setting in which it occurs. The moving of all or part of a monument cannot be allowed except where the safeguarding of that monument demands it or where it is justified by national or international interest of paramount importance.

Article 8

Items of sculpture, painting or decoration which form an integral part of a monument may only be removed from it if this is the sole means of ensuring their preservation.

Restoration

Article 9

The process of restoration is a highly specialized operation. Its aim is to preserve and reveal the aesthetic and historic value of the monument and is based on respect for original material and authentic documents. It must stop at the point where conjecture begins, and in this case moreover any extra work which is indispensable must be distinct from the architectural composition and must bear a contemporary stamp. The restoration in any case must be preceded and followed by an archaeological and historical study of the monument.

Article 10

Where traditional techniques prove inadequate, the consolidation of a monument can be achieved by the use of any modern technique for conservation and construction, the efficacy of which has been shown by scientific data and proved by experience.

Article 11

The valid contributions of all periods to the building of a monument must be respected, since unity of style is not the aim of a restoration. When a building includes the superimposed work of different periods, the revealing of the underlying state can only be justified in exceptional circumstances and when what is removed is of little interest and the material which is brought to light is of great historical, archaeological or aesthetic value, and its state of preservation good enough to justify the action. Evaluation of the importance of the elements involved and the decision as to what may be destroyed cannot rest solely on the individual in charge of the work.

Article 12

Replacements of missing parts must integrate harmoniously with the whole, but at the same time must be distinguishable from the original so that restoration does not falsify the artistic or historic evidence.

Article 13

Additions cannot be allowed except in so far as they do not detract from the interesting parts of the building, its traditional setting, the balance of its composition and its relation with its surroundings.

Historic sites

Article 14

The sites of monuments must be the object of special care in order to safeguard their integrity and ensure that they are cleared and presented in a seemly manner. The work of conservation and restoration carried out in such places should be inspired by the principles set forth in the foregoing articles.

Excavations

Article 15

Excavations should be carried out in accordance with scientific standards and the recommendation defining international principles to be applied in the case of archaeological excavation adopted by UNESCO in 1956.

Ruins must be maintained and measures necessary for the permanent conservation and protection of architectural features and of objects discovered must be taken. Furthermore, every means must be taken to facilitate the understanding of the monument and to reveal it without ever distorting its meaning.

All reconstruction work should however be ruled out "*a priori.*" Only anastylosis, that is to say, the reassembling of existing but dismembered parts can be permitted. The material used for integration should always be recognizable and its use should be the least that will ensure the conservation of a monument and the reinstatement of its form.

Publication

Article 16

In all works of preservation, restoration or excavation, there should always be precise documentation in the form of analytical and critical reports, illustrated with drawings and photographs. Every stage of the work of clearing, consolidation, rearrangement and integration, as well as technical and formal features identified during the course of the work, should be included. This record should be placed in the archives of a public institution and made available to research workers. It is recommended that the report should be published.

European Convention on the Protection of the Archaeological Heritage (Revised)

Council of Europe

Source: Council of Europe (1992) *European Convention on the Protection of the Archaeological Heritage*, Valletta 1992.

THE MEMBER STATES of the Council of Europe and the other States party to the European Cultural Convention signatory hereto, [...]
Have agreed as follows:

Definition of the archaeological heritage

Article 1

1. The aim of this (revised) Convention is to protect the archaeological heritage as a source of the European collective memory and as an instrument for historical and scientific study.
2. To this end shall be considered to be elements of the archaeological heritage all remains and objects and any other traces of mankind from past epochs:

[...]

3. The archaeological heritage shall include structures, constructions, groups of buildings, developed sites, moveable objects, monuments of other kinds as well as their context, whether situated on land or under water.

Identification of the heritage and measures for protection

Article 2

Each Party undertakes to institute, by means appropriate to the State in question, a legal system for the protection of the archaeological heritage, making provision for:

i. the maintenance of an inventory of its archaeological heritage and the designation of protected monuments and areas;
ii. the creation of archaeological reserves, even where there are no visible remains on the ground or under water, for the preservation of material evidence to be studied by later generations;
iii. the mandatory reporting to the competent authorities by a finder of the chance discovery of elements of the archaeological heritage and making them available for examination.

Article 3

To preserve the archaeological heritage and guarantee the scientific significance of archaeological research work, each Party undertakes:

i. to apply procedures for the authorisation and supervision of excavation and other archaeological activities in such a way as:
   a. to prevent any illicit excavation or removal of elements of the archaeological heritage;
   b. to ensure that archaeological excavations and prospecting are undertaken in a scientific manner and provided that:
      – non-destructive methods of investigation are applied wherever possible;
      – the elements of the archaeological heritage are not uncovered or left exposed during or after excavation without provision being made for their proper preservation, conservation and management;
ii. to ensure that excavations and other potentially destructive techniques are carried out only by qualified, specially authorised persons;
iii. to subject to specific prior authorisation, whenever foreseen by the domestic law of the State, the use of metal detectors and any other detection equipment or process for archaeological investigation.

Article 4

Each Party undertakes to implement measures for the physical protection of the archaeological heritage, making provision, as circumstances demand:

i. for the acquisition or protection by other appropriate means by the authorities of areas intended to constitute archaeological reserves;
ii. for the conservation and maintenance of the archaeological heritage, preferably *in situ*;
iii. for appropriate storage places for archaeological remains which have been removed from their original location.

Integrated conservation of the archaeological heritage

Article 5

Each Party undertakes:

i. to seek to reconcile and combine the respective requirements of archaeology and development plans by ensuring that archaeologists participate in planning policies designed to ensure well-balanced strategies for the protection, conservation and enhancement of sites of archaeological interest;
ii. in the various stages of development schemes;
iii. to ensure that archaeologists, town and regional planners systematically consult one another in order to permit;
iv. the modification of development plans likely to have adverse effects on the archaeological heritage;
v. the allocation of sufficient time and resources for an appropriate scientific study to be made of the site and for its findings to be published;
vi. to ensure that environmental impact assessments and the resulting decisions involve full consideration of archaeological sites and their settings;
vii. to make provision, when elements of the archaeological heritage have been found during development work, for their conservation *in situ* when feasible;
viii. to ensure that the opening of archaeological sites to the public, especially any structural arrangements necessary for the reception of large numbers of visitors, does not adversely affect the archaeological and scientific character of such sites and their surroundings.

Financing of archaeological research and conservation

Article 6

Each Party undertakes:

i. to arrange for public financial support for archaeological research from national, regional and local authorities in accordance with their respective competence;
ii. to increase the material resources for rescue archaeology:
   a. by taking suitable measures to ensure that provision is made in major public or private development schemes for covering, from public sector or private sector resources, as appropriate, the total costs of any necessary related archaeological operations;
   b. by making provision in the budget relating to these schemes in the same way as for the impact studies necessitated by environmental and regional planning precautions, for preliminary archaeological study and prospection, for a scientific summary record as well as for the full publication and recording of the findings.

Collection and dissemination of scientific information

Article 7

For the purpose of facilitating the study of, and dissemination of knowledge about, archaeological discoveries, each Party undertakes:

i. to make or bring up to date surveys, inventories and maps of archaeological sites in the areas within its jurisdiction;
ii. to take all practical measures to ensure the drafting, following archaeological operations, of a publishable scientific summary record before the necessary comprehensive publication of specialised studies.

Article 8

Each Party undertakes:

i. to facilitate the national and international exchange of elements of the archaeological heritage for professional scientific purposes while taking appropriate steps to ensure that such circulation in no way prejudices the cultural and scientific value of those elements;
ii. to promote the pooling of information on archaeological research and excavations in progress and to contribute to the organisation of international research programmes.

Promotion of public awareness

Article 9

Each Party undertakes:

i. to conduct educational actions with a view to rousing and developing an awareness in public opinion of the value of the archaeological heritage for understanding the past and of the threats to this heritage;
ii. to promote public access to important elements of its archaeological heritage, especially sites, and encourage the display to the public of suitable selections of archaeological objects.

Prevention of the illicit circulation of elements of the archaeological heritage

Article 10

Each Party undertakes:

i. to arrange for the relevant public authorities and for scientific institutions to pool information on any illicit excavations identified;

ii. to inform the competent authorities in the State of origin which is a Party to this Convention of any offer suspected of coming either from illicit excavations or unlawfully from official excavations, and to provide the necessary details thereof;
iii. to take such steps as are necessary to ensure that museums and similar institutions whose acquisition policy is under State control do not acquire elements of the archaeological heritage suspected of coming from uncontrolled finds or illicit excavations or unlawfully from official excavations;
iv. as regards museums and similar institutions located in the territory of a Party but the acquisition policy of which is not under State control, to convey to them the text of this (revised) Convention;
v. to spare no effort to ensure respect by the said museums and institutions for the principles set out in paragraph iii above;
vi. to restrict, as far as possible, by education, information, vigilance and cooperation, the transfer of elements of the archaeological heritage obtained from uncontrolled finds or illicit excavations or unlawfully from official excavations.

Article 11

Nothing in this (revised) Convention shall affect existing or future bilateral or multilateral treaties between Parties, concerning the illicit circulation of elements of the archaeological heritage or their restitution to the rightful owner.

Mutual technical and scientific assistance

Article 12

The Parties undertake:

i. to afford mutual technical and scientific assistance through the pooling of experience and exchanges of experts in matters concerning the archaeological heritage;
ii. to encourage, under the relevant national legislation or international agreements binding them, exchanges of specialists in the preservation of the archaeological heritage, including those responsible for further training.

Chapter 5.4

The Nara Document on Authenticity

UNESCO

Source: UNESCO (1994) *Nara Document on Authenticity*.

Preamble

[...]

3.

THE NARA DOCUMENT ON AUTHENTICITY is conceived in the spirit of the Charter of Venice, 1964, and builds on it and extends it in response to the expanding scope of cultural heritage concerns and interests in our contemporary world.

4.

In a world that is increasingly subject to the forces of globalization and homogenization, and in a world in which the search for cultural identity is sometimes pursued through aggressive nationalism and the suppression of the cultures of minorities, the essential contribution made by the consideration of authenticity in conservation practice is to clarify and illuminate the collective memory of humanity.

Cultural diversity and heritage diversity

5.

The diversity of cultures and heritage in our world is an irreplaceable source of spiritual and intellectual richness for all humankind. The protection and enhancement of cultural and heritage diversity in our world should be actively promoted as an essential aspect of human development.

6.

Cultural heritage diversity exists in time and space, and demands respect for other cultures and all aspects of their belief systems. In cases where cultural values appear to be in conflict, respect for cultural diversity demands acknowledgment of the legitimacy of the cultural values of all parties.

7.

All cultures and societies are rooted in the particular forms and means of tangible and intangible expression which constitute their heritage, and these should be respected.

8.

It is important to underline a fundamental principle of UNESCO, to the effect that the cultural heritage of each is the cultural heritage of all. Responsibility for cultural heritage and the management of it belongs, in the first place, to the cultural community that has generated it, and subsequently to that which cares for it. However, in addition to these responsibilities, adherence to the international charters and conventions developed for conservation of cultural heritage also obliges consideration of the principles and responsibilities flowing from them. Balancing their own requirements with those of other cultural communities is, for each community, highly desirable, provided achieving this balance does not undermine their fundamental cultural values.

Values and authenticity

9.

Conservation of cultural heritage in all its forms and historical periods is rooted in the values attributed to the heritage. Our ability to understand these values depends, in part, on the degree to which information sources about these values may be understood as credible or truthful. Knowledge and understanding of these sources of information, in relation to original and subsequent characteristics of the cultural heritage, and their meaning, is a requisite basis for assessing all aspects of authenticity.

10.

Authenticity, considered in this way and affirmed in the Charter of Venice, appears as the essential qualifying factor concerning values. The understanding of authenticity plays a fundamental role in all scientific studies of the cultural heritage, in conservation and restoration planning, as well as within the inscription procedures used for the World Heritage Convention and other cultural heritage inventories.

11.

All judgements about values attributed to cultural properties as well as the credibility of related information sources may differ from culture to culture, and even within the same culture. It is thus not possible to base judgements of values and authenticity within fixed criteria. On the contrary, the respect due to all cultures requires that heritage properties must be considered and judged within the cultural contexts to which they belong.

12.

Therefore, it is of the highest importance and urgency that, within each culture, recognition be accorded to the specific nature of its heritage values and the credibility and truthfulness of related information sources.

13.

Depending on the nature of the cultural heritage, its cultural context, and its evolution through time, authenticity judgements may be linked to the worth of a great variety of sources of information. Aspects of the sources may include form and design, materials and substance, use and function, traditions and techniques, location and setting, and spirit and feeling, and other internal and external factors. The use of these sources permits elaboration of the specific artistic, historic, social, and scientific dimensions of the cultural heritage being examined.

Appendix 1

Suggestions for follow-up (proposed by H. Stovel)

1.

Respect for cultural and heritage diversity requires conscious efforts to avoid imposing mechanistic formulae or standardized procedures in attempting to define or determine authenticity of particular monuments and sites.

2.

Efforts to determine authenticity in a manner respectful of cultures and heritage diversity requires approaches which encourage cultures to develop analytical processes and tools specific to their nature and needs. Such approaches may have several aspects in common:

- efforts to ensure assessment of authenticity involve multidisciplinary collaboration and the appropriate utilization of all available expertise and knowledge;
- efforts to ensure attributed values are truly representative of a culture and the diversity of its interests, in particular monuments and sites;
- efforts to document clearly the particular nature of authenticity for monuments and sites as a practical guide to future treatment and monitoring;
- efforts to update authenticity assessments in light of changing values and circumstances.

3.

Particularly important are efforts to ensure that attributed values are respected, and that their determination includes efforts to build, as far as possible, a multidisciplinary and community consensus concerning these values.

4.

Approaches should also build on and facilitate international co-operation among all those with an interest in conservation of cultural heritage, in order to improve global respect and understanding for the diverse expressions and values of each culture.

5.

Continuation and extension of this dialogue to the various regions and cultures of the world is a prerequisite to increasing the practical value of consideration of authenticity in the conservation of the common heritage of humankind.

6.

Increasing awareness within the public of this fundamental dimension of heritage is an absolute necessity in order to arrive at concrete measures for safeguarding the vestiges of the past. This means developing greater understanding of the values represented by the cultural properties themselves, as well as respecting the role such monuments and sites play in contemporary society.

Appendix 2: Definitions

Conservation

All efforts designed to understand cultural heritage, know its history and meaning, ensure its material safeguard and, as required, its presentation, restoration and enhancement. (Cultural heritage is understood to include monuments, groups of buildings and sites of cultural value as defined in article one of the World Heritage Convention).

Chapter 5.5

The Burra Charter (1999)

Australian National Committee of ICOMOS

Source: Australia ICOMOS (1999) *The Burra Charter*.

Preamble

[...]

THE BURRA CHARTER PROVIDES guidance for the conservation and management of places of cultural significance (cultural heritage places), and is based on the knowledge and experience of Australia ICOMOS members.

[...]

What places does the Charter apply to?

The Charter can be applied to all types of places of cultural significance including natural, indigenous and historic places with cultural values.

[...]

Why conserve?

Places of cultural significance enrich people's lives, often providing a deep and inspirational sense of connection to community and landscape, to the past and to lived experiences. They are historical records, that are important as tangible expressions of Australian identity and experience. Places of cultural significance reflect the diversity of our communities, telling us about who we are and the past that has formed us and the Australian landscape. They are irreplaceable and precious.

These places of cultural significance must be conserved for present and future generations.

The Burra Charter advocates a cautious approach to change: do as much as necessary to care for the place and to make it useable, but otherwise change it as little as possible so that its cultural significance is retained.

Articles

Article 1. Definitions

For the purposes of this Charter:

1.1 *Place* means site, area, land, landscape, building or other work, group of buildings or other works, and may include components, contents, spaces and views.

1.2 *Cultural significance* means aesthetic, historic, scientific, social or spiritual value for past, present or future generations.

Cultural significance is embodied in the place itself, its fabric, setting, use, associations, meanings, records, related place and related objects.

Places may have a range of values for different individuals or groups.

1.3 *Fabric* means all the physical material of the *place* including components, fixtures, contents, and objects.

1.4 *Conservation* means all the processes of looking after a *place* so as to retain its *cultural significance*.

1.5 *Maintenance* means the continuous protective care of the *fabric* and *setting* of a *place*, and is to be distinguished from repair. Repair involves restoration or reconstruction.

1.6 *Preservation* means maintaining the *fabric* of a *place* in its existing state and retarding deterioration.

1.7 *Restoration* means returning the existing *fabric* of a *place* to a known earlier state by removing accretions or by reassembling existing components without the introduction of new material.

1.8 *Reconstruction* means returning a *place* to a known earlier state and is distinguished from *restoration* by the introduction of new material into the *fabric*.

1.9 *Adaptation* means modifying a *place* to suit the existing use or a proposed use.

1.10 *Use* means the functions of a place, as well as the activities and practices that may occur at the place.

1.11 *Compatible* use means a use which respects the *cultural significance* of a *place*. Such a use involves no, or minimal, impact on cultural significance.

1.12 *Setting* means the area around a *place*, which may include the visual catchment.

1.13 *Related place* means a place that contributes to the cultural *significance* of another place.

1.14 *Related object* means an object that contributes to the *cultural significance* of a *place* but is not at the place.

1.15 *Associations* mean the special connections that exist between people and a *place*.

1.16 *Meanings* denote what a *place* signifies, indicates, evokes or expresses.

1.17 *Interpretation* means all the ways of presenting the *cultural significance* of a *place*.

Conservation principles

Article 2. Conservation and management

2.1 *Places of cultural significance* should be conserved.

2.2 The aim of *conservation* is to retain the *cultural significance* of a *place*.

2.3 *Conservation* is an integral part of good management of *places* of *cultural significance*.

2.4 *Places* of *cultural significance* should be safeguarded and not put at risk or left in a vulnerable state.

Article 3. Cautious approach

3.1 *Conservation* is based on a respect for the existing *fabric*, *use*, *associations* and *meanings*. It requires a cautious approach of changing as much as necessary but as little as possible.

3.2 Changes to a *place* should not distort the physical or other evidence it provides, nor be based on conjecture.

Article 4. Knowledge, skills and techniques

4.1 *Conservation* should make use of all the knowledge, skills and disciplines which can contribute to the study and care of the *place*.

4.2 Traditional techniques and materials are preferred for the *conservation* of significant *fabric*. In some circumstances modern techniques and materials which offer substantial conservation benefits may be appropriate.

Article 5. Values

5.1 *Conservation* of a *place* should identify and take into consideration all aspects of cultural and natural significance without unwarranted emphasis on any one value at the expense of others.

5.2 Relative degrees of *cultural significance* may lead to different *conservation* actions at a place.

Article 6. Burra Charter process

6.1 The *cultural significance* of *a place* and other issues affecting its future are best understood by a sequence of collecting and analysing information before making decisions. Understanding cultural significance comes first, then development of policy and finally management of the place in accordance with the policy.

6.2 The policy for managing a place must be *based on* an understanding of its *cultural significance*.

6.3 Policy development should also include consideration of other factors affecting the future *of a place* such as the owner's needs, resources, external constraints and its physical condition.

Article 7. Use

7.1 Where the *use* of a place is of *cultural significance* it should be retained.

7.2 A *place* should have a *compatible* use.

Article 8. Setting

Conservation requires the retention of an appropriate visual *setting* and other relationships that contribute to the *cultural significance* of the *place*.

New construction, demolition, intrusions or other changes which would adversely affect the setting or relationships are not appropriate.

Article 9. Location

9.1 The physical location of a *place is* part of its *cultural significance*. A building, work or other component of a place should remain in its historical location. Relocation is generally unacceptable unless this is the sole practical means of ensuring its survival.

9.2 Some buildings, works or other components of *places* were designed to be readily removable or already have a history of relocation. Provided such buildings, works or other components do not have significant links with their present location, removal may be appropriate.

9.3 If any building, work or other component is moved, it should be moved to an appropriate location and given an appropriate use. Such action should not be to the detriment of any *place* of *cultural significance*.

Article 10. Contents

Contents, fixtures and objects which contribute to the *cultural significance* of a *place* should be retained at that place. Their removal is unacceptable unless it is: the sole means of ensuring their security and *preservation*; on a temporary basis for treatment or exhibition; for cultural reasons; for health and safety; or to protect the place. Such contents, fixtures and objects should be returned where circumstances permit and it is culturally appropriate.

Article 11. Related places and objects

The contribution which *related places* and *related objects* make to the *cultural significance* of the place should be retained.

Article 12. Participation

Conservation, *interpretation* and management of a *place* should provide for the participation of people for whom the place has special *associations* and *meanings*, or who have social, spiritual or other cultural responsibilities for the place.

Article 13. Co-existence of cultural values

Co-existence of cultural values should be recognised, respected and encouraged, especially in cases where they conflict.

Conservation processes

Article 14. Conservation processes

Conservation may, according to circumstance, include the processes of: retention or reintroduction of a *use*; retention of *associations* and *meanings*; *maintenance, preservation, restoration, reconstruction, adaptation* and *interpretation*; and will commonly include a combination of more than one of these.

Article 15. Change

15.1 Change may be necessary to retain *cultural significance*, but is undesirable where it reduces cultural significance. The amount of change to a *place* should be guided by the *cultural significance* of the place and its appropriate *interpretation*.

15.2 Changes which reduce *cultural significance* should be reversible, and be reversed when circumstances permit.

15.3 Demolition of significant *fabric* of a *place* is generally not acceptable. However, in some cases minor demolition may be appropriate as part of *conservation*. Removed significant fabric should be reinstated when circumstances permit.

15.4 The contributions of all aspects of *cultural significance* of a *place* should be respected. If a place includes *fabric*, *uses*, *associations* or *meanings* of different periods, or different aspects of cultural significance, emphasising or interpreting one period or aspect at the expense of another can only be justified when what is left out, removed or diminished is of slight cultural significance and that which is emphasised or interpreted is of much greater cultural significance.

Article 16. Maintenance

Maintenance is fundamental to *conservation* and should be undertaken where *fabric* is of *cultural significance* and its maintenance is necessary to retain that *cultural significance*.

Article 17. Preservation

Preservation is appropriate where the existing *fabric* or its condition constitutes evidence of *cultural significance*, or where insufficient evidence is available to allow other *conservation* processes to be carried out.

Article 18. Restoration and reconstruction

Restoration and *reconstruction* should reveal culturally significant aspects of the *place*.

Article 19. Restoration

Restoration is appropriate only if there is sufficient evidence of an earlier state of the *fabric*.

Article 20. Reconstruction

20.1 *Reconstruction* is appropriate only where a *place* is incomplete through damage or alteration, and only where there is sufficient evidence to reproduce an earlier state of the *fabric*. In rare cases, reconstruction may also be appropriate as part of a use or practice that retains *the cultural significance* of the place.

20.2 *Reconstruction* should be identifiable on close inspection or through additional *interpretation*.

Article 21. Adaptation

21.1 *Adaptation* is acceptable only where the adaptation has minimal impact on the *cultural significance* of the place.

21.2 *Adaptation* should involve minimal change to significant fabric, achieved only after considering alternatives.

Article 22. New work

22.1 New work such as additions to the place may be acceptable where it does not distort or obscure the *cultural significance* of the place, or detract from its *interpretation* and appreciation.

22.2 New work should be readily identifiable as such.

Article 23. Conserving use

Continuing, modifying or reinstating a significant *use* may be appropriate and preferred forms of *conservation*.

Article 24. Retaining associations and meanings

24.1 Significant *associations* between people and a *place* should be respected, retained and not obscured. Opportunities for the *interpretation*, commemoration and celebration of these associations should be investigated and implemented.

24.2 Significant *meanings*, including spiritual values, of a *place* should be respected. Opportunities for the continuation or revival of these meanings should be investigated and implemented.

Article 25. Interpretation

The *cultural significance* of many places is not readily apparent, and should be explained by *interpretation*. Interpretation should enhance understanding and enjoyment, and be culturally appropriate.

Conservation practice

Article 26. Applying the Burra Charter process

26.1 Work on a *place* should be preceded by studies to understand the place which should include analysis of physical, documentary, oral and other evidence, drawing on appropriate knowledge, skills and disciplines.

26.2 Written statements of *cultural significance* and policy for the *place* should be prepared, justified and accompanied by supporting evidence. The statements of significance and policy should be incorporated into a management plan for the place.

26.3 Groups and individuals with *associations* with a place as well as those involved in its management should be provided with opportunities to contribute to and participate in understanding the *cultural significance* of the place. Where appropriate they should also have opportunities to participate in its *conservation* and management.

Article 27. Managing change

27.1 The impact of proposed changes on the *cultural significance of a place* should be analysed with reference to the statement of significance and the policy for managing the place. It may be necessary to modify proposed changes following analysis to better retain cultural significance.

27.2 Existing *fabric*, *use*, *associations* and *meanings* should be adequately recorded before any changes are made to the *place*.

Article 28. Disturbance of fabric

28.1 Disturbance of significant *fabric* for study, or to obtain evidence, should be minimised. Study of *a place* by any disturbance of the fabric, including archaeological excavation, should only be undertaken to provide data essential for decisions on the *conservation* of the place, or to obtain important evidence about to be lost or made inaccessible.

28.2 Investigation of a place which requires disturbance of the *fabric*, apart from that necessary to make decisions, may be appropriate provided that it is consistent with the policy for the place. Such investigation should be based on important research questions which have potential to substantially add to knowledge, which cannot be answered in other ways and which minimises disturbance of significant fabric.

Article 29. Responsibility for decisions

The organisations and individuals responsible for management decisions should be named and specific responsibility taken for each such decision.

Article 30. Direction, supervision and implementation

Competent direction and supervision should be maintained at all stages, and any changes should be implemented by people with appropriate knowledge and skills.

Article 31. Documenting evidence and decisions

A log of new evidence and additional decisions should be kept.

Article 32. Records

32.1 The records associated with the *conservation* of a *place* should be placed in a permanent archive and made publicly available, subject to requirements of security and privacy, and where this is culturally appropriate.

32.2 Records about the history of a *place* should be protected and made publicly available, subject to requirements of security and privacy, and where this is culturally appropriate.

Article 33. Removed fabric

Significant *fabric* which has been removed from a *place* including contents, fixtures and objects, should be catalogued, and protected in accordance with its *cultural significance*.

Where possible and culturally appropriate, removed significant fabric including contents, fixtures and objects, should be kept at the place.

Article 34. Resources

Adequate resources should be provided for conservation.

THE BURRA CHARTER (1999)

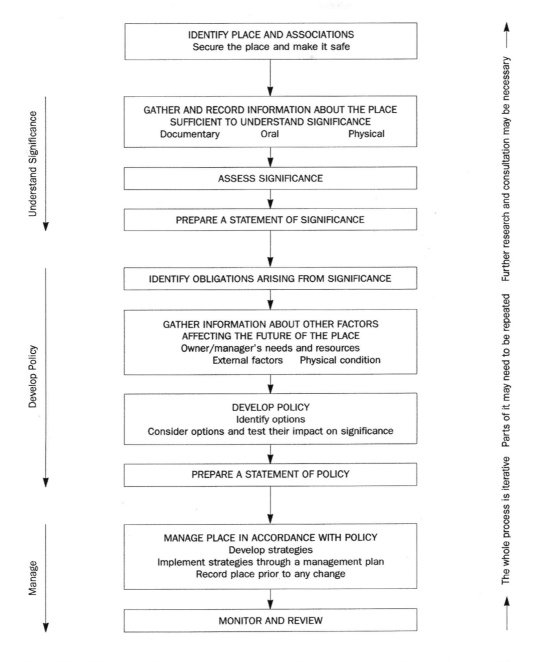

Figure 5.5.1 The Burra Charter process: sequence of investigations, decisions and actions. The 1999 Charter has been suspended. The updated 2013 version can be viewed at http://australia.icomos.org/publications/burra-charter-practice-notes/.

Problems of decay and conservation measures by site type

Chapter 6

Decay and mitigation of stone ruins

Introduction

Ruins were defined by Thompson (1981: 9) as a roofless shell, 'the shell may stand to roof height or exist only as a foundation (or even merely as an archaeological fossil in the subsoil)'. In Britain, they are normally formed of stone, often mortared and represent the final decay phase of every building, wall or other stone construction erected by humankind. Their presence primarily speaks of:

- The organised society that built them. Details of the walling and its architectural features provide a history of the building; a biography of its making, its use and its loss.
- The decay that overtakes all the works of man reducing them to rubble; the sublime power of nature that overwhelms the creations of even the greatest human civilisations to leave only picturesque ruins.

Ruins are the archetypal mnemonic evoking powerful feelings of loss, ancestry and beauty; an Anglo-Saxon poet looking down on the decaying Roman ruins of the city of Bath wrote:

> Splendid is the masonry – the fates destroy it;
> the strongest buildings crashed, the work of giants moulders away.
> The roofs have fallen, the towers are in ruins,
> the barred gate is broken. There is frost on the lime,
> the gapping roofs are shattered and decayed,
> and sapped by old age.
>
> (Mackie 1934: 198–9)

Since the start of antiquarian research, ruins have provided an enormous volume of detail about the built past; building forms and architectural features defining civilisations and periods of the past (Doric, Ionic and Corinthian capitals to columns). Nowadays, the stone of the buildings provides evidence of provenance, and thus trade. The shaping of the stone, the composition of the mortar and the construction of the structure provide evidence of the engineering, mathematical and technical expertise of its builders, the carved and pigmented decoration speak of the artistic influences of the constructing culture, while the size, complexity and number of buildings speak to the resources available to their creators. The use to which the buildings were put provides the principal evidence about what activities took place in the past on that site. This is the detail through which we define, describe and document the past. The disbelief by the Rhodesian colonial government that black Africans were capable of constructing the stone ruins of Great Zimbabwe demonstrates that we draw substantial inferences about the technical and social sophistication of the peoples who create substantial ruins and this evidence has the power to force us to re-evaluate the past (Bahn 1996: 176–7; Webber 2005).

In Britain, large numbers of stone ruins were created at specific points in the past, often the period following one of stone construction such as in the fourth and fifth centuries with the decline of Roman Britain and in the sixteenth century following the dissolution of the monasteries. Major changes in social attitude, beliefs or political power invariably lead to the abandonment of buildings, the containers and symbols of the rejected ideas and values. In countries such as Russia or Ireland, the burnt out mansions of a previous elite can provide a stark and powerful reminder to a contested past of the nineteenth and twentieth centuries. Thompson (1981: 14) suggested that it was over 100 years before monastic remains in Britain could be viewed with the dispassionate eye of the historian rather than a religious threat. It has been suggested that it takes at least three to four generations (so the present generation do not have direct contact with someone who was functionally affected by it) to move from a symbol of oppression to become something old, venerable and ancestral (Haug 2001; Caple 2010); in the case of some buildings, it may take far longer.

Decay

The principal agents of destruction of ruins are human beings, who constantly demolish and rebuild. Rain, frost and vegetation also degrade structures, burying the base of the walls of buildings in the rubble of the roof and upper wall structures. The severity of all these agencies in north-western Europe is demonstrated by the small number of Roman buildings that remain standing above ground in contrast to the survival of extensive cities in the semi-desert of North Africa. Ruins are complex objects that invariably have a long history of construction, use, decay or later reuse, and finally conservation processes. It is important to try to recover the limited evidence for these events, as well as preserve them, even if only traces of walls now remain. In Chapter 6.1, Ashurst and Shalom (2007) illustrate the biography and range of conservation problems a building can typically acquire. The decay processes of stone are described in Table 3.0.1 and Chapter 10. The degradation and loss of mortar, the frost damage to stone, and cracking of walls usually due to differential loading of subsidence of foundations are among the most common problems seen affecting ruined stone buildings in Britain. Elsewhere in the world, seismic activity has severely damaged masonry buildings (Fielden 1987), with many notable examples in the Mediterranean region. Evidence and critical evaluation of the structures, their performance in seismic events, and subsequent conservation has been collected (see www.niker.eu) to aid future efforts to preserve such structures *in situ*.

History of the perception of ruins in Britain

The ruin was a key metaphor in the Renaissance world for what happens when the world ceased to be ordered and controlled. Fascination with ancient ruins, initially classical but later 'Gothick', set in the natural landscape continued and can be traced through the eighteenth century, from the gardens of William Kent and later Lancelot 'Capability' Brown, through the engravings of Samuel and Nathaniel Buck (1724–1742), to the scholarship of Stukeley and other antiquarians (Piggott 1976). By the 1750s, the philosophical concepts of the picturesque and the sublime were being explored by Burke, but it was the late eighteenth-century work by Gilpin (1782), *Observations on the River Wye, and Several Parts of South Wales, etc. Relative Chiefly to Picturesque Beauty; Made in the Summer of the Year 1770*, which gave an identifiable visual form to the picturesque. Circa 1770–1850, the Romantic movement, seen primarily in Britain through the literature of Wordsworth, Tennyson, Sir Walter Scott and Byron, created an intellectual climate in which the ruins of the past were regarded as things of beauty, stimuli to the mind, a focus for emotion and empathy. Piggott (1976: 122) has argued that improvements in the practicalities of travel (turnpike roads, improved draft horses and lightweight carriages) and the discouraging effect that the French Revolution and later Napoleon had on British travel in Europe, greatly increased the ability to travel and experience the picturesque in Britain in the late eighteenth and early nineteenth centuries.

This creation of value attached to ruins, led to the incorporation of ruins into garden and landscape settings such as Fountains Abbey, which was 'added' into the water gardens of Studley Royal by William Aislabie in 1767. At Newton House in Carmarthenshire, as in many other cases, the gardens were laid out to draw the eye to the existing ruins of Dynefwr Castle (Rees and Caple 2007: 21, 40). Such valuation led to the preservation of many classical and medieval ruins. However, the selective ruination of existing buildings to increase their aesthetic appeal and the creation of fake ruins, often out of parts of original buildings as in the case of Shobdon, Herefordshire (Thompson 1981: 17), and the Hermitage and Merlin's Cave at Richmond Lodge, Surrey (Piggott 1976: 119), demonstrated that what was valued was the aesthetic of the picturesque, the idea of an imagined past, not the reality of the past.

The religious revival of the early nineteenth century following the Church Building Act of 1818, the establishment of the Oxford Movement from 1833, and the activities of the architectural societies in Oxford (1839) and Cambridge (1840) resulted in the construction of new churches and, above all, the restoration of many churches that had suffered sad neglect through the eighteenth century. The restoration undertaken was not the modern usage of the word, but that of Violett-le-Duc: 'Restoration – The word and the thing are modern. To restore a building is not to maintain, repair or even remake it; it is to re-establish it in a complete state which can never have existed at any given moment' (Violett-le-Duc 1858–1868; Thompson 2006: 89–93). This reconstruction of many churches was carried out with the arrogant zeal of missionaries converting church buildings to an idealised High Gothic architectural form. The stripping away of the evidence of the past led to a backlash by the Romantic Movement, Ruskin's *Seven Lamps of Architecture* (1849) inspiring William Morris and the foundation of SPAB, which, from 1877, emphasised the virtue of the original structure, the evidence of the past rather than just the idea (see Chapter 5).

This preference for preservation in the 'as found' form evolved into the orthodoxy that was practised by the Office of Works (Works Department), the section within 'The Office of Woods, Forests, Land Revenues, Works and Buildings', the British government department dealing with ruins, which came into its care from the Irish Church Act of 1869 (Irish ecclesiastic ruins) (Thompson 2006: 35), the 1882 Ancient Monuments Protection Act (British prehistoric ruins) and the 1913 Ancient Monuments Consolidation and Amendment Act (British medieval ruins). The Office of Works started conservation of ruins after the picturesque and romantic movements had passed their zenith, though there remained many concerned at the scale of engineering work necessary to preserve the ruins (Ashurst and Burns 2007: 85). The Office of Works approach was not, however, the overtly visible 'tile' repairs favoured by SPAB (Thompson 2006: 66), but a less obtrusive style often utilising additional 'core work' to support, protect and preserve existing remains and ensure their legibility. The value of original stonework may not have been appreciated by some of the original restorers of the nineteenth century, but it was certainly appreciated by others. Detailed recording of original masonry was actively promulgated by RIBA in their publication *Conservation of Ancient Monuments and Remains* of 1865 (Jokilehto 1999: 182). Even the exuberant work of William Burges for the Marquis of Bute, who, at Castell Coch, arguably undertook the most extensive and imaginative reconstruction of any British monument, clearly outlined and preserved the original Roman stonework at Cardiff Castle (see Figure 6.0.1). This sequence of changing values and emphasis in the preservation and conservation of ruins seen in Britain between the eighteenth and twenty-first centuries is played out in a similar fashion throughout the countries of the world (Jokilehto 1999: 186–209).

Ruins conserved/restored/reconstructed

Religious ruins and buildings

Repairs to religious buildings have been seen as meretricious acts in Buddhism and most other major religions since time in memoriam. While this has ensured the survival of some buildings, it has resulted in unrecorded work, uncritical repair and restoration that has swept away the evidence of earlier buildings. Examples include the nineteenth-century repairs to churches in Britain by the Camden Group and the repair of *stupas* in Sri Lanka in the 1930s (Wijesuriya 2001: 257).

Tourism

The power and image of the ruin are often powerful national symbols and draw tourists and their associated financial benefits. This encourages increasingly extensive and ultimately fanciful restoration/reconstruction to try to stimulate greater visitor interest and spending. This can lead to a backlash, a rejection of 'Disneyfied' remains in favour of greater value for the original evidential ruins – precious evidence of the past to be accurately preserved. Across the decades, we have continued to oscillate between these extremes.

Historic buildings

Historic buildings have a roof and so keep out the extremes of the weather. The more benign conditions within a roofed building help preserve many internal fragile features – floors, mosaics, wall paintings, decorated and carved surfaces – especially when executed in unstable stone such as gypsum or Purbeck marble. Ruins exposed to the weather cannot preserve such features from swift decay. When faced with such fragile features, it is possible to add a roof to a ruin and transform it into an historic building. Such buildings, though protective, are

DECAY AND MITIGATION OF STONE RUINS 225

Figure 6.0.1 Roman stonework at Cardiff Castle outlined during the nineteenth-century restoration work of the Marquis of Bute and William Burges.
Source: Photograph by the author

expensive to maintain but are an asset capable of use for habitation, work or other activities, and as such can generate income to pay for maintenance. Such buildings can consequently be used or sold to private individuals or organisations; this will ensure they are maintained and that they cease to be a drain on the public purse, though there is usually a trade-off, accepting some damage or loss of the historic fabric (adding services means holes in walls at the very least) in order to maintain functionality and preserve other rare and fragile aspects of the building. In ruins that remain unroofed, the evocative power of the ruin and its history, which includes its ruination, is displayed for visitor instruction; however, fragile features such as wall paintings cannot survive. When faced with preserving a ruin with fragile remains, options revolve around converting into an historic building, erecting a shelter (see Chapter 14), reburying it (see Chapter 15), removing the fragile features (mosaic or wall painting) to a museum or accepting its gradual decay and loss. In each case, it is about balancing what is lost against what is gained, though to do this it is necessary to make accurate predictions about the risk and benefits of each approach projected decades into the future.

In practice: ruin to visitable monument

The practice of taking a ruin (an often picturesque, unstable structure whose past and fabric is undeciphered) and transforming it into a visitable monument (a stable structure that can inform the viewer of its past) is a series of decisions and processes; each separate action needs to be carefully considered, but it is also essential to take a holistic view of what is done to the structure. Thompson (1981: 27) suggests that the aim is to give the visitor 'a fuller understanding of the ruin', which he describes as 'a constant objective at all times', but there is also the requirement to preserve (and record) the evidence of the past. There is invariably a sensitivity by practitioners to the (often unstated) aesthetic component, which harks back to the beauty of the ruin recognising that it is socially valued because of its picturesque qualities, and efforts are made to ensure that the resultant monument preserves/invokes those visually valued qualities. Authenticity and beauty are not the same thing (Thompson 1981: 64), and thus choices must be made, as shown in the debate over Tintern Abbey (Ashurst and Burns 2007: 85) (see Chapter 6.2). The evidence of the past is unique and irreplaceable; aesthetic qualities (beauty or the picturesque) are transient, culturally contexted qualities that can be created as well as lost. That said, the evocative quality of many ruins is the reason they have survived up to this point, and the present visual impact of the monument may well be a key element to the continued survival of the evidence.

Prior to any work commencing, an informed decision to preserve/conserve the ruin/monument is normally made and such decisions should only be made following acquisition of all the relevant information (Clark 2001) (see Chapter 5, section on values). Stubbs (1995), following Fitch (1990), outlined the range of options that could be considered (see Table 6.0.1).

In cases where the ruins are to be displayed, the sequence of actions would normally include:

- The structure is recorded in detail, so there is a clear fixed point of knowledge about what evidence was present in the structure. Any unintentional damage and loss of information through subsequent processes will at least be known from this original record. Ideally, this comprises a detailed stone-by-stone drawing or rectified photographs and accurate plan and elevation drawings with key features marked. The stone and mortar should be sampled and analysed (Abrey 2007). Recording should continue during clearing and conservation of the monument so that all the features present in the building fabric are fully documented. Interpretation should occur alongside the recording, so that a building biography is constructed understanding how the building developed from its origins, through its use, to its decay. The sequence of changing rooflines, alterations to windows and doors needs to be understood, and evidence in the masonry sought. Ephemeral traces are often only recognised and recorded when prompted by the questions raised by interpretation.
- Identify and understand the decay processes. Undertake investigation to determine if there are structural problems, any active wall movement, and if any materials are particularly susceptible to decay, particularly areas of previous conservation. This may include some excavation and some long-term monitoring. Cracking is present in many walls for many reasons; it should be recorded and investigated (e.g. with dated tell tales and, where appropriate, by an architect or structural engineer).

Table 6.0.1 Examples of different approaches to preserving and displaying ancient remains

Approach	Sites
Preserved	
Sites remain unexcavated	Unexcavated sections of Pompeii, Italy Tomb of Emperor Qin Shi Huang, China Builth Castle, Wales
Backfilled sites after excavation	Rose Theatre, London San Diego Presidio, California, USA
Backfilled sites occasionally unearthed	Woodchester, Gloucester, England Rock art sites in Scandinavia
Above ground ruins left 'as found'	Wigmore Castle (most of it)
Temporarily protected (roofed) site 'as found'	Flag Fen
Part preserved, part restored	
Stabilised ruins	Machu Picchu, Peru Dryslwyn Castle, Wales Coventry Cathedral (Medieval), England Mycenae, Greece
Stabilised ruin with associated museum	Paestum, Italy Skara Brae, Orkneys, Scotland
Stabilised ruin with (1) projected outline of the original building (2) small section restored	Benjamin Franklin's House, Philadelphia (1) Knossos, Crete (2) Mount Grace Priory, Teeside, England (2) Pompeii (excavated), Italy (2)
Stabilised ruin beneath roof or substantial shelter	Casa Grande, Arizona, USA Fishbourne Palace, Sussex, England Villa Romana del Casale, Piazza Armerina, Sicily Çatalhöyük, Turkey
Ruins incorporated within later structure (1) or garden/landscape (2)	Theatre of Marcellus, Rome (1) Roman Baths, Bath, England (1) Fountains Abbey (Medieval) and Studley Royal (eighteenth century) (2)
Anastylosis	Library at Ephesus, Turkey Temple of Trajan, Pergamon, Turkey
Restored	
Restored ruins	Cardiff Castle and Castell Coch, South Wales Temple of Hatshepsut, Deir el Bahari, Egypt Colonia Ulpia Traiana, Xanten, Germany
Relocated buildings	Abu Simbel, Egypt Temple of Dendur, Metropolitan Museum, New York Obelisk Ramesses II, Place de la Concorde, Paris
Reconstructions	Colonial Williamsburg, Virginia, USA Castell Henllys, Pembrokeshire, Wales Stari Most (bridge at Mostar), Bosnia Hertzegovina

Source: Based on Stubbs (1995)

- Devise a conservation plan that has the support of all parties who value the site (stakeholders) that secures the resources to complete the work and ensures sustainable management and maintenance in the long term.
- To be able to see and understand what is present in the ruins often involves removal of 'accretions', obscuring later material that may comprise: the accumulated soil of years, vegetation, graffiti, later temporary structures such as chicken sheds, and even substantial constructions such as pig sties from nineteenth- and/or twentieth-century farm use. The more permanent and the older these later additions, the more questionable their removal since these later structures are all part of the monument history, though they obscure its earlier form. In Britain, the removal of seventeenth- to nineteenth-century domestic accommodation, industrial facilities and 'folly' features (added to make the ruin picturesque) was often undertaken in the early twentieth century but was rarely done by the late twentieth century. As the present imperceptibly becomes the past and becomes increasingly rare, so it becomes valued and deemed worthy of preservation. Articulating the values associated with the various elements of the monument (see Chapter 5) helps define what is worthy of protection/retention, though there is always an element of subjectivity. Anything removed should have been fully recorded. Notions of 'not removing *any* of the traces of the history of the site' are often untenable as the complex clutter of later accretions and earlier restorations invariably prevent understanding of the ruin. Such removal need not occur at sites not intended for public display.
- Make the monument stable (i.e. structurally sound) so that it will not fall down or disintegrate damaging its visitors. Structural problems must normally be dealt with first; the ruin and its walls must be secure before conservation of its surfaces and decorative details can take place.
- Consolidate the key architectural features of the monument (e.g. support if unstable).
- Protect the features of the monument that cannot be made stable (things can be reburied) or given shelter (this requires realistic assessment of threat, vandalism, looting, accident, weathering, vegetation, etc.).
- If original features are present but fallen or displaced, they may be rebuilt. This process, anastylosis, ranges from replacing single fallen stones to the re-erections of substantial sections of buildings facilitated with appropriate supporting structure (Stubbs 1995; Vacharopoulou 2006). The only form of restoration clearly approved by the Venice Charter 1964, anastylosis has been widely practised in the Mediterranean region, as in the Celsus Library at Ephesus (Jokilehto 1999: 310–11). Some practitioners have undertaken considerable areas of restoration under the guise of anastylosis.
- Restoration of elements to convey the understanding of the monument. The modern expectation of restoration is that it will only be undertaken for elements that it is certain were part of the original. The level of certainty is the key issue, and this varies from one architect/heritage organisation to another. The situation is made more complex by the desire of some owners and heritage bodies to provide a more complete and engaging experience for the visitor, often in an effort to encourage visitation and increased visitor spending.
- Language and the definition of terms continue to be a problem for this subject (see Table 0.1). Though in common usage, restoration is considered returning a building or object (partially or completely) to its original form with a high degree of certainty (reconstruction perhaps where there is less certainty in the reconstructed form); the Burra Charter definitions state 'restoration' can *only* contain original materials (i.e.

anastylosis), while 'reconstruction' is considered returning a building or object partially or completely to its known (certain) original form with some new materials used (Stovel 2001). The term 'recreation' is used where there is less certainty over the rebuilt form. These definitions were followed by English Heritage in 2001 (Woolfitt 2007). However, Stanley-Price (2009) and Molina-Montes (1982) have shown that during the last 100 years, there has been a considerable difference between what is said in the international charters and what occurs in practice. They note that what are often described as reconstructions or restorations go ahead, often in highly speculative form, as the structures created are: national symbols, have continuing functional use, have an educational and research role, aid tourism, because 'visitors love them' and through income help preserve the site. Governments, individual landowners and heritage agencies who can afford to finance 'visitor-friendly' 'restorations' find these arguments more convincing than the concerns raised by conservation professionals about accuracy/authenticity. Sites from Tintern Abbey, whose south arcade columns were taken down, steelwork installed to preserve the upper levels of walling and were rebuilt as original (see Chapter 6.2), to Sir Arthur Evans' reconstruction/recreation of the palace at Knossos, demonstrate the range of activities described as 'restoration' as early as the 1920s. To what extent should any restoration/reconstruction/recreation be understood and readable by the visitor is a key issue; too close to the original and we deceive, too distant and we impair the readability and aesthetic impact of the monument. Decorative detail is normally omitted from any newly added restoration/reconstruction work.
- Appropriate additional construction may take place on a site to ensure public access, safety, for information purposes and on selected sites for facilities for visitors. These are normally clearly discernible from the original fabric of the ruin, but traditionally sympathetic materials with appropriate colours and textures are chosen.

Presentation

Beyond the representation of the historic fabric of the ruin, issues relating to presenting it as a monument fall into two categories (Thompson 1981: 29):

- Requirements to satisfy the visitor's intellectual needs, the ability to see and understand the monument means in practice:
  - Access paths, steps and bridges to enable visitors to see the site.
  - Protective rails and grills to prevent access or toppling over, hand rails to aid access on uneven steps or ground.
  - Presentation of buried features (e.g. walls of the barracks at Caerleon), or those that were wood and have decayed away or have been robbed out, is normally achieved with appropriate surfacing (e.g. paving, gravel, cobbles, rebuilt walls, etc.). The risk of complexity and confusing the visitor has to be balanced against the need to display truth.
  - Notice boards/information panels, carefully located to avoid damaging or obscuring important archaeology, and to be both visible but not obtrusive, now contain far more information than their early twentieth-century predecessors. Again, accuracy, detail and complexity are balanced against the need for simplification and clarity. Signs degrade due to weather and vandalism and need to be replaced occasionally.

The changing understanding of history and continuing research also necessitates replacement.
- Lawns or other 'background' flooring is essential if access to the remains is to be facilitated. The lawns are rarely mistaken for an original surface, and they do not crack and need replacement like paving, thus they are often a highly appropriate surface, though they do require frequent maintenance, cutting and occasional repair. However, they give any site an institutional look, which is less fashionable in the twenty-first century than the twentieth. They are, in temperate climates, often one of the least troublesome and most cost-effective solutions to providing a surface for a monument.

- Requirements to satisfy the physical needs of the visitor such as car parks, toilets and refreshments. The presence of such facilities is costly and increases the visitor numbers at a monument. They should only be established when the monument is capable of absorbing that number of visitors without sustaining physical damage (carrying capacity) (see Chapter 12). Such facilities normally require human support (to clean toilets, make and serve beverages, etc.), and the cost of such facilities and human support requires financial return. Thus, entrance charges may be made at such sites, and souvenirs, games and books are often sold, as well as refreshments, in order to recoup cost.

Guidebooks are created for all well-visited monuments, and contain more background information than their predecessors of the 1930s and 1950s, when it was assumed the visitor had good background knowledge and a discerning eye. Increasingly audio guides are used, requiring less imagination from the visitor, who invariably follows a narrative – more a radio play than a lecture. The advent of mobile phones, portable computers, tablets and similar devices now allows the visitor to download information and hear audio tours on their own device even at remote sites via the mobile phone network. Though the Internet can provide a useful resource for visitors to acquire large volumes of information, some of it can be inaccurate and misleading. The previous role of the national heritage agency or owner of the site as the authoritative source of the interpretation of the site is increasingly challenged by views of the past. This can lead to useful vigorous debate, it can also lead to confusion, especially for visitors whose limited knowledge about history means that they have no framework of understanding of the past onto which the new pieces of information can be attached.

In practice: technical realities

In undertaking preservation of ruins, many technical issues must be overcome, from recording the ruin and erecting temporary supports preventing collapse, to the composition of the mortar used to repoint, and the material from which dowels used for various forms of wall stitching should be made. Many of these issues are covered in Ashurst's *Conservation of Ruins* (2007), from which Chapter 6.2 is an edited extract. Two levels of work are seen in practice: conservation at the level of a structure, often the focus of books on conserving historic buildings such as Fielden (2003), and at the small-scale level of decay of individual pieces of stone or small areas of walling. The question of the decay of stone is discussed by authors such as Price (1996), Doehne and Price (2010) and in Chapter 10 and Table 3.0.1. Treatments revolve around either consolidation of stone for example using silanes, lime treatments, epoxy resins or other materials or the replacement of highly weathered pieces of original stone with near identical replacements. Replacement leads to ethical questions; it facilitates preservation of the building and its visual elements but sacrifices the original stone. The replaced stone will be stronger, and if so desired its shaping can give an indication of the original face or architectural details of the building. It initially looks new and often stands proud of its surroundings, but eventually weathers over time. Attempts to distress/age new stone are rarely successful and are usually considered ethically dubious. Frequent campaigns of restoration lead to building facades formed of a patchwork of stone with different levels of weathering, a unity of sorts.

The increasing problem faced by stone ruins are the threats posed by earlier conservation work; many of the initial materials used for conservation work, cement mortar (Ashurst and Burns 2007: 93, 98–9, 129) and iron or steel dowels, have not only proved ineffective, but made the situation considerably worse (How 1999: 37–41). In almost all cases, the only solution is to, where possible, remove the conservation material and replace it with something that is effective but also stable in the long term in the environment endured by the ancient remains.

While the conservation work on most ruins in Britain follows the careful approach of the Office of Works from circa 1900 onwards, raising the loose stones at the top of the wall and rebedding them, or taking down loose face stones, remortaring them into the wall core and repointing, it is inevitable that the stones do not go back exactly into their original position. The repointed wall is never quite 'as found'. This was demonstrated when detailed drawings of the stonework both 'as found' and following 'consolidation and repointing' were undertaken at Dryslwyn Castle in Carmarthenshire, conserved during the 1980s (see Figure 6.0.2). This shows that although key features appear the same, it is not possible to totally preserve stone

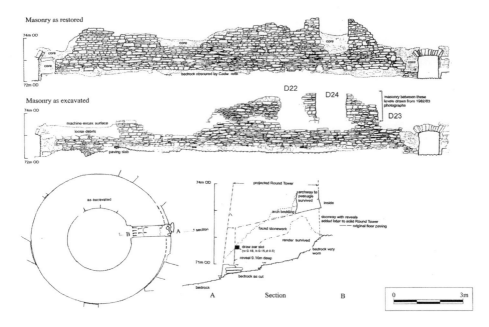

Figure 6.0.2 Internal elevation of Round Tower (Area D) of Dryslwyn Castle, Carmarthenshire, drawn by Mr R.F. Caple circa 1982 and 1986.

Source: Caple (2007: 60)

ruins accurately 'as found, in situ'. This must be true for almost every conserved ancient stone ruin in Britain. The act of consolidation and repointing, which is often described as preservation, necessitates change, and caution should be used over the archaeological interpretation of any remains where there is evidence, such as repointing, or repair. Wherever remains have been exposed for some time, unrecorded conservation work will often have taken place. It is, however, clear that if conservation actions such as repointing were not undertaken, within a few decades the walling would collapse and the information would be lost forever.

Repointing, consolidation and replacement of stonework are not the only approaches possible for preserving the stone remains in situ. Temporary measures (such as application of a shelter coat – a weak lime coating can be applied to protect degrading stone surface, though it will need to be replaced at regular intervals) can be used. Steps to reduce the rate of stone decay can be subtle, and simple ways of reducing the extreme effects of the weather utilised. On the Isle of the Dead, Port Arthur Penal Colony, Tasmania, the rate of stone decay was shown to be related to the extremes of temperature and moisture cycling (going through the crystallisation point of sodium chloride), leading the north side of gravestones to suffer extensive flaking of the surface (efflorescence), while there was none on the south side. Conservation measures involved planting shade trees to ensure both sides of the stone were shaded, so eliminating the extreme temperature and associated relative humidity cycling (Thorn and Piper 1996).

Decorated surfaces

The surfaces of walls, floors and ceilings, usually interior, were frequently given a surface coating, often decorated with coloured images and designs. These ranged from simple monochrome patterns to complex scenic wall paintings. Such decorated surfaces, especially frescos and mosaics are found surviving on the lower parts of walls and floors of the ruins of Roman and medieval buildings, as at Pompeii or the Dover Painted House (Philp 1989), where they have been protected, buried under the rubble of upper parts of the walls and ceilings. Similar painted decorations occur on cave surfaces (see Chapter 10) and on earth brick structures such as Çatalhöyük (see Chapter 7). These decorated surfaces cannot normally survive exposure to weather for long periods without severe degradation, and in the nineteenth and early twentieth centuries many were reburied or removed to museums. In many instances, as at Pompeii, efforts to display wall paintings and mosaics *in situ* in ruined buildings have led to shelters being built over them (see Chapter 13). The conservation of wall paintings in historic buildings has a substantial literature (Mora *et al.* 1984; McDonald 1996; Gowing and Heritage 2003). Cather (2003) has emphasised the need for accurate diagnosis of the causes of decay if these fragile surface decorations are to be successfully conserved as many early attempts at conservation have struggled to be effective in the long term.

The future

After well over 100 years of public acquisition, excavation and presentation of ruins, there are a large number of monuments in public ownership available to visit in Britain and throughout Europe. The increasing standards of display and costs of presentation as well as the recent decline in government funding for heritage activities around Europe have meant that the sustainability of ruins/monuments has become a significant concern. Heritage authorities often struggle to maintain monuments in safe and visitable condition, which has resulted in the need for a selective application of resources and an increasing diversity of approaches to stone ruins. Approaches include:

- Selection of some sites as 'flagship' sites with extensive visitor facilities and events, while others are preserved *in situ* as they stand, without facilities.
- Selection of some sites for reburial. The US Park Service has started reburying some Native American pueblo sites such as Chetro Ketl and Pueblo Bonito (see Chapter 14.3).
- Large-scale excavation of sites such as castles, which would result in revealing new ruins, has largely ceased in Britain. A more sustainable approach, tried in the late 1990s at Wigmore Castle (Coppack 1999) (see Chapter 6.3), was to 'preserve as found', not to excavate the site, but leave it as a ruin. This maintained the natural ecology of the site, ensured the historic fabric was safe, but provided virtually no visitor facilities and limited signage. Avoiding substantial archaeological excavation meant there was limited walling to repoint, so lowering the cost of presenting the monument for public visitation, the natural grass and tree growth may be more sustainable at lower cost than substantial lawns. Access to a few specific areas was prevented, and thus English Heritage stepped back from the aim of 'a fuller understanding of the ruin'. To preserve a colony of bats undisturbed and to ensure public safety a doorway was blocked preventing visitor access, elsewhere core-work was raised above the appropriate level in a number of ground floor window openings, so avoiding the visual intrusion of grilles and rails to maintain the visual impression of a 'ruin', but again ensuring public safety (Coppack 1999: 68). This goes well beyond the text of the Venice Charter 1964, but recognises the cultural significance of the site as a ruin and natural habitat – as understood in *The Nara Document on Authenticity* and *The Burra Charter 1999*.

Bibliography

Abrey, G. (2007) 'Condition surveys of masonry ruins', in J. Ashurst (ed.), *Conservation of Ruins*, London: Butterworth-Heinemann, pp. 44–81.
Ashurst, J. (2007) *Conservation of Ruins*, London: Butterworth Heinemann.
Ashurst, J. and Burns, C. (2007) 'Philosophy, technology and craft', in J. Ashurst (ed.), *Conservation of Ruins*, London: Butterworth-Heinemann, pp. 82–145.
Ashurst, J. and Shalom, A. (2007) 'Short story: the demise, discovery, destruction and salvation of a ruin', in J. Ashurst (ed.), *Conservation of Ruins*, London: Butterworth-Heinemann, pp. xxx–xlii.
Bahn, P. (1996) *The Cambridge Illustrated History of Archaeology*, Cambridge: Cambridge University Press.
Caple, C. (2007) *Excavations at Dryslwyn Castle 1980–1995*, Society for Medieval Archaeology Monograph No. 26, London: Society for Medieval Archaeology.
Caple, C. (2010) 'Ancestor artefacts – ancestor materials', *Oxford Journal of Archaeology*, 29(3): 305–18.
Cather, S. (2003) 'Assessing causes and mechanisms of detrimental change to wall paintings', in W. Gowing and A. Heritage (eds), *Conserving the Painted Past: Developing Approaches to Wall Painting Conservation*, London: James & James, pp. 64–71.
Clark, K. (2001) *Informed Conservation: Understanding Historic Buildings and Their Landscapes for Conservation*, London: English Heritage.
Coppack, G. (1999) 'Setting and structure: the conservation of Wigmore Castle', in G. Chitty and D. Baker (eds), *Managing Historic Sites and Buildings*, London: Routledge, pp. 61–70.
Doehne, E. and Price, C. (2010) *Stone Conservation: An Overview of Current Research*, 2nd edn, Los Angeles, CA: GCI.
Fielden, B.M. (1987) *Between Two Earthquakes: Cultural Property in Seismic Zones*, Rome: ICCROM.
Fielden, B.M. (2003) *Conservation of Historic Buildings*, 3rd edn, Oxford: Architectural Press.
Fitch, J.M. (1990) *Historic Preservation: Curatorial Management of the Built World*, 2nd edn, Charlottesville, VI: University of Virginia, pp. 293–306.

Gilpin, W. (1782) *Observations on the River Wye, and Several Parts of South Wales, etc. Relative Chiefly to Picturesque Beauty; Made in the Summer of the Year 1770*, London: Printed for R. Blamire, in the Strand.

Gowing, R. and Heritage, A. (2003) *Conserving the Painted Past: Developing Approaches to Wall Painting Conservation*, London: James & James.

Haug, A. (2001) 'Constituting the past – forming the present: the role of material culture in the Augustinian period', *Journal of the History of Collections*, 13(2): 111–23.

How, C. (1999) 'Stability and survival', in J. Ashurst (ed.), *Conservation of Ruins*, London: Butterworth-Heinemann, pp. 10–43.

Jokilehto, J. (1999) *A History of Architectural Conservation*, Oxford: Butterworth-Heinemann.

Mackie, W.S. (1934) *The Exeter Book, Part II: Poems IX–XXXII*, London: Oxford University Press.

McDonald, J.K. (1996) *House of Eternity: The Tomb of Nefertari*, Los Angeles, CA: Getty Conservation Institute & J. Paul Getty.

Molina-Montes, A. (1982) 'Archaeological buildings: representation or misrepresentation', in E.H. Boone (ed.), *Falsifications and Misrepresentations of Pre-Columbian Art*, Washington, DC: Dumbarton Oaks, pp. 125–41.

Mora, P., Mora, L. and Philippot, P. (1984) *Conservation of Wall Painting*, London: Butterworths.

Philp, B. (1989) *The Roman House with Bacchic Murals at Dover*, Dover: Kent Archaeological Research Unit.

Piggott, S. (1976) *Ruins in a Landscape: Essays in Antiquarianism*, Edinburgh: Edinburgh University Press.

Price, C. (1996) *Stone Conservation: An Overview of Current Research*, Santa Monica, CA: GCI.

Rees, S.E. and Caple, C. (2007) *Dinefwr Castle Dryslwyn Castle*, 2nd edn, Cardiff: Cadw.

Ruskin, J. (1849) *The Seven Lamps of Architecture*, London: Smith, Elder.

Stanley-Price, N. (2009) 'The reconstruction of ruins: principles and practice', in A. Richmond and A. Bracker (eds), *Conservation Principles, Dilemmas and Uncomfortable Truths*, London: Butterworth-Heinemann, pp. 32–46.

Stovel, H. (2001) 'The Riga charter on authenticity and historical reconstruction in relationship to cultural heritage (Riga, Latvia, October 2000)', *Conservation and Management of Archaeological Sites*, 4(4): 240–4.

Stubbs, J.H. (1995) 'Protection and presentation of excavated structures', in N.P. Stanley Price (ed.), *Conservation on Archaeological Excavations*, Rome: ICCROM, pp. 73–90.

Thompson, M. (1981) *Ruins: Their Preservation and Display*, London: British Museum.

Thompson, M. (2006) *Ruins Reused: Changing Attitudes to Ruins Since the Late Eighteenth Century*, Kings Lynn: Heritage.

Thorn, A. and Piper, A. (1996) 'The Isle of the Dead: an integrated approach to the management and natural protection of an archaeological site', in A. Roy and P. Smith (eds), *Archaeological Conservation and Its Consequences*, preprints of the contributions to the Copenhagen Congress, 26–30 August 1996, London: IIC, pp. 188–92.

Vacharopoulou, K. (2006) 'Conservation of classical monuments: a study of anastylosis, with case studies from Greece and Turkey', unpublished PhD dissertation, University College London.

Violett-le-Duc, E.E. (1858–1868) *Dictionnaire raisonné de l'architecture française du 11e au 16e siècle*, Paris: Bance.

Webber, N. (2005) *The Preservation of Great Zimbabwe: Your Monument Our Shrine*, Rome: ICCROM.

Wijesuriya, G. (2001) 'Pious vandals' restoration or destruction in Sri Lanka', in R. Layton, P.G. Stone and J. Thomas (eds), *Destruction and Conservation of Cultural Property*, London: Routledge, pp. 256–63.

Woolfitt, C. (2007) 'Preventive conservation of ruins: reconstruction, reburial and enclosure', in J. Ashurst (ed.), *Conservation of Ruins*, London: Butterworth-Heinemann, pp. 146–93.

Chapter 6.1

Short story
The demise, discovery, destruction and salvation of a ruin

John Ashurst and Asi Shalom

Source: Ashurst, J. and Shalom, A. (2007) 'Short story: the demise, discovery, destruction and salvation of a ruin', in J. Ashurst (ed.), *Conservation of Ruins*, London: Butterworth Heinemann, pp. xxx–xlii.

THIS STORY SHOWS HOW one small building, part of an ancient settlement, was abandoned, neglected, and fell into a ruin state. This regression slowed as the building became buried, finally becoming largely stable until modern times, when it was uncovered as part of an archaeological project. Exposed and recorded, the site was left again and its regression continued rapidly. Poor quality interventions exacerbated its demise. Finally, intelligent conservation was carried out and the building was re-buried as the best means of ensuring its survival.

1 The complete building

A small cult temple was constructed high on the hillside above a small town located on the water's edge. It was constructed of the local limestone with composite walls 0.75 m thick. The internal space was covered with a stone vault capped with lightweight lime concrete and a pitched tiled roof. The internal surfaces were covered in plaster and richly painted. The floor was covered with limestone, ceramic and marble mosaic. The town and its temple were abandoned following a minor eruption of the nearby volcano and the silting up of the waterway which brought trade to the town.

2 Phase one deterioration

After a few years of disuse roof tiles become loose and fall. The weak fill of lime and tufa above the vault attracts soil forming plants, and their roots exploit fine cracks in the concrete and invade the joints of the vault. Externally, soil is gradually washed down against the upper retaining wall and is scoured from under the shallow foundation of

Figure 6.1.1 The complete building.

Figure 6.1.2 Phase one deterioration.

the lower wall. Water begins to have access to the heart of the walls, moving between the tails of the stones and the core.

3 Phase two deterioration

Earth tremors cause the undermined low wall to lean forward and the unrestrained vault to crack along its length, causing many of the roof tiles to slide to the ground. This is followed by the collapse of the centre of the vault which allows large stones to fall, in places smashing the mosaic floor. Plaster at floor level becomes intermittently saturated, softens and loses its decorated surface. Water is able to pour through the open roof and settle over the floor area.

4 Phase three deterioration

There is now a progressive loosening of the vault stones, which depend now only on the adhesive qualities of the mortar to remain in position. Further collapse of the

Figure 6.1.3 Phase two deterioration.

Figure 6.1.4 Phase three deterioration.

weakened vault creates piles of stone and debris on the floor. Water now has free access to the decorated wall plaster. Accumulation of soil and stone washed down from the hill above bring about the collapse of the top courses of the upper wall, adding to the accumulation of stone within the building. Some of the fallen stone carries with it the decorative painted plaster frieze.

5 Phase four deterioration

There is now little more to fall. Accumulations of stone and soil create relatively stable conditions over the ruined temple. However, deep rooting trees and shrubs readily colonise the loose debris and, as they continue to grow, exploit the wall cores. Small mammals and reptiles occupy the site with its numerous natural cavities. This is the site in the condition found by the archaeological team. Priorities have to be established and time and cost estimates prepared for the work of uncovering and recording. A minimal budget is provided for temporary supports and partial back filling.

Figure 6.1.5 Phase four deterioration.

The likelihood is that this small contingency sum will be spent during the excavation and nothing will be left for protection.

6 Archaeology as an informing force

The site is studied contextually and specifically, carefully recorded and systematically excavated. The stratification, construction, materials, artefacts and sequence of building and destruction become clear. After a period of further analysis reports are prepared and archived, perhaps suggesting a further season of excavation if funds are available. No money is left for any temporary protection, and it is confidently predicted that not much deterioration can take place in one year. The site is left in a dangerous condition and is regularly visited by souvenir hunters.

7 Archaeology as a destructive force

The site has provided all the information considered necessary for the historic record and is left abandoned. No money can be made available for further excavation and a period of neglect begins. Excavated material from the interior of the temple had provided a counterfort against the pressure of soil, loose rock and water moving down the hillside. Now the spoil has been removed, the rear wall collapses. Water ponds under the foot of the lower wall encouraging its subsidence. Water moving through the composite walls loosens the face work from its core. Water ponds on the mosaic floor and micro-organisms begin to colonise the painted plaster surfaces. Cut roots of vegetation growing on the wall begin to support new growth. Small mammals return to the site and begin to burrow into loose fill. The plaster is totally unprotected and detaches from the walls. Within a few years nothing significant will be left on the site for further study and re-appraisal.

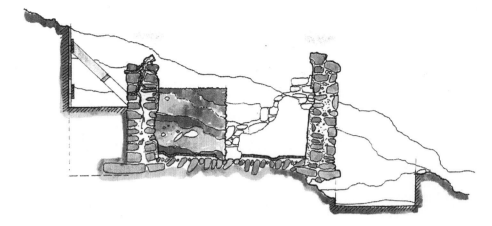

Figure 6.1.6 Archaeology as an informing force.

Figure 6.1.7 Archaeology as a destructive force.

8 Ignorant repair as a destructive force

In an attempt to consolidate the excavated building and leave it open to view, the responsibility for the site passes to a maintenance team with no experience other than general building repair. The walls are capped with cement based mortar and open joints are packed with cement grout and mortar. Fallen stones are picked up and set back on the wall heads with no understanding of their original provenance. Cement mortar is also used to form fillets against broken plaster edges and to patch lacunae in the mosaic floor. The plaster edges are painted with water soluble adhesive. The lower wall is underpinned with stone and concrete block. Water still collects in all the low spots of the site. Drainage channels are formed along the base of the walls and are lined in cement mortar. This kind of work not only completely confuses the surviving evidence of the original building but plays a real part in encouraging its destruction with the use of totally incompatible and inappropriate materials.

Figure 6.1.8 Ignorant repair as a destructive force.

9 Correct conservation as a benign intervention

If the site is considered important enough to leave open, perhaps because it is part of a tourist route, good conservation practice can be used to protect the excavated building, always providing there are adequate funds to carry out conservation maintenance for the indefinite future. Alternatively, the site may need to be temporarily consolidated because the archaeological investigation is not complete. Loose stones remaining in situ can be wedged with stone pins and a weak, compatible lime mortar. Small roots can be removed and large, woody growths cut back as close as possible to the surface of the masonry. Open joints and wall caps can be consolidated with compatible lime mortar, often a putty lime with ceramic powder. Water collecting hollows in the mosaic floor can be covered with geo-textile membrane and levelled with sand. Walls which are leaning or have inadequate support can be buttressed with sand bags. Decisions need to be made about who carries out this work. The archaeologists may need to carry out immediate emergency support works. Full conservation work needs to be carried out by trained conservators.

Figure 6.1.9 Correct conservation as a benign intervention.

10 Reburial

Where no funds are available for adequate conservation works and especially when the future of the site is uncertain, careful reburial after recording is often the wisest option, even when there is local opposition to the idea. Even reburial, however, will require some of the protective support and intervention of the kind which can be carried out by the archaeologists. The whole of the excavated area needs to be covered with generously lapped geo-textile membrane before returning the spoil to the site. Providing there is a generous covering of soil over the walls there is no reason why their outline should not be readable above the ground, and there may be significant benefits in being able to see the position of the building. In some situations temporary land drainage may be installed to divert water from sensitive areas as part of the reburial plan. This protection recreates the relatively stable conditions in which the ruined building survived for many centuries.

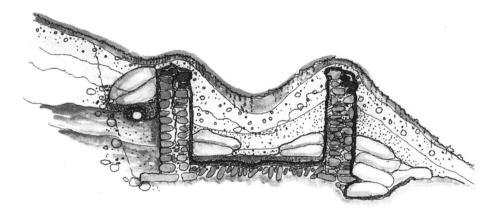

Figure 6.1.10 Reburial.

Chapter 6.2

Philosophy, technology and craft

John Ashurst and Colin Burns

Source: Ashurst, J. and Burns, C. (2007) 'Philosophy, technology and craft', in J. Ashurst (ed.), *Conservation of Ruins*, London: Butterworth Heinemann, pp. 82–145.

THE LIVING, HISTORIC BUILDING must be repaired to keep it habitable and secure, so that even when minimum works are carried out there are always aspects of restoration involved. The ruin is different; its partial destruction and the reasons for that destruction are part of its story, to be conserved. On an untouched site, the conservation team is 'first at the scene of the crime'. The exact way walls are found and the arrangement of fallen material are important to record and to preserve if the story is not to be altered for future generations. Even sites once consolidated can still, to the observant eye, contain evidence not previously noticed or understood, evidence which can be secured and made legible for the first time.

[...]

An initially slow advance of awareness and concern (about ruined ancient monuments) was significantly changed with the appointment of Charles Peers as Inspector of Ancient Monuments in 1910, [...] who began a process of systematic recording and reporting, and established a specialist works division for the repair and maintenance of monuments under the architect Frank Baines. Most importantly, Peers was concerned with establishing specific common standards for the maintenance of monuments in State care. In particular:

> ... maintenance must avoid, as far as possible, anything which can be considered in the nature of restoration, to do nothing which could impair the archaeological interest of the monuments and to confine themselves rigorously to such works as may be necessary to ensure their stability, to accentuate their interest and to perpetuate their existence in the form in which they have come down to us. [1]

In legislative terms, a philosophy of 'preserve as found' had formally and officially arrived.

PHILOSOPHY, TECHNOLOGY AND CRAFT 243

Figure 6.2.1 The west front of Tintern Abbey *c.*1860. This view is typical of the 'romantic ruin' that caught the imagination of Wordsworth and other poets. The heavy ivy mantles conceal the potentially disastrous development of several major structural problems, including the collapse of the south wall of the nave.

[...]

Tintern Abbey is picturesquely set in the wooded Wye valley of South Wales, built over a period of some 50 years, commencing in 1269. Following dissolution in 1535 it was, as was usual, stripped of its lead roof covering shortly afterwards, thus beginning the slow process of decay and eventual collapse of its roof, vault and tower, and the mantling of its walls in ivy. The romantic appeal of Tintern was much enhanced by artists and writers of the eighteenth and nineteenth centuries, and it was this legacy which seemed, to critics of the Office of Works (and there were many) in the early twentieth century, to be so needlessly and carelessly degraded.

William Woodward wrote to the *Daily Express* in July 1921:

> It is acknowledged that Tintern was the loveliest of our ruined abbeys, and so it is upon this particular ruin that the Office of Works has bestowed its benign influence. It has not been satisfied by the unnecessary stripping the walls of their ivy and wild roses, but it has introduced its favourite steel and concrete work as if it were complying with a London County Council Dangerous Structures Act.

But the ivy canopies were not only concealing but contributing to the further demise of the ruined buildings. Frank Baines was very positive on the subject and is famously quoted as saying:

> There is no more pernicious weed in the country than ivy. I once used to go about with a small saw, and whenever I saw ivy I cut its throat. [2]

One of the first structural analysts of the substantial ruins of Tintern at the time of the First World War was William Harvey, whose studies of Tintern, Rievaulx, Westminster and St Paul's Cathedral were published by the *Architectural Press* in 1925, [3] advocating the essential practice of knowing the whole building to understand its movements and the reason for distortion and fracturing. Two major areas of concern were identified at Tintern, once the ivy was removed. The first was a progressive westward movement of the north chancel wall, towards the great arch of the missing tower and the overhanging broken end of the north arcade of the nave (see Figure 6.2.2). Local repairs were not able to contain this westwards movement, as the north-west pier distorted and developed a pattern of fine stress cracks. The drift of its masonry piers in the chancel to the west could only be restrained by the installation of the reinforced wall head beams shown in Figure 6.2.3. The corbelled masonry of the nave arcade could only be supported by the installation of the steel ledgers shown in Figure 6.2.4.

The second major potential collapse was of the south wall of the nave. There it was found that the head of the wall, at its centre point, had a lean to the north of just over half a metre. The instability of the wall was confirmed by cracking patterns. Two options to correct the problem were considered: either to replace temporary timber shoring on the north side erected by the Office of Works (Figure 6.2.5), with masonry buttresses, or to devise a method of tying back the head of the walls. This second option

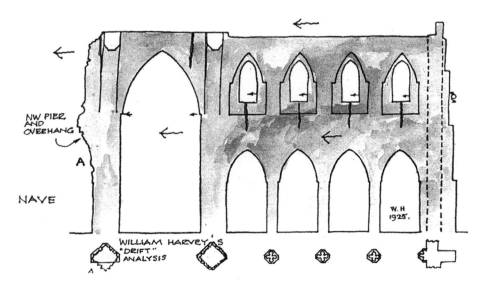

Figure 6.2.2 William Harvey's drawing of the north chancel wall showing the drift of the masonry to the west.

PHILOSOPHY, TECHNOLOGY AND CRAFT 245

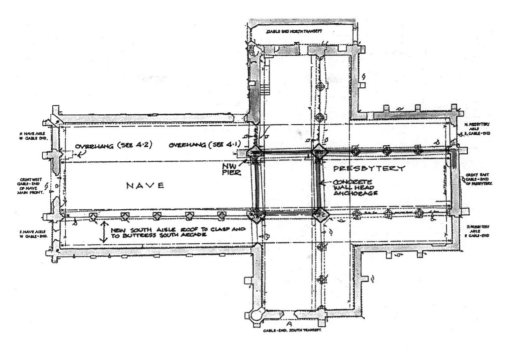

Figure 6.2.3 William Harvey's drawn plan showing the proposed installation of reinforced concrete wall head beam linked to a ring beam at the head of the tower.

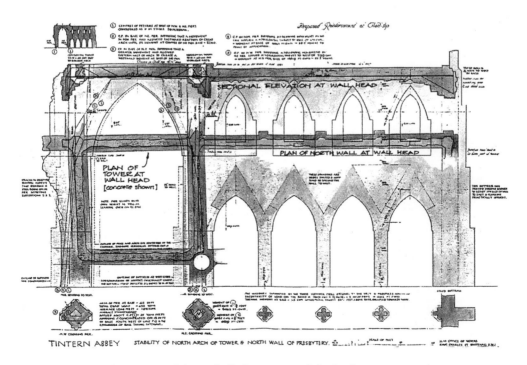

Figure 6.2.4 Reinforcement of the corbelled masonry of the broken nave arcade.

Figure 6.2.5 Tintern Abbey – north-west pier showing timber shoring under broken nave arcade. This overhanging masonry was repaired in the manner shown in Figure 6.2.6.

was selected both for reasons of avoiding visual intrusion in the nave and through fears of possible settlement of massive buttresses which would exacerbate the problem.

The proposal to tie back the wall head was made distinctly more feasible by the presence of a south aisle which once had a single pitch roof. Replacement of this roof, whose line was clearly evident at east and west, would enable a system of reinforcement to be introduced. A lattice girder was installed to restrain the nave walls and bolted through the nave wall without attempting to correct the distortion. The lattice girder was finally covered with oak rafters and tile-stones, leaving the soffit exposed. A secondary operation involved the substituting of the heavy timber shores with brick masonry supports to enable the shattered masonry of some of the piers to be strengthened by cutting out and inserting steel stanchions within the core of the nave piers; the steel was subsequently concealed by replacing original stones, or new stones where the originals had been shattered, and the brick supports removed.

These were the engineering works that so enraged William Woodward and others in the 1920s, but illustrate the ingenuity and care which were taken to transform a dangerous structure into a stable ruin. A certain pride developed based on the ability of architects, engineers and masons to execute major and minor works that were subsequently not easily detectable.

[. . .]

PHILOSOPHY, TECHNOLOGY AND CRAFT 247

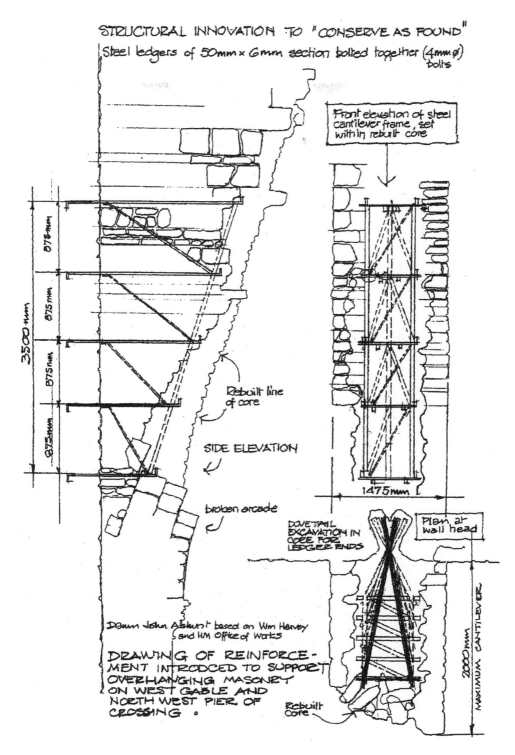

Figure 6.2.6 Reinforcement required to support overhanging masonry – Tintern Abbey.

Context and definitions

The most often repeated phrase in historic fabric conservation must be 'conserve as found with minimum intervention'.

'Conserving as found' is, of course, a philosophy whose implementation is governed, at least in part, by the nature and condition of the site, but it should influence every decision and remain as the ideal goal. In particular, essential conserving works should never introduce speculative restoration, or damage or alter evidence of the original buildings, or conceal the cause and character of their past deterioration and collapse.

'Minimum intervention' is the other familiar guiding principle for conservators of ruins, as for conservation of more complete historic buildings. Unfortunately, fundamental as the principle is, 'minimum intervention' cannot always mean doing very little, and a virtue should not be made of it where more serious intervention is actually needed. Largely worthless, low-key interventions are really only placebos, and may be illustrated by, for instance, the tamping and pointing of fractures without analysing the cause of fracturing, or installing an anchor within a crack or a bulging wall when what is needed is a programme of recording, taking down and rebuilding 'as found'.

[...]

Structural archaeology

The informed, visual examination of any structure, but particularly an historic ruin, will usually enable some, and perhaps a great deal, of its building history to be deduced.

[...]

Structural archaeology is quite distinct from structural analysis, which is based on a study of the structural content and condition [5] its evidence is final and incontrovertible, overriding even archival record. Typical features occurring and to be looked for in the ruined structure may be listed as follows:

- Straight vertical joints
- Toothed joints
- Random joints
- Straight horizontal joints
- Inserted openings
- Shadow lines indicative of the removal or decay of a feature
- Surface cavities such as putlog holes or lost fixings
- Assembly marks
- Changes in wall thickness
- Changes in construction type
- Changes in materials (see Figures 6.2.7 and 6.2.8).

The last category may be immediately obvious but more often is rather subtle in character, especially in the case of mortar or plaster. Long exposure to, and experience of, the materials can become very important if evidence is not to be unwittingly destroyed.

[...]

PHILOSOPHY, TECHNOLOGY AND CRAFT

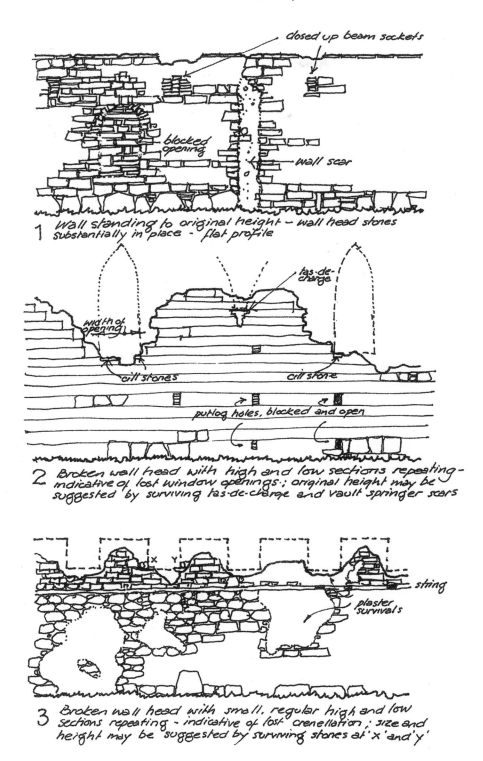

Figure 6.2.7 Ruin profiles. Broken wall heads.

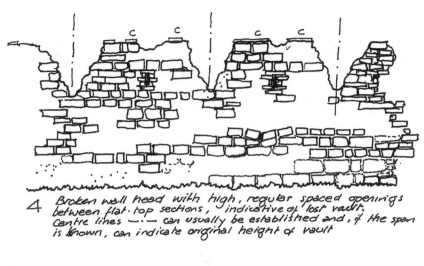

4 Broken wall head with high, regular spaced openings between flat-top sections, indicative of lost vault. Centre lines —·— can usually be established and, if the span is known, can indicate original height of vault

5 Irregular broken wall head with range of windows, leaving a wide variety of masonry heights and overhangs; original height uncertain but may be detectable in core

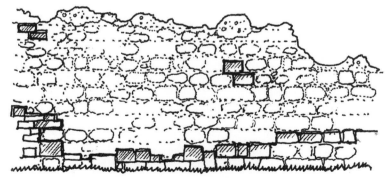

6 Irregular broken wall head surviving only in core work; indicator of well built core, commonly characterised by course lines, compaction layers and stone tail impressions, all of which enable a picture of the stone facing to be read. Walls of core are often — mistakenly — capped in hard, impervious stone and mortar, which quickly degrade the original faces below

Figure 6.2.8 Broken wall heads in masonry and core.

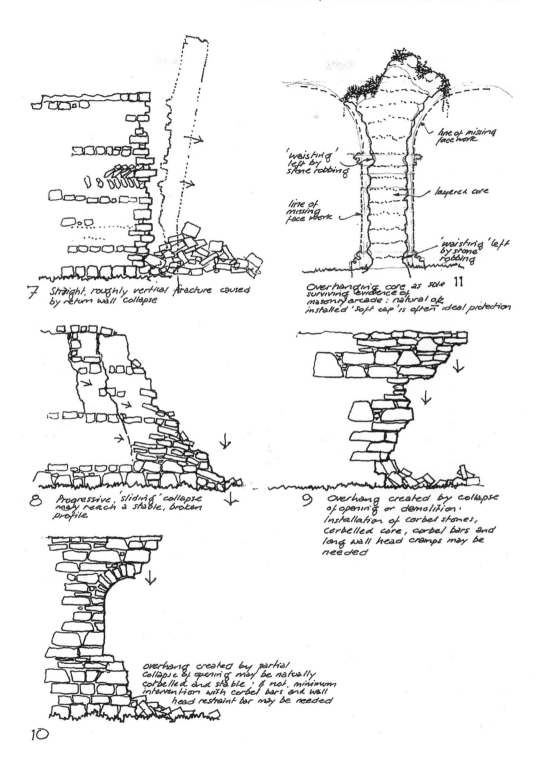

Figure 6.2.9 End profile and overhangs.

Temporary supports and protection

A condition survey, or even a more basic, preliminary survey, will identify parts of a building and its site which are at risk and which may present immediate dangers. In this category might be, for instance, seriously leaning walls, new or spreading fractures, bulging facework with open joints, displaced stones at high level or major landslips. Conditions of this kind often require immediate intervention both to support, contain and protect the ruin from further loss, and to protect visitors, legitimate or not, from injury and possible loss of life.

[...]

On some sites, removal of vegetation is required in order to inspect the masonry and make some assessment of its condition. This operation requires more care and understanding than is generally appreciated, and should in any case be preceded by consideration of the ecological impact removal will entail.

Well-developed plants such as mature ivy (*Hedera helix*) are often found to be clasping and supporting unstable areas of masonry, so that premature or injudicious removal can result in local collapse and injury. Where trees have established themselves in the masonry, the usual approach is to cut them back to within 600 mm of the building face; however, consideration must always be given to effects that the release of the applied loading may have on the wall as the weight of the tree is removed. To avoid local collapses it may be necessary to install some temporary support to vulnerable areas before trees are cut.

A common practice in removing ivy is to cut out a metre section of the plant close to the ground to allow the plant to die on the wall and to poison the root.

[...]

Wall tops

Where walls still stand to their original height, the exposed and untouched wall tops of a rum are often a rich source of information. Evidence of corbels or corbel tables, wall plates, tie beams, water outlets and even roof coverings may be present within a matrix of loose masonry and vegetation. Probably nowhere are structural archaeology and stability found in such an intimate and fragile relationship.

[...]

Broken wall heads may still be indicative of original, complete forms, such as crenellations, gables or towers.

Walls that have been reduced to low levels, standing only a metre or less above present ground levels, often appear to have very little evidence indeed of their original scale and form. [...] Evidence of door openings, buttresses, straight joints indicative of alterations or additions, plaster or tile fragments, changes in materials or construction methods may still survive and must be protected and made as legible as possible by the consolidation process. Maintaining the character of the masonry construction is vital; the size, shape and relationship of core to facework must reflect the 'as found' condition. Very-low-lying walls are particularly vulnerable, in some contexts, to flooding, frost damage, foot traffic, vegetation and stone robbing (see Figure 6.2.10).

All categories of wall may, of course, have been partly or comprehensively conserved in the past. Pre-treated sites of this kind can present particular problems, relating, for instance, to the use of cement-based mortar in joints and cappings, the modification of

PHILOSOPHY, TECHNOLOGY AND CRAFT 253

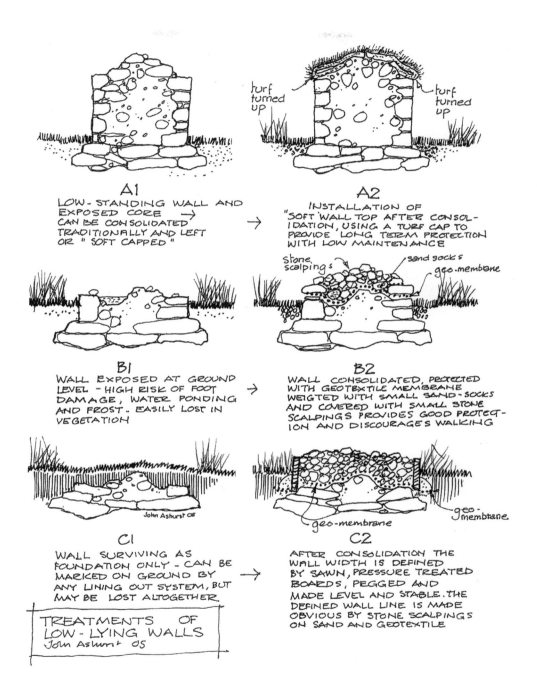

Figure 6.2.10 Treatments of low-lying walls.

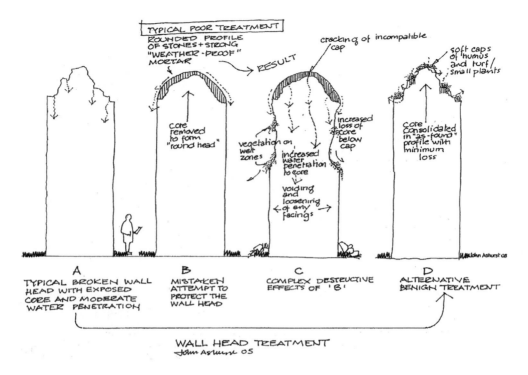

Figure 6.2.11 Wall head treatments.

profiles to shed water and speculative (or accurate) areas of reconstruction. One of the most common problems is the deterioration of original work immediately below cement-rich wall cappings and the detachment of areas of facework pointed in cement-rich mortar (see Figure 6.2.11). Only rarely do detailed records of such work survive even if they were ever made. The recording of past interventions, and of new ones, must become a part of the site's archive, securely stored and easily retrieved. The 'unpicking' of previous work, where of poor or damaging quality, and reconsolidation of the original construction is a common requirement.

The approach and methods for consolidating previously untouched wall heads is suggested as follows. Where present, vegetation should be removed, as previously described. Where there is an intention to reinstate a 'soft' or natural capping to a wall head, the soil, root mats and small plants can be set aside and kept in suitable conditions for re-laying. Enough must be removed to a level where structural and archaeological assessments and recording can be carried out.

Recording should consist of photographs at all stages of progress and should make use of planning frames in preparation for consolidation.

Planning frames are used to record the positions of each stone forming the faces of the wall and the arrangement of exposed core, the aim being to enable the masonry to be put back in exactly the same positions as found. Carried out correctly, the consolidation work will not confuse interpretation of the structure in the future. The consolidation work will thus include any fractures, distortions or leaning and avoid the mistake of 'correcting' or 'restoring'.

[. . .] The outline and locations of each stone are drawn with indelible markers onto the plastic film, and each one is numbered. As the loose stones are lifted from the walls they are cleaned by a bristle brushing and identified by a number corresponding to the number in the planning frame. With the exception of its uppermost course, this number is marked on the top bed of the stone. The marking system should make use of waterproof markers or paint, all of which, except the top course, will be hidden within the wall when rebuilt. The top course can be marked on the bottom bed. The marking system enables the stones to be replaced in their original positions. When the loose, marked stones are taken down they are stacked neatly on the scaffold, ready for rebuilding. As the process of cleaning off, marking, lifting down and stacking proceeds, roots and soil within the walls are removed. Substantial roots are normally followed down into the wall by unpicking masonry until they no longer present a problem, but not all traces of root need to be removed. Fine roots can remain buried within the wall where, without light, they are unlikely to grow. The extent to which a wall head is taken down depends on a number of factors, including the size and arrangement of the masonry units, condition of the original mortars, extent of root invasion and displacement of masonry. As always, experience is essential to decision-making. The exposed wall head is prepared for resetting face stones and core by brushing down and, if available, removing small, loose material with an industrial vacuum cleaner, followed by washing with clean water. Rebuilding proceeds using a well-designed bedding mortar (see 'Mortar'). The position and alignment of each stone are checked with the planning frame and any profiles that were made during dismantling, until the work has been raised to its original position. There is a general acceptance that the finished wall head can be modified from the original 'as found' position to eliminate the risk of rainwater 'ponding', providing that this does not affect or alter any archaeological features that exist within the masonry. If, however, it is intended to reinstate root mats, soil and plants, the ponding issue is not as relevant. On occasion, new soil and seeds representative of the site's natural ecology are installed to provide a 'soft top' which acts as a benign sponge-like covering. The benefits of such a capping can be seen on many 'natural' sites. English Heritage found this of sufficient significance to carry out research into the beneficial effects of 'soft tops' as opposed to traditional hard cappings [4] (see Figure 6.2.12).

Broken wall ends and core facework

[. . .]

The term 'core facework' is often used to describe situations where the facing masonry has been robbed or lost and the core of the wall is now exposed as a 'face'. Broken composite wall ends always involve 'core facework', but the stone facings are often lost from large areas of wall extending back from the break, or quite independently of it. 'Core facework' is thus a very important element in masonry conservation.

[. . .]

The profiles of broken wall ends generally fall into three categories. The first is largely vertical, and may occur, for instance, at a straight joint or where a gable wall had been very inadequately bonded to the return walls. The second is ramped, or stepped back, often the pattern of progressive collapse, and sometimes achieving reasonable stability. The third is overhanging, a potentially dangerous situation commonly resulting

Figure 6.2.12 Perfect protection for this roofless ruin is provided by a mature mat of turf and wild flowers. This natural covering can hardly be improved on, and if the masonry below is stable, should be left alone.

from the collapse of a large window head, or a vault, leaving high-level masonry in a cantilevered position.

Undertaking the consolidation work of masonry in these reduced circumstances requires a proper understanding of the way stones can be corbelled out and counterbalanced in dry masonry. Mortar should never be relied on to achieve stability as a substitute for this understanding. In situations where balance cannot be reached, structural assistance can be provided by incorporating non-ferrous metals in the form of restraining cramps, dowels, corbel bars or column and plate supports.

Fractures

[...]

Some fractures are stable, and no further movement is likely to take place provided a maintenance plan is in place and is acted upon. Typically, some fractures are partly filled with debris. Live or suspect live fractures will usually require some form of monitoring in order to understand the causes of movement and to enable the correct mitigating procedures to be designed and installed. These may involve some underpinning, or underpinning and bridging areas of subsidence, and may sometimes require the insertion of wall-head beams or ring beams of tile or lime concrete. More commonly, large fractures such as those occurring a few metres from a wall end, with displacement on one side of the fracture, may require physical stitching across them; this is achieved by removing facework and core to form slots across the fracture at intervals. The slots are used to receive suitably shaped long stones, or non-ferrous metal bars with turned-down ends or stainless steel threaded bars set in resin dovetails, or lime concrete stitches. All stitches are intended to prevent further movement in the future.

[...]

Whether the fracture is fine or wide, it is important to pack and tamp or grout them with lime mortar to prevent further degradation of the wall core by denying water access. Grout and mortar should be kept back from the face to a sufficient depth to create a shadow line within the old fracture, so that the overall appearance is unchanged after the weakness has been resolved within the core of the wall.

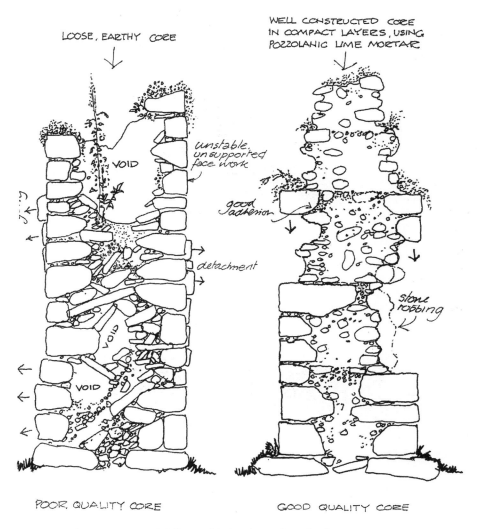

Figure 6.2.13 Characteristics of different kinds of core in ruined contexts.

Voids in walls

Long-term exposure of wall heads, especially where fractures are present, can result in the creation of voids within the core of the wall. Such voids are not limited to ruins, but are particularly common in roofless structures and may house tenants such as bats, birds or snakes, who will require consideration before any remedial work is commenced. In the first decades of conservation work on ancient monuments in Britain, these voids were filled with cement grout (liquid mortar) introduced by a gravity feed system. The principles used were sound and the stability achieved in many cases undisputed, but unfortunately the choice of material sometimes contributed new problems without completely resolving the original ones.

[...]

Void patterns within walls are difficult to determine accurately by survey. The distribution system for invasive water within a thick wall core can be very complex. In spite of this, entry and exit points can be observed and should be recorded. A simple process of sounding the wall faces with a hammer will indicate some of the void locations close to the face, and the removal of a face stone in a suspect area will be even more informative. More sophisticated systems such as using gamma or X-ray or ultrasonic testing are sometimes advocated, but the time and cost and, especially, the potential benefits should be carefully considered against their true value. In all remedial works procedures the simplest means possible to achieve the required result should be selected.

[...]

To further establish voids at greater depths and to determine their extent and direction, water can be fed into the wall using a hosepipe. Flushing with water in this manner has a number of benefits. It will escape the core from either face and indicates the bottoms of tracks or voids within the wall. These are marked as grout injection points. Loose dust and debris is flushed from the wall during this operation and the core is well wetted, ready for the grouting process.

The entire wall or walls are tested in this manner. Any large areas of masonry not showing signs of leaking during the process can be deep drilled through joints on a grid system of 0.5 m vertically, 1.0 m horizontally, and staggered in order to connect with long voids which will act as both grout injection and proving holes during the works.

All marked water escape points are fitted with plastic tubes set into the wall that are of a diameter to accept the grout injection nozzles. Repointing of the wall or walls can now take place and in doing so the plastic tubes are fixed into the masonry.

Grout is always introduced from the base of a wall, not from the top. This important practice is to avoid blocking through air locking and to prevent fine debris working down and closing up the voids. For this reason, it is sensible to plan repointing at open joints from the bottom upwards, so that the mortar can gain enough strength to contain the grout without leakage. In some circumstances the open joints can be plugged with foam backer rod or some alternative packing and repointed after grouting.

Introduction of grout is ideally carried out using a simple diaphragm pump which works by pushing and pulling the operating lever (see Figure 6.2.14).

A pressure gauge is fitted to the pump and this, during pumping, should hardly register, as introduction of grout into the wall needs to allow for the grout to spread slowly and horizontally along the wall, rather than creating a vertical head of grout

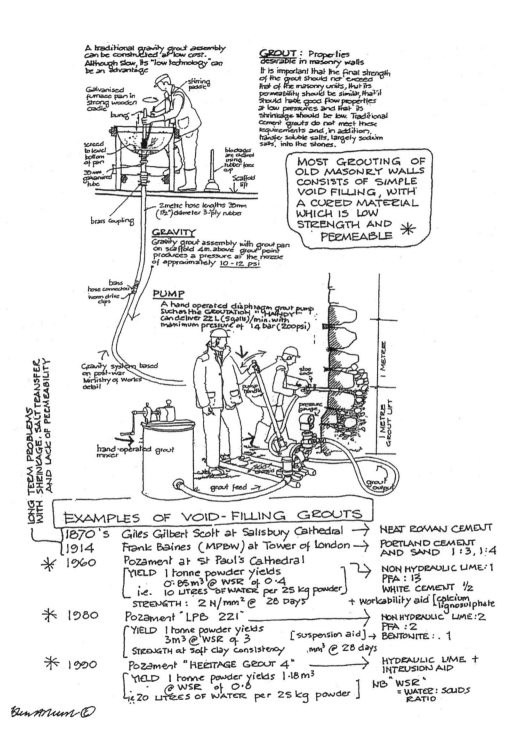

Figure 6.2.14 Grouting masonry walls.

locally at the injection point and then allowing it to spread along the voids within the wall.

The lift heights for grouting will vary on buildings. Large granite ashlars with a fine joint system could be raised 1.5–2.0 m in one day. Alternatively, small stones in a weak mortar should not be raised above 0.5 m without the risk of hydrostatic pressure moving faces away from the core. Decisions on height of grout per day can only be taken on site and must be based on extensive previous experience.

If possible, each lift of grout introduced to a wall should be left for one day before resuming grouting. This is in order to give the grout time to dewater and stabilise before more grout is added to the wall. Grout continues in this manner until the head of the wall is reached. At this stage it is advisable to apply a head of grout to the upper proving holes, to compensate for the reduction in volume of grout due to de-watering within the voids. Quantities of grout taken up at each injection point should be recorded to provide an indication of the volumes filled.

On completion of grouting and after a period of three to four days, the plastic sleeves can be removed and the injection points can be deep tamped and pointed.

Stone replacement

Within the philosophical context already described it is unusual to find any substantial replacements of new stone. All stones, in whatever condition and especially any that have to be replaced, must be recorded and evaluated. All types need to be petrographically identified and provenanced as closely as possible, and archaeological evidence such as lifting tenons, quarry-working marks, tooling, identification marks and mortices must be recorded [. . .] (they are) necessary, to support [. . .] the rule of 'like with like' is generally thought to be appropriate. In many cases this can amount to no more than geological compatibility, because original sources of stone are often no longer available. Matching colour, grain size and texture are thought to be important in the repair of any masonry buildings, but in the conservation of old, weathered masonry the overriding objective must be to so modify the situation in the wall that its life expectancy is significantly increased.

[. . .]

Replacements should normally be 100 or 150 mm on bed, and sometimes longer, depending on their functions, but the face dimensions (L and H) should match those of the lost stone as closely as possible and, most importantly, should be set to the original face line on the building (see Figure 6.2.15). In weathered and decayed masonry, this means that the new stone will project, often forming a ledge on the top bed and creating a shadow line under its bottom bed. In spite of this, there should be no deviation from this rule or the evidence of the original face line and its profiles will be lost, and the authors of future replacements denied essential information.

[. . .]

Replacement stone should always be identifiable, and there is a tradition of incising the date of placement on new stone. In some situations stone replacement within ruins may be structurally necessary and a stylistic difference may be made to differentiate new from old.

In cases where severely decayed masonry is in need of local replacement, an alternative to whole block indenting may be the use of tiles. The Society for the

Figure 6.2.15 This replacement stone has been set in a damaged medieval entrance arch still used by vehicular traffic. The stone is the correct chamfered profile taken from the head of the arch and is placed in its correct line in the jamb. Although the new stone projects from the weathered masonry no mortar weatherings are used; instead the stone has a very slight fall on its top bed and a pencil-round arris. Providing the bedding mortar is deep and well packed this stone will shed water effectively. Guildford, Surrey, UK.

Protection of Ancient Buildings in England has for decades recommended the use of coursed clay tiles for philosophical reasons, in both hydraulic lime and cement and lime. The argument for this approach is that structural support can be introduced in a way that does not compromise the truth, even if the tile repairs were rendered, as they often were. An example of such a repair is at Guildford Castle, carried out in 1914.

The importance of this technique is primarily in its compatibility with the ancient fabric. Porous, permeable tiles of clay or weathered stone set in porous, permeable mortars are receptive to water vapour movement and the passage of salts in solution; they do not create new crises for the beleaguered walls in which they are set and can, in later years, be replaced. Unlike new stone or brick they can be expected to perform in a truly sacrificial role for the benefit of the old work they are trying to sustain.

Stone repairs

The retention, rather than the replacement, of the stones or bricks in a ruin should be an obvious choice. Old techniques of repairing stones included the 'tinning' of open fractures by running in liquid cement, joining detached fragments with shellac or clasping elements such as mullions and tracery with copper tape. Minimum replacement is frequently coupled with techniques of filling small lacunae with mortar ('dental repairs'), or with small pieces of stone or tile within the boundaries of an old stone ('piecing-in'), or of drilling and stitching fractured stones. The design of appropriate mortar fills must follow the general principles set out under 'mortar specification for joints', but in the repair context it is even more crucial to have good water vapour permeability and moduli of elasticity in addition to good texture and good, stable colour in both wet and dry conditions. Dental repairs, like stone repairs, should always be sacrificial and records of their composition must be retained so that future repair material can be repeated or modified.

Fractures in individual stones often require a method of stitching. The use of adhesives alone is not particularly recommended, unless the repair is very small, and should never be used on interfaces exceeding 10 mm² as they form barriers to water movement and can encourage local build-ups of salts. Stitching involves drilling across the fracture, blowing out the debris with a drinking straw or rubber 'puffer', flushing out with water and a suitably sized bottle brush, and grouting in a 'stitch', pre-cut and first fitted dry. Micro-stitching of this kind is best carried out with twisted strands of copper wire (two or three strands can be twisted together using a hand or power drill and then cut to size). Slightly larger stitching can be carried out using purpose-made ceramic pins or T-bars, which have the benefit of being highly compatible with porous stones or ceramic. Very fine stitching can be executed with carbon-fibre pins. In most cases, stitches can be satisfactorily grouted in hydraulic lime.

Mortar

Where ancient ruined masonry is mortared the mortar may be based on lime, soil or gypsum, or on some combination of these three. If a modern artificial cement is present, usually a type of Portland cement, in pre-1850 buildings, it belongs almost without exception to previous and inappropriate programmes of remedial work. [. . .] Most prominent among these are cracking of both joints and stones or bricks, lifting of consolidated wall heads, increased decay rates to stone, plaster, earth walls or mosaics caused by accelerated wetting and drying of salt contaminated water, and increased incidence of frost damage in cold, wet climates. Simply put, there is an inherent and fatal incompatibility between cement and lime-mortared construction, which no amount of theorising or modification will eliminate.

[. . .]

The composite wall, already described, consisting of two masonry skins enclosing a core of stone and mortar, is the most common, traditional form of load-bearing wall, but variations in construction are very numerous and these variations have a profound effect on how walls behave when they are broken and exposed to the weather.

[. . .]

- Make a visual inspection of the mortars on site; look for individual characteristics of colour, texture and weathering, and for differences; where possible, identify earlier interventions; look for and record areas of failure or apparent risk and areas of decaying stone or bricks.
- Take samples of unweathered mortar for record and analysis; this is much simpler matter from wall cores than from joints, but the aim is to remove samples that have not been significantly altered. Each sample should be kept in a sealable bag or jar clearly and indelibly labelled with the name of the site, the location of the site and a description of the mortar sample, preferably supported by a photographic reference and a record of the date and who took the sample.
- Design a mortar that will protect the masonry without creating new problems and that will be visually harmonious with the other mortars on site. This should take account of the original aggregates used and recorded from samples, but analysis should not be used as the basis of a new specification, which is for a mortar

whose role is to perform alongside weathered and altered stones, bricks or earth. The condition of the old masonry must always be the first consideration, the role of the mortar the second and the exposure of the mortar the third.
- Prepare trial batches of mortars and look at them in the context of the site. Prepare method statements for the preparation of the remedial mortars using the site conditions to 'fine-tune' the way the mortar is treated and finished. When completed, these trials and the mortar specification should become a part of the permanent record of the site and are essential for future conservation and maintenance. Without such records no useful lessons can be learnt in the future.

Decisions need to be made on how new mortar should look. The traditional 'like with like' approach, although visually satisfying, may need some adjustment if the new work is to be distinguishable from the old. The last stage of well-executed joint filling is to tamp or wash the mortar face to match the weathered texture of old surviving mortar, or it may be profiled to match an original profile.

[. . .]

Critical to the success of mortar, mortar repair or plaster repair is the curing process. Whatever mortar is used it will almost certainly fail if it dries too quickly for a proper carbonation process to take place. The first essential is to make sure that the backing for mortar or plaster is made adequately damp. In practical terms this means that enough water will have been applied to the surface to avoid any significant suction on the new material. The surface should not glisten with water but it should refuse to take any more. Once the new mortar has been placed it needs to be screened, ideally with plastic film that retains humidity better than any open textured material. [. . .] During the day intermittent fine spraying of mortar surfaces is recommended to keep them in a slightly damp condition over a period of 7–10 days. Without this initial care a great deal of time and effort will be wasted, as the mortar will either shrink and crack or will carbonate rapidly on the surface, sealing mortar behind which will never gain adequate strength.

Replacement mortar materials

[. . .]

Non-hydraulic lime ('air lime') and hydraulic lime ('water lime') with pozzolans such as ceramic powder to promote set and react with available free lime are the usual binder materials for replacement mortars.

[. . .]

Two mortar categories are proposed in Tables 6.2.1 and 6.2.2. The first, Type A, is based on a non-hydraulic lime in the form of putty, with a pozzolan additive to provide a weak hydraulic set. Three pozzolans are suggested, one wood ash and the other crushed ceramic tile or brick, and the third one a metakaolin. True pozzolan could also be included but variations in reactivity are so wide that to do so is not helpful. The purpose of adding pozzolan, following an ancient tradition which survives to the present day, is to provide a relatively weak hydraulic set. The weakest of these was often achieved by reaction of some of the lime in the kiln with the ash or slag from the fuel used in the combustion process. The second category, Type B, is based on natural

Table 6.2.1 Mortar type 'A' – lime putty and pozzolan

	Mix designation		
	A1	A2	A3
Mature lime putty	1.0	1.0	1.0
Aggregate – hard, angular	1.5	1.0	1.0
Aggregate – rough, porous	1.5	1.5	1.5
Aggregate – metakaolin	–	–	0.1
Aggregate – ceramic	–	1.0	–
Aggregate – wood ash	1.0	–	–

Note: A1 = weakest; A3 = strongest.

Table 6.2.2 Mortar type 'B' – hydraulic lime

	Mix designation		
	B1	B2	B3
NHL2	1.0	–	–
NHL3.5	–	1.0	–
NHL5	–	–	1.0
Aggregate – hard, angular	1.5	1.0	1.0
Aggregate – rough, porous	1.0	1.0	1.0
Aggregate – ceramic	–	–	0.5

Note: B1 = weakest; B3 = strongest

hydraulic lime using the European standards to describe them as NHL2 (approximating 'feebly hydraulic'), NHL3.5 (approximating 'moderately hydraulic') and NHL5 (approximating 'eminently hydraulic'). In one case the addition of a pozzolan is suggested to react with some of the free lime present after the hydraulic set has taken place.

Description of mortar constituents

- *Lime putty.* This should be putty prepared from quicklime stored in an airtight tub or under water for a minimum of six months. Aged putties well in excess of one year old are particularly desirable for the weaker mixes. The putty must be in a stiff, plastic state when it is gauged, to avoid inaccuracies when batching. A stiff putty yields significantly more lime than the same volume of a loose, wet putty.
- *Aggregate – hard, angular.* This describes a clean, sharp grit-sand, well graded to suit the appearance of the mortar being matched.
- *Aggregate – rough, porous.* This describes aggregate with a pore structure that will assist carbonation of the mortar and improve its resistance to salt crystallisation and to freeze–thaw damage. Typically, this would be broken, graded limestone or brick, but could include particles of slag and other porous material.
- *Pozzolan – metakaolin.* This product may not be available in every country, but is a useful material. China clay fired at approximately 800° C produces material that

will react rapidly with calcium hydroxide to provide a hydraulic set. Strength gains continue over quite a long period. Quantities in excess of one-tenth of the lime binder are not recommended.
- *Pozzolan – ceramic.* Following Roman tradition, this pozzolan is typically a low-fired brick or tile powder fired at relatively low temperatures (c.1,000° C) ground to a fine powder (passing a 75-micron sieve). Grinding to provide fresh broken surfaces can be useful. Proportions are normally 1:1 with the binder.
- *Pozzolan – wood ash.* The weakest of the pozzolans is a difficult material to quantify, and like all additives must be subject to preliminary trials. The great advantage is that ash is universally available. Great care should be taken in using any other forms of fuel ash with unknown soluble salt contents and unknown reactivity.
- *Natural hydraulic limes – NHL2, NHL3.5 and NHL5.* Natural hydraulic limes are becoming increasingly available, with France being the current major supplier.

The mortars in Tables 6.2.1 and 6.2.2 are arranged according to their strength; thus, the weakest mortar is A1 and the strongest is B3. The weakest mortar able to perform the intended function without creating new problems for historic fabric should always be selected.

Grout materials

Non-hydraulic lime ('air lime') and hydraulic limes ('water limes') in combination with pozzolans such as pulverised fuel ash (pfa) or fine powdered ceramic with suspension aids such as bentonite are the usual solids used in grouting. Although, in the past, cement was extensively and almost exclusively used, it should now be eliminated from grouts for historic masonry. Some mix proportions are shown in Figure 6.2.15.

Unmortared walls

Many examples of unmortared masonry survive from a wide range of cultures, time and geographical distribution. These may be highly sophisticated or very primitive, but all required skill and experience to construct, whether water-washed boulders at Tel Dan (see Figure 6.2.17), irregularly split slate slabs at Trei'r Ceiri, carefully fitted polygonal stones at Cuzco (see Figure 6.2.16) or the seamless ashlar of classical Greece. The principal threats to such construction, depending on location, are stone robbing, seismic movement, subsidence and acts of war. Not being mortar dependent at all, they are often extremely durable and stable. The contrast between dry-built and mortared construction is particularly interesting in wet, cold climates; there is little that water movement (aside from scouring at the wall base) can do to unmortared walls, and freezing presents few problems because of the free-draining nature of the construction. Some dry-built construction was packed with earth to keep out wind and rain, but these materials in such a context are nonstructural and usually lost through time and weathering. Some were also plastered with clay, lime- or gypsum-based plasters.

The most important and perhaps obvious point to make in conservation work is that mortar and grout must never be introduced. Such interference with the natural wetting and drying rhythms in the wall will be damaging and may result in localised

Figure 6.2.16 Massive, unmortared stones at Cuzco illustrate some of the most accurately worked masonry seen anywhere, and virtually indestructible except through severe seismic activity, deliberate demolition or artillery fire.

collapse, quite apart from falsifying the evidence. If locally bulging or leaning wall sections require help, they must be carefully recorded and marked before taking down and rebuilding using the planning frame. Iron cramps run in lead and bronze cramps were both used in dry-built ashlar. Occasionally, these need replacing in phosphor bronze or stainless steel, with preference given to bronze alloy where the installations are likely to be seen. If new stones are introduced into ashlar the work must carefully match the precision of the original.

[. . .]

Plaster

Plaster often survives in ruins, sometimes to the extent that it still has a protective role for the masonry, sometimes only as small coatings of gesso on architectural moulding, sometimes as the last indication of a decorative scheme, coloured or polished; its value in dating a structure or in indicating the original character of the building or a room within it is often considerable. [. . .] The most vulnerable plasters in the context of a ruin are those based on clay-earth (mud undercoats or full plasters) and those based on gypsum, especially in wet climates. Both are readily degraded in water and suffer surface softening and attrition followed by detachment, often soon after exposure if they are not protected by paint or lime-wash. Well-carbonated lime plasters, non-hydraulic as well as hydraulic, can have surprising tenacity and durability, and natural cement and artificial cement stuccos commonly only fail due to cracking, detachment and freezing of trapped water, although these failures may be exacerbated by a history of soluble salt crystallisation.

In the context of the ruin, conservation activity includes the installation of small roof covers attached to the wall to throw water clear of the plaster (see Figure 6.2.17),

Figure 6.2.17 Masonry of water-washed boulders at Tel Dan, northern Israel. Upper courses rebuilt.

removal of organic soiling with biocide and small steam guns, removal of any impermeable cement-based mortar edge fillets or patches, flushing and grouting detachments and fractures, and installing lime mortar edge fillets and fills in lacunae.

[. . .]

Weak surfaces can sometimes be consolidated with multiple applications of lime water and, where appropriate, protected with finely screened limewash, gauged with a small percentage of casein.

Floors

Solid floors exposed by the loss of roofs are challenged in the same way as wall heads and internal wall surfaces; they were not intended to be weathering surfaces. The most vulnerable are those of rammed earth, with or without a plaster finish. These are very quickly destroyed by rain and the root systems of plants, although evidence sometimes survives close to the protected base of walls or where the floor was covered with fallen debris. Floors of this kind, after recording, must be covered if they are to be retained in dry, ventilated conditions. Even when the floor finish is missing there may be layers of compacted material below, indicative of the original floor level and even of the missing finish type. Once recorded these compacted layers normally need to be protected by back-filling.

Well-fired brick or tile and stone slabs or cobbles are the most durable finishes and may, with judicious pointing in hydraulic lime and sand, lifting and rebedding where necessary to avoid hollows where ponding can take place, weather well in exposed contexts.

Floors such as Roman or Byzantine mosaic, or medieval floor tiles, present particular problems in the context of ruins. They may have been damaged by fallen masonry roof tiles or timber and may survive in localised areas with unsupported edges, becoming loose through exposure to weather. They are vulnerable to plant growth and organic soiling and salt deposits, and to hollows developing in the supporting base, leading to subsidence and water collection. They are, perhaps more than any other artefact on the ruin site, at risk from souvenir hunters. Unfortunately, many of these floors have been badly treated by uninformed custodians, and both mosaics and tiles have been grouted and even bedded in strong cement-based mortar to try to secure them. In cold, wet zones this treatment can have disastrous effects on clay floor tiles, and on ceramic and limestone tesserae, with the ancient fabric acting sacrificially to the mortar; similarly, in sites where soluble salts migrate to the floor surface, ceramic, limestone and marble will again suffer casualties while the mortar survives.

Notes and references

1. Peers, C. (1931). The treatment of old buildings. *RIBA Journal*.
2. Baines, F. (1924). From an address to the Northern Polytechnic Department on the Preservation of Ancient Monuments and Historic Buildings, 3 December.
3. Harvey, W. (1925). *The Preservation of St Paul's Cathedral and Other Famous Buildings: A Text Book on the New Science of Conservation*. The Architectural Press.
4. Viles, H., Groves, C. and Wood, C. (2002). 'Soft wall capping experiments.' *English Heritage Research Transactions*, Volume II.
5. How, C. (2007). 'Stability and Survival.' In J. Ashurst, *Conservation of Ruins*. London: Butterworth Heinemann, 11–43.

Chapter 6.3

Setting and structure
The conservation of Wigmore Castle

Glyn Coppack

Source: Coppack, G. (1999) 'Setting and structure: the conservation of Wigmore Castle', in G. Chitty and D. Baker (eds), *Managing Historic Sites and Buildings*, London: Routledge, pp. 61–70.

WIGMORE CASTLE, one of the greatest castles of the Welsh March and the principal castle of the Mortimer dynasty, is one of the few major castles in Britain that has not been conserved since it was abandoned in the sixteenth century (see Figure 6.3.1). Allowed to decay naturally for four centuries, it remains a substantial ruin within an area of historic woodland pasture, apparently little changed since it was recorded by the Buck brothers in the early 1730s, [...] a remarkable archaeological resource with buildings buried by their own collapse to approximately first floor level. Although many parts of the site had stabilised quite naturally, others have remained unstable, and a section of the curtain wall fell as recently as 1988 (Shoesmith 1987, 3).

A Scheduled Ancient Monument, Wigmore had been identified as being at risk by English Heritage in a survey that placed it historically and archaeologically as the most significant unconserved castle of the Welsh March (Streeten 1993). [...] the present owner, John Gaunt, placed the site in the guardianship of the Secretary of State for National Heritage in November 1995.

The condition of the site

[...] the structures that are visible today date predominantly from the thirteenth and early fourteenth centuries, the period of the Mortimers' greatest power and the castle's greatest extent. The castle was built of a local mud-stone with dressings of a soft sandstone, originally 'plastered' to protect it from weathering. Most of the 'plaster' had gone and the masonry was generally eroded, though it still contained many archaeological features. Wall tops were protected by a dense mat of vegetation that contained a number of rare species of fern but also briars and small trees that were starting to destabilise the masonry (see Figure 6.3.2), as well as dense ivy that had been cut at ground level and was now well rooted into the upper walls. [...] In most areas, the

Figure 6.3.1 Wigmore Castle from the south prior to being taken into guardianship.
Source: From Coppack (1999)

Figure 6.3.2 The north wall of the shell keep before repair.
Source: Image Glyn Coppack

earthworks of buried buildings were at least partially obscured and it was difficult to 'read' the site. [. . .]

The philosophy of repair

Theory

Wigmore Castle was untouched, and therefore an ideal site for developing a philosophy of repair tailored to suit its needs and to reflect current developments in conservation practice. So often, repair is constrained by what has been done in the past, however well intentioned that work was. The policy of 'conserve as found', an expression that dates from the days of Sir Charles Peers and Sir Frank Baines in the first half of this century, has been taken to mean different things to each generation, to the extent that 'conservation' is often in fact no more than replication with some if not all of the original elements, and 'found' reflects the expectation of the time or the idiosyncrasies of the conservator. What it has never meant is the leaving of a monument as close to its state as originally found, which is also consistent with its long-term stabilisation and public access, yet this is what a site like Wigmore requires.

[. . .] At Wigmore, the site itself provided the basis of the repair strategy, its state and component parts being the only factors that controlled the approach adopted. Immediately before the site was taken into guardianship, a full photographic survey was made of all of the surviving masonry, followed by a fully digitised photogrammetric and rectified photographic survey which has formed the basis of all subsequent work. A topographic survey was made of the whole of the site, including outworks not in guardianship, and a detailed ecological survey followed. [. . .] surviving elements of the castle were not as fragile as they looked, [. . .] and they supported an extensive and important ecosystem that was more fragile than the ruins. It was also obvious, and had been for some time, that there were serious structural problems that might require massive intervention, including extensive ground disturbance, unless a more sensitive approach could be developed. [. . .] The site, effectively, presented a unique opportunity to develop the least intrusive techniques of repair and presentation, based on the site itself and designed to enhance its qualities. For once, it was possible to 'conserve as found' with the minimum amount of reconstruction and intervention, to set the standard for the future repair of ruined structures, and to monitor the effectiveness of the approach adopted.

Practice

Repair was to be done by contract, which required the preparation of a full specification of works before the site could be properly examined. Most of the higher masonry was obscured by ivy which could not be removed without destabilising the ruins, and only limited access to examine the upper levels was possible. The only way in which work could be specified was to identify a series of appropriate treatments, which included perhaps more taking down and resetting than was actually going to be necessary, and applying these as it seemed appropriate from the photogrammetric survey drawings by examining what could be seen of the masonry from ground level. This approach requires a great deal of experience if it is to be at all meaningful and a close working relationship between curator, architect and civil engineer. [...]

To ensure that the specification was realistic and to identify more precisely what problems would be encountered in the course of the works, a section of the east curtain wall was scaffolded, stripped of ivy, and used as a test-bed for different conservation techniques. The area chosen seemed fairly typical, with a fragile wall-head, exposed core, and a well-preserved outer face. [...]

Archaeology

The decision to preserve the castle's archaeology undisturbed was taken long before the site came into guardianship. [...] Some excavation was unavoidable, to inform the civil engineers about stability and levels, and to provide access for repair. [...]

The first trench to be dug, a section inside the south curtain of the outer bailey, revealed some 9 m (30 ft) of buried deposits, a timber kitchen of the twelfth century, [...] but preserving its archaeology intact for future research was the option followed. [...] Only one further area will be excavated in the course of conservation, the east tower, a thirteenth-century corner tower that has become detached from the curtain wall and is slowly subsiding into the ditch. After reinforcement and repair, this tower will be backfilled and displayed at its current level. [...]

The main thrust of the archaeological research will be the detailed recording and analysis of the surviving masonry, carried out immediately in advance of conservation and in the course of repair, to standards set by the Central Archaeological Service of English Heritage, [...] It was determined before the main contract began by carrying out an experimental area of recording on the east curtain wall to different levels and standards. [...] The archaeologists who record the masonry 'as found' will also record it 'as repaired', so that a consistent record is made. The 'as repaired' drawings will provide the record against which the effectiveness of repair can be audited as well as making a positive record of all interventions.

The repair of masonry

Because the surviving ruins at Wigmore were the product of a continuing process of collapse, many parts of the site remain unsupported and unstable, and if not restrained will ultimately fall. [...] In the 1640s, sections of curtain wall were destroyed, either by mining or explosives, leaving stress fractures in the surviving structure that had widened with water penetration. More recently, tree roots have been the problem, though many of the trees were felled after the damage had been done. As their roots had rotted out, water was again able to penetrate the core. This was the cause of the collapse of a section of the south curtain in 1988 and of the instability of the east tower. Stone robbing has removed large areas of the inner face of the curtain wall, again exposing corework. Elsewhere there has been rather desultory robbing of quoins and dressings, leaving rubble walling exposed to weathering and slow collapse. Remarkably, the remaining structures were reasonably sound, the original mortar had survived well, and only the wall tops were friable, the result of root penetration. The ivy, though rooted into the walls, had in fact preserved more than it had destroyed.

Minimum intervention requires an acceptance that masonry will not be entirely repointed and capped to run off water. It also means that there will be a continuing need to monitor the site and carry out small-scale repairs as they are needed. [. . .] Where support was needed for over-hanging masonry, it was provided by under-building with new stone in preference to building-in support into the existing fabric. The fallen face of the south curtain will be rebuilt to protect its surviving core and inner face, and where walls have cracked they will simply be stitched and grouted with mortar that is no harder than the original bedding mortar. It is only at the wall-head that a minimalist approach will not work. The experimental stripping of a part of the east curtain wall demonstrated that parts of the parapet and wall-walk had survived, well protected by the vegetation that had colonised the site from shortly after its abandonment. It could be preserved as it was found and made secure with the minimum of taking down, but it was too fragile to leave exposed. The natural soft capping had worked very effectively for 400 years, and its return to the wall-top would continue the process of preservation. It would mean, however, covering the wall-walk and parapet again, so important features of the site would not remain visible after repair. The alternative would have been to rebuild the whole of the wall-top, which would then be didactic but not historic. Consistency required that it be left as it was found, its grass and fern capping restored, and its form can now be seen only in the archaeological record.

Perhaps a typical area is the south tower, an early fourteenth-century residential tower on two storeys over a partially vaulted basement that houses a small bat colony. Generally, its rubble work was sound and required very little repointing. [. . .] only failed mortar and voids were to be repointed, using a lime putty mortar matched to the original. Where stone had failed, as it had in some areas, it was to be replaced with new matching stone quarried locally or recovered from the tons of rubble that littered the site, laid to matching courses. Unsupported rere-arches were to be supported with new ashlar quoins and voussoirs cut to the dimensions identified by their surviving bedding rather than packing up voids with slates or rubble. Below the grass capping on the walls, the wall-head survives for the most part, together with a part of the parapet.

[. . .] The intention is to stabilise high-level masonry, and not necessarily to repair it to the extent that it is stronger than the undamaged masonry at a lower level. The wall-heads will be left very much as they are found, perpetuating the evidence they contain of roof structure, wall-walks and water spouts. As with the east curtain wall, however, these features will be largely invisible after repair.

The vaulted basement of the tower, [. . .] was virtually intact. Access to it was restricted to the summer months as it was a recorded bat roost. [. . .] Here, it was decided that the protection of the bat colony was more important than public access. On an open site, no grille would survive in the door (case) for more than a few weeks, [. . .] After the basement and the stair were recorded, the vault was supported on permanent scaffolding, the door blocked to within 15 cm (6 in) of its lintel, and the stair backfilled. [. . .] The only other modification to the site was to be the adding of additional core to the base of robbed ground-level window openings to raise their cills, openings that would otherwise require grilles to ensure the safety of visitors.

The soft landscape

[...] most of the site comprises buried buildings defined by their earthworks in a landscape that had been developed as rough pasture since at least the early eighteenth century but that had not been grazed or managed for a number of years. [...]

The soft landscape at Wigmore protects the buried elements of the site as well as providing substantial information on the planning of the castle. It also provides the only public access to the ruins.

[...] The existing tree-cover will be maintained, and managed effectively; some of the young saplings are being retained to strengthen the existing planting and provide for the future. [...] The first requirement, on the advice of an ecologist, however, was to recover the coarse pasture land from the invading scrub, opening up the recently colonised parts of the outer and inner baileys for both sheep and public access. Blackthorn and nettles have an important part to play in controlling public access, and are far less intrusive than fencing in areas that would otherwise be unsafe. Paths around the site could be identified by differential cutting, dangerous holes filled, and the screes of loose masonry removed. An important element in the approach to public access was the decision that not all parts of the site would be easily accessible, though where access was allowed it would have to be safe. [...] No parts of the site can be described as disability-friendly. In the inner bailey, on top of a steep motte, some steps built up on the surface in order to reduce gradients will be the only positive intervention in the landscape. As with the conservation of the structure, this goes against existing policies of maximising public access and information capture. At Wigmore, it was accepted that the setting of the castle and its ecosystem were no less important than public access; their protection was central to the display of the ruins.

The castle is, of course, only one element of a much larger whole, and must be treated as such. To the east, the village of Wigmore is a planned town with an important pre-Conquest church, whilst to the north are substantial remains of Wigmore Abbey, the Augustinian house established as the Mortimers' mausoleum. It is part of a much greater whole, the frontier with Wales and a base for the English colonisation of that country. Its conservation and display must be seen in that wider context and it must not be separated from that context by modern intervention. It is for this reason that access to the site will be by foot only from the village itself, with no intrusive car park or visitor facilities close to the castle, which must remain a central feature of a remarkable and important landscape, uncluttered and unspoiled.

[...]

References

Coppack, G. (1999). 'Setting and structure: the conservation of Wigmore Castle', in G. Chitty and D. Baker (eds), *Managing Historic Sites and Buildings*, London: Routledge, pp. 61–70.
Shoesmith, R. (1987). 'Neglect and decay: Wigmore Castle – home of the Mortimers.' *Rescue News* 42: 3.
Streeten, A.D.F. (1993). 'Medieval Castles in the Central Marches: an Archaeological Management Review', unpublished paper presented to the Ancient Monuments Advisory Committee, London: English Heritage.

Chapter 7

Decay and mitigation of earthen architecture remains

Earthen architecture

EARLY ANTIQUARIANS WHO EXPLORED the ancient civilisations of Egypt and Mesopotamia found that all that remained of many of the great cities mentioned in ancient texts such as the Old Testament were decayed ruins of sun dried mud bricks (adobe). Later explorers of the Indus Valley and central Asia similarly found great cities reduced to low mounds of earth; the decayed remains of mud brick.

Earthen architecture encompasses a wide range of building types: mud bricks (adobe), rammed earth (pise), cob, even turf. Though normally referred to as earth, in almost all cases except turf the material used is subsoil, the mineral soil beneath the topsoil with low levels of organic material (see B and C horizons in Figure 3.2.1). Though water may be added to the soil to make it malleable, the water soon evaporates to leave a small amount present in the soil, which holds the soil particles together (Jaquin and Augarde 2012: 29–33). The degree of compaction of the earth, the size of the particles and their ratio, together with the presence of small amounts of fibrous organic material and small amounts of deposited mineral, determine the properties of the earthen architecture material (Warren 1999). Provided that the appropriate quantity of water remains present in the soil, the structural integrity of the construction remains.

The basic construction techniques are variants on four basic forms:

- *Rammed earth (pise, al taub, tapial, pakhsa, brayed earth)*: wall built up from layers of soil placed between wooden shuttering (formwork) compressed by hammering, tamping or human trampling to form a solid compressed mass. Typical walls are 200–800 mm wide with little added to the earth, just enough water to make it deformable, the compaction level is high. The shuttering is moved and the process repeated until full height walls are built (Cooke 2010: 9; Jaquin and Augarde 2012: 5–9). This creates a monolithic wall structure with horizontal banding derived from the differential compaction of the 'lifts' or layers of rammed earth.

- *Cob (placed earth)*: earth mixed with water, organic material (dung, straw, hair) and sand or crushed rock material, laid in a succession of layers and left to dry, it builds gradually into a wall. The edges are usually cut back to form the vertical wall face (Cooke 2010: 9–10; Jaquin and Augarde 2012: 5–9). A monolithic wall without much evident layering is created.
- *Adobe (mud/unfired brick, cut or pressed block)*: earth often with added organic material (dung, straw) pressed into an open form or mould to create a block. These are left to dry, then mortared together, using the same mud mixture, to form walls. Early 'bricks' (and more recent ethnographic examples) were spherical or ovoid shapes (e.g. plano-convex bricks) of third-millennium Mesopotamia, later almost universally replaced by rectangular block form; eventually, blocks of standard size were used. More recently, earth is often compressed into a mould to form a block, often with additives such as lime or cement (Cooke 2010: 8–9; Jaquin and Augarde 2012: 9–11). The walls are usually plastered so the core structure is not visible. This technique was and still is the most widely used form of earthen architecture, normally used in the arid environments of the Middle East and Asia. Whole houses, mosques and city walls can be made of adobe; it can also be used to form panels within a wooden framework.
- *Wattle and daub*: earth as mud with animal dung or fibrous vegetable matter daubed over both sides of a fine network of woven timber laths, branches or plant stems within a larger structural wooden framework that carries the weight of the roof. This form is seen in temperate countries, such as Britain and Chile, and tropical countries, such as Sri Lanka (Agnew and Taylor 1990: 106,112) where timber is readily available.

Ancient earthen architecture requires wooden lintels or arches over doorways and windows. Roofs were typically constructed of rammed earth or blocks of earth on a layer of branches supported on timber beams resting on the tops of the earth walls. Historically, calcium rich earths were often used or additives such as lime (nowadays cement) have been added to earth as stabilisers to provide additional strength. Earth plasters/renders are often applied to the exterior of the wall, especially of adobe constructions to protect the wall core, some contain additives such as blood to increase water resistance (Cooke 2010: 13). Specifically, waterproof coatings such as limewash can also be applied. Earthen walls that do not utilise wooden framing are usually thick (typically 0.5–3 m).

Earthen architecture is one of the earliest forms of construction seen in almost all ancient civilisations; Mesopotamia, Egypt, China and India, 10 per cent of the buildings on the UNESCO World Heritage list are earthen construction (Correia and Fernandes 2006). Most examples of earthen architecture we currently see are from dry climates where adobe, pise and cob dry quickly. Low levels of rainfall are absorbed and then later evaporate off the earth roofs; large downpours of water can run off flat roofs that invariably have drains or gullies. As long as the water does not pond on the flat roof, then the structure should not collapse. For added protection, the tops of the walls and roofs are often given greater water resistance (fired brick, bitumen coating, etc.). Earthen structures function well in temperate climates such as Britain and North America, where pitched roofs of thatch, slate, split stone or lead on a sturdy wooden framework ensure that the earthen walls beneath remain dry. Eaves often project beyond the wall to throw water well away from the structure. It is essential that all earthen structures are repaired and maintained.

Decay of earthen architecture

Cracking

Earthen construction is a non-ductile material that has good strength in compression but little shear or tensile strength. Consequently, when the ground is unstable, due to poor foundations, earthquakes or as a result of becoming damp and compressing, earthen walls often crack. Uneven application of load, from flooring beams or the presence of doors or windows also leads to cracking. To preserve such structures, it is essential to understand the reason for the cracking and address that structural problem, providing stable foundations, drying and solidifying wet or unstable ground, removing load, altering its distribution or providing appropriate support (even infilling doors and window openings) before focusing on other decay factors. Even if cracks are filled or the sides are tied together, unless the differential load acting on them is adjusted they will return to tear the building apart (Jaquin and Augarde 2012: 37–42, 54–60).

Water

When there is too much water, the structural integrity of the earth is lost and particles form a suspension and flow away. Surfaces that become wet, such as wall tops, exhibit cracking and where water flows over the earth structure it will cut gullies into the surface, widening and deepening cracks. It will also support vegetation resulting in root damage. The repeated wetting and drying of earthen walls cause expansion and contraction of clays, so breaking apart the compacted earth particles reducing them to dust. At the base of the wall, rising damp or rain splash leads to loss of wall substance, undercutting the wall. Foundations unaffected by water can greatly aid the longevity of such walls. Impervious coatings of cement or similar can cause water build-up within the earth resulting in a loss of strength behind the cement leading to cracking and the coating falling off in sheets (Jaquin and Augarde 2012: 43–8, 64–8). Where roofs are lost and the rammed or placed earth or mud brick is regularly washed by rainwater, it appears to melt. The washed out earth builds up around the base of the walls until the lower parts of the wall are completely buried and little more than undulating ground surface is left; the lower parts of the walls remain intact protected by such an environment. Archaeological excavations in Asia and the Middle East have frequently unearthed the lower levels of the walls of ancient buildings, revealing villages, towns, even cities such as Panjakent (ancient Sogdiana) and Merv. When such remains are uncovered, unless protected, they promptly resume the decay and build-up process.

Crystallisation

Water transports soluble salts, especially up from the ground as rising damp. The precipitation of such salts at evaporative surfaces (efflorescence and cryptoflorescence) can damage the wall surface and repeated wetting and drying cycles and associated crystallisation can degrade the lower parts of walls, leading to considerable loss of substance and the formation of cavities in the surface. In areas such as southern Iraq, this can continue and reduce whole buildings to dust. Crystallisation also occurs with frost formation. If earthen walls become soaked with liquid (free) water and it freezes, then ice crystals can grow and break apart the agglomerated soil. This combination of circumstance is rare. In places such as the Himalayas and central

Asia, where there is use of earth architecture and frequently cold conditions, the climate is dry, and thus liquid (free) water is rare.

Other decay processes

The expansion and contraction of soil particles from wetting and drying can cause the compacted earth to lose its coherence/strength and crumble. Physical contact from humans or animals and erosion from wind can also lead to loss of earth wall substance.

Many of the decay processes in earthen architecture are synergistic. The bases of walls are affected by water splash and damp rising from the ground, resulting in wetting and drying cycles and/or salt crystallisation that leads to cavity formation and the weakening and collapse of walls. Zones of wetting and drying at the tops of walls, effects of expansion from heating and cooling, erosion by wind lead to the loss of coherence and earthen walling crumbles to soil. The range of processes and their cumulative effect has been clearly described in a series of drawings by Louise Cooke (2010: 39–42) (see Chapter 7.1).

Composition

The widespread occurrence of earthen architecture throughout the world indicates that a wide range of soil compositions are capable of forming solid walling. Analytical programmes (Austin 1990; Coffman *et al.* 1990) have confirmed this, with values of 89–27 per cent sand (mainly quartz and feldspars), 68–8 per cent silt and 15–1 per cent clay (Austin 1990: 422) being recorded for earthen walling. In general, there are around equal proportions of expansive clays (smectite [montmorillonite] and mixed layer illite/smectite) and non-expansive clays (kaolinite, illite and chlorite). The relatively low clay content, especially limited expandable clays, ensures that the soil does not shrink and crack apart too easily. Some sources suggest higher levels of clay are used, but such sources may not distinguish between clays and silts (Cooke 2010: 12). Austin (1990) suggests that the adobe of the south-western USA and Mexico contains a high level of dissolved calcium minerals in the soil water, which results in precipitation of calcium minerals that play an important part in binding together adobe. The presence of fibrous additives, such as hair, or chemical binders, such as blood or lime, varies between and within cultures. Jaquin and Augarde (2012) show that water bridges between soil particles and the associated surface tension provide a significant force pulling the particles together. Thus, water content of the earth is crucial in maintaining the strength of the earth wall. Processes that lead to the pores filling with water (lack of surface tension) lead to loss of cohesion of the earth particles, while it becomes friable when extremely dry.

Conservation

Archaeologists of the late nineteenth and twentieth centuries exposed numerous earthen architectural remains, including large areas of major ancient cities such as Mohenjo-daro and Merv. These sites now have very extensive and highly visible decay problems. This has led to the urgent quest for simple, cheap conservation solutions that will preserve these remains *in situ*. Ideally, a method that preserves the visual form of these remains as excavated in perpetuity. Difficulties in finding conservation solutions led to the formation of a number of international committees such as ICOMOS International Scientific Committee on Earthen Architectural Heritage (http://isceah.icomos.org/index.php?option=com_content&task=view

&id=11&Itemid=16) and led to a number of projects and initiatives such as Terra and GAIA funded by organisations such as the GCI (www.getty.edu/conservation/our_projects/field_projects/earthen/; www.getty.edu/conservation/our_projects/field_projects/adobe/).

Many such research activities and publications have been undertaken in association with organisations such as CRATerre, who are concerned with modern use of earthen architecture, which is extensive. The published results of research and conservation work on earthen architecture have given rise to a substantial literature on this subject (Getty Conservation Institute 2002; Avrami et al. 2008).

A number of different approaches to the conservation of earthen architecture can be distinguished.

Repair and reconstruction

Many historic structures still contain occupants, functioning as buildings: libraries, mosques, forts, museums, heritage centres and, above all, as dwellings, from the pueblos of New Mexico to the houses of the Dakhleh Oasis, Egypt (Schijns 2008). For these buildings, the focus remains on repair and maintenance to ensure the continuing functionality of the building. Experience has shown that modern materials such as cement are invariably disastrous for repairs as they are barriers to water (vapour) movement leading to saturation of earth behind the cement, resulting in cracks in walling, mortar render detaching from the wall surface and the ends of roof beams (viga) rotting (Garrison 1990: 55). In contrast, repair with mudbrick or rammed earth has normally proved an effective form of renovation. This has emphasised the need for accurate identification of materials and an awareness of the way in which buildings of earthen construction work.

Problems with salts, water splashing, damp and erosion at the base of buildings are invariably greatly reduced with improvements in surface or subsurface drainage, which channels water away from the sensitive earthen architecture to locations where it can safely pool, evaporate or run off. The constant repair of earthen architecture to keep it weatherproof with traditional materials, removing outer layers of degraded plaster/render and re-rendering/re-plastering the original wall core or recoating in fresh limewash, results in difficulty in distinguishing later repair activity from original material. While this preserves the wall core, it provides a new veneer, obscuring the original and aged appearance in favour of functional integrity. It can be suggested this is not easily reconciled with the aims of conservation, as articulated through documents such as the Venice Charter (see Chapter 5.2) (Correia and Fernandes 2006; Cooke 2010). However, Ruskin and Morris had long considered that maintenance was the only acceptable form of conservation (see Chapter 5.1). These grandfathers of conservation always sought to venerate traditional crafts considering their truth and integrity important – for them, valuable as it was, the historic fabric was not the only consideration. More recent charters such as Nara (see Chapter 5.4) and Burra (see Chapter 5.5), as well as the UNESCO 2003 Convention for the Safeguarding of Intangible Cultural Heritage, recognise that heritage goes beyond the physical fabric to value the intangible nature of a place or a social activity, and this includes 'traditional craftsmanship' and 'customary practices'. Recoating is undoubtedly a traditional approach to preserving earthen structures.

Capping and encapsulation

In the case of archaeological earthen ruins, structures without roofs or current occupants, there is a focus on preservation of the original material and the visual appearance of the ruined remains. The tops of exposed walls invariably suffer active erosion from rainfall. Two differing protective approaches are used; the top of the wall can be capped with:

- Materials resistant to erosion, in particular the effects of rainfall, such as fired bricks. Resistant capping materials may project over the structure and attempt to throw water away from the wall faces.
- Materials intended to decay and be replaced, often modern adobe (Caperton 1990; Cooke 2010: 86–91). Marker materials are sometimes introduced between the new sacrificial capping and original materials, which might otherwise be indistinguishable, in order to identify the research valued original material.

The earthen walls sometimes suffer erosion immediately beneath the hard capping layer. The continued decay of capped walls led to encapsulation; the covering of historic earthen architectures on all exposed surfaces with new earth material, either plaster or a thicker layer of adobe blocks. Marker materials are often used to indicate the boundary between original and the encapsulating material. Encapsulation obscures the original historic material, but does protect and preserve it.

Consolidation

The earth of the architecture can potentially be strengthened through the deposition of a consolidating material. Examples include ethyl silicate and other silanes, polyisocyanates (Selwitz *et al.* 1990), potassium silicate (Zuixiong 1990) and acrylic copolymers (Sramek and Losos 1990). The composition of the earth and the decay mechanism determine if any such consolidant is effective. Some consolidants have proven effective for some earths in some decay situations, but the same consolidants fail in other situations. Consolidants can create additional problems introducing moisture barriers, soluble salts and are often irreversible and cannot be removed, though experiments are continuing. Consolidation is often considered a highly desirable conservation approach since it preserves 'original' material and its original appearance. However, 'to date, no viable chemical consolidants have been found that do not cause further damage to unstabilised earth walls' (Jaquin and Augarde 2012: 70). This view is also echoed by Cooke (2010) in a recent review of the subject and long-term experiments at Fort Seldon (New Mexico, USA). Literature in this area can be deceptive since the results of conservation work are often published as soon as they have been completed in order to give a positive profile to the project. Few papers have been published that report, 10 or 20 years later, on how the conservation measures have stood the test of time. Where they do, the results often reveal problems or failures (Chiari 1990).

Decorative surfaces

As with stone structures (see Chapter 6), the internal wall surfaces of earthen buildings are often decorated with plastered and painted surfaces. Even early sites such as Çatalhöyük have multiple layers of painted plaster on earthen walling (Matero and Moss 2004: 217).

This material is fragile, subject to the threats of damage already described, as well as physical damage in use and risks of an interface in a buried environment. Controlling moisture levels to avoid shrinkage and delamination from desiccation or salt damage when dry are challenging problems, leading many to rebury such decorative surfaces after recording (Matero and Moss 2004).

Backfilling (see Chapter 14)

Replacing earth around ruined walls to protect them was initially routinely practised between excavation seasons, in order to protect those ruined walls. In recent years, the excellent preservation of walls treated in this manner has been in stark contrast to the poor conditions of those walls exposed to weathering. Consequently, backfilling, which, when done in a planned manner to preserve the remains should be called reburial (see Chapter 14), has become increasingly utilised as a more permanent protection measure (Cooke 2010: 79–85). Geotextile, a form of stabilising stable polymer mesh (Ingold and Miller 1990), typically polypropylene or polyester, is sometimes placed at (or very near) the interface to mark original material, though care is needed to ensure that this does not alter drainage patterns. The soil for backfilling at such sites is often formed from degraded adobe (collapsed upper parts of the walls), and thus has the same chemical composition as the walls it surrounds, creating a chemically stable environment. Care is taken to avoid forming soil that is too compressed or too loose. It is contoured to encourage drainage away from walls and out of buildings (e.g. through doorways to avoid ponding in the base of houses and other structures). Examples of backfilling/reburial of earthen structures include Fort Seldon (Caperton 1990), Merv (Cooke 2010: Appendix 6) and the San Diego Presidio (Calarco 2000). Historic earthen architecture ruins below the soil surface are safe from frost, salts, wind erosion and the depredations of humans. Steps need to be taken to avoid subsurface threats such as root damage (ensuring no deep-rooted trees develop on the burial site) and that neither soluble salts nor water build up in the buried earthen architecture, through ensuring that there is similar porosity between surrounding soil and the earthen remains.

Shelters and drainage (see Chapter 13)

Where the archaeological remains have a high social value and need to be visible, protective structures can be erected over the remains to protect them from the erosive effects of wind and rain. However, roofs or shelters are invariably visually intrusive and problems of salt crystallisation, vegetation and algae growth can remain. Surface or subsurface drainage, which channels water away from the sensitive earthen architecture to locations where it can safely pool, evaporate or run off, is essential where shelters are erected so they do not protect one part of the site and damage others.

Seismic threat

The brittle nature of earthen structures means that they are frequently structurally damaged in seismic events. Several aspects of earthen architecture, low thick walls, wooden beamed roofs, wooden lintels above windows and door openings, a few small window and door openings and buttressed walls, all increase seismic resistance and may have evolved in many local earthen architectures to resist such threats. In very seismically active areas such as Kashmir, Turkey, Yemen, Nepal and Yugoslavia, large lintels and additional wooden horizontal beams within the walls are extensively used to reduce the risk of wall collapse (Langerbach 1990; Sumanov 1990; D'Ayala 2009; Tony Wilkinson pers. comm.). Recent adaptations of earthen building such as the additions of upper stories and larger window and door openings, as seen, for example, in some buildings in California, have reduced the capacity of earthen architecture to survive seismic events (Kimbro 1990; Sanchez and Allen 1990). The loss of historic buildings to seismic events, such as the earthquakes at Bam (Iran) in 2003 and Northridge California in 1994 has encouraged the development of measures to make existing historic earthen structures better able to withstand seismic events (Tolles et al. 2000, 2002; Hardy et al. 2009). The insertion (retrofitting) of bond (tie or collar) beams resting on the top of adobe walls to take the weight of the roof structures and distribute the load evenly over the whole wall reduces the likelihood of structural collapse (Kimbro 1990; Sanchez and Allen 1990; Tolles et al. 2000; Webster 2009) and is one of the most unobtrusive and effective methods used. Measures such as regular maintenance (pointing in mud or lime etc.) avoiding cement repairs (which induce areas of weakness) (D'Ayala 2009) and adding fibres such as jute to adobe all increase crack and collapse resistance in buildings undergoing seismic events. Insertion of horizontal and vertical reinforcement (high or low tech – wires, bamboo, polymer mesh, stainless steel wires) around or within walls (wall core rods) improves seismic resistance. More substantial measures such as encircling cracked structures with fabric or polymer meshes, which can be hidden by cutting chases into the walls around the structure to bury them within the walls are also possible (Dowling and Samali 2009; Islam and Iwashita 2009; Torrealva et al. 2009; Tolles 2009). However, there is a risk of the loss of a substantial amount of historic fabric. This has been described as resulting in 'the Vietnam approach', practically destroying what you value in an effort to save it (Langerbach 1989: 32; Sanchez and Allen 1990: 350).

In practice

Excavation followed by decades of exposure has left sites such as Mohenjo-daro and Merv, built partially or completely of earthen architecture, slowly degrading as a result of weathering, damp and soluble salt problems. Recent projects such as Ajina Tepe in Tajikistan (Fodde et al. 2007) (see Chapter 7.2) have, rather than excavating new sites, tackled already partially exposed sites and undertaken holistic research, recording and conservation programmes. The need to leave some of the site as an exposed monument to the past, a focus for visitors and locals alike means that some walls require capping and encapsulation so they will survive, but much of the rest of the site will be reburied. Guardians are employed to ensure maintenance is carried out and to dissuade others from vandalising/treasure hunting the site. Education programmes explain the value and antiquity of the sites and the continuation of traditional earthen architectural building techniques for use in maintenance and repair of the site is actively encouraged. Those working with earthen architecture are moving beyond the 'quick-fix' consolidation approach that has proved a chimera, to a more long-term strategy, seeking to start to reduce the existing problems through reburial and encapsulation, and raising local value of the site so local resources are drawn into site protection. Crucially, there is recognition that, given the friable nature of exposed earthen architecture, there must be an active maintenance regime if such remains are to be successfully preserved *in situ*.

Bibliography

Agnew, N. and Taylor, M. (1990) *Adobe 90, 1990 Proceedings of the 6th International Conference on the Conservation of Earthen Architecture, Las Cruces, New Mexico*, Los Angeles, CA: GCI.

Austin, G.S. (1990) 'Adobe and related building materials in New Mexico, USA', in N. Agnew, M. Taylor and A.A. Balderramma (eds), *Adobe 90 Preprints 6th International Conference on the Conservation of Earthen Architecture, Las Cruces, New Mexico*, Los Angeles, CA: GCI, pp. 417–23.

Avrami, E., Guillaud, H. and Hardy, M. (2008) *Terra Literature Review: An Overview of Earthen Architecture Conservation*, Los Angeles, CA: GCI.

Calarco, D.A. (2000) 'San Diego Royal Presidio: conservation of an earthen architecture archaeological site', in International Conference on the Study and Conservation of Earthen Architecture (ed.), *Terra 2000, 8th International Conference on the Study and Conservation of Earthen Architecture, Torquay, Devon, UK, May 2000*, London: James & James, pp. 20–5.

Caperton, T. (1990) 'Fort Seldon ruins conservation', in N. Agnew, M. Taylor and A.A. Balderramma (eds), *Adobe 90 Preprints 6th International Conference on the Conservation of Earthen Architecture, Las Cruces, New Mexico*, Los Angeles, CA: GCI, pp. 209–11.

Chiari, G. (1990) 'Chemical surface treatments and capping techniques of earthen structures: a long term evaluation', in N. Agnew, M. Taylor and A.A. Balderramma (eds), *Adobe 90 Preprints 6th International Conference on the Conservation of Earthen Architecture, Las Cruces, New Mexico*, Los Angeles, CA: GCI, pp. 267–73.

Coffman, R., Agnew, N., Austin, G. et al. (1990) 'Adobe mineralogy: characterisation of adobes from around the world', in N. Agnew, M. Taylor and A.A. Balderramma (eds), *Adobe 90 Preprints 6th International Conference on the Conservation of Earthen Architecture, Las Cruces, New Mexico*, Los Angeles, CA: GCI, pp. 424–9.

Cooke, L. (2010) *Conservation Approaches to Earthen Architecture in Archaeological Contexts*, BAR International Series 2147, Oxford: Archaeopress.

Correia, M. and Fernandes, M. (2006) 'The conservation of earth architecture: the contribution of Brandi's theory', in J.D. Rodrigues and J.M. Mimoso (eds), *Theory and Practice in Conservation: A Tribute to Cesare Brandi, International Seminar*, Lisbon: National Laboratory of Civil Engineering.

D'Ayala, D. (2009) 'Seismic vulnerability and conservation strategies for Lalitpur minor heritage', in M. Hardy, C. Cancino and G. Ostergren (eds), *Proceedings of the Getty Seismic Adobe Project 2006 Colloquium*, Los Angeles, CA: GCI, pp. 120–34.

Dowling, D. and Samali, B. (2009) 'Low-cost and low-tech reinforcement systems for improved earthquake resistance of mud brick buildings', in M. Hardy, C. Cancino and G. Ostergren (eds), *Proceedings of the Getty Seismic Adobe Project 2006 Colloquium*, Los Angeles, CA: GCI, pp. 23–33.

Fodde, E., Watanabe, K. and Fujii, Y. (2007) 'Preservation of earthen sites in remote areas: the Buddhist monastery of Ajina Tepa, Tajikistan', *Conservation and Management of Archaeological Sites*, 9(4): 194–218.

Garrison, J.W. (1990) 'The evolution of adobe construction systems in the Southwest (USA) and related conservation issues', in N. Agnew, M. Taylor and A.A. Balderramma (eds), *Adobe 90 Preprints 6th International Conference on the Conservation of Earthen Architecture, Las Cruces, New Mexico*, Los Angeles, CA: GCI, pp. 53–6.

Getty Conservation Institute (2002) *Terra Bibliography*, GCI Project Bibliography Series, Los Angeles, CA: GCI.

Hardy, M., Cancino, C. and Ostergren, G. (eds) (2009) *Proceedings of the Getty Seismic Adobe Project 2006 Colloquium*, Los Angeles, CA: GCI.

Ingold, T.S. and Miller, K.S. (1990) *Geotextiles Handbook*, Telford: ICE.

Islam, M.S. and Iwashita, K. (2009) 'Seismic response of fiber-reinforced and stabilized adobe structures', in M. Hardy, C. Cancino and G. Ostergren (eds), *Proceedings of the Getty Seismic Adobe Project 2006 Colloquium*, Los Angeles, CA: GCI, pp. 101–8.

Jaquin, P. and Augarde, C. (2012) *Earth Building: History, Science and Conservation*, Bracknell: IHS BRE Press.

Kimbro, E.E. (1990) 'The impact of the 1989 Loma Prieta earthquake on historic adobe structures in Santa Cruz County, California', in N. Agnew, M. Taylor and A.A. Balderramma (eds), *Adobe 90 Preprints 6th International Conference on the Conservation of Earthen Architecture, Las Cruces, New Mexico*, Los Angeles, CA: GCI, pp. 327–31.

Langerbach, R. (1989) 'Bricks, mortar and earthquakes', *APT Bulletin*, 21(389): 32.

Langerbach, R. (1990) 'Of Taqand Dhajji: the earthquake resistant mud and brick architecture of Kashmir', in N. Agnew, M. Taylor and A.A. Balderramma (eds), *Adobe 90, Proceedings of the 6th International Conference on the Conservation of Earthen Architecture, Las Cruces, New Mexico*, Los Angeles, CA: GCI, pp. 92–8.

Matero, F. and Moss, E. (2004) 'Temporary site protection for earthen walls and murals at Çatalhöyük, Turkey', *Conservation and Managements of Archaeological Sites*, 6(3–4): 213–27.

Sanchez, G. and Allen, D. (1990) 'Seismic strengthening of historic adobe structures in California: an overview', in N. Agnew, M. Taylor and A.A. Balderramma (eds), *Adobe 90, Preprints 6th International Conference on the Conservation of Earthen Architecture, Las Cruces, New Mexico*, Los Angeles, CA: GCI, pp. 348–56.

Schijns, W. (2008) *Vernacular Mud Brick Architecture in the Dakhleh Oasis, Egypt*, Oxford: Oxbow Books.

Selwitz, C., Coffman, R. and Agnew, N. (1990) 'The Getty Research Project at Fort Selden III: an evaluation of the application of chemical consolidants to test walls', in N. Agnew, M. Taylor and A.A. Balderramma (eds), *Adobe 90, Preprints 6th International Conference on the Conservation of Earthen Architecture, Las Cruces, New Mexico*, Los Angeles, CA: GCI, pp. 255–60.

Sramek, J. and Losos, L. (1990) 'An outline of mud brick structures conservation at Abusir', in N. Agnew, M. Taylor and A.A. Balderramma (eds), *Adobe 90, Preprints 6th International Conference on the Conservation of Earthen Architecture, Las Cruces, New Mexico*, Los Angeles, CA: GCI, pp. 449–54.

Sumanov, L. (1990) 'Traditional sun-baked (adobe) brick structures in Macedonia', in N. Agnew, M. Taylor and A.A. Balderramma (eds), *Adobe 90, Preprints 6th International Conference on the Conservation of Earthen Architecture, Las Cruces, New Mexico*, Los Angeles, CA: GCI, pp. 131–6.

Tolles, E.L. (2009) 'Seismic retrofit applications of Getty seismic adobe project technology to historic adobe buildings', in M. Hardy, C. Cancino and G. Ostergren (eds), *Proceedings of the Getty Seismic Adobe Project 2006 Colloquium*, Los Angeles, CA: GCI, pp. 159–64.

Tolles, E.L., Kimbro, E.E., Webster, F.A. et al. (2000) *Seismic Stabilization of Historic Adobe Structures: Final Report of the Getty Seismic Adobe Project*, GCI Scientific Program Reports, Los Angeles, CA: GCI, available at: www.getty.edu/conservation/publications/pdf_publications/seismicstabilization.pdf (accessed August 2014).

Tolles, E.L., Kimbro, E.E. and Ginell, W.S. (2002) *Planning and Engineering Guidelines for the Seismic Retrofitting of Historic Adobe Structures*, Los Angeles, CA: GCI.

Torrealva, D., Neumannand, J.V. and Blondet, M. (2009) 'Too earthquake resistant design criteria and testing of adobe buildings at Pontificia Universidad Católica del Perú', in M. Hardy, C. Cancino and G. Ostergren (eds), *Proceedings of the Getty Seismic Adobe Project 2006 Colloquium*, Los Angeles, CA: GCI, pp. 3–10.

Warren, J. (1999) *Conservation of Earth Structures*, London: Butterworth-Heinemann.

Webster, F.A. (2009) 'Application of stability-based retrofit measures on some historic and older adobe buildings in California', in M. Hardy, C. Cancino and G. Ostergren (eds), *Proceedings of the Getty Seismic Adobe Project 2006 Colloquium*, Los Angeles, CA: GCI, pp. 147–58.

Zuixiong, L. (1990) 'Consolidation of a Neolithic earthen site with potassium silicate', in N. Agnew, M. Taylor and A.A. Balderramma (eds), *Adobe 90, Preprints, 6th International Conference on the Conservation of Earthen Architecture, Las Cruces, New Mexico*, Los Angeles, CA: GCI, pp. 295–301.

Chapter 7.1

Conservation approaches to earthen architecture in archaeological contexts

Louise Cooke

Source: Cooke, L. (2010) *Conservation Approaches to Earthen Architecture in Archaeological Contexts*, BAR International Series 2147, Oxford: Archaeopress, pp. 39–42.

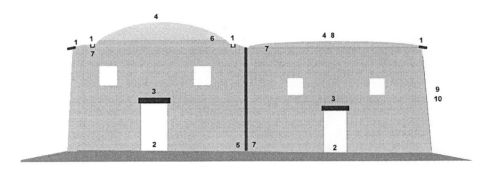

Figure 7.1.1 Maintenance of earthen architecture.

1. Wide drainage spouts of wood or ceramic are installed on rooftops (to drain horizontal surfaces) [. . .]. Regular maintenance checks, and where necessary repair are essential for these to remain functioning, [. . .]. Simple preventive measures such as checking gutters, and removing vegetation growth are important to prolong the life of an earth structure.
2. Regular (and daily) maintenance associated with the cleaning of areas more prone to gather dirt, such as cooking areas, ovens and thresholds – in these places daily maintenance might be through the application of a thin wash of earth plaster or earth and water.
3. Replastering of interior and exterior walls – the renewal and reworking of the surface, particularly in mudbrick structures where the exterior surface is coated in earthen plasters and renders, and for the interior of structures to keep them clean and functioning.

4. Roof maintenance of flat and domed and barrel roofs, through the use of earth plasters on top of the existing surface (which has been swept clear of debris).
5&6. More substantial repairs to wall bases, roofs and walltops through the cutting out of the damaged zone, and the insertion of replacement materials – depending on the area of the structure damaged this may again be coated in an earth plaster.
7. More substantial repair may routinely be required for stepped areas leading to roofs, areas of the external surface affected by dripping rainwater or to the base of undercut walls.
8. Re-compaction of the top layer of earthen roofs following precipitation, in some instances utilising roof rolling stones.

[...]

10. Patterns of maintenance and renewal may develop cultural or socio-religious significance, and they are planned in association with annual festivities etc.

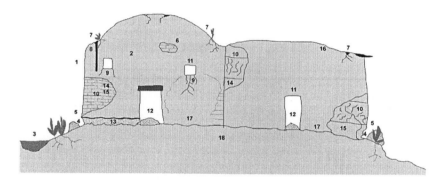

Figure 7.1.2 Erosion factors affecting un-maintained earthen architecture.

1. Causes of environmental deterioration are active, and earthen architecture is in a constant state of change.
2. Wind and wind blown sand cause differential surface erosion through abrasion, whilst precipitation washes fines out and obscures the surface of the structure.
3. Water trapped at the base of the occupation mound raises humidity in a zone at the base of the building.
4. Capillary action takes place at the base of the building, and is exaggerated at the corners; the resulting piles of loose and spalled material raise higher the zone of potential damage.
5. Falling water creates a zone of damage at the base of the walls through splash back.
6. Extreme diurnal and annual temperature and climatic variation leads to the mechanical breakdown of the constituent parts of earthen material, resulting in erosion to the surface.
7. Lack of maintenance to the earthen roof allows the creation of cracks and water infiltration into the dome, increasing the risk of structural collapse at the junction between the dome and the vertical wall, in addition water run-off thins the top of the earth dome. In other areas lack of maintenance contributes to vegetation growth and the use of the eroding earthen material by insects and nesting birds.

8. Lack of maintenance to original drainage gullies results in erosion of the surface, first through the creation of runnels, and latterly through more substantial gullies.
9. Lack of maintenance and repair leads to construction imposed stresses through the structure; in particular rainwater gullies are quick to form at the base of voids, such as windows and doors.
10&15. Detachment of the earthen plaster/render from the surface e.g. through mechanical weathering, of the structure exposes the wall core and earthen substrate to further damage from the effects of freeze/thaw, wind erosion and moisture. Through the exposure of the earthen substrate the rammed or placed earth lifts may deteriorate differentially, and insects and animals may utilise weaknesses in the earthen material.
11. Zones around voids, such as windows and doors, gradually erode to become thinner and wider, resulting in gradual enlargement through time.
12. As a result of loose collapsed materials, moisture becomes trapped in the interior, raising humidity and accelerating rates of erosion.
13. Capillary action leads to undercutting, and at the base of the structure surface detachment of the earthen plaster exposes fired bricks used in the original structure as a capillary break. The robbing of the fired bricks from the base removes the capillary barrier and increases the rate and height of capillary movement up the wall.
14. Stresses are imposed by the variation in the original material used for construction, such as the variation between mud bricks and mud mortar, and between the separate lifts in the rammed/placed earth structure.
16. Robbing and/or bio-deterioration of timbers from flat roofs leads to a rapid acceleration in erosion through the exposure of the wall tops to falling water and further erosion. Deterioration is accelerated through robbing and recycling of earthen material for incorporation in new construction or as fertiliser for agricultural fields.
17. Detachment of the earthen plaster/render from the base of the surface of the structure exposes the wall core and earthen substrate to more extensive damage from capillary action.
18. The processes of erosion and deposition lead to the accumulation of loose, more porous material both within the structure and in a zone on the immediate exterior. The moisture trapped in these erosion mounds moves the zone of evaporation up the remaining upstanding walls, and contributes to zones of undercutting higher up the structure. The more loose and moist materials also attract vegetation, altering humidity regimes, and further attracting insects and animals to the eroding structure.

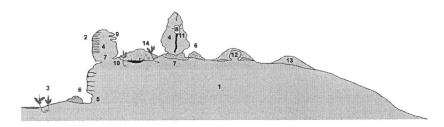

Figure 7.1.3 Erosion factors affecting eroded but still extant earthen architecture.

1. Causes of environmental deterioration are active, and the eroded earthen architecture is in a constant state of change.
2. Wind and wind blown sand cause differential erosion through abrasion damaging the upstanding earthen architecture, and by altering the shape and profile of the erosion mound through time.
3. Water trapped at the base of the occupation mound raises humidity in a zone at the base of the eroding building and mound.
4. Extreme diurnal and annual temperature and climatic variation leads to the mechanical breakdown of the constituent parts of earthen material, resulting in erosion to the surface.
5. Precipitation creates a zone of damage at the base of the walls through splash back.
6. Capillary action takes place at the base of the upstanding earthen structure and the resulting piles of loose and spalled material raise higher the zone of damage, and generate a deeper, and more extensive zone of damage.
7. Extensive damage to the base of the wall through undercutting alters the loading characteristics of the extant wall, making it more liable to dramatic collapse, under the influence of dynamic wind loads.
8. Birds nest in weak spots in earthen structure, such as original voids, and/or zones of differential erosion between mortar and mud bricks, the resulting phosphate rich surface deposits from bird excrement alter the chemical composition of the surface creating a zone with an increased propensity for erosion.
9. Insects such as hornets and wasps nest in earthen architecture, reworking the earthen material and re-depositing it in glass-like honeycomb structures.
10. Animals and reptiles excavate burrows and nests; the deposition of faeces alters the chemical and physical properties of the surface. In addition larger animals, such as camels, rub on exposed upstanding earthen walls and cause abrasion.
11. The original construction and design impose stresses through the extant structure, in particular extensive run-off gullies formed at the base of the original windows channel run-off down the surface of the structure. Zones around voids, such as windows and doors, become thinner and wider, resulting in gradual enlargement through time.
12. Falling water washes fines out and obscures the surface of the structure, this results in the thinning and shortening of the walls. Surface run-off and wind erosion result in the movement of the eroded earthen material over the site and contribute to the exposure, covering up, and burial of earthen walls.
13. Continued surface erosion of extant walls eventually results in the formation of low mounds, associated with prevailing wind direction, and direction of surface run-off.
14. Vegetation may add stability to the erosion material, and erosion mound, whilst other vegetation, such as tamarisk may contribute to changing moisture regimes on the surface, whilst the extensive root systems of desert plants can damage buried earthen material.

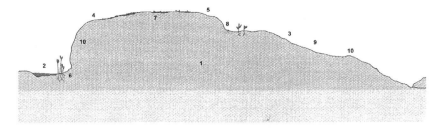

Figure 7.1.4 Erosion factors affecting unexcavated archaeological sites.

1. Causes of environmental deterioration are active, and the eroded archaeological site is in a constant state of change, altering the shape and degree of preservation of the unexcavated archaeological strata.
2. The proximity to stagnant water increases the overall porosity and looseness of the eroded earthen material, this creates an erosive matrix, which may be washed away as a result of surface run-off and wind erosion.
3. Wind and wind blown sand cause differential erosion, and through abrasion alter the shape and profile of the erosion mound through time.
4. Extreme diurnal and annual temperature and climatic variation leads to the mechanical breakdown of the constituent parts of earthen material, resulting in erosion to the surface.
5. Capillary action results in the deposition of salts at the surface or subsurface.
6. Vegetation growth is encouraged by proximity to water. Vegetation damages unexcavated earthen architecture as a result of root damage, and changes in microclimate association with water vapor and humidity on the surface.
7. Low lying grassy vegetation adds stability to gentle slopes and surfaces dependent on climate and local environment.
8. Animals, birds, insect and reptiles burrow into the softer eroded earthen material, adding chemical variation to the surface through waste deposits.
9. Gullying is caused by surface run-off across the loose erosive matrix down the eroded hill slope through hill wash.
10. 'Tell-creep' occurs through the erosion on the wind buffeted side of the slope creating a zone which is poorly preserved, in contrast tell-creep alongside surface run-off re-deposits materials and creates a zone of the erosion mound which is better protected.

Preservation of earthen sites in remote areas

The Buddhist Monastery of Ajina Tepa, Tajikistan

Enrico Fodde, Kunio Watanabe and Yukiyasu Fujii

Source: Fodde, E., Watanabe, K. and Fujii Y. (2007) 'Preservation of earthen sites in remote areas: the Buddhist Monastery of Ajina Tepa, Tajikistan', *Conservation and Management of Archaeological Sites*, 9(4): 194–218.

[...]

Introduction

CENTRAL ASIA HOLDS a great variety of earthen archaeological sites, most of them located in remote areas. Before the collapse of the Soviet Union archaeological excavations were neither followed by conservation work nor by backfilling, and often work was carried out in haste without any standard documentation. However, the site of Ajina Tepa is unique in the context of Central Asia (see Figure 7.2.1). Comprehensive and systematic excavation campaigns were undertaken between 1961 and 1975, under the supervision of Moscow's Institute of Oriental Studies of the Russian Academy of Sciences, which employed the most up-to-date excavation and documentation techniques. The wealth of information that was produced is manifest not only in the Russian and English monographs (Litvinskij & Zejmal 1971, 2004), but also in the extensive archival material.

A UNESCO/Japan Trust Fund for the Preservation of World Cultural Heritage project, entitled Preservation of the Buddhist Monastery of Ajina Tepa, Tajikistan (Heritage of the Ancient Silk Roads), was started in 2005 and will be completed in 2008.

[...]

A house neighbouring the site was chosen as a base for the practical conservation work and as accommodation for the national and international experts. The house

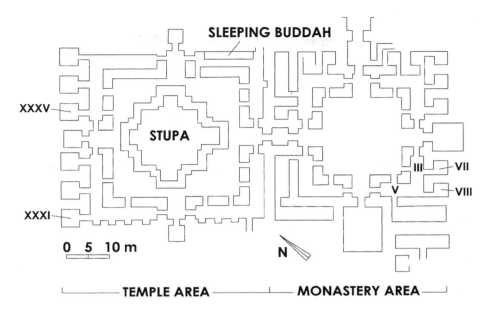

Figure 7.2.1 Schematic plan of the monastery of Ajina Tepa. Numbering refers to points discussed in this paper. [. . .] The plan is characterized by thick walls (up to 2.4 m) decorated with wall paintings and sculptures of the Buddha and bodhisattvas, now kept in the National Museum of Tajikistan.

Source: After Litvinskij and Zejmal (2004: 20)

owner was selected as guardian for the site, his role being useful especially during the winter months when no activity is carried out at the site. A car, essential for transporting both people and conservation materials, was purchased.

[. . .]

A laboratory for the analysis of earthen material was set up in the National Museum of Antiquities of Tajikistan, where a room was allocated for the purpose. [. . .] Training is one of the main components of the project and it was carried out in the form of empirical testing and laboratory analysis, in order to introduce current principles of conservation science and transfer the skills to young conservators and students. Tests proved to be essential for a proper understanding of the behaviour of earthen materials, and soil and historic sample characterization was necessary before physical testing.

[. . .]

Description of the monastery

Litvinskij and Zejmal (2004, 21) define the monastery of Ajina Tepa as a typical seventh to eighth centuries AD combination of two distinct parts, *vihāra* (monastic area) and *caitya* (temple area): the monastery (characterized by an open courtyard measuring 19 × 19 m, with *cellae* facing four elbow-shaped access passages, or *īwān*), and the temple (with a similar arrangement of four *īwān* facing the *cellae*, but with a massive terraced stupa in the courtyard). The discovery and excavation of the 13 m long Buddha in lying position in one of the corridors of the temple area was particularly important for the study of the spread of Buddhism in Central Asia. Depictions of the Buddha in *parinirvanasana* (symbolizing his mortal passing and his last stage from the cycle of rebirth) are widespread in Southeast Asia and Sri Lanka, but are quite rare in Central Asia (McArthur 2002, 107). The first attempts to conserve the statue, which was made of earth, were made in 1961. It was then cut into 92 pieces and transported to the National Museum of Antiquities in Dushanbe (Masov *et al.* 2005, 167). Here it was conserved by a group of experts under the leadership of P.I. Kostrov from the Hermitage Museum in Saint Petersburg and since 2001 it has been part of the permanent exhibition of the National Museum. After the destruction of the Bamiyan Buddhas in Afghanistan, this is currently the largest statue of the Buddha in Central Asia.

[...]

Walling material

Mudbrick and *pakhsa* (rammed earth) were both employed in the construction of the monastery walls, although *pakhsa* is seldom found at the lower wall levels. The tendency in Ajina Tepa is to find from five to eight courses of mudbrick at the base of the wall and several courses of *pakhsa* blocks on top. This is not a traditional method in western Central Asia, but it is rather typical in fifth to seventh century AD Bactria and Tukharistan (Litvinskij and Zejmal 1971, 223). Furthermore, Litvinskij and Zejmal (2004, 54) explain that this method was necessary to allow the construction of niches at the base of the walls, a simplified task if mudbrick is used. Roofing was constructed with barrel vaults, without formwork. It is likely that, for structural reasons, vaulting was made with bricks richer in straw in order to reduce the vertical component of the force. Mudbrick cannot take bending or shearing so the vault was built following the catenary, thus eliminating all bending and allowing the material to work only under compression. Walls were plastered with mud plaster (*saman*) in thick layers (Litvinskij and Zejmal 1971, 223; 2004, 56).

The present state of conservation of the site does not allow proper measurement of the original dimensions of the mudbrick and *pakhsa* blocks. However, Litvinskij and Zejmal (2004, 26) stated that at the time of excavation the *pakhsa* blocks measured 0.70 × 0.78 × 0.80 m, and that the mudbricks measured 0.10–0.12 × 0.25 × 0.50 m. Other mudbricks surveyed by Litvinskij measured 0.05 × 0.20 × 0.50 m. Fired brick was found in the core of the stupa and for paving the main courtyard path; these bricks measured 0.035–0.06 × 0.31–0.54 × 0.26–0.40 m. Fired brick was also found, used as paving material for two small *cellae* (XXXI and XXXV), for pavingstairs and walks, as a cladding material for wall bases, and for doorways (Litvinskij and Zejmal 1971, 223). The inner walls were 2.2 m thick, whilst the outer walls were 3.4 m. No clear foundation method was employed in Ajina Tepa. Generally, a *pakhsa* platform of 0.15–0.20 m was built at floor level, although occasionally a layer of red clay was applied as a footing (Litvinskij and Zejmal 2004, 55).

Historic repair methods

The excavation report by Litvinskij contains descriptions of building techniques, but he also found archaeological evidence to suggest that changes and repair work had been carried out in several parts of the building, mainly due to the collapse of the vaults.

In some cases this may have been caused by miscalculations of wall thickness in relation to the load of the vaults, with consequential collapse. This is probably true for Period I of the monastery. Repair and renovation work also extended to the wall paintings. Decayed earthen sculptures were sometimes found reused as repair material within the masonry (Litvinskij and Zejmal 2004, 20). More serious structural faults were repaired by adding *pakhsa* buttresses, such as those found in the inner wall of section V.

Main conservation threats

In order to have an overview of the main causes of deterioration, a survey was carried out in 2006 before starting conservation. This indicated the most common symptoms of decay as being: the collection of debris at the wall bases, the appearance of a soft or hard crust of clay, grass growth (some with deep roots), coving (undercutting), animal, insect and human damage, water channels, salts crystallization, cracks, and missing parts of walls. The fact that none of the walls considered in this study was previously conserved adds value to the research because it shows the behaviour of exposed earth walls in a natural environment.

The study shows that the main causes of decay can be broadly classified as: vegetation damage, rheological (water flow), man-made, and soluble salts.

Vegetation damage

The site is characterized by a substantial amount of flora, which grows between the wall structures and on top of the walls. The vegetation is represented by succulent plants and prickly desert grass, which vary from shallow to deep-rooted. It was soon clear that one of the most urgent needs was the management of the deep-rooted grass that grows on top of the structures. It causes serious collapse of structural parts, mainly due to the long and wide root system.

Rheological (water-flow) damage

Earthen structures are mechanically eroded by water, accentuated by the lack of water drainage systems. The lack of capping or sheltering of excavated walls can cause irreversible damage. In addition, washed-out soil often collects at the base of walls. The patterns of decay produced can be described as discrete erosion channels and general erosion due to rain washing.

Man-made damage

The most urgent conservation action in Ajina Tepa resulted from damage to the site caused by visitors walking on earthen walls. Shovel marks were also frequently found on the historic earthen structures, as local people used the walls as a quarry for mudbrick making. In 2006, in order to protect the site from man-made decay, a fence of circa 600 m was constructed.

In addition, the decaying old pedestrian bridge that led to the site was not safe and it was decided to build a new one (dimensions 1.2 × 14 m) to allow safe access for visitors, site staff and conservation materials.

Soluble salts damage

Coving (undercutting) is a typical decay symptom of earthen walls, especially when they are not supported by a plinth. The combination of soluble salts rising from the ground and wind erosion destabilizes the earthen material. Salts can effloresce on the surface of the wall base and when this is accompanied by the combined action of wind and windblown silt, the area affected by efflorescence is easily eroded (Fodde 2007b). When this is repeated several times, the section of the wall base can become thinner and eventually lose its load-bearing capacity, causing collapse.

Direct inspection of several structures of the site showed that the rate of decay was high and urgent conservation work was needed.

Preparatory work

One of the most useful tools for the management of conservation work at this site was the action plan. This document, continuously updated, was used together with the work plan as a reference for the numerous activities of the project.

Drainage plan

Before drafting the drainage plan, the site was monitored in the winter (November to March) and wet areas were mapped. The following information was collected:

- *Rainfall data*, to understand the amount of collected water and the evaporation rate (heavy storms are carefully studied and the amount of water compared with the rooms' capacities).
- *Temperature* (especially useful for freeze and thaw cycles).
- *Changes in the ground topography* (creation of gullies and channels by rain).

This study was carried out through photographic documentation and topographic mapping. The drainage plan is an essential tool for the removal/redirection of water away from foundations and structures, for both the inner and outer areas of the site. Monitoring also helps to predict the impact of worst possible cases (for example, one week of repeated storms). To aid drainage, it was suggested that the water be redirected/dispersed into small catchments, as it was very unlikely that it could be managed otherwise.

Study of local sources of clay

Local sources of clay were inspected and samples taken. Interviews and questionnaires were undertaken with local craftsmen to identify the nearest soil quarries. Samples were analysed in the laboratory to assess compatibility with the historic fabric of the monastery. The detailed study of the building materials enabled a better understanding of their traditional use and conservation. This preparatory work was essential for the selection of repair materials.

Selective removal of vegetation, monitoring, and damage recording

In order to understand the influence of vegetation on the earthen structures, it was decided to select one area that was overgrown with vegetation. This was regularly cleaned of all plants and grass, and photographs were taken to monitor vegetation growth. These data were compared with a similar structure that was left untouched.

Spoil heaps removal

Removal of spoil heaps was carried out in 2006 by hand and light machinery. This work was supervised by an archaeologist.

Analytical work

The aim of the work was to provide information on the building materials used in the Buddhist monastery. It is important to stress that during the experimental analysis the information provided by the archaeologists and the study of building techniques were complementary. [. . .] An interdisciplinary approach is therefore necessary for this type of research:

- comparison between mudbrick sizes
- study of building techniques (including *pakhsa*)
- laboratory analysis of historic building materials and comparison of wall masses
- laboratory analysis and assessment of materials employed for the building of the shelter coat
- analysis of natural samples surrounding the monastery area in order to understand the origin of the material used for the construction of the structure itself
- study and assessment of material to be employed for the future repair of the monastery.

Careful examination of the archaeological structures often shows different layers and reuse of old mortars or renders in the historic mix. Sampling was therefore preceded by visual inspection: a necessary tool for understanding and identifying the historic fabric, and for selecting samples that were representative of the wall mass or structure under study. It was also important that sample collection was carried out without seriously damaging the historic fabric.

Results of laboratory analysis

All of the analytical work was undertaken following the established protocols (Fodde 2007a). A total of 20 samples of historic mudbrick and 20 samples of historic *pakhsa* were analysed, and the results are provided here. Soluble salts were found in a concentration of 3.7 per cent in mudbrick and 6.6 per cent in *pakhsa* samples. This difference in content could not be explained, as the material used for their manufacture seems to be similar in origin (see granulometry, Figure 7.2.2). Mineral composition studied by X-ray diffraction (XRD) by Saitama University and the analysed samples showed high salinity in *pakhsa* samples compared with other sites in the Chuy Valley (Kyrgyzstan): for Krasnaya Rechka, Burana, and Ak Beshim the average soluble salts content was 3.8 per cent (Fodde *et al.* 2008). As for other Central Asian sites, at Otrar (Kazakhstan) the average salts content of earthen materials was 5.6 per cent.

Carbonates were found in all of the tested samples from Ajina Tepa and the average value was 24.7 per cent for mudbrick and 24.6 per cent for *pakhsa*. The conjecture is that the predominant acid-soluble element of the tested samples was calcium carbonate, [. . .] The particle size distribution for mudbrick was: clay (14.7 per cent), silt (64.9 per cent), sand (19.9 per cent), and gravel (0.5 per cent); in contrast, the particle-size distribution for *pakhsa* was: clay (14.2 per cent), silt (57.3 per cent), sand (26.1 per cent), and gravel (2.4 per cent).

Physical tests were carried out comparing the behaviour of historic samples with those of the possible repair material. The erosion test showed that the average perforation time for mudbrick samples was 0.19 minutes and for *pakhsa* samples, 0.13 minutes. A wetting and drying test gave the average percentage of lost material after the fifth cycle as 9.8 per cent for mudbrick, compared with 7.0 per cent for *pakhsa*. A shrinkage test provided a clear difference between mudbrick (3.1 per cent) and *pakhsa* (2.4 per cent). A freeze and thaw test could not be carried out due to a lack of freezing equipment.

Reference areas were calculated for both mudbrick and *pakhsa* (see Figure 7.2.2). These showed a slight difference, suggesting flexibility in the type of soil being used. The two reference areas were used to compare the granulometry curves of possible repair materials. [. . .]

A problem faced by the conservator of earthen buildings and sites today is that of selecting a repair material that follows the requirements given in the ICOMOS charters, such as that for the *Protection and Management of the Archaeological Heritage* (1990). These include sacrificial interventions, reversibility, minimal intervention, repairing like with like, etc. In order to achieve this fundamental aim, a sophisticated understanding of the materiality of the object or structure to be conserved is required. Conservation papers that explain analytical work often give no scientific explanation as to whether the repair material will follow these requirements. A new method was proposed by Fodde (2007a) for the requirement of sacrificial interventions, but more work needs to be done: the method was developed using a simple field laboratory and it is planned to repeat it with more sophisticated analysis.

Construction and monitoring of test walls

Eight test walls were built in the project house yard, following the method already carried out in Kyrgyzstan (Fodde 2007a). Test walls, measuring 1.20 × 1.20 × 0.38 m (height, width, depth), were constructed with mudbrick (measuring 0.34 × 0.16 × 0.10 m). The construction of the test walls was inspired by the principle that the testing of conservation materials should not be carried out on historic materials. It was also dictated by the necessity of studying the best-performing material for the conservation of the site. This will be essential for testing the repair material after proper analysis in the laboratory. Monitoring of wall decay will be designed to record the following parameters: colour change, erosion, cross-sections, coving (undercutting), moisture, photographic documentation, extent of cracks, and weather. The data will be recorded after 3, 6, 12, and 24 months from the construction of the walls.

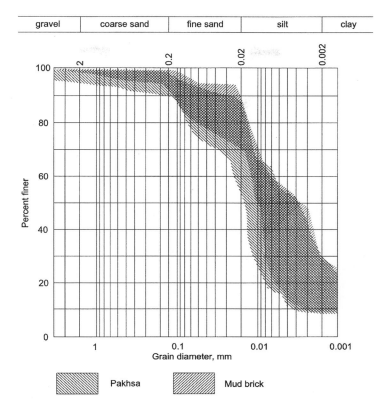

Figure 7.2.2 Diagram showing grading envelope or reference area for historic *pakhsa* and mudbrick. The usefulness of a recommended zone derives from the fact that those soils which comply with it are more likely to behave satisfactorily than those which do not. The employment of this guidance zone is of great use, especially for comparing it with the granulometry curves of the repair materials. Comparison between the two reference areas reveals a slight difference between the range of soils employed in *pakhsa* and in mudbrick.

Source: Picture by Enrico Fodde

Documentation

Extensive documentation work and training has been undertaken since the beginning of the project. Training has taken place in the archiving of documents, the analysis and evaluation of archival photographs of structures (relevant to conservation), and of excavation reports (relevant to conservation). In addition, there has been training in the cataloguing and listing of objects and finds, topographical surveying, purchasing of satellite images, archaeological investigation, site interpretation, 3-D mapping and the detailed study of important structures (sections and rectified elevations).

[. . .]

Three-dimensional documentation of earthen masses

The photogrammetric documentation of elevations was undertaken before, during, and after conservation. The method employed, 3-D visualization of masses from digital stereo photographs, was of great assistance to the project. A topographical map of the site was also constructed using photogrammetry, together with total station recording.

Designing proformas for condition recording

Condition recording of structures was undertaken using drawing conventions for damage assessment, authentication, and intervention records (Figures 7.2.3 and 7.2.4). The conventions were designed following work carried out on other sites, such as Otrar (Kazakhstan), Krasnaya Rechka (Kyrgyzstan) and Mohenjo-Daro (Pakistan) (Fodde 2007b, 2008b). This essential tool was accompanied by a sketch sheet and a bullet-point sheet, to be used as a guide for the completion of the proformas. The structure of the form covered: description of the object, examination of historic documents (photographs, archival material, etc.), previous interventions, summary of damage report (with reference to graphic material), diagnostic summary, intervention proposal, intervention action, and recommendations for future monitoring and maintenance.

Collection of climatic data

One of the future tasks for the project will be the creation of a computer database of old and new weather station data, and the interpretation of this data (hopefully involving the weather station department of Kurgan Tybe). The following data is of prime importance:

- *diurnal maximum and minimum temperature*: this provides information on the expansion and contraction of materials, efflorescence, subflorescence, hygroscopicity of salts and evaporation rates
- *diurnal maximum and minimum relative humidity*: this provides information on evaporation rates, hygroscopicity, increase in structure weight, wetting and drying cycles, efflorescence and subflorescence phenomena
- *rainfall data*: this provides information on the erosion of wall surfaces, ground erosion, gullies, underground tunnels, holes, increase in weight of the wall, bulging, wetting and drying cycles and settlement (that may create cracks and eventual wall collapse).

Geological survey

A geological survey of two inspection wells, to a depth of 10 m, is planned: this will provide data on geological stratification, ground water level, and the future possibility of monitoring of seasonal changes.

Conservation activities

Cleaning work and temporary conservation

Before undertaking any conservation activity, those walls that were covered in debris were inspected by the archaeological team. Cleaning was undertaken by removing the debris that covered the structures to check the extent of the walls. When full

Drawing Convention

№	Symbol	Description (English)	Description (Russian)
1		Grass	Травянистые растения с коротким корнем
2		Grass with deep roots	Растения с длинным корнем
3		Hole (made by animals)	Большие норы
4		Hole (made by insects)	Норки насекомых
5		Wide portion of missing wall	Пещерообразное углубление
6		Hard crust of clay	Корковый оплыв
7		Soft crust of clay	Рыхлый оплыв
8		Crack	Трещины
9		Border between historic material and repair work	Граница между древней и консервационной стеной
10		Rising damp	Сырые участки
11		Geotextile	Геотекстиль
12		Salt crystallization	Высолы
13		Man-made damage	Человеческий фактор
14		Decayed mortar	Разрушение кладочного раствора
15		Flaking (mud brick)	Отслоение поверхности
16		Lychens	Лишайник
17		Decayed repair brickwork	Разрушение консервационной кладки
18		Fired brick	Обожженный кирпич
19		Mud brick	Сырцовый кирпич
20		Replaced mud brick	Консервационный сырцовый кирпич
21		Missing mud mortar	Сохранившийся древний раствор
22		Preferential channels	След от стока воды
23		Graffiti	Современные надписи на кирпиче
24		Cultural layer	Культурный слой
25		New mud plaster	Консервационная обмазка
26		Charcoal	Кусочки древесной золы
27		Carbonates	Карбонаты
28		Crushed fired brick	Цемянка
29		Coving	Рюмочное разрушение
30		Mud brick sample	Отбор проб кирпича
31		Mud mortar sample	Отбор проб раствора
32		Collection of debris at base of wall	Насыпь
33		Infill sand layer	Консервационный песок
34		Decayed repair plaster	Разрушение консервационной обмазки

Figure 7.2.3 Drawing conventions in English and Russian employed for the documentation of damage and conservation threats.
Source: Picture by Enrico Fodde

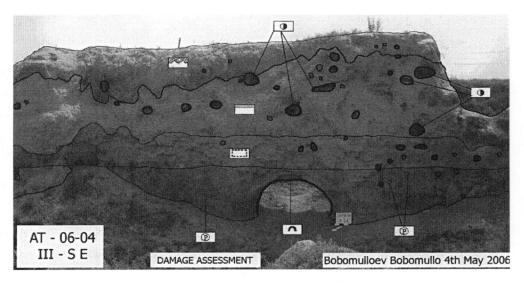

Figure 7.2.4 Documentation of damage using the conventions in Figure 7.2.3.
Source: Picture by Enrico Fodde

conservation could not be achieved before the winter, structures were temporarily protected by backfilling, until the next favourable season.

Reburial activities

One urgent conservation activity at Ajina Tepa was the reburial of endangered structures. The first important step was that any reburial activity should be preceded by the identification and sourcing of appropriate materials. Employing local sand and soil in repair work has many advantages, not least of which is that the sources for the original materials were traditionally close to the site. Reburial should take place after proper testing, cleaning, documentation, collection of information on the structures (coursing details, material analysis), application of a separation layer, and the designing of a monitoring programme. During the original excavations at Ajina Tepa reburial was never contemplated as a conservation measure. This is similar to what has been experienced in other countries, and awareness-raising and training are necessary to make the technique acceptable, both ethically and to avoid psychological barriers.

Monitoring conservation work

A programme of monitoring of the conservation work has been devised, enabling repeatability. This includes the insertion of plastic pins in the conservation work to measure erosion, and laboratory analysis of conservation material to measure the migration of salts (to be carried out by collecting samples vertically, at given intervals, in order to measure the moisture and salts content). In addition, useful information on the behaviour of conservation interventions is provided by visual inspections and regular photographic documentation.

Repair of eroded walls and shelter coating

The manufacture of mudbricks for conservation started as soon as the selection of repair material was concluded in the field laboratory. Conservation work was concentrated in the monastery area, where the most endangered structures were located (see Figures 7.2.5–7.2.7). The first area to be tackled was corridors III and V. Here, archaeological cleaning was carried out under the supervision of an archaeologist. The main aim was to structurally consolidate the wall between corridor III and VII–VIII. A shelter coat was applied, following specific stages. The first stage was the preparation of drainage slopes, so that rainwater would not reach the base of the walls. Then a shallow trench (0.2 m deep) was dug along the wall and filled with a conglomerate of gravel and salts-free soil. The mix was rammed, to give a solid ground on which to lay the shelter coat masonry. No geofabric was employed as a separation layer between the historic structures and the shelter coat because in Tajikistan there is a strong bias against such material: it is felt that it could encourage rising damp and that its future use would be too expensive for any local project. However, the mudbricks used in the shelter coat are clearly identifiable as a modern intervention. Filling the gap between the mudbrick skin and the historic fabric was conducted with dry soil. Plastering of the encapsulation, with a mix of soil and straw, then followed. In some cases windows were left to expose the historic fabric as a didactic approach to the shelter coating. This method was

EARTHEN SITES IN REMOTE AREAS

Figure 7.2.5 Local master builders and labourers, trained during the project, applying a shelter coat of mudbrick to the most endangered walls (2007). Due to the height of some of the walls shelter coats had to be made quite thick at the base. The rationale of this conservation intervention was that the historic structure would carry the minimum load and that the coat would be self-supporting.

Source: Picture by Enrico Fodde

Figure 7.2.6 Shelter coating of mud plaster following the morphology of the earthen walls. In some cases windows were left to expose the original fabric, a didactic guide to the work done.

Source: Picture by Malka Budanaeva

Figure 7.2.7 The structural consolidation of leaning walls was undertaken with thick mudbrick buttresses. These have the advantage of being reversible and easily readable as a new intervention (2006). Work in progress.

Source: Picture by Enrico Fodde

successfully employed in another UNESCO project in the Upper Chuy Valley in Kyrgyzstan (Fodde 2008a).

Buttress construction

Some of the leaning walls were so fragile that it was necessary to build mudbrick buttresses to avoid the total collapse of the historic fabric (see Figure 7.2.7). This was done as an urgent conservation measure before shelter coating the wall.

Maintenance activity after an unfavourable 'rainy season'

It is expected that after the rainy season not only the historic parts but also the conservation work may need maintenance. A budget for the yearly maintenance of the site has been allocated, which will be carried out on completion of the project. This will also include landscaping work and terrain modelling. This is considered as routine work for the proper conservation of the site.

Conclusion

Several benefits of the work to the site can be identified. Urgent conservation was tackled immediately and this included the repair of heavily eroded and tilting structures. More routine repair work was carried out where needed. Site presentation was improved in terms of fencing, access bridge construction, and the repair of the path. It should also be mentioned that documentation was undertaken of the entire site before and after conservation, so that it could be referenced by future conservators. Follow-up work will include maintenance schedules of both the historic fabric and the repair work.

Apart from carrying out documentation and physical conservation at the site, another important outcome of the project was the improvement in skills of the Tajik experts and the building up of a national capacity for the conservation and management of earthen archaeological sites. This is of great importance to Tajikistan, especially when considering the shortage of skills that resulted after its independence from the former USSR and the subsequent civil war, when the majority of heritage experts fled the country. In addition, the country still lacks an appropriate infrastructure, or conservation institutes or department, although recently the Tajik government has started to move to address this situation.

Bibliography

Fodde, E. (2007a). 'Analytical methods for the conservation of the Buddhist Temple II of Krasnaya Rechka, Kyrgyzstan.' *Conservation and Management of Archaeological Sites* 8(3): 136–153.

Fodde, E. (2007b). 'Fired brick and sulphate attack: the case of Moenjodaro, Pakistan.' *Journal of Architectural Conservation* 13(1): 69–80.

Fodde, E. (2008a). 'Structural faults in earthen archaeological sites in Central Asia: analysis and repair methods.' In D. d'Ayala and E. Fodde (eds), *Sixth International Conference on Structural Analysis of Historic Construction*. London: Taylor & Francis, 1415–1422.

Fodde, E. (2008b) 'Fired brick conservation in the Kyrgyz silk roads: the case of Burana's Mausoleum 4.' *Journal of Architectural Conservation* 14(1): 77–94.

Fodde, E., K. Watanabe and Y. Fujii (2008). 'Conservation and documentation of the Buddhist monastery of AjinaTepa, Tajikistan: heritage of the silk roads.' In L. Rainer, A. Bass Rivera and D. Gandreau (eds), *Terra 2008, 10th International Conference on the Study and Conservation of Earthen Architecture*. Los Angeles: Getty Conservation Institute, 171–176.

Litvinskij, B. and T.I. Zejmal (1971). *Adjina Tepa. Architektura, Jivopis, Skultura*. Moscow: Izdatelstvo Iskusstvo.

Litvinskij, B. and T.I. Zejmal (2004). *The Buddhist monastery of Ajina Tepa, Tajikistan*. Rome: ISIAO.

McArthur, M. (2002). *Reading Buddhist Art*. London: Thames and Hudson.

Masov, R., S. Bobomulloev and M. Bubnova (2005). *National Museum of Tajikistan: the album*. Dushanbe: National Museum of Tajikistan.

Chapter 8

Decay and mitigation of earthworks

Earthworks: protection and decay

EARTHWORKS, NORMALLY COMPRISING BANKS, platforms or mounds of earth and/or stone, usually with associated ditches, are the most common form of ancient monument. They are present in all corners of the world where there has been human activity, from the 150 miles of Offa's Dyke dividing eighth-century Mercian England from Wales, to the remains of the windbreaks created by early twentieth-century explorers in the Antarctic (Barr and Chaplin 2004). Earthwork sites in Britain and Europe are most usually seen as defences outlining a habitation site (hill forts, castles), land divisions (dykes, field boundaries), transport (Roman roads), agricultural sites (medieval ridge and furrow), habitation (deserted prehistoric and medieval villages), industrial sites (mine pits, mills), funerary monuments (long barrows and round barrows) and monumental-scale ritual sites (henges, cursus). These most numerous and ubiquitous monuments are principally at risk from the natural forces of erosion and people who seek to use the ground they occupy for new activities – such as agriculture (livestock, ploughing, forestry), quarries or roads (see Chapter 2). The perceived ubiquity and numerousness of these sites meant that in the recent past, they had a low social value, and thus little protection. In the UK, prior to 1882, the only method to ensure that an ancient earthwork was not destroyed was to own it, Sir John Lubbock having to purchase parts of Avebury to protect the site from development, while as late as 1924 Alexander Keiller purchased Windmill Hill to prevent the construction of a wireless station on the ancient monument (Champion 1996: 49; Hunter 1996: 8). The increasing value of earthworks as part of the nation's past was emphasised in the 1882 Ancient Monuments Protection Act when almost all of the 50 Roman and prehistoric monuments in the schedule attached to the act were, in part or whole, earthworks (Thompson 2006: 97–9) (see Chapter 4).

The focus of this chapter is on the earthwork monument itself. Other aspects of the site, such as the artefacts and buried archaeology deposits, are discussed in Chapter 9.

DECAY AND MITIGATION OF EARTHWORKS

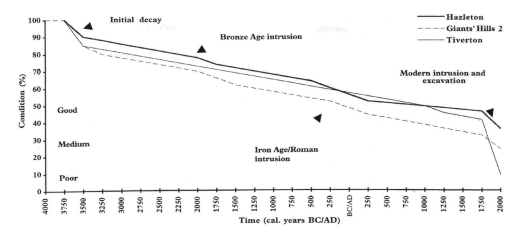

Figure 8.0.1 A decay profile based on excavated data from the long barrows at Hazelton, Giants Hill and Tiverton.

Source: Darvill and Fulton (1998: 19)

Survival

Darvill and Fulton (1998) suggested that earthworks in England suffered two significant periods of decay (see Figure 8.0.1).

Initial decay phase

Immediately after their construction, during their period of use, earthworks suffer trampling and solifluction (downslope movement of exposed soil), leading to rapid erosion. The mound and/or ditch profiles erode or collapse quickly losing steepness, they vegetate and stabilise as shown by the experimental earthworks at Overton Down and Wareham (see Figures 3.3.1 and 3.3.2).

Slow decay phase

Subsequent decay is slow. If the monument has value to that society, it will be preserved through one of two mechanisms:

- High social value leads to repeated use and continued erosion, but also active repair/conservation.
- Lower social value is still sufficient to prevent active vandalism, damage or reuse of the site. In this condition, it has become 'sacred ground', often left to nature, a form of preservation (*in situ*) by neglect. If ungrazed, this often leads the site to become covered in trees (see Figure 8.0.2).

Aurel Stein noted examples of such social valuation in Central Asia at the start of the twentieth century:

Shami Sope, a withered old man of about ninety, had heard from his father and grandfather, who had both died at a great age, that the little mound had ever been respected by the folk of Somiya as a hallowed spot not to be touched by the plough share. Some unknown spirit is supposed to have sat upon this spot, and evil would befall those who should touch the ground. The name of the saint is forgotten and the villagers would not assert whether he rests under the mound or not. But the people of Somiya never pass without saying a prayer, and according to the testimony of Shami Sope and his forebears, they have clung to this custom for the last two centuries.

(Stein 1903: 265–6)

The enigmatic nature of earthworks allows each generation to write their own story (or adapt earlier stories) about these monuments, so enabling them to have a value to the present. This malleability has enabled some prehistoric earthworks to remain valued to the present day, where that value is now articulated as protection in law. Social veneration was effectively the principal means of protecting ancient monuments prior to the creation of heritage protection legislation (see Chapter 4).

Later (final) decay phase

When the monument has lost social value (e.g. because a new social group occupies the land or the memory has faded), it is incorporated back into the landscape and is utilised as a functional resource. Roman roads were used as quarries and prehistoric barrows were later ploughed flat for agriculture; the ability to be part of a large easily ploughed field had become the site's greatest attribute. Hence, many earthworks became badly degraded or were lost completely.

Slope

There is a substantial literature on creating stable modern earthworks, especially for road and rail construction (Kézdi and Rétháti 1988). Reported failures in earthworks (Greenwood *et al*. 1985; McGowan 1985) emphasise the importance of water content and soil type when considering the stability of earthworks. The experimental earthwork on the chalk at Overton Down and observations of the boulder clay earthworks on Hadrian's Wall suggest slopes below 20° from the horizontal are normally stable, steeper and the risk of erosion increases. However, the sand of the Wareham earthwork declined from 14° to 7° to achieve stability (Rimmington 2004: 4), thus soil type is crucial. Beyond gradient, the water content of the soil (which, when high, leads to mobility of clay even within shallow banks) and disturbance to the toe of the bank can lead to landslip (Greenwood *et al*. 1985; Parsons and Perry 1985). Such features remain relevant to archaeological earthworks, where changes in rainfall or drainage can lead to structural failure.

Earthworks as agents of preservation

The demise of organic materials beneath the Overton Down and Wareham earthworks, the cotton and linen quickly, the oak and hazel wood more slowly, demonstrates that organic artefacts and ecofacts normally decay beneath earthworks (see Chapter 3.3). However, the formation of a mound of soil can, depending on the nature of the soil, the size of the mound and processes such as iron pan formation, create a barrier to the diffusion of oxygen or oxygenated water, leaving the material in the centre of the mound in a deoxygenated environment, thus preserving it. This was seen beneath Silbury Hill, where vegetation buried when the mound was erected in the Bronze Age was reported in the excavations to the centre of the mound in the 1950s to still be undecayed and green – its chlorophyll still preserved (Canti *et al.* 2004). This preservative quality of earthworks made of clay was evidenced by the preservation of Viking ships beneath mounds at Tune, Gokstad and Osberg, in contrast to the mound of sand and gravel at Borre in 1850–1852, where little trace of the boat remained (see Chapter 1). The ability of ditches to collect and retain water can lead to waterlogged conditions in sunken features such as pit shafts, graves and ditches at earthwork sites, again leading to preservative oxygen-free (anoxic) conditions and the preservation of organic artefacts and ecofacts (see Chapter 11).

Agents of earthwork erosion

Cultivation

Ploughing has continued to be the scourge of earthworks, highlighted by numerous writers (Hinchcliffe and Schadla-Hall 1980; Darvill 1987: 128; Lambrick 2004). Coles (1987) (see Chapter 2.1) identified the damage caused to earthworks by both the intensification of agriculture in the decades following World War II, while losses from ploughing between 1955 and 1995 were documented in detail by Darvill and Fulton (1998). Examples such as the damage to the Hopeton Earthworks (Ohio) have been documented in the USA (US Army Corps of Engineers 1992: 1.30). The larger the ploughs and the deeper they go, the greater the damage. Centuries of ploughing have often left archaeological remains such as barrows and castle mottes, places venerated in antiquity, covered with trees, isolated islands in a sea of intensive agriculture, devoid of archaeological context (see Figure 8.0.2). Modern experimentation and monitoring of 'real' monuments shows cultivation (regardless of the type of ploughing) removes between 1 and 3 cm per year from the height of prehistoric earthworks (Oxford Archaeology 2010).

Vegetation

The presence of trees over many earthworks has in recent centuries saved them from obliteration from ploughing. Normally 80–90 per cent of tree roots are within 0.6 m of the surface and are rarely found below 2 m (Crow and Moffat 2005: 105). Since it is normally large volumes of root activity that tear earthworks apart, surface features such as stone revetted banks and shallow sites such as deserted medieval villages are most at risk from the root growth from small trees and shrubs, pushing out the revetting stones and disturbing stratified deposits (Jones 2003: 194). Individual tree roots, particularly those with deeper taproots such as apple and oak, can disturb and damage deeper archaeological remains; the roots of mature trees in Trajan's Park (Rome) were found, at a distance of 30 m from the tree and a depth of 15 m below the surface, to be tearing apart the subterranean vaults of Nero's imperial residence, which lies beneath the park (Caneva *et al.* 2006). Shallow rooted trees such as beech potentially damage sites through windthrow; mature trees blown over by the wind tearing up archaeological remains in their root plates (typically 4–6 m diameter

Figure 8.0.2 The isolated motte of Castell Dyffryn Mawr, Pembrokeshire, covered with trees. The surrounding bank and ditches of the bailey have long since been ploughed away.

Source: Photograph by the author

and 1–1.5 m deep) when they are wrenched from the soil. The species of tree and the nature of the soil determine depth of rooting (Crow 2005). Banks, barrows and other raised earthworks are most at threat from shallow root and windthrow damage. Excessive shade from trees can kill grass and lead to increased erosion. Where damage from tree roots is considered a threat, felling the tree and allowing the roots to die *in situ* is considered to lead to least disturbance, though regrowth of the tree needs to be prevented through use of herbicides or repeated removal of young growth. Appropriate siviculture, such as coppicing, will reduce depth of roots and thinning will reduce the likelihood of windthrow, but wholesale clearing of trees can lead to soil destabilisation and soil loss, as at Caesar's Camp, Bracknell, Berkshire (Crow and Moffat 2005: 108). In modern forestry practice, it is the tracked vehicles responsible for logging and clearing, as well as drainage activities, that tear the ground surface apart, damaging shallow stratigraphy and archaeological remains (Jackson 1978; Wildesen 1982; Darvill 1987: 98–9; White 1994: 104) (see Chapter 9.1). Trees, especially conifers, can also have a desiccating effect on the surrounding soil, potentially damaging to waterlogged deposits. Widely spaced deciduous trees desiccate at a level closer to that of grassland (Crow and Moffat 2005: 105). Though a couple of studies have suggested that tree growth is less damaging to sites than cultivation (Crow and Moffat 2005: 107), the potential damage that tree roots can do to a site is recognised, and the UK Forestry Commission Guidelines require that trees are not planted on archaeological sites and in a 20 m buffer zone around them (Forestry Commission 1995). This emphasises the need to accurately locate ancient earthworks, have them correctly mapped and their full extent determined prior to afforestation. Any ancient monument glades and earthworks under existing tree cover should be incorporated into forest management plans (Forest District Conservation Plans) so that existing glades are maintained and cleared of saplings (Crow 2004). Existing sites already covered with trees need to be managed to restrict root growth and minimise the risk of windthrow damage.

Other forms of vegetation especially scrub can also have a damaging effect. Bracken, whose rhizomes disturb soil to a depth of 40 cm, can be particularly damaging to archaeological deposits near the present ground surface (Rees and Mills 1999). Gerrard (1999) encountered up to 275 rhizomes per m^2 in his excavation of prehistoric hut circles in Dartmoor. Difficulties in controlling bracken often require the use of otherwise undesirable herbicides (Berry and Brown 1994: 90–1, 109; Rimmington 2004: 81). In temperate climates, grass and other shallow-rooted vegetation is normally considered the most desirable form of vegetation over archaeological sites, 'a well maintained grassland is the best landscape environment for the preservation of archaeological remains' (Darvill 1987: 88), though mechanisms for regular grazing (in the spring and early summer to take the young growth shoots) or cutting need to be established to prevent larger woody stemmed plants (scrub) and trees taking over (Rimmington 2004: 8, 43). You cannot actively manage sites you cannot see. Mowing by hand is expensive and can result in damage to any stone features (see Figure 8.0.3); consequently, animal grazing is often preferred, though this can lead to problems of erosion (see below).

Rye grasses are used to form hard-wearing turf for well-visited monuments such as Stonehenge (Rimmington 2004: 38–40), which attracted 870,000 visitors in 1999; however, a 'sports field' maintenance regime, involving regular cutting, aeration, feeding, repair of breaches and rotating pathways over a larger area to provide recovery time for the grass, are invariably necessary for the most heavily used sites (Wimble 1994). The most intensively damaged and used areas may need a cellular polymer structure such as Golpla® into which grass can grow, but which prevents physical damage/loss of the soil surface. For less intensively visited sites, native grassland species that utilise poorer soils may be more appropriate (Jones 1998).

The faster growth of vegetation in 'jungle' conditions can lead to enhanced vegetation growth rates and potentially greater damage to earthworks in tropical environments. Root damage can appear dramatic on masonry monuments, but earthworks are greatly affected. On upland and semi-arid sites or those suffering industrial pollution, vegetation cover is often

Figure 8.0.3 Gravestone outside York station. Numerous chips have been knocked off the gravestone from the regular passage of lawnmowers.

Source: Photograph by the author

absent or ephemeral, and the effects of water, sun and wind can result in high levels of erosion. Consequently, preventing vegetation loss and establishing revegetation programmes are often highly appropriate mitigation measures. Catastrophic vegetation loss, such as fires, like that which swept over Fylingdales Moor (North Yorkshire) in 2003, can reveal and expose to extensive erosion earthwork monuments that are normally hidden and protected by vegetation (Vyner 2009).

Animal 'attack'

The raised mound of an earthwork offers a potential home to burrowing animals such as rabbits and badgers (Darvill and Fulton 1998: 138; Dunwell and Trout 1999; Rimmington 2004: 59–70), and a potential windbreak to sheep, cattle and other grazers. A single rabbit hole can represent up to 8 m of burrow and 1.6 m^3 of removed soil (Rimmington 2001: 17). Where the vegetation surface is broken through animal trample (poaching), dust bowls form and constant use maintains, extends (sheet erosion) and deepens such features (see Figure 8.0.4). Gateways, fence lines, rubbing posts, water troughs, salt licks, regular movement routes (stock tracking), pinch points, sheltered areas in the lee of trees or structures, all suffer erosion once the vegetation cover is broken; water and wind erosion of the soil enhance and deepen such features, leading to significant damage to ancient earthworks. The full range of erosive problems associated with earthworks in Britain and their conservation is discussed in *Managing Earthwork Monuments* (Rimmington 2004) and *Erosion on Archaeological Earthworks: Its Prevention, Control and Repair* (Berry and Brown 1994), with a useful summary by Streeten (1994) (see Chapter 8.1). The experience in Cambridge, Yorkshire and elsewhere shows that grazing is one of the most efficient ways to manage the grass cover, though there do need to be controls such as using fenced areas and only issuing grazing licences for specific periods,

Figure 8.0.4 Cattle scrape in a twelfth-century ringwork castle, Castell Pengawsai, Pembrokeshire.

Source: Photograph by the author

specific types and numbers of stock. Grazing licences should be set at levels which avoid significant risk of erosion. Heavy grazing by larger heavier cattle can be particularly damaging (Jones 1998: 293); sheep or mixed species grazing may be preferable. In wild areas such as Dartmoor, fences are socially and visually unacceptable leading to greater risk of uncontrolled animal erosion (Berry and Brown 1994: 79, 85, 90).

Visitation

This is the eternal heritage paradox; you want people to come and learn about the monuments (earthworks) of the ancient past, but their interest in and visitation to those monuments potentially leads to wear and damage of the site (Berry and Brown 1994; Darvill and Fulton 1998: 138). Public awareness of the presence of visible and complete deserted medieval and prehistoric villages on Bodmin Moor and Dartmoor has led to increased visitation and erosion damage of the fragile acid upland moorland soil (Darvill 1987: 105–16; 148–63). Human movement over the monument can erode and wear through the turf, creating gullies in the soil where water pools leading to even faster soil degradation and vegetation loss. The erosion is usually most concentrated on unofficial paths (desire lines), around steps; notice boards, gateways, styles, entrances, seats, tables, viewpoints and toilet and refreshment facilities where visitor activity is focussed (Thackray 1994: 103–5). It becomes important to manage visitor numbers and movement as soon as active erosion features start to emerge (see Chapter 12). Experiments at Stonehenge (Wimble 1994) showed that on grassland 50 times more damage is done on wet than dry ground. The benefits of a hard-wearing rye grass for paths that appear natural but resistant to wear are clear; however, soil and vegetation type, topography, climate and use/activity all affect the capacity of any surface to withstand wear. Suppressing visitor numbers to reduce erosion damage can be achieved through:

- Reducing the size of the car park and increasing its distance from the site, as done by the National Trust at Badbury Rings (Dorset) (Thackray 1994: 108).
- Eliminating focal points, as practised by the Yorkshire Dales National Park Authority, who have not provided information boards at popular, errodable sites such as Ingleborough (Yorkshire) (White 1994: 95).

The National Parks and other UK heritage organisations have suggested that where there is a conflict between preservation of the heritage and visitation by the public, both stated aims of these organisations, the Precautionary or 'Sandford' Principle, applies:

> National Park Authorities can do much to reconcile public enjoyment with the preservation of natural beauty by good planning and management and the main emphasis must continue to be on this approach wherever possible. But even so, there will be situations where the two purposes are irreconcilable . . . Where this happens, priority must be given to the conservation of natural beauty.
> (Lord Sandford, 1974 – Chair of the National Parks Policy Review Committee)

This was, for example, the reason that public access inside the stones at Stonehenge ceased in 1978 (Cathersides 2001) and in 2014 is still restricted, through an application process, to only 26 people per day.

On unfenced sites such as earthworks on the semi-arid ranges of the USA or the arctic regions of Canada, USA and Russia, off-road vehicles are the cause of significant damage to earthworks (Wildesen 1982: 70; US Army Corps of Engineers 1992: 1.18).

The earliest antiquarians to the 'nighthawks' of the present day have realised that earthworks mark the site of ancient settlements or burials and as such often contain valuable artefacts (see Chapter 1). The deliberate looting of artefacts from such sites (Hutt *et al.* 1992; Dobinson and Denison 1995) is a problem throughout the world. Proximity to roads was identified as one of the key factors in the vandalism and looting of sites in the USA; the site of Albany Mounds, located beside Route 84 and hidden by 8 ft high prairie grass, has suffered extensive looting (US Army Corps of Engineers 1992: I.12, I.13, 5.1). The remoteness of sites, limited personnel, lack of priority by law enforcement agencies, complexity of legally proving wrongdoing and high costs make detection, apprehension and prosecution difficult (Reed and Schreiner 2000). At remote sites, signs can protect against unintentional visitor damage to the remains, though they can sometimes attract deliberate damage, to both the remains and the sign. Their presence is important in aiding prosecution for deliberate damage of sites, as ignorance of the value of the remains cannot be maintained. Signs were shown to be more effective as a deterrent when accompanied with a barrier (fence, bank, ditch, brash and at the Fort Hood army range, barbed wire) (US Army Corps of Engineers 1992: I.18, VI.1, X.1). Where there is a breakdown of law and order, as in conflict situations, the risk of looting rises dramatically (see Chapter 2); those sites with earthworks or ruins attract most attention from looters, whether driven by poverty or greed.

Military activity

Since the invention of the firearm, banks and ditches, ancient or modern, have been used as protection. Military use can sometimes act to preserve earthworks preventing farming and visitation. The earthworks are, however, at risk of damage by explosives, being altered to improve or reduce their protective capacities or from vehicle damage. The development and use of tanks and tracked vehicles since the First World War has greatly increased the risk of damage to earthworks from such vehicles (Morgan-Evans 1992). The urgent demands of war have led to considerable damage of earthworks throughout Europe and the Middle East; of past cultures have no value to the military commanders of the present. The creation of trenches and banks during conflict has damaged existing monuments, but also created new ones. Arguably, the banks and ditches of the hillforts of the Iron Age of Europe and the trenches of the First World War represent the most iconic features of these periods of conflict. Damage can also occur indirectly through developments such as roads, runways and building construction undertaken in support of a war effort (Robertson and Schofield 2000), and even more indirectly through the national need for increased agricultural production, which occurred in Britain during the Napoleonic, First and Second World Wars. This resulted in large numbers of prehistoric, Roman and medieval earthworks being ploughed up for food production, with little or no archaeological record of the damage.

Water

See Chapter 9.

Earthwork conservation

The fact that vegetation forms naturally on the surface of soil, in all but desert regions, and stabilises it, means that unlike the buildings or rock surfaces that simply erode under the effects of weather, earthwork surfaces can often more accurately be considered as biological systems capable of self-repair. If the eroding force can be slowed or stopped, vegetation will re-establish and stabilise the surface, recreating a tough protective skin. Streeten (1994) (see Chapter 8.1) outlines the methodological approach and types of measures typically employed by English Heritage during the 1980s when dealing with earthworks and seen in expanded form in *Managing Earthwork Monuments* (Rimmington 2004). These can be summarised as:

- Create a 'Condition Assessment' record of the nature of the monument and its state of decay at a specific moment in time (photographs, diagrams, etc.) (Rimmington 2004: 14–24). Identify the forces damaging the monument and plan how to stop or reduce them and stabilise the monument, where appropriate repairing existing damage with the aim of returning the monument to a condition that can be maintained and sustained.
- Removal or reduction of controllable erosive forces – including ploughing, wild animals, grazing animals, people (horses and riders, cyclists, walkers, motorists, motorcyclists) using management agreements, legal protection, fences or signs.
- Repair any damage done to the monument – ideally using natural materials (biodegradable) sympathetic to the ecology and soil of the monument. The aim of the conservation work is to prevent further damage and ensure readability of the monument (restored where necessary, and we can be certain of the earthwork's original form). Erosion scars are typically filled with stone topped with soil and then turfed, all chosen to be appropriate to the soil, geology and ecology of the area. This approach has been enacted at sites throughout Britain, including Castleshaw (North Yorkshire) (White 1994: 95–101), Whitesheet Hill and Figsbury Rings (Wiltshire) (Thackray 1994: 107; McGlade 2001). The truth of this 'restoration' is provided through a full record of the extent of the damage and leaving marker materials (gravel or modern marker artefacts), most usually geotextiles (Haygarth 1994; Kavazanjian 2004), at the eroded surface before any material is added, so future archaeologists can be clear and certain about the extent of erosion and subsequent repair (Thackray 1994: 108).
- Soil movement can be restrained through use of geotextiles pinned into place, different forms of geotextile giving differing types of protection (filtering, retention, protection, encouraging/retarding root growth); some are retained in place, while others are biodegradable and have limited lifespan (Haygarth 1994; Kavazanjian 2004).
- Prevent reoccurrence of animal or human erosion through the erection of fences, walls or cover areas with cut vegetation (brash) to ensure animals or people stay off the damaged/repaired area, resting the areas while the vegetation recovers. Where possible, remove foci of activity: notices, seats, steps, tables and facilities (where people congregate) and gates, fences and shelter (where animals congregate) from archaeologically sensitive areas, as these invariably result in erosion zones. Where there are unintended paths (desire lines) created by people, cycles, horses, motorcycles and other vehicles, these should be removed, prevented, obscured or adopted and toughened up. If the volume of users is small, they may be dispersed evenly over the whole monument; large numbers will require dedicated paths formed from appropriate hard-wearing materials (Rimmington 2004: 30–4). Drainage improvements will avoid damp areas on paths and vehicular trackways, which is where most damage is done.

- Establish regular monitoring procedures; it is essential to know when sites are actively eroding and when they are static, or slowly improving. This is typically achieved by visits from field wardens, who both monitor the condition of the site and ensure contact with the landowner, so emphasising to them the value of the site to the wider community. Regular recording (digital photographs, drawings, measurements, levels and profiles across paths and gullies) of potentially erodible features is undertaken to ascertain the impact of use. There is a need for permanent fixed reference points on every monument to which all such monitoring is tied, and it is essential that accurate records of the monitoring are kept (Jones 2003: 195–6).
- Establish regular maintenance procedures. Costs are, in the initial phase of repair, usually low and features such as an earthworks vegetated surface can often self-repair, if protected from continued wear. When erosion is extensive and large volumes of material have to be brought to site, costs are high, as in the case of monuments on the Brecon Beacons, where repair of substantial erosion scars on remote sites required large amounts of materials to be brought in by helicopter. The provision of maintenance for sites is the most efficient means to preserve archaeological remains but it is difficult for many organisations working in a constantly changing managerial and personnel environment to achieve.
- There is a need to obtain legal permission from state heritage agencies to actively intervene with any earthwork protected by legislation. In Britain, this means scheduled monument consent even to undertake preservation work on any scheduled monument. Some forms of legal protection, such as environmental protection (SSSI status or equivalent), may limit what conservation work can be done, such as preventing use of hard-wearing grass species in favour of fragile local flora.
- Sustaining earthworks on farmland only occurs through non-cultivational agricultural activity such as using the land for pasture and grazing with low levels of stock (Oxford Archaeology 2010). English Heritage have, through their COSMIC initiative, been developing management tools for assessing and managing risk to scheduled ancient monuments in arable cultivation (Humble 2010). This is part of their 'Heritage at Risk' strategy, which publishes an annual register of the most threatened sites in England, so identifying and highlighting the archaeological and historic remains at greatest risk. From 1979 (Ancient Monument and Archaeological Areas Act), the statutory heritage agencies of England and Wales have been able to enter into management agreements with farmers for three to five year periods to facilitate use of appropriate benign farming practices and control of vegetation and burrowing animals in exchange for payments. This can represent a cheaper option than acquiring the monument and placing it under state care (guardianship). Wider schemes such as Countryside Stewardship Scheme and Environmentally Sensitive Areas Scheme both now superseded by the Environmental Stewardship Scheme (and Glastir replacing Tir Gofal in Wales) support farming in an environmentally sensitive way (Mcinnes 1993: 252; Berry and Brown 1995; Berry 2001). Beneficially, all such schemes require the creation of a management plan. These are national or EU schemes that reflect the change from intensive agriculture, which characterised European farming after the Second World War, to a more environmental sensitive approach by the 1990s. Initially intended for nature conservation, cultural remains are increasingly seen as part of a sensitively managed landscape. Funding for such schemes is subject to changes in political social thinking. This more environmentally aware approach is also established in other areas of landscape use such as forestry and military practices ranges, where

agreements for the preservation and management of archaeological monuments, as well as areas crucial to plants and animals, are increasingly being practised (Mcinnes 1993). Heritage agencies such as English Heritage, Cadw and Historic Scotland are very aware of their legal responsibilities to the natural world (Harding 1995) and frequently commission ecological surveys of their sites to identify the extent and nature of the plant and animal species present on sites. Identifying both the valuable (scarce) organisms present and the ecosystem that supports them potentially leads to cooperatively working with organisations such as English Nature, to establish an integrated approach to preserve both the valuable archaeological and natural resources (Berry and Brown 1995). Many sites in the UK are both Scheduled Ancient Monuments (SAM) and Sites of Special Scientific Interest (SSSI), protecting cultural heritage and ecological resources.

In practice

To effectively implement conservation or preservation of earthworks, the appropriate form of financial, social and regulatory support needs to be in place. It needs to be locally applied and sensitive to local realities. Excessive regulation can act to prevent action and thus increase damage. Someone must have the responsibility, the resources and the knowledge to monitor and prevent damage and enact preventive and/or remedial measures. Solutions must be sensitive to environmental considerations and the economic realities of farming and heritage tourism. In an effort to clarify responsibilities and engender appropriate actions at appropriate times, organisations such as the National Trust have created management plans, agreed with national heritage agencies, for all the significant archaeological monuments in their control (Thackray 1994).

Particularly challenging conservation problems are still provided by earthworks such as sections of First World War trenches. Examples have been preserved in a number of places, for instance by the Canadians at Vimy and Beamont-Hamel, as memorials to the dead of the Great War. The rotting of wood, downslope movement and the arrival of vegetation, leads to the collapse of trenches and dugouts, and the beautification and softening of the visual impact of the site. As the original is lost, it must either be replaced to keep the visual impact, and we accept that a site 100 years after its creation has little original material in it (fake/reconstruction), or the original is preserved and the dramatic impact of the site is lost. What is the most significant aspect of this site, the visual appearance of the battlefield or the preservation of original material (Bull and Panton 2001)?

Bibliography

Barr, S. and Chaplin, P. (2004) *Cultural Heritage in the Arctic and Antarctic Regions*, Oslo: ICOMOS & IPHC.
Berry, A.Q. (2001) 'Resourcing of management objectives: the opportunities of agri-environmental schemes', in D. McGlade (ed.), *Erosion Control on Archaeological Earthworks and Recreational Paths*, Morpeth: Northumberland County Council, pp. 63–8.
Berry, A.Q. and Brown, I.W. (eds) (1994) *Erosion on Archaeological Earthworks: Its Prevention, Control and Repair*, Mold: Clwyd County Council.
Berry, A.Q. and Brown, I.W. (eds) (1995) *Managing Ancient Monuments: An Integrated Approach*, Mold: Clwyd County Council.
Bull, N. and Panton, D. (2001) 'Conservation of historic battlefield terrain: drafting the Vimy Charter', in P.W.M. Freeman and A. Pollard (eds), *Fields of Conflict: Progress and Prospect in Battlefield Archaeology*, BAR International Series 958, Oxford: Archaeopress, pp. 269–73.
Caneva, G., Ceschin, S. and De Marco, G. (2006) 'Mapping the risk of damage from tree roots for the conservation of archaeological sites', *Conservation and Management of Archaeological Sites*, 7(3): 163–70.

Canti, M.G., Campell, G., Robinson, D. et al. (2004) *Site Formation, Preservation and Remedial Measures at Silbury Hill*, English Heritage Report, available at: http://services.english-heritage.org.uk/ResearchReports Pdfs/061-2004.pdf (accessed April 2016).

Cathersides, A. (2001) 'The restoration of the grassland setting at Stonehenge', in D. McGlade (ed.), *Erosion Control on Archaeological Earthworks and Recreational Paths*, Morpeth: Northumberland County Council, pp. 25–30.

Champion, T. (1996) 'Protecting the monuments: archaeological legislation from the 1882 Act to PPG 16', in M. Hunter (ed.), *Preserving the Past*, Stroud: Alan Sutton, pp. 38–56.

Coles, J.M. (1987) 'The preservation of archaeological sites by environmental intervention', in H. Hodges (ed.), *In-Situ Archaeological Conservation*, Mexico: Instituto Nacional de Antropologia e Historia & J. Paul Getty Trust, pp. 32–55.

Crow, P. (2004) *Trees and Forestry on Archaeological Sites in the UK: A Review Document*, Forest Research, Forestry Commission, available at: www.forestry.gov.uk/fr/INFD-5W2J4W (accessed September 2014).

Crow, P. (2005) *The Influence of Soils and Species on Tree Root Depth*, Forestry Commission, available at: www.forestry.gov.uk/fr/INFD-5W2J4W (accessed September 2014).

Crow, P. and Moffatt, A.J. (2005) 'The management of the archaeological resources in UK wooded landscapes. An environmental perspective', *Conservation and Management of Archaeological Sites*, 7(2): 103–16.

Darvill, T. (1987) *Ancient Monuments in the Countryside: An Archaeological Management Review*, London: English Heritage.

Darvill, T. and Fulton, A. (1998) *The Monuments at Risk Survey of England 1995*, London: Bournemouth University and English Heritage.

Dobinson, C. and Denison, S. (1995) *Metal Detecting and Archaeology in England*, York: CBA and English Heritage.

Dunwell, A.J. and Trout, R.C. (1999) *Burrowing Animals and Archaeology*, Historic Scotland Technical Advice Note 16, Edinburgh: Historic Scotland, available at: http://conservation.historic-scotland.gov.uk/publication-detail.htm?pubid=8546 (accessed September 2014).

Forestry Commission (1995) *Forests and Archaeology Guidelines*, London: HMSO.

Gerrard, S. (1999) *The Dartmoor Archaeology and Bracken Project: Interim Report for the 1999 Season*, Wembworthy, Devon: S. Gerrard.

Greenwood, J.R., Holt, D.A. and Herrick, G.W. (1985) 'Shallow slopes in highway embankments constructed of over consolidated clay', in The Institution of Civil Engineers (ed.), *Failures in Earthworks*, London: Thomas Telford, pp. 79–92.

Harding, P.T. (1995) 'Data for nature conservation in statutory and voluntary heritage agencies', in A.Q. Berry and I.W. Brown (eds), *Managing Ancient Monuments: An Integrated Approach*, Mold: Clwyd County Council, pp. 1–15.

Haygarth, S. (1994) 'Product listing', in A.Q. Berry and I.W. Brown (eds), *Erosion on Archaeological Earthworks: Its Prevention, Control and Repair*, Mold: Clwyd County Council, pp. 115–59.

Hinchcliffe, J. and Schadla-Hall, R.T. (eds) (1980) *The Past under the Plough*, London: DoE.

Humble, J. (2010) 'Assessing and managing risk: the Scheduled Monuments at Risk (SMAR) and Conservation of Scheduled Monuments in Cultivation (COSMIC) projects, England', in S. Trow, V. Holyoak and E. Byrnes (eds), *Heritage Management of Farmed and Forested Landscapes in Europe*, EAC Occasional Paper, Brussels: European Archaeological Council, pp. 95–103.

Hunter, M. (1996) 'Introduction: the fitful rise of British preservation', in M. Hunter (ed.), *Preserving the Past: The Rise of Heritage in Modern Britain*, Stroud: Alan Sutton, pp. 1–16.

Hutt, S., Jones, E.W. and McAllister, M.E. (1992) *Archaeological Resource Protection*, Washington, DC: The Preservation Press.

Jackson, A.M. (1978) *Forestry and Archaeology: A Study of Field Monuments in South West Scotland*, Hertford: The British Archaeological Trust.

Jones, K.L. (1998) 'The state of large earthwork sites in the United Kingdom', *Antiquity*, 72: 293–307.

Jones, K.L. (2003) 'Advances and issues in prehistoric archaeological site stabilisation', *Bulletin of the Indo-Pacific Prehistory*, 23: 191–200.

Kavazanjian, E. (2004) 'The use of geosynthetics for archaeological site reburial', *Conservation and Managements of Archaeological Sites*, 6(3–4): 377–93.

Kézdi, A. and Rétháti, L. (1988) *Handbook of Soil Mechanics Vol. 3: Soil Mechanics, Earthworks, Foundations and Highway Engineering*, Amsterdam: Elsevier.

Lambrick, G. (2004) 'The management of archaeological sites in arable landscapes', in T. Nixon (ed.), *Preserving Archaeological Remains In-Situ?*, London: Museum of London Archaeological Service, pp. 188–96.

McGlade, D. (ed.) (2001) *Erosion Control on Archaeological Earthworks and Recreational Paths*, Morpeth: Northumberland County Council.

McGowan, A. (1985) 'Excavated slopes in fissured fills', in The Institution of Civil Engineers (ed.), *Failures in Earthworks*, London: Thomas Telford, pp. 1–14.

Mcinnes, L. (1993) 'Archaeology as land use', in J. Hunter and I. Ralston (eds), *Archaeological Resource Management in the UK*, Stroud: Alan Sutton, pp. 243–55.

Morgan-Evans, D. (1992) 'The paradox of Salisbury Plain', in L. Macinnes and C.R. Wickham-Jones (eds), *All Natural Things: Archaeology and the Green Debate*, Oxford: Oxbow Books, pp. 176–9.

Oxford Archaeology (2010) *Trials to Identify Soil Cultivation Practices to Minimise the Impact on Archaeological Sites*, Defra project no: BD1705, Effects of Arable Cultivation on Archaeology (EH project no: 3874), known collectively as: 'Trials', available at: http://randd.defra.gov.uk/Default.aspx?Menu=Menu&Module=More&Location=None&Completed=0&ProjectID=12496 (accessed February 2015).

Parsons, A.W. and Perry, J. (1985) 'Slope stability problems in aging highway earthworks', in The Institution of Civil Engineers (ed.), *Failures in Earthworks*, London: Thomas Telford, pp. 63–78.

Reed, J. and Schreiner, J. (2000) 'Technologies against looting and vandalism', in R.A. Williamson and P.R. Nickens (eds), *Science and Technology in Historic Preservation*, New York: Kluwer Academic, pp. 291–308.

Rees, T. and Mills, C. (1999) *Bracken and Archaeology, Technical Advice Note 17*, Edinburgh: Historic Scotland, available at: http://conservation.historic-scotland.gov.uk/publication-detail.htm?pubid=8547 (accessed September 2014).

Rimmington, N. (2001) 'Proactive earthwork management on Hadrian's Wall world heritage site', in D. McGlade (ed.), *Erosion Control on Archaeological Earthworks and Recreational Paths*, Morpeth: Northumberland County Council, pp. 15–18.

Rimmington, J.N. (2004) *Managing Earthwork Monuments*, London: English Heritage, available at: www.helm.org.uk/guidance-library/managing-earthwork-monuments/sectionc-managementissues.pdf (accessed September 2014).

Robertson, M. and Schofield, J. (2000) 'Monuments in wartime: conservation policy in practice 1939–45', *Conservation Bulletin*, 37: 16–19.

Stein, A. (1903) *Sand Buried Ruins of Khotan*, London: Unwin.

Streeten, A. (1994) 'Managing ancient earthworks: diagnosis, cure and prevention of erosion', in A.Q. Berry and I.W. Brown (eds), *Erosion on Archaeological Earthworks: Its Prevention, Control and Repair*, Mold: Clwyd County Council, pp. 5–15.

Thackray, D. (1994) 'The management of monuments and erosion control on National Trust properties', in A.Q. Berry and I.W. Brown (eds), *Erosion on Archaeological Earthworks: Its Prevention, Control and Repair*, Mold: Clwyd County Council, pp. 103–10.

Thompson, M. (2006) *Ruins Reused: Changing Attitudes to Ruins Since the Late Eighteenth Century*, Kings Lynn: Heritage.

US Army Corps of Engineers (1992) *The Archeological Sites Protection and Preservation Notebook*, Vicksburg, MS: US Army Engineer Waterways Experiment Station.

Vyner, B. (2009) 'Fylingdales Moor: a lost landscape rises from the ashes', *Current Archaeology*, 226: 20–7.

White, R. (1994) 'Combating erosion in the Yorkshire Dales National Park', in A.Q. Berry and I.W. Brown (eds), *Erosion on Archaeological Earthworks: Its Prevention, Control and Repair*, Mold: Clwyd County Council, pp. 93–101.

Wildesen, L.E. (1982) 'The study of impacts on archaeological sites', *Advances in Archaeological Method and Theory*, 5: 51–96.

Wimble, A.A. (1994) 'Problems of wear and tear on English heritage sites', in A.Q. Berry and I.W. Brown (eds), *Erosion on Archaeological Earthworks: Its Prevention, Control and Repair*, Mold: Clwyd County Council, pp. 17–23.

Chapter 8.1

Managing ancient earthworks
Diagnosis, cure and prevention of erosion

Anthony D.F. Streeten

Source: Streeten, A. (1994) 'Managing ancient earthworks: diagnosis, cure and prevention of erosion', in A.Q. Berry and I.W. Brown (eds), *Erosion on Archaeological Earthworks: Its Prevention, Control and Repair*, Mold: Clwyd County Council, pp. 5–15.

Introduction

AMONG SOME FOURTEEN THOUSAND scheduled monuments in England, around 60% comprise earthworks in various states of survival and condition. These and other important unscheduled monuments deserve positive management to ensure their continued preservation. The extent to which this objective can be achieved, however, depends both upon the availability of resources to meet defined needs and above all upon the commitment of landowners to manage ancient monuments within an appropriate regime of land-use.

[. . .]

Drawing upon analogies with medical practice, the needs of archaeological conservation demand balance between preventative treatment and the cure of identified ailments. The correct diagnosis of observed and potential causes of deterioration is an essential requirement for the effective management of ancient earthworks.

[. . .] Recording and understanding are prerequisites for proper management, while the monitoring and review of completed work is essential for the continuing refinement of management prescriptions and repair techniques. It is axiomatic that the benefits of simple, cheap and effective preventative measures can be equally valuable and, in the long term, more cost-effective than large-scale interventions to protect or reinstate damaged monuments.

English Heritage has an enabling role in fulfilling the duty to preserve ancient monuments. [. . .] Regular visits by Field Monument Wardens, usually every two to three years, serve a dual purpose:

- to monitor the condition of scheduled monuments; and
- to encourage, through personal contact, the positive attitude and commitment of landowners.

The prevention of damage may sometimes be achieved informally through enlightened farming practice, especially where this can be encouraged under relevant prescriptions for Environmentally Sensitive Areas, whilst other monuments may benefit from the formal definition of management prescriptions and financial provision under a Management Agreement (Ancient Monuments Act 1979 [AMAAA]—Section 17) or other arrangements. For larger projects a "monuments grant" may be offered for the reinstatement of earthworks (AMAAA—Section 24). Standards of specification and workmanship can be safeguarded through the legislative requirement to obtain consent for works of repair to scheduled monuments (AMAAA—Section 2).

Increasingly, there are also opportunities for encouraging positive management of ancient monuments within the wider sphere of landscape conservation, notably in Environmentally Sensitive Areas (ESAs) and through the Countryside Stewardship Scheme. Although the former may include optional conservation plans, such initiatives are relevant mainly to the prevention or mitigation of earthwork erosion rather than to major schemes of repair or reinstatement. [...]

Aims and objectives

Principal aims for the management and repair of ancient earthworks include:

- understanding monuments and their significance;
- ensuring the physical preservation of important archaeological remains, whether visible or invisible;
- maintaining, and where appropriate enhancing, the visual clarity of monuments as legible examples of their class.

Informed archaeological judgements made in fulfilment of these aims rely upon the existence of structured management records. Related objectives therefore comprise:

- monitoring the condition of monuments;
- recording, using topographical, photographic and geophysical surveys;
- sampling and investigation when opportunities arise without recourse to excavation.

Accurate topographical surveys are needed for archaeological interpretations, for the definition of management zones and for the specification and recording of repairs. Photography is an appropriate means of monitoring objectively any changes which may occur in the condition of earthworks.

The initial stage of recording in a management plan thus underpins the definition of suitable management regimes; assists with taking the decision for intervention; and, contributes to the recognition of opportunities for enhanced appreciation of monuments and their associated landscapes.

Specific objectives for the management of individual monuments are best considered after a suitable period of monitoring. Understanding seasonal and other changing patterns and intensities of erosion will invariably contribute to an informed diagnosis. In fulfilment of the strategic objective to make effective use of limited resources, reliable assessments of the severity, position and likely permanence of earthwork erosion must be made in order that its archaeological impact may be judged correctly.

Diagnosis

Natural erosion

Natural deterioration may occur as a consequence of vegetation cover and may result from the effects of weather and ground conditions.

Issues of vegetation management on ancient monuments are of wider relevance to archaeological conservation than the specific concerns for earthwork erosion. Observations may nevertheless reveal, for example, the connection between scrub encroachment and the consequential invasion of burrowing animals. Tree roots may likewise destabilise steep-sided earthworks, rendering them vulnerable to the effects of weather or attrition by livestock. The damage caused by windthrow on the tree-covered monuments may be severe, but the consequential effects of erosion scars are likely to extend beyond the initial impact of uprooting.

Distinction can be drawn between the effects of weather and ground conditions. The former may contribute to geographical and seasonal trends, while the latter reflects more localised factors of topography, geology and soils. Attrition by wind and rain may be potent agents of erosion on certain soils, whilst conditions of drought may weaken thin protective grass cover—say on the crest of a stone or earthen rampart—resulting in vulnerability to further natural erosion or damage from the passage of people and animals. The condition of a monument can likewise be affected by off-site factors, notably changes in land-use or vegetation in adjacent areas affecting wind force, water run-off and the displacement of grazing, etc.

The stability of ancient monuments may also be affected by movements such as solifluxion or even landslip, or by the encroachment of shifting watercourses. Geotechnical assessments may indicate complex processes of the kind observed on the scheduled Roman site at New Weir, Kenchester, situated on the banks of the River Wye in Herefordshire (N.G.R. SO 431 479), where geological factors have resulted in a combination of both landslip and river encroachment.

Animals

Grazing has important benefits for maintaining healthy protective turf on field monuments, yet poaching by livestock and the disturbance caused by burrowing animals can be detrimental to the needs of archaeological preservation. Damage caused by livestock may be linked to the form of a particular monument, or it may be due respectively to soil conditions or to the species of animal and the intensity of stocking. Problems may be exacerbated by pressure points arising from the inappropriate location of gates or feeding troughs adjacent to vulnerable earthworks. Trees and scrub affording shade, shelter or even a rubbing post for livestock may intensify the attrition of fragile surfaces, whilst even stable monuments may become vulnerable when grazed in wet weather.

The principal categories of erosion by animals are trample and scarring, the physical archaeological impact of which depends upon severity and position. Elongated poaching scars are generally disfiguring to the visual amenity of ancient earthworks. Significant losses of archaeological evidence, however, may be confined to severe cases of destabilisation, or encroachment upon sensitive features, including the revetments, postholes and buried soils commonly associated in particular with defensive earthworks.

It is also important to establish the rate of erosion, since what can appear upon initial inspection to be severe and threatening may prove to be very long-standing and largely benign. In other cases, disintegration may be rapid, or the rate of deterioration may suddenly accelerate, perhaps as a consequence of changes in farming practice.

People

The deleterious effects of certain land uses upon ancient monuments are well rehearsed elsewhere (Darvill, 1987). [. . .]

The most severe problems of pedestrian erosion occur in urban areas and on intensively visited monuments in the countryside. Recreational land uses for horse-riding, golf courses, rallying or even metal-detecting feature prominently in the diagnosis of earthwork erosion. Neither are archaeologists and countryside managers immune from criticism. The blight of former archaeological investigations left exposed without backfilling invariably extends the risk of erosion beyond the original limits of excavation. Ill-conceived exploitation of amenity potential in countryside management can also increase significantly the attrition of fragile earthworks. Illustrations of these management problems may be found where the Offa's Dyke Long Distance Path (LDP) coincides with the monument itself, resulting in compaction, degradation and even displacement of the earthwork, especially on its crest and in the vicinity of gates and stiles. Inappropriate siting of picnic amenities affording panoramic views from the crest of an Iron Age rampart provides another example of damage to buried features and consequential erosion at a pressure point (see Figure 8.1.1).

Figure 8.1.1 Dinedor Camp, Hereford and Worcester N.G.R. SO 524 363. Inappropriate siting of picnic tables on the crest of an Iron Age rampart may have damaged buried remains and has encouraged pressure point erosion. This table, installed without scheduled monument consent, was subsequently removed, carefully.

Vehicle damage to earthworks may be associated with the advancing margin of adjoining fields or with land uses such as forestry. Severance may be caused by breaches for access to fields and farms. Once tracks are established, there then arises the further risk of encroachment and erosion at the margins. Scars caused by cyclists are likewise familiar on publicly accessible monuments, whilst particular concerns emerge in the case of rally driving across fragile earthworks. The direct archaeological impact of vehicle damage can be variable, but in addition to its disfiguring appearance, the breakdown of protective ground cover inevitably leaves fragile surfaces more vulnerable to other forms of natural erosion or degradation by livestock.

Cure

Land management

Capacity for the natural regeneration of ground cover in response to seasonal weather patterns reinforces the need for monitoring before justifying investment in repairs to earthwork monuments. Small erosion scars and areas of trample have an observable tendency to migrate as a consequence of land-use and then often to heal themselves. Monuments with a thin soil cover suffering from the effects of drought may require no more than a period of rain to rejuvenate the grass. Identifying and eliminating the causes of erosion may thus be a sufficient prescription for the regeneration of protective cover.

The correct choice and appropriate control of grazing is immensely important for the effective management of field monuments. Suitable stocking densities need to be determined in the light of experience and observation of individual sites and regulated according to prevailing ground conditions in wet and dry weather. High stocking levels on unenclosed areas of a monument even for short periods can be especially damaging owing to patterns of livestock congregation and movement. Temporary protection of erosion scars using electric fences or by laying brash—pegged where necessary in exposed locations—can be an effective means of encouraging regeneration.

Approaches to vegetation management are conditioned by particular circumstances on each monument. Subject to a balanced consideration of nature conservation interests, the removal or pruning of trees to minimise the risk of windthrow and the control of scrub to alleviate pressure points of shelter and shade for livestock are positive initiatives often undertaken willingly by enlightened landowners. More ambitious schemes might also include replacement tree planting away from the monuments for reasons of appearance and management of stock. Conversely, the retention or even encouragement of scrub growth may be beneficial for deterring livestock from vulnerable areas. On an earthwork enclosure, for example, the management plan might prescribe clearance of the interior for reasons of effective management and visual clarity, yet retaining undergrowth on parts of the rampart to discourage livestock trample and scarring.

Mitigating the archaeologically damaging effects of burrowing animals is likely to involve persistent control, the effectiveness of which may be limited where infestation occurs from adjoining land, perhaps in different ownership. Artificial methods of control may also need to be accompanied by the clearance of undergrowth not only to reduce the protection of vermin from birds of prey, but also to encourage the regeneration of grass on badly voided earthworks. As with vegetation management, however, sensitivity to the interests of nature conservation is required. The suitable treatment of vegetation is conditioned by informed diagnosis of the circumstances leading to erosion.

Simple techniques for temporary protection against livestock erosion apply equally to discouraging the damaging effects of pedestrians, horse-riders and cyclists. On rural sites, a barrier of brash, the discrete redirection of a thoroughfare or the strategic retention and enhancement of undergrowth are all cheaper and less visually intrusive than either temporary or permanent fencing. Sites managed specifically for the appreciation of visitors may require more sophisticated treatment, and on publicly accessible, yet unmanned, monuments even the most ingenious methods of regulation may be insufficient to curtail persistent desire lines, unauthorised activities or vandalism. It is a matter of judgement when the failure of routine management necessitates the provision of protective installations such as paths or steps.

Repairs and reinstatement

Interventions can vary in scale from simple and largely preventative repair of small erosion scars through to extensive reinstatements intended to stabilise an earthwork and protect against significant losses of archaeological evidence. The need for reinstatement arises when active erosion is deep enough to degrade the contours of a monument, with priority for action accorded to instances where identifiable archaeological features are at risk.

Among the principles of repair applied to the conservation of historic buildings, criteria which are also of particular relevance to the repair and reinstatement of field monuments include "avoiding unnecessary damage", "adopting proven techniques", "truth to materials" and "the restoration of lost features". The avoidance of damage, for example, presupposes that sources of material for reinstatement will safeguard against damaging interference with primary archaeological deposits which are themselves intended for preservation.

Material might thus be salvaged in exceptional circumstances from identifiable scree associated with recent erosion of the monument itself; alternatively and more commonly, materials will be obtained from appropriate sources away from the areas of archaeological interest. There is a presumption, too, that so far as is practicable, repair techniques should avoid penetration of undamaged and hitherto undisturbed material within the earthwork.

When adopting proven techniques for the repair of historic buildings, it has been explained that:

> Repair techniques should match or be compatible with existing materials and methods of construction, in order to preserve the appearance and historic integrity of the building or monument, and to ensure that the work has an appropriate life. Exceptions should only be considered where the existing fabric has failed because of inherent defects ... New methods and techniques should only be used where they have proved themselves over a sufficient period and where traditional alternatives cannot be identified.
>
> (Brereton, 1991)

For the majority of repairs and reinstatements on ancient earthworks, appropriate methods will include the application of traditional techniques; the choice of local soils and compatible seed mixes; and the specification of biodegradable materials for reinforcement. Environmental considerations, notably on Sites of Special Scientific Interest and in Environmentally Sensitive Areas, are indeed likely to require very careful specification and selection of soils and seed mixes for use in the repair of erosion. In archaeological terms, too, intervention can be minimised by the application of laid turves, or the choice of biodegradable reinforcement in the form of concealed timber retaining boards, soil-filled sacks and jute netting for stabilising exposed surfaces (see Figures 8.1.2 and 8.1.3). For the landowner carrying out such work themselves there is an added advantage that these materials are likely to be available around the farm without recourse to specialist suppliers.

Figure 8.1.2 Herefordshire Beacon N.G.R. SO 760 400. Repairing erosion scars on the medieval motte within this Iron Age hillfort in 1991, using local soil brought by tractor from outside the monument. A thin layer of sand defines the base of the scar, which was then packed with soil behind pegged retaining boards and reseeded in a manner compatible with indigenous grasses of the Malvern Hills.

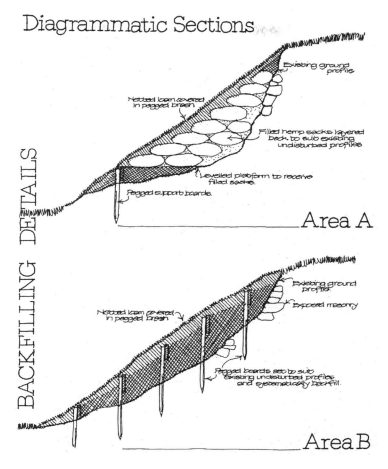

Figure 8.1.3 Bryn Amwlg Castle, Shropshire N.G.R. SO 167 846. Specification for modest earthwork repairs intended to safeguard archaeological stratigraphy and masonry remains exposed by erosion. This drawing and an accompanying written specification were used for obtaining quotations and for a scheduled monument consent application.

Source: Permission granted by David Duckham of Purcell Architects, successors to S.T. Walker and Partners, Birmingham

The issue of "truth to materials" raises matters of archaeological principle relevant to the wider philosophy of conserving field monuments. Should synthetic materials and composites be introduced to the archaeological record, and to what extent should there be a conscious effort to distinguish repairs from the undisturbed composition of a monument? So far as choice of materials is concerned, there can be no prescriptive generalisation, but by analogy with building conservation there clearly need be no objection in principle to the introduction of new materials where these are regarded as an essential and unavoidable means of preservation.

For the physical definition of repairs, it can be argued on the one hand that stratigraphy will be apparent to future excavators and that in any event adequate records made at the time of repair should indicate precisely the location and nature of the work.

Conversely, there are sound arguments for including in the reinstatement of eroded earthworks a "signature lens" of distinctive material (e.g. sand) at the bottom of the infill. Intended incidentally for the avoidance of doubt in the minds of future excavators, the primary purpose of this approach is to ensure legibility in the event of future exposure by erosion, indicating unambiguously to those monitoring the condition of the monument that previously undisturbed horizons are, once again, becoming vulnerable to deterioration. The efficacy of this approach has yet to be tested by systematic review of past applications, and the extent to which material such as a thin layer of sand might be predicted to survive as a visible element of stratigraphy certainly remains a matter for useful experimental assessment.

Similar considerations apply to the appearance of completed earthwork reinstatements. Should minimum standards of intervention be applied only so far as is necessary to protect and stabilise vulnerable areas, or should there also be an attempt to restore the appearance of a monument? In some cases, the two approaches are synonymous, but elsewhere, decisions of principle must be taken on many monuments displaying a history of visible healed erosion scars. In such cases, the argument for restoration to a "smoothed" profile is not persuasive. Cost and priorities, too, are unlikely to favour more than the minimum needed for protection and stability. Safeguards for visual amenity can best be assured by truth to materials rather than by an over-zealous commitment to the faithful replication of what are inevitably the arbitrary surviving profiles. Attention is best directed to the suitable specification of turf or grass seed and to the avoidance of unsightly wire netting which is seldom effective in protecting reinstated surfaces.

Installations

Constructions to mitigate the erosion of ancient earthworks include both new installations and the removal and replacement of existing ones. They range from fencing to the provision of paths and steps for visitors, or the construction of defences against encroaching watercourses. For the majority of private landowners, financial assistance is needed to encourage and facilitate this type of work. Unlike the repair or reinstatement of erosion scars, such installations remain as visible additions to the monument or its environs and thus require sensitive visual treatment.

The alleviation of eroded pressure points may be achieved by moving gates, stiles and feeding troughs, or by the realignment of fences. Notwithstanding the frequent coincidence of field and property boundaries with linear earthworks, worthwhile negotiations may achieve the removal of fences from the crest of a rampart to one side or the other. This can best be achieved when renewal is necessary and, in the case of scheduled monuments, with the opportunity for review in the context of statutory consent. The risk of physical damage arising from the unsupervised replacement of fence posts might thus be avoided and, on grazing land, positive benefits can be derived from mitigating the effects of livestock trample and scarring against a boundary fence.

Entirely new fences may be needed either to prevent the access of livestock on fragile monuments or to establish grazing compartments capable of management under a regime of conservation different from the surrounding pasture. Access gates are required both for grazing and for the control of scrub on monuments which are taken out of grazing. Optimum alignments for new fences away from archaeologically sensitive areas require the negotiation of an appropriate balance between satisfactory appearance and the understandable reluctance of farmers to yield significant areas of improved pasture to the less intensive regimes prescribed for grazing the earthworks. In landscapes characterised by drystone walling, the erection of fences may be unacceptable and certainly the decision to erect and maintain new fences can only be justified where alternative approaches have been discounted. On arable land, bollards may be erected to resist plough encroachment upon islands containing surviving field monuments. To be sufficiently robust, these installations can be unsightly and always remain vulnerable to accidental, or even deliberate, damage.

Installations to prevent erosion on intensively visited monuments and for the alleviation of natural erosion constitute a specialist aspect of monument management beyond the scope of detailed discussion in this brief summary. The same principles of repair, however, apply here as for earthwork reinstatement. Archaeological damage can be avoided by ensuring that construction is reversible and that steps, for example, are built off existing surfaces without cutting deeply into undisturbed levels of the monument.

A decision often has to be made whether to dissipate or to concentrate pedestrian and vehicular wear on a monument. In this context, synthetic geotextiles may be used appropriately for ground reinforcement as inconspicuous alternatives to natural, but visually intrusive, surface materials. On other occasions, however, monitoring of desire lines can reveal the unavoidable need for permanent installations in preference to more widespread erosion. In the case of revetment against the encroachment of fast-flowing watercourses, the use of gabions capable of acquiring a mantle of vegetation is invariably preferable to the construction of concrete or even stone retaining walls so as not to compromise the setting of visible earthworks or ruined structures.

Prevention

Monitoring and the informed preparation and implementation of management plans hold the key to the prevention as well as cure of earthwork erosion. Simple management prescriptions for ancient monuments are, moreover, generally compatible with the wider objectives of environmental conservation.

Among the standard clauses used in English Heritage management agreements, the following examples illustrate the type of preventative treatments which can be applied:

- maintain a healthy grass cover on the monument; or
- maintain the monument under permanent pasture. Any pasture renewal to be carried out by non-destructive means which do not disturb the ground surface of the monument;
- control weeds and burrowing animals;
- control stock levels to prevent the breakdown of grass cover if the site of the monument is periodically grazed. Reseed any eroded patches;
- control scrub and sapling growth by cutting down to ground level leaving the roots *in situ* to avoid disturbing archaeological layers;
- remove dead trees only when ground conditions are dry, leave roots *in situ*;
- ensure that any stockproof fencing is maintained in good condition;
- maintain the bollards surrounding the site in good condition;

- ensure that any ploughing operations in areas adjacent to the monument are kept at least 'n' metres from the perimeter of the monument.

Certain wider issues of land-use planning are nevertheless also relevant for safeguarding the erosion of fragile earthworks. In rural areas, the preferred designation of a Public Right of Way would always avoid traversing precipitous earthworks, whilst regard for operational consequences is a material consideration in the choice of location for new farm buildings. In urban areas and on their fringes, the effects of development can have implications both for the setting and for the management of earthwork monuments. The apparent benefits of designation as public open space may sometimes be outweighed by a preference for fragile monuments to remain within the curtilage of private landowners. For monuments in public ownership, there is a legitimate expectation of commitment to positive management in fulfilment of suitable development plan policies (English Heritage 1992).

Organisation

Experience with encouraging the kind of positive management needed to safeguard the erosion of ancient earthworks has highlighted the essential components of successful schemes. The checklist includes:

- participation of a willing landowner, occupier or third party;
- adequate financial provision;
- concise, unambiguous specification;
- arrangements for archaeological recording;
- involvement of a motivated workforce;
- safeguarding maintenance through continuity of management;
- monitoring standards of work and the effectiveness of specified treatments.

[. . .]

References

AMAAA *Ancient Monuments and Archaeological Areas Act, 1979*. www.legislation.gov.uk/ukpga/1979/46 (accessed January 2015).

Brereton, C. (1991) *The Repair of Historic Buildings: Advice on Principles and Methods*. London: English Heritage.

Darvill, T.C. (1987) *Ancient Monuments in the Countryside: an Archaeological Management Review*. London: Historic Buildings and Monuments Commission for England.

English Heritage (1992) *Development Plan Policies for Archaeology*. London: English Heritage.

PPG 16 *Planning Policy Guidance Note 16: Archaeology and Planning*. Department of the Environment, 1990. http://webarchive.nationalarchives.gov.uk/20120919132719/http://www.communities.gov.uk/documents/planningandbuilding/pdf/156777.pdf (accessed January 2015).

Chapter 9

Decay and mitigation of fragile and buried sites

Sites

'**F**RAGILE SITE' IS USED HERE to refer to those sites that have no, or virtually no, stratigraphy. They comprise scatters of occupation debris or symbolic representations on the ground surface (geoglyphs), archaeological information that can be damaged or lost by a single ploughing event.

'Buried site' is used here to define those sites that have no visible surface trace, no monument, either earthwork or masonry, but stratified archaeological remains buried within the ground.

These types of site come in many different forms.

Fragile sites

- Many fragile sites are located in deserts or semi-arid climates – since these are the areas that have long undisturbed surfaces. In such arid regions, especially Australia, and the semi-desert and plains of the United States, aeolian or fluvial erosive activities have removed soil and sand particles, leaving the larger stones and human occupation debris to settle and form a stony (desert) pavement layer containing archaeological artefacts, a surface scatter of archaeological material devoid of stratigraphy (Hayden 1965). Many Australian Aboriginal hearth or camp sites are of this 'deflated' form (Shiner 2008). In locations that have been reoccupied several times in different periods by different tribes, or people undertaking different activities, a single complex assemblage of artefacts with multiple origins that is difficult to interpret is created (Schiffer 1987).
- In temperate Europe, Asia and some Mediterranean areas, substantial occupation sites with layered stratigraphic sequences have, as a result of stone robbing or ploughing, been reduced to a scatter of cultural material on the surface. In some cases, all the stratigraphic context has been lost, leaving just concentrations of lithic flakes from stone tool manufacture or ceramic sherds from occupation activities. Field walking projects

such as the Boeotian Project (Bintliff 2007) have shown that such distributions can provide information on the location, character and dates of the occupation. In other cases, substantial stratified archaeological remains are still buried beneath the surface scatter.

- Sites that are the result of short-lived events, fairs, markets, and battles. They posses little or no stratigraphy just a scatter of objects in the topsoil, though the nature of the artefacts and their spatial relationship provides crucial information about the nature and organisation of short-lived activities. Fieldwalking and survey by Newman at Marston Moor in the 1970s (Newman 1981) and later metal detector and detailed surveys coordinated by Fox and Scott at the Little Bighorn (Scott *et al*. 1989; Fox 1993), and Foard at Edgehill (Foard 2012), showed that it was possible to recover and map artefacts (principally lead shot, bullets, cartridge cases and buttons) from battlefields in which firearms were used. This can enable battlefield events and combatants to be identified and located.

Single dropped or deposited finds such as those recovered during metal detecting and reported in England and Wales through the PAS scheme only provide information about the artefact type; their preservation '*in situ*' serves no purpose. Only where stratigraphy survives or there are groups or caches of coins or other objects, deposited for ritual purposes (e.g. in a pool), or hoarded and intended for later retrieval is there an archaeological context and meaning.

- True ephemeral sites, created for a single day or event, remaining undisturbed (buried) since that event. Human footprint sites often fall into this broad category, such as the early hominid footprints at Laetoli (see Chapter 14.1). The Palaeolithic footprints in the beach mud at Happisburgh (Ashton 2012) and the footprints from the Mesolithic discovered in the muds of the Severn estuary (Aldhouse-Green *et al*. 1993) were both swept away by the tide after only a few weeks' exposure – fragile indeed.
- Snow patch sites of Scandinavia, northern Canada, Alaska, Siberia and the Alpine regions occur where permanent patches of snow have attracted animals seeking water or to escape insects, and with them human hunters, whose debris has been preserved, frozen in the enduring snow. Each winter the patches grow, and each summer retreat, so by late summer the debris of millennia of hunting activities, arrow heads, arrows, parts of bows, etc., are scattered on the mountainside around the remaining snow patch.
- Exposed surface sites such as geoglyphs used for ritual activity, such as White Horse at Uffington or the Nazca lines, intended to be visible but fragile and capable of being destroyed by a single ploughing or vandalism event.

Buried sites

- Occupation, ritual, transport, industrial and defensive sites created from prehistory to the present formed primarily from wood that has rotted or earthworks that have been ploughed flat or buried. These sites can have substantial stratified archaeological remains, some of which are only present as the varying colours and textures of soil whose shape and location derive from the constructions created in the ancient past (features). Buried, they are frequently only identified and delineated by geophysics, the extent of crop marks or excavation (Renfrew and Bahn 1991: Chapter 3). Without a surface monument, they are often unexpectedly encountered during development such as road construction, quarrying, etc.

- Substantial sites, often with stone walling and earthworks, buried in deeply stratified sites – typically in urban environments. No surface trace remains to argue for preservation.
- Burials and graves that are without an earthwork or headstone. Such sites normally only emerge from excavation or geophysical survey. The fragile site equivalent would be excarnation sites, where bones are all that remains of bodies left on the surface to degrade naturally; however, these are rare.

All these sites leave little or no trace on the surface of the ground. Much of their value is in the artefacts of the past and their associated relationships. They are the most numerous type of site but are the most difficult to preserve *in situ* – as they have no monument to act as a focus for interest or education of later generations (low amenity value). They may have a significant symbolic value, such as battlefields, which are visited by later generations, though without the focus of physical remains, these traditional places of veneration may not be in the original location. In many cases, interest in the site comes largely from archaeologists and historians (high academic/historic value). With no monument to repair, protection of the surviving archaeological evidence is the primary focus of the preservation effort. Unlike masonry or adobe structures, no restoration activities need be considered. The lack of stratigraphy on fragile sites places emphasis on the artefacts and their spatial relationship as the only meaningful information available.

Damage and destruction

Impacts, measurable change on archaeological remains can be human-made or natural (see Chapters 2 and 8), Schiffer's 'c' or 'n' transforms (1976) (Schiffer and Gumerman 1977: 297). In addition to the damage or loss of archaeological features, they can take the form of damaging the artefacts, removal of the artefacts or disturbance of the relationship of the artefacts so as to reduce or eliminate their archaeological information. With no surface presence, visitation to fragile and buried sites is rare, thus damage of these sites is focused on natural erosive agencies such as wind and water, deliberate looting of sites or alternative land use.

Artefact decay, seen in chemical, physical and biological terms in Table 3.0.1, has been expressed by Chris Mathewson in a simpler form that relates the survival of commonly seen categories of archaeological materials and information (site components) to site conditions (see Figure 9.0.1) (Mathewson and Gonzalez 1988). This matrix indentifies surface weathering, where there are cyclic wet/dry and freeze/thaw events, as some of the most damaging to archaeological artefacts. This emphasises the preservative effects of burial/reburial. This matrix can aid mitigation activities within the reburial process, for example indicating that where shell is present, the reburial soil needs to be neutral or basic if the shell is not to be lost through acid dissolution. Physical damage to artefacts is principally caused by machine-based impacts (Hayden 1965; Wildesen 1982; Haase 1983), especially ploughing (Haldenby and Richards 2010), a process that also aerates the soil, greatly increasing the rates of corrosion of iron and other metal artefacts (Galliano *et al.* 1998; Gerwin *et al.* 1998). Even under soil, when compressed by machinery or vehicles, artefacts are broken, though the thickness of the ceramic, depth of burial and the nature of the soil are more important in determining the strain experienced by the object, and thus the likelihood of breaking rather than the stress (load) applied to the soil surface (Mathewson *et al.* 1992; US Army Corps of Engineers 1992: II.5). Plates to spread load, depths greater than 4 ft/1.2 m, and non-deformable stony and sandy soils increase protection.

332 DECAY AND CONSERVATION MEASURES

SITE CONDITIONS	Animal Bones	Shell	Plants, Ecofacts	Charcoal	Crystalline Lithics	Granular Lithics	Ceramics	Features	Soil Attributes	Metals	Context	Rock Art	Isotopic Content
Cyclic Wet-Dry	A	A	A	A	A	A	A	A	A	A	N	A	A
Continuously Dry	E	E	E	E	N	E	N	N	N	E	N	E	E
Continuously Wet, Anaerobic	E	E	E	A	A	A	A	A	A	A	N	A	A
Continuously Wet, Aerobic	A	A	A	A	N	A	A	A	A	A	N	A	A
Cyclic Freeze-Thaw	A	A	A	A	A	A	A	A	A	N	A	A	A
Freeze	A	A	A	A	N	A	N	A	N	E	N	A	E
Thaw	N	N	N	N	N	A	N	N	A	N	A	N	A
Compression	A	A	A	A	N	N	A	A	A	N	A	N	N
Movement	N	N	N	A	N	N	N	A	A	N	A	N	N
Erosion	A	A	A	A	A	A	A	A	A	A	A	A	A
Deposition/Sedimentation	E	E	E	E	E	E	E	E	E	E	E	E	E
Microorganisms	A	N	A	A	N	N	N	N	N	A	A	A	A
Macroorganisms	A	A	A	A	N	A	N	A	A	N	A	N	N
Vegetation	N	N	N	N	N	N	N	A	A	N	A	A	N
Human Intrusion	A	A	A	A	A	A	A	A	A	A	A	A	A
Acidic Environment	A	A	E	N	N	A	N	N	A	A	N	A	N
Basic Environment	E	E	A	N	N	E	N	N	A	A	N	A	N
Oxidizing Environment	A	A	A	A	N	N	N	A	A	A	N	N	A

Notes
E = Condition Enhances Preservation/Reduces Decay
A = Condition Accelerates Decay
N = Condition is Neutral or Has No Effect
☐ = Site Components and Conditions

Figure 9.0.1 Mathewson's matrix of differing site information sources against the decay mechanisms that can afflict them.

Source: Mathewson and Gonzalez (1988)

All the activities described in Chapter 2 will have a significant impact on fragile scatters or buried deposits, and are thus damaging all the key artefact relationships. Wildesen (1982) (see Chapter 9.1) provides detailed evidence showing that activities such as forestry and logging, brush cutting, vehicle traffic, even downslope movement, lead to the loss of artefacts or the destruction of their relationship with each other and the site. Loss of vegetation leads to aeolian and fluvial soil erosion of sites, especially in arid and semi-arid regions, leading to loss of archaeological deposits and the accumulation of materials from multiple occupation phases. Fire can strip vegetation leading to considerable soil erosion and exposing stones containing petroglyphs to the public, who investigate, damage or loot the exposed decorated stones (Vyner 2009; ERA n.d.). Vegetation is as much a protector for its capacity to obscure or insulate and reduce the impact of weather. While the roots of vegetation, especially trees and bracken, can be damaging to shallow stratigraphy (see Chapter 8), vegetation management regimes that preserve grassland and moors in upland Britain are seen as preservative for even fragile archaeological remains (Mcinnes 1993: 144); the intensively cultivated lowlands are frequently damaging as ploughing removes the stratigraphy and alters the relationship between the finds (Darvill 1987: 87, 128). Other mechanisms, such as burrowing animals, damage buried sites as stratigraphic relationships are ruined by vertical and horizontal displacement of artefacts (see Chapter 8) (Bocek 1986; Dunwell and Trout 1999).

The use of metal detecting has led to detection of objects and discovery of sites where there are no surface indications of remains. Such detection can be positive – reporting finds, leading to the identification and excavation or protection of sites, it may be a tool to lead to the survey of battlefield material (Dobinson and Denison 1995; Foard 2012) – or it can lead to the looting and destruction of archaeological remains (see Chapters 2 and 8). A more recent risk with surface exposed and shallow stratified sites is the risk of modern contamination. While this may be dumping of modern rubbish on some unvalued sites, the high spiritual values associated with sites in Chaco Canyon have drawn many visitors to these sites, where they have deliberately inserted modern objects into the ground as offerings or charms, intended for retrieval once they have gained spiritual energy from the site (Finn 1997). This compromises the archaeological integrity of such sites. Similar concerns are now being voiced about period re-enactment on traditional battle sites, which are becoming contaminated with accurate modern replica weaponry fragments (Battlefields Trust n.d.).

Throughout their history, humans have camped and settled beside water – coast, lake, river or stream (Darvill 1987: 59). The water has subsequently become a potentially active agent of decay, eroding the often fragile surviving archaeological remains. In the US, heritage authorities have been active in protecting Native American sites from water body erosion (US Army Corps of Engineers 1992; Nickens 2000). Small flows of water lead to gully formation, loss of soil and erosion of the monument. Any and all fast-moving water flows or wave actions can wear away soil, either through their shear erosive power or through saturation of the ground, causing the soil particles to lose coherence, leading to soil flow and loss (Darvill and Fulton 1998: 137). There is gradual loss of sites to coastal erosion (Darvill 1987: 51–63) at sites such as Brean Down (Bell 1990). More destructive events, especially storms, cyclones, hurricanes and tsunamis, can completely eliminate coastal sites (Bird 1992). Predicted climate changes would suggest that larger numbers of more extreme weather events can be expected, resulting in more flash flooding events in arid regions and greater storm damage in coastal regions in future years.

Values and protection

A simplified values-based approach, outlined in Chapter 5, is essentially that proposed by most modern authors (e.g. Nickens 2000: 326) for planning preservation of fragile or buried sites. While recognition of intangible values are helpful for preserving 'traditional' sites such as reputed battlefields, the lack of visible surface remains presents a challenge to implementing protection. Steps normally include:

- identification and evaluation of the site and its significance;
- identification and understanding of the (erosive) agent(s) affecting the site;
- selection of the most appropriate preservation strategy and technologies;
- implementation of the selected protection approach;
- establishing monitoring and maintenance procedures; and
- publication of the results.

(Nickens 2000: 326)

Where there is a decision to take action (and after assessment the decision may be not to take action), three strategies are evident in seeking to preserve ephemeral/fragile archaeological remains:

- Control or prevent visitation/control land use.
- Physically protect (blanket) (reburial).
- 'Preservation by record' – this is a euphemism for the loss of the archaeological remains of which some form of record has been made. This record is a proxy, a useful substitute, but this is not meaningfully preservation as only a few fragmentary finds are ever retained.

Legal protection

In many cases, ephemeral sites such as graves, battlefields and meeting places have been preserved through the absence of human activity, either as the result of the site being 'lost' to consciousness or having a social significance, which meant they were considered 'special', and social tradition required that they were not used for normal agricultural or building activities (see Chapter 8).

The modern articulation of social value is the creation of legal protection for a site (see Chapter 4). However, legal instruments must be specific, and a boundary must exist or be created to define the protected space. Existing boundaries are often adopted, though these are sometimes seen to be later creations and do not accurately represent the original edge of the site. For buried sites with no monument, accurate delineation through geophysics or small-scale excavation is often necessary if legal measures are to be effectively applied to preserve the complete site.

If a site is fragile and can be lost through a single ploughing event, protection must be at a level that controls land use. For scattered and fragile sites, the type of protection that most effectively prevents uncontrolled land use is often that associated with nature conservation, such as the UK's SSSI status. Only the fragility of plants and ecosystems corresponds with that of the spatial and stratigraphic relationship of ancient artefacts. Similarly, reducing the movement of water and oxygen through the soil (e.g. by stopping ploughing and fertiliser application) can be a significant first step in minimising the level of corrosion rates of iron and copper alloy artefacts at deeper sites (see Chapter 3).

The extensive nature of battlefield or surface ritual sites or the frequency of sites in certain areas has often resulted in their protection in 'conservation areas', national parks or archaeological parks (e.g. Coa Valley, Portugal) (Fernandes 2007). Again, only where there are legal controls that allow heritage authorities control of land usage will there be effective preservation of fragile and superficial sites. Where they are established, 'parks' can also help preserve the natural landscape features that may be important features in people's 'heritage' and explain the siting of settlements and ritual sites (see Introduction). In semi-arid, tundra and upland regions, large areas of 'wilderness' can sometimes be established as parks, to preserve landscape and their associated fragile monuments; however, such measures are limited by high land costs in the intensively farmed and almost entirely man-made landscape of much of lowland Europe. This is seen in the efforts to preserve waterlogged archaeological remains throughout north-western Europe (see Chapter 11). The high cost of land purchase and associated subsequent management has encouraged heritage authorities in Britain and Europe to promote the use of a range of modern schemes for taking land out of farming production (see Chapter 8), though most schemes are focused on identifiable monuments. In locations such as mountains, tundra or semi-arid environments, it may be necessary to protect fragile sites from excessive visitation as described for earthworks (see Chapter 8) and rock art sites (see Chapter 10).

Physical protection

Though legal protection is principally used to minimise threats to fragile and buried sites from human beings, natural threats, especially from aeolian and fluvial erosion, require physical protection measures for the site. Previous authors, especially those working in the USA, have compiled examples of effective practice in providing physical protection for sites from a range of erosive threats (US Army Corps of Engineers 1992; Jones 1994). Though a conceptual approach with a holistic appreciation of the issues is widely advocated, in almost all cases the cost of the protective measures is a crucial factor in determining what work is done (Nickens 2000: 317–20; Jones 2003). Recent efforts have focussed on accurate assessment of the erosive force (sea, wind) and implementation of the appropriate deflection and deposition systems, creating salt marshes rather than sea walls (English Heritage 2003) (see Chapter 14). Resisting them is a costly battle you will ultimately lose.

Hydraulic erosion

Preservation measures focus on removing water in the form of drainage to avoid saturation, creating soft ground leading to earthwork failures or erosion zones. Small water forces can be deflected using stone or wood to reinforce banking, as in the case of preventing Kingsdale Beck eroding the 'Apron Full of Stones' cairn (White 1994: 94–5); such activities move the point of force/impact to another part of the bank that does not contain culturally sensitive material. Where there are shorelines, the erosive forces of water are strong, and thus while geotextile and sediment may soft shield the site, concrete blocks or stone boulders (riprap) are sometimes required to prevent physical damage and prevent the loss of the soft coating (Nickens 2000). At Llangorse Cranog (Wales) and Voyageurs National Park (Minnesota, USA), geotextile was used to trap sediment protected by stone or concrete rubble (riprap) to create a stable shoreline (Lynott 1989; Davies, pers. comm.), while at Roods Creek Mounds, Georgia, sheet piling was needed to protect the site (US Army Corps of Engineers 1992: III.3). Though there are a number of examples of barriers to protect sites from coastal erosion, such as the sea wall of gabions (stone-filled steel mesh cubes) at New Brunswick, Canada (US Army Corps of Engineers 1992: III.1), or that protecting the prehistoric Orcadian village of Skara Brae, it is recognised that hard barriers such as sea walls are expensive to maintain, and often unsustainable in the long term. Consequently, in the UK, there has been a move away from 'hard' protection measures from the sea to alternatives:

- Absorbing impact through establishing salt marshes or similar coastal fringe environment in what are described as 'Managed Realignment Schemes' (English Heritage 2003).
- Recording and monitoring the archaeology in threatened areas, including excavation of sites ahead of erosion, as in the case of Seahenge, a prehistoric timber circle uncovered by the tide on a swiftly eroding beach at Holme-next-the-Sea, Lincolnshire, Norfolk (Miles

2000; Watson 2005). Both Cadw and Historic Scotland currently (2013) have active programmes often using local volunteers to map areas of sea erosion of cliffs and record exposed archaeological features. Where appropriate, they are excavated ahead of loss, as at Angle Bay, Pembrokeshire, where early medieval Christian burials have been eroding out of the cliff (Groom et al. 2011).

In the USA, Germany, Switzerland, Austria and the UK, freshwater shoreline planting, especially of willow, is seen as particularly effective in preventing lacustrine and riverine shoreline erosion dissipating the energy of the moving water and encouraging sediment build-up (see Chapter 11). With costs of between 6 per cent and 25 per cent of the hard engineering solutions (US Army Corps of Engineers 1992: V.2), it is currently considered the most cost-effective method of shoreline protection.

Aeolian erosion

Wind can strip desiccated soils in arid and semi-arid regions, exposing both fragile and buried sites. Soil or sand deposited to bury and protect archaeological remains can be stripped off within months and erosion resumed. Systems such as vegetation or fences can deflect the erosive winds and lead to deposition of material (soil or sand) on the site, so protecting it. They are the preferred response, but wind and weather patterns must be understood and systems monitored and maintained if they are to be effective. Examples of this approach are seen at Aboriginal burial and midden sites such as Snaggy Bend (Clark and Hope 1985) and Nundera Point (Sneison et al. 1986). In both cases, the importance (value) of archaeological information (stratified deposits, midden material, archaeological features and human bones) is initially established, including plans of the extent of the human burials and multiple midden layers and accurate dating of the site. An evidence-based appreciation of the threats to these remains was then established; subsequently, appropriate strategies to prevent further erosion taking place were formulated and the resources found to implement these actions. At Nundera, there was a continuing destructive threat of aeolian erosion, but installing sand dune forming fencing at the appropriate heights and distances meant that it reduced surface wind speed leading to sand drop and thus dune formation rather than erosion, ensuring the exposed site was reburied.

Either accurate modelling of the erosion forces (see Figure 9.0.2) or local knowledge, experience and observation can lead to the erection of barriers of the correct type and size to achieve the desired sand build-up and site protection. It is also essential to establish vegetation tolerant of the conditions and native to the area to secure the sand/soil surfaces. Throughout much of Europe and North America, a vegetative and thus self-repairing system is often the most resistant surface to protect archaeological remains. As with earthwork erosion, regular maintenance and adjustment of protection measures is the key to successful preservation (Sneison et al. 1986).

Other

Physical damage from vegetation and burrowing wild and farmed animals is also a significant threat to fragile and buried sites (see Chapter 8). Mitigation measures are usually more difficult to apply effectively to the large areas of some fragile sites.

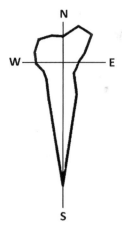

Figure 9.0.2 Wind Rose: monitoring the direction of wind for a year enables a diagram that shows the percentage of time (distance from the centre) the wind comes from a particular direction. In this case, from the caves of Mogao, China, fencing is located out beyond the site to catch the wind, which comes predominantly from the south, so it drops its sand and does not blow it into the valley and the caves in the cliff face.

Source: Wanfu et al. (2010)

Chemical control

The concept of a benign (chemical) burial environment (Caple 2004) is rarely mentioned as the focus is on the physical form of monuments, rather than the artefacts they contain. Drawing from the chemistry of the burial environment (see Chapter 3), ideas for establishing a benign environment include:

- Since artefacts will be near equilibrium of their long-standing burial environment, minimal loss will occur if that environment is maintained, so the less change, the more benign.
- Not increasing oxygenation of the soil (e.g. avoiding ploughing – leave land as pasture – or improving drainage). This will lead to lower oxygen levels, so maintaining low levels of decay for organics and metals (Galliano et al. 1998; Gerwin et al. 1998).
- Avoiding adding salts or minerals such as some fertilisers or road salt to soils as this will reduce the likelihood of increased corrosion levels or mineral precipitation, with resultant surface damage in oxic soils.

Excavation, collection and record

If there are insufficient resources to preserve archaeological remains (low value to society), or the technology is not sufficiently well developed/reliable to preserve them, they are excavated and recorded. The record is always an imperfect facsimile of reality and thus should be as complete as possible (as resources allow).

In the case of surface finds, given the fragility of the remains, if there is any threat and it is not possible to leave the remains totally undisturbed, there is a case for excavation/ collection. While this is not preservation *in situ*, it is a pragmatic response to the realities of the fragile nature of the environment. Global warming has led to greater retreats in recent years in the snow patch sites of Scandinavia, northern Canada, Alaska, Siberia and the Alpine regions; wooden artefact fragments, preserved in the snow and ice for millennia, are being revealed (Callanan 2013). Such fragile artefacts have barely a few years of exposure before freeze/thaw cycles, and fungal activity will degrade and eventually destroy them. Preservation *in situ* is not realistically possible, thus accurate survey, detailed record, collection, artefact conservation and museum storage represent the only viable option. The collection of archaeological material from soil surface sites has proved difficult to interpret correctly, biased as it is by the decay of materials and selective collection process (Haase 1983; Bintliff 2000; Shiner 2008). The most accurate understanding is achieved by collecting all material, including coarse pottery, building materials, charcoal, corroded ironwork and industrial materials, as well as more discernible artefacts and fine pottery, so that the collection is held together and analysed completely (Windmiller and Huckell 1973). The materials from field walking or metal detector surveys are less frequently analysed and published than archaeological excavations.

In the case of buried sites, since these archaeological remains lack any surface monument, they are frequently encountered during modern construction work. Planning procedures (see Chapter 4) in most European countries now require pre-construction assessment of the presence of buried archaeological remains, ensuring they can be assessed and either excavated and recorded or preserved *in situ*. However, when they emerge during construction work, given the economic imperative of the construction work, they are normally quickly excavated, recorded and removed.

Urban and development sites

> Conflicts of interest will arise between the need to preserve nationally important archaeological remains and the need to allow our towns to thrive and develop. Historic urban areas cannot be fossilized, but equally, economic growth must not rob the future of its past.
>
> (Wainwright 1993: 418)

Most of the preceding comments have been focused on fragile surface sites normally found in remote and rural locations. However, urban archaeology sites are invariably also buried remains with no visible surface monument. The high social and financial value of land in towns and cities is a reflection of the desire to live and work, build and rebuild, in such locations. Consequently, cities such as York, London, Durham and Bergen have extensive stratified archaeological remains typically 1–5 m deep, formed from the detritus of living and construction over hundreds of years of human occupation. It is, therefore, no surprise that it is in these locations that the conflict between development and preservation of archaeological remains *in situ* has often come to a head, as in the case of the Rose Theatre site (see Chapter 11.1) (Corfield 2004).

Major urban developments are usually sited to avoid existing heritage sites, given their legal protection and the poor publicity that results from attempting to destroy much-loved heritage. The high prevalence of archaeological remains within cities and the high cost of making changes late in the construction process (Davis *et al.* 2004: 5) has created an emphasis on involving archaeologists at the pre-planning/design stage of development projects, so significant archaeological remains are avoided (Davis *et al.* 2004). All UK heritage and planning authorities encourage this approach. Recovering archaeological information (initially desk-based assessments using HER, borehole, test pit and other information), alongside geological and soil data, allows archaeological assessment of the likelihood of any archaeological remains being present, as well as their extent, nature, significance and likely state of preservation. This is required by the planning process (Department for Communities and Local Government 2012), though these factors are best incorporated into the pre-application planning and design process, so that the building design is adapted to take account of any likely planning restrictions. Many English towns such as Bristol, Carlisle, Boston, Nantwich, Droitwich and Berwick-upon-Tweed have mapped their waterlogged deposits and their archaeological significance as part of the National Heritage Protection Plan, in an effort to facilitate appropriate development and avoid loss of the waterlogged archaeological remains. Planning permission is then sought by the developer, with a clear assessment of the likely nature of archaeological remains to be encountered and a proposal of how they will be preserved/recorded. The subsequent planning permission will detail the nature of the extent of archaeological work required as the planning authority seeks to balance the competing interests.

Many different outcomes/solutions can occur; they include:

- Archaeological remains are so important that permission to develop is refused and the remains are preserved intact, though they may not be investigated or any steps taken to ensure they are preserved.
- Development is permitted with specified measures to preserve as much of the remains as possible. One solution to preserve as much archaeology *in situ* as possible and avoid the expense and delay of total excavation is using appropriate foundations (Tilley 2001):
    - *Piling*: usually high cost used to support multistorey buildings, there are many forms of piling available (Davis *et al.* 2004: 56–61; Environment Agency 2006; English Heritage 2007). It will depend on the nature of the ground and building being constructed and the costs as to the type of piling chosen. The unstable made-up ground of many cities often makes piling the preferred option. This is particularly true when there are waterlogged deposits (see Chapter 11), where piling down to firmer clay layers below the waterlogged layers is often considered essential. Excavations around *in situ* piles at locations such as Farrier Street site, Worcester, have shown limited disturbance, up to 0.3 m around a 0.1 m square pre-stressed concrete pile driven directly into the ground (Dalwood *et al.* 1994: 108–11). This created a 3 per cent loss of archaeological area of the site due to piling. A figure of 5 per cent loss of archaeological deposit was seen as acceptable at York, and while not endlessly repeatable, has become an accepted norm in development in towns and cities in the UK (Davis *et al.* 2004: 25).
    - *Raft*: a wide shallow 'raft' foundation of reinforced concrete can spread the load over a large area. Usually used for single- or two-storey buildings over ground such as soft clay, alluvial deposits and compressible fill. Normally cheaper than piling and more expensive than burial. Incidents such as calcium sulphate precipitation, ground shrinkage and void formation noted at 44–45 Parliament Street, York (Davis *et al.* 2002), suggest that degradative processes can sometimes continue beneath the concrete foundations of buildings without anyone being aware of the loss of archaeological information until the building is demolished.

- *Burial*: the practice of burying sites, located near the soil surface beneath layers of soil or sand, to physically protect them, with buildings, roads, railways or other developments constructed above the protective layer, is sometimes seen as cheaper than archaeological excavation and its associated report (US Army Corps of Engineers 1992: III.8), though some form of archaeological assessment is invariably undertaken before such sites are buried. Experimental work has documented the extent of displacement of artefacts from high levels of surface loading, such as the vertical displacement of artefacts by 20–30 mm caused by a 75 ft high overlying bank (US Army Corps of Engineers 1992: II.3), and the extent and ceramic breakage as a result of different soils, loading, orientation and bridging structures (Mathewson *et al.* 1992). Concerns have also been shown about the changing soil chemistry of archaeological deposits from new overburdens.

- Develop without restriction. A watching brief is often maintained to ensure that any unexpected archaeological remains are recorded.
- The archaeological remains are to be recorded via excavation and removed. Building foundations are usually designed to minimise such archaeological work to reduce expense (see above).

In some instances, archaeological remains are unexpectedly encountered during excavation, or are more extensive or important than was initially appreciated. If they are of sufficient significance, they can either be reburied and preserved *in situ* beneath the building, as in the case of the Rose Theatre (Corfield 2004), or made visible to the public, as in the case of the Roman amphitheatre of Roman London, fragments of which are preserved in the geographical original location within the concrete basements of the London Guildhall (Ganiaris and Bateman 2004). In most cases, they are excavated, recorded and removed with the limited time and resources available.

Bibliography

Aldhouse-Green, S.R.H., Whittle, A.W.R., Allen, J.R.L. *et al.* (1993) 'Prehistoric human footprints from the Severn estuary at Uskmouth and Magor Pill, Gwent, Wales', *Archaeologia Cambrensis*, CXLI: 14–55.

Ashton, N. (2012) 'One million years UK: new from Happisburgh: footprints', *British Archaeology*, March/April: 20–1.

Battlefields Trust (n.d.) *Battlefield Threats: A Policy Approach*, available at: www.battlefields trust.com/cms/upload/docs/343/20141204managing_battlefield_threats_policy_paper_final.pdf (accessed January 2016).

Bell, M. (1990) *Brean Down Excavations 1983–1987*, London: Historic Buildings and Monuments Commission.

Bintliff, J. (2000) 'Beyond dates on the map: future directions for surface artefact survey in Greece', in J. Bintliff, M. Kuna and N. Vendova (eds), *The Future of Surface Artefact Survey in Europe*, Sheffield: Sheffield Academic Press, pp. 3–20.

Bintliff, J. (2007) *Testing the Hinterland: The Work of the Boeotia Survey (1989–1991)*, Cambridge: McDonald Institute for Archaeological Research.

Bird, M.K. (1992) 'The impact of tropical cyclones on the archaeological record: an Australian example', *Archaeology in Oceania*, 27(2): 75–86.

Bocek, B. (1986) 'Rodent ecology and burrowing behavior: predicted effects on archaeological site formation', *American Antiquity*, 51(3): 589–603.

Callanan, M. (2013) 'Melting snow patches reveal neolithic archery', *Antiquity*, 87: 728–45.

Caple, C. (2004) 'Towards a benign reburial context: the chemistry of the burial environment', *Conservation and Management of Archaeological Sites*, 6(3–4): 155–66.

Clark, P. and Hope, J. (1985) 'Aboriginal burials and shell middens at Snaggy Bend and other sites on the Central Murray River', *Australian Archaeology*, 20: 68–89.

Corfield, M. (2004) 'Saving the Rose Theatre: England's first managed and monitored reburial', *Conservation and Managements of Archaeological Sites*, 6(3–4): 305–14.

Dalwood, C.H., Buteux, V.A. and Darlington, J. (1994) 'Excavations at Farrier Street and other sites north of the city wall, Worcester 1988–1992', *Transactions of the Worcestershire Archaeological Society*, Third Series, 14: 75–114.

Darvill, T. (1987) *Ancient Monuments in the Countryside: An Archaeological Management Review*, London: English Heritage.

Darvill, T. and Fulton, A. (1998) *The Monuments at Risk Survey of England 1995*, London: Bournemouth University and English Heritage.

Davis, M.J., Gdaniec, K.L.A., Brice, M. et al. (2004) *Mitigation of Construction Impact on Archaeological Remains*, London: English Heritage.

Davis, M., Hall, A., Kenward, H. et al. (2002) 'Preservation of urban archaeological deposits: monitoring and characterisation of archaeological deposits at Marks & Spencer, 44–45 Parliament Street, York', *Internet Archaeology*, 11, available at: http://intarch.ac.uk/journal/issue11/oxley_index.html (accessed September 2014).

Department for Communities and Local Government (2012) *National Planning Policy Framework*, London: Department for Communities and Local Government.

Dobinson, C. and Denison, S. (1995) *Metal Detecting and Archaeology in England*, York: CBA and English Heritage.

Dunwell, A.J. and Trout, R.C. (1999) *Burrowing Animals and Archaeology*, Historic Scotland Technical Advice Note 16, Edinburgh: Historic Scotland, available at: http://conservation.historic-scotland.gov.uk/publication-detail.htm?pubid=8546 (accessed September 2014).

English Heritage (2003) *Coastal Defence and the Historic Environment*, London: English Heritage, available at: www.english-heritage.org.uk/publications/coastal-defence-and-the-historic-environment/ (accessed September 2014).

English Heritage (2007) *Piling and Archaeology*, London: English Heritage, available at: www.english-heritage.org.uk/publications/piling-and-archaeology/ (accessed September 2014).

Environment Agency (2006) *Piling in Layered Ground: Risks to Groundwater and Archaeology*, Rotherham: The Environment Agency, available at: www.gov.uk/government/uploads/system/uploads/attachment_data/file/290536/scho0906bllu-e-e.pdf (accessed September 2014).

ERA (n.d.) *England's Rock Art*, available at: http://archaeologydataservice.ac.uk/era/section/record_manage/rm_manage_fylingdales.jsf (accessed September 2014).

Fernandes, A.P.B. (2007) 'The conservation programme of the Coa Valley Archaeological Park: philosophy, objectives and action', *Conservation and Management of Archaeological Sites*, 9(2): 71–96.

Finn, C. (1997) '"Leaving more than footprints": modern votive offerings at Chaco Canyon prehistoric site', *Antiquity*, 71: 169–78.

Foard, G. (2012) *Battlefield Archaeology of the English Civil War*, BAR British Series 570, Oxford: Archaeopress.

Fox, R.A. (1993) *Archaeology, History and Custer's Last Battle*, Norman, OK and London: University of Oklahoma Press.

Galliano, F., Werner, G. and Menzel, K. (1998) 'Monitoring of metal corrosion and soil solution at two excavation sites and in the laboratory', in W. Mourey and L. Robbiola (eds), *Metal 98: Proceedings of the International Conference on Metals Conservation*, London: James & James, pp. 87–91.

Ganiaris, H. and Bateman, N. (2004) 'From arena to art gallery: the preservation of London's Roman amphitheatre in-situ', in T. Nixon (ed.), *Preserving Archaeological Remains In-Situ?*, London: Museum of London Archaeological Service, pp. 198–201.

Gerwin, W., Scharff, W. and Baumhauer, R. (1998) 'Corrosive decay of archaeological metal finds from different soils and effects of environmental pollution', in W. Mourey and L. Robbiola (eds), *Metal 98: Proceedings of the International Conference on Metals Conservation*, London: James & James, pp. 100–5.

Groom, P., Schlee, D., Hughes, G. et al. (2011) 'Two early medieval cemeteries in Pembrokeshire: Brownslade Barrow and West Angle Bay', *Archaeologia Cambrensis*, 160: 133–204.

Haase, W.R. (1983) 'Mitigation of chaining impacts to archaeological sites', *Journal of Range Management*, 36(2): 158–60.

Haldenby, D. and Richards, J.D. (2010) 'Charting the effects of plough damage using metal-detected assemblages', *Antiquity*, 84: 1151–62.

Hayden, J.H. (1965) 'Fragile pattern areas', *American Antiquity*, 31: 273–6.

Jones, K.L. (1994) *Archaeological Site Stabilisation and Reconstruction in the United States*, Winston Churchill Memorial Fellowship Report 1993, New Zealand Department of Conservation Science and Research Internal Report No. 45, Wellington, New Zealand: New Zealand Department of Conservation Science and Research.

Jones, K.L. (2003) 'Advances and issues in prehistoric archaeological site stabilisation', *Bulletin of the Indo-Pacific Prehistory*, 23: 191–200.

Lynott, M.J. (1989) 'Stabilization of shoreline archaeological sites at Voyagers National Park', *American Antiquity*, 54: 792–801.

Mathewson, C. and Gonzalez, T. (1988) 'Protection and preservation of archaeological sites through burial', in P.G. Marinos and G. Koukis (eds), *The Engineering Geology of Ancient Works, Monuments and Historical Sites: Preservation and Protection, Volume 1*, Rotterdam: Balkema, pp. 519–26.

Mathewson, C., Gonzalez, T. and Eblen, J.S. (1992) *Burial as a Method of Archaeological Site Protection*, Vicksburg, MS: US Army Engineer Waterways Experiment Station, NTIS No. ADA247685.

Mcinnes, L. (1993) 'Archaeology as land use', in J. Hunter and I. Ralston (eds), *Archaeological Resource Management in the UK*, Stroud: Alan Sutton, pp. 243–55.

Miles, D. (2000) 'Holme timber circle', *Conservation Bulletin*, 37: 6–7.

Newman, P. (1981) *Battle of Marston Moor 1644*, Chichester: Bird.

Nickens, P. (2000) 'Technologies for in-place protection and long-term conservation of archaeological sites', in R.A. Williamson and P.R. Nickens (eds), *Science and Technology in Historic Preservation*, New York: Klewer Academic, pp. 309–32.

Renfrew, C. and Bahn, P. (1991) *Archaeology, Theories, Methods and Practice*, London: Thames & Hudson.

Schiffer, M.B. (1987) *Formation Processes of the Archaeological Record*, Albuquerque, NM: University of New Mexico Press.

Schiffer, M.B. and Gumerman, G.J. (1977) *Conservation Archaeology: A Guide for Cultural Resource Management Studies*, London: Academic Press.

Scott, D.D., Fox, R.A., Jr., Connor, M.A. et al. (1989) *Archaeological Perspectives on the Battle of the Little Bighorn*, Norman, OK and London: University of Oklahoma Press.

Shiner, J. (2008) *Place as Occupational Histories*, BAR International Series 1763, Oxford: Archaeopress.

Sneison, W.J., Sullivan, M.E. and Preece, N.D. (1986) 'Nundera Point: an experiment in stabilising a foredune shell midden', *Australian Archaeology*, 23: 25–41.

Tilley, G.P. (2001) 'Engineering methods of minimising damage and preserving archaeological remains in situ', in M. Corfield, P. Hinton, T. Nixon and M. Pollard (eds), *Preserving Archaeological Remains In-Situ*, London: Museum of London Archaeological Service and Bradford University, pp. 1–7.

US Army Corps of Engineers (1992) *The Archeological Sites Protection and Preservation Notebook*, Vicksburg, MS: US Army Engineer Waterways Experiment Station.

Vyner, B. (2009) 'Fylingdales Moor: a lost landscape rises from the ashes', *Current Archaeology*, 226: 20–7.

Wainwright, G. (1993) 'The management of change: archaeology and planning', *Antiquity*, 67: 416–21.

Wanfu, W., Tao, W., Weimin, Z. et al. (2010) 'Research and application methods for comprehensive control of wind-borne sand at the Mogao Grottoes', in N. Agnew (ed.), *Conservation of Ancient Sites on the Silk Road: Proceedings of the Second International Conference on the Conservation of Grotto Sites*, Los Angeles, CA: GCI, pp. 358–64.

Watson, C. (2005) *Seahenge: An Archaeological Conundrum*, London: English Heritage.

White, R. (1994) 'Combating erosion in the Yorkshire Dales National Park', in A.Q. Berry and I.W. Brown (eds), *Erosion on Archaeological Earthworks: Its Prevention, Control and Repair*, Mold: Clwyd County Council, pp. 93–101.

Wildesen, L.E. (1982) 'The study of impacts on archaeological sites', *Advances in Archaeological Method and Theory*, 5: 51–96.

Windmiller, R. and Huckell, B.B. (1973) 'Desert culture sites near Mormon Lake, Northern Arizona', *Kiva*, 39(2): 199–211.

Chapter 9.1

The study of impacts on archaeological sites

Leslie E. Wildesen

Source: Wildesen, L.E. (1982) 'The study of impacts on archaeological sites', *Advances in Archaeological Method and Theory*, 5: 51–96.

Introduction

[...]

Studies of artifact movement

AFTER REDMAN AND WATSON (1970) explicitly tested the relationship of surface to subsurface materials by conducting excavations on prehistoric mounds in Turkey, archaeologists began to examine the actual movement of artifacts on surfaces and to attribute such movement to various causes (impact agents), particularly geomorphological processes and agricultural and other human activities. The issue of congruence between surface and subsurface assemblages also is beginning to receive the attention it deserves (Baker 1978; Hughes and Lampert 1977; Lewarch and O'Brien 1981). Clearly, whatever the 'original' relationship between surface and subsurface expressions of site content, the present relationship depends on the amount, direction, and selectivity or distribution of impacts causing transfer of artifacts on the site surface.

Kirkby and Kirkby (1976) proposed a geomorphological model to account for the natural movement of ceramic sherds through time within and across the surface of prehistoric house mounds in semi-arid environments. On the basis of their model and data on sherd sizes, densities, and locations at archaeological sites in southern Mexico and southwestern Iran, they concluded that 'over a 500-year period sherds less than 4 cm can be displaced by up to 5 m on slopes as low as 1 to 3 degrees' and that 'larger sherds of 4–8 cm are displaced on similar slopes by less than 1 m' (1976: 240–241). They propose that geomorphic processes such as wetting and drying or freeze-thaw cycles, although present, probably only impact artifact location in the top 50 cm of a site, and that 'small, random disturbances tend to diffuse coarse material in all directions outwards from areas' of concentration, rather than directionally (1976: 241). They conclude that 'these geomorphic processes produce only very slow mixing of material which is probably always less significant than the rate at which the mound material is being eroded' (1976: 241).

Rick (1976) also investigated natural downslope movement of artifacts, including stone, bone, and ceramics, by analyzing materials collected from the surface of a long variable slope below a rock shelter in Peru. He suggests that 'if there is a finite upper weight limit in a given material, then there is a slope angle below which that material will not be moved' called the critical angle (1976: 142). For example, his data show that 'no significant number of projectile points' occurs in sample units with slopes less than 20° (1976: 143). Artifact distribution and downslope movement are influenced by environmental factors such as paleoclimate, vegetation cover, and the thickness and stratigraphy of the archaeological site from which the materials are derived (Rick 1976: 143).

After 4 years, the experimental earthwork at Overton Down showed evidence of erosion and downslope movement of surface materials; the crest had sunk 16.5 cm, with a concomitant compressing of the inner layers of the mound (Jewell and Dimbleby 1966: 323). Although their text does not mention internal movement of artifacts placed in the earthwork during construction, it does indicate (1966: Figure 1) that some such movement took place between 2 and 4 years after mound construction.

The impacts caused by human actions such as plowing may be more or less severe than those caused by nature. For example, Talmage *et al.* (1977: 24) quoted a study of a Maryland site by Robertson as showing that 'plowing disturbs artifacts more than had previously been expected based on prior archaeological investigations of plowed sites.' Yet Redman and Watson's mounds had been plowed for years, and they concluded

> though there is probably some lateral displacement, we do not believe it to be very great: calculations based on a random walk simulation . . . suggested that even with three thousand plowings, movement [of artifacts] would be five meters or less.
>
> (1970: 280)

In fact, Binford *et al.* (1970: 7) used plowing as a method to help define site boundaries and to reveal 'something of the internal structure of the site' at Hatchery West. Roper's (1976) study of the impacts of plowing at the Airport site in Illinois seems to bear out these latter studies. She estimated the mean lateral displacement of biface fragments on the surface of the Airport site to be 2.07–4.12 m; she believes that amount of movement is not enough to 'distort spatial relationships' significantly (1976: 373). [. . .]

Several studies have been conducted to examine the impacts of specific kinds of ground-disturbing projects on archaeological materials, with particular attention paid to artifact movements on ground surfaces. Roney, in an unpublished study of grazing impacts, concluded that horizontal displacement of artifacts by cows 'was less severe than had been anticipated,' and would 'probably leave intact spatial patterns relating to activity areas and isolation of individual campsites, but could obscure very fine patterning, as might be of interest in a study of motor habits' (1977: 15). Roney suggests that moister soil might cause greater potential artifact displacement due to increased vertical mixing, and that artifacts might actually stick to the hooves of milling cattle, and be transported out of the area.

[...]
Gallagher (1978) used steel washers to simulate artifacts in a study of the impacts of 'scarification' in southern Idaho. 'To scarify' is defined as 'to loosen the top soil in preparation for regenerating' a timber stand (Mifflin and Lysons 1979: 17); it is usually done with a bulldozer, often with a toothed blade. Gallagher placed 396 steel washers in 99 postholes on a 6 × 6 foot (1.8 × 1.8 m) grid over the area; four washers were in each posthole, on the surface of the mineral soil, and at depths of 1, 3, and 6 inches (2.5, 7.6, and 15.2 cm). He reports that 14% of the surface washers had been horizontally displaced, 5% were vertically displaced, and 36% were lost altogether (not recovered even with the aid of a metal detector). The average horizontal displacement was 20.5 inches (52 cm); the average vertical displacement was 2.6 inches (6.6 cm) (1978: 294). Smaller percentages of the more deeply buried washers were displaced, but 10% of those buried at the 6-inch (15.2 cm) depth were not recovered. As with the chaining project studied by DeBloois et al. (1975), the impacts from scarification were not uniform: 'Some areas were heavily disturbed, while others were apparently untouched' (Gallagher 1978: 293).

Wood (1979) reports on a study of the impacts caused by crushing brush (principally sagebrush and other unpalatable species) on grazing areas west of Prescott, Arizona. He cites studies by DeBloois et al. (1975) and Gallagher (1978) to propose that artifact damage per se 'appears to be less of a factor in data loss than dislocation,' at least 'until the artifacts are so badly damaged as to be unrecognizable' (1979: 29).

[...]

Phillips (1980), in an unpublished study of the impacts of tractor yarding of logs over a natural and cultural lag deposit of basalt, cryptocrystalline silica, and obsidian in eastern Oregon, [...] concluded

> vertical displacement was greatest in deeper soils with low bulk density and fine particle size. Horizontal displacement was greatest in the primary skid trails, deck and slash piling activities. Form modification [of cultural materials] was greatest in the rocky soils and least in low density ash/basalt soils.
> (1980: 8)

Studies of internal changes in sites

Aside from studies of the movement of surface artifacts, few experiments have been conducted to determine the nature and severity of impacts on archaeological sites themselves, whether from natural or cultural causes. In North America, artificial sites have been constructed as teaching aids for classes in archaeological field methods, but little quantitative work has been reported (see Ascher 1970; Chilcott and Deetz 1964).

[...]

Roger Parsons and his coworkers have used archaeological sites in the Midwest and the West Coast as 'soil genesis benchmarks' to provide limiting dates for the study of soil profile development (Parsons 1962; Parsons et al. 1962; Reckendorf and Parsons 1966), but no archaeologists have studied the impacts of pedogensis on the integrity of the archaeological record. Mattingly and Williams (1962) report on changes in chemical properties of soils buried since Roman times in England, again using the archaeological site to provide a limiting date for their study, but did not assess the impacts of prolonged burial on the archaeological sediments or their cultural contents.

The Overton Down experiment, mentioned previously, was designed to obtain quantitative data on natural processes because 'monuments are continually being modified by nature and ... evidence of weathering, denudation, and silting can be as informative as the artifacts sometimes found in them' (Ashbee and Cornwall 1961: 129).

[...]

Qualitative and semiquantitative studies of site morphology can provide useful hypotheses for model building. Cook (1963: 333) suggests that the 'degree of surface weathering' might shed light on the age of artificially constructed mounds in western Mexico; Jewell and Dimbleby's work in England (1966) confirms that mound morphology does in fact change in measurable ways through time. Building upon these studies, Kirkby and Kirkby (1976) described a model to account for geomorphic processes acting on house mounds in arid environments. They suggested that a mound profile approximates a normal curve over time, and that 'the absolute heights [at different times] of the mound can be seen to depend on both its original size and shape, but the spreading out of the mound ... is independent of these factors' (1976: 233). They cautioned that the use of the slope profile as a relative dating tool depends on both the original size of the house mound and the local climate; in Iran, such a mound might retain surface expression for up to 2,000 years, whereas in Oaxaca, it might survive for only 500 to 800 years (1976: 236).

Human beings can alter their living space while they are occupying it, as Ascher (1968), Schiffer (1976, 1977), and others have pointed out. Schiffer's A–S and S–S processes treat those aspects of scavenging, reuse, and exchange as they operate within living communities (the 'systemic context'). Matthews (1965) points out that a zone of disturbance travels upward in a stratified archaeological site; as humans occupy it, deposits accumulate and the 'surface' rises. Both objects and sediments are subject to this upward migration through time. Although Matthews describes the type of impact, and something of its behavior, we are given no data on severity of mixing, its rate or extent, or on how its presence actually affects our ability to recover the systemic context of the cultural material so transferred.

As with studies of impacts on artifacts, most recent studies on sites describe percentages or numbers of sites impacted, or state the impact agent or type that results in damage or destruction. Papers by Clewlow *et al.* (1971), Davis (1972), Medford (1972), Moratto (1973), Newman (1971), Palacios and Johnson (1976), Schiffer and House (1975a, 1975b), and Traylor *et al.* (1979) provide good examples of this approach. But all impact types can be classified as either burial, transfer, removal, or alteration regardless of the nature of the impact agent. All of these disturbances to the archaeological record, whether caused by natural or cultural processes, can and should be described. As Talmage *et al.* (1977) suggest, it is the *regularities* of these impacts that are important; few studies treat these regularities in any systematic or comprehensive way.

[...]

Studies of fire impacts

Barnes (1939) provided a classic description of the morphological changes in stone artifacts when subjected to fire, and made 'pot-lid fracture' a term in the vocabulary of every archaeologist who deals with lithics. Yet virtually nothing has been published on the impacts of fire on archaeological materials since his time. Unpublished proposals, single-issue contract reports or staff papers, and abstracts of papers presented at by-invitation-only meetings constitute the bulk of the 'literature' at this time (e.g., Eisler *et al.* 1978; Fenn *et al.* n.d.; Kelly and Mayberry 1979; Manuel 1980; see also Switzer 1974). Traylor *et al.* (1979) discovered that fire altered the morphology of adobe bricks, but observed that the major impacts resulted from heavy machinery (mixing and transport of surface sediments and artifacts) and from vandalism by fire fighters (removal of artifacts).

Summary

Aside from removal of specimens or sediments altogether, extensive disturbance of strata or specimen location is the most detrimental impact the archaeological record can suffer. Studies of artifact movement already have been described; very few quantitative studies of actual surface disturbance due to human agents (the 'ground-disturbing project' or the vandal) have been conducted. Many reports state that sites are, in fact, disturbed, but few archaeological studies provide any specifics. [. . .]

Studies of impacts to soils and sediments

A great deal of research has been conducted by environmental scientists in order to answer the question 'how much?' with respect to erosion, compaction, disturbance, and sedimentation association with modern land-disturbing activities such as timber harvest, grazing, and recreation. In contrast to most archaeological studies, these studies go beyond identifying impact type, and approach assessments of impact degree, extent, and duration in quantitative terms.

Compaction studies

Compaction of sediments can be measured in kilograms per square meter or by before-and-after measurements of soil bulk density and/or pore space. Compaction can be caused by any of several impact agents: heavy machinery, animals (including humans), and natural deposition. Compaction on an archaeological site may alter the nature of the sediments, and the inferences that can be drawn from them. It may also alter relationships among imbedded artifacts, and in some cases damage the artifacts themselves (especially bones and ceramics). Research on compaction has been conducted by recreation specialists, soil scientists, and logging engineers, with varying and sometimes contradictory results.

For example, visitor use at campgrounds and on trails results in increased compaction on heavily used areas (Brown *et al.* 1977; Liddle 1975; Merriam and Smith 1974). Liddle (1975: 24) reports as much as 0.68 g/cm^3 increase in bulk density on English walking paths over that of adjacent undisturbed sediments. Merriam and Smith (1974: 629) report, however, that compaction amounts seem to level off after several years, and that further increases do not occur. Not surprisingly, the amount of use and the type and amount of initial vegetation cover appear to determine the amount of impact at any specific locality. Soil moisture, initial bulk density, and soil texture (especially the type and percentage of clay particles) affect the degree of compaction noted in these and other studies.

Grazing by large animals also may cause compaction to occur, but the amounts of measurable change vary widely, and other factors such as slope, soil texture, and initial bulk density play an important role in determining the degree of impact (see, e.g., Currie and Gary 1978; Read 1957; Rich and Reynolds 1963).

Several studies of compaction conducted by logging specialists have especially interesting implications for archaeological impact analysis. For instance, although some studies show little variation in soil bulk density after several passes with heavy equipment, Kuennen *et al.* (1979) found that compaction varied with depth, and that maximum compaction in their Montana study units occurred from 4 to 16 inches (10 to 41 cm) below the surface. They suggest (1979: 5) that the nature of the parent material and genetic soil horizons are primary factors affecting the depth of compaction. Duration of compaction impacts is as little as 18 years in Virginia (Hatchell and Ralston 1971) but may last over 55 years in the Willamette Valley of Oregon (Power 1974). Froelich (1978) and King and Haines (1979) report that compaction increases with the number of passes by the equipment, and that soil moisture and soil texture affect the results of their tests.

The amount of compaction may vary in different parts of a site, and depends on at least four factors: (*a*) the nature of the impact agent, (*b*) the distribution of the compacting activity (i.e., whether it is confined to logging skid trails, or spread widely over the site area), (*c*) the number of separate 'impact events' (e.g., passes by a tractor), and (*d*) the nature of the site sediments and included cultural materials. The question *how much* compaction constitutes an adverse effect cannot be answered without reference to these factors.

Erosion studies

Numerous studies and syntheses exist that treat the erosional impacts of ground-disturbing projects, especially in the context of pollution abatement (see, e.g., Environmental Protection Agency 1976; McDonald *et al.* 1977). McDonald *et al.* (1977: 7) distinguish between erosion hazard and erosion potential in a way that is useful to archaeologists: 'Erosion hazard is an inherent property of the site while erosion potential relates to the effect of ... activities upon that site.' That is, erosion *hazard* relates to n-transforms, and erosion *potential* to c-transforms (Schiffer 1972, 1976). Based on this distinction, many versions of a *universal soil loss equation* (USLE) have been developed for estimating the erosion potential of certain activities, especially farming practices on cropland in the Midwest (see, e.g., U.S. Department of Agriculture 1978); Curtis *et al.* (1977: 2) point out that the USLE can be used to predict erosion from 'skid trails, temporary roads, landings, burns, grazing, game and recreation areas, and planting sites on forested lands' as well. They include tables and graphs for computing the values of each factor in the equation for woodland situations.

Roads and road construction usually cause the greatest erosional impact of any ground-disturbing activity, as several studies have shown, and as some archaeologists seem to recognize. For instance, Lyneis *et al.* (1980: 78) cite studies showing that 38% of the historic and prehistoric trail system in Death Valley National Monument has been destroyed by sheet and gully erosion since 1910, when the first roads were constructed near the trails (Hunt and Mabey 1966). Similarly, Megahan (1976: 22) points out that in forested areas, it is 'not simply the cutting of timber,' but the entire 'logging operation,' including access road construction, that creates undesirable disturbance. Resulting changes may include disruption of soil structure, removal of protective vegetation, increased raindrop impact, and possibly reduced infiltration rates.

[...]

Surface mixing studies

Severe and widespread disturbance (mixing and transfer) of archaeological sediments can wreak havoc with interpretations of the internal structure of archaeological sites. Aside from the few studies of the impacts of various activities on surface movement of artifacts, no large-scale experiments on soil mixing have been conducted by archaeologists. The forestry literature, however, is replete with studies of surface disturbance of soils in a timber harvest unit caused by various logging practices. [...]

Most investigators report *extent*, as measured by the percentage of area subjected to disturbance, and also make an attempt to provide explicit, measurable criteria for *severity* of impact, although their definitions for each category of severity may differ. Each of the definitions in Table 9.1.1, however different from the others, provides operational criteria for assigning observable impacts to a specific category, either by defining a measurable threshold (e.g., greater than 5 cm) or by providing an 'either-or' criterion (e.g., mineral soil either is, or is not, exposed). By contrast, an otherwise useful study by Gallagher (1978), an archaeologist, includes no such criteria; 'severe disturbance,' for example, is defined as 'mixing . . . over a wide area . . . [involving] considerable depths' with the result that 'archaeological features would be extensively disturbed' and 'interpretability would be reduced to a minimum' (1978: 297). The main questions have been begged: How wide is a 'wide area'? How deep is 'considerable depth'? Most important, what is meant by 'extensively disturbed'?

Table 9.1.1 Definitions of surface disturbance categories

Category	Definition
Severe	Removal of litter, disturbance of soil >2.5 cm deep (Wooldridge 1960: 371).
	Removal of the litter, A horizon, and a portion of the B horizon; burial of the soil surface by at least 0.25 m of soil material; or severe compaction of the mineral soil (Utzig and Herring 1975: 61).
	Where A horizons are disrupted sufficiently to expose B horizons (Patric and Gorman 1978: 33).
	Surface soil removed and subsoil exposed (Klock 1975: 80; Dyrness 1967: 2).
Moderate	Removal of litter, soil disturbed to <2.5 cm depth (Wooldridge 1960: 371).
Slight	No removal of litter or soil (Wooldridge 1960: 371).
	Litter disrupted sufficiently to expose, partly or wholly, mineral soil (Patric and Gorman 1978: 33).
	Litter removed, soil exposed; litter and soil mixed 50–50; soil on top of litter or slash (Dyrness 1967: 2).
	Undisturbed litter and topsoil still in place (Klock 1975: 80).
	Litter; no compaction (Dyrness 1967: 2).

The results of 23 studies of degree and extent of surface disturbance associated with different log-yarding systems were presented in Wildesen (1982: Table 2.2) (after Wildesen 1977). Haupt (1960) points out that factors such as the number of stems cut, whether an area is clear-cut or cut selectively, and the size of the tractor used for yarding affect the amount of surface bared during yarding. Because of the interaction of these factors, and the relationship of tractor size to the number of skid roads and haul roads needed, there is no simple formula to determine which method of cutting or yarding is *the least* disruptive to surface soils. As Klock's (1975: 81) data suggest, 'adding the area of roads necessary for some cable skidding operations could raise the total area of severe soil surface disturbances to more than 50%,' although Patric and Gorman (1978: 34) assert that even with such additional area included, less than 3% of their study area in West Virginia would have exhibited 'severe' disturbance (see also, Brown 1973; DeByle 1976; Hope 1979; Silen and Gratkowski 1953; Smith and Wass 1976).

[. . .]

Studies of fire

Fire is a potent impact agent, not only for the damage it can cause directly, but also because it interacts with other impact agents to encourage or enhance their actions. Fire is known to cause destruction of organic matter in surface soils (Dyrness *et al.* 1957; Fenn *et al.* 1976; Packer and Williams 1976) and to alter other chemical properties of soils such as pH, cation exchange capacity, and percentage of nitrogen, potassium, and sulfur (DeBano *et al.* 1977).

Fire also creates enhanced erosion potential, especially in arid environments (Beaufait *et al.* 1975; DeBano 1977), and may increase a tendency toward compaction (Packer and Williams 1976). Wells and his coworkers (1979: 16) sum up the current knowledge of fire impacts to soils as follows:

> Fire influences soil physical properties and erosion to a degree depending upon the intensity of the fire, the proportion of the overstory and understory vegetation destroyed, forest floor consumed, heating of the soil, proportion of the area burned, and frequency of fire occurrence. [In addition,] the changes wrought vary greatly with the conditions of the soil, forest floor, topography, and climate.

Studies of vandalism on archaeological sites

No discussion of impacts to the archaeological record can omit a description of the actions of vandals. Vandalism, including the results of thoughtless activities such as indiscriminate use of off-road vehicles (ORVs), takes an enormous toll on archaeological sites each year. This is especially true in the western United States, where estimates of numbers of sites severely damaged run upwards of one third of the total site inventory (Lyneis *et al.* 1980). Only recently have any studies of the actual magnitude of damage from vandalism been undertaken. As yet, comprehensive data on the actual type, extent, and degree of impacts do not exist.

Several studies have been conducted in the western United States to ascertain the amount of vandalism that occurs to archaeological resources on federal lands. Williams

(1978: 36) points out that different resource types are subject to differential vandalism, with rock art sites being the most vulnerable, followed by open camps or chipping stations, stone or adobe-walled dwellings, historic buildings, and rock-shelters and caves, in that order. His study area included nine states in the 'intermountain west'; his data show that the kind of sites most subject to vandalism vary by subregion within this broad area. Williams lists four 'vulnerability factors' which seem to influence the amount and type of vandalism: resources that are well known, show signs of previous vandalism, receive high visitor use, or are obviously deteriorated are targets for further vandalistic acts (1978: 49). He develops a 'profile' of the typical vandal, based on characteristics reported by various federal land managers and archaeologists (1978: 57, 60, 61, 63): Most vandals are over 30, vandalize in groups, are males from smaller towns (less than 25,000 people), are probably local residents or travel less than 100 miles to commit their acts of vandalism, and are repeaters (1978: 71). Motives for archaeological and historical vandalism seem to be desire for personal acquisition of artifacts, followed by ignorance (of the law or of the destruction caused to the archaeological record), curiosity, recreation, profit, showing off, rebellion, and carelessness, in that order (1978: 67). Increases in the rate of vandalism seem to be associated with an increased awareness of cultural resources, coupled with easy access and lax law enforcement; decreases in the trend seem to be associated with areas where the resources are scanty and law enforcement is vigilant. Williams suggests (1978: 13) that 'cultural resource vandalism ... seems to be on the whole a characteristically different "type" of depreciative activity' than other kinds, in part because collecting is a primary motive, rather than simple destruction per se. Therefore, archaeological vandals are likely to be 'more methodical in their approach and older ... than the youths damaging school buildings' (Williams 1978: 13).

McAllister (1979) provides support for the idea that archaeological vandals are methodical; he lists some of the special tools such persons use to make their work more efficient and to help them escape detection by authorities. Among them are bottomless tents; aircraft spotters with radio communications to the vandals on the ground; special probes to locate burials without having to remove a lot of overburden; helicopter transportation in and out of the target area; and use of heavy equipment to move the greatest amount of dirt in the least amount of time (1979: 35–36). Such tools are not inexpensive, and their use requires planning and attention to logistics beyond that expected of the casual recreationist. Of the known sites in McAllister's northern Arizona study area, 50% showed damage by vandals; in some subareas as many as 80% of the known sites were vandalized.

Lyneis *et al.* (1980) studied vandalism and natural impacts on archaeological resources in the California Desert Conservation Area, administered by the Bureau of Land Management in southeastern California. They found that accessibility of sites to population centers and roads was a major factor in the damage suffered from vandalism, and that different site types suffer different amounts and kinds of vandalism. For instance, only 36% of the aboriginal village sites are listed as in 'good' condition, whereas 48% of the caves or rock-shelters are so listed (Lyneis *et al.* 1980: 49). Overall, 38% of the rock features (alignments and ground figures) show damage by off-road vehicles (ORVs), and 25% of the rock art panels show damage by vandals (removal, use as shooting target, or enhanced exfoliation resulting from building campfires against the rock) (1980: 49).

[...]

Lyneis *et al.* (1980: 2) point out that not only does the use of ORVs increase the accessibility of vulnerable sites and damage some sites simply from traveling over them, but there is a synergistic effect of ORV use on fragile desert pavement soils: Because the efficacy of wind as an erosive force depends on the degree of armoring on desert surfaces, destruction of vegetation and desert pavement by wheeled vehicles increases the danger of destruction by wind erosion (Lyneis *et al.* 1980: 76). In addition, most sites damaged by human actions (vandalism or ORV use) are on slopes less than 6° (Lyneis *et al.* 1980: 76). Coupled with the fact that 50% of the desert is within 1.6 km of a road, and 95% is within 4.8 km of a road, it seems unlikely that land managers will be able to limit access in order to reduce vandalism (Lyneis *et al.* 1980: 78).

Sheridan (1979) summarizes much recent research on the impacts ORVs cause to natural resources. In addition to disruption of vegetation cover and the resulting increases in erosion, several studies report severe compaction on ORV trails, in some cases up to 1 m deep (Snyder *et al.* 1976; Webb *et al.* 1978). Thus, for compaction as an impact type, although the extent may be limited to trails, it certainly is severe, and it may not be reversible.

Behavioral studies of other kinds of vandalism do not provide much encouragement for those who would control archaeological vandalism, although Harrison's (1976: 474) definition of vandalism is relevant to archaeological studies: Vandalism is 'any willful act of physical damage that lowers the aesthetic or economic value of an object or area. In contrast to other categories of depreciative behavior, vandalism results in visible scars.' Harrison lists exposure, access, and facility condition as three physical factors influencing the incidence of vandalism, and confirms that most acts of vandalism are performed by repeaters.

Clark *et al.* (1971: 9) found that 'more than 80 percent of the depreciative acts observed were committed when other people were present' and 'in more than 90 percent of these cases, no perceptible reaction by adjacent campers could be observed'. But part of the problem seems to be, as Clark (1976: 65) points out, that

> many times an act of vandalism as defined by a manager may be very appropriate [behavior] from a user perspective. In some cases, recreationists who have little contact with the environment may really not know what is defined as vandalism by managers. In other cases they may know but disagree.

Harrison corroborates this point by suggesting that many acts of severe vandalism are 'a result of thoughtlessness or ignorance on the part of visitors, and offenders seldom view their damage as vandalism' (1976: 479).

Recent successful efforts to obtain new federal legislation applicable to 'pot hunting' on public lands merely highlight the extent of this problem. In view of the fact that only archaeologists seem to consider surface collecting vandalism, the controversy over new antiquities legislation only points up what a poor job the profession has done in educating the public in the importance of *context* to interpretations from archaeological data (see Collins 1980; Collins and Green 1978; Grayson 1976; U.S. Congress 1979).

The study of motives of archaeological vandals, and the actual damage they cause is in its infancy. Without more detailed data, archaeologists cannot hope to develop effective measures to prevent or counteract vandalism. Inappropriately targeted educational programs will not work; fences and arrests are usually too late; and before-and-after studies of the archaeological resources themselves are nonexistent. As with other impact agents and types, it is clear that we need more specific, quantitative data on vandalism.

[...]

References

Ascher, R. (1968). 'Time's arrow and the archeology of a contemporary community.' In K.C. Chang (ed.) *Settlement Archaeology*. Palo Alto, California: National Press Books, 43–52.

Ascher, R. (1970). 'CUES I: design and construction of an experimental archaeological structure.' *American Antiquity* 35 (2): 215–216.

Ashbee, P. and I.W. Cornwall (1961). 'An experiment in field archaeology.' *Antiquity* 35: 129–134.

Baker, C.M. (1978). 'The size effect: an explanation of variability in surface artifact assemblage content.' *American Antiquity* 43 (2): 288–293.

Barnes, A.S. (1939). 'The differences between natural and human flaking on prehistoric flint implements.' *American Anthropologist* 41 (1): 99–112.

Beaufait, W.R., C.E. Hardy, and W.C. Fischer (1975). 'Broadcast burning in larch-fir clear cuts: the Miller Creek-Newman Ridge study.' U.S. Department of Agriculture, Forest Service Research Paper I__–175.

Binford, L.R., S.R. Binford, R. Whallon *et al.* (1970). 'Archaeology at Hatchery West.' *Society for American Archaeology Memoir* No. 24.

Brown, G.W. (1973). 'The impact of timber harvest on soil and water resources.' *Extension Bulletin* 827. Corvallis: Oregon State University.

Brown, J.H., Jr., S.P. Kalisz, and W.R. Wright (1977). 'Effects of recreational use on forested sites.' *Environmental Geology* 1 (5): 425–431.

Chilcott, J.H., and J. Deetz (1964). 'The construction and uses of a laboratory archaeological site.' *American Antiquity* 29 (3): 328–337.

Clark, R.N. (1976). 'Control of vandalism in recreation areas—fact, fiction, or folklore?' In *Vandalism and outdoor recreation*. U.S. Department of Agriculture Forest Service General Technical Report PSW-17, 62–72.

Clark, R.N., J.C. Hendee, and F.L. Campbell (1971). 'Depreciative behavior in forest campgrounds: an exploratory study.' Pacific Northwest Forest and Range Experiment Station Research Note PNW–161.

Clewlow, C.W. Jr., P.S. Hallinan and R.D. Ambro (1971). 'A crisis in archaeology.' *American Antiquity* 36 (4): 472–473.

Collins, R.B. (1980). 'The meaning behind ARPA: how the act is meant to work.' U.S. Department of Agriculture, Forest Service *Cultural Resource Report* No. 32: 1–9.

Collins, R.B. and D.F. Green (1978). 'A proposal to modernize the American Antiquities Act.' *Science* 202: 1055–1059.

Cook, S.F. (1963). 'Erosion morphology and occupation history in western Mexico.' *University of California Anthropological Record* 17: 281–334.

Currie, P.O. and H.L. Gary (1978). 'Grazing and logging effects on soil surface changes in central Colorado ponderosa pine type.' *Journal of Soil and Water Conservation* 33 (4): 176–178.

Curtis, N.M. Jr., A.G. Darrach and W.J. Sauerwein (1977). 'Estimating sheet-rill erosion and sediment yield on disturbed western forest and woodlands.' *U.S. Department of Agriculture, Soil Conservation Service Technical Note No. 10*, Woodland.

Davis, H. (1972). 'The crisis in American archaeology.' *Science* 175: 267–272.

DeBano, L.F. (1977). 'Influence of forest practices on water yield, channel stability, erosion, and sedimentation in the southwest.' In, *Proceedings of the Society of American Foresters National Convention*, Albuquerque. Washington, D.C.: Society of American Foresters, 74–78.

DeBano, L.F., P.H. Dunn and C.E. Conrad (1977). 'Fire's effect on physical and chemical properties of chaparral soils.' In, *Proceedings of the Symposium on the Environmental*

Consequences of Fire and Fuel Management in Mediterranean Ecosystems, Palo Alto. U.S. Department of Agriculture Forest Service, General Technical Report WO-3, 65–74.

DeBloois, E.I., D.F. Green and H.G. Wylie (1975). 'A test of the impact of pinyon-juniper chaining on archaeological sites.' In, *The Pinyon-Juniper ecosystem: a symposium, May 1975*. Logan, Utah: Utah State University, College of Natural Resources, 153–161.

DeByle, N.V. (1976). 'Fire, logging and debris disposal effects on soil and water in northern coniferous forests.' In, *Proceedings of the XVI International Union of Forest Research Organizations World Congress*, Oslo. 201–212.

Dyrness, C.T. (1967). 'Soil surface conditions following skyline logging.' *U.S. Department of Agriculture, Forest Service Research Note* PNW-55.

Dyrness, C.T., C.T. Youngberg and R.H. Ruth (1957). 'Some effects of logging and slash burning on physical soil properties in the Corvallis watershed.' *U.S. Department of Agriculture Forest Service Research Paper* No. 19. Pacific Northwest Forest and Range Experiment Station.

Eisler, D., D. Parrella, and L. Spencer (1978). 'Report on the investigation and analysis of cultural resources, Young's Butte fire, Paulina Ranger District, Ochoco National Forest.' Unpublished report. Prineville, Oregon: Ochoco National Forest.

Environmental Protection Agency (1976). *Forest harvest, residue treatment, reforestation, and protection of water quality*. EPA 910/0-76-020.

Fenn, D.B., G.J. Gogue and R.E. Burge (1976). 'Effects of campfires on soil properties.' *National Park Service Ecological Services Bulletin* No. 5. U.S. Department of Interior.

Fenn, D.B., R. Kelly, and K. Davis (n.d.). 'Evaluation of effects of controlled burning and wildfires on surficial archeological resources.' Unpublished report, San Francisco: National Park Service.

Froelich, H.A. (1978). 'Soil compaction from low ground-pressure, torsion suspension logging vehicles on three forest soils.' *Oregon State University Forest Research Lab Research Paper* 36. Corvallis.

Gallagher, J.G. (1978). 'Scarification and cultural resources: an experiment to evaluate serotinous lodgepole pine forest regeneration techniques.' *Plains Anthropologist* 23 (82): 289–299.

Grayson, D. (1976). 'A review of recent attempts to prosecute Antiquities Act violations in Oregon.' *Tebiwa* 18 (2): 59–64.

Harrison, A. (1976). 'Problems: vandalism and depreciative behavior.' In G.W. Sharpe (ed.) *Interpreting the environment*. New York: Wiley, 473–495.

Hatchell, G.E. and C.W. Ralston (1971). 'Natural recovery of surface soils disturbed in logging.' *Tree Planters Notes* 22(2): 5–9.

Haupt, H.F. (1960). 'Variation in areal disturbance produced by harvesting methods in ponderosa pine.' *Journal of Forestry* 58 (8): 634–639.

Hope, S.M. (1979). 'Surface disturbance in relation to highlead logging.' Unpublished M.A. thesis, Department of Forestry, University of Washington, Seattle.

Hughes, P.J. and R.J. Lampert (1977). 'Occupational disturbance and types of archaeological deposit.' *Journal of Archaeological Science* 4 (2): 135–140.

Hunt, C.B. and D.R. Mabey (1966). 'Stratigraphy and structure, Death Valley, California.' *U.S. Geological Survey Professional Paper* 494-A.

Jewell, P.A. and G.W. Dimbleby (eds) (1966). 'The experimental earthwork on Overton Down, Wiltshire, England: the first four years.' *Proceedings of the Prehistoric Society* 32 (11): 313–342.

Kelly, R.E. and J. Mayberry (1979). 'Trial by fire: effects of NPS burn programs upon archeological resources.' *Abstract, 2nd Conference on Scientific Research in the National Parks*, San Francisco.

King, T. and S. Haines (1979). 'Soil compaction absent in plantation thinning.' *U.S. Department of Agriculture Southern Forest Experiment Station Research Note* SO-251.

Kirkby, A. and M.J. Kirkby (1976). 'Geomorphic processes and the surface survey of archaeological sites in semi-arid areas.' In D.A. Davidson and M.L. Schackley (eds), *Geoarchaeology*. Boulder, Colorado: Westview Press, 229–253.

Klock, G.O. (1975). 'Impact of five post fire salvage logging systems on soils and vegetation.' *Journal of Soil and Water Conservation* 30 (2): 78–81.

Kuennen, L., G. Edson, and T.V. Tolle (1979). 'Soil compaction due to timber harvest activities.' U.S. Department of Agriculture, Forest Service Northern Region, *Soil Air and Water Notes* 79–73.

Lewarch, D.E. and M.J. O'Brien (1981). 'The expanding role of surface assemblages in archaeological research.' In M.B. Schiffer (ed.), *Advances in archaeological method and theory* (Vol. 4). New York: Academic Press, 297–342.

Liddle, M.J. (1975). 'A selective review of the ecological effects of human trampling on natural ecosystems.' *Biological Conservation* 7: 17–36.

Lyneis, M.M., D.L. Weide, and E. Warren (1980). *Impacts: damage to cultural resources in the California desert*. Department of Anthropology, University of Nevada, Las Vegas.

Manuel, D. (1980). 'Prescribed burning and its effects on cultural resources within the Diablo and Sierra de Salinas mountain ranges of the interior central coast of central California.' Unpublished report, Bureau of Land Management, Folsom. District Office, California.

Matthews, J.M. (1965). 'Stratigraphic disturbance: the human element.' *Antiquity* 39: 295–298.

Mattingly, G.E.G. and R.J.B. Williams (1962). 'A note on the chemical analysis of a soil buried since Roman times.' *Journal of Soil Science* 13(2): 254–258.

McAllister, M.E. (1979). 'Pothunting on National Forest lands in Arizona: an overview of the current situation.' In D.F. Green and S. LeBlanc (eds), *Vandalism of cultural resources: the growing threat to our nation's Heritage*. U.S. Department of Agriculture Forest Service Southwestern Region, *Cultural Resource Report* No. 28, 29–48.

McDonald, R., G. Alward, W. Arlen et al. (1977). 'Silvicultural activities and non-point pollution abatement: a cost-effectiveness analysis procedure.' *Environmental Protection Agency Report No. EPA 600/8 77 018*, Washington D.C.

Medford, L.D. (1972). 'Agricultural destruction of archeological sites in northeast Arkansas.' *Arkansas Archeological Survey, Research Series* 3: 41–82.

Megahan, W.F. (1976). 'Effects of forest cultural treatments upon streamflow.' In *Proceedings of the 1975 Forest Acts Dilemma Symposium*. Montana Forest and Conservation Experiment Station, University of Montana, 14–34.

Merriam, L.C. and C.K. Smith (1974). 'Visitor impact on newly developed campsites in the Boundary Waters Canoe Area.' *Journal of Forestry* 72: 627–630.

Mifflin, R.W. and Lysons, H.H. (1979) *Glossary of Forest Engineering Terms*, Portland, Oregon: US Department of Agriculture, Forest Service, Pacific Northwest Forest and Range Experiment Station.

Moratto, M.J. (1973). 'Archeology in the far west.' *The Missouri Archaeologist* 35 (1–2): 19–32.

Newman, T.M. (1971). 'The crisis in Oregon archeology.' *Tebiwa* 14 (1): 1–3.

Packer, P.E. and B.D. Williams (1976). 'Logging and prescribed burning effects on the hydrologic and soil stability behavior of larch/Douglas-fir forests in the northern Rocky Mountains.' In *Proceedings of the Montana Tall Timbers Fire Ecology Conference and Fire and Land Management Symposium* No. 14, 1974. Tallahassee, Florida: Tall Timbers Research Station, 465–479.

Palacios, V. and R.L. Johnson (1976). 'An overview of archaeology and the law: seventy years of unexploited protection for prehistoric resources.' *Notre Dame Lawyer* 51: 706–721.

Parsons, R.B. (1962). 'Indian mounds of northeast Iowa as soil genesis benchmarks.' *Journal of the Iowa Archeological Society* 12 (2): 1–70.

Parsons, R.B., W.H. Scholtes and F.F. Riecken (1962). 'Soils of Indian mounds in northeastern Iowa as benchmarks for studies of soil genesis.' *Soil Science Society of America Proceedings* 26: 491–496.

Patric, J.H. and J.L. Gorman (1978). 'Soil disturbance caused by skyline cable logging on steep slopes in West Virginia.' *Journal of Soil and Water Conservation* 33 (1): 2–35.

Phillips, B. (1980). 'An analysis of a timber harvesting operation's impact and effects on a basalt lithic scatter in N.E. Oregon: a synopsis.' Unpublished report, Bureau of Land Management State Office, Portland.

Power, W.E. (1974). 'Effects and observations of soil compaction in the Salem district.' *U.S. Department of the Interior, Bureau of Land Management Technical Note* 256, Oregon.

Read, R.A. (1957). 'Effect of livestock concentration on surface-soil porosity within shelterbelts.' *Journal of Forestry* 55: 529–530.

Reckendorf, F.F. and R.B. Parsons (1966). 'Soil development over a hearth in Willamette Valley, Oregon.' *Northwest Science* 40 (2): 46–55.

Redman, C.L. and P.J. Watson (1970). 'Systematic, intensive surface collection.' *American Antiquity* 35 (3): 279–291.

Rich, L.R. and J.G. Reynolds (1963). 'Grazing in relation to runoff and erosion on some chaparral watersheds of central Arizona.' *Journal of Range Management* 16: 322–326.

Rick, J.W. (1976). 'Downslope movement and archaeological intrasite spatial analysis.' *American Antiquity* 41 (2): 133–144.

Roney, J. (1977). 'Livestock and lithics: the effects of trampling' Unpublished report, Bureau of Land Management, Nevada State Office.

Roper, D.C. (1976). 'Lateral displacement of artifacts due to plowing.' *American Antiquity* 41 (3): 372–375.

Schiffer, M.B. (1972). 'Archaeological context and systemic context.' *American Antiquity* 37 (2): 156–165.

Schiffer, M.B. (1976). *Behavioral archeology*. New York: Academic Press.

Schiffer, M.B. (1977). 'Toward a unified science of the cultural past.' In S. South (ed,), *Research strategies in historical archeology*. New York: Academic Press, 13–40.

Schiffer, M.B. and J.H. House (1975a). 'Direct impacts of the channelization project on the archeological resources.' In M.B. Schiffer and J.H. House (eds), *The Cache River archeological project, Arkansas Archeological Survey, Research Series No. 8*, 273–275.

Schiffer, M.B. and J.H. House (1975b). 'Indirect impacts of the channelization project on the archeological resources.' In M.B. Schiffer and J.H. House (eds), *The Cache River archeological project, Arkansas Archeological Survey, Research Series No. 8*, 277–282.

Sheridan, D. (1979). *Off-road vehicles on public land*. Washington, D.C.: Council on Environmental Quality.

Silen, R.R. and H.J. Gratkowski (1953). 'An estimate of the amount of road in the staggered setting system of clearcutting.' *Pacific Northwest Forest and Range Experiment Station Research Note* No. 92.

Smith, R.B. and E.F. Wass (1976). 'Soil disturbance, vegetative cover and regeneration on clearcuts in the Nelson Forest District, British Columbia.' *Canada Pacific Forest Research Center Information Report* BC-X-151. Fisheries and Environment Canada, Canadian Forestry Service.

Snyder, C.T., D.G. Frickel, R.F. Hadley et al. (1976). 'Effects of off-road vehicle use on the hydrology and landscape of arid environments in central and southern California. *Water Resources Investigations* 76–99. ' U.S. Geological Survey.

Switzer, R.R. (1974). 'The effects of forest fire on archaeological sites in Mesa Verde National Park, Colorado.' *The Artifact* 12: 1–8.

Talmage, V., O. Chesler, and Interagency Archeological Services staff (1977). *The importance of small, surface, and disturbed sites as sources of significant archeological data*. Cultural Resource Management Studies. National Park Service, Washington, D.C.

Traylor, D., L. Hubbell, N. Wood et al. (1979). 'The La Mesa fire study: investigation of fire and fire suppression impact on cultural resources in Bandelier National Monument.' Unpublished report, National Park Service, Santa Fe.

United States Congress (1979). *House report* No. 96-311.

United States Department of Agriculture (1978). 'Predicting rainfall erosion losses.' *Agricultural Handbook* No. 537. Washington, D.C: U.S. Government Printing Office.

Utzig, G., and L. Herring (1975). 'Forest harvesting impacts at high elevations: five case studies.' *British Columbia Forest Service Research Note* No. 72.

Webb, R.H., H.C. Ragland, W.H. Godwin et al. (1978). 'Environmental effects of soil property changes with off-road vehicle use.' *Environmental Management* 2 (3): 219–233.

Wells, C.G. et al. (1979). *Effects of fire on soil: a state-of-knowledge review, U.S. Department of Agriculture, Forest Service General Technical Report* WO-7.

Wildesen, L.E. (1977). 'Analysis of project-related impacts on archaeological resources.' Unpublished manuscript Pacific Northwest Region, U.S. Department of Agriculture, Forest Service.

Wildesen, L.E. (1982) 'The study of impacts on archaeological sites', *Advances in Archaeological Method and Theory*, 5: 51–96.

Williams, L.R. (1978). 'Vandalism to cultural resources of the Rocky Mountain west.' *Cultural Resources Report* No. 21. U.S. Department of Agriculture, Forest Service, Southwestern Region, Albuquerque, New Mexico.

Wood, J.S. (1979). 'Chaparral conversion and cultural resources on the Prescott National Forest: an experimental study of the impacts of surface mechanical treatment by Marden brush-crusher.' *Cultural Resource Report* No. 27. U.S. Department of Agriculture, Forest Service, Southwestern Region, Albuquerque, New Mexico.

Wooldridge, D.D. (1960). 'Watershed disturbance from tractor and skyline crane logging.' *Journal of Forestry* 58 (5): 369–372.

Chapter 10

Decay and mitigation of rock art and cave sites

Definition

Depictions, whether *pictograms* (images of recognisable things, such as human beings or animals), *ideograms* (symbols with discernible meaning) or *psychograms* (images/symbols without meaning), have occasionally survived either as *petroglyphs* (pecked or engraved into the stone surface) or *pictographs*, which are either *drawn* (applied dried pigments, e.g. burnt end of a stick making a charcoal mark) or *painted* (wet pigment applied often with a binder) on to a rock surface (Anati 2010). Some incised petroglyph designs have pigment added to highlight them. The term rock art is used for convenience to refer to pictographs and petroglyphs, though rock imagery may be more appropriate (Dean et al. 2006: 11). Given the age of many rock art images, the detailed meaning may never be known to us, and ethnographic evidence indicates that meanings change over time. The presence of offerings left at some sites indicates that these images facilitated communication with supernatural powers, a tradition that continues to the present day (Bahn 2010: 160–9; Dean, pers. comm.). Ethnographic parallels suggest that specific ceremonies, shamanistic rituals, vision quests, initiations and activities such as circumcision may have taken place at these sites, which can have great social value/meaning. The currently degraded state of images can make them difficult to accurately read (RAR 1996: 55) and record (see Figure 10.0.1); their symbolic nature makes them difficult to understand. Differences between the experiences of their creators and those of present-day viewers make them difficult to interpret accurately.

Though some pigments and binders from cave art have been dated by C^{14} AMS as well as OSL dating of quartz grains (Aubert 2012), frequently it is the nature of the depicted image that is the evidence for dating, thus horses in American art indicate their creation post-European contact. The nature of the images and the style of their depiction often indicate the cultural affiliations of the artist.

Pictographs normally only survive on the internal surfaces of caves, shelters, tombs or buildings. Large groups of pictographs are seen in the Upper Palaeolithic caves of Europe, mainly France and Spain. More recently, images have been created by Native American and

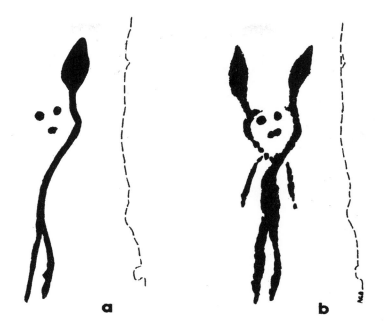

Figure 10.0.1 (a) Peterborough petroglyph as initially recorded and as infilled with wax crayon, identified as a picture of a snake and three snake eggs. (b) The same petroglyph as it appears when examined closely and recorded (photographed) in oblique light (Bahn et al. 1995).

Source: Image courtesy of Robert G. Bednarik

Australian Aboriginal peoples in shelters, rather than caves. Petroglyphs have been executed by many cultures; those in Scandinavia, Europe and North America have been the most extensively studied. They survive on exposed and protected rock surfaces, on bedrock and on smaller boulders, decreasing in size to eventually be portable decoration/sculpture. Though the earliest pictographs are applied directly to the rock surface, later civilisations in Egypt, China and India painted the art on lime, gypsum or clay plastered on to the walls of rock-cut tombs and buildings (see Chapter 6).

The archaeological value of the image is often so high that efforts are made to preserve it *in situ*. In some cases, the intangible cultural values (beliefs) preclude actions to preserve the ancient image, either allowing it to degrade or be remade (repainted). Expressed simply, the traditional 'Western' approach to rock images was as art; the image was everything. In some early cases, images were cut out and removed to museums; later, structures or barriers were erected to protect the images. For Aboriginal and other native cultures, the images are part of the landscape and the culture; separating them from the landscape removes their meaning/purpose, as does disconnecting them from dances or ceremonies, their social context (Mowaljarlai et al. 1988). Rock art sites have been extensively studied (ICOMOS 2012) and are sometimes one of the few remaining traces of long vanished cultures. In 2002, there were 13 sites or groups of rock art sites in the World Heritage List (Clottes 2002).

The present distribution of pictographs and petroglyphs is principally a function of differential preservation and not their original presence. Pictographs are nowadays largely confined to caves or rock shelters; Bahn (1986) and others have suggested that originally, graved, drawn and painted images were present throughout the landscape, and many external petroglyph sites were originally pictographs whose pigment has subsequently weathered away. The vast majority of such glyphs in Britain are now present in the harder sandstones and metamorphic and igneous rocks of the north and west of Britain; few are seen in the clay, chalk and limestone of the south and east. They may well have been present in prehistory, but have since degraded and been lost, as have the numerous examples that would have originally been present on wood and other perishable materials.

Decay and damage

Decay processes can break up or spall off the exterior surface of the rock of the pictographs/petroglyphs or they can damage, remove or obscure the pigment (and any associated binder) of pictographs. Anything that touches (impacts) the surface dislodges pigment or damages the rock surface. Many attempts to preserve images have failed due to poor characterisation of the rock, inadequate understanding of the decay processes or a lack of resources. The problems of decay, especially problems of 'negative human impacts', have been described and imaged by authors such as Rosenfeld (1988), Lambert (1994), Bahn (2010) and Darvill and Fernandes (2014), and other references in ICOMOS (2012).

Principal natural decay processes include:

- *Freeze thaw*: growth of ice crystals in pores and microcracks beneath the surface. Rocks with uneven pore sizes grow a few large ice crystals, which tend to spall off the surface of the rock; those with even pore sizes have numerous smaller ice crystals, which is far less damaging. This process is responsible for the scree slopes of mountains, and can thus be highly damaging. However, the presence of petroglyphs and the marks of glaciers on rock surfaces that have suffered repeated freeze/thaw cycles over thousands of years does mean that it is not damaging in every case.
- *Soluble salts*: salts that readily dissolve in water (such as sodium chloride) are drawn to the rock surface where the water evaporates and the salts crystallise. This can occur on the surface (efflorescence), gradually breaking it up, or it can occur beneath the surface in cracks and fissures (cryptoflorescence), causing the surface to spall off. The relative humidity of the air in the cave/shelter will determine the evaporation rate. A stable relative humidity = low evaporation rate and few salts form; fluctuating relative humidity is much, much more damaging.
- *Crust formation*: very gradually, minerals with low solubility can be drawn to the rock surface through wetting and evaporation processes. These can redeposit the mineral (cement) in the exterior layers of rock (case), hardening the surface but weakening the area behind which, depending on the rate and extent of the cement movement, can lead to detachment of the rock (contour scaling). Alternatively, the minerals can be drawn out and deposited on the surface of the rock, forming a crust. Minerals deposited on the surface include:
  - Calcium carbonate, which covers the surface and any associated images in a white crust (*maladie blanche*) is a common problem in limestone caves. Changes in the temperature and carbon dioxide levels in the cave can lead to the precipitation of calcium carbonate out of solution.
  - Silica, which builds up very gradually, often forms a transparent layer that can bind pigments to the surface and protect them, though it can also be white and obscure the image.

- Iron oxides create a red, orange or yellow crust in or on the surface.
- Gypsum (calcium sulphate) covers the surface in a white crust.

Where these minerals incorporate dust, they form a black crust.
- *Water flow*: running over the surface can wear away the surface of the rock, dislodging rock grains and dissolving minerals. Dripping from roofs or overhanging trees, it wears away the surface. Low levels of water seepage can lead to surface mineral formation; in limestone rocks, this leads to stalagmite and stalactite formation.
- *Dust*: driven by wind or kicked up by people and animals deposits on cave and shelter walls, obscuring the images. Where mineral cement exudes from the rock, this dust can become a permanently obscuring surface crust.
- *Bacterial growth*: bacteria are present on the surface of the rock; where there is nutrient-rich water available, bacterial levels increase. Bacteria can excrete oxalic acid, leading to the gradual formation of oxalate mineral crusts, such as whewellite, on the rock surface. They can also excrete 2-ketogluconic acid, which solubilises silica (Rosenfeld 1988: 39). The types and number of bacteria present will depend on the rock and environmental conditions, but their actions are very slow.
- *Algae*: grow on wet/damp rock surfaces and where there is a light source present. They can cover surfaces and obscure images very quickly (St. Clair and Seaward 2004).
- *Lichens (symbiotic combination of fungi and algae)*: similar to algae, though lichens are normally seen on exterior surfaces and can tolerate drier conditions. They penetrate pores and fissures, forming a very thin reaction zone (nm scale) with the rock surface; they damage more extensively if actively removed (Florian 1978; St. Clair and Seaward 2004).
- *Mosses, plants*: various forms of plant can live on rock surfaces; again, light and a source of water is needed to sustain life. Higher plants have root systems that can tear rock surfaces apart; trees are especially damaging.
- *Birds, bats and insects*: live on rock surfaces either in crevices or forming nests on the surface. They can obscure images with nests or excreta.
- *Cattle, sheep, goats and many wild animals*: live in caves and shelters and abrade images off walls as they scratch or rub up against the rock or lick it to obtain salts. The presence of animals can lead to a build-up of excreta or soil, burying the lower parts of images resulting in their demise.

Much damage has been done by human interaction. In addition to the total loss of sites through quarrying or development (see Chapter 2), damage occurs through:

- *Touching*: in visited caves, touching by numerous visitors wears away the fragile paint or rock surface.
- *Occupation*: rubbing against the walls wearing off images, people living in the cave can lead to a build-up of soil, burying the lower parts of images, resulting in their demise.
- *Fire*: in the cave for light or heat, scorch the rock surface that spalls off or is covered with soot. Where fire is set or occurs naturally in the landscape, exposed rock surfaces fracture due to heat expansion leaving them friable and susceptible to freeze thaw and other forms of damage, as occurred at Fylingdales Moor (Lee 2010).
- *Vandalism*: deliberate mutilation of the surface, usually graffiti, the reasons for which are human and social. Bahn (2010) provides many examples of deliberate damage.
- *Looting*: removing the image for personal gratification or financial gain.

- *Highlighting*: some shallow petroglyphs are picked out by chalk or paint to make them clearer to visitors; this prevents any possibility of identifying any original pigment and potentially physically damages the image (Bednarik 1987). It should be noted that visitors to rock art sometimes highlight the design themselves if it is obscure, to aid their own appreciation of the art as well as that of others.
- *Rubbing or moulding*: attempting to copy petroglyph images, rubbings or moulding have often been made. This damages the images; rubbing wears away and pressure flakes off the rock surface. This is particularly true for moulding the image; moulding compounds such as rubber latex can grip and pull out the rock grains from the image surface, while silicon rubber can also leave a residue. Any remaining original pigment could be pulled out of these glyphs through such techniques and/or contaminants introduced (Bahn 2010: 180–84).
- *Conservation*: attempts to preserve the images end up damaging them; for example, application of chemicals to kill plant or algal growth may lead to soluble salt problems.
- *Visitors*: viewing pictographs in caves has led to the introduction of lights, and the presence of visitors raises the temperature and increases the carbon dioxide content, as well as bringing microbes (fungal and algal spores) with them and kicking up dust. All of this can sometimes lead to algal and fungal growth on the rock surface and the formation of calcium carbonate crusts, which obscure the very images they came to see.

Given the severity of human impacts, remoteness from human beings is often a key reason for the survival of rock art sites.

Damage is often synergistic (i.e. one decay mechanism or product triggers another, leading to a damaging cascade effect). In many cases, sequences of decay are triggered by sudden short-term changes, such as the fire that swept over the Fylingdales Moor in North Yorkshire in 2003, exposing nearly 200 rocks with petroglyphs. Some were damaged by the heat, while many more, denuded of vegetation, were exposed to the synergistic depredations of inquisitive visitors and the effects of weathering. This led to the need for quick accurate recording of the petroglyphs, and there were efforts to hide (overturning, burying or removing) decorated stones in an effort to 'preserve' them. The protective nature of the vegetative mat and the potentially damaging effect of flail cutters that in earlier years had cut down the heather for harvesting or creating firebreaks became evident (Sharpe *et al.* 2008: 21; Lee 2010).

Exposed exterior petroglyphs

Mitigation

In the second half of the twentieth century, many newly emergent and resource-poor countries in desert and semi-desert areas, such as Algeria, struggled to cope with a vast number of fragile rock art sites present in the country (Hachid 1987). The importance of these sites for creating national identity was often reflected in the laws passed to protect the sites, but with few personnel to enforce the law, limited knowledge of the new laws, few trained personnel to evaluate the sites and limited resources to protect or conserve them, the ability to preserve such sites was limited. Without detailed records of all sites in a usable archive, it was/is not possible to identify the most important sites and focus the limited resources available on them. For all heritage authorities, the loss of many rock art sites to vandalism or natural decay has emphasised that the greatest need that exposed petroglyph sites have is for accurate recording and the establishment of permanent archives for those records. It can be argued that it is important to make information publicly available (e.g. websites such as the England's Rock Art website, http://archaeologydataservice.ac.uk/era/, Trust for African Rock Art or the UCLA Rock Archive). Finding and recording rock art can be achieved by volunteers as well as professionals (Barnett and Sharpe 2010). Accurate recording requires survey to record the location, written description using standardised terminology, drawings of the images and photography, and ideally stereoscopic pairs of photographs to provide a basic 3D image (Bryan 2010). All petroglyphs should be photographed in raking light in several orientations in order to reveal the shallow surface indentations, ideally with multiple images for Reflective Transformation Imaging. Infrared and UV images of pictographs may reveal more information as some pigments adsorb IR radiation or fluoresce under UV light. Since moulding process can potentially cause damage to petroglyphs, non-contact photographic recording is preferred to minimise risk to the object. If direct record needs to be made, permanent marker on transparent (polyester) film is preferable. Despite its high cost, a full record is increasingly being seen as best provided by a laser-scanned image, since this record is a detailed 3D image, capable of being used to accurately monitor degradation or create 3D physical images for display using CAM systems or 3D printers. It is possible to create replicas and bury or remove original stones if there are persistent problems with active erosion or vandalism. Trained volunteers are increasingly used to record petroglyphs, so building up large databases of rock art (Clottes 2006; Barnett and Sharpe 2010) that can include assessments of the rock art condition and the risks it faces.

Mitigation: controlling visitation

The balance between preservation through remoteness and the need to raise awareness of rock art sites, and so increase their value to justify funding for protection of sites, is demonstrated by efforts to protect the rock art sites of the Sierra de San Francisco, Baja, California (de la Luz Gutierrez *et al*. 1996). Here, a National Park was established to allow local controls on access to the rock art sites to be established/enforced. A classification of sites was established to both control and enable access. Some already well-known and easily reached sites were designated Category I and could be publicly visited. Fences and walkways were installed to guide the visitors. Category II sites were only visitable using mules and with guides. The size of parties and camping facilities were limited. Category III sites required permission (requested at least six months in advance) before they could be visited, and Category IV sites were only able to be visited by accredited researchers with formal permission. The grading of these sites derived from the cultural importance as well as the fragility of the site. As the beneficial effect of remoteness reduced, so the protection from the law and regulation was increasingly used.

In general, petroglyph sites are managed by fencing to keep animals out, erecting rails to keep visitors from walking on the rock surface, and notices to inform visitors about the meaning and extent of the images and make them aware of the protected nature of the site. Rails act as psychological barriers defining the permitted and the not permitted areas. Limiting their size and height and placing them in an appropriate position avoids visual intrusion and visitor antagonism but provides guidance that is heeded by the vast majority of the visiting public. Providing clear details about the site (true nature of the images, date and culture that created them and an indication of what the rock means, to the extent we understand it) seems to aid positive visitor response (Lambert 1994: 37–40; Darvill *et al*. 2000: 138–9). Information helps them to value what they are seeing. Since rock art sites often occur in groups, archaeological parks, as at Alta (Norway) or Coa (Portugal), have been created to protect and promote such groups (Clottes 2002: 132). Alternatively, walks between groups of local sites, with associated signs, leaflets and other facilities, have been developed, as at Fylingdales, North York Moors (UK) (Lee 2010: 101). Erecting buildings over petroglyph sites, as at Peterborough (Canada) and Besovy Sledki (Russia), remains controversial since it dissociates the glyphs from their landscape. It only occurs where the continued preservation of the site is threatened, though it did not prove effective at Aspeberget in Sweden (Bahn and Hygen 1996). At such sites, there is a great increase in the potential for public viewing and education (Bahn et al. 1995; RAR 1996; Wainwright 1996; Wainwright et al. 1997).

Managing expectation

In Scandinavian countries, chalking or painting petroglyph designs to enable them to be seen is considered acceptable; in others, such as the UK, it is not (Bahn et al. 1995; RAR 1996). Some Scandinavian sites such as Aspeberget in Sweden and Østfold in Norway have had paint applied to pick out the glyphs. This practice is considered part of a role of educating and engaging local people with petroglyphs. Given the large number of petroglyphs, their proximity to large numbers of people, and with no other form of safeguarding that could be afforded, maintaining the social valuation of this art is the only effective method of protection available. That said, painting only occurs on around 4 per cent of sites, and such practices are generally decreasing (Hygen 1996; Clottes 2006: 9). At Bulgandry, Gosford (Australia) and at one example from Peterborough (Canada), the glyphs were cleaned, removing colouring material, though the cleaned images then clearly stood out from the background rock. Repeated chalking, painting or cleaning will damage the surface, as will walking over rocks to undertake these activities, there is concern that if authorities do not make the image visible, the public will take matters into their own hands. This happened at Bulgandry, and visitors significantly damaged the images as they highlighted them (Lambert 1994: 56–7; Hygen 1996; Darvill et al. 2000: 137–8). Colouring/highlighting selected images (Hygen 1996), removing modern crayon and other colouring materials (Wainwright 1996) or leaving the present colouring materials *in situ* but preventing any further colouring (RAR 1996) have all been advocated. The removal of paint, crayon or chalk graffiti from over petroglyphs or marker pen, soot, mud or other pigments from pictographs in cave and shelter sites is one of the primary activities of conservators at rock art sites (Rosenfeld 1988; Dean et al. 2006).

Cleaning

Especially with external glyphs, weathering erosion continues and low levels of decay must continue to be expected. 'It's often inappropriate and frankly pointless to try and stave off natural deterioration' (Dean et al. 2006: 11). Before any substantial conservation intervention, there is always a need to document the extent and rate of decay. This will help to justify considerable conservation expenditure, lead to clearly defined aims for any conservation actions and prevent subsequent discussion happening without a clear appreciation of the 'what would have happened if nothing was done' scenario (Bahn et al. 1995; RAR 1996; Wainwright 1996; Wainwright et al. 1997).

The current approach of English Heritage to exposed rock art sites is to 'leave as found' (Sharpe et al. 2008). Visitors are encouraged not to clean rocks (e.g. by removing lichen from the surface) or enhance the visibility of glyphs by chalking the images or taking rubbings, as sites have been damaged or worn away from such activities (Lambert 1994: 48). There is evidence that lichen, which certainly can be visually intrusive, is both damaging to the surface of some rocks (Rosenfeld 1988: 64) and protective for others (Jefferson and Jefferson 2010); however, lichen removal can often damage or weaken the stone surface. It is increasingly appreciated that rock surfaces exposed to the weather build up a hardened surface that protects them, and exposed glyphs should therefore be left exposed for public visitation. Equally, those that are covered with turf or vegetation should similarly be left covered; exposing these to make a larger monument may well lead to increased rates of decay, as the rock surface may have been weakened by root action and chemical decay and cannot now stand exposure to weather without accelerated rates of degradation. Surviving glyphs have invariably reached some form of equilibrium with their surrounding environment, exposed to weather or buried beneath the soil. Any disturbance, whether physical, chemical or biological, can start a phase of accelerated decay until a new equilibrium is established – though this may only be after considerable damage has been done to the surface.

Pictographs and petroglyphs in shelters and caves

Lascaux

The saga of attempts to preserve the images in this cave echo loud and long in the short history of preservation *in situ*. The cave contains over 150 paintings and 1,500 engravings, created in a single sequence c.17,000 years ago, which were protected soon after their creation by a rock collapse at the cave entrance that sealed the site. After discovery in 1940, the cave was soon open to the public and maintained as a public attraction for 23 years. The installation of lighting and, in 1958, air conditioning meant that by 1960, the images were being enjoyed by up to 2,000 visitors a day (Delluc and Delluc 1984). Subsequently, the presence of a green algal biofilm over the surfaces (*maladie verte*) led to the closure of the cave to the public in 1963. Treated with formalin solution, the algal growth was suppressed, and thereafter 25 people per week were permitted to visit the cave. However, the cave was by then starting to exhibit evidence of calcite crystal growth (*maladie blanche*) over its walls, a product of the high CO_2 levels from visitors. It was subsequently permanently closed to the public in 1972. In 2001, there was an outbreak of the fungus *Fusarium solani* and the allied bacterium *Pseudomonas fluorescens* associated with the earth and clay bank surfaces in the cave. These were treated with applications of quicklime and antibiotics. Subsequently, black stains on the ceiling, which had noticeably increased by 2007, were identified as melanised fungi. In more recent tests, a wide range of fungi (Aspergillus niger, *Penicillium spp*) and bacteria (*Ralstonia spp*. and *Pseudomonas spp.*) have been found in the cave, as well as higher forms of life, amoebae and arthropods. Researchers are now aware that caves have microbiological ecosystems that adapt to changing conditions (Bastian and Alabouvette 2009); once the public are admitted to a cave, the preservative ecosystem is lost, and one adapted to human presence (light, heat, high humidity, high carbon dioxide levels and human detritus), which may imperil the art, slowly establishes. Similar problems have been noted at the cave of Altamira, which had reduced visitor numbers from 1982 and was closed permanently in 2002 because of phototrophic microorganisms on the painting surfaces. At Altamira, chemicals have not been used; excluding light, and carbon and nitrogen sources to re-establish the preserving conditions, has been the approach (Saiz-Jimenez *et al.* 2011). It remains difficult to make an effective assessment of the threat that visitors pose to cave ecosystems and what, if any, represents a safe level of visitation. Since in France many caves are owned privately or by local communities, who derive economic benefits from visitors, there is clearly a direct conflict between employment (wealth creation) and the preservation of the paintings. The cave site at Pech Merle had a limit of 700 people per day set by the French Ministry of Culture (68,000–69,000 visitors in 1985) (Lorblanchet 1986), though most other cave sites had much lower visitor limits of 35–500 per day; at Niaux, it is as few as 20 per day (Clottes and Chippindale 1999).

Vandalism: graffiti and looting

Graffiti (visual communication that uses words, symbols or images inscribed, drawn or painted on to surfaces, not initially/formally intended for such inscription) is usually seen as an assertion of personal identity or belief by the less powerful members of society (Macdonald 2002; Baird and Taylor 2011). Graffiti occurs where it can be privately created but has a public audience – public toilets or the inconspicuous corners of public areas. It often attracts responses – a dialogue (Baird and Taylor 2011: 7–8). It also occurs where other graffiti is present, which may be the reason numerous rock art sites have attracted modern graffiti, whose perpetrators presumably understand the ancient pictographs and petroglyphs in their own cultural envelope as graffiti, and feel able to add and comment on the previous image (enter the dialogue).

There are a variety of views on how to deal with this problem. Some suggest that keeping sites secret will prevent their defacement, while others suggest that if sites are well known, the regular passage of visitors will police the site and prevent opportunities for graffiti (Gale and Jacobs 1987; Marymor 2001). There is some evidence that providing alternative means of expressions, such as a book, can lead to a reduction in graffiti (Lambert 1994: 36; Darvill *et al*. 2000: 136). Most of the efforts of rock art conservators, such as Claire Dean working in North America, are spent removing graffiti (Rosenfeld 1988; Dean *et al*. 2006). Though Australian sites were plagued by graffiti in the mid-twentieth century, by the early years of the twenty-first century the problems of graffiti had reduced, probably as a result of education, as well as laws with stiff legal penalties that were actively enforced (Dean *et al*. 2006). Volunteers or part-time employees can monitor sites, and have been shown to reduce vandalism and graffiti (Dean *et al*. 2006). The second form of vandalism is looting (for personal gratification or financial gain) (Bahn 2010: 176–80), where the image is cut out or damaged trying.

The imposition of graffiti on sites must be clearly distinguished from the remaking (repainting) of images at traditional sites by practitioners of the beliefs that are represented by the images. Samples with over 40 layers of paint in a 5 mm thick fragment sampled from the Kimberley's (Australia) (Rosenfeld 1988: 11) attest the repeated nature of this practice. The modern-day repainting of the historic Wandjina figures in the Kimberley area (Australia) circa 1987 by unemployed Aboriginal teenagers, under tutelage by tribal elders, was described by Bowdler (1988), but raised issues about how such actions should be instigated, who should approve them and on what basis.

Mitigation at cave sites

Given the problems of deliberate damage highlighted above (Bahn 2010) and damage caused unintentionally by large numbers of visitors revealed by Lascaux, the first line of defence is to keep the location of the cave art site secret (Dragovich 1986: 144; Bahn 2010: 184). Even if sites are known, it is possible to hide them again by removing signs, removing tracks and not providing any mention of them in publicly available information. This was successfully enacted at Carnarvon Gorge in Queensland, but attempts to hide access to the Feast Group petroglyph at Gosford, New South Wales, failed (Lambert 1994: 35; Darvill *et al*. 2000: 132). Once discovered, there is urgency to record the images in detail and protect them as quickly as possible in case of vandalism, looting or damage, as happened to the image of a reindeer discovered in 2011 scratched in a barely accessible part of a cave on the Gower Peninsula in South Wales. This was the oldest piece of Palaeolithic art identified in the UK, but it was vandalised before it could be fully recorded and even before its location was publicly revealed or it could be protected (Stonepages 2012). This demonstrates the reluctant necessity for protecting caves containing rock art with unsightly locked steel doors and grills at the entrances, as well as placing severe restrictions on the dissemination of information. In France in 1986, there were 135 caves with Palaeolithic art; only 24 were open to the public (Clottes 1986). While closed cave systems can be sealed with gates and grilles, Bahn (1986) has suggested that looters can and sometimes do force access into some of these caves. While such gates may be effective in the narrow-entranced caves of France, the more open caves and shelters of North America and Australia can make limited use of this technique; instead, they must use mesh screening across the front of the rock surface to protect the art from being touched (Lambert 1994: 40). Conceptually, it is preferable not to 'jail' the art behind bars and mesh; it fails to preserve any sense of place and the other aspirations of the Burra Charter (see Chapter 5.5). In practice, there may be few other options, and bars and meshes can always be removed at a later date. Indigenous peoples using the cave art as part of their culture may have strong views, either on restricting access to the images or making the location public.

Heritage authorities are often prepared to allow cave locations to remain secret, or for them to be securely locked and public access denied, provided that there are alternative caves that facilitate public visitation. Remote locations help keep some sites secret and secure; often those sites closer to human access or those that are already known and have facilities and a reputation are pragmatically often the ones chosen for public visitation. To protect the art at visited cave and rock art sites, but allow visitors reasonably close to the images, walkways have been installed at a number of sites such as Alta (Norway), Cresswell Craggs (UK), Carnarvon Gorge (Australia) and Tandjiesberg (South Africa) (Lambert 1994: 41–5; Darvill *et al*. 2000: 134–6). These allow control of the exact distance between the visitor and the art. Walkways need to be well designed, with places to photograph and study the art. They also need to be sturdy, secure, long-lasting and safe to use; consequently, they are more expensive than rails, meshes or grills. They also preserve the cave floor deposits, as at Mulka's Cave (Rossi and Webb 2007) (see Chapter 12.1), which are fragile and threatened by wear and loss from the footfall of numerous visitors (Deacon 1995). Control can also be achieved through ensuring people go through the cave in guided parties. At such sites, a low rail or similar barrier in front of the art is used to guide with the minimum of visual intrusion. In restricted places where the art could be touched or brushed, metal grills over the art allow it to be seen but prevent intentional/unintentional touching (Lambert 1994: 35–7; Darvill *et al*. 2000: 133–4). In all cave sites, you only need to illuminate the art when visitors are present. This can be achieved by giving visitors torches or lights on helmets, or where permanent lighting is installed it can be switched on or off by guides or triggered by infrared devices detecting the heat or movement of people. The absence of light reduces the risk of algal growth.

The increasing body of evidence regarding the problems that visitors can cause in the stable cave environments, from Altamira to Mogao, in 2010 (Maekawa et al. 2010) has led to drastically reduced numbers allowed to visit the actual caves and the emergence and popularity of reproductions. In the case of Lascaux, a replica cave (Lascaux II) was created in a nearby quarry, exactly replicating in textured and pigmented concrete parts of the original cave with exact copies of the paintings (Delluc and Delluc 1984). Opened in 1983, by 1986 it was being visited by 300,000 people a year, indicating the interest in cave art. Other sites have developed alternative visitor experiences; the Parc Pyrénéen d'Art Préhistorique near the cave of Niaux explores the meaning and making of prehistoric rock art (Clottes and Chippindale 1999), though such attractions require costly investment; alternatively, virtual tours are available from the websites of a number of caves.

The more the visitors value the art and understand its fragility, the lower the need for protection and the lower the risk to the site posed by visitors. Thus, most cave sites attempt to both protect the art and educate the visiting public. Information and understanding can be provided through notices on site. In locations with a museum or visitor centre, films or exhibitions can inform in more detail before the visitor sees the cave. The most expensive but meaningful education is provided verbally by a guide. The more education that can be achieved, the less the need for protection; the less education, the more need for protection. It is far harder to educate large numbers of people passing through the attraction quickly, but much easier with a small group and a dedicated guide.

Conservation

Early attempts to retain the paint flaking from surfaces by impregnating with a consolidant have often failed to solve the problem in the longer term. Where that consolidant blocked the pores of the plaster or stone and sealed the surface, the situation often became worse, not better. Pressure to solve problems quickly and cheaply leads to the wrong answers and makes the situation worse. Only full understanding of the processes of decay will lead to a long-term resolution of the problems. Modern approaches focus on accurately identifying the agents and mechanisms of decay, and mitigation focuses on blocking or preventing the agents of decay impacting the pictographs and petroglyphs. The importance of maintaining a stable environment in tombs and caves and the impossibility of doing that with large numbers of visitors is becoming appreciated. Direct treatment of pigmented surfaces is rarely considered appropriate. Preference is always given to removing agents of decay, not only visitors, but also water flowing over the surface.

In 1978–1979 at the cave of Niaux (Ariège), there was a loss of images as a result of increased water flow (Bahn 1986, 2010). Though a natural phenomenon, activities that can trigger increased water flows (inappropriate farming methods) or alter water quality, e.g. raising nutrient or soluble salts levels (from fertilisers, road salt, etc.) or microbial levels (from faecal matter contamination), should be avoided. To counter threats of water running over image surfaces, artificial driplines can, where appropriate, be created in the vicinity of the image, using materials such as silicon rubber, to deflect the water (Rosenfeld 1988; Darvill et al. 2000).

Mogao Grottos

Not all cave sites have pictographs or petroglyphs images on the rock surface; some have layers of plaster (mud, gypsum or lime) covering the native rock, such as ancient Egyptian tombs, of which one of the best studied is that of Nefertari (Getty Conservation Institute 1992). Less well known but equally challenging, at over 250 locations principally along the Silk Road in eastern China there are groups of grottos, caves dug into the soft rock that form temples for Buddhist worship constructed principally between the Han and Tang Dynasties (second to ninth centuries AD), though they continued to be constructed and used well into the Qing Dynasty. They have extensive carved stone sculpture and painted decoration; many have mud plaster with a white kaolin outer coat, which is painted and covers the cave walls. The largest group occurs in the Dunhuang area, with a particular concentration at Mogao. Conservation by the Chinese government has been ongoing at this site since the 1940s (Jinshi 1997). More recently, multinational teams, including Getty Conservation Institute, have been involved (Agnew 1997, 2010). The challenges faced at the site include the crumbling cliff face, detaching paint, dust and erosion. In particular, efflorescent salts in the upper cave levels (a mixed salt solution, principally halite – sodium chloride – with a deliquescence point of 67 per cent) mean that in periods of rain or with large numbers of visitors, the relative humidity becomes high enough to start dissolution and recrystallisation cycles, leading to efflorescence on the surface of paint or plaster and disrupting the decoration, pushing it from the walls. As it is not possible to isolate the native rock from the natural water in its pores, like the rock-cut tombs of Egypt and the prehistoric caves of Europe, visitation will need to be heavily controlled if the paint or plaster is to be prevented from flaking off the walls. Earlier attempts at consolidation with polymers have failed to solve the problem (Agnew *et al.* 2010) and only more holistic solutions, which reproduce the stable environments that helped preserve the cave paintings for hundreds of years, appear likely to provide long-term preservation *in situ*.

Conclusion

The economic paradox for heritage – visitors can potentially damage the archaeological remains but visitors are required to generate funding to preserve the remains – is particularly acute for cave art. The arguments for excluding or severely limiting public access to some sites appear inescapable. Alternatively, external petroglyph sites demonstrate *par excellence* the problems of small archaeological sites widely dispersed over the landscape; they are challenging for a professional heritage agency to identify, protect and maintain in a cost-effective manner. Large-scale public awareness and education leading to social valuation would appear to be one approach. This can involve, or lead to, the use of volunteers to record and assess sites, run archives and engage in regular visitation and even basic maintenance.

Bibliography

Agnew, N. (ed.) (1997) *Conservation of Ancient Sites on the Silk Road: Proceedings of an International Conference on the Conservation of Grotto Sites*, Los Angeles, CA: Getty Conservation Institute.

Agnew, N. (ed.) (2010) *Conservation of Ancient Sites on the Silk Road: Proceedings of the Second International Conference on the Conservation of Grotto Sites*, Los Angeles, CA: Getty Conservation Institute.

Agnew, N., Maekawa, S. and Wei, S. (2010) 'Causes and mechanisms of deterioration and damage in Cave 85', in N. Agnew (ed.), *Conservation of Ancient Sites on the Silk Road: Proceedings of the Second International Conference on the Conservation of Grotto Sites*, Los Angeles, CA: Getty Conservation Institute, pp. 412–29.

Anati, E. (2010) *World Rock Art: The Primordial Language*, Oxford: Archaeopress.

Aubert, M. (2012) 'A review of rock art dating in the Kimberley, Western Australia', *Journal of Archaeological Science*, 39(3): 573–7.

Bahn, P. (1986) 'Comments', *Rock Art Research*, 3(2): 144–6.

Bahn, P. (2010) 'Mustn't crumble', in P. Bahn (ed.), *Prehistoric Rock Art: Polemics and Progress*, Cambridge: Cambridge University Press, pp. 170–97.

Bahn, P.G. Bednarik, R.G. and Steinbring., J. (1995) 'The Peterborough Petroglyph site: reflections on massive intervention in rock art', *Rock Art Research*, 12(1): 29–41.

Bahn, P.G. and Hygen, A-S. (1996) 'More on massive intervention: the Aspeberget Structure', *Rock Art Research*, 13(2): 137–8.

Baird, J.A. and Taylor, C. (2011) 'Ancient graffiti in context', in J.A. Baird and C. Taylor (eds), *Ancient Graffiti in Context*, London: Routledge, pp. 1–17.

Barnett, T. and Sharpe, K. (eds) (2010) *Carving a Future for British Rock Art: New Directions for Research, Management and Presentation*, Oxford: Oxbow.

Bastian, F. and Alabouvette, C. (2009) 'Lights and shadows on the conservation of a rock art cave: the case of Lascaux Cave', *International Journal of Speleology*, 38(1): 55–60.

Bednarik, R.G. (1987) 'The chalking of petrographs: a response', *La Pintura*, 15(2–3): 12–13.

Bowdler, S. (1988) 'Repainting Australian rock art', *Antiquity*, 62: 517–23.

Bryan, P.G. (2010) 'Three dimensional rock art recording: a lower cost "photogrammetric" approach revelations', in T. Barnett and K. Sharpe (eds), *Carving a Future for British Rock Art: New Directions for Research, Management and Presentation*, Oxford: Oxbow, pp. 2–10.

Clottes, J. (1986) 'Comments by Jean Clottes', *Rock Art Research*, 3(2) 148–9.

Clottes, J. (2002) *World Rock Art*, Los Angeles, CA: Getty.

Clottes, J. (2006) 'Rock art today', *The Getty Conservation Institute Newsletter*, 21(3): 5–9.

Clottes, J. and Chippindale, C. (1999) 'The Parc Pyrénéen d'Art Préhistorique, France: beyond replica and re-enactment in interpreting the ancient past', in P.G. Stone and P. Planel (eds), *The Constructed Past: Experimental Archaeology, Education and the Public*, London: Routledge, pp. 194–205.

Darvill, T. and Fernandes, A.P.B. (2014) *Open-Air Rock Art Conservation and Management*, London: Routledge.

Darvill, T., Ucko, P. and Gibson, A. (2000) *Rock Art Pilot Project*, London: English Heritage, Bournemouth University, Institute of Archaeology – UCL.

de la Luz Gutierrez, M., Hambleton, E., Hyland, J. et al. (1996) 'The management of World Heritage Sites in remote areas: the Sierra de San Francisco, Baja, California, Mexico', *Conservation and Managements of Archaeological Sites*, 1: 209–25.

Deacon, J. (1995) 'Promotion of a neglected heritage at Stone Age sites in the Western Cape, South Africa', *Conservation and Managements of Archaeological Sites*, 1: 75–86.

Dean, J.C., Flood, J., Van Tilburg, J.A. et al. (2006) 'Preserving a worldwide heritage: a discussion about rock art conservation', *The Getty Conservation Institute Newsletter*, 21(3): 10–15.

Delluc, B. and Delluc, G. (1984) 'Lascaux: a faithful copy', *Antiquity*, 58: 194–6.

Dragovich, D. (1986) 'A plague of locusts or manna from heaven? Tourists and conservation of cave art in southern France', *Rock Art Research*, 3(2): 141–4.

England's Rock Art (n.d.). http://archaeologydataservice.ac.uk/era/ (accessed August 2014).

Florian, M.L.E. (1978) 'A review: the lichen role in rock art – dating deterioration and control', in C. Pearson (ed.), *Conservation of Rock Art: Proceedings of an International Workshop on the Conservation of Rock Art, Perth, September 1977*, Sydney: ICCM, pp. 95–8.

Gale, F. and Jacobs, J.M. (1987) *Tourists and the National Estate: Procedures to Protect Australia's Heritage*, Canberra: Australian Government Publishing Service.

Getty Conservation Institute (1992) *In the Tomb of Nefertari: Conservation of the Wall Paintings*, Marina del Ray, CA: J. Paul Getty Museum.

Hachid, M. (1987) 'In situ archaeological heritage in Algeria: challenges and resources', in H. Hodges (ed.), *In-Situ Archaeological Conservation*, Mexico: Instituto Nacional de Antropologia e Historia & J. Paul Getty Trust, pp. 24–31.

Hygen, A-S. (1996) 'Conservation, intervention or destruction of rock art? Some Scandinavian experiences', *Rock Art Research*, 13(1): 49–52.

ICOMOS (2012) *Rock Art: A Bibliography*, Paris: ICOMOS, available at: www.icomos.org/en/home-doc/516-rock-art-bib2012 (accessed August 2014).

Jefferson, P. and Jefferson, D. (2010) 'Prehistoric rock art: a petrographic and geological assessment of the stone in order to identify the possible factors affecting the durability of the exposed carvings', in T. Barnett and K. Sharpe (eds), *Carving a Future for British Rock Art: New Directions for Research, Management and Presentation*, Oxford: Oxbow, pp. 102–22.

Jinshi, F. (1997) 'Fifty years of protection of the Dunhuang Grottoes', in N. Agnew (ed.), *Conservation of Ancient Sites on the Silk Road: Proceedings of an International Conference on the Conservation of Grotto Sites*, Los Angeles: Getty Conservation Institute, pp. 12–22.

Lambert, D. (1994) *Conserving Australian Rock Art: A Manual for Site Managers*, Canberra: Aboriginal Studies Press.

Lee, G. (2010) 'The Fylingdales fire site: archaeological revelations', in T. Barnett and K. Sharpe (eds), *Carving a Future for British Rock Art: New Directions for Research, Management and Presentation*, Oxford: Oxbow, pp. 94–101.

Lorblanchet, M. (1986) 'Comments by Michel Lorblanchet', *Rock Art Research*, 3(2): 152–5.

Macdonald, N. (2002) *The Graffiti Subculture: Youth, Masculinity and Identity in London and New York*, Basingstoke: Palgrave.

Maekawa, S., Gang, I., Ping, X. *et al.* (2010) 'Origins of moisture affecting the wall paintings in Cave 85', in N. Agnew (ed.), *Conservation of Ancient Sites on the Silk Road: Proceedings of the Second International Conference on the Conservation of Grotto Sites*, Los Angeles, CA: Getty Conservation Institute, pp. 464–70.

Marymor, L. (2001) *ARARA Guidelines for Managers of Rock Art Sites on Public Lands: Public Access*, available at: www.arara.org/Guidelines_Managers_Public_Lands.pdf (accessed September 2014).

Mowaljarlai, D., Vinnicombe, P., Ward, G.K. *et al.* (1988) 'Repainting images on rock art in Australia and the maintenance of Aboriginal culture', *Antiquity*, 62: 690–6.

RAR (1996) 'RAR debates', *Rock Art Research*, 13(1): 47–60.

Rosenfeld, A. (1988) *Rock Art Conservation in Australia*, Canberra: Australian Government Publishing Service.

Rossi, A. and Webb, R.E. (2007) 'The consequences of allowing unrestricted tourist access at an Aboriginal site in a fragile environment: the erosive effect of trampling', *Conservation and Management of Archaeological Sites*, 9(4): 219–36.

Saiz-Jimenez, C., Cuezva, S., Jurado, V. *et al.* (2011) 'Palaeolithic art in peril: policy and science collide at Altamira Cave', *Science*, 334: 42–3.

Sharpe, K., Barnett, T. and Rushton, S. (2008) *The Prehistoric Rock Art of England: Recording, Managing and Enjoying our Carved Heritage*, London: English Heritage.

St. Clair, L. and Seaward, M. (eds) (2004) *Biodeterioration of Stone Surfaces: Lichens and Biofilms as Weathering Agents of Rock and Cultural Heritage*, Dordrecht: Kluwer Academic.

Stonepages (2012) *Stronger Protection to Welsh Cave Art Site After Vandalism*, available at: www.stonepages.com/news/archives/004785.html (accessed August 2014).

Wainwright, I.N.M. (1996) 'Structure protects rock art in Petroglyphs Provincial Park, Ontario, Canada', *Rock Art Research*, 13(1): 52–3.

Wainwright, I.N.M., Sears, H. and Michalski, S. (1997) 'Design of a rock art protective structure at Petroglyphs Provincial Park, Ontario, Canada', *Journal of the Canadian Association for Conservation*, 22: 53–76.

Chapter 10.1

The consequences of allowing unrestricted tourist access at an Aboriginal site in a fragile environment
The erosive effect of trampling

Alana M. Rossi and R. Esmée Webb

Source: Rossi, A. and Webb, R.E. (2007) 'The consequences of allowing unrestricted tourist access at an Aboriginal site in a fragile environment: the erosive effect of trampling', *Conservation and Management of Archaeological Sites,* 9(4): 219–36.

Introduction

MULKA'S CAVE LIES 18 km north of Hyden and 300 km south-east of Perth on the eastern edge of the Wheatbelt in the Southwest of Western Australia (see Figure 10.1.1). The region is underlain by the Yilgarn Block, a massive craton of Late Precambrian shield. [...] The landscape is topographically monotonous: gently rolling expanses of very thick nutrient-deficient colluvium through which granite domes, such as The Humps, protrude for up to 100 m, forming notable landmarks.

Mulka's Cave is one of a number of massive boulders that weathered off The Humps in the early Tertiary (Twidale & Bourne 2004). Subsequently, the interior of the boulder eroded away, creating a large cavern whose walls and ceiling are covered in Aboriginal artwork, predominantly red and white hand stencils and handprints, plus some linear paintings. When the artwork first came to the attention of non-Aboriginal people is not known, but the cave was certainly visited in the late nineteenth century; some of the graffiti can be dated to 1893–1894. Visitors were probably rare before 1920, however, when Hyden was founded. Davidson, an American anthropologist, did visit the cave in the 1930s, but his research into the rock art of Western Australia had little, if any, impact on the general public, who were not, at that time, particularly interested in Aboriginal culture. In January 1951, however, Day (1951) described Mulka's Cave in *The West Australian* newspaper, bringing it to public attention as a place worth seeing. How many intrepid travellers visited the site during the next twenty years is unknown,

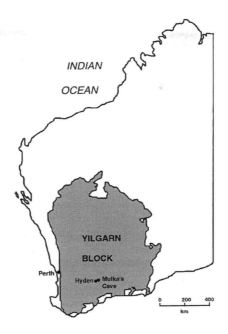

Figure 10.1.1 Location of Hyden on the Yilgarn Block, a craton of Archaean granite, in south-central Western Australia.

because no records were kept, but numbers were probably low because the site was then well off the beaten track. When the Western Australian Aboriginal Heritage Act became law in 1972, a Department of Aboriginal Sites (DAS) with responsibility for recording and maintaining places of cultural significance was created at the Western Australian Museum. Mulka's Cave (DIA site 5842) was entered onto the Permanent Register of Western Australian Aboriginal Sites soon after, as DAS staff began an audit of known sites. Randolph (1973) visited the site, then called Bates Cave, and stated that only two or three carloads of people were coming to the site annually.

In line with DAS policy at the time, which did not include Aboriginal consultation but did aim to make white Australians aware of the importance of Aboriginal sites, Mulka's Cave was opened to the general public in the 1970s. This was long before the Native Title Act (1999) became law or Land Councils were set up to represent Aboriginal people. Moreover, Aboriginal people did not then live in Hyden, but local (white) residents encouraged tourists to visit Mulka's Cave. They sought to attract visitors to their town by aggressively promoting Wave Rock, a natural granite weathering feature, as worth seeing. Mulka's Cave is 15 km north of Wave Rock.

[...]

DAS staff visited Mulka's Cave from time to time throughout the 1970s and 1980s. Like many Aboriginal sites in the Southwest, its walls were defaced with racist graffiti when land rights first became an issue in the 1960s and 1970s. As much as possible of the graffiti was removed (Randolph 1973; Haydock & Rodda 1986), and a low wooden post-and-rail fence, an explanatory sign, and a visitors' book were installed. A pamphlet about the site was produced and freely available in Hyden and other towns in the region.

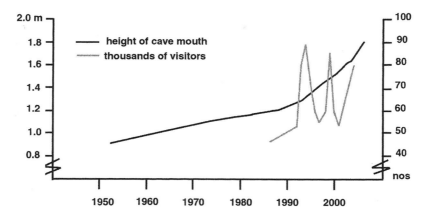

Figure 10.1.2 Estimated rate of erosion at the cave mouth graphed against visitor numbers.

By the late 1980s, however, DAS realized that the environs of Mulka's Cave were deteriorating due to over-visitation (Rodda 1989), although the full extent of the erosion was not appreciated. Nothing was done to halt the degradation, however, because the Western Australian government decided to remove DAS from the Museum and incorporate its personnel into the Aboriginal Affairs Department, now called the Department of Indigenous Affairs (DIA). In the process, staff were shed and those who remained found their freedom to conduct fieldwork curtailed. They enforcedly became bureaucrats, unable regularly to monitor sites like Mulka's Cave. Hence, conditions at the site continued to deteriorate while tourist numbers increased by an order of magnitude (see Figure 10.1.2).

In 2003–2004, tourist organizations in Hyden successfully sought funding from Canberra to upgrade the infrastructure at Mulka's Cave. A rock art researcher was asked to devise a management plan (Gunn 2003). He recommended moving the car park away from the site, installing a boardwalk in front of the cave, creating new interpretive signs, constructing walking tracks to other features of the site complex and revegetating denuded areas. An Aboriginal Steering Committee was set up by the DIA that included members of all the families with historic links to Mulka's Cave. This committee had to approve each stage of the management plan before it could be implemented. The artwork was recorded in detail in 2004 (Gunn 2006). Serventy (1952) had only published a brief description. Gunn (2006) recorded 275 hand stencils, 40 sprayed areas, 37 handprints, 23 paintings, three drawings and an object stencil. He considered the artwork to be (comparatively) 'ordinary' because hand stencils are ubiquitous across southern Australia. In 2005 the Mulka's Cave Aboriginal Steering Committee approved the installation of an elevated walkway, designed by a consultant who had undertaken similar work at other Western Australian sites, both Aboriginal and non-Aboriginal, that are open to the public. Tourists would, thereafter, be confined to the walkway. Once the Steering Committee had approved the walkway design, the Minister of Indigenous Affairs gave his consent, under Section 18 of the Heritage Act, for the work to proceed. The walkway was installed by a private contractor. The aim was to protect the ground surface outside the cave from pedestrian traffic while better informing visitors of the significance of the site by putting several signs, carrying up-to-date and culturally appropriate information, whose wording was approved by the Steering Committee, on a viewing platform.

Our involvement in the Mulka's Cave project began after all the management decisions had been made. In 2004, Rossi, then a recent graduate, helped Gunn record the artwork. In 2006, the Mulka's Cave Aboriginal Steering Committee agreed that, under Webb's supervision, Rossi could study the artefacts found during the ground disturbance necessary before the walkway was installed and could test pit other parts of the site. Her research focuses on how the entire site complex was used by Aboriginal people in the archaeological past. [...] As required by the Minister of Indigenous Affairs in his Letter of Consent, Webb, an experienced archaeologist, monitored the installation of the walkway. Representatives of the Aboriginal families with historic links to Mulka's Cave assisted the installer. When the new walkway was officially opened, by the local member of federal parliament, in October 2006, a senior woman from those families gave a 'welcome to country' and thanked everyone who had been involved in the project, including us.

The walkway is made from steel (see Figure 10.1.3A). It is raised about 0.3 m above the ground. A drain has been installed at the cave mouth (see Figure 10.1.3B), to funnel

Figure 10.1.3 Four views of the walkway installed at Mulka's Cave (May 2006). A – steel walkway, raised about 0.3 m above the ground; B – drain installed at the cave mouth; C – rainwater funnelled out onto the flats below the cave; D – rubber matting, 6 mm thick, on the floor of the cave to protect the remaining deposits, with consolidated sediment between the end of the walkway and the matting.

rainwater falling over the entrance out onto the flats below the cave (see Figure 10.1.3C). The installer decided to put rubber matting 6 mm thick on the floor of the cave to protect the remaining deposits and prevent further erosion. The sediment was consolidated between the end of the walkway and the matting (see Figure 10.1.3D). These measures should prevent further erosion of the sediments at the cave mouth and beneath the walkway and allow the groundcover on the talus to regenerate. Sheoak (*Allocasuarina huegeliana*) seedlings, the locally dominant tree, have also been planted over the slope outside the cave. Further planting may be undertaken in future, by local landcare groups, as and when funds become available. It is hoped that as the sheoaks become established an understorey of low *Melaleuca*, *Thryptomene*, and *Verticordia* shrubs, and forbs, will regenerate naturally. Their roots should stabilize the ground surface. That they may also disturb any Aboriginal stone artefacts that the sediment contains is unavoidable. We have argued elsewhere (Webb & Rossi 2008) that 10–15 m^3 of sediment has been transported from inside the cave to the slope outside over the past fifty years, forming a layer about 300 mm thick that attenuates down slope. The context, and significance, of the stone artefacts it contains has, of course, been destroyed. We therefore consider their possible further disturbance by tree roots to be insignificant. No Aboriginal artefacts were found in the area where the pipes discharge. It is sufficiently well vegetated that outflow, which is considerable during rainstorms, should not cause erosion. Before the walkway was installed, the artefacts on the surface of the talus were collected as part of Rossi's study of the site; excavation of the postholes for the walkway supports showed that artefacts were rarely found more than 150 mm below the present surface of the talus. Whether any archaeological material remains *in situ* in the cave is unknown.

In passing, we would note that the extent of the management work undertaken at Mulka's Cave is unusual for Western Australian Aboriginal sites, but every aspect of the project was approved by the Mulka's Cave Aboriginal Steering Committee before it was implemented. Most of the sites known to us that are open to the public have only the minimal infrastructure previously in place at Mulka's Cave: an explanatory sign and a low wooden post-and-rail fence; usually installed in the 1970s–1980s, before DAS became DIA. In particular, grilles have not been placed over the artwork at any of the decorated shelters; a common practice in other Australian states (Clark 2002). As a result, we believe, most Western Australian art sites are fairly free of graffiti. Whereas, at art sites with grilles we have visited in Victoria and New South Wales, the presence of a barrier seems to engender graffiti; for example, at Bunjils and Billimina, discussed by Clark (2002). Heritage managers might like to bear this point in mind when considering whether to install grilles at the sites in their care. Having got in, trespassers seem to feel the need to commemorate their prowess by writing their names on the walls. Some of the more accessible art sites in Southwestern Australia were defaced with racist graffiti in the 1960s–1970s, as noted above. It was removed by DAS conservators (Haydock & Rodda 1986). New graffiti have not appeared, but the sites are rarely visited, except by DIA staff or other professionals. Indeed, most Western Australian Aboriginal sites are protected by their relative inaccessibility. Those that are not now on private property, to which the landowners can and do deny the general public access, are off the beaten track and poorly, if at all, signposted. These less accessible sites are, and should remain, unspoiled. Thus, the old DAS policy, which might

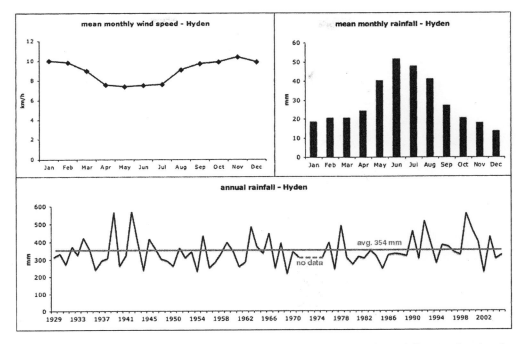

Figure 10.1.4 Monthly wind speed and rainfall patterns and annual rainfall at Hyden for the last seventy years.
Source: Bureau of Meteorology data

be described as benign neglect, was and is clearly effective at preventing vandalism at rarely visited sites. It cannot address the problems inherent to opening sites to tourists, however.

This paper considers one aspect of those problems by discussing the evidence for sediment erosion within and without Mulka's Cave during the last fifty years; caused, we believe, by uncontrolled tourist access to a site where the passage of numerous feet in a confined space has had irreversibly deleterious effects. The aridity of the regional environment is important to understanding why tourism has impacted Mulka's Cave so disastrously. Although The Humps is now surrounded by farmland, it really lies on the western edge of the Western Desert. The regional climate is extra dry Mediterranean (Beard 1981). That is: hot, dry summers and cool, moist winters, although rain can fall at any time of year. Mean annual rainfall at Hyden is 345 mm, but the actual amount received varies greatly from year to year (see Figure 10.1.4). Temperatures range from diurnal maxima of 48° C in summer to nocturnal minima of –5° C in winter. Visitor numbers at Mulka's Cave peak during the April and October school holidays (DAS, unpublished data). Before the walkway was installed, tourists visiting the cave in April, when it has often not rained for six months, probably had the greatest impact on the site because the ground is then devegetated, facilitating erosion. The frequent, lengthy droughts are also important because the ground cover may not regenerate at all in spring, if little rain falls during the winter months, but the tourists keep on coming. Ahern (1991) noted similar problems at Stonehenge, Wiltshire, England.

The erosive effects of tourism

As noted above, few tourists visited Mulka's Cave before the 1970s. In the last thirty years, however, with improved roads, the prevalence of four-wheel-drive vehicles, increased leisure and disposable income and the intense promotion of Wave Rock, the number of people visiting Mulka's Cave has increased greatly (see Figure 10.1.2). Unfortunately, this increase coincided with the administrative changes that made it difficult for DIA staff to monitor the site. Had the cave been inspected between 1989 and 2003, we are sure the severity of the erosion would have been noticed and steps would have been taken to arrest it sooner, highlighting why heritage managers need to monitor much-visited sites regularly.

When Rossi compared the photographs she took of Mulka's Cave in April 2004 with those taken in May 2006, the shape of the cave mouth had visibly changed; prompting her to examine earlier pictures of the cave that could be dated (Day 1951; Serventy 1952; Randolph 1973; Bowdler *et al.* 1989; Rodda 1989). Figure 10.1.5 is the result of that research: the shape of the cave mouth was traced from the photographs taken in 2004 and 2006 and the tracings were superimposed. They were aligned along the edge of the overhang and matched for scale. Then tracings were made from older pictures of the cave mouth and added to the composite image. They were scaled and matched to the composite image by aligning at least two features we do not think have moved over time, [...] Fortunately, before the walkway was installed, most photographs were taken from approximately the same spot, which gave an optimal impression of the cave mouth; making superimposition comparatively easy.

From Figure 10.1.5, we conclude that by 1988, when the Bowdler *et al.* (1989) test excavated the floor deposits just inside the dripline, about 0.5 m of sediment had been eroded from the 1952 level, the earliest datable pictures known. That is, an erosion rate of about 15 mm/yr, on average. By 2004, another 0.5 m of deposit had been lost and the erosion rate had doubled to 30 mm/yr, on average. Moreover, the erosion channel in front of the cave had deepened and widened and all trace of the test pit had disappeared; making it difficult, if not impossible, to reassess the age of the deposits within the cave. [...] That the rate of sediment erosion would have continued to accelerate had the walkway not been installed is suggested by the amount of deposit lost between 2004 and 2006 and the fact that the slope outside the cave was probed to a depth of one metre in 2006 without reaching bedrock. Furthermore, since about 1990, the rate of erosion has increased even when tourist numbers have dropped (Figure 10.1.5), suggesting that the integrity (cohesiveness) of the sediment has been damaged beyond repair.

Discussion

We believe that trampling is the main agent of erosion at Mulka's Cave (Rossi & Webb 2008). Although the cave is large, 15 m × 9 m × 2.5 m high (Gunn 2006), there are very few places where visitors can stand comfortably to view the artwork because the interior is filled with boulders; [...] These restrictions affect people's behaviour within and without the cave, but were not a major problem when fewer tourists visited the site. We [...] have noted that, when in the cave, independent travellers tend to find a spot where they can view most of the artwork and stand relatively still, discussing it

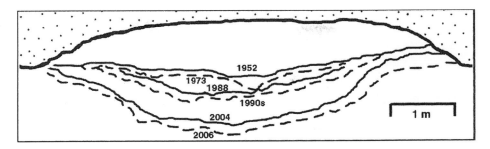

Figure 10.1.5 Reconstruction of the ground level within Mulka's Cave between 1952 and 2006.
Source: Based on Day (1951), Serventy (1952), Randolph (1973), Bowdler *et al.* (1989) and our own photographs

with their companions and taking photographs. These people appear to be genuinely interested in Aboriginal cultural heritage; some even asked us questions about the site when they realized we were working there. This type of visitor usually takes time to read all the signs on the new viewing platform. Visitors on commercial tours, many of whom do not seem to understand English, behave differently. Before the walkway and new signs were installed, their guides tended to hustle them into and out of the cave quite quickly. The guides gave their own interpretations of the artwork. Judging by the 'commentaries' we have overheard, they knew little about Aboriginal culture. Now, the guide often remains by his bus and leaves his tour group to visit on their own. How much the foreign visitors understood of the spiel they used to get we do not know, but we have noticed that they now look at the signs only if one of their number reads English. Because they are numerous, often as many as thirty, and the space within the cave is restricted, the people in these groups are in constant motion, as they jostle for room to take photographs, sometimes of each other, rather than of the artwork. We believe it is the constant movement of visitors' feet, particularly those in tour groups, that has eroded the floor deposits.

We searched the archaeological literature for comparative data on erosion caused by over-visitation at tourist-accessible sites and the approaches employed to arrest it. [...] Authors who have discussed erosion caused by over-visitation include Ahern (1991), Lee (1994; Lee & Wilson 2004), Deacon (1995), Schmidt and Spence (1999), Williams (1999), Phillips (2003), and Davis (2004). They all advocate site-specific solutions that include those employed at Mulka's Cave: revegetation of eroded or denuded areas, restricting access to designated pathways and, if necessary, the installation of elevated boardwalks, but they were all averse to sealing pathways, unless it was the only way to halt erosion, because it can make sites look too 'managed'. [...] Ahern (1991) noted that the sealed pathways at Stonehenge were to be removed. All the paths at Mulka's Cave are made from compacted ferruginous pea gravel; the natural substrate.

[...]

The effect that trampling can have on unconsolidated surfaces was investigated by Gager and Conacher (2001). They showed that the erosion caused by walkers using the access tracks in Kalamunda National Park, on the eastern outskirts of Perth, was worst on tracks that ran straight down a slope. Moreover, where granite outcropped less than 50 m upslope of a track, the surrounding ground remained saturated for several days after rain, facilitating solifluction and channelling. Ahern (1991) noted that grass was easily deracinated and destroyed by visitors' feet when the underlying ground was waterlogged. At Mulka's Cave, the old access track ran straight upslope to the cave mouth and granite outcrops all around; preconditions facilitating erosion. [. . .] These factors were clearly in play outside Mulka's Cave before the walkway was installed.

[. . .]

Because the entrance to Mulka's Cave is quite constricted, the people in tour groups cannot all enter at once. Before the walkway was installed, they used to mill around on the talus, before and after viewing the artwork: now they are confined to the walkway. The constant passage of their feet used to prevent the groundcover on the talus from regenerating in winter, leaving the friable sandy deposits vulnerable to erosion by wind and water all year round. A similar problem was noted at Gordion, an early city in central Turkey (Schmidt & Spence 1999), where the climate is equally arid. There, erosion due to over-visitation was tackled by planting the denuded areas with local species, despite the possibility of spoiling the 'look' of the site by over-intervention. Ahern (1991) noted that erosion increased at Stonehenge during dry weather. There, the problem was solved by planting grass, an impractical option at Gordion and Mulka's Cave.

[. . .]

Now that the talus has been planted with seedling trees and covered with dead brushwood, to discourage visitors from straying and to protect the seedlings, we expect the erosion to abate. The tendency for visitors to ignore made paths and create their own, more direct, routes was curtailed at Opepe (Williams 1999) and Mauao (Phillips 2003), Maori *pa* in New Zealand, and at Cawthorne Roman Camps, North Yorkshire, England (Lee 1994; Lee & Wilson 2004), by fencing the worst-affected areas. So far that solution has proved unnecessary at Mulka's Cave. Visitors are effectively confined to the walkway.

While we believe that trampling is the main cause of sediment translocation at Mulka's Cave, the erosive effect of rain also needs to be considered; particularly once visitation was sufficiently frequent to inhibit plant growth. [. . .] Because granite is impermeable, when it rains at The Humps water pours over the present entrance to Mulka's Cave, eroding the external deposits. Erosion is greater in summer than winter because the talus deposits are then very dry and devegetated, so sediment-loaded surface runoff is high. In winter, rain is more likely to be absorbed because the ground is already damp. As Figure 10.1.4 shows, [. . .] abundant rain has only fallen six times in the last 70 years. The amounts received in January 1990, March 1992, and January 2000 are particularly relevant to our argument because by the late 1980s it was obvious that the environs of Mulka's Cave were becoming devegetated due to over-visitation (Rodda 1989). We believe those falls would have been particularly erosive because of their volume (over 200 mm in 2000) and the time of year when they fell. Abundant rain in May or August will be less erosive because it is more likely to be absorbed. Figures 10.1.2 and 10.1.5 show that erosion of the cave deposits increased markedly between 1900 and 2004, when visitation also increased. As much sediment was lost in those fourteen years as in the previous forty due, we believe, to increased visitation coupled with the erosive power of torrential rain.

Conclusion

This study of the erosive effect of visitors' feet illustrates one of the dilemmas that plagues cultural tourism, particularly in a state as vast and sparsely populated as Western Australia. There is a fine line between wanting people to understand and appreciate places of cultural significance and letting them spoil sites simply by visiting them. Is it preferable if one fairly ordinary site is visited by droves of tourists, who are 'controlled', thereby preserving and conserving more important sites, to which access can easily be denied because they are on private property or difficult to find? Or would tourism have fewer deleterious effects if more sites were made accessible, thereby spreading visitor numbers and reducing their impact at individual sites? Or would opening more sites to visitation merely add to the number of sites impacted? Or should all sites be closed, possibly precipitating vandalism by people who think they have a right to go anywhere they please? Lee (1994; Lee & Wilson 2004), Williams (1999) and Phillips (2003) have all discussed these issues; while Moncrieff (2000) considered visitor impact on granite domes from a nature conservation perspective. None of these authors reached firm conclusions, apart from the need for regular monitoring; [...] In Western Australia, discussion on access issues as they appertain to Aboriginal sites is in its infancy because few are open to tourism. When a site is open, or is to be opened, discussion *must* involve the landowner, the relevant Aboriginal people, Land Council and/or native title representative body, the Department of Indigenous Affairs and local residents, both Aboriginal and non-Aboriginal. All these stakeholders were consulted about Mulka's Cave.

The remoteness of most Western Australian Aboriginal sites makes the prevention of vandalism almost impossible; while the effects of over-visitation are difficult to monitor, even at sites that are relatively close to towns, unless a ranger is employed to oversee visitor behaviour (Clark 2002). This has yet to be done at any of the Aboriginal sites in Western Australia we have visited, even Mulka's Cave; but that site is lucky. It is near Hyden and local residents, admittedly non-Aboriginal, are interested in its maintenance, so the effectiveness of the new infrastructure in controlling tourist behaviour can be monitored. Only time will tell how successful the walkway has been in arresting soil erosion, but the initial signs are promising. [...] We last visited Mulka's Cave in March 2008. The rubber matting was still in place and appeared to be working well and most of the seedling trees were surviving, after one of the driest summers for decades. We believe, therefore, that the new infrastructure is performing as intended.

We hope this study of the erosive effects of trampling will prompt the guardians of other archaeological sites in fragile environments to monitor soil erosion, to consider the impact tourist numbers are having on the sites in their care and spur them to take any mitigative action required sooner rather than later.

Bibliography

Ahern, K. (1991). 'Visitor wear and tear of cultural landscapes: recommendations for Stonehenge.' *Cultural Resource Management* 14 (vi): 24–26.

Beard, J.S. (1981). *Swan, Explanatory notes to sheet 7 of the 1:1,000,000 Vegetation Survey of Western Australia*. Perth: University of Western Australia Press.

Bowdler, S., J. Harris, A. Murphy *et al.* (1989). 'Test excavation at Mulka's Cave (Bate's Cave) near Hyden, Western Australia.' Unpublished report to the Department of Aboriginal Sites, Western Australian Museum, Perth.

Clark, I.D. (2002). 'Rock art sites in Victoria, Australia: a management history framework.' *Tourism Management* 23: 455–64.

Davis, M. (2004). 'A study into the mitigation of construction impact on archaeological remains.' In T. Nixon (ed), *Preserving archaeological remains in situ?* London: Museum of London Archaeology Service, 224–29.

Day, R.B. (1951). 'The Humps beyond Hyden.' *The West Australian*, 27 January 1951.

Deacon, J. (1995). 'Promotion of a neglected heritage at Stone Age sites in the Western Cape, South Africa.' *Conservation and Management of Archaeological Sites* 1: 75–86.

Gager, P.R. and A.J. Conacher (2001). 'Erosion of access tracks in Kalamunda National Park, Western Australia: causes and management implications.' *Australian Geographer* 32: 343–57.

Gunn, R.G. (2003). *Mulka's Cave Aboriginal rock art site: a discussion of management options*. Report to the Department of Indigenous Affairs, Perth.

Gunn, R.G. (2006). *Mulka's Cave Aboriginal rock art site: its context and content*. Records of the Western Australian Museum 23: 19–41.

Haydock, P. and J. Rodda (1986). *A survey of rock art conservation in the Murchison/Wheatbelt area of WA: a study of past treatments and new methods of measurement and site management*. Report to the Department of Aboriginal Sites, Western Australian Museum, Perth.

Lee, G. (1994). 'Erosion control on Cawthorne Roman Camps.' In A.Q. Berry and I.W. Brown (eds), *Erosion on archaeological earthworks: its prevention, control and repair*. Mold: Clwyd County Council, 87–92.

Lee, G. and P. Wilson (2004). 'Cawthorne Camps (North Yorkshire): damage and survival.' In T. Nixon (ed), *Preserving archaeological remains in situ?* London: Museum of London Archaeology Service, 173–78.

Moncrieff, D. (2000). 'Managing tourism and recreation on Wheatbelt granite outcrops.' *Journal of the Royal Society of Western Australia* 83: 187–96.

Phillips, K.J.S. (2003). *Preliminary archaeological survey and identification of threats to archaeological resources at Mauao Historic Reserve, Tauranga*. Report to Tauranga District Council, Tauranga, New Zealand.

Randolph, P. (1973). *Bates Cave, Hyden*. Report to the Department of Aboriginal Sites, Western Australian Museum, Perth.

Rodda, J. (1989). *Mulka's Cave site management project*. Report to the Western Australian Heritage Commission and the Department of Aboriginal Sites, Western Australian Museum, Perth.

Rossi, A.M. and R.E. Webb (2008). 'The erosive effect of tourism at an Aboriginal rock art site on the western edge of the arid zone in south-western Australia.' *Antiquity* 82 (315), available at: www.antiquity.ac.uk/ProjGall/rossi/index.html.

Schmidt, K. and C. Spence (1999). 'Highlights from the Cultural Site Management Workshop, Monday 26 April 1999.' *Sustainable Development* 24: 1–2.

Serventy, V. (1952). 'Cave paintings near York and Hyden.' *The Western Australian Naturalist* 13: 121–30.

Twidale, C.R. and J.A. Bourne (2004). 'Notes on the geomorphology of The Humps, near Hyden, Western Australia.' *Journal of the Royal Society of Western Australia* 87: 123–33.

Webb, R.E. and Rossi, A.M. (2008). 'How was Mulka's Cave, an Aboriginal rock art site near Hyden, in south-central Western Australia, used by the people who decorated its walls, when the present entrance was much smaller?' *Records of the Western Australian Museum* 24: 307–18.

Williams, A.M. (1999). *Threats to archaeological features within the redoubt and village area of Opepe Bush Scenic and Historic Reserve, Taupo*. Science and Research Internal Report 168, Department of Conservation, Wellington, New Zealand.

Chapter 11

Decay and mitigation of waterlogged sites

Deposits, remains and survival

WATERLOGGED DEPOSITS ARE soils saturated with water; without any oxygen present, they are anoxic and are often referred to as anaerobic or stagnant. Such conditions are present in the bottoms of many ditches, pits and wells, beside most rivers, lakes and other bodies of water (including the seabed), as well as bogs. Waterlogged conditions arise because:

- The water does not move/drain freely (impeded drainage), either due to a barrier or a soil such as clay with low hydraulic conductivity (i.e. the water cannot move through the soil quickly).
- The oxygen in the water/soil has been consumed by aerobic organisms such as Basidiomycete fungi, which consume cellulosic materials such as wood, leading to anoxic conditions.
- Oxygen diffuses very slowly through water.

In such soils, organic material does not decay quickly, leading to soils rich in partially degraded organic material such as peats. Such organic soils absorb and hold water like a sponge and are often saturated with water (Holden et al. 2006). Since human occupation often occurred beside water sources, archaeological evidence of human occupation is often preserved in waterlogged deposits, from Neolithic Alpine lake villages to the medieval and Roman remains under major European cities (almost all of which are on rivers). In this reducing environment, wood and other organic materials are preserved and metal does not corrode (see Table 3.0.1). The wood does continue to degrade very slowly due to anaerobic bacteria and the depolymerisation action of water (hydrolysis). This weakens the wood and other organic materials, whose cellular structure is supported when saturated with water, but which collapse, shrink and break up when they dry out. The presence of sulphate reducing bacteria (SRB) in most soils means that as reducing conditions establish, sulphide ions are created, leading to the production of minerals such as iron sulphide, which are often present in waterlogged wood. The metals present will either remain uncorroded or possess a thin black iron or copper sulphide deposit; other minerals such as siderite (iron carbonate) and vivianite (iron phosphate) can also be present depending on the chemistry of the environment. Glass, ceramic and stone are largely undegraded in this environment but poorly fired prehistoric ceramics often become soft. However, upon excavation, the exposed metalwork starts to corrode and the wood and other organic material lose water, they shrink, warp, crack and crumble. Excavated artefacts of metal and inorganic materials could be dried off and stored in museums; however, waterlogged wood and other organics presented a challenge. Two long-term options existed:

- *Conserve*: remove the waterlogged wooden artefacts from their deposits, and replace the water with less volatile materials to support the cell structure while avoiding the stresses from evaporation that cause cellular collapse.
- *Preserve* in situ/*rebury*: maintain or recreate the waterlogged conditions that:
    - ensure a water saturated environment; and
    - ensure maintenance/recreation of a reducing environment.

The difficulties of conserving wet organic objects in the nineteenth and early twentieth centuries is why many museums are filled with metal, ceramics and stone objects. Though successful conservation treatments for waterlogged organics have been widespread since the 1970s generating many small wooden and leather objects – bowls, tools, weapons, shoes and toys for display – the cost has remained high. Many European countries have also now conserved a number of large, high-profile wood objects, usually boats, which are on display – e.g. Mary Rose (England), Wasa (Sweden), Roskilde Viking Ships (Denmark), and Gokstad, Oseberg and Tune Viking ships (Norway). The high costs of conservation and display now mean that unless the specimen is unusually complete or impressive, such objects are increasingly likely to be preserved *in situ* or reburied (e.g. Shardlow Boat II) (Williams 2008a). The large numbers of objects thrown into pools or mires in antiquity, such as the Iron Age deposits at Nydam (Gregory and Matthiesen 2012), are so numerous and costly to conserve that they too are often left preserved *in situ*. Other waterlogged features such as the bases of houses, palisades and wooden defences, wharves, quays and trackways have significance and meaning derived from their location and European heritage authorities, often citing the *European Convention on the Protection of the Archaeological Heritage* (Council of Europe n.d.), normally seek to preserve such features *in situ*.

Monitoring

Water enters soil systems either as meteoric water (i.e. rainwater, directly onto the ground, indirectly through rivers and streams), where it acquires dissolved minerals, or as groundwater, present in the lower levels of soil. Meteoric water is oxygenated (oxic) and percolates downwards; groundwater rises from below and may be oxygenated or anoxic. Above the groundwater, the soil is wet, drawing water up by capillary action. This capillary fringe may be saturated at its base but is less than saturated at higher levels. The level of groundwater is normally measured as height below surface (or above/below Ordinance Datum) and determined using a porous/perforated ended pipe sunk into the ground (standpipe, piezometer, borehole, dipwell). A number of different measuring devices have been used to measure the height of the water from the top of the pipe (Davis 1998), whose relative height can be determined using a GPS device or survey. The top of the water marks either the top of the groundwater or the top of a suspended (perched) water table (saturated deposits such as peat). Such suspended water tables are common in the complex layers of soil in human occupation areas. Above the saturated layers the water or moisture content of the soil is measured either by weighing and drying and reweighing a soil sample (weight of water against weight of soil expressed as a percentage) or determined using equipment such as moisture cells, neutron probes (Davis 1998) or, more recently, TMR (Time Domain Reflectometry) (Smit et al. 2006), and capacitance techniques such as Theta probes. Though organic archaeological remains are preserved in saturated anoxic conditions, as the moisture content falls, so does the quality of the waterlogged archaeological remains.

In the UK in the mid-1980s, events such as the loss of the waterlogged prehistoric timbers surviving in the base of ditches at Etton as a result of lowering the water table to facilitate quarrying of sand and gravel (French and Taylor 1985), but the preservation of a section of the Neolithic dated Sweet Track (see Chapter 2.1) running across the Somerset Levels alerted heritage authorities to the possibility of preserving valuable waterlogged archaeological deposits *in situ*, through maintaining the level of the 'groundwater' in relation to the archaeological remains. However, the drainage and subsequent rewetting of the site of Sutton Common led to modelling of the water table using a grid of 50 piezometers, which demonstrated the constantly changing 3D subsurface topography of the water table. We are now more aware that the water table level is influenced by a range of factors: the hydraulic conductivity of the various soil layers, the surface topography and the rate and location of recharge (water input) sources, which is dependent on the weather and varies with the season (Chapman and Cheetham 2002; Cheetham 2004). This has been defined as water balance by Corfield (2007: 144). Using appropriate software, hydraulic conductivity data and water table information, 3D models of water flows can be created (Welch and Thomas 1998). Such complexity has highlighted the risks of interpreting large archaeological sites with water table data from a single point.

Following the monitoring of water chemistry from dipwell samples at the Rose and Globe Theatres and the use of *in situ* electrodes and datalogger by Caple and colleagues (Caple and Dungworth 1998) (see Chapter 11.1), the importance of water chemistry, especially redox, to survival of archaeological remains began to be appreciated. Monitoring since the late 1990s has, where possible, normally included redox potential or dissolved oxygen content, as well as pH, temperature (essential to correct other readings) and conductivity (a measure of dissolved salts) or concentrations of specific ions (nitrate, sulphate, sulphide, etc.). Readings may come from electrodes directly inserted into the ground or from water samples removed from piezometers/dipwells. By 2012, more than 39 sites in England had been monitored as part of preservation *in situ* work since the mid-1990s (Williams 2012), and many more in Norway, Denmark and the Netherlands.

The stability of minerals and thus the burial chemistry of soil was shown in Chapter 3 to be usefully described on Eh-pH or Pourbaix diagrams. This monitoring of redox (Eh) and pH conditions can thus be predictive of the archaeological materials that will survive (Corfield 2007: 150), which organisms will be active and which minerals will form/not form (Caple et al. 1997) (see Table 11.0.1).

As there remain concerns by some workers in this field about determining redox potential (Eh) over long periods using redox probes, an alternative is to measure the relative concentrations of oxidised/reduced species (NO_3^-, Fe^{3+}, Fe^{2+}, S^{2-}, NH_4^+) or minerals present in sediment samples, as was done at Trondheim (Petersén and Bergersen 2012).

386 DECAY AND CONSERVATION MEASURES

Table 11.0.1 Oxidising/reducing environment

Description	Species present/absent	Redox value (mV)	Microbes
Oxidising	Oxygen	400 plus	Aerobes
Mildly reducing	NO_3^-, Mn^{4+} decline	100 to 400	Facultative anaerobes
Reducing		−100 to 100	Facultative anaerobes and obligate anaerobes
Highly reducing	SO_4^{2-}, Fe^{3+} disappear S^{2-}, NH_4^+, Fe^{2+}, CH_4 appear	−400 to −100	Obligate anaerobes

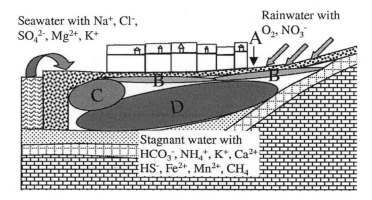

Figure 11.0.1 Model of hydrology and water chemistry of Bryggen, Bergen.
Source: Matthiesen (2008: 1386)

The monitored parameters in the water chemistry can be related to the survival of the archaeological materials. For example, reducing conditions (<100 mV) have been correlated with the survival of waterlogged organic material and uncorroded metal. Lower redox values usually occur at lower depths. A rise in redox level can be associated with an increase in oxygenated water entering the system and correlated with rainfall (Caple and Dungworth 1998; Lillie *et al*. 2008: 1897–8); this will lead to decay of organic material, even if the ground remains saturated.

There can be substantial spatial variation in the chemistry of soils; for example, work on the relatively homogeneous agricultural topsoils has shown pH values ranging from 4.5 to 7 in a single field (0.45 ha), suggesting that 'soil pH can vary by 2 units over very small distances' (Cresser *et al*. 1993). The stratigraphic variation in the soil often corresponds to differences in composition – organic matter, porosity, etc. – and results in variable levels of water content and water chemistry, including redox values with depth (Matthiesen *et al*. 2008: 166, Figure 3). In order to accurately characterise the water chemistry of Bryggen, the made-up ground of the old medieval waterfront area of Bergen, samples were obtained from 14 boreholes and modelled. This accurately described the changing water chemistry with depth in this area and revealed unusual inputs such as degrading bone and mortar from archaeological remains. Crucially, it showed how water chemistry could be correlated with water sources/inputs, leading to the identification of areas influenced by rainwater (B), seawater (C) and stagnant water (D) (see Figure 11.0.1).

It demonstrated that the flow rate of oxygenated rainwater entering the system was responsible for the decline in organic material in the waterlogged deposits, and thus the gradual loss and shrinkage of these deposits, which is occurring at 1–8 mm a year. Thus, water chemistry can be used to predict the likelihood of survival of archaeological remains (de Beer et al. 2008, 2012; Matthiesen 2008; Matthiesen et al. 2008). Similar multi-borehole/sampling site appraisals (e.g. Must Farm and Nantwich) are required if a detailed understanding of the water level and chemistry is to be achieved and lead to the planned preservation of waterlogged archaeological remains (Malim and Panter 2012).

Understanding the threats: monitoring in practice

Published examples of monitoring allow correlations between burial environments and specific conditions and events to be observed (see Table 11.0.2).

The monitoring in cities such as York, Parliament Street (Davis et al. 2002), Nantwich (Malim and Panter 2012), Trondheim (Peacock 2002; Petersén and Bergersen 2012), even at Must Farm in Cambridgeshire, shows that often we are not seeing preservation of organic archaeological remains due to groundwater saturation (indicated by piezometers) but by raised/perched/suspended water tables and the capillary fringe (tension saturated zone) above the groundwater. This means that not just groundwater level, but moisture content measurements, are becoming increasingly important. Since the medieval period, seasonal fluctuations in groundwater level re-saturated the ground and/or rainwater has slowly percolated down from the surface and kept these perched water tables wet. However, it now appears likely that the paving, asphalting and concreting over of European cities in the nineteenth century and the development of sewers to take away water has created a profound change, drying our subsoil city environment (Malim and Panter 2012: 431). Though loss from leaking pipes and

Table 11.0.2 Reported burial environment of selected urban and rural sites

Site	Reference
Urban sites	
Parliament Street, York	Davis et al. (2002)
Rose Theatre, London	Corfield (2004)
Schulzgate, Trondheim	Peacock (2002)
Tower of London	Keevil et al. (2004)
Langgate, Tønsberg	Reed (2004)
Bryggen, Bergen	Matthiesen (2008), Matthiesen et al. (2008)
Rural sites	
Sweet Track, Somerset	Brunning et al. (2000)
Sutton Common	Cheetham (2004), Chapman and Cheetham (2002)
Schokland	Huisman and Mauro (2012)
Over	French (2004)
Scottish Crannogs	Lillie et al. (2008)

sewers may be seen as recharging saturated ground (Holden et al. 2006: 72), on balance the upper layers of the organic rich, previously waterlogged, deposits are drying out, shrinking and turning brown as the organic material decays, as was noted at Parliament Street in York (Davis et al. 2002) and described by Kenward and Hall (2004). This suggests that the rich organic deposits beneath many cities and the archaeological remains they hold are in peril.

Urban and rural sites such as York (Davis et al. 2002), Market Deeping (Cambridgeshire) (Corfield 2007) or the Somerset Levels (Brunning et al. 2000) normally show a rise in the water table during the winter, as a result of increased rainfall and a drop in water table during the summer as the soil loses water through evaporation and transpiration. Where oxygenated rainwater feeds into the waterlogged levels, this causes the redox levels to rise in the winter (specific days of heavy rainfall are correlated with rises in oxygen, and thus Eh level) (Matthiesen et al. 2008: 168, Figure 4), while during the summer, the rise in temperature and biological activity in the upper levels of the soil, and lack of recharge of oxygenated rainfall, lead to lower oxygen levels and the waterlogged deposits become more reducing (Holden et al. 2006: 75). Since the IPCC predictions of climate change for the UK suggest there will be both wetter winters and drier summers, leading to greater fluctuations in water level, greater loss of reduced conditions in anoxic saturated environments can clearly be expected.

Waterlogged sediments typically have pH between 6.0 and 7.5, depending on the local geology and water chemistry inputs. However, the oxidation of soil that has previously been saturated and anoxic leads to acidification both in the laboratory (Caple et al. 1997) and in the field (Huisman and Theunissen 2008; Lillie et al. 2008: 1896). This acidity is seen visually as the oxidation and loss of pyrite (iron sulphide) and deposition of gypsum (calcium sulphate) (Huisman and Mauro 2012). This sequence of conditions leads to aggressive degradation of materials such as shell and bone (Kars et al. 2004). Conductivity levels in saturated soils describe the levels of dissolved minerals, which can indicate if the water is of meteoric or groundwater origin and indicate the presence of contamination (>600 µS/cm) with fertilisers (Caple et al. 1997).

In addition to determining physical factors such as water table level and hydrological capacities of the soils, water chemistry (plus buffering and reaction capacity with mineral, organic and clay particles) should be complemented with assays of biological activity. The millions of different species of fungi and bacteria present in the soil mean that it is not normally possible to identify and measure the quantity of specific micro-organisms in the soil directly (Hopkins 1998), so proxies are used, such as: the degradation of known materials over time typically using cotton strip or modern wood samples (Harrison et al. 1988), determining the total biomass in the soil, ATP determination (Ausmus 1973), or determining the level of extracellular enzyme activity (Lillie et al. 2012). Biological organisms can be differentially distributed or active through the soil, as shown by the variation in methane production in ombrotrophic bogs in Canada (Brown 1995). This may be in response to differing chemical or physical conditions in the burial environment; however, it emphasises the need for multiple sampling, especially with depth.

There are two reasons for incurring the costs of monitoring:

- *For research*: to understand what is happening to a burial environment and why.
- *For preservation*: to monitor key variables to ensure a site burial environment remains preservative. In such cases, there should be a clear plan about what interventions will take place should the environment cease to be preservative.

At sites such as Bryggen in Bergen and Nydam, the monitoring is feeding into research and the future care of the sites (Loska and Christensson 2012). However, as Williams (2012) has shown in the UK, monitoring has often been used as a condition of planning consent. Factors such as:

- the preservative conditions prior to development are invariably not known;
- the archaeological deposits have not been partially excavated so their value has not been established;
- there is no resource or plan to amend the environment of the site should the environment cease to be saturated and anoxic;
- there are few documented examples to show how specific mitigation strategies influence burial conditions; and
- the monitoring is only funded for a short period.

These realities mean that the capacity of monitoring to aid the preservation of waterlogged archaeological remains is often severely compromised.

Loss of waterlogged conditions

From the MAREW date (see Chapter 2), Robert van de Noort has suggested that 78 per cent of the ancient monuments present in England's wetlands in 1950 had been destroyed by 2000 (van de Noort et al. 2002). The principal threats to these archaeological remains are (see Chapter 2):

- The lowering of a water table to facilitate activities such as gravel and sand abstraction leads to drying out and destruction of waterlogged deposits and their archaeological organic materials. At Over (Cambridgeshire), abstraction over 500 m away lowered the water table and destroyed archaeological wood remains (French and Taylor 1985: 151; French 2004).
- Where water levels are maintained but oxygenated surface waters reach the peaty deposits containing archaeological organic remains, aerobic microbial reactions consume all organic material, leading to shrinkage of the ground. Bryggen in Bergen is sinking by between 1 and 8 mm per year and the pasture lands of the Somerset Levels by 10–20 mm (Christensson et al. 2008: 117; Brunning 2012).
- As peaty soil dries following ploughing, the light organic material is lost through wind erosion as dust.

These effects are often combined, leading the cultivated peat soils of the Somerset Levels to suffer 10–40 mm loss per year (Brunning 2012). The Somerset Levels has seen ground levels reduced by over 4 m, which leaves prehistoric sites around less than 1 m below the present ground surface (van de Noort et al. 2002) and archaeological remains such as Glastonbury Lake Village drying out and disintegrating or being consumed through microbial decay (Brunning 2008; Jones and Bell 2012).

In Denmark, the prehistoric trackway at Speghoeje Mose in central Jutland was 'protected' by stopping peat cutting 3 m either side of the 'monument', but with the ground on either side cut to 0.5 m below the trackway level, it will have drained, dried and been lost (Coles 1995: 86). Other Danish sites such as Sjellebro, Central Jutland, and Ravening

Bridge, Central Jutland, had legal protection, but this is totally ineffective for sites whose remains are wooden structures in waterlogged deposits, since such protection cannot stop drainage of surrounding lands and the loss of archaeological wooden remains to decay. Similarly, legal protection cannot prevent the seasonal drop in water table at many of the sites in Schokland in Holland, with its World Heritage Status, which are consequently annually under threat (Huisman and Mauro 2012).

In the urban environment, the threat is principally from development, as shown by sites such as the Rose Theatre (see Chapter 14.2) (Corfield 2004; Hughes 2004). Where development is approved, if the waterlogged deposits and associated archaeology are not removed by excavation, the buildings are normally constructed on piles driven through waterlogged ground (see Chapter 9). There is immediate threat from distortion of the ground around the pile, English Heritage (2007) suggesting up to 0.5 m around the pile, Huisman *et al*. (2011) suggesting deformation in wet ground was between ×1 and ×2 the width of the pile beyond the pile (Environment Agency 2006), though other figures have also been suggested (see Chapter 9). There is also a longer-term risk of piles piercing perched water tables (Environment Agency 2006), causing loss of anoxic water, so permitting the ingress of oxygenated water resulting in the loss of waterlogged archaeological remains, as appears to be happening following the construction of a hotel with a deep basement in Bryggen, Bergen (de Beer *et al*. 2008).

Preservation *in situ* and mitigation

Mitigation requires the retention or reintroduction of saturated anoxic conditions. This starts with the elimination of factors causing the loss or decline of such conditions (e.g. water abstraction from sand and gravel quarrying, arable agriculture, restriction and eventual cessation of peat cutting, which is planned for 2030 in the UK) (DEFRA 2010). Where more active steps are taken, it is important to distinguish between:

- preservation *in situ*, discussed in this chapter, where an excavation has uncovered waterlogged deposits, which are believed to be extensive and steps are taken to preserve all these still buried archaeological remains; and
- reburial, discussed in Chapter 14, where a specific site is excavated, uncovered and recorded, followed by active steps to recreate appropriate burial conditions.

Inevitably, there is considerable overlap between these two categories. The difference is largely to do with extent of the site and the affected area, the backfilling/reburial material. An example of preservation *in situ*, where extensive deposits are believed to exist but have only been sampled by excavation, but mitigation measures have been enacted to preserve the whole deposit is seen at Nydam (Gregory and Matthiesen 2012).

Rural sites

Saturation of the layers containing waterlogged archaeological remains is normally achieved by:

- Introducing water over or on to the remains from above. This may be pumped on (from mains or natural sources), as occurs at the Rose Theatre (see Chapter 14.2), or by

creating a lake or reservoir of water that flows down through the site, as is suggested occurs at Flag Fen (Prior and Bamforth 2010). If the water applied to saturate the ground contains dissolved oxygen, organic materials will continue to be consumed, so it should ideally be deoxygenated or from a naturally stagnant water source. Often, no such steps are taken.
- Raising the level of water to surround the remains by retarding drainage. This may be deliberate sealing of soil drains, ditches and natural watercourses, as seen at Fiskerton (Williams et al. 2008b), or stopping water abstraction from wells and boreholes. Since drainage occurs through hydraulic conductivity of the soil on all sides, creating impermeable sides – e.g. through the construction of clay banks (bunds) or burying an impermeable polymer barrier (polythene sheet) – as at Stonea Camp (Coles 1995: 80) reduces loss through this mechanism. Water is also lost through evaporation or transpiration, which can be reduced by controlling plant growth, eliminating trees that are normally associated with higher levels of transpiration, covering the ground with stones or geotextiles that can suppress vegetative growth and avoiding open water surfaces that have high evaporation rates.
- Both of the above are sometimes used, as occurs at the 500 m length of Sweet Track preserved by English Heritage in 1983 (see Chapter 2.1) (Brunning et al. 2000). Similarly, the trackway at Corlea, County Longford in Ireland, was isolated with an impermeable membrane and the water table around it raised to keep an 80 m stretch saturated, water supplied from artificial lakes created for the purpose (Coles 1995: 81–2).

The issues of mitigating the environment were first tackled in the UK at the Sweet Track on the Somerset Levels (see Chapter 2.1). Recent assessment has shown that given the low hydraulic conductivity of peat (<1 cm/day), irrigation ditches or leaky pipes bringing recharge water need to be located within 10–15 m of the archaeological remains if they are to effectively maintain saturation (i.e. deliver more water than is lost through evapotranspiration) (Brunning et al. 2000: 14).

While these solutions protect sites and short sections of trackway, they are no solution for the kilometres of other prehistoric trackways that fan across boggy landscapes such as the Somerset Levels. To do that, one needs to raise the level of the water table across a large area, mitigation not at site level, but at the scale of landscape. Such an approach means working with drainage boards to control water levels and requires farmers to switch from profitable arable framing to grazing animals utilising flood meadows, activities that will need to be supported by compensation for any loss of earnings. This approach has been tried by English Heritage and English Nature in the area around the Sweet Track site/Shapwick Heath National Nature Reserve. Elsewhere in Europe, similar schemes that create areas of permanently raised water table centred on archaeological remains have been attempted at Åmose, West Zealand, Denmark (Coles 1995: 88) and at Schokland (Huisman and Mauro 2012: 410). These are expensive, requiring land purchase or compensation for loss of earnings, and should be (but are not always) accompanied by monitoring to ensure appropriate water levels and anoxic conditions are formed around the archaeological remains. Such large schemes often require funds beyond those available for archaeology. Other agencies, especially those involved in nature conservation, also are concerned to preserve wetlands and have larger funds available. In 2004, Bryony Coles (2004) explored schemes in a number of other European countries (see Chapter 11.2), showing how it was possible to mitigate large areas using the larger resources available through nature conservation and the European Union.

The key agreement as far as wetlands is concerned is the Ramsar Convention (Carp 1972; Ramsar Convention website). This treaty, whose signatories include the UK, all major European countries and the USA, is geared to preserving wetland habitat for wildlife, but this does include consideration of cultural (and thus heritage) activities.

Urban sites

See Chapter 9, 'Urban sites', and Chapter 14.2 (Corfield 2004).

Lacustrine sites

The loss of waterlogged sites occurring both now and in the past at locations such as the Alpine lake villages is substantial. The lowering of many Alpine lakes in the nineteenth century led to the discovery of approximately 750 'pile dwellings' wooden prehistoric sites, preserved under the water and lacustrine silts that had built up over the last 3,000 years. Around Lake Leman, of the 75 sites identified when the lake was lowered, by the 1990s only 60 could be found; of these, only 27 had surviving wooden posts and only 11 surviving archaeological deposits. This loss derives from a combination of drying out, fungal activity, ploughing and wave action from the lowered lake level. Many of these sites at the shore edge are now being protected by erecting soft barriers such as planting willows to diffuse wave action and encouraging vegetation and soil build-up. Sites beneath the lake surface are being buried beneath layers of geotextile and gravel or gravel filled sacks, which helped to resist wave and current action and encouraged sedimentation (Coles 1995: 89–92; Hafner 2008; Heumüller 2012).

Present and future practice

Guidelines for monitoring and describing preservation of archaeological sites *in situ* have been published by the Netherlands (Smit *et al*. 2006) and Norway (Riksantikvaren and NIKU n.d.). The Norwegians used a simple table that crucially differentiates between soil/burial conditions: dry (A), partially or occasionally saturated (B) and fully saturated (C), and a 0–5 scale for preservation conditions. The Dutch emphasise the need for a baseline of information about a site, appropriate to the level of preservation and material present on the site, which can include highly detailed micromorphological as well as monitoring work. The Danes, Norwegians and Dutch recognise that a significant element of their heritage exists as waterlogged wood and associated cultural material (historic towns, ships and sacrificial artefact deposits) and that saturated anoxic conditions must be maintained to preserve their national cultural heritage. Resources to achieve such control or compensate adjacent landowners for modifying their activities must be measured against the value of the protected archaeological remains. Where the legal system is based on the rights of landowners, it remains difficult to enforce control of groundwater levels and quality within their lands. Local authority meetings associated with granting planning permission are normally the only forum where the social valuation of archaeological remains can be measured against financial resources and the rights of the landowners.

Monitoring at sites that have had areas excavated and reburied, such as Nydam, Illerup Ådal (Tjelldén *et al.* 2012), Sweet Track and the Rose Theatre, indicates that they are still saturated and anoxic, a proxy that assures us that the archaeological remains are preserved. This is no small thing, since so many sites despite legal protection have no protection for their preservative burial environment and are, or appear to be, likely to decay (e.g. Glastonbury Lake Village) (Brunning 2008; Jones and Bell 2012). Given the substantial resources required to preserve such sites, this means selecting a few key sites and focusing resources on them. It will also require data from multiple sampling points, modelling the hydrology and water chemistry over a number of years to accurately understand the threats to the site conditions and resources to mitigate them. Some form of subsequent monitoring and maintenance of the site will be required in the long term to ensure appropriate burial conditions are sustained. Only through such measures are archaeological remains in waterlogged conditions truly preserved *in situ*.

Bibliography

Ausmus, B.S. (1973) 'The use of the ATP Assay in terrestrial decomposition studies', *Bulletins from the Ecological Research Committee*, No. 17, Modern Methods in the Study of Microbial Ecology, pp. 223–34.

Brown, A.D. (1995) 'Carbon cycling in peat and the implications for the rehabilitation of bogs', in M. Cox, V. Straker and D. Taylor (eds), *Wetlands, Archaeology and Nature Conservation*, London: HMSO, pp. 99–107.

Brunning, R. (2008) 'How does monitoring fit into a wider strategy? A multi-site example from a rural wetland', in H. Kars and R.M. van Heeringen (eds), *Preserving Archaeological Remains In Situ: Proceedings of the 3rd Conference 7–9 December 2006, Amsterdam*, Geoarchaeological and Bioarchaeological Studies 10, Amsterdam: Vrije Universiteit Amsterdam, pp. 217–25.

Brunning, R. (2012) 'Partial solutions to partially understood problems: the experience of in-situ monitoring and preservation in Somerset's Peatlands', *Conservation and Management of Archaeological Sites*, 14(1–4): 397–405.

Brunning, R., Hogan, D., Jones, J. *et al.* (2000) 'Saving the Sweet Track: the in situ preservation of a Neolithic wooden trackway, Somerset, UK', *Conservation and Management of Archaeological Sites*, 4: 3–20.

Caple, C. and Dungworth, D. (1998) 'Waterlogged anoxic archaeological burial environments', *English Heritage Ancient Monuments Laboratory Report Series*, 22/98.

Caple, C., Dungworth, D. and Clogg, P. (1997) 'The assessment and protection of archaeological organic materials', in P. Hoffmann, T. Grant, J.A. Spriggs and T. Daley (eds), *Proceedings of the 6th Waterlogged Organic Archaeological Materials Conference, York 1996*, Bremerhaven: ICOMM-CC – WOAM Working Group, pp. 57–72.

Carp, E. (ed.) (1972) *Proceedings, International Conference on the Conservation of Wetlands and Waterfowl, Ramsar, Iran, 30 January–3 February 1971*, Slimbridge, UK: International Wildfowl Research Bureau.

Chapman, H. and Cheetham, J.L. (2002) 'Monitoring and modelling saturation as a proxy indicator for in situ preservation in wetlands: a GIS based approach', *Journal of Archaeological Science*, 29: 277–89.

Cheetham, J.L. (2004) 'An assessment of the potential for in situ preservation of buried organic archaeological remains at Sutton Common, South Yorkshire', unpublished PhD thesis, Hull University.

Christensson, A., Dunlop, A.R., Matthiesen, H. *et al.* (2008) 'Safeguarding a World Heritage Site: Bryggen in Bergen, Norway', in H. Kars and R.M. van Heeringen (eds), *Preserving Archaeological Remains in Situ: Proceedings of the 3rd Conference 7–9 December 2006, Amsterdam*, Geoarchaeological and Bio-archaeological Studies 10, Amsterdam: Vrije Universiteit Amsterdam, pp. 111–22.Coles, B. (1995) *Wetland Management: A Survey for English Heritage*, Warp Occasional Paper No. 9, Exeter: Wetland Archaeology Research Project.

Coles, B. (2004) 'Steps towards the heritage management of wetlands in Europe', *Journal of Wetland Archaeology*, 4: 183–98.

Corfield M. (2004) 'Saving the Rose Theatre. England's first managed and monitored reburial', *Conservation and Managements of Archaeological Sites*, 6(3–4): 305–14.

Corfield, M. (2007) 'Wetland science', in M. Lille and S. Ellis (eds), *Wetland Archaeology and Environments: Regional Issues, Global Perspectives*, Oxford: Oxbow, 143–55.

Council of Europe (n.d.) *Conventions Website*, available at: http://conventions.coe.int/Treaty/en/Treaties/Html/143.htm (accessed August 2014).

Cresser, M., Killham, K. and Edwards, A. (1993) *Soil Chemistry and Its Applications*, Cambridge Environmental Chemistry Series 5, Cambridge Cambridge University Press.

Davis, N. (1998) 'In situ monitoring of wet archaeological environments: a review of available monitoring technologies', in M. Corfield, P., Hinton, T. Nixon and M. Pollard (eds), *Preserving Archaeological Remains in Situ*, London: Museum of London, University of Bradford, pp. 121–5.

Davis, M., Hall, A., Kenward, H. et al. (2002) 'Preservation of urban archaeological deposits: monitoring and characterisation of archaeological deposits at Marks and Spencer, 44–45 Parliament Street, York', *Internet Archaeology*, 11, available at: http://intarch.ac.uk/journal/issue11/oxley_index.html (accessed August 2014).

de Beer, H., Christensson, A., Jensen, J.A. et al. (2008) 'Bryggen World Heritage Site: a numerical groundwater model to support archaeological prospection strategies', in H. Kars and R.M. van Heeringen (eds), *Preserving Archaeological Remains in Situ: Proceedings of the 3rd Conference 7–9 December 2006, Amsterdam*, Geoarchaeological and Bioarchaeological Studies 10, Amsterdam: Vrije Universiteit Amsterdam, pp. 95–100.

de Beer, H., Matthiesen, H. and Christensson, A. (2012) 'Quantification and visualisation of in situ degradation at the World Heritage Site Bryggen in Bergen, Norway', *Conservation and Management of Archaeological Sites*, 14(1–4): 215–27.

DEFRA (2010) *The Natural Choice: Securing the Value of Nature*, London: H.M. Government.

English Heritage (2007) *Piling and Archaeology*, London: English Heritage, available at: www.english-heritage.org.uk/publications/piling-and-archaeology/ (accessed September 2014).

Environment Agency (2006) *Piling in Layered Ground: Risks to Groundwater and Archaeology*, Rotherham: The Environment Agency, available at: www.gov.uk/government/uploads/system/uploads/attachment_data/file/290536/scho0906bllu-e-e.pdf (accessed September 2014).

French, C. (2004) 'Hydrological monitoring of an alluviated landscape in the Lower Great Ouse Valley at Over, Cambridgeshire: results of the gravel extraction', *Environmental Archaeology*, 9: 1–12.

French, C. and Taylor, M. (1985) 'Desiccation and destruction: the immediate effects of dewatering at Etton, Cambridgeshire, England', *Oxford Journal of Archaeology*, 4: 139–55.

Gregory, D. and Matthiesen, H. (2012) 'Nydam Mose: in situ preservation at work', *Conservation and Management of Archaeological Sites*, 14(1–4): 479–86.

Hafner, A. (2008) 'In situ preservation of submerged prehistoric settlements in lakes of the Alpine region. Anti-erosion measures at sites in Lake Bienne, Switzerland', in H. Kars and R.M. van Heeringen (eds), *Preserving Archaeological Remains in Situ: Proceedings of the 3rd Conference 7–9 December 2006, Amsterdam*, Geoarchaeological and Bioarchaeological Studies 10, Amsterdam: Vrije Universiteit Amsterdam, pp. 245–51.

Harrison, A.R., Latter, P.M. and Walton, D.W.H. (1988) *Cotton Strip Assay: An Index of Decomposition in Soils*, Cumbria: NERC, Institute for Terrestrial Ecology, available at: http://nora.nerc.ac.uk/4949/1/24%2520-%2520Cotton%2520Strip.pdf (accessed September 2014).

Heumüller, M. (2012) 'Erosion and archaeological heritage protection in Lake Constance and Lake Zurich: the Interreg IV project', *Conservation and Management of Archaeological Sites*, 14(1–4): 48–59.

Holden, J., West, L.J., Howard, A.J. et al. (2006) 'Hydrological controls of in situ preservation of waterlogged archaeological deposits', *Earth-Science Reviews*, 78: 59–83.

Hopkins, D.W. (1998) 'The biology of the burial environment', in M. Corfield, P. Hinton, T. Nixon and M. Pollard (eds), *Preserving Archaeological Remains In-Situ*, London: Museum of London Archaeological Service and Bradford University, pp. 73–85.

Hughes, R. (2004) 'Design and decision on five development sites in London: Governor's House, Millennium Footbridge, Alder Castle, Plantation Place and Park Lane, Croydon', in T. Nixon (ed.), *Preserving Archaeological Remains In-Situ?*, London: Museum of London Archaeological Service, pp. 98–136.

Huisman, D.J. and Theunissen, E.M. (2008) 'Too good to be true: the unexpectedly good condition of the Nieuwe-Dordrecht Neolithic trackway and its implications', in H. Kars and R.M. van Heeringen (eds), *Preserving Archaeological Remains in Situ: Proceedings of the 3rd Conference 7–9 December 2006, Amsterdam*, Geoarchaeological and Bioarchaeological Studies 10, Amsterdam: Vrije Universiteit Amsterdam, pp. 15–27.

Huisman, D.J., Muller, A. and van Doesburg, J. (2011) 'Investigating the impact of concrete driven piles on the archaeological record using soil micromorphology: three case studies from the Netherlands', *Conservation and Management of Archaeological Sites*, 13(1): 8–30.

Huisman, D.J. and Mauro, G. (2012) 'The never ending story? The lessons of fifteen years of archaeological monitoring at the former Island of Schokland', *Conservation and Management of Archaeological Sites*, 14(1–4): 406–28.

Jones, M. and Bell, M. (2012) 'In situ preservation of wetland heritage: hydrological and chemical change in the burial environment of the Somerset Levels, UK', *Conservation and Management of Archaeological Sites*, 14(1–4): 115–25.

Kars, H., Collins, M., Jans, M. et al. (2004) 'Bone as an indicator in the in-situ degradation of archaeological heritage. Two examples: Apigliano, Italy and Aartswoud, the Netherlands', in T. Nixon (ed.), *Preserving Archaeological Remains In Situ?*, London: Museum of London, pp. 11–17.

Keevil, G., Hogan, D., Davis, M. et al. (2004) 'Waterlogged archaeological remains, environmental conditions and preservation in situ: a case study from the Tower of London', in T. Nixon (ed.), *Preserving Archaeological Remains In-Situ?*, London: Museum of London Archaeological Service, pp. 137–42.

Kenward, H. and Hall, A. (2004) 'Actively decaying or just poorly preserved? Can we tell when plant and invertebrate remains in urban archaeological deposits decayed?', in T. Nixon (ed.), *Preserving Archaeological Remains In-Situ?*, London: Museum of London Archaeological Service, pp. 4–10.

Lillie, M., Smith, R., Reed, J. et al. (2008) 'Southwest Scottish Crannogs: using in situ studies to assess preservation in wetland archaeological contexts', *Journal of Archaeological Science*, 35: 1886–900.

Lillie, M., Soler, I. and Smith, R. (2012) 'Lowland floodplain responses to extreme flood events: long term studies and short term microbial community response to water environment impacts', *Conservation and Management of Archaeological Sites*, 14(1–4): 126–49.

Loska, A. and Christensson, A. (2012) 'Take the right decision everybody', *Conservation and Management of Archaeological Sites*, 14(1–4): 294–302.

Malim, T. and Panter, I. (2012) 'Is preservation in situ an unacceptable option for development control? Can monitoring prove the continued preservation of waterlogged deposits?', *Conservation and Management of Archaeological Sites*, 14(1–4): 29–41.

Matthiesen, H. (2008) 'Detailed chemical analyses of groundwater as a tool for monitoring urban archaeological deposits: results from Bryggen in Bergen', *Journal of Archaeological Science*, 35: 1378–88.

Matthiesen, H., Dunlop, A.R., Jensen, J.A. et al. (2008) 'Monitoring of preservation conditions and evaluation of decay rates of urban deposits: results from the first five years of monitoring at Bryggen in Bergen', in H. Kars and R.M. van Heeringen (eds), *Preserving Archaeological Remains in Situ: Proceedings of the 3rd Conference 7–9 December 2006, Amsterdam*, Geoarchaeological and Bioarchaeological Studies 10, Amsterdam: Vrije Universiteit Amsterdam, pp. 163–80.

Peacock, E. (2002) *Monitoring in Situ Archaeological Deposits at Schultzgt, 3–7, Trondheim, Norway (1996–2001)*, Rapport Arckeologisk Serie 2002-1, Trondheim: NTNU.

Petersén, A. and Bergersen, O. (2012) 'An assessment of the status and condition of archaeological remains preserved in situ in the medieval town of Trondheim based on archaeochemical investigations conducted during the period 2007–2010', *Conservation and Management of Archaeological Sites*, 14(1–4): 228–38.

Prior, F. and Bamforth, M. (2010) *Flag Fen, Peterborough: Excavation and Research 1995–2007*, Oxford: Archaeopress.

Ramsar Convention (2013) *Manual*, 6th edn, available at: www.ramsar.org/sites/default/files/documents/library/manual6-2013-e.pdf (accessed December 2014).

Reed, I. (2004) 'Deposit monitoring in Tonsberg, Norway', in T. Nixon (ed.), *Preserving Archaeological Remains In-Situ?*, London: Museum of London Archaeological Service, pp. 87–90.

Riksantikvaren and NIKU (n.d.) *The Monitoring Manual. Procedures and Guidelines for the Monitoring, Recording and Preservation Management of Urban Archaeological Deposit*, available at: www.riksantikvaren.no/filestore/Veileder komp.pdf (accessed September 2014).

Smit, A., van Heeringen, R.M. and Theunissen, E.M. (2006) *Archaeological Monitoring Standard. Guidelines for the Non-Destructive Recording and Monitoring of the Physical Quality of Archaeological Sites and Monuments*, Nederlandse Archaeologische Rapporten 33, Amersfoort: National Service for Archaeology, Cultural Landscape and Built Heritage.

Tjelldén, A.K.E., Kristiansen, S.M. and Botfeldt, K.B. (2012) 'Preservation status and priorities for in situ monitoring of the weapon sacrifice in Illerup Ådal, Denmark', *Conservation and Management of Archaeological Sites*, 14(1–4): 150–8.

van de Noort, R., Fletcher, W., Thomas, G. et al. (2002) *Monuments at Risk in England's Wetlands*, Exeter: English Heritage and Exeter University.

Welch, J. and Thomas, S. (1998) 'Groundwater modelling of waterlogged archaeological deposits', in M. Corfield, P. Hinton, T. Nixon and M. Pollard (eds), *Preserving Archaeological Remains In-Situ*, London: Museum of London Archaeological Service and Bradford University, pp. 16–20.

Williams, J. (2012) 'Thirty years of monitoring in England: what have we learnt?', *Conservation and Management of Archaeological Sites*, 14(1–4): 442–57.

Williams, J., Bacon, H.M., Onions, B. et al. (2008a) 'The second Shardlow Boat: economic drivers or heritage policy?', in H. Kars and R.M. van Heeringen (eds), *Preserving Archaeological Remains in Situ: Proceedings of the 3rd Conference 7–9 December 2006, Amsterdam*, Geoarchaeological and Bioarchaeological Studies 10, Amsterdam: Vrije Universiteit Amsterdam, pp. 317–25.

Williams, J., Fell, V., Graham, K. et al. (2008b) 'Re-watering of the Iron Age Causeway at Fiskerton, England', in H. Kars and R.M. van Heeringen (eds), *Preserving Archaeological Remains in Situ: Proceedings of the 3rd Conference 7–9 December 2006, Amsterdam*, Geoarchaeological and Bioarchaeological Studies 10, Amsterdam: Vrije Universiteit Amsterdam, pp. 181–97.

Chapter 11.1

Results of the characterisation of the anoxic waterlogged environments which preserve archaeological organic materials

Chris Caple, David Dungworth and Phil Clogg

Source: Caple, C., Dungworth, D. and Clogg, P. (1997) 'Results of the characterisation of the anoxic waterlogged environments which preserve archaeological organic materials', in P. Hoffmann, T. Grant, J.A. Spriggs and T. Daley (eds), *Proceedings of the 6th Waterlogged Organic Archaeological Materials Conference, York 1996*, pp. 57–72.

Introduction

ENGLAND'S NATIONAL STRATEGY for dealing with archaeological remains is now primarily one of 'preservation in situ' wherever possible. [1] Thus there is now a need to focus away from archaeological excavation to preservation strategies. It may be questioned whether there is currently sufficient information to implement this policy confidently. With regard to waterlogged anoxic environments, it has already been suggested that there is insufficient data to make informed choices about the means of preserving these deposits. [2, 3] This was highlighted by the problems encountered in preserving the Rose and Globe theatres. [4, 5] In both cases, the burial conditions that have preserved these wooden buildings since the 16th century were not analysed and remain unknown. Thus the means of preserving them subsequent to excavation, or indeed even of assessing the degree of success of the preservation regime (reburial in saturated sand), remains unknown. This highlights the problem of having neither a baseline of knowledge about archaeologically important waterlogged anoxic deposits nor proven methods for analysing and characterising such deposits. Indeed, no freshwater terrestrial waterlogged anoxic environment containing archaeological material from Britain has ever been defined in biological, physical and chemical terms.

Recent research

In order to answer these concerns English Heritage has undertaken research on the methods for monitoring and preserving water-tables. [6, 7] They have also supported research in Durham [8, 9, 36] which has sought to define the overall chemical balance of anoxic waterlogged burial environments. It has been suggested [2, 3] that this chemical balance may as important as water level in determining the survival of waterlogged archaeological organic material since oxygenation is as crucial a step as dehydration in the destruction of waterlogged remains. [10] The chemistry of these environments is complex and research at Durham has concentrated on obtaining a holistic view through monitoring of the oxidation/reduction state, the pH and the level of ionised species within the burial environment. This has produced the first picture of the overall chemical balance in some of the most important waterlogged archaeological deposits in Britain.

Anoxic waterlogged deposits

Although there has been work on anoxic soil and water environments, this derives largely from studies of hypolimnic waters; [11, 12, 13] paddyfield soils; [14, 15, 16] other anoxic agricultural soils; [17, 18] and studies of peat bogs and mires. [19] This work provides a general picture of anoxic deposits as oxygenless reducing environments, with ion species present in reduced form with sulphides and other reduced form minerals, together with low levels of anaerobic micro-organisms and large volumes of organic material preserved within an otherwise homogeneous sediment.

Characteristic factors of anoxic waterlogged environments

The swift fall in the concentration of oxidising species present in the soil following the creation of a waterlogged environment, is due to their consumption by soil chemical reactions and aerobic micro-organisms. The lack of oxygen suppresses aerobic micro-organisms and the production of oxidising species. Consequently there is a rise in the concentration of anaerobic micro-organisms and in the production of reducing species. A number of major changes in ion species, together with their causative mechanism have been summarised by Caple. [2, 3] The build-up of reducing species will eventually level off as it suppresses the productive output of the relevant microbes. The chemical balance of the environment is both determined by, and is a product of, the microbial presences. Thus the chemical balance effectively characterises the environment. The extent of reducing ion species present is collectively measured as oxidation/reduction potential (Eh).

Of all the chemical reactions within the aqueous conditions the most common are those involving proton (H^+) loss or gain. The proton balance or pH equilibrium within anoxic soils is controlled by chemical equilibria such as the ferric hydroxide/ferrous iron equilibria, ammonium dissociation and bicarbonate dissociation. [12] Other factors affecting pH include the acidifying effect of the breakdown of organic matter, aluminium and iron coordination complexes which give a buffering effect at pH below 5, and the reactions which control the Eh level. Clay particles act as cation exchangers and may be particularly important in proton absorption. Organic matter will also be an important proton buffering material particularly in ombrotrophic environments.

Many other highly soluble ions are present within the aqueous environment. Each of the wide range of chemical equilibria within any burial environment can be measured using ion specific electrodes (ISE). This can be a complex procedure, since many factors affect accurate concentration determination. A simpler overall indicator level of the overall ionic concentration is obtained through conductivity.

The nature of the water which feeds into the deposit is normally the determining factor in the level of ionic species present within the liquid of the burial environment. This is, however, modified by the physical and chemical nature of the sediment, the particle size, and the ion exchange capacity of the particle surface. This will also prove an important factor in determining the overall capacity of any given anoxic waterlogged deposit to remain anoxic since such cation exchange sites will also act as reservoirs of reduced ion species.

The Durham research project

Initial research [8, 9] established that the burial environment could be defined using a Water Quality Monitoring (WQM) system monitoring standard parameters: temperature, pH, Eh, conductivity and relevant Ion Specific Electrodes (ISE) connected to a data logger. Experiments have been conducted using Solomat Water Quality Monitoring systems which utilise a data logger and electrode interface MPM 4000, MPM 4007 in conjunction with temperature compensated probes for: pH (403 PH), Eh (405 PH ORP) and conductivity (703 US), plus a number of ISEs for monitoring specific chemical equilibria (sulphide and ammonium). The probes attached to 3 m of cabling, are directly inserted into the deposit whilst the data logger remains at the surface, in a waterproof container, storing data. This system when run from an associated battery can store all the data from 6 probes monitored every 20 minutes for up to 31 days.

The archaeological sites

- Vale of Pickering: A lowland peat deposit from a post glacial lake which has suffered terrestrialisation. The important Mesolithic archaeological site of Starr Carr, together with several similar sites have been recovered from the paleoshoreline. Later drainage for agriculture has lowered the water-table and exposed much of the upper levels of archaeology. The lower levels have their water level maintained by the freshwater run off from the surrounding hills.
- Flag Fen: A lowland peaty soil formed in an inlet or shallow valley which flooded during the Late Bronze and Iron Age. This inlet was crossed by a palisade alignment with an associated platform. This wooden monument was used for ritual deposition. This site has been left above the water-table by deepening drainage dykes. Part of the site has been saved by creating an artificial lake above the archaeological organic remains and allowing the water to drain down through the site.
- Sweet Track: A Neolithic trackway which crosses the Somerset Levels, a low lying marsh which has been extensively dug for peat since the Roman period. Part of the Sweet Track is preserved in the Shapwick Heath nature reserve which has tried to maintain the burial environment by retarding drainage and pumping on water to regularly flood the site. The effectiveness of this preservation regime has been questioned. [26]
- Woodhall: A Medieval, 13th century, moated manor site in the floodplain of the river Aire. This site has a deep moat, cut into the cambic gley soil of the floodplain,

which has remained flooded since the medieval period and has slowly filled with discarded material and vegetative growth.
- Pict's Knowe: A Neolithic henge monument in a low lying Scottish valley, whose ditch was recut in the Iron Age when rising water levels flooded the site. The site appears to have remained flooded until recent drainage for agricultural use started to affect the site.
- Bull Wharf: Part of the Medieval, 12th century, London riverfront. It is composed of riverine silts, wooden piled structures and dumped fills. Many of the large riverfront timbers have remained intact on this site, though the poor survival of small organic artefacts initially led the excavators to speculate that it may have undergone periods of drying.
- Over: A free draining low lying river gravel site with a pelo-alluvial gley soil in the valley of the river Great Ouse in Cambridgeshire. There are several Bronze Age barrows in the vicinity. The site was monitored through the base of a borehole 10–30 m away from the archaeological features.
- Lanchester: Small natural hollow in the glacial clay of a North Pennine valley filled with a soil rich in decaying vegetable matter. It contains no archaeological material but has similar soil conditions to many archaeological sites, and was available both as a permanent monitoring site and the source of samples for laboratory work.

Results

When the conductivity and pH electrodes of the Water Quality Monitoring system are inserted into the anoxic waterlogged environment, they come to equilibrium quickly. The redox potential (Eh) comes to equilibrium more slowly, and normally only gives consistent readings after approximately 72 hours. In some locations it can take from 7 to 10 days to reach equilibrium (see Figure 11.1.1). This indicates that the system is sensitive enough to monitor the disturbance which it causes to the environment from its insertion. It also indicates that single or spot readings of such environments will be incorrect, and longer monitoring periods, for a minimum of 72 hours, are required to produce accurate Eh readings.

The long-term monitoring of conductivity levels shows a gentle rise in values in almost all stagnant environments, typically an increase of 10 microsiemens over a 5 day period was seen for a low conductivity solution such as rainwater. This is due to the normal gradual seepage of electrolyte from the pH and Ion Specific Electrodes. Account must be taken of this factor when examining conductivity readings running over a period of several days.

As a result of these two factors a period of 7 to 10 days was established as the appropriate for monitoring the conditions on the archaeological sites which were investigated. Results indicated that no additional information was gained when longer periods of monitoring 20–30 days were undertaken.

The repeated monitoring of the site at Lanchester, which has a burial environment identical to larger archaeologically important sites, has demonstrated the consistency and reproducibility of this form of monitoring (see Figure 11.1.2).

The pH levels of the majority of archaeological sites, were in the near neutral region of 6.0–7.2 (see Figure 11.1.2). This indicates that despite several of the sites being largely composed of degraded organic material, the clays and mineral particles as well as the

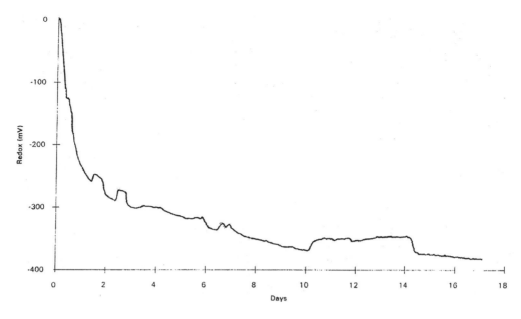

Figure 11.1.1 The redox potential (Eh) readings (mV) following insertion of the monitoring probe into the anoxic waterlogged burial environment at Lanchester.

organic material act to buffer the pH of the environment to these levels. These pH levels agree well with the best previous data obtained for Coppergate (7.0–7.6) and Piecebridge (6.6–7.8). [20]

Where additional monitoring was undertaken at a number of ombrotrophic upland peat bogs Widdybank Moss and Cauldehole, which are rainwater fed, mineral deficient and where the vegetous matter is primarily *Sphagnum*, much lower pH levels were recorded. Wether Hill, a drained upland acid soil showed similarly low pH levels.

Site	*pH*
Widdybank Moss	3.0
Cauldehole Moss	4.5
Wether Hill	4.0

These values indicated the greater acidity from upland sites which was suggested by the earlier readings of pH of 5.3–5.6 for the highly organic ditch fill of the Roman fort of Vindolanda high on the Pennine uplands near Hadrian's Wall. [21]

It is noticeable that the sites with the 'best' preservation of organic material in this study are Flag Fen and Woodhall, which together with our test site at Lanchester have low Eh Values of −200 to −400 mV. The still well preserved archaeological material at the Sweet Track (Sweet Track 2) and Vale of Pickering (Vale of Pickering 2) sites, also have low Eh values, −100 to −200 mV. In the soil of those same sites which has either dried out (Sweet Track 1) or been subject to oxygenated water (Vale of Pickering 1) the soils have become oxidising i.e. have positive Eh values, and archaeological organic materials are no longer being preserved. If the results from the dipwell at Over are typical

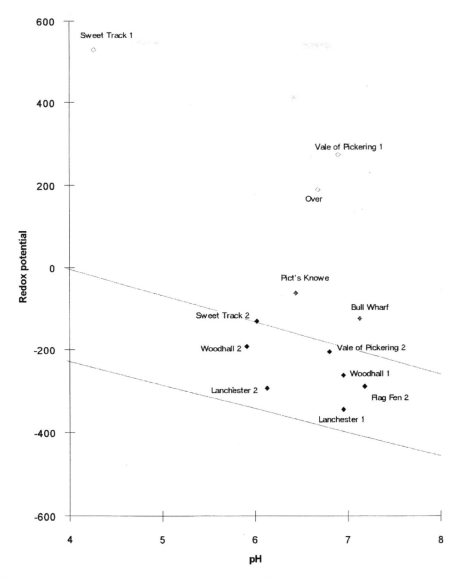

Figure 11.1.2 Representative Eh and pH values for waterlogged anoxic environments from archaeological sites monitored 'in situ' using a Water Quality Monitoring system.

of that archaeological site, one would expect little or no archaeological organic material to survive within the Bronze Age barrows on the site.

In sites where there are near zero Eh levels, such as Pict's Know or Bull Wharf, the archaeological organic material present appears to be starting to degrade. Thus the Eh levels of a site appear to correlate directly with the level of preservation of organic material.

Much existing work on analysing water chemistry and water level has been undertaken with the use of dipwells. These are usually pipes pushed into augured holes in the ground in which water collects from the deposits at the base of the pipe. This water is then sampled. Often the initial water is removed (purged) and when the tube refills it is sampled. Data from dipwell samples of the Lanchester site (see Figure 11.1.3) indicate that samples from dipwells, however they are obtained, do not describe the burial conditions, particularly Eh, as accurately as the monitoring probes of the Water Quality Monitoring system directly inserted into the anoxic waterlogged deposit.

The conductivity levels in the monitored burial environments, which are summarised in Table 11.1.1, appear to accurately indicate the type of water input to the sites. The upland sites with only rainwater input (3) have low values (4, 5), those sites with rain water running through a relatively undisturbed and uncultivated soil have only slightly higher vales (6, 7, 8, 9) similar to those seen in stream waters (2). Those sites in the east of England which are fed by groundwater from soils with high levels of agriculture and associated fertiliser pollution (10, 11, 12) have the highest levels of conductivity.

Further research will be needed to see whether such water inputs are having an effect on archaeological organic materials. However, it may be predicted that the presence of such high levels of dissolved minerals would greatly raise the rate of decay should such archaeological organic material become subject to aerobic conditions.

In laboratory experiments anoxic waterlogged sediment from Lanchester which were stored in plastic bags became acidic, though its Eh rose only slightly. This is presumably due to the diffusion of oxygen through the polythene bag and oxidation of the sample. If this process is allowed to continue and the water content declines, due to the loss of water vapour, the resultant sample becomes desiccated and oxidised (dried mud). It appears, however, to retain its acidic nature.

The monitoring of the drying out process in a continuous experiment revealed (see Figure 11.1.4) that there are clearly at least two separate processes. The Eh rises with declining water content. A separate acidification due to oxidation reaction then occurs. This may be followed by a further rise in Eh. If the sample is rehydrated, then the process

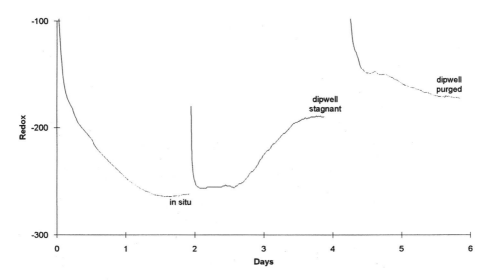

Figure 11.1.3 The Eh readings for 'in situ' monitoring and for samples removed immediately and after purging from a dipwell, in the anoxic deposits at Lanchester.

Table 11.1.1 Conductivity levels, in microsiemens, of various waters and waterlogged anoxic burial environments

	Sample/site	Conductivity (microsiemens)
1	Tap water	180–200
2	Stream water	500–600
3	Rain	30–100
4	Widdybank Moss	30
5	Cauldehole Moss	120
6	Pict's Knowe	200
7	Sweet Track	250
8	Lanchester	800
9	Vale of Pickering	800
10	Flag Fen	900–1,300
11	Woodhall	1,500
12	Over	1,700

is reversed with decline in Eh and subsequently a decline in acidity. These reactions fit well with those proposed by Ponnamperuma [27] for waterlogging and dehydration of acidic soils.

If the sample of anoxic waterlogged sediment from Lanchester is monitored with oxygenated water flowing over it, there is little reaction. A slight loss of conductivity may indicate the diffusion of ionic species from the sediment to the flowing fresh water. If the oxygenated water flows through the anoxic deposit (see Figure 11.1.5), as it would if it were pumped onto a drying deposit to maintain the water level, then the Eh rises dramatically making the sample aerobic. The pH initially falls, as the sample oxidises, but the acidic species appear soluble and are slowly washed out of the sample. This mechanism may explain the oxidised near neutral pH of the Vale of Pickering 1 monitoring site.

Discussion

The redox and pH values determined in this survey correspond well with the values for waterlogged soils and peat bogs, sulphate reducing bacteria and iron sulphide mineral stability encountered by Bass Becking, Kaplan and Moore [28] (see Figure 3.4.4). [...] This also matches well the observed phenomena of the presence of iron pyrites and the detection of hydrogen sulphide in several of these archaeological waterlogged anoxic burial environments (see Figure 3.4.5). This both provides confidence that the measured values correspond well to the existing body of knowledge and accurately describe the realities which we observe in the field.

If natural environments are regarded as simple systems it is possible to plot the measured Eh and pH values against the stability of specific chemical equilibria e.g. bicarbonate dissociation or mineral stability equilibria such as the ferrous ion/ferric hydroxide system ($Fe^{2+}/Fe(OH)_3$) [29] [17] [...] The $Fe^{2+}/Fe(OH)_3$ system accurately describes the decrease of pH upon oxidation as ferrous ions oxidise and adsorb hydroxide ions, from the dissociation of water, to form hydrated iron oxides so releasing

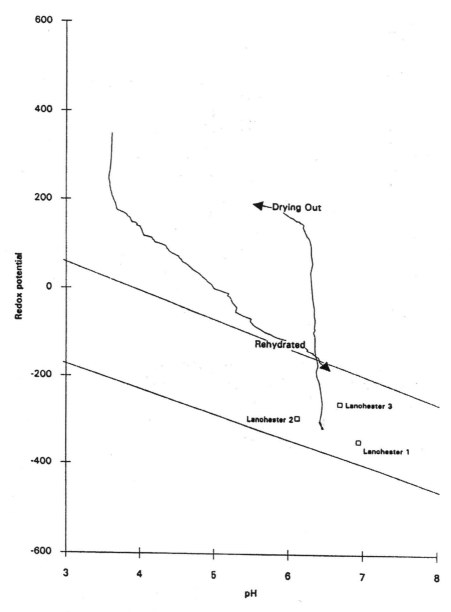

Figure 11.1.4 Changes in the Eh and pH of sediment samples from Lanchester which are undergoing dehydration and rehydration.

H+ ions. It also describes the rise in pH upon inundation and the creation of anoxia as the dissociation of ferric hydroxide to ferrous ions releasing hydroxide ions to neutralise H. Not all observed data [30] corresponds with such a simple system and in ombrotrophic peat bogs more complex chemical equilibria such as the presence of organic iron complexes have to be postulated, in order to explain all the observed data. The lack of complete accurate definitions of the composition of the soil and

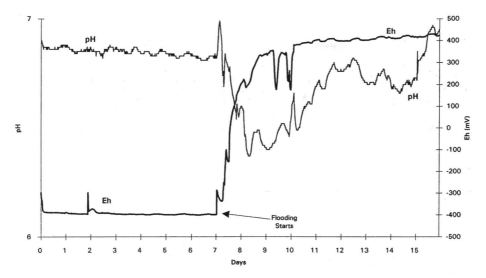

Figure 11.1.5 The changes in Eh and pH of an anoxic waterlogged sediment sample from Lanchester which has oxygenated water flowing over it for days 0–6 and through it for days 7–15.

groundwater, in particular the form of the iron minerals present, prevents definitive interpretations being advanced.

Recent work by Brown [33] has emphasised the variable nature of anoxic 'boggy' waterlogged deposits with regard to the distribution of detected methane production. [...] Similarly substantial levels of variation in all monitorable variables, most notably redox potential have been noted in paddy field soils. [34] [...]

The transient nature of some factors affecting the Eh and pH levels have also been documented. The effect of rainfall was noted in raising the Eh level in our own data from Pict's Knowe, [36] whilst the work of Haavisto [37] showed substantial changes in redox potential and Gosling and Baker [38] showed substantial changes in pH, consequent upon periods of rainfall. The latter case demonstrated the risk of creation of an acid sulphate soil [39] in a soil where there is constantly rising and falling water-table as the sulphur is cycled between sulphide forms in anoxic conditions and highly acidic sulphuric acid upon oxidation. The fluctuating water-tables identified by Corfield [2] on some sites could risk developing into this aggressive chemical state. On other sites this may alternatively be seen in a far more benign form with the oxygenated water flushing away the soluble acidic components leaving a neutral soil depleted in sulphur compounds as may be the case at the monitoring site Vale of Pickering 1.

Conclusions

The Water Quality Monitoring system appears capable of successfully monitoring anoxic waterlogged environments for the parameters of pH, redox and conductivity. These appear to be the most appropriate variables with which to initially characterise such burial environments. The monitoring at a number of sites has established the first published values for Eh and pH for the anoxic burial environments of a series of British archaeological sites. A simple correlation between redox level and degree of preservation of archaeological organic material can be observed. The pH of the burial environment has been shown to be influenced by the water input, the nature of the sediment and the degree of oxidation of the deposit. Comparison of the monitoring system with the traditional monitoring method of dipwells has shown that increased accuracy is obtainable with Water Quality Monitoring systems.

A protocol for using Water Quality Monitoring systems for analysing waterlogged anoxic deposits has been established. [...] Simple experiments with drying of samples and inundation with oxygenated water have indicated the detrimental nature of such occurrences, which can be accurately documented with Water Quality Monitoring systems. The complexity within these process: separate oxidation reactions to raise the Eh of the sample and depress its pH, can be successfully detected with Water Quality Monitoring systems.

Bibliography

1. English Heritage, 1991. *Exploring our Past, Strategies for the Archaeology of England*. HBMC, London.
2. Caple, C., 1993. Defining a reburial environment: research problems in characterising waterlogged anaerobic environments. *Proceedings of the 5th ICOM Group on Wet Organic Archaeological Materials Conference, South Portland, Maine*. ed. P. Hoffmann, 407–421.
3. Caple, C., 1994. Reburial of waterlogged wood, the problems and potential of this conservation technique. *International Biodeterioration and Biodegredation* (1994), 61–72.
4. Ashurst, J., Ballaam, N. and Foley, K., 1989. The Rose Theatre, Overcoming the Technical Preservation Problems. *Conservation Bulletin* 9, English Heritage.
5. Biddle, M., 1995. *'What future for British Archaeology'* the opening address to the 8th IFA Conference, Bradford 1984. Oxbow, 1995.
6. Corfield, M., 1993. Monitoring the condition of waterlogged archaeological sites. *Proceedings of the 5th ICOM Group on Wet Organic Archaeological Materials Conference, South Portland, Maine*. ed. P. Hoffmann, 423–436.
7. Coles, B., 1995. *Wetland Management a Survey for English Heritage*, WARP, Exeter.
8. Caple, C., and Dungworth, D., in press (a). Monitoring Wetland Burial Environments. *Conservation Science* 1995. James & James, Edinburgh.
9. Caple, C, and Dungworth, D., in press (b). Investigations into Waterlogged Burial Environments. *Archaeological Science Conference* 1995. Liverpool.
10. Bouteljie, J.B., and Goransson, B., 1972. Decay in wood constructions below the ground water table. *Biodeterioration of Materials*, eds A.H. Walters and E. Hueck van der Plas.
11. Davison, W., 1977. Sampling and handling procedures for the polarographic measurement of oxygen in hypolimnetic waters. *Freshwater Biology* 7 (1977), 393–401.
12. Davison, W., 1980. Studies of chemical speciation in naturally anoxic basins. *Freshwater Biological Association Annual Report* 48, (1980), 393–401.
13. Gwynfryn Jones, J., 1985. Decomposition in lake sediments: bacterial action and interaction. *Freshwater Biological Association Annual Report* 53 (1985).
14. Gong, Z., 1983. Pedogenesis of paddy soil and its significance in soil classification. *Soil Science* 135, 5–10.
15. Jeffery, J., 1961. Defining the state of reduction of a paddy soil. *Journal of Soil Science* 12, 172–179.
16. Jeffery, J., 1961. Measuring the state of reduction of a waterlogged soil. *Journal of Soil Science* 12, 317–325.
17. Ross, S., 1989. *Soil Processes*. London.

18   Killham, O.W., and Alexander, M., 1984. A basis for organic matter accumulation in soils under anaerobiosis. *Soil Science* 137, (6), 419–427.
19   Verhoeven, J., 1992. Fens and Bogs in the Netherlands: Vegitation, History, Nutrient Dynamics and Conservation. *Geobotany* 18. Kluwer Academic Publishers, Amsterdam.
20   Hunter, K., 1980. A study to determine the possibility of testing archaeological soils for factors influencing the preservation of artefacts. Unpublished dissertation, Dept of Archaeology, University of Durham.
21   Seawood, M., 1976. *The Vindolanda Environment.* Newcastle upon Tyne.

[...]

25   Dickinson, C.H., 1983. Micro-organisms in Peatlands. *Ecosystems of the World 4A: Mires, Swamp, Bog, Fen and Moor: General Studies.* ed A.J.P. Gore. Elsevier Scientific Publishing, Amsterdam.
26   Cox, M.J., Jones, E.B.G. and Hogan, D.V., 1995. Wetside curation and monitoring in the Somerset Levels and Moors. *Science & Site* eds J. Beavis and K. Barker. School of Conservation Sciences Bournmouth University, Bournmouth, 78–92.
27   Ponnamperuma, F.N., 1972. The Chemistry of Submerged Soils. *Advances in Agronomy* 24, 29–96.
28   Bass Becking, L.G.M., Kaplan, I.R. and Moore, D., 1960. Limits of the natural environment in terms of pH and oxidation-reduction potential. *The Journal of Geology* 68, 3, 243–284.
29   Greenland, D.J. and Hayes, M.H.B., 1981. *The Chemistry of Soil Processes.* Wiley, Chichester.
30   Freeman, C., Lock, M.A. and Reynolds, B., 1993. Climatic change and the release of immobilized nutrients from Welsh riparian wetland soils. *Ecological Engineering* 2, 367–373.
31   Pollard, AM., 1995. Groundwater Modelling in Archaeology – The Need and the Potential. *Science & Site* eds J. Beavis and K. Barker, School of Conservation Sciences Bournmouth University, Bournmouth, 93–98.
32   Weiner, S., Goldberg, P. and Bar-Yousef, O., 1993. Bone diagenesis using Fourier transform infrared spectrometry: studies of localized variations in mineral and matrix. *Second Workshop on Bone Diagenesis*, Academic Press, Oxford.
33   Brown, A.D., 1995. Carbon cycling in peat and the implications for the rehabilitation of bogs. *Wetlands Archaeology and Nature Conservation.* eds. M. Cox, V. Straker and D. Taylor, HMSO, London, 99–107.
34   Grant, C.J., 1965. Soil characteristics associated with the wet cultivation of rice. *Mineral Nutrition of the Rice Plant.* Johns Hopkins Press, Baltimore, 15–28.

[...]

36   Caple, C., forthcoming. Parameters for Monitoring Anoxic Environments. *Proceedings of the Preservation of Archaeological Remains In Situ Conference, London 1996.*
37   Haavisto, V.F., 1974. Effects of a heavy rainfall on redox potential and acidity of a waterlogged peat. *Journal of Canadian Soil Science* 54, 1333–135.
38   Gosling, L.M. and Baker, S.J., 1980. Acidity fluctuations at a broardland site in Norfolk. *Journal of Applied Ecology* 17, 479–490.
39   Bloomfield, C. and Coulter, J.K., 1973. Genesis and management of acid sulphate soils. *Advanced Agronomy* 25, 265–326.

Chapter 11.2

Steps towards the heritage management of wetlands in Europe

Bryony Coles

Source: Coles, B. (2004) 'Steps towards the heritage management of wetlands in Europe', *Journal of Wetland Archaeology*, 4: 183–98.

IN WESTERN AND NORTHWESTERN EUROPE there is a long history of wetland drainage, a process often referred to, somewhat erroneously, as 'reclamation'. There is almost certainly an equally long history of opposition to drainage, but it is only from the mid to later 20th century that attempts to halt the process have become effective. Neither drainage nor opposition have been motivated primarily by concerns for the wetland archaeological heritage, but rather by economic, social and political factors. It is against this background that recent moves to protect the wetland heritage should be considered. In this paper, three case studies from different parts of Europe will be examined to explore the influence of external and local factors on attempts to protect and manage wetlands of known archaeological significance. The extent of local involvement in the process and the significance of a sense of 'ownership' of the heritage will then be assessed.

In Britain, the first groups to press for the protection of wetland environments came from a background of interest in nature conservation. One of the first nature reserves to be established was in East Anglia at Wicken Fen which was acquired in 1899 by the National Trust. At much the same date, in the southwest of England the Glastonbury Antiquarian Society bought the field containing the late prehistoric wetland settlement known as the Glastonbury Lake Village. While protection of wetlands for their nature conservation interest developed slowly throughout the 20th century, it was to be many years before a similar development took place on the archaeological side.

From the mid 20th century, in part linked with wetland loss following recovery from the two World Wars and with the first effects of Common Market agricultural policies, conservation groups concerned with the protection of birds began to stress the importance of wetland habitats. Many species of migrating bird depend on wetlands as feeding grounds along their migration routes, or for winter feeding, or during their breeding season. The conservation groups recognised that international agreement and cooperative action was needed to protect the birds, whose seasonal moves between breeding and over-wintering grounds paid no attention to human territorial boundaries. Pressure for the protection of birds at an international level led to the first Convention on Wetlands held in Ramsar in Iran in 1971. By the end of the century, 123 countries had signed as Parties to the Convention, thereby committing to the wise use of their national wetland resources, to the designation and management of wetlands of international importance within their national borders, and to international cooperation to protect wetlands (Davidson 2001).

Meanwhile, archaeologists of the mid to later 20th century who worked in wetland conditions were mainly concerned with the rescue or salvage excavation of threatened sites. The scale and complexity of investigations expanded as the interdisciplinarity of wetland archaeology was explored, as the developments which prompted excavation grew in scale, and as funding increased thanks to legislation requiring developers to support excavation. Leaders in the field of modern, scientific rescue excavations on a large scale were undoubtedly the Swiss, whose investigations of prehistoric settlements ahead of motorway development along the shores of their lakes were funded by a tax on vehicle fuel, and the archaeologists of Baden-Württemberg in southern Germany were not far behind (Schlichtherle 2001). Thus, multidisciplinary developments in wetland archaeology around the Alpine lakes came to influence a number of other European countries.

Wetland survey for the purpose of informing planning decisions and the development of management strategies was pioneered by English Heritage from the mid 1970s (Coles 1995). In the course of the first English Heritage surveys in the Somerset Levels and the Fens, it became apparent that the wetland archaeological heritage faced some of the same threats as the natural heritage, and that similar action would be needed to protect archaeological sites as to protect rare species and their wetland habitats. In Somerset, English Heritage and English Nature took joint action in the early 1980s to secure a nature reserve of national importance which also contained an internationally significant archaeological site (Brunning 1999). In the later 20th century, several other European countries began wetland survey with a view to creating an inventory of their wetland heritage that would inform management strategies. In much of Europe, however, the character and extent of the archaeological resource remain unknown, and its survival therefore a matter of concern. In 1994, an international meeting was held at Marigny in eastern France, which recognised the need for greater knowledge, and explored common concerns and common strategies for archaeology and nature conservation (Ramseyer and Roulière-Lambert 1996). In 2000, at the first symposium of the European Archaeology Council, a similar theme was discussed, and in the publication of the symposium, the possibilities of cooperation between archaeologists and the Ramsar Convention on Wetlands were further explored (Coles and Olivier 2001).

The clear messages to emerge from these discussions were that de-watering was the major threat to wetland habitats and wetland archaeology alike, and that successful management required control of water level and water quality which could be achieved when working with a large block of wetland but not at the level of individual small sites. Other threats varied from region to region, depending on the local character of wetlands, local traditions of land ownership and exploitation, and the interplay of local

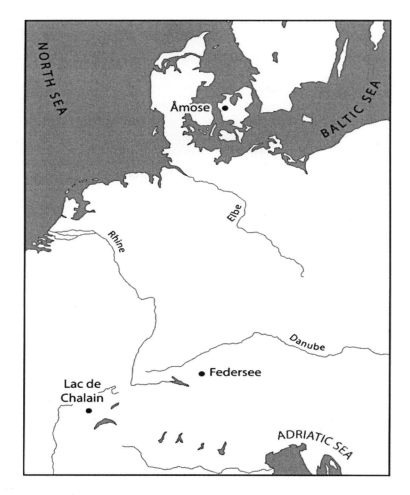

Figure 11.2.1 Map of Western Europe to show the location of the three case studies discussed in the text.
Source: Drawn by M.J. Rouillard

and external factors. These aspects will now be considered through the examination of three case studies, from Denmark, Germany and France (see Figure 11.2.1) where management schemes have been developed to protect wetland archaeology.

The Åmose, Zealand, Denmark (Fischer 1999, 2001) (see Figure 11.2.2)

In southern Scandinavia, intensive drainage of wetlands has developed over the last two centuries, to make land available for agriculture and to allow peat cutting for fuel, the latter being particularly important during and immediately following World War II. In the process of wetland destruction much important archaeological and palaeo-environmental evidence was retrieved, but there were also undoubtedly great losses. In recent decades, new threats have come through the heavy use of fertilisers in farming

Figure 11.2.2 Archaeological and palaeoenvironmental investigations at Muldbjerg I in the Åmose, directed by Troels-Smith (1954). Note the intensified exploitation of peat already underway beyond the site, which prompted this and other excavations.
Source: Photo: Troels-Smith

and through pervasive airborne pollution, both of which have a detrimental effect on water quality and hasten the decay of buried waterlogged organic materials.

The Åmose is a large river-valley bog in western Zealand, where drainage in the 1940s revealed archaeological sites of the Late Palaeolithic, Mesolithic and Neolithic, dating from c.10000 BC to c.3000 BC, and spanning the transition from foraging to farming economies. The material evidence was exceptionally well preserved and embedded in peat which provided a well stratified record of environmental change over the millennia of human presence in the wetland. This allowed a pioneering combination of archaeological and palaeoenvironmental investigations which came to characterise Scandinavian archaeology in the eyes of the world, as exemplified in Fischer and Kristiansen (2002).

[...]

Drainage continued, arable cultivation increased, deep ploughing was introduced, and the exposed peat surface wasted away at a rate of up to 4 cm per year. It was not until the 1980s that survey and several small excavations by Anders Fischer and colleagues, working for the National Forest and Nature Agency, demonstrated that there remained areas of peat containing several hundred sites of archaeological and palaeo-environmental significance. The uppermost material was degraded while the better-preserved deposits were at risk because of the continuing drainage, ploughing and use of agricultural fertilisers.

Having assessed the situation in the Åmose, the National Forest and Nature Agency argued that the cultural heritage of the area as a whole was of international significance, and should be protected as such. The argument for area protection was mainly based on the practical need to control water levels and water quality over a large area, even for the protection of scattered individual sites. By taking the area approach, one advantage would be the protection of buried sites which had not been located in the survey, which were likely to be of higher quality than sites which had been exposed. The approach also ensured the protection of the landscapes contemporary with the sites, the significance of which was not necessarily appreciated by most archaeologists until recently. The area identified for an immediate management initiative, the Kongemose area, covered 230 hectares (c.550 acres).

Following four years of legal discussions, a scheme was agreed for the 230 hectares to become a reserve. The landowner was paid c.£500,000 to relinquish his rights to cultivate the land within the reserve, and the drains were blocked to allow natural re-wetting of the ground. Parts of the Konge-Åmose Reserve have been set aside for nature conservation, some low-lying areas have flooded and become shallow lakes, and elsewhere there is pasture for cattle. The cattle are an important element in the management scheme because they eat tree seedlings and prevent unwanted tree growth. The milk from the cows can be marketed as organic (biological) since no fertilisers are used within the protected zone, and it has the additional cachet of coming from a heritage and nature reserve.

By the year 2000, the Konge-Åmose Reserve had developed sufficiently for discussions to begin on a second, more ambitious scheme for an enlarged reserve of 4,000 hectares. There were two main reasons for this initiative. First, a sufficiently high groundwater level could not be reached and maintained throughout the Kongemose Reserve without raising the level of the Åmose river, which borders the reserve, and which itself has been artificially lowered. Second, the initial Kongemose reserve includes only part of the archaeologically-rich Åmose area which is threatened by drainage and ploughing. The proposals for an enlarged reserve included provision for a wider range of activities within the protected zone, and particularly involved more sections of the local community through low intensity recreational uses. Landowners around the original reserve, having witnessed the positive benefits of the first scheme, expressed an interest in the new proposals, as did local politicians and community groups. Writing at the end of 2000, Fischer expressed his view that the development of the enlarged reserve had both local and national support (Fischer 2001). The main obstacle which he foresaw lay in the agricultural policies of the European Union, which lay outside the control of Danish archaeologists and were likely to alter without reference to the impact on wetland heritage management. His conclusion: that lobbying on a pan-European scale was required for the effective protection of the wetland cultural heritage.

The Federsee, Baden-Württemberg, Germany (Schlichtherle and Strobel 1999; Schlichtherle 2001) (see Figure 11.2.3)

The Federsee is a lake in southern Germany which has been gradually shrinking since the end of the last glaciation and its former shorelines are marked by successive phases of human settlement. Peat formed in the marshes around the lake margins as the water body diminished, and drainage of these wetlands from the 1780s onwards has enabled farming and the spread of settlement and accelerated the further shrinking of the lake. By the 1870s, prehistoric settlements preserved in the shoreline peats began to be

Figure 11.2.3 Aerial view of the Federsee, showing the area of the shrunken lake in the foreground, with the peat-moor zone of archaeological and nature conservation interest clearly visible surrounding the remaining water-body.
Source: Photo: O. Braasch, Landesdenkmalamt Baden-Württemberg

recognised and excavated, and in the 1920s there was an influential programme of research excavations around the lake. The investigations demonstrated that the waterlogged peat had preserved wooden structures and a wide range of artefacts, including organic objects, from settlements of farming peoples dating to the Neolithic and Bronze Age. A number of the sites soon became classics of European prehistory. In the years immediately before and during World War II the archaeology of the Federsee was manipulated for political ends, and this may partly explain the low level of investigation in the following decades.

In the 1980s, the State Archaeological Service of Baden-Württemberg began a programme of survey and excavation in the Federsee wetlands, led by Helmut Schlichtherle and Dieter Planck. Their aim was to establish what remained of the archaeological heritage of the region, and to assess its condition and potential for long-term preservation. The small-scale excavations revealed settlement remains with good evidence for their environmental context, good preservation of organic materials, and the potential to establish well dated sequences for the associated artefacts. These results demonstrated that the wetland archaeology of the Federsee remained significant at a European level. It was also apparent that some of the sites were becoming desiccated and for several it was only a matter of years before little would be left but lithics and other durable inorganic materials.

By 1985, the State Archaeological Service was working to coordinate efforts to protect the remaining Federsee wetlands, by bringing together a range of organisations with interests in the area. These included archaeology and nature conservation bodies, as one might expect, and also agricultural groups, water engineers and the Baden-Württemberg Finance Ministry. One of the first steps taken was to draw up an inventory of the known archaeology, flora and fauna of the Federsee wetlands, leading to an impressive list of 18 prehistoric settlements, over 40 logboats, 700 plant species, 265 bird species and 3,300 hectares of remaining wetland. Armed with this knowledge, areas were identified for preservation on the basis of containing buried prehistoric settlements in good condition, and ground surface conditions favourable to the development of a nature reserve.

With the support of the Finance Ministry and funds from the State Lottery and the European Union, any land in the locality which came up for sale was bought, whether or not it lay within a protection zone. Grants from the European Union for land purchase, planning and conservation work totalled $c.£1.5$ million (3.2 million DM) in the years 1996–2000. Another $c.£2.4$ million (5 million DM) came from the Finance Ministry specifically to fund "acquisition of archaeological monuments". The approach to land acquisition meant many sales were initiated by the landowners, rather than being requested by the conservation group. The conservation group then began a programme of land exchange, offering the arable fields and *grünland* (pasture and meadowland) they had bought both within and outside the protection zone for land within the core areas of archaeological and nature conservation interest. This was a particularly successful strategy, more so than direct purchase, since many landowners who would not have wanted to sell up were prepared to exchange fields, which allowed them to continue farming as before whilst also contributing to the protection of the cultural heritage. Grazing and mowing could continue in designated areas within the protection zone, with subsidies to the farmers to encourage them to adapt their methods to the benefit of ecological diversity.

The archaeological wealth of most wetlands is not visible, since organic material must remain buried and waterlogged to survive. Similarly, many wetland plants and animals are hard to see or inaccessible. In the Federsee protection zone, therefore, a combined archaeology and nature conservation visitor area has been designated, with museums, reconstructions, information panels and guided walks. By the year 2000 there were over 13,000 visitors a year, drawn from the immediate area, the wider region and abroad.

The long-term aim for the Federsee is to enlarge the protection zone to 2,900 hectares ($c.6,000$ acres) of wetland of archaeological and ecological significance. The broad-based support which was sought from an early stage, by bringing together all the different groups with an interest in the area, should help in achieving that aim. However, the future depends in large part on European Union agricultural policies, where change could affect the continuation of the land purchase scheme, and the subsidies for wetland-friendly farming.

The Lac de Chalain, Jura, France (Pétrequin and Pétrequin 2000; Pétrequin 2001) (see Figure 11.2.4)

The Lac de Chalain is one of a number of small lakes in eastern France whose rich archaeological heritage was first recognised in the later 19th century. Thereafter, for much of the 20th century, the lake was neglected by archaeologists, and it was not until

Figure 11.2.4 Aerial view of the Lac de Chalain. The shoreline discussed in the text is that in the centre of the photograph, and it is here that holidaymakers, farmers, fishermen and archaeologists all have an interest in use of the zone straddling lake and hinterland.

Source: Photo: P. Pétrequin

the 1970s that interest revived. The renewed investigations, led by Pierre Pétrequin and Anne-Marie Pétrequin, recorded 34 prehistoric settlements around the lake which is only a little over 3 km long by 1 km wide. The sites are dated from the mid-sixth to the early first millennium BC. Settlement was not continuous throughout this long period but for the Neolithic in particular there are long sequences when the patterns of occupation and population dynamics can be traced with considerable precision. The presence of ceramics and other artefacts in well-dated contexts has provided reference chronologies for archaeological studies beyond the immediate region. At the same time, the lake shore deposits provide well-stratified sequences of data for environmental reconstruction, enabling the evolving settlement history to be placed in the wider landscape context. Thus the archaeology of Chalain is significant for European prehistory as well as on the local and regional scales.

By the 1980s it was apparent that the remaining sites faced a number of threats, and would not survive beyond the short to medium term unless steps were taken to protect them. The more serious of the problems included drainage for agriculture which was lowering the local water table and a hydroelectric scheme which caused fluctuations in the level of the lake and erosion of the shores. Prehistoric sites near the surface were affected by both processes, and by holidaymakers who swam and boated in the lake and used the shore as a beach. In addition, there were proposals to develop the local tourist industry further, to boost the local economy at a time of changing holiday patterns and flagging agricultural returns.

In 1986 the first steps were made for the protection of one of the richest stretches, in archaeological terms, of the Chalain shoreline. Archaeologists and other scientists with local interests came together with regional heritage protection groups and the Chalain Community Council to discuss possible measures. In 1989 an agreement was signed with the hydroelectricity company to minimise fluctuations in lake levels. By the same year, the archaeological zone was fenced off, both along the landward side and through the lake waters, so that holidaymakers and others would no longer trample the soft waterlogged ground and damage the surface cultural deposits. In 1992 the legal protection of the designated zone was enhanced. In 1993 practical measures were taken to halt erosion and stabilise the shoreline by laying bags of clayey soil on a geotextile base and planting them with vegetation to help retain the protective blanket of soil. Meanwhile, state funds became available for a programme of land purchase in archaeologically rich areas. Ownership was vested in the Community Council which thereby became responsible for maintenance. These steps were accompanied by efforts to make the invisible cultural heritage accessible to the local communities and to visitors through displays, experimental house reconstructions, and a range of well illustrated and interesting publications.

By the mid 1990s, however, the scheme began to falter and fall apart. The Community Council was not carrying out maintenance of the protected zone, and the fence was not kept in repair. It seems that the Council's withdrawal was in protest at the archaeologists having thwarted their plans for the development of a large visitor centre and restaurant on the lake shore. The archaeologists, who had indeed objected to the proposed developments, felt they had had to do so because the proposed site was in the middle of the protection zone. Other local groups and individuals were upset because their former activities had been disrupted by the archaeological protection scheme, which restricted farming and fishing and catering for the summer visitors. The archaeologists were unhappy because they felt they had borne the brunt of the work, and of the complaints, with little help from the other scientific groups, including those concerned with nature conservation. Meanwhile, the vegetation planted to consolidate the shoreline was growing more vigorously than anticipated, with no one accepting responsibility for its control. In this unpromising situation, land purchase was brought to a halt in the late 1990s and management effectively ceased.

In the year 2000, state funds became available for an intensive survey of the designated archaeological protection zone, which was $c.60$ hectares in extent. This yielded a large amount of new archaeological and environmental evidence which, it was hoped, would provide the impetus to bring all the interested parties back to the negotiating table, prepared to develop a management scheme that would reconcile their conflicting interests.

Discussion: steps forward and steps back?

It is too early to claim that any of the wetland management schemes described above have either succeeded or failed. However, the projects in the Åmose and the Federsee appear more promising than the Lac de Chalain scheme. The following points may have some bearing on the ways in which the different situations have developed, and on future prospects.

Physical context and existing exploitation strategies

- The Åmose and Federsee protection zones were both former wetlands predominantly under arable and pasture at the outset of negotiations. The Lac de Chalain zone covered lake, former shoreline wetland under pasture and arable hinterland, with fishing and the holiday trade as additional exploitation strategies.
- The initial protection zone in the Åmose covered 230 hectares with 4,000 proposed for the future. In the Federsee the proposal is for 2,900 hectares. The Lac de Chalain zone covers 60 hectares.

[...]

Archaeological profiles

- It is difficult to determine quite how the international profile of the archaeology of a site or region affects the development of a strategy for management of the cultural heritage, but it seems likely that it does influence local as well as national perceptions.
- The archaeology of the Federsee has come to widespread public attention [...] sites excavated in the 1920s have become classics of the archaeological literature, particularly for the Neolithic [...]
- The evidence from the Åmose, [...] several of the sites have become embedded in the European construct of the Mesolithic. [...]
- The archaeology of the Lac de Chalain [...] does not have the international profile of the Åmose or the Federsee.

Economic aspects

- On the Lac de Chalain, the pressure of traditional activities, including the holiday trade, led to the exclusion of people from the archaeological protection zone. [...] the physical presence of a fence may have discouraged the local communities from developing a sense of ownership and responsibility [...]
- [...] Åmose [...] the single landowner was generously compensated for relinquishing the right to arable [...] and the use of the area for cattle grazing.
- The Federsee changes in agricultural exploitation have probably caused least upheaval [...]

Links with nature conservation

- The ecological value of a wetland can contribute to schemes for protection of the cultural heritage, through support from nature conservation groups and by attracting support from different sectors of the public.
- Groups engaged in protection of the natural wetland heritage have several decades' more experience than archaeologists in this field. They work at many different levels, from international to local, and increasingly they stress the need to work with local communities and their traditional methods of wetland exploitation.

Nothing is static in the worlds of heritage management and nature conservation. [...]

References

Brunning, R. (1999). 'The *in situ* preservation of the Sweet Track.' In Coles, B., J. Coles and M. Schou J_rgensen (eds), *Bog Bodies, Sacred Sites and Wetland Archaeology*, WARP Occasional Paper 12. Exeter: WARP, 33–38.

Coles, B. (1995). *Wetland Management. A survey for English Heritage*, WARP Occasional Paper 9. Exeter: WARP.

Coles, B. and A. Olivier (eds) (2001). *The Heritage Management of Wetlands in Europe*, EAC Occasional Paper 1, WARP Occasional Paper 16. Brussels and Exeter: EAC and WARP.

Davidson, N. (2001). 'A Foreword from the Ramsar Convention on Wetlands.' In B. Coles and A. Olivier (eds), *The Heritage Management of Wetlands in Europe*, EAC Occasional Paper 1, WARP Occasional Paper 16. Brussels and Exeter: EAC and WARP.

Fischer, A. (1999). 'Stone Age Åmose. Stored in museum boxes and preserved in the living bog.' In Coles, B., J. Coles and Schou J_rgensen (eds), *Bog Bodies, Sacred Sites and Wetland Archaeology*, WARP Occasional Paper 12. Exeter: WARP, 85–92.

Fischer, A. (2001). 'Scandinavia.' In Coles, B. and A. Olivier (eds) *The Heritage Management of Wetlands in Europe*, EAC Occasional Paper 1, WARP Occasional Paper 16. Brussels and Exeter: EAC and WARP, 47–54.

Fischer, A. and K. Kristiansen (eds) (2002). *The Neolithisation of Denmark – 150 years of debate*. Sheffield: John Collis Publications.

Pétrequin, P. (2001). 'Gestion du patrimoine archéologique en milieu humide: le cas de la France et des lacs de Chalain et de Clairvaux.' In B. Coles and A. Olivier (eds), *The Heritage Management of Wetlands in Europe*, EAC Occasional Paper 1, WARP Occasional Paper 16. Brussels and Exeter: EAC and WARP, 117–124.

Pétrequin, P. and A.M. Pétrequin (2000). '*Chalain et Clairvaux. 4000 ans d'habitat lacustre. Itinéraire, Franche-Comté.*' Editions du Patrimoine et MAE editeurs, ERTI.

Ramseyer, D. and M.J. Roulière-Lambert (eds) (1996). '*Archéologie et érosion. Mesures de protection pourla sauvegarde des sites lacustres et palustres,*' Actes de la rencontre de Marigny-Lac de Chalain. Lons-le-Saunier: Centre Jurassien du Patrimoine.

Schlichtherle, H. and M.u.A. Strobel (1999) *Archaeology and Protection of Nature in the Federsee Bog*, Catalogue to the exhibition in the European Council. Strasbourg.

Schlichtherle, H. (2001). 'Schutz und management archaologischer Denkmale im Bodensee und Federsee.' In B. Coles and A. Olivier (eds), *The Heritage Management of Wetlands in Europe*, EAC Occasional Paper 1, WARP Occasional Paper 16. Brussels and Exeter: EAC and WARP, 125–132.

Generic mitigation measures

Visitor and land management

Chapter 12

Generic mitigation measures
Visitor management

Conservation through raising value

PRESERVATION ACTIVITIES, IDENTIFYING and mitigating the physical threats to archaeological remains, often require substantial resources, and additional further funding is required maintain the site thereafter. The remains must have sufficient value to individuals, local, regional or national organisations that they will make the required resources available. Value can be raised by heightening the significance of the remains to a small number of individuals or generally increasing the number of people and organisations who appreciate the remains; in practice, attempts are made to do both. It is often possible to raise value through or during the preservation process. In practice, steps taken to increase the value of the remains involve increasing:

- *Knowledge*: the more that is known about a site, when it existed, who lived there, what events or activities occurred on the site (historical value), the more people relate to the site and value it, seeing it not just as history, but part of their heritage (Lowenthal 1996). Undertaking research, such as surveying the site or undertaking archaeological excavation, raises awareness about the site and emphasises its importance. Involvement of local people in these activities or through regular lectures or tours can transmit that importance to the wider community. If knowledge about the site is transmitted (shared/taught) to a large number of people, the more chance of at least some valuing the site. Educating a wider audience can take place using a large number of methods and at many different educational levels: school visits, site tours, lectures, TV, radio, newspapers, books, articles in academic journals, articles in popular magazines, the Internet. Some can be targeted to specific groups (e.g. local historical societies); others to a more general audience through the mass media. As people may encounter more than one of these sources of information, different messages can be given, making the site more complex and involving.
- *Activities*: if the site plays a role in the life of the local community, or a specialist group, then they are more likely to value it (communal or social value). If events are held at

the site, then people are constantly reminded of its existence, damage is noticed and repaired. Activity may be visits by tourists, walking the dog, the local village fete, barbecues, concerts, Easter egg hunts or a nature watch. In all these activities, people will exchange information about the site (education) and its value grows. There are dangers from too many people, leading to damage of the site and encouraging the development of facilities (e.g. laying power and water to the site), which may harm the physical remains (see Chapter 8).

The value of sites gradually declines for each succeeding generation unless they are actively re-enforced and re-transmitted. In almost all cases, this means people – either local people involved in activities on the site or visitors coming to see the site. A balance must be established between the use and damage to the site and a high value, or the risk of little activity and a low value.

Visitors: value

Visitors to archaeological remains bring several 'benefits':

- Direct spending of money at the monument (admission, guidebooks, refreshments, souvenirs).
- Indirect spending in the local area (accommodation, meals, transport, gifts).
- Valuing the site (they talk about it and tell others = more visitors, if one group of people think a site is important then so will others, high visitor numbers encourage investment in the site and local facilities) (see above).

The financial benefits come to local businesses and heritage organisations. It is often the case that the presence of large numbers of visitors leads to investment in the site – part of which will aid preservation of the remains, but this is not guaranteed.

Visitors damage archaeological remains:

- *Deliberate damage*: looting, graffiti, souveniring (see Chapter 10).
- *Unconscious damage*: wearing away surfaces (see Chapter 8), changing the environment in caves (see Chapter 10).
- *Indirect damage*: building improved facilities, paths and access improvements, poor-quality conservation and restoration (see Chapter 6).

There is a balance to be struck between the benefits derived from visitors and the losses from visitation:

Many historic houses, villages, churches and so on could not be kept in a proper state of repair without tourist money . . . and given a reasonable influx of tourist money it is usually possible . . . to keep the tourist nuisance at an acceptable level.
(Beck and Bryan 1971: xxi)

The economic benefits of tourism to communities have proved compelling for most communities. However, this does not always translate into benefit to the remains, which are often the responsibility of different organisations.

The dual requirement to both preserve the archaeological remains and ensure that the ancient sites are available for education and enjoyment, or words to that effect, form the basis for most heritage legislation around the world. However, without management and control, archaeological remains could be 'loved to death' by their visitors. Consequently, management of the site focuses both on managing activities to minimise damage but maximising value and seeking to attract an appropriate number of people to the site (Goldilocks number) – too many and the site is damaged; too few and their impact is insufficient to raise the perceived value of the site. The impact of visitors on sites has already been discussed in Chapters 8 and 10. The principal conceptual tool for assessing and managing visitors in relation to preservation of archaeological remains is carrying capacity.

Carrying capacity

The concept of carrying capacity, the number of individuals an environment can support without detriment (significant negative impact), was coined in the nineteenth century. It became more widely used from the 1960s in ecology and human population research, in particular wildlife and range management studies, to describe the number of animals a given area could support without negative impact of the environment. Wagar (1964) recognised that the concept could be applied to recreational visitors to wilderness lands and, from the 1980s, tourism carrying capacity (TCC) referred to the number of tourists an area could take without physical, social, economic or cultural negative impact (Mathieson and Wall 1982). It was also applied to individual heritage sites. As far as preservation *in situ* is concerned, we are concerned with the number of visitors a given site can take without significant physical impact on the archaeological remains. However, there are clearly difficulties in defining carrying capacity in a realistic site situation: the differences in susceptibility of different parts of the monument to damage (depending on materials and mechanism), variations in susceptibility depending on the season and the weather, the question of what is a 'significant' impact (who decides and what measures are used). There is also variability due to the impacts of different types of visitor, Loubser (2001) making the distinction between 'soft' visitors (self-motivated, informed individuals or small groups who are self-sufficient), who invariably have minimal impact on the sites and are respectful of the remains, and 'hard' visitors (seek comfort, information, facilities). Carrying capacity remains a useful concept since the relationship of 'more visitors more damage, fewer visitors less damage' is widely observed (Butler 2002), but given the variability noted above a single number is unlikely to be accurate. In practice, a single number is used for administrative convenience, as in the case of visiting prehistoric French caves or walking inside the stones at Stonehenge. Such numbers are usually based on experience of previous visitor behaviour and the precautionary principle (see Chapter 8), but have been varied, usually responding to the political necessity of some public access. Ideally a number just below the lowest number of visitors at which damage is detected is used as the stated carrying capacity, though it may vary with the season, weather conditions, visitor type etc. Carrying capacity is not an end in itself; it is a means to an end, maximising visitation to archaeological remains, with the educational and financial benefit that flows from that, but without damaging the archaeological value (integrity) of the remains.

In a crude form, carrying capacity has been enacted in the past, such as banning tourists from the area immediately beside the stones at Stonehenge in 1978 due to damage to the stones and surrounding ground (Bainbridge 1979). Similar steps were taken in caves such as Lascaux housing Palaeolithic art (see Chapter 10), but such responses have invariably occurred once damage is already quite severe.

In modern heritage practice, approaches such as limits of acceptable change (LAC) (Stankey et al. 1985) enacted in frameworks such as visitor experience and resource protection (VERP) (National Park Service 1997) have been seen as a useful way of applying the concept of carrying capacity. It can be summarised as:

- Specify desired future (resource) conditions.
- Identification of indicators (of resource conditions).
- Specify standards (of acceptable conditions).
- Develop monitoring (of the indicators).
- Develop management actions (to ensure that standards are maintained).

Qualitative goals such as the desired site conditions are defined in terms of quantifiable indicators (such as specific damage); these are monitored and compared against defined standards (which can act as trigger points), leading to actions to mitigate the damage and ensure the quality of the remains is restored/maintained.

At present, many sites suffering from visitor degradation are in the process of defining quantifiable indicators, setting appropriate standards and having a management plan to define mitigation measures when agreed trigger points are crossed. Sites such as earthworks typically monitor damage as turf rupture (measured or photographed from a fixed point), path or gully erosion (measured depth or changed profile). Attempts are being made at sites such as the caves at Jenolan, Australia (Mackay 2010), and at Mogao, China (Demas et al. 2010) (see Chapter 12.1), to use relative humidity and carbon dioxide levels as definable quantifiable indicators and set appropriate standards. These could give much more dynamic responses, constantly measuring a number of indicators and advising authorities on visitor numbers dictated by the most susceptible variable in the changing condition of the monument and its environment or weather conditions.

Mitigation

Mitigation measures related to visitors appropriate to earthworks were described in Chapter 8; those applicable for cave environments were described in Chapter 10. Generic measures to reduce visitor numbers include:

- Discourage visitation; cease all publicity, remove signage, remove car parking and transport links (bus stops), remove facilities such as toilets and cafes, only allow guided tours or prebooked visits, increase admission price.
- Deflect visitation, encourage people to visit 'flagship' or 'honeypot' sites, those that can absorb visitors without significant damage to the site, and where quality of the visit can be ensured.
- Controlling visitor numbers present in the monument at any one time minimises the risks of crowding, pilfering and vandalism, and above all from damage resulting from brushing against objects or collision with them, a particular concern in historic houses. Timed tickets, as practised at Mr Straws' House, Worksop (National Trust property), minimises these problems.

- Limiting the number of people who can visit the remains over a given period of time, usually a year. This can be achieved by reducing opening hours, reducing the times in the year when the site is open, closing the monument once smaller weekly or monthly visitor number quotas have been met and closing the monument in bad weather. These measures are particularly appropriate to limiting the wear damage on biologically self-repairing systems such as turf (i.e. earthworks).

Sites such as Steel Riggs on Hadrian's Wall endured 500,000 visits annually, which resulted in considerable erosion. Removing all publicity and emphasising other sites reduced visitor numbers, so avoiding the need to close the site to protect it (Butler 2002).

Bibliography

Bainbridge, S. (1979) *Restrictions at Stonehenge: The Reactions of Visitors to Limitations in Access: Report of a Survey*, London: HMSO.

Beck, B. and Bryan, F. (1971) 'This other Eden: a study of tourist in Britain', *The Economist*, 240: 66–83 and supplement following 60.

Butler, R.W. (2002) 'Issues in applying carrying capacity concepts: examples from the United Kingdom', WWF Hellas Conference on Methods for Tourism Carrying Capacity Measurement and Visitor Management in Protected Areas: Presentations and Conclusions, Athens, 31 May–1 June.

Demas, M., Maekawa, S., Bell, J. *et al.* (2010) 'Sustainable visitation at the Mogao Grottoes: a methodology for visitor carrying capacity', in N. Agnew (ed.), *Conservation of Ancient Sites on the Silk Road: Proceedings of the Second International Conference on the Conservation of Grotto Sites*, Los Angeles, CA: Getty Conservation Institute, pp. 160–9.

Loubser, J. (2001) 'Management planning for conservation', in D.S. Whitely (ed.), *Handbook of Rock Art Research*, Walnut Creek, CA: AltaMira Press.

Lowenthal, D. (1996) *Possessed by the Past*, New York: The Free Press.

Mackay, R. (2010) 'Special and environmental monitoring as a tool for managing visitor impact at Jenolan Caves, Australia', in N. Agnew (ed.), *Conservation of Ancient Sites on the Silk Road: Proceedings of the Second International Conference on the Conservation of Grotto Sites*, Los Angeles, CA: Getty Conservation Institute, pp. 170–8.

Mathieson, A. and Wall, G. (1982) *Tourism: Economic, Physical and Social Impacts*, London: Longman.

National Park Service (1997) *The Visitor Experience and Resource Protection (VERP) Framework: A Handbook for Planners and Managers*, Denver: Denver Service Centre, National Park Service, US Dept. of the Interior, available at: http://planning.nps.gov/document/verphandbook.pdf (accessed June 2014).

Stankey, G.H., Cole, N.D., Lucas, R.C. *et al.* (1985) 'The limits of acceptable change (LAC) system for wilderness planning, USDA Forest Service', General Technical Report no. INT. 176, Ogden, UT: Intermountain Forest and Range Experiment Station, Forest Service, US Dept. of Agriculture, available at: www.fs.fed.us/cdt/carrying_capacity/lac_system_for_wilderness_planning_1985_GTR_INT_176.pdf (accessed June 2014).

Wagar, J.A. (1964) *The Carrying Capacity of Wild Lands for Recreation*, Forest Science, Monograph 7, Washington, DC: Society of American Foresters.

Chapter 12.1

Sustainable visitation at the Mogao Grottoes
A methodology for visitor carrying capacity

Martha Demas, Shin Maekawa, Jonathan Bell, and Neville Agnew

Source: Demas, M., Maekawa, S., Bell, J. *et al.* (2010) 'Sustainable visitation at the Mogao Grottoes: a methodology for visitor carrying capacity', in N. Agnew (ed.), *Conservation of Ancient Sites on the Silk Road,* Los Angeles, CA: Getty Conservation Institute, pp. 160–9.

[. . .]

AT THE MOGAO GROTTOES, visitor numbers have risen steadily since the 1980s and site managers have faced increasing pressure from local authorities and businesses to encourage more tourism. The direct and indirect impacts of visitation on the primary cultural resource of the site, the 492 painted caves, have not been determined previously, raising concerns for irreparable damage from increased visitation. For this reason, a carrying capacity study commenced in 2001 to determine the impact of visitation on the caves and inform management practices in order to prevent deterioration and ensure the quality of the visitor experience. The study, which addresses one of the principal objectives of the master plan for the site, is a joint undertaking of the Getty Conservation Institute (GCI) and the Dunhuang Academy (DA) and is part of a larger initiative to apply the China Principles at the Mogao Grottoes (Agnew *et al.* 2006).

Defining the parameters of the carrying capacity study

The carrying capacity for a heritage site is defined not as an immutable number of visitors that a site can safely accommodate but rather in terms of the parameters necessary to prevent deterioration of the resource while maintaining a predetermined threshold of visitor safety, satisfaction, and education. This involves consideration of a number of variables: management capabilities and limitations, including services and infrastructure; various impacts to a site, their relationship to visitation, and methods to monitor them; the degree of change or impact that is acceptable at a site; and the means by which a site's values will be protected and the quality of the visitor experience maintained while allowing flexibility to meet changing conditions. The complexities inherent in this undertaking required that clear parameters be established at the outset of the study. For Mogao, these parameters are as follows:

- Values to be protected. The ultimate aim of establishing carrying capacity is to protect the primary cultural and natural values of the site (the wall paintings and sculpture of the grottoes and the landscape) as well as the quality of the experience of visitors, who come to Mogao because of those values.
- Limits of acceptable change. This concept defines the degree of change or impact that will be tolerated for the resource and the visitors. As the wall paintings and sculpture in the caves are the primary cultural resource of the site and are nonrenewable, no detectable change due to visitation is acceptable. Some level of impact to the landscape and to the quality of visitor experience during peak periods is unavoidable but can be mitigated or reversed through good planning and management.
- Current management policies and use zones. Existing management policies and practices relevant to carrying capacity are the number of guides, tour size and numbers, opening hours, and so on. Current use zones are the Grotto Zone (see Figure 12.1.1), where the decorated caves are excavated into the cliff face, and the Visitor Use Zone, where visitor facilities and exhibition buildings are located. This study is aimed primarily at the Grotto Zone.
- Time of greatest threat. This is the summer peak period of visitation, from May through October, including the two national holiday weeks in May and October. During this period, management and the grottoes themselves are often overwhelmed by visitors, and environmental conditions pose the greatest danger. The experience of visitors is also most heavily affected at this time.

Based on the above parameters, the carrying capacity for the Mogao Grottoes site was defined as follows:

- Daily maximum number of people who can visit the Grotto Zone without any resulting alteration or damage to the wall paintings and sculpture. Any damage or deterioration to the wall paintings due to visitation is irreversible and unacceptable. Determining a safe number of visitors to the caves and the conditions of visitation lies at the core of the carrying capacity study.
- Maximum number of people who can be accommodated in the Visitor Use Zone without unacceptable change or intrusion to the landscape and setting of the site. The desert landscape setting of the grottoes includes the natural environment (mountains, sand dunes, trees, river) as well as cultural features (stupas, historic buildings, the cliff face with caves), all of which contribute significantly to the values of the site and are integral to the experience of the visitor. The landscape and setting are affected mainly by visual intrusions (buildings and parking lots) related to visitor services, and there is a direct relationship between visitor numbers and the buildings needed to service them.

Figure 12.1.1 The Grotto Zone is the protected, narrow strip along the cliff face into which the caves were carved, many of which are open to public visitation.
Source: Photo: J. Paul Getty Trust

- Maximum number of people who can use the site daily while maintaining the quality of the visitor experience, visitor safety, and the ability of management to effectively meet visitor requirements. The relationship of visitors to the primary cultural and natural values, to the staff, and to the information and services provided constitutes the visitor experience of the site. A temporary decline in visitor satisfaction may be tolerated because the condition is reversible with good management and adjustment of visitor numbers; however, there can be no tolerance for diminished visitor safety.

In sum, the carrying capacity for the Mogao Grottoes is the maximum number of visitors who can use the site daily over the six-month peak visitation period of May through October without risk of damage to the wall paintings and sculpture, without unacceptable change to the setting and natural environment, and while ensuring visitor safety and satisfaction. Establishing the carrying capacity for the Grotto Zone is the priority, as it constitutes the primary cultural resource and is the focus of this study. [. . .]

Methodology of the carrying capacity study

The methodology developed for this study is adapted from the Visitor Experience and Resource Protection (VERP) model developed by the U.S. National Park Service for natural sites. It consists of two main stages (VERP 1997; Merced River Plan 2000).

Stage 1: assessment and analysis

[...] Five distinct steps progress from defining the problem to determining the conditions that will limit visitation. [...]

Identifying issues that have an impact on the site and visitors

The most critical issue impacting the preservation of the wall paintings is active or ongoing deterioration. By this is meant that the mechanisms leading to decay are active or can be activated under certain conditions, one of which is elevated humidity, caused by the cave doors being open for visitation, allowing outside air to enter (see Figure 12.1.2). For visitors, key issues to consider are acceptable carbon dioxide (CO_2) levels and comfortable physical space requirements.

Identifying key indicators to monitor change

Indicators measure the status or 'health' of the resource. For the wall paintings, the main indicator of ongoing problems is evidence of hygroscopic salt-related deterioration (see Figure 12.1.2, right), but any detectable change in the wall paintings is indicative of undesired conditions and requires a management response. For visitors, the main indicators are a decline in satisfaction, as measured in surveys repeated over time,

Figure 12.1.2 Ongoing deterioration of the wall paintings (a severe example, right) can be activated by elevated external humidity entering the caves, especially during periodic rain events in the summer months (left).
Source: Photos: J. Paul Getty Trust

complaints to guides about crowding, and incidents of fainting due to bad air quality and high CO_2 levels.

Defining desired conditions

The desired condition for the wall paintings is stability, meaning no change in their current state. This requires a stable environment that does not activate the mechanisms of deterioration, namely deliquescent salts, and prevention of physical damage by visitors. For visitor safety and comfort, CO_2 concentrations must be maintained at or below internationally accepted levels, and the allocated space per person for visitation should be sufficient to ensure that crowding is not a factor.

Designing and implementing a research and assessment strategy

The aim of the research and assessment strategy was to determine the mechanisms of deterioration, the link between deterioration and visitation, and the safety and comfort levels for visitors. This is the largest and most complex component of the carrying capacity study. The research strategy integrates analytical investigations in the laboratory, environmental monitoring and research, deterioration monitoring, assessment of condition and visitation potential for each cave, and visitor-related research and surveys. Together, these components of the study provide information on the following:

- the presence, types, and distribution of active deterioration in the caves;
- the conditions for activating this deterioration;
- the role of natural (i.e., not mechanically driven) air exchange with the outside, as measured by number of air changes per hour (ACH), in accelerating or mitigating deterioration, rise of relative humidity (RH), and CO_2 buildup; and
- the basis for determining risk to the wall paintings from visitation, to visitors themselves from CO_2 buildup, and to the visitor experience from crowding and other factors.

The six basic components of the research and assessment strategy are described in some detail below. These are the basis for determining the limiting conditions.

Analytical investigations

It was confirmed from the joint DA-GCI project in cave 85 that ongoing deterioration in the wall paintings is due mainly to hygroscopic salts and their response to fluctuations in humidity (i.e., deliquescence of salts as humidity rises and recrystallization as it falls). This cycle of deliquescence-recrystaliization occurs repeatedly over time as cave humidity changes and ultimately results in damage to the wall paintings. To understand this phenomenon, it was necessary to identify the salt species and the deliquescent relative humidity. Laboratory investigations showed that Mogao salts, primarily sodium chloride (NaCl) with minor amounts of other salt species, begin to absorb detectable amounts of water vapor at approximately 67 percent RH (pure NaCl deliquesces at 75 percent RH) (see Figure 12.1.3). Practically, this means that 67 percent RH is the critical point at which deterioration is activated in susceptible caves, though time is also important: the

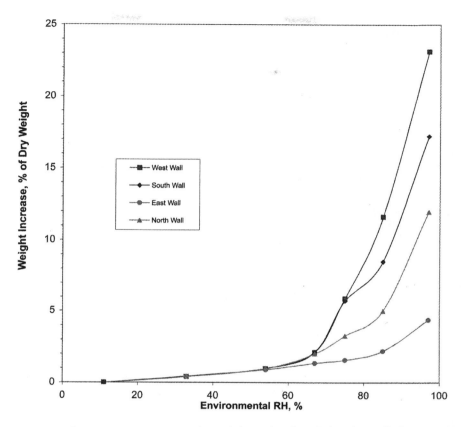

Figure 12.1.3 Laboratory investigations showed that salts identified in the wall plaster at Mogao (in this example, from cave 98) begin to absorb a large amount of water vapor at approximately 67 percent RH. Note that the west wall—adjacent to the body of the rock—contains the highest percentage of salts in most caves and thus the quickest uptake of moisture.

longer cave RH remains above 67 percent, the more moisture is absorbed (depending on the amount of salts) and the greater the potential for damage. For purposes of managing the caves, the RH threshold for visitation has been conservatively set at 62 percent.

Salt concentrations in caves vary and thus have different rate responses to fluctuating RH. To understand the effect of salt concentration and the progression of deterioration, painted clay coupons that simulate the structure, composition, and pigments of the wall paintings and loaded with different amounts of salts were manufactured. Half of each coupon was also sprayed with a 2 percent solution of polyvinyl acetate (PVAC), previously used at Mogao as a treatment for flaking wall paintings. Once complete, the coupons were subjected to cycling at 25 and 85 percent RH in an environmental chamber to ensure thorough deliquescence and crystallization of the salts during each cycle. Coupons were examined after each drying cycle, that is, when recrystallization and any resulting damage occur (see Figure 12.1.4), and changes were recorded photographically and through written description. Coupons representative of progressive deterioration were withdrawn and stored in a desiccator at a low RH to prevent further change.

Figure 12.1.4 Clay coupon, simulating the structure, composition, and pigments of the wall paintings, showing typical salt-related deterioration after 26 cycles of high and low RH fluctuations in an environmental chamber.
Source: Photo: J. Paul Getty Trust

An index of deterioration was then established that correlated with number of cycles and percentage of salt. The coupons that make up this index serve as a model for the development of salt-related deterioration in painted clay and exhibit many of the same patterns and types of conditions present in the wall paintings (e.g., cracking, flaking, plaster powdering). The coupons will also serve as reference for uncycled coupons placed in the caves as long-term deterioration monitors, as discussed in Deterioration Monitoring below.

Environmental research and modeling

Environmental monitoring is pivotal to making the link between visitation and mechanisms of deterioration in the caves. The objective is to determine the separate effects on the cave microenvironments of visitors (i.e., people in the caves) on the one hand and visitation (i.e., the opening and closing of cave doors) on the other, building on previous environmental monitoring and testing.

Since 1991, environmental monitoring has involved:

- monitoring of the exterior climate [. . .]
- recording air temperature, relative humidity, and surface temperature in four test caves, [. . .]
- experiments to understand the effect of visitors on the microenvironment (Maekawa 1996) [. . .]
- experiments to determine the air exchange rate under varying conditions: doors opened, closed; visited, not visited; and the time required for the cave microenvironment to return to baseline
- spot monitoring in selected caves of CO_2, RH, and temperature during periods of peak visitation.

The air change rate, or ACH, is the number of times in one hour that the interior air is mixed with an equal volume of exterior air. Air change rate is measured by decay of a tracer gas released in the cave. There is no single, fixed value for cave's ACH. The range of ACH values found for a particular cave depends on whether the doors are opened or closed, on the temperature difference between exterior and interior, on exterior wind speed and direction, and on cave characteristics such as size, architectural configuration, and area of door opening. ACH values drop markedly when cave doors are closed or when visitors block the entryway.

Air exchange with the exterior purges the cave of water vapor and CO_2 emitted by visitors and, likewise, may bring in high humidity from outside until the exchange process equilibrates interior and outside air. A continuously visited cave has its doors open throughout the visitation day (an eight-hour period) such that a return to the cave's environmental baseline (i.e., the situation without visitation and the door closed) is possible only during the closed period at night (sixteen hours). During the summer period, the external atmospheric humidity rises and experiences periodic spikes due to rain events, typically reaching 85 percent. Elevated relative humidity may persist for several days depending on the duration of the rain and humid conditions, resulting in greater quantity of moisture absorbed by the salts and, consequently, greater damage upon drying. The surface temperature of the cave walls, always substantially cooler than exterior air in summer, is also integral to determining the relative humidity at the surface of the paintings and the potential for salt deliquescence. As air temperature cools at the wall surface, relative humidity rises, meaning that exterior air does not need excessive humidity to create undesired conditions for the paintings.

Caves with high air exchange may be expected to override the influence of visitors on relative humidity (approximately 5 percent) and CO_2 buildup. However, in caves where air exchange is low, the increase in relative humidity and CO_2 can be significant during peak months. The lowest ACH values, either measured in situ or calculated from an empirical formula (based on measured ACH values as a function of cave volume and similar measured caves), are used to determine the potential for elevated CO_2 levels in each cave. Statistical values based on environmental data collected over a number of years indicate how many days per month over the summer period those caves with active deterioration will likely require closure because of infiltrating high ambient humidity. Table 12.1.1 illustrates that on the average over the monitored five-and-a-half-year period, 68 percent RH was exceeded less than 5 percent (36 hours) of the month of July; however, in any single year a relative humidity higher than 68 percent can occur for a longer period as the climate varies from year to year.

Deterioration monitoring

Methods of monitoring for visitor-induced deterioration were established and put in place in four environmentally monitored test caves in 2002. Areas of active deterioration are monitored photographically (see Figure 12.1.2), through written observations, and by collection and weighing of fine particles of plaster and, rarely, paint flakes fallen from the walls. Two of these caves were closed to visitation as control caves, and two were subject to routine visitation, allowing for comparison in the rate of change of unvisited and visited caves.

Table 12.1.1 Summer monthly percentile rank of surface relative humidity at the west wall of cave 29 based on data collected over a five-and-a-half-year period

Month	7.2 hours per month RH exceeded	36 hours per month RH exceeded	72 hours per month RH exceeded
May	56%	43%	35%
June	83%	55%	43%
July	84%	68%	59%
August	81%	62%	52%
September	60%	47%	35%

Salt-laden clay coupons identical to those cycled in the lab were installed in the caves to determine their feasibility for use as long-term deterioration monitoring tools. If and when the coupons show signs of deterioration, they will be compared to the reference deterioration index produced in the lab and assigned a rank of severity. The coupons are intended to supplement in situ inspection and provide standardized monitors for deterioration, over the long term, in susceptible caves.

Visitor management research and assessment

Visitor-related research and assessment have focused on three areas: visitor behavior and satisfaction; appropriate physical capacity or occupancy (for the usable area of the main chamber of each open cave) (see Figure 12.1.5) and CO_2 safety levels; and current visitor management policies and capacity.

Since 2002 visitor surveys and observations have been conducted by the Dunhuang Academy and the Australian Department of the Environment and Heritage to assess visitor behavior and satisfaction. Poor air quality and high CO_2 have long been a source of discomfort for visitors in the summer months. Acceptable limits for physical capacity (2 persons per square meter) and CO_2 levels (not to exceed 1,500 parts per million [ppm]) were established based on bibliographic research and industry standards. These values become critical parameters for defining the limiting conditions (ASHRAE 2007; Doorne 2000).

'Management capacity' refers to the ability of management to protect the caves and to service the visitors in the Grotto Zone. [. . .]

Assessment of cave physical condition and visitation potential

An assessment of physical condition and visitation potential is being undertaken for each of the 492 painted caves at Mogao. The principal objective is to determine which caves may be opened to visitation as a function of their physical condition (assessment of risk level to the wall paintings from visitation) and visitation potential (cultural significance, safety and access, physical capacity, and capacity set by the CO_2 limit). The CO_2 capacity of a cave is defined (for purposes of this study) as the number of visits of twenty-five persons that the cave can accommodate such that the CO_2 concentration does not exceed 1,500 ppm. In addition, the assessment will serve to plan for regular monitoring of the caves and periodic reevaluation of risk status.

Figure 12.1.5 The physical capacity of a cave, based on usable area of the main chamber, varies markedly, with many caves being too small to handle a group of twenty-five persons. Inevitably, groups tend to cluster close to the guides and the main focal points.
Source: Photo: Richard Ross © J. Paul Getty Trust

A principal purpose of the risk assessment is to determine those caves that are at risk from visitation due to the salt-related mechanisms of deterioration. Those caves require careful monitoring and temporary closure under certain exterior environmental conditions. Other risks from visitation include the potential impact of humidity fluctuations or air movement on fragile paint layers (e.g., severe flaking) and mechanical damage from visitors touching the paintings. The risk assessment is used to establish a provisional carrying capacity and is the first stage in a process to ensure that there is no present or future impact from visitation. The preliminary ranking of risk will need to be confirmed and periodically reassessed as part of an ongoing monitoring program. The assessment process will result in a 'portfolio' for each cave comprising a compilation of information on the date, location, size, dimensions, significance, visitation history, safety issues, and previous interventions, in addition to a record of its current physical condition. This information will become part of an integrated management system for both visitor management and conservation planning to be defined in Stage 2 of the carrying capacity study.

Defining the limiting conditions: The limiting conditions are the parameters that will restrict visitation to each cave and that may require management responses. They are derived from the research and assessment strategy discussed above and may be characterized as either 'winnowing' or 'restricting' conditions. The winnowers—principally significance, safety and access, and physical capacity but also including an unacceptable level of risk to the wall paintings—provide clear thresholds that must be met for caves to be open to visitors for purposes of establishing the initial carrying capacity. These conditions thus winnow, or separate out, the caves currently suitable for visitation from those that cannot be visited.

The restricting conditions, which are applied to the winnowed caves, are risk to wall paintings, CO_2 capacity, and management capacity. Risk to wall paintings and CO_2 capacity will restrict visitation in certain caves under specific conditions but will not prevent their use. Management capacity, limited by factors such as tour group size, number of guides, and hours of opening will also play a role in restricting the total number of visitors that can be accommodated in a single day.

All of these limiting conditions are potentially amenable to mitigation strategies, which might allow a higher threshold of visitation. Some of these strategies may be viable in the short term (e.g., the use of smaller tour group size to allow for visitation of smaller caves), but others may require a period of investigation, testing, and monitoring to determine their efficacy (e.g., the use of fans to increase air exchange, which may create new risks, or undertaking conservation of caves at unacceptable risk). [. . .]

Stage 2: response

In the response stage of the methodology the limiting conditions described above are used to establish the carrying capacity of the grottoes. Each open cave will have a maximum number of possible tour groups per hour, based on the CO_2 limit and natural air change rates. For a number of reasons, forced air exchange is not considered practicable or desirable. These numbers will be adjusted further due to periodic climatic events (e.g., rain), requiring open caves at risk to be temporarily closed. The carrying capacity of the Grotto Zone will therefore vary as a consequence of management responses to environmental changes or a change in visitor management capacities and policies (e.g., size of groups, opening hours, or number of guides).

Long-term monitoring and management tools are needed for sustainable visitor capacity. Ongoing monitoring of the wall paintings and cave microenvironments will be necessary to determine if and when change occurs. Methods of monitoring that will trigger management responses, such as real-time data capture and display of the environment within selected caves, are in development by the Dunhuang Academy. In addition to such sophisticated monitoring, simple tools are being tested for use. For instance, small papersachets of different dry deliquescent salts (NaBr at 59 percent, KI at 70 percent, and NaCl at 75 percent RH) mixed with water-soluble dyestuff (crystal violet) have proved effective as a relative humidity indicator. Placed inside a cave, these 'sentinels' indicate, by staining the paper, that a particular relative humidity has occurred or has been exceeded. Portable CO_2 readers are also being utilized for spot measurement of CO_2 in selected caves. Condition monitoring, based on the risk assessment and assigned risk level, is designed to provide evidence of ongoing deterioration or damage. When the monitoring indicates change from desired conditions, specific actions need to be defined and set in motion. This will mean closing those caves with active salt-induced deterioration when exterior humidity rises above 62 percent, or reducing the number of daily tours or the period between visits (while keeping doors open to allow natural ventilation to flush the cave) if CO_2 limits are exceeded, or reassigning risk level if deterioration is shown to be continuing.

Concluding remarks

The correlation and interpretation of all the generated data and observations are complex and represent a long-term effort to develop a comprehensive and rational visitor capacity for the open caves over the summer period of high visitation to the site. The initial carrying capacity for the Grotto Zone will need to be validated over time and adjusted as necessary. Management systems will need to be developed that will be responsive to changing conditions, on a daily basis, and staff trained to ensure the upkeep and efficient running of these systems. The Dunhuang Academy has already put some of these systems in place, such as a reservation system, which is critical for managing visitors to the site. Others are in development, such as a visitor flow simulation model, which will determine the most effective way to move visitors through the site, and an off-site visitor orientation center, which will reduce the visual intrusions on the landscape, provide visitors with an introduction to the grottoes, and manage the flow of visitors to the site.

The strength of the carrying capacity study for the Grotto Zone is that it provides an objective, scientific basis for understanding and assessing the impact of visitation on the cultural resource at Mogao—the wall paintings. The difficulty of relating visitor use to impacts has been cited as the primary challenge to applying carrying capacity planning to cultural resources, as distinct from impacts to natural resources, which can be quantified (Valliere and Manning 2003: 237). Although we cannot yet quantify the impact of visitation on the wall paintings, we can use the theoretical model of deterioration to mitigate or prevent it. Continued research and monitoring will be needed to validate and refine our understanding of the causes of deterioration and their relationship to visitor use.

References

Agnew, N., K. Altenburg, M. Demas *et al.* (2006). 'Tourism: A good servant, but a bad master: Strategies for visitor management at Chengde and Mogao, China.' *Historic Environment* 19 (2): 13–19.

ASHRAE (2007). *American National Standard Institute (ANSI)/American Society of Heating, Refrigerating, and Air-Conditioning Engineers (ASHRAE) Standard 62, 1–2007, Ventilation for Acceptable Indoor Air Quality*. Atlanta, GA: American Society of Heating, Refrigerating, and Air-Conditioning Engineers.

Doorne, S. (2000). 'Caves, cultures and crowds: Carrying capacity meets consumer sovereignty.' *Journal of Sustainable Tourism* 8 (2): 116–30.

Maekawa, S. (1996). 'Preventive strategies for reducing the impact of visitors on the microenvironments of caves at the Mogao Grottoes.' In A. Roy and P. Smith (eds), *Archaeological Conservation and Its Consequences: Preprints of the Contributions to the Copenhagen Congress, 26–30 August 1996*. London: International Institute for Conservation of Historic and Artistic Works (IIC), 76–79.

Merced River Plan. (2000). Yosemite National Park. www.nps.gov/archive/YOSE/planning/mrp/2000/final_mpr/html/mrpverp.htm.

Valliere, W. and R. Manning (2003). 'Applying the Visitor Experience and Resource Protection (VERP) framework to cultural resources in the national parks.' In R. Schuster, *Proceedings of the 2002 Northeastern Recreation Research Symposium*. Gen. Tech. Rep. NE-302. Newtown Square, PA: U.S. Department of Agriculture, Forest Service, Northeastern Research Station, 234–38.

VERP (1997). *The Visitor Experience and Resource Protection (VERP) Framework: A Handbook for Planners and Managers*. Washington, DC: U.S. Department of the Interior. National Park Service. http://planning.nps.gov/document/verphandbook.pdf.

Chapter 13

Generic mitigation measures
Shelters

Shelters: introduction

A WIDE VARIETY of archaeological remains are protected by shelters, including:

- Buildings, often those built in stone, containing mosaics such as Brading Villa, Isle of Wight (Edwards *et al.* 2003) and the Orpheus mosaic, Paphos, Cyprus (Stanley-Price 1991) or decorated wall plaster as in the Dover Painted House, Kent (Philp 1989).
- Adobe buildings such as Çatalhöyük (Matero 1999), Tilmen Höyük, Turkey (Musso 2008) or mud mortar and plaster buildings such as the monastery on Sirbani Yas Island, Abu Dhabi (Goodburn Brown *et al.* 2012).
- Petroglyphs at sites such as Peterborough, Canada (Bahn *et al.* 1995; Wainwright *et al.* 1997).
- Excavation sites such as Jingsha (Bai and Zhou 2012) and Blackwater Draw, New Mexico (Fiero 2001), even waterlogged wood remains at Flag Fen, Cambridgeshire (Pryor 2005).

Shelters are created over archaeological remains to fulfil two functions:

- to help preserve them against damage from the weather, principally the effects of rain, frost and sun; and
- to provide access and a suitable environment for visitors to view them.

This dual role means that unlike reburial (see Chapter 14), the ideals of preservation of the archaeological remains have to be compromised to achieve access and visibility. This dual role argues shelters as a conservation rather than purely preservation method (Caple 2009). Visible in their original location, the public can see mosaics and wall paintings as part of a building, the buildings as part of a settlement, settlements and trackways as part of a landscape. The archaeological remains have a context, without the need for words; the visitor can see why they are in that location, what their function is, a much more complete and involving picture of the past.

Shelters provide protection from:

- Freezing – freeze/thaw cycles that physically break apart stone and all other porous materials (see Chapter 10).
- Rain, which washes away water-soluble soil/clay and other material (see Chapter 7).
- Hydration cycles alternating wet and dry, which cause materials to expand and shrink, slowly cracking them apart. On exposed sites, extreme saturation and desiccation happens very quickly.
- Thermal cycles, alternating hot and cold conditions, cause materials to expand and contract quickly, eventually cracking them apart. On exposed sites, the heating and cooling happens very quickly to more extreme temperatures.
- Drying out – wet ground, wet materials such as waterlogged wood or saturated clay lose water to drying atmosphere shrink, crack and break apart. On exposed sites, relentless sun and wind mean that this happens extremely quickly.
- Where shelters have walled sides, they prevent uncontrolled and potentially damaging access by animals and humans to the site.

Shelters signify:

- Value of the archaeological remains; they are important enough to protect. This message is not lost on visitors – whose numbers increase when shelters are erected. At Blackwater Draw Excavations, New Mexico, visitor numbers tripled following the construction of the shelter (Jerome et al. 2001).
- It shows local people that central/regional government and heritage agencies are doing something tangible to protect their heritage. They are not taking the remains away to a distant national museum or reburying them (out of sight, out of mind), but preserving them *in situ* within their physical and social landscape.

Shelters are also a facility that can be opened (an event), in which activities from education to retail opportunities can take place.

But shelters come with a cost: the initial cost of the building, the cost (where appropriate) of staffing the site, the cost of maintaining the visual condition of the remains and the facilities of the site.

History

There is a tradition of building shelters over valued remains such as religious buildings – where it was considered an act of devotion and piety. In Sri Lanka, King Vasabha (170–126 BC) is recorded as having constructed a shelter over an existing stupa 'Jumparama'. Columns still present around other stupas indicate this tradition, continued for centuries. It found voice again in the nineteenth and twentieth centuries, with religious groups pressing the Sri Lankan Department of Antiquities to roof over the sculptures of Buddha that were being unearthed among the ruins of temples in the jungle of Ceylon/Sri Lanka by early archaeologists: 'Construction of a roof over an existing stupa was a protection to the monument and also considered as a further contribution in honour of the Buddha' (Nimal and

De Silva 1986: 272). In many civilisations, early buildings or sacred sites are incorporated into or overlain by later ones: early Mayan temples are found beneath later ones or the Church of the Holy Sepulchre, Jerusalem, built over the tomb of Christ.

In Europe by the nineteenth century, the importance of archaeological remains as 'evidence of the past' had been established and efforts were made to protect these remains and make them visible to scholars. This resulted in the construction of shelters over the archaeological remains, using traditional local building forms, in countries such as Italy and the UK. A thatched cottage building with stone walls was built over the remains of the Roman Villa in Bignor, Kent, between 1811 and 1815 to protect the mosaics. At sites such as Pompeii and Herculaneum, new walls of masonry or brick were constructed on top of the original ruin walls and given traditional roofs of timber beams covered with slates or terracotta tile to protect wall paintings and mosaics beneath. These shelters often gave a good impression of what the original building would have looked like. This approach was particularly used by Amedeo Maiuri, who was responsible for the repair and development of Herculaneum from the 1920s to the 1960s, deliberately mimicking the original Roman roofing and building style. This preserved the 'traditional' ruined cityscape; however, Maiuri's 'ad identicum' work is now considered as blurring the line between shelter and restoration.

In the USA, shelters were placed over a number of valued sites from the early twentieth century (Matero 1999; Cosh 2002; Pesaresi and Rizzi 2007). Many of these early structures were temporary constructions in wood and sheet metal such as the earliest shelters over Casa Grande (1903) (Matero 1999: 205), or the Maesa Verde sites (Fiero 2001). By the 1930s, in both the Americas and Europe, new building materials were starting to be available and there was a conscious desire not to mimic the past, as evidenced by the steel roof construction of Frank Oldfield Jr. over the ruins at Casa Grande. After the Second World War, light, space-frame and tensioned structures were increasingly used, as were modern materials such as glass, steel, polymers, wood composites, aluminium, stainless steel, fabric and a lot of concrete. Using these materials, low-cost, often flat-roofed buildings, which could be quickly erected (prefabricated construction techniques), were widely used to shelter some of the many ruins unearthed by archaeologists in the latter half of the twentieth century. These lighter materials allowed larger cavernous spaces to be created, which enabled large areas of excavation to be protected or ruined buildings to be seen and appreciated in their entirety. Often, the building forms and materials used in these shelters were experimental, and some architects can be accused of constructing 'a memorial to their own ingenuity' (Corfield, cited in Solar 2003: 271) as their designs, though innovative, have often failed in terms of longevity and functionality. Other shelters were often only intended for short-term use, but have continued to function long after their architects and builders had intended.

The principal problem of these low-cost shelters, which became apparent in later years, was that many of the new materials decayed; composite wood rotted, flat roofs leaked, steel corroded flaked paint and dripped rusty water on to the monument and polymers cracked, yellowed and needed replacement. For example, at the Roman villa at Piazza Armerina, Sicily, constructed as part of a 'glasshouse' style shelter circa 1960, the Perspex windows had to be replaced in 1972 and again in 1986 (Stanley-Price and Ponti 2003: 278). Lawrence Durrell, in *Sicilian Carousel*, described this 'glasshouse' shelter as 'a straggling building in dirty white plastic which suggested the demesne of a mad market gardener who was specialising in asparagus' (Stanley-Price and Jokilehto 2001: 34). Construction using modern materials and structures was also not always benign, sometimes cutting into original fabric to secure the structures, such as bolts through the wall at Gela, to secure the glass plates and grooves cut into the original stonework, and to secure Perspex sheet at Heraclea Minoa (Stanley-Price and Jokilehto 2001: 23, 30). Many required large concrete foundations to support the ends of the wires for tensioned structures or seat 'visually unobtrusive' thin steel pillars (Stanley-Price 1991).

Though the majority of site 'shelters' are scattered throughout Europe, during the last 30 years increasing numbers have been constructed in developing countries such as Turkey (Musso 2008), China (Bai and Zhou 2012) and UAE (Goodburn Brown et al. 2012). These countries are seeking to preserve their own newly uncovered archaeological remains and facilitate tourism, but again there is a risk that such short-term economic considerations dictate remains be displayed and often outweigh long-term preservation issues. Despite being a 'conservation' measure, shelters, unlike other conservation treatments such as consolidants or coatings, have rarely been tested or evaluated. With over 200 years of erecting shelters, the statement 'we remain severely hampered by an incomplete understanding of the causes and mechanisms of deterioration and the potential impact of a shelter on the site's environment and, therefore, we are ill equipped to provide architects with a specific conservation brief for the protection of the site' (Roby and Demas 2012: 67–8) can still be made. Recent work assessing the design and performance of shelters over mosaics in England and Israel (Stewart et al. 2006) and of shelters in Italy, where there are more than anywhere else in the world (Laurenti 2006), has provided a great deal more information on the construction and performance of these structures. Previous publications on shelters are summarised in annotated bibliographies (Demas 2001; Roby and Demas 2012), with a number of examples of shelters reported in *Conservation and Management of Archaeological Sites Vol. 5 Special Issue on Protective Shelters* and the PhD of Zaki Aslan at UCL (Aslan 2008). One of the clearest case histories of a site shelter comes from palaeontology: the Lark Quarry, Queensland, Australia (Agnew et al. 1989). Accurate measurements of the environment inside shelters, which have demonstrated the significance of the role and nature of the building in the decay mechanisms, have only been undertaken in recent years (Agnew et al. 1996; Stewart et al. 2004; Laurenti 2006). Architects, builders, archaeologists and heritage managers involved in creating structures had been primarily focused on the visitors to the site or the aesthetics of these structures, assuming that protecting the site against the extremes of weather was sufficient. However, recently, as longer-term decay issues such as algal growth and salt precipitation problems have emerged, conservators have become more actively involved and resources are being made available to assess the protective capacity of these structures (Agnew 2001) (see Chapter 13.1).

Types of shelter

Hundreds of shelters exist of many different forms and materials. They can be grouped on the basis of:

- Form (Schmidt 1988), with two types:
    - Open: a roof supported on pillars with open sides. These are usually cheaper, often temporary structures. The principal variant of this form are examples supported on two or three walls leaving one or two open sides, such as the shelter over the clay-tiled chapel floors at Strata Florida Abbey (Wales) (see Figure 13.0.1).

- Closed: a roof supported on walls that enclose the remains, creating a secure enclosure, such as that over the mosaics at North Leigh Roman Villa (Oxfordshire) (see Figure 13.0.1).
- Lifespan (Solar 2003: 268), with three principal types: temporary, semi-permanent and permanent. However, as many shelters, such as the hexashelter over the Orpheus mosaic at Paphos (Stanley-Price 1991), intended as temporary have become semi-permanent, this is a classification of intention rather than reality.

In practice, there is a continuum of form, of function, of materials and types of construction. Certain combinations of form, function and materials emerge as more common than others (see Table 13.0.1).

Problems with shelters

Problems with shelters often arise from the differences between expectation and reality, especially at the point of their inception. Archaeological remains emerge during excavation, valued by the excavator and local people as a visible sign of their past; they are invariably seen as a valuable resource for educating the younger members of society and having potential to attract tourists, consequently people are loathe to cover them over again. Appreciating that they will degrade if left to the weather, the idea of a shelter is often suggested. With few published examples, people are often unaware of the problems: the costs of creating the shelter, the costs of maintaining and running such facilities, the limited number of visitors it will attract or the continued decay problems of the archaeological remains; consequently, realistic assessment of options, costs or consequences rarely occurs. Sometimes temporary shelters are erected. These often represent short-term thinking, and can be useful to 'buy some time'. A few years further on from initial discovery, local people and politicians are perhaps more aware; the remains will have started to degrade, the cost of maintenance will have become apparent, enthusiasm of local people will have waned and the true level of tourist interest will have become apparent. It is then possible to reassess the value of the remains and consider options such as reburying the site or, if the site has acquired a higher profile and developed a useful educational or tourism role, seek funds to create a more permanent shelter. Many temporary shelters continue long after their envisaged replacement date due to continued expectation of remains being visible, but with no funds for replacement, no resources to remove the shelter and no credible plan for any alternative, the existing shelter remains. Shelter structures must be sufficiently strong to withstand wind, rain and the weight of snowfall; poorly designed and constructed shelters can collapse onto the remains they are there to protect, inflicting great damage (Nimal and De Silva 1986: 276).

Some damage of archaeological remains is almost inevitable when a shelter/building is erected in the middle of a series of archaeological remains; to imagine anything else is naïve. Concrete foundations, typically up to 1 m^3, required to support each post, have to be cut into archaeological deposits for the shelter, as in the case of the shelter over the church on the Early Christian monastery at Sir Bari Island (Goodburn Brown et al. 2012: 256). Damage can be minimised and recorded with good archaeological supervision of the excavation and erection process. There are a number of examples of damage done when erecting shelters, such as at Lark Quarry, where the creation of foundations cut through the dinosaur footprints being protected because there was no appropriate supervision of the builders (Agnew 1989, 2001).

SHELTERS 443

Figure 13.0.1 Shelters at Strata Florida Abbey (Ceredigion) (above) and North Leigh Roman Villa (Oxfordshire) (below).

Source: Photographs by the author

Once erected, a series of longer-term degradation issues gradually emerge. Solar (2003: 266) listed 12 mosaic sites under shelters erected between the 1970s and 1990s in Israel showing these signs of deterioration:

- Human visitors are drawn to the site with increased threat of vandalism and wear.
- Animals, especially insects and reptiles, are attracted for protection (shade or shelter) against the weather (kangaroos at Lark Quarry, wasps and rats at Blackwater Draw).
- Birds and bats come to nest or roost.
- Vegetation opportunities for plants.

Table 13.0.1 Shelter types

Shelter type	Nature of shelter
Unsheltered	Archaeological remains left exposed to the elements, such as the mosaics and building ruins of the Roman city of Italica in Spain. Exposed to the elements with only guard rails and low walls to discourage the public from walking on the mosaics. Some sites may have thermal insulation and water-impermeable covering applied during the winter. Such coverings are removed for the summer tourist season.
Temporary shelter	Supported roof with up to four walls, often erected during or immediately after excavation as a temporary shelter to protect the remains during conservation or until a more permanent shelter can be erected. Typically, a wood or metal frame covered with lightweight fabric or polymer materials. Examples include: simple horticultural growing tunnels (polythene sheet over hemispherical steel tubes) (Barker 1986), hexashelter (knitted polythene shade fabric, later replaced with double layered vinyl fabric, stretched between aluminium spars in a non-planar hexagon with stainless steel tension wires) (Agnew *et al.* 1996), used at the Orpheus mosaic, Nea Paphos (Stanley-Price 1991) and Fort Seldon (USA). The continued use of the hexashelter at Paphos demonstrates yet again that 'temporary' shelters have a way of becoming permanent (Fiero 2001: 62).
Permanent shelter (open)	A roof-only structure open on all sides, erected of wood or metal frame, designed purely to keep the rain and sun off the site, such as the steel roof structure erected in 1932 at Casa Grande to protect earth wall ruins. Such shelters are designed so 'the roofs are high enough, the shelters open enough and the sites low enough so that the shelters do not intrude on the view of the site' (Fiero 2001: 61). A series of adobe buildings at Mesa Verde are protected by such roofs, but they have metal sides, which can be added to create secure structure, or heavy vinyl curtains, which can be drawn around the roofed framework during the winter to provide additional protection (Fiero 2001).
Permanent shelter (<4 sided enclosure)	Roof and one, two or three walls. The open side(s) encourages visitors to view the remains. The structures are often of sturdy construction and utilise one or more walls of the monument. Such structures keep rain, snow and strong winds from the remains, and reduce the length and duration of frost. The leeward side is usually open unless the layout of the site dictates otherwise. An example is the three-sided enclosure at Strata Florida Abbey, Wales, protecting glazed floor tiles *in situ*.
Permanent shelter (shed/greenhouse)	Roof and four sides. There will often be a window in one or more sides for viewing and a door for access. This arrangement controls access and provides higher levels of security than open sided shelters. The structure is usually light and can have a shed-like form with sheet material such as Preservation Hall at Flag Fen (Cambridgeshire) or be glazed on all sides to create a greenhouse, as at the Roman Villa at Piazza Armerina (Stanley-Price and Ponti 2003). In many instances, the building frames are raised over the site walls, giving (intentionally or unintentionally) the volume or form of the original building. Smaller buildings protecting just a decorative fragment or larger barn-like constructions over the whole site are also seen.

Table 13.0.1 continued

Shelter type	Nature of shelter
Permanent shelter (building)	Roof and four sides. The walls are substantial, often existing monument walls built up in brick, blocks or masonry, and given a substantial roof. This may have a flat or sloping roof, usually depending on local building tradition. Door provides access. Such sites are secure. Such sturdy structures are required where there are high winds, high levels of snow or rainfall or security threats. They are often appropriate to the local building tradition, resembling local houses or barns. Examples incude the substantial stone-walled building with steel frame roof protecting the Midhow Chambered Cairn in the Orkney Isles.
Permanent shelter (museum)	Roof and four sides. The walls are substantial, built in brick, blocks or masonry, and given a substantial flat or sloping roof. Door provides access. Such sites also possess interpretation panels, displays of finds in cases, gift shop, cafe, etc. Examples are Brading Roman Villa, Fishbourne Palace or Roman Painted House Museum (Dover). Admission is often charged.

- Salt efflorescence as the ground responds to the new climate in the shelter.
- The site surface breaks up or lifts; thermal or hydrological cycling often helps disassociate it from its substrate.
- Dust whose removal to see the details and colours of mosaics requires constant cleaning with resultant damage to the monument.
- Condensation on the cold ground or shelter frame wets the remains leading to algal growth, discolouration, etc.
- Drainage problems lead to wet ground and algal and salt problems.
- Subsurface fragility or voids lead to structural damage, especially if mosaics are walked on.

At the heart of many of many of these problems is that shelters create their own climate and ecosystem (see Chapter 10). The problems particularly focus on the damp ground inside the shelter:

- If the soil remains damp, drawing moisture from the ground, given the need for light to enable the visitors to view the remains, photosynthetic organisms such as algae and plants will quickly establish. Most common are green algae, which cover and obscure damp surfaces such as the plaster at the base of walls and mosaics. Mosses and higher plants are also seen and may require the use of biocides to inhibit biological growth (Bai and Zhou 2012).
- If damp earth is exposed, it dries, leading to shrinkage and cracking. The evaporation of water from earth and mortar loses coherence and causes dusting of the surface; drying and wetting cycles may cause cracking and surface delamination. Waterlogged sites dry up; organic material shrinks and cracks apart.
- The water coming up from the ground draws with it soluble salts that crystallise on the surface (efflorescence) or just below the surface (cryptoflorescence), slowly tearing apart the surface, especially damaging to stone or mosaic surfaces.

Usually, the only way to create a stable situation in the shelter is to stop moisture coming up from the ground. As in the case of the Orpheus mosaic, Paphos, mosaics are often lifted and relaid on concrete slabs incorporating an impermeable membrane (Stanley-Price 1991). Drying the ground with deep external or internal subsurface drainage can be helpful, but water repellents and sealants have been tried with little long-term success. Given the problems listed above, it has not been possible to preserve and show to the public interesting 'as excavated' archaeological earth surfaces filled with cultural debris for longer than a few months without extensive modification (Waane 1986). One of the few successful attempts to preserve and display original waterlogged timbers *in situ* occurs at the waterlogged Bronze Age wooden trackway site of Flag Fen, Cambridgeshire. A 10 × 10 m square coffer-dam was created around a section of trackway using sheet steel piles isolating the peat and archaeological remains, which are kept wet with ice-cold water sprayed on at regular intervals; this keeps the wood saturated but free of algae. A steel frame building, Preservation Hall, was constructed on top of the piling to facilitate public viewing. At most aerobic sites, wooden structures decayed in antiquity and the educative value of the site is achieved through reconstructing the wooden structures at sites such as Castell Henllys, Pembrokeshire, Wales (Mytum 1986), Yoshinogari in Japan (Mizoguchi 2006) or at Modena, Italy (Cardarelli and Pulini 2008).

In making the remains visible to the public, access over the site for them to view the remains is required. Walking on protected surface such as mosaics is prohibited/discouraged; instead, walkways are normally supported on existing ruined walls, as seen at the Roman Villa at Piazza Armerina, Sicily (Stanley-Price and Ponti 2003). The provision of a shelter gives the impression that the archaeological remains are stable; however, many mosaics remain fragile, often located above unsupported hypocaust systems.

Shelters, like all buildings, require maintenance if they are to continue to function effectively. At Herculaneum, depleting the on-site 'works' team and working in a contract culture made it impossible to maintain shelters erected over the previous 100 years. The ruins subsequently degraded, becoming dangerous, leading to closures of large parts of the site, which resulted in increased tourist numbers on the remaining areas of the site (Pesaresi and Rizzi 2007). Unexpected natural events can precipitate re-evaluations of the site and its shelter, such as the flooding and drainage problems at Brading Roman Villa (Edwards *et al.* 2003). The problems of distance of the sheltered remains from major towns and roads lead to low numbers of visitors and high maintenance costs, which raises questions about the effective use of resources in erecting shelters in remote locations such as Lark Quarry (Agnew *et al.* 1989).

Best practice for preserving archaeological remains under shelters

There is a need to carefully balance the risks of damage to the remains from exposure to the weather against risks of damage by conditions under a shelter, between the different types of shelter and their cost. The cheaper and more flimsy the shelter, the lower its cost but the less protection it provides and the faster it and the remains beneath will decay. In most cases, the more substantial a building, the higher its cost, but it represents a longer and more secure future for the remains.

It can been suggested that the general requirements for a shelter (Agnew 2001; Teutonico 2001; Roby and Demas 2012: 68) include:

- Protect the remains ensuring minimal damage.
- Design that mitigates environmental fluctuation – ideally eliminating condensation.
- Effective drainage so subsurface water is drawn away from the remains.
- Precipitation and surface water is deflected away from the site and does not flow into/over it.
- Prevents microbial growth, deters or prevents birds or bats from nesting, perching or roosting, deters the presence of animals in or under the shelter.
- Reversible so the structure can easily be removed or replaced without damaging the site.
- Avoiding the greenhouse effect; solar gain leading to heating and low RH, cooling at night leading to low temperature and high RH and condensation.
- Construction using stable materials that do not corrode, discolour, embrittle or degrade.

Enclosed shelters often use natural light through windows and skylights to illuminate the archaeological remains. However, the problems of solar gain can lead to excessive heating, coupled with cool nights and large areas of glass, which provide poor insulation, result in fluctuating temperatures and an inability to control humidity. This can lead to condensation and salt efflorescence problems (Stanley-Price and Ponti 2003). The development of computer modelling in the design stage of buildings and the availability of climate data increasingly allow architects to model the likely environment for any proposed shelter. Insulation and ventilation can be simulated to achieve a design that maximises passive climate control. Such an approach is preferable on the grounds of sustainability to using air handling or conditioning systems, which are costly, require maintenance and do sometimes fail. This passive climate control building approach was utilised for the design of a proposed structure over Lot's Basilica, Jordan (Aslan 2001). To undertake such planning, good data on shelter environments, especially moisture levels and temperature, is essential (Stewart *et al.* 2004).

Any agency responsible for creating a shelter that effectively preserves archaeological remains will need to resolve the following issues before starting detailed design and construction work:

- Creating the clear specification/brief for the architect that considers the preservation of the remains. Though each site is different, the decay problems normally include the issues listed above and all need to be considered.
- Any specification should be realistic, taking into consideration the resources available to fund the construction and should involve/be agreed by all 'stakeholders' who value the site.
- There should be a good record of the remains on the site, a reference point for assessing degradation or claims of damage during construction.
- Ensure the architects and builders meet the required specification, including that the work does not damage the site when being carried out. There should be monitoring of key environmental factors after erection of the shelter, as only the monitoring of such data, which is then shown to meet the specification, can constitute an objective measure of the success of the shelter.
- Establish effective maintenance. No building can continue to function indefinitely without maintenance. Ensure an individual, whose work is seen by an oversight committee at which all stakeholders are represented, is responsible for the remains and the shelter. Checks are made that maintenance work is done to an appropriate standard (Agnew *et al.* 1989: 401).

Bibliography

Agnew, N. (2001) 'Methodology, conservation criteria and performance evaluation for archaeological site shelters', *Conservation and Managements of Archaeological Sites*, 5(1–2): 7–18.

Agnew, N., Griffin, H., Wade, M. et al. (1989) 'Strategies and techniques for the preservation of fossil tracksites: an Australian example', in D.D. Gillette and M.G. Lockley (eds), *Dinosaur Tracks and Traces*, Cambridge: Cambridge University Press, pp. 397–407.

Agnew, N., Maekawa, S., Coffman, R. et al. (1996) 'Evaluation of a modular lightweight modular site shelter: quantitative meteorological data and protective indices for the hexashelter', *Conservation and Management of Archaeological Sites*, 1: 139–50.

Aslan, Z. (2001) 'Designing protective structures at archaeological sites: criteria and environmental design methodology for a proposed structure at Lot's Basilica, Jordan', *Journal of Conservation and Museum Studies*, 5(1–2): 73–86.

Aslan, Z. (2008) 'The design of protective structures for the conservation and presentation of archaeological sites', unpublished PhD thesis, University College London.

Bahn, P.G., Bednarik, R.G. and Steinbring, J. (1995) 'The Peterborough petroglyph site: reflections on massive intervention in rock art', *Rock Art Research*, 12(1): 29–41.

Bai, L. and Zhou, Z-L. (2012) 'Issues of in situ conservation at Jinsha, People's Republic of China', *Conservation and Management of Archaeological Sites*, 14(1–4): 263–72.

Barker, P. (1986) 'Temporary shelters and site protection', in N. Stanley-Price (ed.), *Preventive Measures During Excavation and Site Protection (Ghent Conference)*, Rome: ICCROM, pp. 45–50.

Caple, C. (2009) 'The aims of conservation', in A. Braker and A. Richmond (eds), *Principles of Conservation*, London: Elsevier, pp. 25–31.

Cardarelli, A. and Pulini, I. (2008) 'The archaeological park and open air museum at the Middle Bronze Age site of Montale (Modena, Italy)', in N. Marchetti and I. Thuesen (eds), *ARCHAIA: Case Studies on Research Planning, Characterisation, Conservation and Management of Archaeological Sites*, Oxford: Archaeopress, pp. 355–66.

Cosh, S. (2002) 'Cover buildings over Romano-British mosaics', *Mosaic: The Bulletin of the Association for the Study and Preservation of Roman Mosaics (ASPROM)*, 29: 4–8.

Demas, M. (2001) 'Annotated bibliography on protective shelters for archaeological sites', *Conservation and Management of Archaeological Sites*, 5(1 and 2): 91–105.

Edwards, C., Corfield, M., Knight, B. et al. (2003) 'The investigation and conservation of 4th century AFD mosaics at Brading Roman Villa, Isle of Wight, England', in Michaelides (ed.), *Mosaics Make a Site: The Conservation in Situ of Mosaics on Archaeological Sites*, Proceedings of the VIth International Conference of the ICCCM, Rome: ICCM, pp. 101–10.

Fiero, K. (2001) 'Preserving dirt wall structures in Mesa Verde National Park', *Conservation and Management of Archaeological Sites*, 5(1–2): 55–62.

Goodburn Brown, D., Norman, K., Elders, J. et al. (2012) 'Preservation in situ for tourism: an early Christian monastic complex on Sir Bani Yas Island, Western Abu Dhabi, UAE', *Conservation and Management of Archaeological Sites*, 14(1–4): 249–62.

Jerome, P., Taylor, M.R. and Montgomery, J. (2001) 'Evaluation of the protective shelter at Blackwater Draw archaeological site, New Mexico', *Conservation and Management of Archaeological Sites*, 5(1–2): 63–72.

Laurenti, M.C. (ed.) (2006) *Le Coperture Delle Aree Archeologiche: Museo Aperto*, Roma, Italy: Gangemi Editore.

Matero, F. (1999) 'Lessons from the great house: condition and treatment history as prologue to site conservation and management at Casa Grande Ruins National Monument', *Conservation and Management of Archaeological Sites*, 3(4): 203–24.

Mizoguchi, K. (2006) *Archaeology, Society and Identity in Modern Japan*, Cambridge: Cambridge University Press.

Musso, T. (2008) 'Low impact restoration techniques, coverings and fixed devices in an archaeological park: a case study at Tilmen Höyük in Turkey', in N. Marchetti and I. Thuesen (eds), *ARCHIA: Case Studies on Research Planning, Characterisation, Conservation and Management of Archaeological Sites*, Oxford: Archaeopress, pp. 319–40.

Mytum, H. (1986) 'The reconstruction of an Iron Age roundhouse at Castell Henllys, Dyfed', *Bulletin of the Board of Celtic Studies*, 33: 283–90.

Nimal, T.E. and De Silva, P. (1986) 'Roof over a monument: Sri Lankan experience', in N. Stanley-Price (ed.), *Preventive Measures During Excavation and Site Protection*, Rome: ICCROM, pp. 271–9.

Pesaresi, P. and Rizzi, G. (2007) 'New and existing forms of protective shelter at Herculaneum: towards improving the continuous care of the site', *Conservation and Management of Archaeological Sites*, 8(4): 237–52.

Philp, B. (1989) *The Roman House with Bacchic Murals at Dover*, Dover: Kent Archaeological Research Unit.
Pryor, F. (2005) *Flag Fen: Life and Death of a Prehistoric Landscape*, Stroud: Tempus.
Roby, T. and Demas, M. (2012) *Mosaics in Situ: An Overview of Literature on Conservation of Mosaics in Situ*, Los Angeles, CA: Getty Conservation Institute.
Schmidt, H. (1988) *Schutzbauten*, Stuttgart: Konrad Theiss Verlag.
Solar, G. (2003) 'Protective shelters', in Michaelides (ed.), *Mosaics Make a Site: The Conservation in Situ of Mosaics on Archaeological Sites*, Proceedings of the VIth International Conference of the ICCCM, Rome: ICCM, pp. 263–74.
Stanley-Price, N. (ed.) (1991) *The Conservation of the Orpheus Mosaic at Paphos, Cyprus*, Los Angeles, CA: GCI.
Stanley-Price, N.P. and Jokilehto, J. (2001) 'The decision to shelter archaeological sites: three case studies from Sicily', *Conservation and Management of Archaeological Sites*, 5(1–2): 19–34.
Stanley-Price, N. and Ponti, G. (2003) 'Protective enclosures for mosaic floors: a review of Piazza Armerina, Sicily, after forty years', in Michaelides (ed.), *Mosaics Make a Site: The Conservation in Situ of Mosaics on Archaeological Sites*, Proceedings of the VIth International Conference of the ICCCM, Rome: ICCM, pp. 275–87.
Stewart, J.D., Julien, S. and Staniforth, S. (2004) 'An integrated monitoring strategy at Chedworth Roman Villa (Gloucestershire)', in T. Nixon (ed.), *Preserving Archaeological Remains in-Situ?*, London: Museum of London Archaeological Service, pp. 179–87.
Stewart, J.D., Negeur, J. and Demas, M. (2006) 'Assessing the protective function of shelters over mosaics', *Getty Conservation Institute Newsletter*, 21.2 (Spring 2006).
Teutonico, J.M. (2001) 'Protective shelters for archaeological sites in the southwest USA: conclusions and recommendations', *Conservation and Management of Archaeological Sites*, 5(1–2): 87–90.
Waane, S.A.C. (1986) 'Roofs and shelters: the Tanzanian experience', in N. Stanley-Price (ed.), *Preventive Measures During Excavation and Site Protection*, Rome: ICCROM, pp. 245–9.
Wainwright, I.N.M., Sears, H. and Michalski, S. (1997) 'Design of a rock art protective structure at Petroglyphs Provincial Park, Ontario, Canada', *Journal of the Canadian Association for Conservation*, 22: 53–76.

Chapter 13.1

Methodology, conservation criteria and performance evaluation for archaeological site shelters

Neville Agnew

Source: Agnew, N. (2001) 'Methodology, conservation criteria and performance evaluation for archaeological site shelters', *Conservation and Management of Archaeological Sites*, 5(1 *and* 2): 7–18.

[. . .]

Methodology

No FORMAL METHODOLOGY has been developed for sheltering. Typically, in many places shelters have been built as a one-off, ad hoc venture. Consequently several aspects of the process are at risk. Clearly, when sheltering is being undertaken without the basis of prior experience and without a methodology, the risk is amplified. [. . .] The methodology that follows has become accepted as a standard approach to site conservation planning, intervention and management. This method employs a decision-making process that:

- identifies all the values of the site, and orders them by significance
- documents comprehensively the condition of the resource
- identifies the threats and deterioration mechanisms, ranks them in order of severity and, where possible, quantifies the deterioration (so much damage or loss of this or that kind over that much time)
- assesses the management environment of the site, which includes staffing, infrastructure, funding, as well as input from stakeholders to inform and guide decision-making
- considers also options other than sheltering and what their implications for the site might be.

On the basis of these steps the decision whether or not to shelter the site is made. The assessments and decisions above are the key initial steps in the process. Other steps, some of which can occur in parallel, are:

- consideration of how the decision to shelter will fit with the larger objectives of the site's conservation and management
- interim protective measures, such as temporary reburial or sheltering, while the often long and protracted planning, design, approvals and funding stages for a permanent shelter are occurring
- identification of a team with requisite experience and skills
- a process for shelter design review and revision.

Frequently overlooked in the planning process are three vitally important elements:

- assured resources for long-term maintenance of the structure and the site
- supervision of construction: usually construction of a shelter occurs over unprotected (or minimally protected) remains when the site is particularly vulnerable to damage. For example, covering the site with a combustible material, as a temporary protection during construction, has resulted in fires in two instances reported in the literature
- a monitoring plan to determine whether the resource is being effectively protected. Monitoring should focus on the threats and deterioration processes previously identified.

Criteria for protective, aesthetic and interpretive functions

Once the decision to shelter has been made, specific conservation criteria are next established in an iterative process by reviewing again the assessments. By conservation criteria are meant those threats, factors or parameters that need to be addressed in a sustainable way in order that the shelter will preserve the values of the site. In this respect the conservation criteria need to go hand-in-hand with the assessments that resulted in the decision to shelter. Conservation criteria must obviously be communicated clearly to the shelter designer or design team and underpin all aspects of the final design.

A good shelter should:

- function effectively to protect the resource, [...]
- be in harmony with the context of the site and the landscape
- fulfill its interpretive/display function well, [...]
- be capable of being maintained within the resources available, since a shelter cannot, in the end, fulfill its primary function of protection if it is not maintained

[...]

Protective function

In terms of its protective function the shelter must protect against environmental and biological effects (rain, wind, frost, acid precipitation and invasive flora and fauna). A considerable literature exists on environmental and biological impacts, including human (vandalism), on sheltered sites, so these aspects will not be further developed in detail here. [1] Identified threats should be ranked in order of severity, and potential side effects need to be thoroughly assessed as outlined below. Whether a shelter is an open structure or entirely enclosed, and whether ventilation and environmental controls are active or passive, is dictated principally by the nature of the site and especially the identified threats, as well as resources available for its maintenance.

Aesthetic criteria

Regarding the aesthetics of a shelter there are several points to consider. While the scale of the shelter is dictated by that of the site, both lateral and vertical, the aesthetic impact of the shelter in the context of the site itself and the landscape is important. This is not the same as the architecture of the shelter, considered purely from an architectural perspective, though often the two are not sufficiently distinguished. Admiration for the shelter design may overwhelm the more important consideration, that of the appropriateness of the shelter and its relationship to what it protects and the setting. The harmony of the shelter with the site in the landscape is clearly highly subjective, as witness critiques of Minissi's shelter at Piazza Armerina. [2] [. . .] It is unfortunate when the tail wags the dog and the shelter's architecture takes over. No matter how beautiful the architecture of the shelter is in its own right, inevitably it is an impact on the site, and an alien. Therefore, basic design concepts should be applied to an archaeological site in its landscape. These relate to the aesthetics of proportions, colour, texture of materials and to viewscapes. As part of the process the designer should be briefed to consider these relationships, and also alternative designs.

Interpretive function

Similarly, the interpretive functionality of a shelter, while of great importance in many instances (as has been pointed out, typically shelters are built because the site will be visited), should be subordinate to the protective function. Among criteria to be considered are how the visitor will enter and exit the shelter, the routing of walkways and their capacity, the location of the best viewing points, interpretive panels and materials and how these might affect the flow of visitors, and so forth.

Although unlikely to be universally agreed upon, an hierarchy of priorities when considering sheltering is suggested: Protective effectiveness > display/ interpretation functionality > aesthetic of the shelter in context > architectural statement.

The need for thorough process

As stated above, the decision to shelter and conservation criteria are reiterative processes. Not only should these products be the outcome of a thorough methodology, but it is appropriate also to always consider other options besides sheltering. The pressure to shelter can be quite compelling because archaeologists and managing authorities continue to be reluctant to rebury sites. This is a natural consequence of the profession: archaeologists spend time, often years, and money excavating the site and want it revealed, not concealed; authorities have political agendas and pressure from tourism interests to consider. A shelter seems like the answer: it protects and may allow public viewing at the same time. What could be better?

A number of examples, illustrating the need for thorough process and some pitfalls, follow.

Reburial versus sheltering

Laetoli Trackway

Sheltering is sometimes not the best way to preserve a site, however important and worthy of preservation. For example, at the fragile site of the Laetoli hominid trackway in a remote part of Tanzania, various groups had proposed a shelter and public access (as well as other options such as lifting the tracks). The condition and management assessments and conservation criteria for sheltering showed very clearly that a shelter could not fulfill its purpose. The strong recommendation not to shelter was based on considerations such as the rapid weathering of the volcanic tuff, its mechanical weakness, remoteness of the site, lack of infrastructure (water, power, access road), lack of trained personnel, security of the site and inadequate maintenance capability, among other considerations. Consequently, the site was reburied and as part of the project an interpretive display was created with a replica of the trackway at the existing Olduvai Museum some distance away. [3, 4]

Lark Quarry

A contrasting case to that of Laetoli is the Lark Quarry dinosaur stampede trackway site. [5] At this remote site in Queensland, Australia, the decision to shelter was the wrong one. The site, in fact, should have been reburied. The scientific values of the site are considerable: the statement of significance reads, in part, 'it represents the largest concentration of running dinosaur footprints thus far known on earth' and 'it holds a large amount of data regarding the gaits, speeds, sizes and behavior of dinosaurs'. The threats to the site were (and are still today) vandalism from the collection of illicit souvenirs, wetting and drying from sheet flooding and direct rain leading to cracking of the soft mudstone, and erosion. The site is not staffed. The decision to open it to visitors was based upon a number of mistaken premises. These were that visitors would come to the site in considerable numbers and that the site could remain unstaffed, being interpreted only through signs and a brochure. In fact, few visitors make their way to the site which is off the beaten track and once there, many are disappointed by their inability to be able to 'read' the trackway's 4,000 footprints, often superimposed upon each other, and, given the dryness of the semi-desert environment, are often obscured by accumulation of dust in the prints.

That being said, the shelter built in 1979 comprised a pentagonal flat roof set on steel posts in concrete footings (see Figure 13.1.1). There are a number of cautionary lessons to be learned from both the design and the construction of this shelter. The construction work for the shelter was not supervised and damage occurred where one of the concrete footings destroyed a holotype footprint. The straw and plastic protective covering on the surface was not removed during construction and caught fire during welding. This resulted in darkening and exfoliation of the surface. The shelter roof is open at the sides and does not exclude windblown rain and dust. Today we are all aware that the environments created by shelters also attract unwanted guests; at Lark Quarry these were kangaroos, some of which died on the site during prolonged drought. Additionally, flooding of the site occurred from the hillside above the trackway. Vandalism has repeatedly occurred in the form of taking footprints as souvenirs (see Figure 13.1.2).

Figure 13.1.1 Roof at Lark Quarry in 1981, prior to the erection of a perimeter fence to prevent kangaroos sheltering under the roof. Natural lighting is provided by translucent panels and visitors view the tracks from a raised walkway.
Source: Photo: N. Agnew

Figure 13.1.2 Loss of part of the dinosaur trackway at Lark Quarry. Steel support columns for the roof and walkway, set into and on the trackway, are shown at the top of the image.
Source: Photo: N. Agnew

As a result of these and other problems the scientific, and indeed also the interpretive, values of the site were seriously compromised and much conservation work and retrofitting of the shelter had to be undertaken as early as mid-1983. In fact, it is easy to be critical of a shelter such as Lark Quarry which was undertaken by a competent architect, though someone inexperienced with the conservation needs of a fragile palaeontological site in a remote area. There is apparently now a proposal to completely enclose the site in an environmentally controlled building.

In summary, the assessments of Lark Quarry were not thorough and the shelter failed in its primary function. The shelter was designed and built without conservation input or sheltering expertise. Thus, many of the issues were overlooked. As each deterioration problem came up, the shelter required retrofitting as remedy. The methodological process was not in place at that time. The lessons to be learned here are that if the wrong decisions are made early on, there is a multiplier effect with adverse consequences over time.

Stakeholder issues

Of signal importance in the sheltering process is the management assessment that would have taken place during the decision-making stage. There are many facets to this, but one of particular relevance is the need for stakeholder involvement. Fortunately, today there seems to be better awareness of the important role of stakeholders in conservation. Two examples follow where this was overlooked.

Yunju Temple

At Yunju Temple, an ancient Buddhist site near Beijing (not far from the Peking Man fossil site), some 10,000 stone stele inscribed with texts predicting the end of the world, dating from about the 6th century, were excavated and in recent years housed on site in a new underground shelter. This was done, presumably, to mimic the original deliberate burial of stele. This is an interesting hybrid of sheltering and 'reburial' of which a number of other examples exist, e.g. Tubac in Arizona and Atri [6] in Italy. Visitors view the stele, through glass, in their nitrogen-filled underground gallery. The stele are stacked in rows one behind the other and are inaccessible. Scholars of the texts have been outraged by being thwarted in their legitimate desire to be able to examine the inscriptions firsthand.

Siqueiros Mural

Similarly, a proposed shelter for the Siqueiros Mural in Los Angeles ran into trouble some years ago. The Getty Conservation Institute had thought that all the stakeholders had been involved. Protracted review of the design by different commissions of the city took place over many months, yet towards the end of the process other claimants, notably the Los Angeles Conservancy and the California State Historic Preservation Office, emerged as critics of some aspects of the design, including its aesthetic appropriateness to the historic architecture of the streetscape. While this shelter was not built for reasons of cost and other considerations, the entry of these two organizations late in the process necessitated additional design modifications after a further series of meetings.

Soluble salts

Buildup of soluble salts under shelters is often not realized as a consequence of sheltering. Any good shelter will have a rainwater disposal system from the roof and this is obviously an essential requirement, yet capillary rise from soil moisture or ground water, together with lateral migration from the unsheltered surroundings which are wetted by rain, brings soil salts to the surface. Ventilation systems in shelters have the potential to exacerbate this phenomenon by accelerating evaporation from the sheltered surface. If a capillary supply of moisture is feeding this evaporation, the problem is made all the worse. Of course, under the shelter, the accumulation of salts is not reduced by rainfall as the surface is not wetted. The consequences of accumulation of salts on a fragile surface naturally are often quite destructive. This may be an intractable problem, but one which is best addressed by ensuring that site drainage is effective, and capillary rise of moisture is minimized.

Site security

Olduvai Gorge

In poor countries building materials are a valuable commodity. Where sheltered sites are not staffed the shelter itself may become the target, not of vandals but of local people wanting materials. A shelter may literally disappear overnight. This might seem an obvious risk given foresight, yet it happens. The so-called DK site, a two-million-year-old hominid site in the Olduvai Gorge, was sheltered by Mary Leakey in the 1960s or 1970s. Within a short while, the valuable galvanized steel roof was stripped. The shelter has never been repaired and today the site is derelict (see Figure 13.1.3). Other sites in the region have experienced a similar fate. [7]

Figure 13.1.3 Shelter building over the DK hominid site in Olduvai Gorge, Tanzania.
Source: Photo: N. Agnew, © J. Paul Getty Trust

Dust accumulation

Dust accumulation under a shelter is not usually perceived as anything more than a nuisance, one requiring regular removal. Yet dust has quite serious consequences for fragile surfaces, e.g. petroglyphsetched in soft rock, fossil footprints, a mosaic pavement. All of these will be damaged by regular cleaning, to a greater or lesser degree, no matter how carefully done. Additionally, dust obscures the 'readability' of the site, in the case of glyphs or footprints to the extent that the visitor is frustrated. And, furthermore, a dusty surface conveys a lack of care, even if this is a quite erroneous impression.

Unexpected consequences

The unexpected occurs far too frequently in conservation, and site sheltering is no exception to this. With good conservation criteria established and rigorous review of proposals, the consequences of unpleasant surprises can be avoided. The examples above suffice here to illustrate some adverse side effects resulting from failure to follow through the process. Often there is a naïveté when it comes to designing and constructing shelters which translates into a self-deception that the shelter will function well. Perhaps this arises from a natural enthusiasm for the project, the opportunity to create the shelter, and the lack of perceived need for review and critique. Important too, is the mistaken belief that sheltering is not intervening on fabric. The truth is that there is simply not enough prior critical evaluation from every point of view of shelter proposals, whether for unexpected side effects, the shelter's proposed response to deterioration threats and mechanisms, the aesthetics of the shelter in the context of the site and landscape, long-term monitoring and maintenance, staffing, and so on.

Performance evaluation

Almost no research or experimental work has been done on sheltering of archaeological sites and cultural resources. [1] This is interesting because it stands in sharp contrast to other types of conservation interventions. Today one would not think of intervening on a monument with, say, a stone consolidant without it having been tested and evaluated beforehand. Why this situation should be so in the case of shelters is difficult to pinpoint exactly, but probably it is due to the fact that shelters are invariably constructed in response to an immediate need as a once-only enterprise. Subsequently no systematic evaluation is undertaken. A further important point is that shelters are not seen as an intervention in the fabric of the site. This view is, of course, erroneous; shelters may have repercussions both good and bad. As a consequence there is a dearth of quantitative information on the actual performance of shelters, despite the huge number of shelters of all kinds (from sheds to vast site museum shelters) around the world. These could afford a valuable archive for the critical evaluation of sheltering and a research topic in its own right for anyone with the time and resources to undertake such a study, though, as discussed below, without valid performance indicators established at the outset, evaluation can at best be only subjective in most cases. The notion that shelters per se are a good thing and provide housing for homeless sites, and that any shelter is better than no shelter, plays a part in this attitude. Yet the complex issues that emerge on closer examination of the question contradict this notion.

Evaluation means different things to different people, and may result in different criteria, usually subjective, being applied. To some the architecture of the shelter is important, to others the crucial aspects are the aesthetic of the shelter and its relationship to the setting and the landscape, yet to others its function as an interpretive center is the significant consideration, and so on. In the absence of documented or quantitative data on the primary function of the shelter, i.e. its effectiveness in preserving the resource and thereby its values, it is not surprising that discord may reign, as demonstrated by the contentious issues raised by one of the cases discussed below.

Hexashelter at Fort Selden, New Mexico

This experimental shelter (see Figure 13.1.4) was erected specifically to evaluate its effectiveness (or otherwise) in reducing climatic impact. [8] This was done in two ways: by quantitative monitoring of meteorological parameters under the shelter and outside, and by monitoring adobe walls likewise beneath and outside the shelter (see Figure 13.1.4); these were also instrumented. Nearly a year's data were collected before the shelter collapsed from snow load on the membrane roof after an unusually heavy storm. Parameters measured were temperature (air and walls), windspeed, rainfall, and solar radiation. The monitoring walls were photographed regularly. The results were very clear and showed significant reduction in solar radiation, rainfall and windspeed especially (under the shelter). Comparison of the photographic record of the two walls likewise reflected the protective efficacy of the shelter, though no quantitative data were acquired on loss of fabric from the exposed wall.

The point is not that the hexashelter was especially effective, though it was designed as a 'minimalist' shelter. Many other designs would have served as well or better. Rather, it is to show that it is possible to quantitatively monitor a shelter's performance and the condition of the resource fairly simply, provided that an appropriate control is included, in this case the external wall. Although a sophisticated, solar-powered meteorological station was used which logged data every fifteen minutes, simpler recording devices could serve as well in real situations. More important is a means of monitoring the condition of the cultural resource with an appropriate control. In addition to regular standardized photography, preferably under controlled lighting, other techniques appropriate to a particular site may be employed: an erosion meter, sampling for salt accumulation, monitoring biological infestation, and so on.

Peterborough petroglyph shelter

The case of Peterborough in Canada is illustrative of the passions that a shelter can evoke. Was the criticism by Bahn, Bednarik and Steinbring a fair evaluation of the protective structure or an unwarranted attack sustained in the journal *Rock Art Research* (edited by one of these authors)? [10] The case is included here because it is very specific in the criticisms of the shelter and, as such, qualifies as an evaluation of the functioning of a sheltering structure, though unilaterally undertaken. That the tone of the criticisms is uncompromisingly hostile is unfortunate to say the least. Here is a brief summary of the issues raised.

The shelter was built in 1984 to protect a 1,000–2,000 year old petroglyph site of about 80 m^2. [9] In 1995 Bahn et al. published [10] a long and detailed article

Figure 13.1.4 Hexashelter at Fort Selden, New Mexico. The roof is an impervious membrane and the side-panels are a knitted, open-weave synthetic textile.
Source: Photo: N. Agnew, © J. Paul Getty Trust

relentlessly critical of every aspect of the shelter, from the decision process to the design, implementation and its performance. The paper concluded with recommendations that construction of a shelter (over a rock art site) should be undertaken only if:

- the project manager could guarantee an independent, long-term sophisticated monitoring program over many decades.
- guaranteed high-caliber scientific support would be available, and that identifying the threats precisely was essential.
- all adverse information relating to intervention projects be made available.

In a detailed article published in 1997, one of the most comprehensive in the literature on shelters, Wainwright, Sears and Michalski [9] described the design of the structure at Peterborough and the reasons for the decision to shelter the site. The rationale for the design was discussed, as was the form of the building. The authors mentioned prior consultation with the native community; they described earlier studies and documentation, biological, geochemical and geophysical weathering, the petrology of the site, meteorological data, and concluded that damage by frost far outweighed that from other sources. Vandalism was identified as a major threat. They described, at some length, sheltering options and presented the rationale, the exclusion of water, for a totally enclosed shelter. A completely passive design was chosen for reasons of long-term reliability and elimination of costly energy consumption. Access for disabled visitors was included.

The authors emphasized that they were compelled to conclude that sheltering was the only way whereby the site could be preserved. They stated unequivocally that the site has been stabilized and natural weathering prevented.

Apart from the very bitter debate the Peterborough case generated, in which others joined, an important lesson is the complexity of the sheltering issue, one in which compromises must often be made. Among these are the need for thorough studies, and publication, of the threats and deterioration, for continued monitoring and maintenance and, above all, indisputable evidence for the preservation effectiveness of the shelter. The last seems not to have been quantified definitively at Peterborough, though detailed and various monitoring prior to and after construction has been in place. The team responsible for the decision to shelter, its design, implementation, maintenance and condition monitoring also left themselves open to criticism because comprehensive publication on the site's shelter and process, which might have addressed all or most of the criticisms, was delayed for more than a decade.

Conclusions

The approach to sheltering requires a holistic, interdisciplinary approach throughout. Shelters are indeed conservation interventions on the cultural resource, and may, in the absence of a thorough approach, do more harm than good. Of particular importance in the sheltering process is a means of demonstrating, sustained over time, that the shelter is doing its job of preventing deterioration. Good baseline documentation of conditions at the outset is obviously essential if this is to be convincing, but it is difficult or impossible to correlate subsequent conditions of the artefact under the shelter with its protective function without a valid control. The simplest way to monitor the efficacy of the shelter is to establish a control outside the shelter. Often this is possible when, for example, non-heritage fabric is adjacent to or near the shelter. Otherwise, indicator samples can be set up within and outside the shelter. These need not necessarily be large or costly. Monitoring of both the artefact and the control provides direct evidence of the functioning of the shelter. Monitoring can be done photographically and photogrammetrically and/or by other kinds of often simple deterioration markers. Without hard evidence of this kind it is almost impossible to prove that the shelter is performing as it should.

[...]

In summary, thorough assessments, diagnosis of threats and deterioration mechanisms and devising conservation criteria to address the threats are key points in the sheltering enterprise. The process is really no different than for any other conservation intervention, but has often been faulty in the past. Without setting the right course at the beginning things will surely go awry.

References

1. Demas, M. (2001). 'Annotated bibliography on protective shelters for archaeological sites.' *Conservation and Management of Archaeological Sites* 5 (1 *and* 2): 91–105.
2. Stanley-Price, N. and J. Jokilehto (2001). 'The decision to shelter archaeological sites: Three case-studies from Sicily.' *Conservation and Management of Archaeological Sites* 5 (1 *and* 2): 19–34.
3. Demas, M., N. Agnew, S. Waane et al. (1996). 'Preservation of the Laetoli Hominid Trackway in Tanzania.' In, *IIC Preprints of the Contributions of the Copenhagen Congress, Archaeological Conservation and its Consequences, Copenhagen* (1996), 38–42.
4. Agnew, N. and M. Demas (1998). 'Preserving the Laetoli Footprints.' *Scientific American* 279: 44–55.
5. Agnew, N., H. Griffin, M. Wade et al. (1989). 'Strategies and techniques for the preservation of fossil tracksites: an Australian example.' In D.D. Gillette and M.G. Lockley (eds), *Dinosaur Tracks and Traces*. Cambridge: Cambridge University Press.
6. Scichilone, G. (1986). 'The site of the cathedral at Atri: a case study of in situ conservation of archaeological remains.' In, *Preventive Measures During Excavation and Site Protection (Ghent Conference, 6–8 November, 1985)*. Rome: ICCROM, 309–14.
7. Waane, S.A.C. (1986). 'Roofs and shelters: The Tanzanian experience.' In, *Preventive Measures During Excavation and Site Protection (Ghent Conference, 6–8 November, 1985)*. Rome: ICCROM, 245–56.

8 Agnew, N., S. Maekawa, R. Coffman et al. (1996). 'Evaluation of the performance of a lightweight modular site shelter: Quantitative meteorological data and protective indices for the "hexashelter".' *Conservation and Management of Archaeological Sites* 1 (3): 139–50.
9 Wainwright, I.N.M., H. Sears and S. Michalski (1997). 'Design of a rock art protective structure at Petroglyphs Provincial Park, Ontario, Canada.' *Journal of the Canadian Association for Conservation* 22: 53–76. See also: Young, G.S. and I.N.M. Wainwright (1995). 'The control of algal biodeterioration of a marble petroglyph site.' *Studies in Conservation* 40 (2): 82–92; Laver, M.E. and I.N.M. Wainwright (1995). 'An investigation of the dissolution of a marble petroglyph site by acidic precipitation.' *Studies in Conservation* 40 (4): 265–73; Wainwright, I.N.M. (1990). 'Rock painting and petroglyph recording projects in Canada.' *Association for Preservation Technology Bulletin* 22 (1/2): 55–84 [Reprinted in *Ontario Rock Art Conservation Association Newsletter*, (Summer–Autumn 1991): 30–59].
10 Bahn, P.G., R.G. Bednarik and J. Steinbring (1995). 'The Peterborough petroglyph site: reflections on massive intervention in rock art.' *Rock Art Research* 12 (1): 29–41. See also: *Rock Art Research* 13 (1) (1996): 47–60; 14 (1) (1997): 53–8.

Chapter 14

Generic mitigation measures
Reburial

Introduction

THE TERM REBURIAL is widely used and means different things to different people. Three types of reburial can be distinguished:

- *Backfilling*: the reburial of an archaeological site during and immediately after excavation.
- *Conservation reburial*: the deliberate reburial of archaeological remains in their original position, following a 'conservation planning' process (see Chapter 5) with the intention to preserve the remains intact in their present state.
- *Storage reburial*: the deliberate reburial of archaeological remains in a new position (i.e. not *in situ*), in effect using the natural burial environment to preserve archaeological artefacts rather than a museum store.

Backfilling

Buried archaeological remains, whether masonry walls, adobe buildings, corroded metal artefacts or waterlogged wood, invariably come to equilibrium with the surrounding earth. Exposed by excavation to a new 'open air' environment, within minutes the damp soil and archaeological remains start to lose water through evaporation, within hours they have started to dry, shrink, crack and turn to dust. The soil loses colour and it becomes difficult to distinguish archaeological features. Organic archaeological remains, in waterlogged deposits, dry and fragment and turn to dust.

During excavation

In recent years, where appropriate, archaeological practice in northern Europe has been to cover surfaces during excavation and overnight with tarpaulins or black polythene (Barker

1986: 48). This inhibits the drying process, keeping the ground moist, colourful and workable; it also prevents rain or snow washing away archaeological surfaces. The black colour reduces light transmission and the risk of plant growth beneath the polythene. Between excavation seasons, the site will dry, vegetation will take hold and archaeological remains degrade, unless the site is again covered with black polythene or similar. Normal practice is to cover with polythene with a protective layer of soil to act as a thermal and physical barrier, to reduce the risk of frost damage or trampling damage from animals or human visitors and to prevent degradation of the polythene by sunlight. To prevent iron pan formation and other problems that water build-up around polythene creates (saturation, anoxia, pH change and mineral deposition), it is usually pierced (Barker 1982). In recent years, greater attention has been paid to the nature of backfilling (Gibbs 1994).

After excavation

In the past, when excavations had been completed, the archaeologist was faced with three choices:

- Leave the archaeological remains exposed. Early antiquarian archaeologists, wherever they worked in the world, usually left the remains they uncovered visible. This was the point of excavation, to reveal the remains of the past. The grandeur and importance of these visible remains are testament to the skill of the archaeologist and their insight into the past. Schliemann's trench through the tell at Hissarlik/Troy is visible to the present day, with archaeological remains of the different levels poking out beneath the sections. Since reputations were based on the artefacts and sites, archaeologists found time spent backfilling a waste of valuable manpower, so they did not do it. This tradition of leaving remains exposed has been continued by later generations.

    The decay problems noted above continued; indeed, they increased in severity. The longer trenches were left open, the more exposed stone was damaged by freeze thaw and salt efflorescence cycles, which led to even more degraded stone ruins. As the sides of the trenches collapsed and plant life returned, ancient excavation sites were reduced to vegetated humps and hollows of earth: 'It takes about thirty years for a mosaic to completely disappear under a covering of vegetation' (Veloccia 1977: 48).
- Backfill the site – reburying uncovered archaeological remains with the excavated soil (Gibbs 1994; Goodburn Brown and Hughes 1996). Even in the past there were archaeologists who refilled their excavation trenches, some out of a sense of civic or moral responsibility for the condition of the archaeological remains, others as a result of agreements with the landowner. Exposed, degrading archaeological remains, with their implications of lack of care or value, are not an image that modern archaeologists or the heritage agencies wish to project. This, when coupled with the increasing availability and low cost of earth moving machinery from the 1970s onwards, has resulted in an increasing expectation and ability to backfill. Returning the site to the 'as found' state has become a norm in the developed world and can be described as an 'unconscious preservation strategy' (Demas 2004: 137).
- Leave selected archaeological remains exposed by partially backfilling the site. The presence of some remains marks the site as one of antiquity and interest. This often satisfied the concerns of local citizens, who want to 'see' their past, and the archaeologists, who want to 'see' what is there, but minimised the area needing longer-term care and

protection. The remains that are exposed are normally stonework as it is often considered relatively stable or can be conserved.

In the present day, archaeologists rarely decide alone about backfilling their sites; a conscious decision usually involves the archaeologist and one or more of the landowner, the heritage agency, the developer and sometimes a representative from the local community. If substantial remains are uncovered, the discussion usually includes a debate about the possibility of display, with or without a shelter (see Chapter 12). Key issues include:

- Are the remains stable? Can they technically be made stable *in situ* and capable of being safely visited by the public without unacceptably damaging the remains? In cases such as prehistoric rock art in the caves of France, the answer is often no.
- Can the cost of making the remains stable and capable of being visited and the associated cost of maintaining them be afforded (i.e. will the public visit in sufficient numbers to justify the costs)? In cases such as the hominid footprints at Laetoli, the answer was no.

If the answer to any of these questions is no, then the site usually has high archaeological research value, but it cannot at present be used for education/visitation and the emphasis switches to preserving the remains in a manner that maximises the preservation of the information about the past they contain; the site is effectively being 'mothballed', preserving its evidence of the past until either the resources are available to make it available for public display (the value of the site is high enough to attract visitors from far and wide) or the technical conservation expertise to safely stabilise the site for public visitation has been achieved. This preservation is normally achieved through reburial. If this occurs after the appropriate decision-making process (see Chapter 5), then it can be termed conservation reburial.

Conservation reburial

Conservation reburial occurs where a known site is deliberately interred to preserve the archaeological remains, a conscious strategy to prevent any (further) damage from human visitation, vegetation, animals, weathering, etc. Time has normally elapsed after excavation and many more people are involved in the decision than with backfilling. There is detailed consideration of the archaeological value of the remains (i.e. the 'conservation planning' processes outlined in Chapter 5 are followed and a conscious decision is reached). The remains are recorded in detail, the risks to the buried remains are identified and resources to fund appropriate mitigation measures are obtained. The difference between backfilling and conservation reburial is sometimes as little as the consciousness of the decision process and the associated planning. On occasions, there is even little separation in time, between excavation and conservation reburial, as in the case of the Rose Theatre (see Chapter 14.2). It was the identification of decay mechanisms, consultation of stakeholders, assessment of a range of mitigation strategies, allocation of resources and the creation and implementation of a costly conservation reburial plan that made this a true example of conservation reburial.

Given the state of current knowledge, it is not always easy to be certain of the threat posed to archaeological remains by reburial, as in the case of painted rock art that has been both preserved and lost due to burial beneath sand/soil (Lambert 1994: 18–20). It depends on the nature of the material, its decay mechanism, the water content, chemistry and biological activity of the burial soil. In most cases, one of the three following environments is created to try and mitigate the effects of decay: *physically protected*, *waterlogged* and *desiccated* conditions. Despite using different materials, these different burial environments have a common structure, here defined as the 'protective reburial system' and described in the 'Reburial sequence' section. Post-burial, there is a continued responsibility for the reburied remains, which should be monitored – e.g. probes and data loggers to monitor water levels and the chemistry on *waterlogged* sites, moisture levels on *desiccated* sites and sample areas that can be excavated and re-examined at intervals, as at Laetoli (Agnew and Demas 1998), on *physically protected* sites. The protection also extends to maintenance of the burial materials and conditions – e.g. suppressing burrowing animals and the growth of trees and resulting in root damage (Agnew and Demas 1998: 37) and ensuring effective drainage, so avoiding water ponding on adobe and stone ruin sites. Education makes people aware of the nature and meaning of the site, making it valuable, even sacred, to them (Agnew and Demas 1998: 37). This will reduce deliberate human damage (vandalism) to the remains.

As Demas (2004: 143) observed, reburial is mentioned in the 1931 Athens Charter but is not in later charters. This reflects the emphasis that later charters had on public access and restoration, with participants often solely focused on the problems of upstanding stone ruins (see Chapter 5). The increasing emphasis on preservation of a wide range of archaeological remains *in situ*, following the limitations of funding for monument care and high-profile cases, such as the Rose Theatre in the UK and Chaco Canyon sites in the USA, led to increased awareness of the techniques of reburial by the 1990s.

Reburial environments

Physically protected

Here, the threat is usually to fragile but chemically and biologically stable remains such as wall paintings, mosaics, earthen architecture and fragile archaeological layers. These are features that may well be damaged by physical intrusion; visitors, animals, plants (roots), as well as freeze/thaw, hot/cool, wet/dry cycles and loss of substance through wind or water erosion. They would also be damaged by moisture loss and salt crystallisation. This means the primary requirement is physical protection, like that given to earthworks (see Chapter 8) and fragile sites (see Chapter 9) (i.e. a blanket or buffer of material to prevent thermal or moisture variation). Though there are eighteenth- and nineteenth-century examples of ancient buildings preserved by builders or architects, covering them back up with the soil from which they were unearthed (Siddell 2012), one of the first examples where there was a clear perception of preserving remains unscathed under soil and returning to see them again and again was the Orpheus mosaic at Woodchester Roman villa (Gloucestershire). This was excavated and drawn first by Samuel Lysons in 1793, more fully by George Hawker in 1796; it was subsequently reburied under layers of sand, soil and turf and has been uncovered and reburied between six (Smith 1973) and 12 times (Laporte Payne 1935; Cull 2000), for public exhibition, most recently in 1973. By the 1930s archaeologists were well aware of the fragility of mosaics that were left exposed to the weather and at sites such as Jaresh in Jordan routinely backfilled in order to protect them (Stanley-Price 1985: 50). Archaeologists did not normally publish such basic information on excavation practice, and even at the first ICCROM supported International Committee for the Conservation of Mosaics conference in Rome in 1977, conservators focus on interventive techniques, and preservation by reburial is only briefly mentioned (Veloccia 1977: 41). In later meetings, good practice is outlined more fully:

> For some months in winter the mosaic can be covered with a polythene sheet plus 20cms of washed sand, pozzolana, volcanic earth or similar, well sifted material. However it is extremely dangerous to keep an impermeable film on the mosaic for more than a year. This 'protection' in time increases the likelihood of the mosaic to destruction by earthworms, rats, roots, salts or condensation.
>
> For longer periods the mosaic is covered first with a layer of washed sand, pozzolana or expanded clay granules then with well sifted earth which has been mixed with a hormonal type herbicide. A covering of 30cm deep should be used for short periods, 1m deep for long periods. Straw, sawdust and, in general, any organic materials must be avoided entirely.
>
> Herbicide application and/or weeding must be repeated yearly at least and more often if vegetation develops.
>
> (ICCM 1983: 18)

This advice is largely repeated and enhanced in later papers at ICCROM/ICCM and Getty preservation *in situ* conferences (Mora 1995; Roby 2004; Stewart 2004). The pressing needs of exposed and degrading sites often means that reburial solutions have been tried on site without long-term testing; few details of actual practice have been published (Roby 2004). Only limited laboratory testing of reburial methods have been reported (Podany *et al.* 1994). For many sites, especially in the Mediterranean region, the demand for public visibility during the summer tourist season has led to seasonal exposure of many mosaics with the development of temporary 'reburial' systems for overwinter protection.

There are numerous other types of sites that have been physically protected; examples include the hominid footprints at Laetoli (Demas *et al.* 1996; Agnew and Demas 1998) (see Chapter 14.1), adobe structures such as the San Diego Presidio (Colarco 2000) and the ancient city of Merv (Cooke 2007) and wall-plaster sites (Mora 1995; Burch 1997; Moss 1998).

Waterlogged

Here, the threat is to organic materials and metals preserved through waterlogged (wet and anoxic) conditions, most frequently boats, trackways, waterfronts, buildings and ritual deposition sites. Loss of water would cause waterlogged wood to warp, shrink and crack; the presence of oxygen would cause the metals to corrode and the wood to rot. This meant that the primary requirement was the presence of water (Corfield 1996) and anoxic (oxygen-free) conditions (Caple *et al.* 1997) (see Chapter 11). One of the first occasions where there was a conscious attempt to maintain conditions and preserve waterlogged structures were the wrecks uncovered by the Dutch authorities during the Zuider Zee/Ijsselmeer reclamation where the wrecks were surrounded by an impermeable barrier to create a raised water table (Coles 1987) (see Chapter 2.1). Subsequently, in the UK, following the exposure of prehistoric trackways across the Somerset Levels, a section of one of them, the Sweet Track, was preserved *in situ*, in 1984, creating a clay bund around the track area and pumping in water to maintain a raised water table. Subsequently, at UK sites such as Sutton Common, Flag Fen and Fiskerton (Williams *et al.* 2008), measures have been taken to retard drainage or pump water on to the deposits to maintain the water level. The extent of anoxia is either presumed (Flag Fen), tested occasionally (Sweet Track) or frequently monitored (Rose Theatre). Short-term reburial during long breaks in excavation demonstrated in London at sites such as Guildhall and Bramcote Grove (Goodburn Brown and Hughes 1996) that simple covering of the site, without interventive measures or monitoring, resulted in fungal attack of waterlogged wood, so demonstrating the need for ensuring saturated anoxic reburial conditions if waterlogged wood is to be successfully preserved *in situ*. It was the high profile site of the Rose Theatre (London) (Corfield 2004) (see Chapter 14.2), where protests by famous actors and the public on 14 and 15 May 1989 at what was perceived to be the loss of the remaining fragments of an original Shakespearian theatre, which was widely reported in the media, caused planned development work to stop, government funding to be released to compensate the developer, and created time for a redesign of the building and the development of a better preservation solution. It brought home to heritage authorities in the UK the social importance of the remains and the possibilities presented by preservation *in situ*, but also how challenging this could be both in technical terms and the problems of public perception of conservation reburial.

Desiccated

Desiccated conditions have preserved organic material, particularly wood and textiles; the threat is that the introduction of water or high humidity will support the presence of fungi, bacteria or insects that will consume the organic material and mobilise soluble salts, leading to physical break-up of surfaces from efflorescence effects. In reference to the tomb of Tutankhamun, Carter and Mace commented:

> From every point of view it was a thousand pities that this tomb should have suffered from infrequent moisture filtering through fissures in the limestone rock into which it was cut. This moisture saturated the air of its chambers and caused a humid atmosphere to exist therein for what must have been considerable intermittent periods. It not only nourished a fungoid growth and caused a peculiar pink film to be deposited everywhere, but it destroyed practically all the leatherwork by melting it into a black viscid mass. It also caused extensive warping to take place among the varied woods used in the construction of many objects. It also dissolved all adhesive material such as glue, so that the component parts of many articles fell apart. It also resulted in much deterioration of the textiles – an irreparable loss, for among them were rare garments like the tapestry woven linen fabric as well as of needlework.
>
> (Carter and Mace 1924: Vol. III, 151–2)

This emphasises that the primary requirement in desiccated reburial is the retention of desiccated conditions. In most cases, such as Egyptian tombs, the contents were removed to museums for conservation and storage in preservative environments. Early Anasazi desiccated sites, which were also excavated and had finds removed to museums, had stone ruins that still contained wood floors and roofs. These were simply left as found, with no attempt to preserve. However, in recent years, the US National Park Service has been partially reburying a number of the sites in and around Chaco Canyon. It is seeking to recreate the preserving burial conditions at the site of Chaco Canyon, which successfully preserved the mud plasters and the wooden beams of the floors (Ford et al. 2004) (see Chapter 14.3). Shin Makaewa and colleagues have established just how dry the sandy ground needs to be, <5 per cent moisture creating burial conditions of <75 per cent RH, to prevent fungal degradation of the wood (Maekawa 2004). Efforts have focused on monitoring moisture levels and identifying potential water sources, then using membranes, drains, evaporating basins and differential fill levels to ensure the moisture does not reach the organic components. Though backfilling has been used on many desert and semi-desert sites since the 1930s, hoping dry desiccating conditions would re-establish, no active monitoring or measures to control moisture ingress were ever taken. The attempts from circa 2000 at Chaco Canyon (see Chapter 14.3) (Ford et al. 2004) are the first to try to monitor moisture levels and take active steps to control moisture entering the soil and thus achieve 'conservation reburial' in desiccated conditions.

Reburial sequence

Conceptually, reburial seeks to create a buffer between the archaeological remains and the aggressive environment that threatens it (see Figure 14.0.1).

In selecting the buffer material, there are three elements to consider:

- The buffer/environment interface. This will be a tough barrier to deflect the erosive agents of the aggressive environment and/or one that is repaired or self-repairs when it is damaged, so preventing loss of buffer material. If it is not resistant, self-repairing or maintained, the buffer material will be lost.
- The buffer material acts to slow and minimise transfer between the external environment and the archaeological remains. If it is impermeable, there is risk of boundary effects such as water or salts build-up. Consequently, buffers usually maintain gradients, slowing movement of gases, liquids or temperature between the external environment and the buried remains. Buffers should be stable and inert, not releasing any material that would interact with the archaeological remains.
- The buffer/archaeology interface should avoid any detectable impact on the archaeological remains. It should not be too hard and physically damage the remains; it should have similar porosity and chemistry to the remains so that it does not unintentionally become a barrier to water or dissolved minerals.

These buffer layers are effectively those that have previously been described as protecting earthworks (see Chapter 8) and fragile sites (see Chapter 9), soft capping or shelter coats for stone walls (see Chapter 6), fresh earth plaster coating, capping or encapsulation of earthen architecture (see Chapter 7), but in conservation reburial they are at a higher specification, designed to protect specific archaeological remains, such as the Laetoli footprints, and are normally subsurface as it is a less aggressive environment. In practice, several layers and different materials may be required to achieve this 'protective reburial system' (see Figure 14.0.2):

- *Capping layer*: Deposition. This comprises discontinuous obstacles such as vegetation or fencing that will discourage erosive forces such as animals or human beings from trampling over the site. Vegetation, fencing, stones and other structures also slow the erosive forces

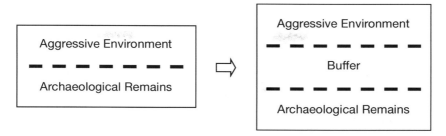

Figure 14.0.1 Reburial protection involves the insertion of a buffer between the erosive agents of an aggressive environment and the archaeological remains.

of wind or water causing them to drop sediment, leading to deposition of an additional buffering layer on the site. Soil/sand catchment systems, specific types of fencing or vegetation can be deliberately erected to create sediment build-up. At Nindera Point, 'sand dune forming fencing' was installed, which prevented aeolian erosion of the dunes and led to sand build-up over the site (Sneison *et al.* 1986: 37). At Laetoli, boulders dissuade animal and human activity on the site, preventing erosion (see Chapter 14.1). There are a variety of fibrous geotextiles, erosion prevention matting and catch fencing that have proved effective in preventing erosion and led to deposition. Often, short-term protection such as biodegradable barriers like burlap sacks filled with oyster shells, hay bales and booms of tethered logs have been found to absorb wave impacts and enable the establishment of vegetation that subsequently provides physical protection and encourages sediment deposition of blanketing soils/sediments to form (Nickens 2000: 321–5). Only vegetation, which is both a self-renewing and self-repairing system, is a long-term solution to the erosion problem, and using native plant species that are well adapted to the local environment is the most ecologically sound approach (Sneison *et al.* 1986; Lin *et al.* 1997). There is, however, a need to monitor and maintain all barriers and depositional protective systems. Vegetation systems may require water and nourishment and may need replacement or selective removal to mitigate excessive growth such as tree roots which can grow to threaten the site.

- *Capping layer*: Protection. This is a tough, hard or self-repairing surface designed to physically resist the erosive force. For waves, it could be stone or concrete block (riprap); for human and animal traffic, it could be vegetation (grass or other small surface rooted species are most usual) designed to protect the layers beneath. The surface of the capping layer is often contoured to deflect erosive forces, most usually to encourage water run-off, away from stone and adobe ruins, into gulleys and drain away from archaeological areas (Cooke 2007: 106). In the case of waterlogged sites, the capping layer prevents evaporation, and on sites at risk from tree growth a bio-barrier (biocide impregnated geotextile) prevents root growth (Agnew and Demas 1988: 36).
- *Buffer (fill) layer*: Usually local soil or sand, often with small stones. This material is often what was removed by excavation (or erosive forces), and as such it had previously established chemical equilibrium with the archaeological remains, an equilibrium that normally re-establishes upon reburial, provided that the backfilled soil originally came from that layer and location. This material provides a cushioning layer, absorbing pressure from above; vehicles or buildings on or over the site. It provides thermal insulation, so avoiding freeze/thaw cycles, provides distance between any erosive agent and the

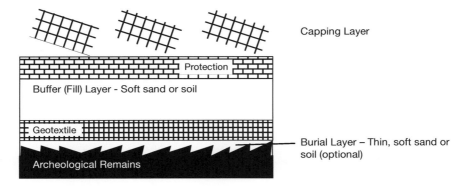

Figure 14.0.2 Conceptual protective reburial system.

archaeological remains, and enables moisture gradients to be established, preventing drying out. The depth will depend on the site and the envisaged site use. New materials that have been used to form this layer include sand, pozzolana, expanded clay pellets and gravel (Demas 2004: 149). Such material should be chemically inert and tested to ensure that there is no deleterious chemical change of or on the archaeological remains, no alteration of pH, no deposition of soluble salts, etc. For example, Buckland sand was used to bury the Rose Theatre since it is composed almost entirely of inert silica with no soluble salts or minerals. Experimentation has demonstrated the need to maintain similar porosity to archaeological remains in the fill/blanket layer in order to maintain moisture flow and avoid salt crystallisation (efflorescence), thus coarse fill materials such as gravel or clay pellets could create air gaps and salt problems in some situations (Podany *et al.* 1994). Sometimes appropriate geotextiles are introduced as part of the buffer layer to help hold the material in place and reduce risk of loss through erosion.

- *Geotextile*: An inert polymer (normally polyester or polypropylene) fabric, either woven or unwoven (bonded by needle punching or by heat), in a variety of thicknesses and textures, which act as physical protection for the archaeological layer and as a marker; an indicator of the presence of the archaeological remains just below. It demonstrates to later investigators that this is not undisturbed ground, but was created during the late twentieth/early twenty-first century. Geotextiles are permeable and do not stop water passing through; examples include Typar® (spun-bonded) and Enkafilter® (needle-punched), though a range of geotextiles are available (Haygarth 1994; Kavazanjian 2004). The fabric facilitates removing the fill layer and protects the remains from physical damage. Very occasional examples of cementing around the geotextile, or root growth along the layer, have been reported. These probably derive from failure to ensure unimpeded moisture movement through fill, geotextile and burial layers.
- *Burial layer*: This thin, optional layer is designed to cushion the archaeological remains from the geotextile, preventing air gaps and filling hollows (since the geotextile is often too stiff to exactly match the contours of the archaeological remains) and protecting, where necessary, the fragile archaeological remains from direct contact with the geotextile (e.g. woven structures not imprinted on to soft waterlogged remains). Fine-sieved local sand or soil with similar porosity and chemistry to the archaeological remains are used to ensure free water movement and ensure no salts or minerals are deposited at this interface.

Reburial sequences such as this are seen in projects from the remains of the Roman amphitheatre at Guildhall in London (Goodburn Brown and Hughes 1996) to the Presidio at San Diego (Colarco 2000). Although a number of reburial projects have been undertaken in recent years, few have been published (Roby 2004); none have been running for long enough to be re-excavated to determine which materials and procedures work or have failed:

> Because of the paucity of data from research projects or long term evaluations of reburial operations, technical design must rely primarily on a theoretical understanding of the properties and behaviour of fill materials and their impact on the burial environment.
>
> (Demas 2004: 148)

Gaseous and sterile

It is appropriate to draw comparison between the reburial through recreating waterlogged, desiccated and physically protective burial conditions and the work on cave environments discussed in Chapter 10. The work at Lascaux and Mogao has shown that to preserve paintings in caves and tombs, the burial environment that had preserved them from the past to the present must be recreated. This means little or no human visitation, a sterile, low-temperature, stable gaseous environment, devoid of light, carbon and nitrogen sources, with constant RH.

Storage reburial

The limited value that some archaeological objects have for display in museums or the high cost or technical difficulty of conservation, coupled with the high research value these objects have for archaeologists, leads to a need for safe storage of such artefacts. This can be achieved in museum stores for objects that are stable stored in dry atmospheric conditions. However, where these fragments are waterlogged timbers, they need storage in wet anoxic conditions, and the most certain way of ensuring such conditions is to rebury these remains in natural waterlogged (wet and anoxic) deposits. Jespersen and her Danish colleagues (1985) expended considerable effort, monitoring the chemistry and biological activity of waterlogged sand deposits, in order to find a suitable site in which to rebury the timbers of the Kollerup Kog. Fry (1996) recounts a more pragmatic solution of a field in Northern Ireland in which a number of dugout canoes have been reburied, without any analysis of soil conditions. He notes that this was, to some degree, a cultural process, since the fieldwork to recover the objects had been costly and there was a desire by the archaeologists, and no doubt the local community, to 'keep them for posterity', but without the resources for conservation, the careful interment in a 'designated' reburial site described as 'safe' meant all people's requirements would be satisfied (Fry 1996). There have also been a number of attempts, such as at Red Bay, Canada (Stewart *et al.* 1995), to store ships' timbers through reburial in the seabed as responses to emergency situations. In recent years, there have been attempts to research and assess appropriate locations for future reburial such as Firestone Copse, Isle of Wight (Hogan *et al.* 2006) and Marstrand Harbour, Sweden, where there has also been research of the effects of reburial on 'fresh' materials and a large quantity of archaeological material was reburied (Peacock *et al.* 2008).

Over the years, given the limited display and storage space in museums, a number of British archaeologists have reburied material on the archaeological sites from which it was recovered, especially architectural stonework from Roman and medieval sites (e.g. Caple 2007: 7), so ensuring its preservation, though without testing, monitoring or undertaking wider consultation; this is perhaps more accurately described as storage by backfill. However, such reburial into already excavated ground, especially on scheduled ancient monuments, provides unique legal protection for the remains, which enjoy the same protection as unexcavated parts of the site and cannot be re-excavated without scheduled monument consent.

Public expectation

As Demas (2004) points out, there are negative public connotations with reburial:

- Archaeologists unearth the past, they don't cover it up; this is counter-intuitive, and archaeologists, politicians and the public react negatively to things running contrary to their expectations.
- As with human burial, anything placed in the ground is seen as likely to decay, thus without further information it appears that the archaeological remains are being destroyed.
- The term reburial is used when human and other remains are returned to groups such as Native Americans under NAGPRA agreements for reburial (Fforde *et al.* 2002). Such material is not intended ever to be retrieved or disturbed again. This again adds to the public expectation that the term represents the loss of archaeological remains.
- Things that are no longer useful are put away or covered up. The concept 'out of site, out of mind' holds true in our daily lives, and reburial can be seen by some in the same context. Thus, if you are local to the site and the remains being 'covered up' by the authorities are meaningful to you, it can appear that they are deleting your past, while no doubt maintaining theirs. These feelings are especially true if these authorities 'burying your heritage' are based far away and are a different race or cultural group.

These issues were certainly present in the case of the San Diego Presidio, where an initial proposal to 'bury' the adobe built structure of the north wing of the presidio, which was one of the first multi-ethnic communities on west coast America, was stopped in the face of adverse public reaction that suggested the city would 'prefer to keep history buried beneath a park . . . covering up its Spanish Mexican roots' (Bauer 1999; Colarco 2000: 23). Subsequently, considerable time and effort went into explaining the decay that occurs to adobe buildings when left unprotected as ruins and the costs of conservation and redisplay, above all demonstrating that the decision was not based on racial grounds, but on preservation and economic considerations. It also sought to show that this was a reversible solution and that there was care taken and cost involved in the conservation reburial process. Subsequently, after a much wider community involvement and creating a new decision-making group that included all stakeholders, the conservation reburial went ahead. Similar issues over the value of the archaeological remains to a particular interest group, a lack of public awareness of the issues involved in conservation reburial, emerged in the Rose Theatre (Corfield 2004). In both cases, the news media proved to be a double-edged sword, both facilitating communication with a wide range of people who may place value in the archaeological remains, potentially drawing them into the decision-making process but also representing divided opinions and extreme views since a conflict or crisis will undoubtedly 'sell more newspapers'.

As yet, there are few, if any, good high-profile examples where sites have undergone conservation reburial and then been unearthed and redisplayed; this type of 'storage' needs to be shown to work and establish that reputation before it is accepted as such.

The total authenticity and integrity of reburied remains stands in marked contrast to the exposed, visited and frequently restored monuments that we all visit. Frequent programmes of work to maintain monuments have involved replacement and restoration work, each valid in their own way, but the cumulative effect is that little of what is now seen is original material. In reference to Chaco Canyon, staff from the National Park Service concluded, 'Perhaps even more disturbing, throughout the period 1950s through the early 1980s, there was an increasing awareness that the repetitive fabric treatments were significantly affecting the authenticity and integrity of the structures' (Ford et al. 2004: 180).

The largest problem in achieving public awareness and support for reburial is that the decay of archaeological remains on exposed surface sites is not something that archaeologists or heritage professionals have highlighted (or want to highlight) to the public, since it could reflect poorly on their present stewardship. Many archaeologists are also unaware of the level of decay and restoration on monuments and the high costs of conserving and maintaining heritage resources. Few archaeology courses include lectures about the different types of decay or explore the economics of repair and maintenance of monuments. Local communities often see archaeological remains as an attractant to tourists and the economic benefit they bring. Covering the remains would reduce or eliminate the tourist trade and its economic benefit. This has certainly been a concern for communities around French Palaeolithic caves, which have had visitor numbers reduced to a trickle (see Chapter 10). At well known sites such as Merv (Cooke 2007) and Aztec Ruins (Bass Rivera et al. 2004) or Chaco Canyon (Ford et al. 2004), partial refilling is being tried to see how well the system works. Thus far, it appears to be reducing maintenance costs and damage to the sites, and not leading to an outcry over the 'loss' of the site, and still enabling local communities to take pride and gain identity from the site and derive economic benefit from it.

The response of different groups to conservation reburial varies. Many Native American groups who have been consulted over the partial reburying of sites at Chaco Canyon (Ford et al. 2004: 181) or Aztec Ruins (Bass Rivera et al. 2004: 287) have not raised any objections. Many see the natural decay processes of nature as the most appropriate thing to happen to the remains of the past. There is little difference in such a world view between the decay processes that occur on exposure to the air and those that occur beneath the soil; they are both natural and both can be seen as preferable to active conservation of the ruins.

In the introduction to this book, it was noted that society requires signifiers, monuments to form the mnemonics to create their past, whether mountains or historic houses – fixed reference points on which a past is based. A simple discrete little notice will not do it; the sign needs to be significant and enter people's visual consciousness, such as the low mound of lava boulders at Laetoli (see Chapter 14.1). Where remains are conservation reburied, there needs to be a strong social signifier to the presence of ancient remains to help ensure future social awareness, valuation and preservation of the site.

Bibliography

Agnew, N. and Demas, M. (1998) 'Preserving the Laetoli footprint', *Scientific American*, September 1998: 26–37.
Barker, P. (1982) *The Techniques of Archaeological Excavation*, 2nd edn, London: Batsford.
Barker, P. (1986) 'Temporary shelter and site protection', in ICCROM (ed.), *Preventive Measures During Excavation and Site Protection. Conference Ghent 6–8 November 1985*, Rome: ICCROM, pp. 45–50.

Bass Rivera, A., Culpepper, B., Barrow, J. et al. (2004) 'Partial reburial of west ruin at Aztec Ruins national monument', *Conservation and Managements of Archaeological Sites*, 6(3–4): 285–94.
Bauer, L.L. (1999) 'Preserving the Presidio should take precedence', Letters to the Editor, *San Diego Union Tribune*, 13 August.
Burch, R. (1997) 'The reburial of wall paintings: a critical assessment of the technique of reburial for the conservation of in situ excavated plasters', unpublished postgraduate diploma dissertation, Courtauld Institute of Art, University of London.
Caple, C. (2007) *Excavations at Dryslwyn Castle 1980–1995*, Society for Medieval Archaeology Monograph, London: Society for Medieval Archaeology No. 26.
Caple, C., Dungworth, D. and Clogg, P. (1997) 'The assessment and protection of archaeological organic materials in waterlogged burial environments', in P. Hoffmann, T. Grant, J.A. Spriggs and T. Daley (eds), *Proceedings of the 6th Waterlogged Organic Archaeological Materials Conference, York 1996*, Bremerhaven: ICCOM-CC WOAM Working Group, pp. 57–52.
Carter, H. and Mace, A.C. (1924) *The Tomb of Tut.ankh.amen* Vol. 1, London: Cassell & Co.
Colarco, D. (2000) 'San Diego Royal Presidio: conservation of an earthen architecture site', in International Conference on the Study and Conservation of Earthen Architecture (ed.), *Terra 2000 Preprints: 8th International Conference on the Study and Conservation of Earthen Architecture, Torquay, Devon, UK (2000)*, London: James & James, pp. 19–25.
Coles, J.M. (1987) 'The preservation of archaeological sites by environmental intervention', in H. Hodges (ed.), *In-Situ Archaeological Conservation*, Mexico: Instituto Nacional de Antropologia e Historia & J. Paul Getty Trust, pp. 32–55.
Cooke, L. (2007) 'The archaeologists challenge or despair: reburial at Merv, Turkmenistan', *Conservation and Managements of Archaeological Sites*, 9(2): 97–112.
Corfield, M. (1996) 'Preventive conservation for archaeological sites', in A. Roy and P. Smith (eds), *Archaeological Conservation and Its Consequences: Preprints of the Contributions to the Copenhagen Congress*, London: IIC, pp. 32–7.
Corfield, M. (2004) 'Saving the Rose Theatre: England's first managed and monitored reburial', *Conservation and Management of Archaeological Sites*, 6(3–4): 305–14.
Cull, J. (2000) *Roman Woodchester: Its Villa and Mosaic*, Andover: Pitkin Unichrome.
Demas, M. (2004) '"Site unseen": the case for reburial of archaeological sites', *Conservation and Management of Archaeological Sites*, 6(3–4): 137–54.
Demas, M., Agnew, N., Waane, S. et al. (1996) 'Preservation of the Laetoli hominid trackway in Tanzania', in A. Roy and P. Smith (eds), *Archaeological Conservation and Its Consequences: 1996 IIC Copenhagen Congress*, London: IIC, pp. 38–42.
Fforde, C., Hubert, J. and Turnbull, P. (eds) (2002) *The Dead and Their Possessions: Repatriation in Principle, Policy and Practice*, London: Routledge.
Ford, D., Demas, M., Agnew, N. et al. (2004) 'Chaco Canyon reburial programme', *Conservation and Management of Archaeological Sites*, 6(3–4): 177–202.
Fry, M.F. (1996) 'Buried but not forgotten: sensitivity in disposing of major archaeological timbers', in A. Roy and P. Smith (eds), *Archaeological Conservation and Its Consequences: Preprints of the Contributions to the Copenhagen Congress*, London: IIC, pp. 52–4.
Gibbs, R. (1994) 'The use of backfill techniques on "dry" and "waterlogged" archaeological sites', unpublished BSc dissertation, University of London.
Goodburn Brown, D. and Hughes, R. (1996) 'A review of some conservation procedures for the reburial of archaeological sites in London', in A. Roy and P. Smith (eds), *Archaeological Conservation and Its Consequences: Preprints of the Contributions to the Copenhagen Congress*, London: IIC, pp. 65–9.
Haygarth, S. (1994) 'Product listing', in A.Q. Berry and I.W. Brown (eds), *Erosion on Archaeological Earthworks: Its Prevention, Control and Repair*, Mold: Clwyd County Council, pp. 115–59.
ICCM (International Committee for the Conservation of Mosaics) (1983) *Mosaics No. 2: Safeguard, Carthage 1978, Perigueux 1980*, Rome: ICCROM.
Hogan, D., Jones, M. and Simpson, P. (2006) *Reburial of Organic Remains: Final Report to English Heritage 2006*, Archaeology Data Service, available at: http://archaeologydataservice.ac.uk/archives/view/reburial_eh_2007/ (accessed September 2014).
Jespersen, K. (1985) 'Extended storage of waterlogged wood in nature', in R. Ramiere and M. Colardelle (eds), *Waterlogged Wood, Study and Conservation: Proceedings of the I.C.O.M. Waterlogged Wood Working Group Conference, Grenoble 1984*, Grenoble: ICCOM-CC Working Group WOAM, pp. 39–54.
Kavazanjian, E. (2004) 'The use of geosynthetics for archaeological site reburial', *Conservation and Management of Archaeological Sites*, 6(3–4): 377–93.

Lambert, D. (1994) *Conserving Australian Rock Art: A Manual for Site Managers*, Canberra: Aboriginal Studies Press.

Laporte Payne, A.A. (1935) *The Roman Villa at Woodchester, Gloucestershire*, Stroud: Arthurs Press.

Lin, P-M., Agnew, N., Yunhe, L. et al. (1997) 'Desert adapted plants for control of windblown sand', in N. Agnew (ed.), *Conservation of Ancient Sites on the Silk Road: Proceedings of an International Conference on the Conservation of Grotto Sites*, Los Angeles, CA: Getty Conservation Institute, pp. 227–34.

Maekawa, S. (2004) 'Monitoring of soil moisture in backfilled soil, for conservation of an ancestral Puebloan great house in Chaco Canyon', *Conservation and Management of Archaeological Sites*, 6(3–4): 315–24.

Mora, P. (1995) 'Conservation of excavated Intonaco, Stucco and mosaics', in N.P. Stanley-Price (ed.), *Conservation on Archaeological Excavations*, 2nd edn, Rome: ICCROM, pp. 91–100.

Moss, E. (1998) 'Protection and environmental control of the plastered mudbrick walls at Çatalhöyük', unpublished MSc thesis, University of Pennsylvania.

Nickens, P. (2000) 'Technologies for in-place protection and long-term conservation of archaeological sites', in R.A. Williamson and P.R. Nickens (eds), *Science and Technology in Historic Preservation*, New York: Kluwer Academic, pp. 309–32.

Peacock, E., Bergstrand, T., Godfrey, I.N. et al. (2008) 'The Marstrand reburial project: overview, phase 1 and future work', in H. Kars and R.M. van Heeringen (eds), *Preserving Archaeological Remains in Situ: Proceedings of the 3rd Conference 7–9 December 2006, Amsterdam*, Geoarchaeological and Bio-archaeological Studies 10, Amsterdam: Vrije Universiteit Amsterdam, pp. 253–63.

Podany, J., Agnew, N. and Demas, M. (1994) 'Preservation of excavated mosaics by reburial: evaluation of some traditional and newly developed materials and techniques', in *Conservation, Protection, Presentation: Fifth Conference of the International Committee for the Conservation of Mosaics, Faro – Conimbriga, 4–8 October 1993. Proceedings (Mosaics 6)*, Lisbon: Instituto Portugues Museus, pp. 1–19.

Roby, T. (2004) 'The reburial of mosaics: an overview of materials and practice', *Conservation and Management of Archaeological Sites*, 6(3–4): 229–36.

Siddell, J. (2012) 'PARIS London: one hundred and fifty years of site preservation', *Conservation and Management of Archaeological Sites*, 14(1–4): 372–83.

Smith, D.J. (1973) *The Great Pavement and Roman Villa at Woodchester, Gloucestershire*, Woodchester: Woodchester Roman Pavement Committee.

Sneison, W.J., Sullivan, M.E. and Preece, N.D. (1986) 'Nundera Point: an experiment in stabilising a foredune Shell Midden', *Australian Archaeology*, 23: 25–41.

Stanley-Price, N. (1985) 'Patterns of survival among some Byzantine floor mosaics in the Levant', in ICCM (ed.), *Mosaics: Conservation in Situ: Aquileia*, Rome: ICCROM, pp. 49–54.

Stewart, J. (2004) 'Conservation of archaeological mosaic pavements by means of reburial', *Conservation and Management of Archaeological Sites*, 6(3–4): 237–46.

Stewart, J., Murdock, L.D. and Waddell, P. (1995) 'Reburial of the Red Bay wreck as a form of preservation and protection of the historic resource', in P. Vandiver, J.R. Druzik, J.L. Galvan Madrid, I.C. Freestone and G.S. Wheeler (eds), *Materials Issues in Art and Archaeology IV*, Material Research Society 352, Pittsburgh: Material Research Society, pp. 791–805.

Veloccia, M.L. (1977) 'Conservation problems of mosaics in situ', in ICCM (ed.), *Mosaics No. 1: Deterioration and Conservation, Rome, November 1977*, Rome: ICCROM, pp. 39–43.

Williams, J., Fell, V., Graham, K. et al. (2008) 'Re-watering of the Iron Age causeway at Fiskerton, England', in H. Kars and R.M. van Heeringen (eds), *Preserving Archaeological Remains in Situ: Proceedings of the 3rd Conference 7–9 December 2006, Amsterdam*, Geoarchaeological and Bioarchaeological Studies 10, Amsterdam: Vrije Universiteit Amsterdam, pp. 181–97.

Chapter 14.1

Preservation of the Laetoli hominid trackway in Tanzania

Martha Demas, Neville Agnew, Simon Waane, Jerry Podany, Angelyn Bass and Donatius Kamamba

Source: Demas, M., Agnew, N., Waane, S., Podany, J., Bass, A. and Kamamba, D. (1996) 'Preservation of the Laetoli hominid trackway in Tanzania', in A. Roy and P. Smith (eds), *Archaeological Conservation and Its Consequences: 1996 IIC Copenhagen Congress*, London: IIC, pp. 38–42.

Introduction

THE PLIOCENE SITE of Laetoli within the Ngorongoro Conservation Area in northwestern Tanzania, some 30 km from the famous site of Olduvai Gorge, preserves both hominid and faunal tracks, as well as both early hominid and animal fossils. It has immense scientific value, particularly for the study of human evolution. The hominid trackway at Site G, one of the many fossil track sites in the area fortuitously preserved within layers of aeolian and airfall volcanic tuff, not only records evidence of the diversity of life in the savannah of east Africa at the time, but provides unique proof of bipedalism in hominids from 3.6 million years ago.

[...]

The trackway was excavated by Dr Mary Leakey in 1978–79. Following excavation and study, it was documented photogram-metrically, molded for casting, and then reburied for protection under a mantle of soil capped with lava boulders intended to serve as an armor against erosion and large animals such as elephants and cattle belonging to the Maasai. [1] What was not realized at the time was that the uncompacted reburial fill, which contained acacia seeds, together with physical protection and moisture retention provided by the boulders, would create a micro-environment conducive to germination and rapid growth of vegetation. Since the site is remote and often inaccessible by vehicle during the wet season, it was seldom visited. Nonetheless, by the late 1980s growth of acacia trees on the reburial mound was being reported. [2] The reports were confirmed in 1992 when a preliminary assessment of the condition of the hominid trackway was undertaken as the initial step in a collaborative project

Figure 14.1.1 Laetoli trackway, Site G. Southern 10 m of the trackway in 1995 after re-excavation of the Footprint Tuff surface, before removal of acacia stumps and excavation of the fill from the footprints. Acacia trees in the southernmost part of the trench (foreground) produced extensive lateral roots, while trees growing in the weathered northern portion developed taproots which penetrated the tuff.

between the Getty Conservation Institute (GCI) and the Antiquities Unit of the Tanzanian Ministry of Education and Culture. At that time, a 3 × 3 m test trench was opened and revealed that roots had penetrated the Footprint Tuff (the multiple layers of volcanic ash in which the tracks were made) and had damaged individual hominid prints (see Figure 14.1.1).

Conservation of this remote and fragile palaeontological site posed complex challenges. Foremost among them was to determine an appropriate strategy for long-term protection. Since the excavation in 1978–79, two different strategies have been proposed for the trackway: *in situ* preservation for presentation to visitors and access to scholars, or lifting and relocating the trackway or individual tracks to a museum.

To keep sites open for the public to visit and for scholarly study is an option selected for many archaeological sites, often through use of shelters. However, experience has shown that this type of preservation is not always effective and may result in deterioration of the site, rather than its preservation.

Fragile, remote sites, such as Laetoli, which are often inaccessible and therefore difficult to monitor and maintain, are frequently not suited to public presentation.

Protecting such sites with a shelter is rarely an adequate solution. The Tanzanian experience has demonstrated the inherent difficulties. [3] Further afield but otherwise more directly comparable is the dinosaur trackway site of Lark Quarry in Australia. In addition to resulting in inadvertent damage to the trackway, efforts to protect this isolated site by a shelter consumed resources not commensurate with subsequent benefits to the site. [4]

The second option, removal of the trackway to a museum, has been advocated as a means of preserving it and allowing access for study. Removal would, however, prove technically difficult and furthermore is incompatible with conservation principles. Although methods may have improved since the unsuccessful removal of a faunal print from Site C during the 1978 season, [5] there are other problems at Laetoli that make removal an undesirable option. Apart from the high cost of lifting the trackway, there would be great risk of damage or loss because of the natural lamination of the tuff (exacerbated by weathering and root penetration), tremendous logistical problems due to the remoteness of the site, and a need for large display space (presently unavailable in Tanzania). Even where museum space is available, if other requirements such as physical support, maintenance and control of the environment cannot be met, damage will result in the long term. [6]

[...] The hominid footprints at Laetoli were impressed in that location 3.6 million years ago, in sight of the Sadiman volcano that produced the multiple layers of ash which formed the Footprint Tuff, and subsequently buried it. When considering the conservation strategy, it was believed that every effort should be made to keep the footprints in their original context. It must also be noted that the association of animal tracks with the hominid footprints is of scientific value, and removing the footprints from their original location would destroy that association.

A third option—namely re-excavation, conservation, documentation and long-term reburial—presented itself as a more feasible and responsible method of conservation. Utilizing reburial as the basis of the conservation strategy, it is the aim of the project to retain the cultural value of the site by preservation *in situ* and to save the remaining scientific value by eliminating causes of damage, and by enhancing what value remains through comprehensive documentation.

The plan to conserve the trackway at Site G entails four phases of activity. Phase 1, completed in 1993, involved detailed assessment of the condition and conservation requirements through partial re-excavation of the 1992 trench. The results and recommendations formed the basis for planning the work for Phases 2–4. Phase 2, in 1994, involved mapping the site; treatment of the 150 trees on the trackway and adjacent to the site with a biodegradable herbicide (Roundup) applied to the stumps; site stabilization measures to control surface water flow during the rainy season and to stop active erosion at the northern end of the trackway; making a new master mold from the 1979 cast of the trackway stored at Olduvai; and meeting with the local Maasai elders to inform them of the objectives of the project and to enlist their support for future protection and monitoring of the site. Phase 3 entails three major campaigns over a three-year period (1995–97) involving re-excavation of the trackway, conservation treatment, documentation, scientific re-study by specialists to answer questions still not fully resolved, and reburial of the trackway in a manner that will ensure its future protection. Phase 4, planned for 1996–97, will see the initial implementation of the maintenance and monitoring program, and the creation of museum exhibits in Tanzania about the trackway. The 1995 campaign, described below, was completed in July and August of that year.

Re-excavation

The primary goal of the re-excavation in the 1995 season was to expose the southernmost 10 m of the trackway in order for conservation, documentation and scientific re-study to be undertaken. For scientific purposes, the southern section is the most important since it preserves approximately 6.8 m of the best hominid prints (29 prints, of which approximately 21 are well defined). Within the excavated area, 37 acacia trees were inventoried and mapped. Re-excavation also revealed the original 1979 excavation trench walls, datum points, and other features that were not well documented in the final publication of the site.

The use of a temporary shelter over the excavated area both enhanced the comfort of those working on the trackway and protected the trackway from direct sunlight.

Conservation and documentation

[...]

Following final excavation and fine cleaning of the hominid and faunal prints and the surrounding tuff surface with wooden tools and soft brushes, a graphic condition survey was undertaken using acetate sheets over 20 × 25 cm (8 × 10 inch) Polaroid photographs. The condition survey recorded loss, fractures, structural weakness and intrusive root growth, as well as adherent overburden or residues of previous treatment.

Damage to three hominid prints from roots occurred in the weathered northern portion of the excavated area, as well as to peripheral areas of the trackway where no hominid or animal prints are found. Treatment of stumps and roots penetrating the tuff involved the following processes: application, where necessary, of a water-based acrylic dispersion (Acrysol WS-24) as a surface consolidant to secure the fragile and disrupted tuff prior to treatment; cutting of roots using a battery-powered, rotary mini-saw; removal or reduction of remaining roots or stumps to a level below the exposed tuff by routing with a mini-router, and by extraction with tweezers where possible; filling the voids left by root removal and areas of overhanging tuff with a viscous mixture of the acrylic dispersion and fumed silica; and lastly, addition of a preservative (pentachlorophenol, 3.8% w/v, in isopropyl alcohol and acetone 1:1 by volume) into holes drilled in remaining root segments. The purpose of the preservative is to discourage insects, particularly termites which are active at the site.

Comparison of the re-excavated hominid footprints with the casts originally made in 1979 showed an obscuring or slight loss of detail. While there may be a number of contributing factors, such as softening of the tuff due to water and subsequent deformation by the weight of the overburden, it was clear that a resin applied in 1979 was primarily responsible. The resin was identified as Bedacryl, poly(butyl methacrylate), commonly used in conservation at that time as an adhesive and consolidant. The Bedacryl also darkened the footprints and surrounding area, and many of the animal prints.

Since Bedacryl obscured both fine texture and the contrast distinctions in the tuff, a decision was made to clean two footprint impressions in order to assist the scientists in their re-study. After several representative test patches had been cleaned and the solubility in acetone of the Bedacryl layer had been determined, the two impressions were prepared for study. Results of the cleaning test showed that where the Bedacryl was thin and overlay a calcite layer or more robust tuff, it could be safely removed using acetone with brushes or by poulticing. However, where the Bedacryl layer had deteriorated and the underlying tuff was adhered to the Bedacryl layer, the use of these methods could result in loss of underlying tuff. Because the resin layer does not appear to present any danger to the trackway, and since removal from the more deteriorated layers found in many of the impressions would pose a risk, it was decided not to extend the cleaning beyond the two footprints.

On completion of the conservation, photogrammetry was undertaken accurately to survey and record the 29 hominid footprints and other salient features on the excavated portion of the surface. The photogrammetric record will be used to generate a contour map of the site to an accuracy of 0.5 mm for the individual hominid prints and 5 mm for the surrounding surface. All information will be stored on a CD-ROM in the AutoCAD and ARC Info formats, and will eventually be integrated into a Geographical Information System (GIS), which will comprise a complete record of the project.

Scientific re-study

[...] During two weeks of the 1995 field campaign, three scientific re-study projects were conducted.

Reburial

Reburial was chosen as the long-term preservation method for the trackway at Laetoli Site G. The reburial system is designed to protect the trackway from deterioration due to exposure and growth of vegetation. This measure, accompanied by routine maintenance, will protect the site for the future and is easily reversible should the decision be taken one day to present the site to the public.

The reburial overburden consists of multiple layers of water-permeable geotextile and Biobarrier, fine granular fill, local soilfill, Enkamat erosion control matting and lava boulders mounded to a height of approximately one metre (see Figure 14.1.2). The function of the composite overburden is to isolate and protect the footprints from vegetation and erosion, and to maintain a stable environment at the Footprint Tuff horizon. The mounded shape, with a gradient of approximately 11–14° on each side, will assure surface run-off while maintaining an adequate slope to allow for re-vegetation by grasses.

The geotextile and Biobarrier function as an horizon marker and barrier against root intrusion into the burial fill. Biobarrier is a polypropylene geotextile studded with nodules that slowly release the root inhibitor trifluralin: a low-toxicity herbicide that is biodegradable, essentially water-insoluble and therefore non-leaching, non-migrating and non-systemic, that is, it will not be absorbed by plant roots or kill plants whose roots contact the nodules. Testing of the Biobarrier close to the site in 1993–94 confirmed that it blocks root growth but does not kill vegetation. The effective life of Biobarrier is dependent upon temperature and depth of burial. Manufacturer's data claim an effective life of 40 years at 20° C average soil temperature and 10 cm depth; at 25° C it has

THE LAETOLI HOMINID TRACKWAY IN TANZANIA 481

Figure 14.1.2 Reburial profile to show six of the ten layers of the composite: coarse sand layer (foreground), second layer of Biobarrier, Enkamat, coarse sand, local soil, and lava boulder capping. The four layers not visible in the photograph are a fine sand layer covering the Footprint Tuff surface, Typar geotextile, a coarse sand layer and the first layer of Biobarrier.

20 years of effective life at the same depth. [7] The Biobarrier is, however, not intended as the primary means of controlling root growth. Regular monitoring and maintenance to remove seedlings will always be the principal method of protecting the site against future intrusion of roots. The geotextiles are a second line of defence should maintenance lapse.

Definitive mineralogical and geological studies of the tuff were conducted by R.L. Hay in 1978–79. [8, 9] Laboratory analysis was undertaken at the GCI to re-examine the geochemistry and composition of the Footprint Tuff in order to determine suitable granular materials for use in the reburial. [. . .] The trackway comprises a calcite-cemented tuff, relatively resistant to embedding (especially when dry), and a weaker, clay-rich tuff susceptible to shrinking and swelling cycles and sand embedding under load. Observations of embedding tests under the environmental scanning electron microscope show that there is greater penetration of the tuff surface by angular grains than by well-rounded sand of similar size.

On the basis of field examination and laboratory testing it was determined that the reburial sand should be chemically stable and consist of rounded, medium- to fine-grained, moderately sorted sand, with sufficient calcium carbonate content to be compatible with the chemical composition of the tuff and to prevent leaching of carbonate from the tuff by rainwater percolating through the reburial fill. Several types of granular material were considered for testing and possible use: the 1979 reburial material (sand from the nearby Garusi River), five samples of river sands from Tanzania, a pure quartz sand and various manufactured, inert materials. After evaluating the composition, properties and performance under load of each sand, and considering the practical aspects of transporting large amounts of material to the site, two local river sands were selected for use in the reburial: a light colored, sub-angular, moderately sorted sand from the Kakesio River; and a dark colored, sub-angular to sub-rounded sand (which is essentially weathered volcanic tuff) from the Garusi River. The two sands were sieved at their source to eliminate organic material, especially acacia seeds, and particles greater than 6.3 mm; further sieving to obtain finer grain sizes was undertaken at the site. Together, the Kakesio River and Garusi River sands meet most of the reburial performance criteria, and provide sufficient color distinction from the Footprint Tuff.

To monitor the reburial conditions, a 2.5 × 2.5 m test trench adjacent to the trackway was backfilled in the same way. This simulation is intended to replicate the conditions of the actual reburied trackway, and will be monitored by partial re-excavation in the future.

[...]

Site protection and maintenance

One of the greatest challenges facing the project is to provide a sustainable maintenance and monitoring program and ensure the security of the site in the long term. Theft of materials used in trial tests has been a problem since the inception of the project in 1993. Continued re-vegetation is inevitable and requires a simple but regular maintenance program to remove new growth. To address these concerns, a strategy has been adopted that emphasizes public awareness, on-site security, and participation and oversight by the local community and the two government agencies responsible for the cultural and natural heritage in the area.

Among the early decisions acted upon was the establishment of an international consultative committee to guide conservation and scientific decisions and to ensure wide representation. This comprises professional representation from both the Tanzanian Antiquities Unit and the GCI, government officials and political representatives from Tanzania, the regional UNESCO representative, and participation of the palaeo-anthropological community so that scientific needs, particularly those concerned with re-study, will be addressed.

Meetings with Maasai elders from the nearby villages of Esere and Endulen were held by project team leaders and representatives of the Antiquities Unit and the Ngorongoro Conservation Area Authority to discuss the cultural and scientific values of the site and to solicit local involvement in its protection. This initiative led, during the 1995 field season, to a traditional ceremony attended by some 100 people in which the trackway was blessed and so adopted into the heritage of the Maasai as a sacred site.

Conclusion

[...]

At Laetoli the success of the appropriate technical solution—reburial—ultimately relies on the commitment of the local population to prevent the effort being thwarted by casual disturbance, and of the government authorities to monitor and maintain the site in the future.

References

1. Leakey, M. and J.M. Harris (1987). *Laetoli. A Pliocene Site in Northern Tanzania.* Oxford: Clarendon Press.
2. Johanson, D.C. and J. Shreeve (1989). *Lucy's Child.* New York: Avon Books, 190.
3. Waane, S.A.C. (1986). 'Roofs and shelters: the Tanzanian experience.' In, *Preventive Measures During Excavation and Site Protection: Ghent Conference. 6–8 November 1985.* Rome: ICCROM, 245–256.
4. Agnew, N., H. Griffin, M. Wade et al. (1989). 'Strategies and techniques for the preservation of fossil tracksites: an Australian example.' In D.D. Gilette and M.G. Lockley (eds), *Dinosaur Tracks and Traces.* Cambridge: Cambridge University Press, 397–407.
5. Jones, P. (1987). 'Appendix D.' In M. Leakey and J.M. Harris, *Laetoli. A Pliocene Site in Northern Tanzania.* Oxford: Clarendon Press, 553.
6. Shelton, S.Y., R.C. Barnett and M.D. Magruder (1993). 'Conservation of a dinosaur trackway exhibit.' *Collection Forum* 9 (1): 117–126.
7. Reemay Inc. (1993). *Biobarrier Root Control System: Technical Applications Manual.* Tennessee: Remay Inc.
8. Hay, R.L. (1978). 'Melilitite-carbonatite tuffs in the Laetoli beds of Tanzania.' *Contributions to Mineralogy and Petrology* 67: 357–367.
9. Hay, R.L. (1987). 'Geology of the Laetoli area.' In M. Leakey and J.M. Harris, *Laetoli. A Pliocene Site in Northern Tanzania.* Oxford: Clarendon Press, 23–47.

Chapter 14.2
———————

Saving the Rose Theatre
England's first managed and monitored reburial

Mike Corfield

Source: Corfield, M. (2004) 'Saving the Rose Theatre: England's first managed and monitored reburial', *Conservation and Management of Archaeological Sites*, 6(3 and 4): 305–14.

Background

DURING THE LAST THIRD of the 16th century London theatres were superseding inn courtyards as places of entertainment, but they were strictly controlled by the Mayor and Aldermen of the City of London, who saw them as a bad influence on good order. There was a more liberal regime south of the River Thames, where inns and brothels abounded in the area known as Bankside. It was here that Philip Henslowe took a lease on the Little Rose Estate and, in partnership with Philip Chomley, built the Rose Theatre in 1587. The Rose was soon followed by the Swan (1595), the Globe (1599) just to the southeast (not on the site of the modern reconstruction to the west of the Rose) and the Hope (1614) to the northwest. The Rose Theatre, which was remodelled in 1592, was bequeathed by Henslowe to his son-in-law Edward Alleyn, a renowned actor of the time. In due course, Alleyn bequeathed the detailed records of the theatre that he and Henslowe had kept to the college he founded, which survives as Dulwich College. It is these records, together with the survival of the ground plan of the theatre, that makes the Rose so important; they provide much of what is known of the Elizabethan theatre.

In March 1603 all London theatres were closed following the death of Queen Elizabeth; they re-opened in May, but were closed again by an outbreak of plague. The Rose did not re-open, and most of its structural components were removed to be used elsewhere. The great significance of the Rose was that it was the place where the great classics of the Elizabethan playwrights were first performed, including those of Christopher Marlowe and William Shakespeare – indeed it is possible that Shakespeare himself performed there. [1]

Geological background

At the time of construction of the theatres, the area of Bankside was low-lying marshland, subject to flooding. During the Mesolithic the River Thames had been a much broader river, with its main course running to the south of the present one. The site of the Rose was then in shallow water between a group of small islands. [2] As the river developed its present course, estuarine blue silty clay first built up on the river gravel to a depth of about 1.0 m, a level that was sufficient to sustain the development of peat beds 1.0–2.0 m thick. Later these were overwhelmed by another build up of silty clay 1.0–1.5 m thick, and it was on this wet surface that the theatre was built. [3] By the 16th century some attempts to drain the land had been made. [. . .] [1] Despite these rudimentary measures, the ground would still have been very damp; indeed, this was a necessary condition because if the ground dried out the clay silts would shrink and large crevices would open up, endangering visitors to the theatre.

Discovery of the theatre

The circumstances surrounding the discovery, excavation and reburial of the remains of the theatre and the surrounding controversies have been reviewed by Wainwright, Biddle, Chippendale, Orrel and Gurr, and Tilley in a special edition of *Antiquity* published in 1989. [4]

In the period 1814–1819 Southwark Bridge was built immediately to the east of the theatre. Its southern approach just missed the site of the Rose but covered part of the site of the nearby Globe. In the 1950s Southbridge House was built on the site of the Rose, on piled foundations that went through the theatre remains. Typically for the period, no archaeological investigations were undertaken and the remains of the theatre were not recognized. In 1988 outline planning permission for redevelopment of the site was granted by Southwark Borough Council and it was agreed that the then Department of Greater London Archaeology of the Museum of London would be allowed two months to investigate the site. Again, this was the normal procedure in the 1970s and 1980s, with archaeological investigations of sites that were not statutorily protected being a matter of agreement between the owners and archaeologists, brokered by local authority archaeologists as part of the planning process. Later in the year the site was sold, with its planning permission, to Imry Merchant Developers (IMD) who agreed to contribute to the costs of excavation. Excavation began in December but it was not until February that evidence of the theatre began to emerge. With the help of English Heritage, an extension of the archaeological work was agreed for a further ten weeks, and a temporary roof was installed so that excavation could continue in wet weather and to enable the public to view the work.

In the area available for excavation, two-thirds of the theatre was revealed and the foundations and associated deposits were found to be very well preserved. In basic form there would have been two concentric, polygonal timber framed walls with thatched roofs, into which galleries for the rich people were built. The stage was to the north and the open space in front of it was the groundling, where the poorer members of the audience stood to watch performances.

[. . .]

There had been great public interest in the site, with leading members of the theatrical profession and Shakespearean historians proclaiming its iconic importance and pressing for it to be fully excavated and the remains preserved. English Heritage were unable to support a proposal for the site to be given statutory protection as this would have restricted its development, costing the government many millions of pounds in compensation. By now, the developers had agreed that the remains would be preserved under their building and had asked their architect to redesign it to give better protection to the site. The new scheme created a basement area with the building supported on huge piles located outside the theatre footprint, spanned by the largest steel beams ever used in London. The government provided £1 million in recognition of the costs incurred, although, later, the developers estimated the overall cost to them was approximately £10 million.

Reburial strategy

The ongoing archaeological work was now focused on the protection of the site, principally to arrest the severe drying that had resulted in deep cracks opening as the clay matrix dried and shrunk. A water-spraying system was installed and the exposed timbers were covered when not being worked on. A scheme for burying the site was devised, based on the need to protect the remains during building work and to maintain the site's integrity until it could be fully excavated and conserved. The anticipated time scale was two to three years.

The key requirements of the burial system were:

- The entire site had to be kept wet. This was necessary to prevent shrinkage of the clay matrix and to keep the organic components fully saturated – the physical stresses imposed by any drying would cause wood to shrink and crack.
- A reducing environment needed to be maintained to minimize biological activity – bacteria, fungi and insects colonize even ancient organic remains and gain sustenance from them.
- The covering should protect the remains from extremes of temperature – at elevated temperatures the possibility of biological and chemical activity would be increased, at low temperatures there is a risk of freezing and consequent damage, while fluctuating temperatures may weaken remains by inducing cycles of expansion and contraction.
- The covering should protect the remains from physical damage or contamination during building operations.
- It should be possible to monitor the water levels and water chemistry.

A variety of covering media were considered, including peat and clay silts. These were rejected on the grounds that the peat would increase the acidity of the water and the clays would be difficult to emplace without leaving air pockets in which oxidation could occur. It would also be difficult to separate the clay from the archaeological surfaces when the site was re-excavated. The chosen system was deemed to be controllable and to be entirely neutral and chemically inert so that the ground environment should not be affected in any way by the burial materials; it is described by Ashurst and colleagues. [5]

- The remains were first covered by Terram 1500, a non-woven polypropylene/polyethylene geotextile with good physical properties and resistance to biological

Figure 14.2.1 The Terram barrier has been laid over the site, the joins sealed with lime mortar and the sand cover is being delivered through a pipeline to minimize activity on the theatre remains.
Source: Image: English Heritage archive

attack. The material was laid in sheets, with upstanding features covered with pieces cut to size. Pits and other cut features were filled with sand to give a roughly level surface. The joins in the Terram were sealed with a weak (1:6) lime/sand mortar. In retrospect, heat sealing or sealing tapes may have been preferable but time was of the essence and the equipment and materials were not so readily available (see Figure 14.2.1).

- The Terram was covered with Buckland sand to a minimum depth of 300 mm over any archaeological remains. The sand was pumped through a pipe to minimize damage to the site from wheeled barrows. It was saturated with water to ensure good compaction and to reduce its oxygen content. Buckland sand is a high-grade silica sand, low in chlorides and carbonates that might present risks to archaeological remains, and is free of iron oxides that may be precipitated if the water chemistry changes. [6]
- 'Leaky pipes' were laid at 1,500 mm intervals over the sand and covered with 12 mm of soft sand blinding. These are small-bore pipes with regular perforations along their length that are used in horticulture to irrigate greenhouses. Their purpose was to ensure that the sand was maintained in a fully saturated state at all times. The water was delivered from the mains supply and there was no filtration or de-ionization. Monitoring points were installed (see Figure 14.2.2):
  o The moisture content was measured at various depths in the sand and at the top of the archaeological surface using gypsum resistance cells. These give a relative measure of soil moisture content expressed in millivolts (mV).

o Dipwells were also installed to record the level of the perched water table above the clay – essentially a mixture of intrusive ground water and any water added through the leaky pipe system.
o Water samples were removed from the dipwells to measure:
  – pH,
  – redox,
  – dissolved oxygen (though these measurements are higher than the actual redox and dissolved oxygen because oxygen is absorbed by the sample as it is removed and analysed),
  – conductivity (as an indicator of dissolved salt content), and
  – temperature as an indicator of chemical or biological activity.

Monitoring has been carried out on a monthly basis and continues. Full analyses of the water chemistry were carried out at the time of the initial installation and have been repeated once since.
• Visqueen 1200 grade polyethylene sheeting was laid to seal the sand cover and this was covered with a 50 mm thick weak concrete mix.

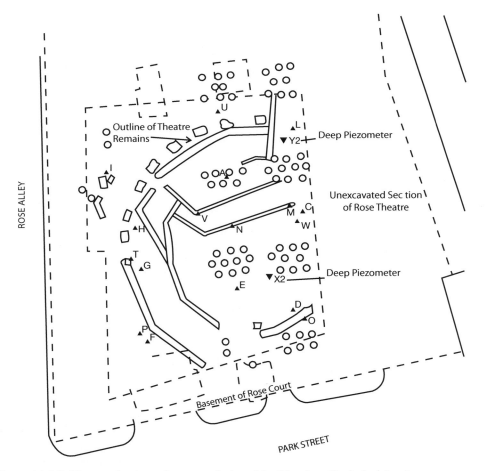

Figure 14.2.2 The monitoring scheme, as designed by Huntings Technical Services.

Performance of the reburial

- Water levels. The water rose quickly to a level where most of the remains were beneath a natural perched water table; by inputting additional water the level was further raised to ensure that the periphery of the theatre was sufficiently wet to prevent shrinkage and deterioration of the wood.
- Soil moisture content. The soil moisture content of the sand lies between 30% at the top to a maximum of about 60% at the bottom. This gives a good level of saturation, ensuring that the clay matrix of the theatre remains is fully saturated (see Figure 14.2.4).
- Redox potential. The redox, as measured, ranged from approximately 500 mV down to approximately –150 mV in places (see Figure 14.2.4). Bearing in mind the sampling method, the redox in the sand was possibly 100 mV lower than the recorded figures, giving a high degree of confidence that within the clay matrix the required reducing conditions were being met. The redox did not show the annual cycle seen elsewhere in wetlands (higher in the summer than in the winter) but the tap water and the river water were closely similar and the peaks and troughs were reflected in the groundwater.
- pH. There is much more variation in the pH levels, but the values at all monitoring points lie between 7 and 8.5, the slightly alkaline conditions reflecting the river and tap water. The tendency towards alkalinity is not a cause for concern and is probably caused by leaching from the concrete cap.
- Conductivity. The conductivity readings show that there is very little input of soluble salts to the reburial site, despite domestic tap water being used to top up the groundwater.

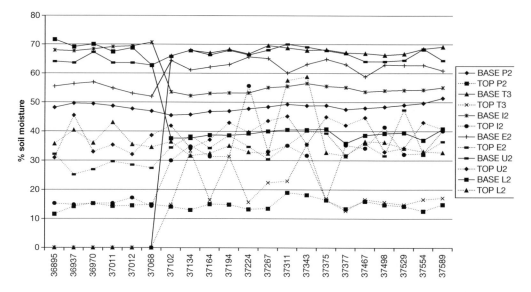

Figure 14.2.3 Soil moisture content measured by TDR (Time Domain Reflectometry), 2001–2002. The traces for the bottom of the access tubes are solid lines and the tops dotted lines. At the bottom of the tubes (i.e. closest to the theatre remains), the soil moisture is mostly above 50%, a level that will ensure that the clay soils are fully saturated.

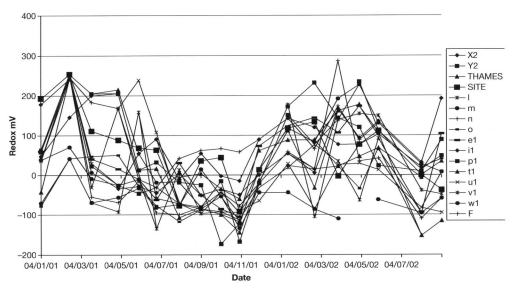

Figure 14.2.4 Redox potential, 1994–1996. The redox is predominantly in the moderately reduced range (+100 to −100 mV) with some excursions into the slightly reduced range (+400 to +100 mV). The sampling methodology involves removal of the sample through the access tube, during which some oxidation occurs.

Since the installation there have been modifications. The water supply depended on frequent visits to the site to check water levels and manually to add water as necessary. In practice, the tap was also used by the occupiers of the building to collect water for a variety of purposes; the pipe was not always re-attached or it was left attached and the tap running, causing flooding of the site. As the site is lower at its centre than at the periphery it is necessary to have a pool of water to ensure adequate saturation of all parts of the theatre remains. Therefore, the pool was used as a balancing reservoir by attaching a metal box with a ball valve to the water tap and locating it at the required depth within the pool. As the water level fell the valve opened and released water until the required level had been reached.

In 1994, 1996 and 2000 it was necessary to replace the soil moisture cells as they had reached the end of their design life. In 2000 the cells were replaced by a time domain reflectometry system (TRIME – Time domain Reflectometry with Intelligent Micro-Elements). Carefully engineered plastic tubes were installed through the sand and into the upper levels of the theatre. A probe, calibrated to the soil type, fits into the tube and is lowered to the depth at which the moisture content is to be measured. Electromagnetic pulses of up to 1 GHz are generated around the TRIME probe and are reflected back. The time taken for the reflection to be received is dependent on the moisture content. Unlike with the resistance cells, the water content can be measured at any depth and the results are given as percentage water content. The method is also more reliable close to saturation point than are the resistance cells. A major disadvantage is that the probes have to be designed for the soil types with which they are to be used but, in the case of a long-term monitoring programme, this should not be a disincentive. [7]

In order to replace the soil moisture cells, 1 m² sondages were dug, with open top and bottom wooden boxes used to prevent the saturated sand from flowing into the excavation, a process that was not entirely successful. It did, however, provide the opportunity to examine the theatre levels and check that all was as predicted. At the periphery (the highest point) the cracks in the clay were still evident at the first opening, but by the second they had closed, indicating that the clay over the entire site was fully saturated. The wood, where it was visible in the sondage, appeared sound, with no evidence of degradation. In particular, a timber post at the periphery of the theatre and therefore at the highest level was in the same condition as the archaeologists remembered. It was not considered necessary to remove samples for detailed examination.

[...]

The use of Buckland sand in the reburial system led to its being specified in other less critical reburials, causing concern because of the costs of using such an expensive material. Silica sands are also very scarce and are classed as strategic minerals, particularly in demand by the glassmaking industry [...]. [6] [8] Canti in 1995 and Davis in 1996 carried out independent studies to identify alternative sands, and jointly analysed twenty different sands to rationalize the test methodology. [9]

[...]

The search for a long-term solution

[...]

The problems at the site of the Rose, where preservation has to be in perpetuity, are formidable. First the clay matrix of the site had to be kept fully saturated to prevent shrinkage. Geotechnical studies had shown that the clay had a water content of 56–83% and that a reduction of water content from 50% to 20% would result in shrinkage of about one-third volumetrically. Even a modest loss of water from 50% to 40% would give 13% shrinkage. If any cracking was sufficiently deep to cause drying of the peat, which has a water content of 226%, the shrinkage would be catastrophic, especially as it would be coupled with chemical and biological degradation. [3, 10] The timber elements of the theatre and organic-based materials mostly had been removed to safe storage, but some remain *in situ*, and still there may be other organic remains buried beneath the excavated surface. If these were exposed, decay would be rapid, both from the physical effects of drying and from biological activity.

[...]

With the remains preserved under a protective cover in the basement of the new building, the objectives of the Rose Theatre Trust (formed by the activists who fought to have the remains excavated and preserved) changed. The Trust's purpose now was to raise support and money for the excavation of the theatre remains and their conservation and display in their original location, to enable the public to see the place where Shakespeare and his contemporaries performed. The *genius loci* was a very important consideration. In the ensuing years the technical problems were discussed at great length and the following option became the preferred solution, both in terms of feasibility and cost.

Excavate the remains and conserve the structural elements and artefacts. Remove the clay down to the gravel terrace base, recording and removing any further archaeological evidence. Form an open-topped concrete enclosure in which a simulated ground surface could be replicated with stable materials. Reinstate the conserved remains in their original spatial positions.

The strategy now is for the site to be excavated only to a sufficient depth to recover all materials associated with the theatre, then to form the open concrete base onto which the conserved remains can be reinstated in their original position. It is therefore important that the entire site remains in an unaltered condition until the remaining technical problems involved in providing a stable support onto which the conserved remains could be located are resolved and the necessary money raised.

Finally, it has to be said that the reburial of the Rose Theatre remains was a strictly temporary measure and was not envisioned to last more than a few years. In this respect it should not be used as an exemplar for other, more permanent, reburials, although the lessons learnt have been valuable. The monitoring programme has led to a realization of the complexities of the ground environment and the development of a wide variety of research at sites elsewhere. Indirectly it led to the two major conferences on 'Preservation of Archaeological Remains *In Situ*' of 1996 and 2001 [12].

References

1. Bowsher, J. (1998). *The Rose Theatre: an archaeological discovery*. London: Museum of London.
2. Sidell, E.J., K.N. Wilkinson, R.G. Scaife et al. (2000). *The Holocene evolution of the London Thames. Archaeological investigations (1991–1998) in advance of the London Underground Limited Jubilee Line Extension*, Museum of London Archaeology Service Monograph 5. London: Museum of London Archaeological Service, 108 – Figure 45.
3. Huntings Land and Environment (1994). 'Investigation of Site Conditions and Repair or Replacement of Monitoring Points [at the Kose Theatre].' Huntings Report R898: HER-07 to English Heritage.
4. Wainwright, G. (1989). 'Saving the Rose.' *Antiquity* 63: 430–435; Biddle, M. (1989). 'The Rose reviewed: a comedy (?) of errors.' *Antiquity* 63: 753–760; Chippendale, C. (1989) 'Editorial.' *Antiquity* 63: 411–413; Orrell, J. and A. Gurr (1989). 'What the Rose can tell us.' *Antiquity* 63: 421–429; Tilley, C. (1989). 'Excavation as theatre.' *Antiquity* 63: 275–280.
5. Ashurst, J., N. Balaam and K. Foley (1989) 'The Rose Theatre.' *Conservation Bulletin* 9, London: English Heritage, 9–10.
6. Manning, D.A.C. (1975). *Introduction to Industrial Minerals*, London: Chapman and Hall.
7. Available at: www.imko.de (accessed October 2003).
8. Department of the Environment (1996). *Provision of Silica Sand in England, Mineral Planning Guidance Note 15*. London: HMSO.
9. Canti, M. and M. Davis (1999). 'Tests and guidelines for the suitability of sands to be used in archaeological site reburial.' *Journal of Archaeological Science* 26: 775–781.
10. Corfield, M. (1998). 'The role of monitoring in the assessment and management of archaeological sites.' In K. Bernick (ed.), *Hidden Dimensions: The Cultural Significance of Wetland Archaeology*. Vancoouver: University of British Columbia Press, 308.
11. Huntings Technical Services (1999). 'Report R1162 to Hollybrook Ltd, Installation of Preservation Backfill at Anchor Terrace Car Park, 1–15 Southwark Bridge Road, London SE1 [site of the Globe Theatre].' Hemel Hempstead: Huntings Technical Services.
12. Corfield, M., P. Hinton, T. Nixon et al. (eds) (1998). *Preserving Archaeological Remains* in situ: *Proceedings of the Conference of 1st April–3rd April 1996*. London: Museum of London Archaeological Services; Nixon, T. (ed.) (2004). *Preserving Archaeological Remains* in situ? *Proceedings of the Second Conference of 12th–14th September 2001*. London: Museum of London Archaeological Services.

Chapter 14.3

Chaco Canyon Reburial Programme

Dabney Ford, Martha Demas, Neville Agnew, Robert Blanchette, Shin Maekawa, Michael Romero Taylor and Katherine Dowdy

Source: Ford, D., Demas, M., Agnew, N. *et al.* (2004) 'Chaco Canyon Reburial Programme', *Conservation and Management of Archaeological Sites*, 6(3 and 4): 177–202.

Introduction

THE MONUMENTAL MASONRY structures and cultural landscape of Chaco Canyon are a lasting testimony to the complex civilization that flourished in the 9th to 12th centuries AD in what is now the southwestern USA. They are also, sadly, a witness to the cumulative impact of decades of exposure on the scientific and interpretive values of archaeological remains. Beginning in the late 1980s, the management of Chaco embarked on an ambitious and far-reaching reburial programme in an effort to stem the tide of deterioration and loss. This paper is a summary of why and how the decision to carry out large-scale reburial was taken and documents the decade-long collaboration between the National Park Service (NPS) and the Getty Conservation Institute (GCI) on reburial methodology and implementation. [...]

The decision to rebury

Chaco Canyon National Monument was established, in the words of the 1907 presidential proclamation, '... to preserve the extensive prehistoric communal ruins ... of extraordinary interest because of their number and their great size ...'. [...] In 1980, the US Congress designated Chaco as a National Historical Park, and expanded the boundaries and protection mandate to over forty major Chaco sites located throughout the Four-Corners region of New Mexico, Colorado, Utah and Arizona. In 1987 Chaco Culture National Historical Park (hereafter referred to as 'the Park', 'Chaco' or 'Chaco Canyon') was inscribed as a World Heritage Site.

Chaco is located in northwestern New Mexico, a high, cool, desert environment (average elevation is 1,900 m) with high diurnal temperature variations and an average annual precipitation (rain and snow) of approximately 22 cm. [...] Tourism now plays an increasingly important role in the local economy.

Archaeological resources within the Park

There are over 4,000 sites recorded in the *c.*14,000 ha of the park. These sites represent some 10,000 years of almost continuous use or occupation with an intense period of building between 850 and 1150 AD. The recorded sites include tens of thousands of rock art images, masonry habitations, earthen architectural mounds, adobe structures, seasonal camps, stone cut stairways, constructed roadways and water control features.

The concentration and variety of these features is remarkable, but overshadowing them are the architectural monuments known as 'great houses' (see Figure 14.3.1). These are complex structures, thought by many scholars to have functioned primarily as public architecture rather than domestic habitations. These huge masonry structures have l-2ha footprints, with enclosed plazas and associated earthen architectural platforms and roads or causeways. The buildings were constructed up to five stories high, with substantial timber roofs and subterranean structures, towers and elevated rooms. As a result of the massive masonry construction, these 1,000-year-old structures retain walls up to 12 m high.

The preservation programme at Chaco

There has been a lengthy history of preservation at Chaco, beginning almost with the first archaeological excavations in the late 1890s. Then, as now, a goal of the excavations was to have sites open to the public, enabling visitors to experience directly the complexity, size, craftsmanship and overwhelming mass and scale of the architecture.

Figure 14.3.1 Aerial view of Pueblo Bonito, the largest of the great houses at Chaco.
Source: Image: G. Aldana iStock

This access, coupled with the remarkable preservation afforded by the arid climate, remote location and protection of the sites by the original descendants, contributed to the National Park and World Heritage designations. Owing to the number and size of these structures, however, preservation became increasingly problematic to achieve.

Of the 4,000 sites, only forty have been excavated, and none completely, and these are included among the approximately 150 structures that comprise the core of the preservation programme [. . .]. The remaining sites are 'passively' maintained through monitoring, fencing and other forms of access restriction. For the structures in the preservation programme to be maintained in good (i.e. stable) condition requires preventive fabric treatment on average cyclic schedules of two to three years. Thus, a minimum of about 15,000 of the total 46,000 m² of exposed masonry requires some type of preventive treatment each year.

From the 1920s through the early 1980s preservation methods focused mainly on replacing eroded fabric 'in-kind' on a cyclic basis. That is, eroded mortar joints were re-pointed with mud or amended mud mortars and eroded stones were replaced with similar stones. Deteriorated wood was only replaced if it threatened the stability of a

Figure 14.3.2 Room 62 in Pueblo Bonito during its excavation in the 1890s.
Source: Image: American Museum of Natural History © New York

Figure 14.3.3 Differential fills in partly reburied or excavated structures result in lateral pressure and salt crystallization on the exposed wall.

Source: Image: courtesy National Park Service, Chaco Culture National Historical Park

structure. This maintenance cycle attempted to suspend the structures in a state of 'ruin', where portions of walls and other architectural features that were never meant to be exposed, such as floors, interior plasters (see Figure 14.3.2), mortars and roofing elements, are constantly exposed to erosive elements.

Although in-kind replacement was effective initially, forces of deterioration multiply. Deeply excavated rooms next to unexcavated ones result in drainage problems, severe horizontal loading on the walls (see Figure 14.3.3) and accelerated loss of mortar and stone on the exposed surface. Moisture infiltration into walls, in combination with freeze–thaw cycles and salt crystallization, accelerates stone and mortar erosion, particularly at bases and tops of walls. The necessary cycle of maintenance became shorter and shorter, and the funding to support these treatments was diminishing. To counteract these trends, harder and more durable mortars replaced the mud mortars in an attempt to extend the period between repair cycles. But under many conditions, particularly in wall bases, these cement-based hard mortars, incompatible as they were with the soft sandstone and original mud mortars, led to severe consequences in the long term. Instead of the mortar joints eroding, large sections of the structural sandstone elements began to fail, and instead of individual stones deteriorating, entire sections of walls eroded and collapsed. Perhaps even more disturbing, throughout the period from the 1950s through the early 1980s, there was an increasing awareness that the repetitive fabric treatments were significantly affecting the authenticity and integrity of structures.

Re-thinking the preservation options

The concern over the impacts of preservation on the architectural, archaeological and cultural integrity of the structures prompted a review and analysis of the preservation programme in the 1980s.

[. . .]

The alternative that responded most comprehensively to the overall assessment of significance, condition and management context was reburial and this would be the focus of the preservation programme as a whole. Partial reburial would be undertaken at selected visited sites, including the great houses, and fourteen excavated sites with no visitor access would be reburied to the level prior to excavation. Partial reburial was not considered appropriate for every great house. Pueblo Bonito, the type-site and cultural icon of Chaco Canyon, was judged to be far too significant in the public mind to consider even partial reburial (although minor backfilling is being undertaken to reduce differential fill levels between adjacent rooms).

Reburial is also an effective, practical and economical treatment for the most threatened structures with the greatest visitation and is a sustainable and relatively low-tech solution to some of the more complex structural problems. Although difficult to calculate cost comparisons, the one-time costs for reburying an average room are estimated to be up to five times the cost of a single routine in-kind fabric treatment. However, the more fragile sections need repair treatment on average every two to five years. Without considering inflation or other factors, such as rising labour and equipment costs, savings are realized within ten to twenty years, and 'fabric savings' are immediate.

Nevertheless, reburial is often problematic for those whose mandate is to interpret sites to the public. Park staff, therefore, consulted with the public and with special interest groups. This is a routine part of the decision-making process for national parks, required by federal environmental laws. During the consultation process the State Historic Preservation Office and the interested public expressed support for long-term preservation, provided access to the resources was not severely limited, and agreed that partial site reburial was an appropriate measure. Consultation with Native American Tribes, who are descendants of the people who built and used the structures, revealed a strong preference for benign neglect as the appropriate treatment (that is, to allow the structures to gradually 'return to the earth'). Recognizing, however, that the Park has a legal mandate to protect and preserve; the ruins, they accepted the proposed reburial plan as a relatively passive intervention to their ancestral places and preferable to treatment-oriented interventions.

[. . .]

The efficacy of reburial

Given the scale of reburial contemplated at Chaco, there was a clear need to demonstrate and document the efficacy of reburial as a preservation strategy. To this end, five rooms were selected at Pueblo Bonito that had been filled either immediately (intentionally through backfilling) or within a few years (through backfill and natural processes of wind-blown sand) after their excavation in the late 19th or early 20th centuries. [1] Selection was also based on the existence of good photographic documentation for purposes of evaluation. These rooms were partially re-excavated in 1992 to determine the condition of original fabric after almost a century in a reburied environment. The results demonstrated unambiguously the beneficial effects of reburial on preservation of stone, mortars and plasters, but they also identified problems (in particular, the deterioration of wood) that would need to be addressed if reburial were to afford maximum preservation of original fabric.

In brief, it was found that the upper 30 cm or so of fill, subject to wet–dry and freeze–thaw cycles, provided only partial protection. Below this level, preservation was somewhat variable, relating to the length of exposure before intentional backfilling or natural processes of deposition but, in general, the mortars, plaster, stone and floor features were in good to excellent condition. In contrast, the walls exposed above the fills had lost almost all of their original mortar and plaster, and revealed stone erosion, loss of construction detail such as chinking patterns and replacement fabric (see Figures 14.3.3 and 14.3.4). In the case of Room 97, walls were a composite of masonry, wood and a type of wattle and daub construction. Nearly 100 years after their excavation and backfilling, the earthen render and mortar were in excellent condition, but the wood in the construction had suffered decay. Wood buried near the surface (the top of the wall was encountered just below the fill surface) suffered from rot and termite infestation, while more deeply buried wood was decayed but in better condition. The only other wood uncovered, a lintel in Room 348, also showed decay. Moisture in the fills (determined from carbide meter and converted to weight-per cent) was highly variable, but tended to increase with depth, from dry conditions at the ground surface through 5wt% at the mid-point to 7.4wt% in the deepest part of trenches. For the fill in Room 97, which contained quantities of stone, the absence of descriptive documentation about the condition of wood at the time of excavation and the unreliability of the carbide meter readings [...], make it difficult to relate the wood deterioration to its burial environment. Clearly the burial environment was less than optimal and moisture and shallow burial conditions played a key role in deterioration.

[...]

Status of the reburial programme

Through the Vanishing Treasures Initiative, [2] sixteen major excavated structures in the park have been partially reburied over the past twelve years. Some 6,000 m^2 of masonry has been reburied, representing about one-eighth of all exposed masonry. The replacement of eroded mortar and stone are now more manageable and the required treatments less invasive. The reburial plan proposes in the next five years to partially rebury an additional eight to ten excavated structures, resulting in about one-quarter of the total exposed fabric in the Park being reburied.

[...]

Figure 14.3.4 Room 62 partially backfilled after excavation and re-excavated in 1992. Note complete loss of plaster above the fill line; the lowest wall niche corresponds to the niche at the centre of the wall in Figure 14.3.2.

Source: Image: K. Dowdy, courtesy National Park Service, Chaco Culture National Historical Park

The case of Chetro Ketl

Chetro Ketl, one of several dozen great houses in Chaco Canyon, was scheduled for partial reburial as part of the reburial programme. Constructed [. . .] over a period of approximately 100 years in the 11th–12th centuries AD, Chetro Ketl, like the other great houses in the canyon, ceased to be used around 1250 AD. Nearly 700 years after abandonment and gradual collapse, the complex was the object of a series of archaeological field school excavations from 1920 to 1937. [3]

Assessment and analysis

The decision to rebury parts of Chetro Ketl was predicated on the overall assessment of significance, condition and management context undertaken for all the sites in the canyon. The summary that follows highlights the salient aspects of the assessment for Chetro Ketl.

Significance

Chetro Ketl is one of the largest and most imposing of the great houses at Chaco. Excavation in the 1920s and 1930s revealed a complex spread over 1.2 ha, preserving evidence of at least four stories, 450–550 rooms, and twelve kivas (circular ceremonial chambers) including a 'great kiva', a colonnaded portico facing the plaza, and a second-storey balcony along its north wall. In addition to its monumentality, Chetro Ketl

Figure 14.3.5 Rooms 54, 53 and 46 during their excavation in 1932. Note the excellent condition of the wood in Room 53, foreground.

Source: Image: Laboratory of Anthropology, © Museum of New Mexico

contains one of the largest stores of original wood elements (predominantly conifers), consisting of over 2,000 primary and secondary roof and ceiling beams, door and vent lintels, and horizontal intramural beams (see Figure 14.3.5). Also preserved are the original ceiling construction in several rooms, and ceiling and wall construction, including painted mud plaster, in one room.

[...]

Condition of the physical fabric

Of all the wood elements in the building, ceiling or roof beams and horizontal poles used for other internal constructions have been most directly exposed to weathering for the sixty to eighty years since their excavation. Many were also impacted by the 1947 flood, and all were susceptible to wet–dry and freeze–thaw cycles from snowmelt during the winter months, and intense solar radiation, rain and high temperatures during summer. Physical deterioration manifests itself as deep longitudinal fissuring and checking on the upper surface, while on the under surface, which remains wet for longer periods of time, fungal decay occurs.

[...]

Response to the assessments

The major challenge at Chetro Ketl was preservation of the wood. In the thirty-six rooms alone of the north-central part of Chetro Ketl that were being considered for reburial (see Figure 14.3.6), nearly 900 pieces of wood were inventoried, of which approximately two-thirds would be within the reburial zone. The options available for preservation of the wood were to do nothing, leaving it exposed to the environment; treat the wood with a preservative and leave it exposed; remove the wood to storage and replace with modern wood; or rebury the wood. The results of continuing to leave the wood exposed would be gradual decay and loss. *In situ* treatment with a preservative was considered but was judged to be both ineffective, because physical deterioration of weathered, exposed wood would not be stopped, and impractical for *in situ* application on such a large scale. [4]

[...]

Reburial design and implementation

[...]

The technical design was premised on the need to maintain moisture content in the fill soil below a level that would support fungal growth (brown, soft and white rot fungi) and termites in the wood (see below for relationship between brown rot and termites). The goal was to achieve a stable, low moisture regime for the wood of not more than 15% by weight.

[...]

Considerations of concern in achieving a low moisture regime were depth of reburial and sources of moisture. The two sources of moisture in the soil are snowmelt and rain water. Over the years, Chaco staff have developed an effective drainage technique to remove rainfall during summer months. This consists of grading and

Figure 14.3.6 Phase 1 rooms prior to reburial. Note position of beams.
Source: Image: M. Demas © J. Paul Getty Trust

compacting the surface from the room walls to PVC drain inlets, which conduct water via buried pipes to a low point beyond the confines of the site. This system works because the soils are sufficiently high in clay to facilitate run-off rather than infiltration. Maintenance of the surface is important and requires twice-yearly checks to regrade and consolidate the surface, [5] remove weeds and inspect the pipes for clogging. With good maintenance and slope of the surface, little rain water penetrates the fill. On the other hand, snowmelt occurs slowly as temperatures rise (with diurnal and seasonal rises in temperature), allowing time for penetration of water, especially at the base of north-oriented walls that are shaded from sunlight. Although a graded surface will assist with snowmelt, it is only partially effective in preventing penetration of moisture. Long experience and testing of soil fills used at Chaco showed that surface moisture from snowmelt is held in the upper zone (approximately 1 m) of clayey soil and does not easily penetrate deeper because of the sealing effect of the smectite clay component. [6]

The fills in most reburied rooms would be 1.8–2.5 m and most of the door and vent lintels would be below the zone of penetration, wetting and drying, and freeze–thaw. The greater challenge was how to limit moisture content and fluctuations in the upper zone of 0.3–1 m of soil where thirty-three beams and nine horizontal poles would be buried (four additional poles, in Room 48, would be at a depth greater than 1 m). Shallow burial of these timbers could not be avoided because of configuration and heights of remaining walls.

[...]

The reburial took place over a four-year period (1994–1997). Although overlapping in time, the two contiguous room blocks selected for reburial are designated Phase 1 (1994–1996) and Phase 2 (1996–1997).

[. . .]

The reburial stratigraphy was as follows, beginning at the bottom and working towards the top of the fill. Figure 14.3.7 also shows the basic stratigraphy of the reburial as it was redesigned in 2003, the only difference being the use of sieved soil adjacent to the membrane and perforation of the inlet drain:

- Horizon marker: all rooms contained some original, unexcavated fill and accumulation of soil over the sixty to seventy years since their excavation. On the surface of these existing fills, a layer of permeable geotextile (Typar®) was laid to serve as an horizon marker.
- Bulk fill: depth of fill placed in individual rooms varied, ranging from 30–60 cm (in Rooms 22–24) to almost 3 m; the majority of rooms had 1.6–2.6 m of fill placed in them. The aim was to raise the level of fills to approximately the same height as the ground surface outside the building and grade the surface in order to control water flow. [. . .] Soil was compacted every 30 cm or so with a weighted roller drum and hand-held steel-plate tamper, but was not sieved and contained large clods of hard clay, which resulted in void spaces between the clods.
- Protection of beams: the thirty-three primary beams and thirteen poles that protruded from the wall face were protected by covering. The reason for the covering was to prevent soil from coming into direct contact with and entering the cracked and fissured wood, which would have exacerbated decay. [7] The non-protruding wood (i.e. lintels) in doors and vents were not treated; the openings were filled with dry-laid masonry to prevent the wood from directly contacting the soil, although the external lintels will have direct contact with soil.

[. . .]

The preferred method of covering was used for all twenty-eight beams and nine horizontal poles in the Phase 2 rooms. This consisted of wrapping the beams and poles in permeable geotextile. A thin, heat-bonded, variety of polypropylene geotextile (Typar®) was selected to avoid water retention adjacent to the wood that can occur in the thick spun-bonded fabrics. A geotextile allows water vapour to pass through and prevents moisture from being trapped, although it is less conformable than the membrane.

[. . .]

- Drainage system: a PVC drainage system (15 cm diameter pipes), of the type routinely used at Chaco, was installed in the upper parts of the fill to direct surface water to inlet drains (see Figure 14.3.7), which carried the water 5 m outside the structure to the north. [. . .]
- Impermeable membrane: a very flexible, impermeable membrane (Tuff-Ply) was laid over the surface of the compacted and graded fill to prevent entry of rainwater and especially snowmelt into the bulk fill. The membrane was cut to accommodate drain inlets and moisture monitoring ports and sealed with silicone rubber. The edges of the membrane were turned up flush against the wall to mitigate entry of moisture, although it was felt that any ingress of moisture would be minimal. In many of the

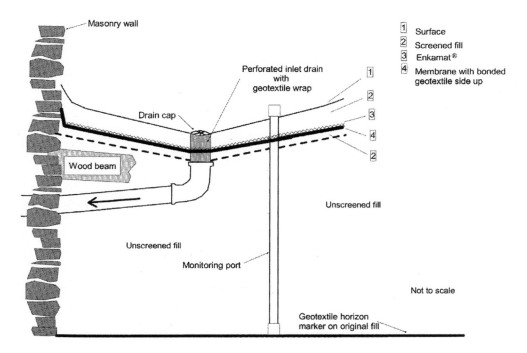

Figure 14.3.7 Basic stratigraphy of the reburial, incorporating features of the redesign for the Phase 1 rooms.
Source: Image: courtesy National Park Service, Chaco Culture National Historical Park

rooms, there was only a shallow layer (5–10 cm) of fill between the top of the beams and the surface membrane.
- Erosion control: Enkamat® (a nylon, three-dimensional, webbed matting) erosion control material was placed above the membrane to provide a protective buffer for the membrane and to hold the final layer of soil.
- Surface fill: the final layer of soil, ranging in depth between 20 and 50 cm, was laid over the membrane and graded towards the collection drains.

Following completion of the reburial (see Figure 14.3.8), the area remains closed to public access, but can be viewed from two vantage points to the east and north of the site.

The use of evaporative or collection basins

Three rooms within the area defined for reburial could not be filled (Rooms 41/43 and 38) because they were located on either side of Room 39, a room containing an original wood ceiling protected by a modern roof; nor could a drainage system be installed, since fills in all other adjacent rooms were at higher levels. Evaporative or collection basins (up to 400-litre capacity) were installed in these rooms to collect surface water from rain and snow. Lack of direct sunlight hinders evaporation of water that collects in these basins, so they actually function more like collection basins, from which water must occasionally be pumped. Infrequent heavy rains (as in October 1994 when

Figure 14.3.8 Phase 1 rooms after reburial, looking west.
Source: Image: M. Demas © J. Paul Getty Trust

22 mm fell) cause overflowing but, for the most part, they are effective in limiting water infiltration into the soil.

Evaluation of the reburial

Phase 1 rooms

- Fill below membrane: the forty one samples of fill below the membrane showed a moisture range from 3.0% to 11.8%, clustering in the 5–8% range. Areas of greatest moisture can be correlated with the inlet pipe in Room 42 and low points in Room 43A where the membrane was incorrectly overlapped allowing run-off to infiltrate below the membrane and create conduits ('piping') in the soil.
- Membrane: examination of the membrane revealed punctures, including near the inlet drain and in one case incorrect overlapping.
- Wood: in all the Phase 1 rooms, before burial, was weathered and splintered, some of it quite fractured. [. . .] The two membrane covered timbers in Room 44 were severely deteriorated by fungal attack and beads of condensation water were observed on the membrane undersurface. The condition of the four closely spaced, deeply buried poles in Room 48 covered by membrane and Enkamat® was variable, one pole was infested with termites, three showed advanced decay and one was dry with no evidence of rot or insect attack. [. . .] In Rooms 45 and 46, the three beams had Enkamat® spacer under the membrane. The beam in Room 46 (west) was well

preserved [...], the Enkamat® around the timber prevented direct contact with condensed moisture [...] and resulted in good preservation. The beam in Room 45 was moderately degraded with severity increasing through its southern half; moisture was noted on the underside of the membrane. [...]

Phase 2 rooms

- Fill below membrane: twenty-five samples of soil were taken below the membrane in Rooms 54, 55, 56 and 59. The soil was dry, with values ranging from 2.7% to 5.7% up to a depth of 2 m. The majority of values were between 4% and 5%.
- Membrane: because the surface fill was removed only in limited areas to take samples and evaluate wood, the membrane was not examined as fully as for the Phase 1 area. No punctures were noted in the areas opened for inspection and moisture values in the north-south profile through Rooms 54–56 confirm that the membrane is functioning as intended.

Figure 14.3.9 Well preserved wood post reburial, Room 59, Chetro Ketl.
Source: N. Agnew © J. Paul Getty Trust

- Wood: because of the dry conditions of the soil and the fact that all timbers were covered with permeable geotextile rather than impermeable membrane, only one beam was evaluated in Room 59. The beam was in excellent condition, with no evidence of additional deterioration after six years of burial (see Figure 14.3.9).

In both reburied areas, it was observed that basal erosion of the wall above the fill line had been reduced. Experience at Chaco has shown that, where there is no drainage system, basal erosion of mortar and stone occurs fairly consistently and rapidly (within a few years) at the fill-wall interface. By excluding or reducing moisture in the fill, the membrane, in conjunction with the drainage system, mitigates capillary rise in the walls leading to basal erosion.

Re-installation of Phase 1 reburial

Following the investigation of the Phase 1 reburial [...] the Drainage was redesigned [...] and the entire area was re-contoured [...]. To replace the easily punctured membrane, a new composite membrane (Griffolyn T-65G) was used, still comfortable, but with better puncture resistance [...]. Soil was sieved to remove the clods of clay and used immediately below and above the membrane to provide a smoother, well compacted and contoured surface [...]. In addition, more exact working specifications were written for the installation crew. These included training and explanation of the characteristics and the performance of the membrane [...].

Discussion and summary

[...]

The deterioration condition of the timbers in Phase 1 can be attributed to a number of interrelated factors. Most important of these was the membrane covering which, when water entered through rents in the isolating room membrane [...] resulted in the moisture being trapped, creating an environment for decay. Clearly it is potentially deleterious to wrap timbers in membrane under such conditions. [...] Wrapping the beams in permeable geotextile allows any trapped moisture [...] to dissipate.

[...]

The Phase 2 reburial differed (from Phase 1) in that all the timbers were covered with geotextile [...] so there should be no moisture trapped by the wrapping. [...] Based on the moisture data in Phase 2 and the investigation of wood in Room 59 the membrane is functioning as intended, but it will be essential to continue monitoring the reburial environment to confirm these results.

[...]

The relationship between Chetro Ketl soils with different moisture contents and relative humidity (RH) gave somewhat different results depending on the soil. Fill soil containing 2.5%–3.0wt% (water) generated 75% RH, but dry samples from undisturbed soil in proximity to Chetro Ketl produced values of 2.4wt%/84% RH and 4.4wt%/91% RH. Soils with these levels of moisture are dry to the touch, powdery and dusty. Factors such as the particle size distribution, clay components, organic content and soluble salts all play a role in the affinity of soil for moisture and hence RH.

[...]
What water content of soil is safe over the long term for buried wood, assuming the absence of liquid water? [...] given the historical survival of buried wood at Chaco, the threshold parameters of 15wt%/75% RH for wood rot fungal growth in air [8] may not necessarily be valid in soil since even the driest soils produce an RH at or above 75%. Nonetheless, more precise values would need to be established through further research. [...] Much more aggressive attack occurs in the presence of liquid water. For these reasons we regard a value of up to 5wt% water in soil for the protection of pre-decayed wood in a burial as reasonably safe and conservative.

[...]

Summary

Preservation challenges at Chaco are exacting. Erosion of stone and mortar caused by salt crystallization (especially at the base of the wall), the pressure of soil on unsupported walls and deterioration of exposed wood are perhaps the three most destructive phenomena affecting the site. These have not yielded to final solutions, but progress has been made in mitigating interventions. This paper has focused on reburial at Chetro Ketl and the difficulty of wood preservation and moisture in a reburial, a problem that manifested itself during the re-excavation of backfilled rooms at Pueblo Bonito.

Wood buried by natural processes after abandonment seven to eight centuries ago had survived well, even though decay was evident in historic photographs and no doubt much was also lost. Unfortunately, very little is known about the original burial conditions that favoured wood preservation. Excavation exposed wood to deterioration. The principal challenge in the reburial at Chetro Ketl was to devise means for the *in situ* preservation of wood, some of it already severely degraded. A balance needed to be struck in the design of the reburial. Most timbers could only be shallowly buried because fill mass was dictated by the variable height of extant walls. On the other hand, re-excavation of rooms in Pueblo Bonito had shown that shallow reburial within the upper wetting and drying zone of soil is not sufficient to ensure survival of the wood. Exclusion of moisture from this zone and maintaining as dry an environment as possible throughout the fill was therefore essential.

[...]

Our initial choice of membrane erred on the side of thinness and flexibility, and it punctured easily during installation. Probably the most significant deficiency in our approach was to overlook the need for good training and supervision of the installation crew, to whom geosynthetics were new materials. Each problem that was manifested in the Phase 1 installation has been addressed in the redesign and reinstallation, but it is clear that this report cannot be the last word on the Chetro Ketl reburial. Periodic monitoring will continue, both of moisture content and by means of retrievable wood samples.

Reburial is a proven intervention, and the decision to use it widely at Chaco as a conservation strategy will undoubtedly achieve the goal of preserving stone, mortar and plaster, and reducing the ultimately damaging cycles of maintenance. The outstanding issue at Chaco remains that of preserving wood in a buried environment. Clearly there is much more research and testing that will be required to meet this challenge. The continued monitoring of the reburial at Chetro Ketl will be critical to this effort.

References

1. Dowdy, K. and M.R. Taylor (1993) 'Investigations into the benefits of site burial in the preservation of prehistoric plasters in archaeological ruins.' In, *7a Conferéncia Internacional sobre o Estudo e Conservacão da Arquitectura de Terra: comunicações: Terra 93*. Lisboa: Direcção Geral Dos Edifícios e Monumentos Nacionais.
2. Vanishing Treasures is an initiative of some forty national parks in the arid western region of the USA to focus preservation efforts on long-term preventative treatments for sites with standing architecture.
3. Lekson, S.H. (ed.), with contributions by J. Dean, P.J. McKenna and R.L. Warren (1983). *The architecture and dendrochronology of Chetro Ketl, Chaco Canyon, New Mexico.* Albuquerque, NM: National Park Service.
4. Water-soluble borates are considered environmentally friendly preservatives. When present in high concentrations, they will limit decay and insect activity, although how well soft-rot fungi would be controlled is unknown. Timbers would have to be impregnated completely, necessitating prolonged immersion. This, in turn, would require that the wood be removed, soaked, dried and reinstated. The chemical effects of borate on degraded wood are also not known, nor are the effects of the leachate on the soil and masonry.
5. Surface 'hardening' by means of a synthetic soil binder has been tried, but found ineffective, as the inevitable foot traffic destroys the integrity of the surface.
6. Maekawa, S. (2004). 'Monitoring of soil moisture in backfilled soil for conservation of an Ancestral Puebloan great house in Chaco Canyon.' *Conservation and Management of Archaeological Sites* 6 (3 *and* 4): 315–324.
7. Blanchette, R., B.W. Held, J.A.Jurgens et al. (2004). 'Wood deterioration in Chacoan great houses of the southwestern United States.' *Conservation and Management of Archaeological Sites* 6 (3 *and* 4): 203–212.
8. Kurt, H. (1986). 'Sorption Isotherms, A Catalogue Technical Report 162/86.' Building Materials Laboratory, The Technical University of Denmark.

Chapter 15

Conclusion

Preservation *in situ*

At its simplest preservation *in situ* can be reduced to answering three questions:

- What have you got? Determine the extent of the site, the nature of the remains (artefacts, buildings and other features), what materials are they made of? Who values this, what do they value about it and why? It is not just the physical remains themselves that are important, but how they are understood and their significance to present-day communities, from local villagers to academic specialists.
- Why does it survive? Determine the extent and nature of decay, the nature of the burial environment and the threats to its continued survival. As shown by the cave art of Lascaux, not understanding what conditions ensured its preservation led to mass visitation and damage to the remains. Only when we accurately understand the nature of the burial environment and the threats to it can we accurately plan mitigation strategies to preserve the remains it surrounds.
- How can it be preserved? Identify mitigation methods that will prevent further decay, secure the resources necessary and implement them. Enhancing the social value of the remains is often the key to securing the resources to sustain preservation into the future, especially for monitoring and maintenance.

When seeking to preserve archaeological remains, whether waterlogged wood, adobe structures, cave art, masonry buildings or scattered artefacts on a battlefield, we draw principally on three mechanisms/traditions:

- *Legislation*: evolves with a society to allow it to exercise a degree of social control and protection, for what society values (in this case, ancient remains), from deliberate damage by members of that society.
- *Scientific knowledge*: has provided insight into the nature and complexity of natural and archaeological materials and their decay processes and potentially enables us to develop appropriate mitigation methods.

- *Conservation*: has given us centuries of experience dealing with the physical remains of the past, balancing the competing requirements to preserve, research and reveal these remains to the public, who have increasingly been the body owning the archaeological remains in Britain and Europe and wanting to see them.

Conclusions

In this book, I have suggested that the past has value for all societies, and that this past is effectively composed of physical remains and the stories, traditions and meanings that connect and explain them, and make them relevant to our present existence (see Introduction). The ancient remains, which have been preserved by accidents of nature and thus come down to us, have given us an expectation that we can preserve archaeological remains for future generations (see Chapter 1). We can identify many of the causes of loss of archaeological sites and artefacts, but human activities, from ploughing to war, are arguably the most destructive (see Chapter 2); they are certainly the most preventable. Since the Age of Enlightenment, human beings have been creating an evidence-based scientific understanding of the world. This not only gives us an accurate and detailed understanding of the past (see Chapter 1), but it enables us to understand the burial medium; how and why archaeological remains are degraded, what soils and burial conditions preserve, and thus we are increasingly able to undertake the preservation of the valued physical remains of our past *in situ* (see Chapter 3). To counter the threat of human destruction, we have developed legal protection, a formalised mechanism of social control, relevant to present-day societies, which, in part, replaces earlier and more informal social valuation and respect for ancient remains (see Chapters 4 and 8). To counter the threat of natural decay (and repair the depredations of human beings), we are developing the discipline of conservation. Since the Renaissance, we have developed methods for physical protection and display (conservation) of archaeological remains (see Chapter 5). However, there have been conflicting requirements to both preserve the physical evidence of the past and to display those remains to inform and educate ourselves (Chapter 5). We have often attempted to do both, but given the aggressive damaging conditions of weathering we have had to place artefacts in museums to preserve and view them, while our exposed ancient sites; castles, temples and pueblos have had to be extensively repaired and restored, and can no longer be considered 'preserved as found' (see Chapter 6, Figure 6.0.3, and Chapter 14, 'Public expectation'). The number of archaeological sites is increasing (geophysics, aerial photography, satellite imaging, metal detecting, and archaeological surveys) but the resources for preserving or displaying them are limited. Scarce resources leave us needing to select which sites to preserve with legislation, which to exploit and which we can only record. We increasingly seek to solve these issues through a detailed valuation process so we understand the significance of these sites (see Chapter 5). This valuation process can also suggest which sites are appropriate (cost-effective, better placed) for preservation and which for restoration or reconstruction work. Increasingly, heritage agencies are starting to use their sites more consciously as collections (Thurley 2013); at some sites, preservation is emphasised, remains being recorded and reburied (see Chapter 14), at others there is an emphasis on display, exploited for educational and economic benefit (see Chapters 12 and 13). In the case of stone structures (see Chapter 6) or earthen architecture (see Chapter 7), exposure leads to active weathering requiring an active programme of maintenance or costly repair and replacement. To fund this, the site must normally have a role as an active highly visited monument or use as a functioning building in the present (i.e. 'use it or lose it'). This puts pressure on authorities and sites to attract tourists and engage in activities on those sites. However, our efforts to preserve sites such as the Palaeolithic art in the caves of France and ancient Egyptian wall paintings in the rock cut tombs of the Valley of the Kings have taught us how fragile these preservative environments are, and how human visitation poses a very significant threat to these sites (see Chapter 10). This lesson is slowly being learnt and applied to other less fragile sites where the capacity to withstand visitors without damaging the site (carrying capacity) is being established and visitor numbers controlled (see Chapters 8 and 12). The need for maintenance and controlling visitation has been emphasised at popular earthwork sites such as Stonehenge (see Chapter 8). Damage to waterlogged sites has shown us that some damage is not visible, but disturbance of the subsurface water levels and chemistry can threaten whole buried ancient landscapes filled with archaeological remains, which we may never get to see (see Chapter 11). We are seeking to become proactive, plotting where waterlogged deposits occur within historic towns, where coastal erosion or earthquakes occur and using that knowledge to record things before they are damaged or lost, or taking steps through planning urban development or managing coastal retreat to minimise loss.

Through the nineteenth and twentieth centuries, we built and filled the museums in Europe; however, in the twenty-first century, we are increasingly focusing on preserving remains *in situ*, embracing the enhanced experience and additional information and meaning about the past that this affords us (see Introduction). On sites that are to be displayed, we battle to learn from nature how to preserve early attempts to crudely consolidate degraded wall paintings and stonework are being replaced with more subtle attempts to control moisture levels and environments. We are seeking to perfect shelters (see Chapter 13), paying more attention to subsoil conditions and building environments so that salts and algae will not flourish. On sites that are to be preserved, we are starting to learn how we can create and maintain preservative burial environments, so we can safely rebury sites and protect as yet unexcavated sites. It is already clear that reburial is not purely a technical process of creating a 'protective reburial system' and monitoring. It will only be successful where a holistic sustainable approach to reburial is taken, as at Laetoli, where, in addition to physical measures, increased social value of the site and maintenance procedures were set in place (see Chapter 14.1). We need to ensure that the lessons of damage we caused through attempts to preserve/conserve in the past are learnt, the values of preservation are appreciated by a wider society, and the skills to preserve *in situ* are developed and practised. Increasing research and education in this subject is the only way this will be achieved.

The challenges

There are limitations on our present and future knowledge and our present and future resources for preservation *in situ*. They stem from the problems of timescale and priority.

Timescale

- *Decay processes* of stone and erosion of earth monuments are often too slow and not sufficiently dramatic to create publicity impact; this makes resources difficult to obtain. Only the damage of fragile wall paintings in tombs and caves has highlighted the fragility of archaeological remains. Slow changes are difficult to measure, and in comparison to the short-term economic changes they are not seen as urgent.

- *Analysis* and publication of results occurs when conservation projects are completed, often helping heritage organisations justify expenditure on sites. There is little or no analysis or publication of the failures or successes of conservation treatments 10, 20 or 50 years after the projects have been completed. Only such analysis will reveal truly effective solutions. There may, however, be organisational concerns that any focus on failures in conservation/preservation (and many things fail after 50 years) would undermine public confidence in heritage agencies and their solutions.
- *Under-tested*: New products and techniques need to be effective for decades. They cannot be realistically tested in the short term and it remains challenging and costly to establish long-term testing regimes. Products are often 'sold' by commercial producers to organisations keen for quick, cheap solutions and they are not appropriate for long-term use in preservation studies. We currently lack the resources to develop our own.
- *Management* of a threat is often a highly responsive solution to a problem, but, like maintenance, many carefully worked out managed solutions are lost with changes of personnel, funding and organisational priority. Organisations have not been around as long as the monuments. It remains unclear if managed solutions are sustainable in the long term.
- *Research* is challenging in natural environments that are highly variable, and thus difficult to accurately characterise, especially over longer periods of time. The long time frames required for preservation *in situ* research are also difficult to achieve with short-term science project funding.

Priority (low)

- *Careers* of archaeologists are not built on the care of monuments but new discoveries and ideas, thus the care of monuments fails to attract the brightest and most assertive students. Resources are therefore often focused on unearthing new discoveries not preserving the old ones. As early as 1904, Flinders Petrie noted the enthusiasm of archaeologists for excavation and recovering artefacts, but their lack of care for the ruins and artefacts they uncover. This continues to the present day.
- *Education* on the preservation of archaeological remains forms only a small part of existing archaeological degrees, usually just a couple of lectures. Though artefact conservation is often covered by specialist degrees and qualifications, very, very few courses teach the preservation of archaeological sites.

Bibliography

Flinders Petrie, W.M. (1904) *Methods and Aims in Archaeology*, London: MacMillan & Co.
Thurley, S. (2013) *Men from the Ministry: How Britain Saved its Heritage*, London: Yale University Press.

Index

academic value of heritage management 165
access, heritage management 168–9
accretions 228, 360–1
accumulation: dust in shelters 457; vegetable mould by worms 105–8
acidic fertilizers 51
acidity 135–6, 398–406
activities, visitor management 421–2
adipocere formation 140–1
adobe construction 276, 290–302
aeolian erosion 336
aerobic environments 95, 101, 135
aesthetic criteria, shelters 452
aesthetic restoration ideal 182
aesthetic values 186
aggregates, mortar 264
agricultural damage 50–3, 75
Ajina Tepa, Tajikistan 290–302
aldehyde tanning 138–40
algal growth on rock art 361
America: Chaco Canyon 493–508; Fort Seldon 458; history of heritage legislation 154–5; Siqueiros Mural 455
Åmose valley, Zealand, Denmark 410–12
Ampato Maiden 19
anaerobic bacteria, breakdown products 135
anaerobic environments 86, 95, 101–2, 135, 140–1, 396–407
anastylosis 184, 228–9
ancestry, early artefacts 6

ancient building burials by worms 106–8
Ancient Monument and Archaeological Areas Act, 1979 145, 151
Ancient Monuments Act, 1931 147, 149, 152
animal damage 310–11, 320–1, 361
animal fibre degradation 96
anoxic environments *see* anaerobic environments
anthropogenic damage 35–8, 43, 59, 293, 311–12, 321–2, 361–2, 372–82
antiquarians 14–16
antiquities trading 156, 203–4
archaeological heritage management 159–78, 408–18
archaeological resource management 171–8
artefacts: corrosion 81–2, 98; density 78–9; forestry and vegetation threats 53–4; heritage legislation 156; holistic approaches 39–41; importance of 4–6; losses 41–4, 55–6, 79–80; Monuments at Risk Survey 70–83; movement 343–5; peat bogs 63–4; trading legislations 156
Athens Charter on the Restoration of Historic Monuments 183
Australia: Burra Charter 186, 209–17; Lark Quarry 453–5; Mulka's Cave 372–82
autohydrolysis in peat bogs 137

backfilling 281, 324–6, 462–4
bacteria 137, 361

Baden-Württemberg, Germany, Federsee 412–14
banks, earthworks 114–15, 117
bedding mortar 255
best practice, shelters 446–7
binding, enzymes/soluble proteins in peat bogs 141
Biobarriers 480–1; *see also* geotextiles
biocidal sprays 51
biological remains 84–8, 110–11, 116–18, 134–42, 399–403
boat at Khufu 17
bog bodies 18–19, 30–4, 134–42
bone degradation 96, 120–1, 122, 136–7
Borum Eshøj, Jutland 18
boundaries, soil horizons 111–12
Britain *see* England; Northern Ireland; Wales
Buddhist monastery at Ajina Tepa 290–302
buffering by dissolved salts 99
buffer materials 468–70, 480–2, 503
Bull Wharf 398–405
burial environments 91–143; biology 101–2; chemistry 99–101, 125–33; corrosion/decay zones 98; denudation 109–10; dissolved salts 99; earthworms 105–8; equilibria 98; Experimental Earthwork Project 113–24; forms of degradation by material 94–6; soil 91–2, 97–8, 109–12, 128–30, 347–50, 372–82; sphagnum peat bogs 134–42; *see also* buried sites
burial mounds 74
buried materials in Experimental Earthwork Project 118–23
buried sites 329–57; artefact movement 343–5; chemical control 337; damage and destruction 331–3; erosion 332–3, 335–6; fire impacts 346–7, 350; forms 330–1; impact studies 343–56; internal changes 345–6; legal protection 334–5; physical protection 335–7; soil 113–14, 347–9; urban developments 338–40; values and protection 333–4; vandalism 350–3
buried soils vs. turf stacks 113–14
Burra Charter, 1999 186, 209–17
buttresses 244–6, 301–2

capping 280, 468–70
carrying capacity 423–4, 426–36
cation sequestration in peat bogs 136–7
causes of piecemeal loss and damage 74–5
causes of wholesale monument losses 71–3
cave sites 358–82, 426–36

cellulosic fibre degradation 96
ceramics 94, 263, 265
Chaco Canyon 493–508
chalky soils 118–23
characterisation, anoxic environments 396–407
Charter for the Protection and Management of the Archaeological Heritage (Lausanne) 153, 185–6
chemical control 337
chemistry: burial environments 99–101, 125–33; waterlogged sites 134–42, 385–7
Chetro Ketl, Chaco Canyon 499–507
China: Xi'an grave complex 18; Yunju Temple 455
Church Building Acts 223–4
Civic Amenities Act, 1967 150, 152
cleaning of petroglyphs 364–5
climate change 38–9
closed shelters 442, 444–5
cob construction 276
collagen 17, 96
collection basins, Chaco Canyon reburial 504–5
collection of information, Malta/Valletta Charter 203
communal values 186
compaction, soils and sediments 347–8
competent authorities, Malta Convention implementation 173–6
complete loss of artefacts 42
composition: earthen architecture 278; sites and decay mechanisms 332; soil 97–8
conductivity: Rose Theatre reburial 489–90; waterlogged sites 398–406; *see also* redox potentials
conservation 59–62, 179–217; agricultural land 51–3; charters 182–6, 194–217; concepts 181–2; earthen architecture 278–81, 285–302; earthworks 313–15, 322–8; fragile sites 335–7; history 179–81; in practice 191, 215–16; principles 211–13; raising value 421–3; restoration 184; rock art 362–5, 366–8; statements of significance 190–1; stone ruins 231–2, 240; theory 179–93; values 186–91; waterlogged sites 390–3; *see also* generic mitigation measures; preservation
conservation-based research and analysis 187–91
Conservation of Nature Act, 1978, Denmark 62

conservation planning 187, 189–91
conservation reburial 462, 464–5
conserving as found 248
consolidation: earthen architecture 280; stone ruins 230–2, 239–40, 254–5
contractors, Malta Convention implementation 173–6
Convention for the Safeguarding of Intangible Heritage 186
conveying understanding of stone ruins 228
copper corrosion rates 81
core facework of stone ruins 255–6
cores of stone walls 255–60
correct conservation of stone ruins 240
corrosion, metals 81–2, 95, 98
corrosion zones 98
Council of Europe 153, 173–6, 185–6, 200–4
cracking of earthen architecture 277
criteria and shelter functions 451–2
CRM *see* cultural resource management
crushed ceramics in lime mortars 263, 265
crust formation on rock art 360
crystallisation in earthen architecture 277
cultivation of earthworks 307
cult temple short story 235–41
cultural diversity, Nara Document on Authenticity 205–6
cultural heritage, World Heritage Convention definition 184–5
cultural resource management (CRM) 162
cultural significance 211–12
curing mortar and plaster 263
Czechoslovakia, Staré Mesto/Mikulcice 58

Dead Sea Scrolls 17
decalcification of bones 137
decay: general forms 94; ideas of 13; Matthewson's matrix 332; *see also* degradation
decay zones 98
decorated surfaces 232, 280–1, 358–71
degradation 86; bacteria 135; bone 96; buried and fragile sites 331–3; cation sequestration 136–7; ceramics 94; earthen architecture remains 277–8; earthworks 304–6; experimental studies 92–7; fragile sites 331–3; glass 94; ignorant repairs 239–40; leather 95–6; metals 81–2, 95, 98; modern materials 93; rock art 360–2; shelters 442–6; stone ruins 94–5, 222, 226, 235–40, 248–58; textiles 96; wood 96; *see also* decay

dehydration of waterlogged sites 389–90
delicate organic remains in near-surface deposits 84–8
delicate remains, biological 85
Denmark: Åmose valley 410–12; bog bodies 18–19, 30–4; Borum Eshøj 18; Conservation of Nature Act, 1978 51, 62; heritage management 167; Tollund man 19, 31–4
density of artefacts, Monuments at Risk Survey 78–9
dental repairs to stone ruins 261
denudation of burial environments 109–10
desiccation 17, 51, 467–8
detection of metals 333
developers, Malta Convention implementation 173–6
development over buried and fragile sites 338–40
diagenesis *see* degradation
dissociation constants 126–30
dissolved salts 57, 99, 294, 360, 455–6
ditches, earthwork changes over time 115–17
divisions of the past 3–5
documentation 297–8, 337–8, 479–80
drainage 62–7, 281, 285, 294, 410–16
dredging and loss of sites 56
Durham Cathedral 191
Durham research project 398–406
dust 361, 457

earthen architecture 275–302; Ajina Tepa 290–302; analysis 295–6; archaeological contexts 285–9; backfilling 281; buttresses 301–2; capping/encapsulation 280; composition 278; conservation 278–81, 285–302; consolidation 280; construction techniques 275–6; decay 277–8; decorative surfaces 280–1; drainage 285, 294; erosion factors 285–9; maintenance 302; in practice 282; reburial 300; reconstruction 279, 296–7, 300–2; repair 279, 300–2; seismic threats 281–2; shelter coatings 280, 300–2; shelters 281
earthworks 50–6, 304–28; backfilling 324–6; bank changes over time 114–15, 117; buried soils 113–14; conservation 313–15, 322–8; decay 304–6; ditch changes over time 115–17; erosion 307–12, 320–2; experimental projects 93, 97, 113–24; installations 326–7; land

management 322–3; management 318–28; as preservation agents 306–7; reinstatement 323–6; repairs 323–6; slopes 306, 324–6; vegetation 307–10
earthworms 105–8, 116
ecofact losses 44
efflourescence 232
Egypt: Great Pyramid 17; Tutankhamun's tomb 18, 26–9
Eh *see* redox potential
electron availability *see* redox potential
encapsulation 280, 300–2
England: Church Building Act, 1818 223; history of heritage legislation 147–54; modern heritage movement 150, 152; National Planning Policy Framework 153–4; National Trust 52; Office of Works 223–4; Peterborough petroglyphs 458–60; Planning Policy Guidance, note 16 151, 153; priorities in monument selection 63; Rose Theatre reburial 484–92; Scheduled Ancient monuments 51–2; Somerset Levels 64–7; York 84–8; *see also* Northern Ireland; Wales
environmental effects of shelters 445–6
environmental interventions, site preservation 48–69
environmentalism, heritage management 161
environmental monitoring of Mogao grottoes 432–3
enzyme binding 141
equilibria of burial environments 98
eroded but extant earthen structures 287–8
erosion: buried and fragile sites 332–3, 335–6; cave sites 372–82; earthen architecture 285–9; earthworks 307–12, 320–2; lake edges 56–7; land 58–9; marine waters 57; rock art 360–2; soil studies 348–9; tourism 378–80; trampling in caves 372–82
estimation of artefact/monument losses 77–83
European Convention on the Protection of the Archaeological Heritage, 1992 153, 185–6, 200–4
European wetlands 63, 408–18
evaluation of shelters 457–60
evaporative basins, Chaco Canyon reburial 504–5
evaporate redox/pH potentials 131–2
evidential values 186
excavations: artefact movement 343–5; backfilling 462–3; buried and fragile sites 337–8; impact studies 343–56; internal changes 345–6; loss of sites 37–8; Pompeii 21–5; potential damage 238–9; Venice Charter 199
Experimental Earthwork Project 93, 97, 113–24
experimental studies of decay 92–7
exterior losses of artefacts 42

farming damage 50–3, 75
fats and adipocere formation in peat 140–1
Federsee, Baden-Württemberg, Germany 412–14
fills, reburials 468–70, 480–2, 503
final decay, earthworks 306
financing under Malta/Valletta Charter 202
fine earth volumes moved by worms 105–6
Finland, water erosion remediation 56
Fiorelli, G. 21–5
fires, impact studies 346–7, 350
Flag Fen 398–405
floors, stone ruins 267–8
forensic analysis of Tollund man 32–4
forestry and loss of sites 53–4
Fort Seldon, America 458
fossilisation, preservation 17
fractures in stone ruins 256–7
fragile sites 329–57; aeolian erosion 336; chemical control 337; damage and destruction 331–3; erosion 332–3, 335–6; forms 329–30; hydraulic erosion 335–6; impact studies 343–56; legal protection 334–5; physical protection 335–7; urban developments 338–40; values and protection 333–4
France: INRAP 175; Lac de Chalain 414–16
freeze thaw, rock art 360
freezing, preservation 19
fresh-water sediment redox/pH potentials 130–1
functions of shelters 438–9

general forms of decay 94
generic mitigation measures 419–509; reburial 462–509; shelters 438–61; visitor management 421–37
geological background, Rose Theatre 485
geotextiles 470, 480–1, 486–7
Germany: Federsee, Baden-Württemberg 412–14; site protections 62
glass degradation 94
Grabungsschutzgebieten 62
gradual natural events and loss of sites 38–9

graffiti, cave art 366
Great Pyramid, Egypt 17
ground truthing experiments 93, 97
grouping of soils by profile-types 112
grout 257–60, 265
Gunhild, Queen of Denmark 31

heritage: definition 5; importance of 1–6; significances 186–91; values 186–91
heritage diversity, Nara Document on Authenticity 205–6
heritage legislation 144–58, 168, 173–6, 183–4, 196–9
heritage management 159–78, 408–18
hexashelters 458
highmoor peat bogs 126–8, 136
historical values 186
history: of conservation 179–81; definition 5; English heritage legislation 147–54; shelters 439–41
holistic approaches to loss of sites 39–41
Holland *see* Netherlands
horizon marking 480–1, 503
horizons 111–12, 480–1, 503
human-caused damage *see* anthropogenic damage
humic acids, peat bogs 137
Hyden, Mulka's Cave 372–82
hydraulic damage *see* water damage
hydraulic lime 263–5
hydrology of waterlogged sites 386–7
hydroxyapatite degradation 96

ICCROM *see* International Centre for the Study of the Preservation and Restoration of Cultural Property
ICOM *see* International Council of Museums
ICOMOS *see* International Council on Monuments and Sites
identification under Malta/Valletta Charter 200–1
ideograms 358–71
ignorant repairs 239–40
impact studies 343–56, 428–36
implementation models of Malta Convention 173–6
initial decay of earthworks 305
INRAP 175
installations, earthwork management 326–7
integrated conservation, Malta/Valletta Charter 202

intellectual needs of visitors, stone ruins 229–30
interfaces 468
internal changes, impact studies 345–6
International Centre for the Study of the Preservation and Restoration of Cultural Property (ICCROM) 182
International Charter for the Conservation and Restoration of Monuments and Sites, 1964 168, 183–4, 196–9
International Council on Monuments and Sites (ICOMOS) 153, 168, 182–6, 196–9, 209–17
International Council of Museums (ICOM) 182
interpretative functions, shelters 452
ion exchange in burial environments 99
Irish Church Act, 1869 224
iron corrosion rates 81

Jura, France, Lac de Chalain 414–16
Jutland, Borum Eshøj 18

Khufu, disassembled boat of 17
knowledge of sites, raising value 421

labile materials 85
laboratory analysis of earthen architecture 295–6
laboratory-based studies of degradation 93
LAC *see* limits of acceptable change
Lac de Chalain, Jura, France 414–16
Lacustrine sites 392
Laetoli trackway, Tanzania 453, 476–83
lake Bienne 56–7
lake Neuchâtel 56–7
Lanchester 398–405
landcut monument damage, Monuments at Risk Survey 75
land erosion, loss of sites 58–9
land management of earthworks 322–3
land planning and archaeological heritage management 167–9
landscapes 48–69, 274, 322–3
Lark Quarry, Australia 453–5
Lausanne Charter for the Protection and Management of the Archaeological Heritage 153, 185–6
leather 95–6, 120–1, 122
legislation 144–58; American history 154–5; buried and fragile sites 334–5; English history 147–54; Malta/Valletta charter

173–6, 185–6, 200–4; national identity 146; object protections 156; protections 144–6; protection through purchase 154; Venice Charter 168, 183–4, 196–9; *see also* charters
lichens, rock art 361
lifespan of shelters 442
lime mortar 255–60
lime plasters 266–7
lime putty 264
lime-rich soils, fossilisation 17
limitations of Experimental Earthwork Project 123–4
limits of acceptable change (LAC) 424
long-term protection through purchase 154
looting of cave art 366
Los Angeles, America, Siqueiros Mural 455
losses of artefacts 35–88
losses of ecofacts 44
losses of monuments 35–88
loss of substance, artefacts 42
Lower Saxony, Germany, wetland drainage 63
low moors peat bog redox/pH potentials 126–8
Luxor, Egypt, Tutankhamun's tomb 18, 26–9

maintenance: Chaco Canyon 495–7, 505–7; earthen architecture 285–9, 302; Laetoli trackway 482
Malta Convention on the Protection of the Archaeological Heritage, 1992 173–6, 185–6, 200–4
management of the archaeological heritage 159–78
management of earthworks 318–28
marine waters: erosion 57; metal degradation 95
masonry walls: grouting 259; Wigmore Castle 272–3
Matthewson's matrix of decay and site composition 332
megalithic tombs 6
metakaolin 263, 264
metal detection 333
metals, degradation 81–2, 95, 98
meteoric waters, redox/pH potentials 126
methodology: conservation planning 189–91; shelters 450–1
microbiology 134–42
Mikulcice, Czechoslovakia 58

military activity, earthworks 312
minerals 17, 99, 126–8
minimum intervention 248
mitigation: generic measures 419–509; reburial 462–509; shelters 438–61; visitor management 424–5; *see also* conservation; preservation
modern heritage movement, England 150, 152
modern materials degradation 93
Mogao grottoes 368–9, 426–36
moisture, shelters 445–6
monitoring: Rose Theatre reburial 488–91; waterlogged sites 384–9
monuments: agricultural damage 50–3; artefact losses 79–82; benefits of losses 44–5; causes of losses 43; corrosion 81–2; English priorities preservation 63; environmental interventions 48–69; forestry and vegetation 53–4; holistic approaches 39–41; Monuments at Risk Survey 70–83; natural events and loss 38–9; part-preservation/restoration 227; presentation 227, 229–30; preservation 227; public interest and conservation 59–62; quarrying 55–6; restoration 227; tourism and urbanism 59; vandalism impacts 350–3; visitors' intellectual needs 229–30
Monuments at Risk Survey (MARS) 70–83; agricultural damage 75; artefact densities 78–9; estimation of losses 77–83; landcut damage 75; piecemeal loss and damage 72–5, 79–80; wholesale losses 71–3, 79–80
mortar: aggregates 264; bedding 255; cement 239–40; constituents 264–5; curing 263; lime 255–60; stone ruins 262–5
mosses, rock art 361
movement of artefacts 343–5
Mulka's Cave 372–82
multivalent cation sequestration in peat bogs 136–7

Nara Document on Authenticity 185–6, 205–8
national identity: heritage legislation 146; heritage management 162–6
National Planning Policy Framework 153–4
National Trust, England 52
natural environment, limits of pH/Eh 125–33
natural events: losses of monuments 43; loss of sites 38–9

natural hydraulic lime 263–5
nature conservation, waterlogged sites 417
Navan, Northern Ireland 55–6
near-surface deposits and organic remains 84–8
Neolithic settlements in Switzerland 56–7
Netherlands, Zuiderzee 59
New Mexico: Chaco Canyon 493–508; Fort Seldon 458
non-collagenous tissue degradation 139–40
non-hydraulic lime 263–5
Northern Ireland, Navan quarry 55–6

objects: heritage legislation 156; loss rates from corrosion 81–2, *see also* artefacts
Office of Works, England 223–4
Olduvai Gorge, Tanzania 456
open shelters 441–2, 444–5
oral tradition 4–5
organic matter: anoxic deposits 86; categories 85; Experimental Earthwork Project 116–18; near-surface deposits 84–8; non-collagenous 139–40; preservation 110–11; sphagnum peat bogs 134–42; tanning in peat 138–41; waterlogged sites 86, 134–42, 399–403
organisational principles for earthwork management 328
organisms, redox/pH potentials 132
Ötzi the Iceman 19
Over, Cambridgeshire 398–405
overgrazing 51–2
Overton Down Experimental Earthwork Project 113–24; buried materials 118–21, 122–3; changing profile 114–17; comparison with Wareham site 122–3
oxidation-reduction potentials *see* redox potentials
oxidising environments: burial biology 101; metal degradation 95

pakhsa 275, 290–302
Parliament Street, York 84–8
part-preservation/restoration 227
the past: divisions 3–5; importance of 1–6
Pazyryk (Scythian) tombs 19
peat bogs 63–4, 126–8, 134–42, 398–406
performance evaluation of shelters 457–60
periodic natural events and loss of sites 38–9
permafrost, preservation 19
Peterborough, petroglyphs shelter 458–60
petroglyphs 358–71, 458–60

pH 99–100, 125–33, 135–6, 385–8, 398–406, 489–90
phases of deterioration, stone buildings 235–8
philosophy of stone ruin repair 242–68
physical condition assessment of cave sites 434–6
physically protected reburial environments 465–6
physical needs of visitors at stone ruins 230
physical protection 17–18, 335–7, 417; *see also* reburial; shelters
pictograms/pictographs 358–71; conservation 362–5, 366–8; Lascaux 365–6; vandalism 366
Pict's Knowe 398–405
piecemeal loss 72–5, 79–80
piecing in, stone 261
pigments, cave art 358–9
piling for urban developments 339
Planning Policy Guidance, note 16 (PPG 16) 151, 153
plant fibre degradation 96
plaster: curing 263; rock art 368–9; stone ruins 266–7
polymeric biphenols, tanning in peat 138
Pompeii 14–15, 21–5
porous rock degradation 94–5
Portland cement 262
post-colonial archaeological heritage management 164
pozzolanic limes 263–5
PPG 16 *see* Planning Policy Guidance, note 16
precipitation of minerals 99
prehistoric drawings, physical protection 17–18
preparatory work at Ajina Tepa temple 294–7
presentation: earthworks 311–12, 321–2; historic buildings 227, 229–30; stone ruins 227, 229–30
preservation: backfilling 462–4; beginnings 6–7; bog bodies 18–19, 30–4; buried and fragile sites 335–7; buried materials 118–23; Chaco Canyon 493–508; conservation reburial 462, 464–5; desiccation 17; earthworks 306–7; Enlightenment rationale 7; environmental interventions 48–69; fossilisation 17; as found 223–4; freezing 19; historic buildings 227; Laetoli trackway 476–83; organic matter 110–11; petroglyphs 362–5, 366–8; physical protection 17–18, 26–9; Pompeii

14–15, 21–5; reburial 59–60, 462–509; resource management 176–8; shelters 438–61; in situ conceptual emergence 7–9; sphagnum peat bogs 18–19, 30–4, 134–42; stone ruins 227, 231–2; storage reburial 462, 471–2; Tollund man 19, 31–4; visitor management 421–37; waterlogged sites 16–17, 62–7, 390–3; Wigmore Castle 269–74; see also conservation
preventative treatments for earthworks 327–8
principles: Ancient Monument and Archaeological Areas Act 145; Burra Charter 211–13; earthwork management 328
profiles: soil 111–12; waterlogged sites 417
proforma design 298
protection: buried and fragile sites 333–7; European Convention 153, 185–6, 200–4; Laetoli trackway 478, 482; Malta/Valletta Charter 200–1; purchases 225; shelters 451–2; through purchase 154; see also conservation; preservation
proteinaceous fibre degradation 96
protein binding in peat bogs 141
psychograms 358–71
publication: Malta/Valletta Charter 203; Venice Charter 199
public awareness, Malta/Valletta Charter 203
public expectations, reburial 472–3
public interests, conservation/preservation 59–62
Pueblo Bonito, Chaco Canyon 494–7
purchase for protection 154, 225

quarrying 55–6, 63–4
Queen Gunhild of Denmark 31
Queensland, Australia, Lark Quarry 453–5

raft foundations, urban developments 339
rain: cave sediment movement 377, 380; redox/pH potentials 126
raised peat bog acidity 136
rammed earth constructions 275, 290–302
rebuilding of stone ruins 255
reburial 462–509; Ajina Tepa temple 300; backfilling 462–4; buffer materials 468–70, 480–2, 503; burial layers 470; buried and fragile sites 340; capping layers 468–70; Chaco Canyon 493–508; conservation reburial 462, 464–5; desiccated sites 467–8; environments 465–8; experiments 93, 97; geotextiles 470; Laetoli trackway 480–2; physically protected environments 465–6; public expectations 472–3; Rose Theatre 486–91; sequence 468–71; shipwrecks 59–60; sterility 471; stone ruins 241; storage reburial 462, 471–2; urban developments 340; waterlogged environments 466–7
Recommendation on International Principles Applicable to Archaeological Excavations 183
reconstruction of earthen architecture 279, 296–7, 300–2
recording buried and fragile sites 337–8
redox potential (Eh): burial environments 99–100; evaporates 131–2; fresh-water sediments 130–1; limits of natural environments 125–33; meteoric waters 126; peat bogs 126–8; Rose Theatre reburial 489–90; soils 128–30; waterlogged sites 385–8, 398–406
reducing environments: anoxic waterlogged sites 396–407; burial biology 101–2; metal degradation 95
re-excavation of Laetoli trackway 479
registration, archaeological heritage management 166–7
reinforcement of Tintern Abbey 245–7
reinstatement of earthworks 323–6
religious buildings 6–7, 223–4, 235–68, 290–302
religious revival, nineteenth century 223–4
remnant colonies on earthworks 53
remortaring stone ruins 231–2
removal of accretions from stone ruins 228
repairs: Chaco Canyon 495–7; earthen architecture 279, 300–2; earthworks 323–6; stone ruins 239–40, 261–2
replacement, stone ruins 231–2, 260–1
repointing stone ruins 231–2
resource management 171–8
restoration: conservation 184; earthworks 323–6; stone ruins 227; Venice Charter 198; Violett-le-Duc 223
rheological damage see water damage
Rhodesian Man 110
risk assessment, Mogao grottoes 434–6
robust remains, biological 85
rock art 358–71; conservation 362–5, 366–8; decay and damage 360–2; Lascaux 365–6; on plaster 368–9; vandalism and looting 366

roofed buildings 224–5
rope, Experimental Earthwork Project 120, 122–3
Rose Theatre, London 484–92
ruins 221–74; *see also* stone ruins
rural sites, waterlogged 387, 390–1
Ruskinian ideal of conservation 181–2
rye grasses 309

salt damage 57, 360, 455–6
salts 57, 99, 294, 360, 455–6
sandy soils, Experimental Earthwork Project 118–23
saturation, waterlogged sites 390–3
Scheduled Ancient monuments, England 51–2, 145
Schleswig-Holstein, site protections 62
scientific assistance/information Malta/Valletta Charter 203–4
scrub vegetation 54, 308–9
Scythian (Pazyryk) tombs 19
sediments 130–1, 347–50, 372–82
seismic threats to earthen architecture 281–2
sequence for reburials 468–71
sequestration of multivalent cations in peat bogs 136–7
Shaanxi Province, China, Xi'an grave complex 18
shallow urban deposit artefact losses, York 84–8
shelter coats 232, 300–2
shelters 438–61; aesthetic criteria 452; best practice 446–7; climate and ecosystem effects 445–6; dust accumulation 457; earthen architecture 281; functions 438–9; history 439–41; interpretative functions 452; methodology 450–1; performance evaluation 457–60; problems 442–6; protective function criteria 451–2; site security 456; soluble salts 455–6; stakeholder issues 455; thorough processes 452–7; types 441–2, 444–5; unexpected consequences 457; uses 438
shipwrecks 56, 59–60
short story of a ruined cult temple 235–41
significance of shelters 439
Siqueiros Mural, America 455
site security, shelters 456
slopes, earthworks 306, 324–6
Society for the Protection of Ancient Buildings (SPAB) 180–2, 194–5

soil: composition 97–8; denudation 109–10; impact studies 347–50; organic matter preservation 110–11; profiles 111–12; redox/pH potentials 128–30; stability fields 129; stratigraphy 91–2; trampling 372–82
soluble protein binding, peat bogs 141
soluble salts 57, 99, 294, 360, 455–6
Somerset Levels, England 64–7
SPAB *see* Society for the Protection of Ancient Buildings
spatial variations, waterlogged sites 386–7
sphagnol hypothesis 134–5
sphagnum peat bogs 18–19, 30–4, 126–8, 134–42
splitting of rocks 94–5
stability fields: non-metallic compounds in peat 127; soils 129
stages of conservation-based research and analysis 188
stakeholder issues, shelters 455
Staré Mesto, Czechoslovakia 58
statements of significance 190–1
sterility, reburial 471
stitching, stone repairs 261–2
stomach contents analysis, Tollund man 34
stone degradation 94–5
Stonehenge 169
stone ruins 221–74; conservation 227–9, 231–2, 240; consolidation 230–2, 239–40, 254–5; cult temple story 235–41; decay 222, 226, 235–40, 248–58; decorated surfaces 232; floors 267–8; future practice 232–3; grout 257–60, 265; historic buildings 224–5; ignorant repairs 239–40; mortar 262–5; phases of deterioration 235–8; philosophy, technology and craft 242–68; plaster 266–7; presentation 226–30; reburial 241; reinforcement 245–7; religious ruins 223–4, 235–68; repairs 261–2; replacement 231–2, 260–1; repointing 231–2; restoration 227; stitching 261–2; structural analysis 244–7; structural archaeology 248–51; technical issues 230–2; tourism 224; walls 252–60, 265–7
storage reburial 462, 471–2
stratigraphy 84–8, 91–2, 111–12
structural analysis 244–7
structural archaeology 248–51
substantial loss of artefacts 42
surface disturbance categories 349
surface losses 41–2
surface mixing studies 349–50

survival 13–34
Sweden: Ancient Monument Act, 1942 51; Royal Proclamation of 1666 159
Sweet Track 64–7, 398–405
Switzerland, water erosion remediation 56–7

Tajikistan, Ajina Tepa 290–302
tanned leather degradation 95–6
tanning in peat bogs 138–41
Tanzania: Laetoli Trackway 453, 476–83; Olduvai Gorge 456
technical assistance under Malta/Valletta Charter 204
technologies, stone ruin repair 242–68
temporary conservation, Ajina Tepa temple 298–302
temporary supports, stone ruins 252
textile degradation 96, 121–22
threats 35–88; anthropogenic causes 35–8; environmental interventions 48–69; holistic approaches 39–41; Monuments at Risk Survey 70–83; natural events 38–9; near-surface deposits 84–8; pressures on sites 49–67; quarrying 55–6; tourism and urbanism 59; water erosion 56–7; waterlogged sites 387–90
Tintern Abbey 242–7
Tollund man 19, 31–4
tomb of Tutankhamun 18, 26–9
tourism 165, 168–9, 224, 311–12, 321–2, 378–80
Town and Country Planning Acts, England 149–50, 152
trade in antiquities 156, 203–4
trampling 372–82
tree planting 74, 307–8
truth to materials 325
Tutankhamun's tomb 18, 26–9
types of shelters 441–2, 444–5

UK Climate Impacts Programme (UKCIP) 39
unconsolidated surface trampling 372–82
underwater artefacts 56, 59–60; *see also* waterlogged sites
UN Environmental Programme (UNEP) 161
UNESCO *see* United Nations Educational, Scientific and Cultural Organisation
unexcavated earthen architecture erosion 289
unexpected consequences of shelters 457
United Nations Educational, Scientific and Cultural Organisation (UNESCO) 182–6, 205–8

un-maintained earthen structures 286–7
unmortared walls 265–7
unroofed buildings 225
urban development 84–8, 338–40
urban waterlogged sites 387, 392
uses of shelters 438

Vale of Pickering 398–405
Valletta Convention on the Protection of the Archaeological Heritage, 1992 173–6, 185–6, 200–4
values: buried and fragile sites 333–4; conservation 186–91; Nara Document on Authenticity 206–7
value of visitors 422–3
vandalism 350–3
Vanishing Treasures Initiative 498
vegetable mould formation by worms 105–8
vegetation 53–4, 293, 295, 307–10, 361
Venice Charter for the Conservation and Restoration of Monuments and Sites, 1964 168, 183–4, 196–9
VERP *see* visitor experience and resource protection
Victorian Society, England 152
Violett-le-Duc restoration 223
visitor experience and resource protection (VERP) 424, 428–36
visitor management 421–37; carrying capacity 423–4, 426–36; impact studies 428–36; mitigation 424–5; Mogao grottoes 426–36; monitoring 429–30, 432–6
void-filling grouts 258–60
volumes of fine earth moved by worms 105–6

Wales, Tintern Abbey 242–7
walls, stone ruins 252–60
Wareham Experimental Earthwork Project 113–24
water damage: Ajina Tepa temple 293, 294, 302; buried and fragile sites 335–6; cave sediments 377, 380; earthen architecture 277; loss of sites 56–7; rock art 360–1; shelters 445–6
waterlogged sites 383–418; characterisation 396–407, 417; dehydration 389–90; deposits, remains and survival 383–4; drainage 410–16; Durham research project 398–406; economic aspects 417; European 63–7, 408–18; experiments 97; hydrology 386–7; monitoring 384–9; nature

conservation 417; pH and redox potentials 385–8, 398–406; physical protection 417; preservation 16–17, 390–3; reburial 466–7; rural 387, 390–1; threats 387–90; urban 387, 392; Water Quality Monitoring 398–406
Water Quality Monitoring (WQM) 398–406
wattle and daub 276
weak lime coatings 232
wetlands: drainage and loss of sites 62–7; European 63–7, 408–18; *see also* waterlogged sites
wholesale losses 71–3, 79–80
Wigmore Castle 269–74
wind damage 336

wood 96, 120–1, 122, 506–7
wood ash, lime mortars 263, 265
Woodhall 398–405
World Heritage Convention, 1972 184–5
worms 105–8, 116
WQM *see* Water Quality Monitoring

Xi'an grave complex 18

yeasts, peat bogs 136
York, near-surface organic remains 84–8
Yunju Temple, China 455

Zealand, Denmark, Åmose valley 410–12
Zuiderzee, Netherlands 59